International Business Negotiations

INTERNATIONAL BUSINESS AND MANAGEMENT SERIES

Series Editor: Pervez Ghauri

Forthcoming titles

HENNART & THOMAS
Global Competitive Strategies

SHAFIK
International Privatization

Other titles of interest

FATEMI
International Trade in the 21st Century

FATEMI
The North American Free Trade Agreement

KOSTECKI & FEHERVARY
Services in the Transition Economies

KREININ
Contemporary Issues in Commercial Policy

MONCARZ
International Trade and the New Economic Order

MOROSINI
Cross-Cultural Acquisitions and Alliances

Related journals — sample copies available on request

European Management Journal
International Business Review
International Journal of Research in Marketing
Long Range Planning
Scandinavian Journal of Management

International Business Negotiations

Edited by

PERVEZ N. GHAURI AND JEAN-CLAUDE USUNIER

PERGAMON

UK   Elsevier Science Ltd, The Boulevard, Langford Lane, Kidlington, Oxford OX5 1GB, UK

USA   Elsevier Science Inc., 660 White Plains Road, Tarrytown, New York 10591-5153, USA

JAPAN   Elsevier Science (Japan), Tsunashima Building Annex, 3-20-12 Yushim Bunkyo-ku, Tokyo 113, Japan

First edition 1996

British Library Cataloguing in Publication Data

International business negotiations
   I. Ghauri, Pervez N., 1948 –   II. Usunier, Jean-Claude
   658.4'5

ISBN 0 08 042775 8

Library of Congress Cataloging-in-Publication Data

International business negotiations / edited Pervez N. Ghauri and Jean
  -Claude Usunier. – 1st ed.
     p.   cm. – (International business and management series)
  Includes index.
  ISBN 0–08–042775–8 (hardcover)
    1. Negotiation in business. 2. International trade. 3. Export
  marketing. 4. Joint ventures. 5. Foreign licensing agreements.
  6. Corporate culture. I. Ghauri, Pervez N., 1948–
  II. Usunier, Jean-Claude. III. Series.
  HD58.6.I58 1996   96–35060
  658.4–dc20   CIP

Printed and Bound in Great Britain by Redwood Books Ltd.

Contents

Part I

Part II

WITHDRAWN

v

Contents

Part III

Part IV

Series Editor's Preface

International business has proved in recent years to be the most dynamic area of business studies. The world economy is becoming globalized, as new blocs and relationships emerge to create a radically different business environment. We have seen the increasing importance of the European Union, the opening up of most of the former centrally planned economies, and a phenomenal growth in emerging markets. All these changes present new challenges and opportunities for academics and practising managers, and highlight the need for more research and publication. This will enhance our understanding of the realities of competition within an increasingly interdependent, yet culturally diverse, business world.

Most universities and business schools now offer international business programmes, at least at graduate level: an MSc in International Business or a Master's degree in International Management. All MBA programmes claim to offer an "international" MBA. Academics and business leaders have both come to appreciate the importance of preparing future managers for the complexities of the new world order.

Consequently, the volume of academic research in international business has increased significantly. Like most business and management literature, it tends to be dominated by a North American perspective, while actual practice varies dramatically and continually adapts to new circumstances. However, as medieval traders, nineteenth-century entrepreneurs and twentieth-century corporations each adopted very different approaches according to the nature of their eras and their own individual perceptions, so the approaches adopted in contemporary international business must reflect the realities of the world in which we live.

The aim of this series is to apply a truly international perspective to the study of international business, with a special emphasis on management and marketing issues. While existing series cover other areas such as finance and economics, there are very few publications covering these issues systematically, apart from the two journals *International Business Review* and *Journal of International Business Studies*. The International Business and Management Series deals with such topics as globalization, international business negotiations, cross-cultural communication, entry strategies, doing business in different regions, and future trends. Work on competition, the development of international business theory, methodological issues, the results of empirical studies and the findings of practitioners, also fall within its brief.

Throughout, the intention is to provide up-to-date guidance to students and practitioners of international business, and to advance the frontiers of knowledge in this fast-developing field.

University of Groningen,
The Netherlands

PERVEZ N. GHAURI

Editors' Preface

Business negotiations are increasingly recognized as a full part of the managerial process, highly relevant to the implementation of business strategies. Traditionally, most of the business literature has focused on strategy formulation on the one hand and management systems and procedures on the other. There is now more emphasis on "how to do" rather than simply "what to do", implying an increased emphasis on relationships with clients, agents and partners as a key success factor in the implementation process. International marketers are now more and more business negotiators, who constantly discuss deals across borders with a variety of people, ranging from consumers to intermediaries and even competitors.

The dramatic growth of international trade over the last five decades has been not only in terms of volume but in complexity as well: service offerings are now mixed with products, and technology often plays a central role as an object of the exchange. Deals are not only made through discussions of a bundle of physical attributes and a price; they are also drafted between merchants and business people from different countries having different objectives and cultural backgrounds. Establishing, maintaining and fostering relationships is therefore of prime importance for the market transaction to take place. It is more and more recognized that international trade is not only a matter of price and product but also of people who manage a complex relational process. Business negotiations occupy a prominent place in international trade because any transaction is in some way negotiated even though on a limited range of issues. Within the relational process some more complex deals are worth consideration in more detail, not only sales agreements but also the discussion of agency and distribution contracts in foreign markets and the negotiation of joint ventures and licensing agreements.

Given the considerable growth in alliances, partnerships and technology deals across borders, finding the right partner(s) and developing an adequate framework for conducting the relationship with them are now considered key success factors. Technology often plays a major role in such deals and this could mislead people into believing that the whole negotiation process is principally an engineers' discussion based on rational and scientific facts. In fact, technical complexity intermingles with human complexity to render such negotiation processes difficult to manage. Complexity is probably one of the main features of this kind of negotiation exercise: partners come from quite diverse national and cultural backgrounds, do not share the same native language, yet still have a major interest in dealing with each other.

A considerable amount of literature is available on negotiations, some of it also on business negotiations but the field of international business negotiations is quite neglected. Some studies on negotiations with different regions or countries such as the Middle East, Japan and China are available. However, there is no book on this topic that discusses international business negotiations in a comprehensive manner.

As the body of literature has been growing in the field of international business negotiations for the last fifteen years, we believe it is now appropriate to give a comprehensive overview of the knowledge which has been so developed. Some twenty authors have contributed to this edited volume, some of them coming from academia, some from business companies, while most of them have been involved both in research and in the practice of negotiation at international level. The reason for compiling this book is that we want our readers to use it as a tool for increasing their knowledge and effectiveness in negotiation; the path towards achieving this is threefold: (i) understanding the process of international business negotiations; (ii) developing knowledge of the issues at stake and the main variables; (iii) developing skills for being a successful international negotiator.

The book is divided into four parts: (I) general aspects of international negotiations; (II) culture and international business negotiations; (III) the negotiation of specific kinds of agreements; (IV) a regional approach to international business negotiations.

The first part is designed to cover the basics of international business negotiations. Chapter 1 gives an overview of international business negotiations and proposes a model which is used further in the text. This introductory chapter is followed by a discussion of how national culture, organizational culture and personality impact buyer-seller interactions; it sets in perspective the respective roles of country, corporate and individual variables in shaping negotiation behaviour at the international level. Chapter 3 presents a model of the negotiation process with different strategies, going back to the fundamental theoretical approaches of negotiation to highlight how they apply in the international area. The fourth chapter is illustrative and shows the kind of mismatch which may occur in international business negotiations, when business people coming from various countries interact with each other.

Culture is a major determinant of strategies and tactics in international business negotiation, because negotiations involve communication, time, and power and these variables differ across cultures. The second part deals with various aspects of culture which have an impact on the negotiation of business at international level, starting with a chapter which gives an overview of these influences. Chapter 6 presents the most widely used framework for describing national cultures, Hofstede's four dimensions of culture, and discusses their influence on international business negotiations. The three following chapters are dedicated to issues which have a quite significant cross-cultural variance: issues in cross-cultural communication and what they imply for international negotiators (Chapter 7), how people view time and deal with it in business negotiations which are suffused with time-loaded aspects such as dates, planning, scheduling, etc., (Chapter 8) and finally, the role of atmosphere in negotiations (Chapter 9).

The third part is orientated towards the content of the deals being negotiated. The first three chapters present the agreements to be discussed by the parties: international sales and export transactions; agency and distributorship agreements; licensing agreements and international joint ventures. Chapter 13 deals with the negotiation of a project which is both a complex sale and, frequently, an episode in an on-going relationship. Chapter 14 deals with mergers and acquisitions in the European Union, and shows how cooperative negotiation works as an asset for the future venture.

The fourth part of the book has a more regional focus, looking at how negotiations should be managed with people from various important areas, though it also builds on cultural factors as well as content-oriented aspects of international business negotiations. We could not be exhaustive here and decided to concentrate on major countries and areas which make up a quite significant part of world trade. Chapter 15 deals with the IBM-Mexico microcomputer investment negotiations, a case in complex negotiations involving a large multinational company and a host government in a Latin American country. Chapter 16 explores the specifics of the negotiation in Eastern and Central Europe, where the political and economic environment has been subject to tremendous changes over the last five years. The following two chapters are dedicated to North–South business negotiations, emphasizing the interaction between Japanese and Americans (Chapter 17) and offering a comparative perspective on how East Asians negotiate, based on insights about Japanese, Chinese and Korean negotiators (Chapter 18). The final chapter of the book is normative and prescriptive in nature; it indicates some general guidelines for effectively negotiating international business.

This is not a general book on negotiation. It focuses on its international business aspects and should therefore be read with cross-border business deals constantly in mind. References can be found at the end of each chapter which lead to more general approaches to business negotiations. The first two parts should be read by all with an interest in the subject, since they deal with basic aspects of international business negotiation. For the third and fourth parts it is up to readers to decide which kind of agreements and which areas of the world they wish to focus on.

Most chapters have both a conceptual content and illustrative examples. This is designed to help readers who have not been personally involved in such situations to figure out how the concepts described operate in practice. For those readers who have professional experience of international business negotiations, the book can also be used to re-read situations, that is, to provide them with insights on why a particular negotiation developed in a certain way. It may serve too as a base for preparing some negotiation in a specific area of the world, or with partners from certain cultures, or when negotiating certaing types of agreements.

We would like to thank all the contributors in this volume who made it possible to cover a broad range of issues related to international business negotiations. Our grateful appreciation goes also to Tony Seward of Elsevier Science who has been instrumental in publishing this book and to Ellen M. Flikkema who helped us in typing and other editorial routines. Any errors and shortcomings remain our responsibility.

PERVEZ N. GHAURI   JEAN-CLAUDE USUNIER

Groningen   *Strasbourg*

List of Tables and Figures

List of Tables and Figures

The Contributors

Viviane de Beaufort is Professor of Law and European Institutions at ESSEC, France. Completing her law education at the University of Paris-Sorbonne, she has published many articles on European institutions in law and public policy journals. She has just edited a book on the European Union transformation (*Maastricht II, la Copie à Réviser*). She also wrote a book on the acquisition of companies in Europe (*Acquérir une Enytreprise en Europe*). Her current research is about M&As in Europe.

Ian McCall consults in cross-border management, having previously been a government official marketing tropical products, a sales/marketing manager in the sugar engineering business and a lecturer on international management. He conducts courses on international business and negotiation and communication in business schools in Finland, France, Sweden and the United Kingdom and has published books and journal articles in these areas.

Michael J. Copeland (B.Sc. in Political Science from Xavier University) served as a Military Officer in the US Army for four years and then joined the Human Resources Department at Procter & Gamble. In 1980 Mr Copeland designed a transfer technology support for Japan for Procter & Gamble. From 1981 he was responsible for all international relocation systems. In 1988 Mr Copeland was responsible for managing Training and High Potential Development Systems for Procter & Gamble's International Divisions.

Bernard Cova is Professor, EAP, Paris and Associate Research Director, IRE, Institut de Recherche de l'Enterprise in Lyon. He received his Doctorate from the University of Paris Dauphine, and specializes in the study for the implications of the postmodern on marketing theory and practice. He manages a European research programme on Project Marketing and Systems Selling supported by major industrial companies. His latest book is *Stratégies d'incertitude*, which traces different scenari for companies facing uncertainty.

Christophe Dupont is at present Director of LEARN (a laboratory devoted to research and applied studies on negotiation) hosted by the Lille (ESC) Business School. Professor Dupont's career has been mostly spent on international affairs, teaching and training. He is a member of the International Advisory Board of the *Negotiation Journal* and has published a number of articles and books, among which *La négociation: conduite, théorie, applications* (Dallog 1994), is now in its fourth edition.

Pervez N. Ghauri earned his Ph.D. from the Department of Business Studies, University of Uppsala in Sweden where he also taught for more than ten years. After that he worked in the Norwegian School of Management for about five years as Professor of Marketing. At present, he is working as Professor of Marketing at the Faculty of Management and Organisation, University of Gronigen, The Netherlands. He has vast experience of teaching graduate and executive programmes and is founding editor of *International Business Review*. He has published widely on marketing and international business topics.

John L. Graham is presently Professor of International Business and Marketing and Associate Dean of the Graduate School of Management at the University of California, Irvine. Graham's primary professional interests are concerned with international business negotiations. Graham has published extensively in both academic and management journals including the *Harvard Business Review*, the *Journal of Marketing*, *Strategic Management Journal*, *Marketing Science*, the *Journal of Consumer Research*, the *Journal of International Business Studies*.

Geert Hofstede is Emeritus Professor of Organizational Anthropology and International Management from Maastricht University, The Netherlands. He holds a Masters level degree in Mechanical Engineering from Delft Technical University, and a doctorate in Social Psychology from the University of Groningen. He worked in industry in roles varying from production worker to Director of Human Resources. He founded and managed the Personnel Research department of IBM Europe, and was a Faculty meemberat IMD, Lausanne, Switzerland: INSEAD, Fontainebleau, France; the European Institute for Advanced Studies in Management, Brussels, Belgium, and IIASA, Laxenburg, Austria. His best known books are *The Game of Budget Control* (1967), *Culture's Consequences* (1980), and *Cultures and Organizations: Software of the Mind* (1991).

Sudhir H. Kalé, Ph.D. is Associate Professor of Business Administration in the College of Business at Bond University, Gold Coast, Australia. He has previously served on the faculty at the University of Illinois, Arizona State University, and the University of South Carolina. Dr. Kalé's current research investigates the impact of individual personality and temperament on dyadic interactions in the international context. His work has been published in *Journal of Marketing Research*, *Journal of Marketing*, *Journal of Applied Psychology* and *International Marketing Review*. Professor Kalé also conducts training programmes for managers all over the world on topics such as behavioral dimensions of selling, applications of the Myers-Briggs Type indicator in management, and corporate culture.

Alain Pekar Lempereur is Professor of Law and Negotiation at ESSEC, France. As a Fulbright Fellow, he got his Doctorate in Juridical Sciences from

Harvard Law School, specializing in conflict resolution and the use of argument. He has published several articles in scholarly journals and has edited three books on persuasion (*L'Homme et la Rhétorique; Figures et Conflits Rhétoriques*) and on argumentation (*Argumentation. Colloque de Cerisy*). He is now focusing his attention on various methods of negotiation and mediation in Europe.

Florence Mazet has been a Researcher and a Lecturer at IRE-Group ESC Lyon since 1989. Her research interests include the marketing of firms selling package deals and projects-to-order and the offering strategies of industrial firms. She has participated for four years in the second IMP project on industrial network relationships.

Vernon Parker, ARCS, B.Sc, CPA, EPA. After graduating in Chemistry from the Royal College of Science, London, in 1960, he trained for the patent profession in Abel & Imray, Chartered Patent Agents, London, and then joined Imperial Chemical Industries PLC Group. Over the ensuing 30 years he has held various positions in several businesses of ICI involving responsibility for intellectual property, licensing, technology transfer and engineering contracts. For several years he was a member of the Institution of Chemical Engineers Working Group on Contract for Process Plant and has lectured on IP issues, licensing and technology transfer, engineering contracts and Industry/University cooperation at various fora. He is the author of the book *Licensing Technology and Patents* published by the I.Chem.E. in 1991. He is presently Manager of the ICI Explosives Group Technical Centre in Scotland and is the IP Coordinator and Technology Licensing Manager for the global ICI explosives business.

Robert Salle is Professor, Groupe ESC Lyon, and Research Director, IRE, Institut de Recherche de l'Entreprise in Lyon. He is currently the Head of the Scientific Development team of IRE. He has been researching in the field of industrial marketing for over 15 years (member of the IMP Group since 1979) and is currently focusing on the themes of capital-project marketing, key-account management and the management of supplier-customer relationships.

Yoshihiro Sano is currently the President of Pacific Alliance Group, a consulting firm specializing in cross-border mergers and acquisitions, joint ventures, and investment opportunities in the United States and Japan. He is formerly a principal in charge of International Business Services of Ernst & Young and has done extensive consulting work on strategic planning feasibility and mergers and acquisitions.

Camille P. Schuster (Ph.D. in Communication from the Ohio State University) is a Professor of Marketing at Xavier University. Dr Schuster was the Director of the Roanoke Office of the Virginia Center for World Trade, she founded and was the first Director of the Center for International Business at Xavier University, and is a member of the Southern Ohio District Export Council. In addition to consulting for companies, Dr Schuster has published research in the areas of international marketing in the *Journal of Global Marketing, Journal of Public Policy and Marketing and Industrial Marketing Management.*

Rosalie L. Tung holds a Chair in International Business at Simon Fraser University, Canada. She is an authority on international management and the author of eight books and over fifty publications on international human resource management, comparative manageent, and international business negotiations. She is involved in management development and consulting around the world.

Sabine Urban is a Professor at Strasbourg University (Robert Schuman) and heads the CESAG (Centre of Managerial Research)/IECS Strasbourg which is affiliated to it. She teaches international economics and corporate strategies in several universities both in France and abroad, and is in charge of the International Commerce degree at the IECS Strasbourg. She sits on the board of several industrial and financial firms. Her main research fields are international business and the European economy; she is author and co-author of numerous publications in these fields.

Jean-Claude Usunier is Professor of Marketing and International Business at Université Louis-Pasteur (Strasbourg, France). His research deals mostly with cross-cultural comparisons and the study of intercultural encounters in international marketing, with special emphasis on the behavioral skills to be developed by the international marketer. He has published several books and over thirty articles in journals.

Stephen E. Weiss, a negotiation specialist, is Associate Professor of Policy and International Business, and Director of the International MBA Program at the Schulich School of Business, York University, in Toronto,.Canada. He has also held faculty positions at the University of Pennsylvania, New York University's Stern School of Business, and Dartmouth College's Tuck School of Business. In addition to his academic responsibilities, Weiss has lectured and conducted programs on negotiation for business, government, and education groups in Asia, Western Europe, and Latin America as well as North America.

Part I

CHAPTER 1

Introduction

PERVEZ GHAURI

The Nature of Business Negotiation

Negotiation is a basic human activity. It is a process we undertake in everyday activities to manage our relationships, such as between a husband and wife, children and parents, employers and employees, buyers and sellers and business associates. In some of these negotiations, the stakes are not that high and we do not have to pre-plan the process and the outcome, but in some cases, such as business relationships, the stakes are high and we have to prepare, plan and negotiate more carefully. This volume deals, in particular with the latter type of negotiation. In business relationships, parties negotiate because they think they can influence the process in such a way that they can get a better deal than simply accepting or rejecting what the other party is offering. Business negotiation is a voluntary process and parties can, at any time, quit the process. Negotiation is, thus, a voluntary process of give and take where both parties modify their offers and expectations in order to come closer to each other.

In literature, sometimes "bargaining" and "negotiation" are used interchangeably. But in our opinion, they mean different things. *Bargaining* is more like haggling in a typical "bazaar" setting, or in so-called competitive bargaining or distributive bargaining. Here, the objective of the parties is to maximize their own benefit, quite often at the expense of the other party. It refers to a typical win–lose negotiation, where the resources are limited or fixed, and everybody wants to maximize his share of the resources. Parties are therefore more competitive and opportunistic. They normally do not like to share information with the other party unless they have to, and they want to get the maximum information on and from the other party. Although this view on negotiation is out-dated, it is still practiced and studied in some situations such as labor management negotiations (Walton & McKersie 1965).

On the other hand *negotiation*, also called "integrative bargaining", refers to win–win negotiation where both or all parties involved can end up with equally beneficial or attractive outcomes. In other words, everyone can win. It is more related to a problem-solving approach, where both parties involved perceive the

Pervez Ghauri

process of negotiation as a process to find a solution to a common problem. In integrative bargaining however, if negotiations are not properly handled, both parties can end up with a jointly inferior deal. With negotiation, it is possible for both parties to achieve their objectives and one party's gain is not dependent upon the other party's concession. Business negotiation is considered by many authors as being this type of negotiation (Fisher & Ury 1991, Pruitt 1983, Ghauri 1983, Ghauri 1986 and Lewicki *et al.* 1994).

Some characteristics of this type of negotiation are:

- Open information flow between the parties. In this case, both sides sincerely disclose their objectives and listen to the other party's objectives in order to find a match between the two.
- A search for a solution that meets the objectives of both parties.
- Parties understand that they do have common as well as conflicting objectives and that they have to find a way to achieve, as much as possible, common and complementary objectives that are acceptable to both sides.
- To achieve the above, both parties sincerely and truly try to understand each other's point of view.

The above characteristics are, in fact, opposite to distributive bargaining. That means that the process of negotiation in a problem-solving situation is completely different from a process of distributive bargaining. In the problem-solving negotiation, parties have to look for a solution which is beneficial and acceptable to both sides: a win–win solution. In fact, they look for a jointly optimal outcome, which cannot be achieved unless the parties have this problem-solving approach.

In international business settings, the development of the negotiation process and how parties perceive the relationship are crucial. This process is influenced by some facts and factors beyond the negotiation process in question. The cultural differences that exist on several levels form one of the most important factors: on a national level, cultural differences at the level of different countries; on an organizational level, different type of organizations, depending upon their home country and industry, have different cultures; and on an individual level, individuals involved in the process of negotiation have different cultural backgrounds not only due to different countries and organizations but also due to their professional backgrounds, such as engineers vs. marketing people. Cultural differences create a challenge to the negotiators involved, and demand understanding as well as flexibility. An ability to assess these differences and properly handle the consequences is essential for success in international business negotiations. This process is also of a dynamic nature and can move in a positive as well as a negative direction at any time, for example, after or during each session. This dynamism is characterized as "atmosphere" in our world. The atmosphere not only explains the perceptions of the parties but also the progress of the process. The more the parties understand and adapt to each other, the more positive the atmosphere around the process, and the more parties are willing to compromise and see common benefits.

4

A Framework for International Business Negotiation

An overall framework for business negotiation has three groups of variables: background factors, the process and the atmosphere. Since the negotiation process is inherently dynamic, a certain perception of the parties or a particular development in the process may influence a change in the background factors.

Background factors

This group of variables serves as a background to the process. It influences the process of negotiation and the atmosphere. The effect of different variables on the process and its different stages varies in intensity. One of these variables may influence one stage positively and another negatively. A positive influence means that the process saves time and continues smoothly, while a negative influence causes delay and hindrances. Background factors include objectives, environment, market position, third parties and negotiators.

Objectives are defined as the end stage each party desires to achieve. They are often classified as common, conflicting or complementary. For example, parties have a common interest in as much as both want a successful transaction to take place. At the same time, their interests may conflict, since profit to one is cost to the other. In terms of complementary interest, buyers in international deals are concerned with acquiring the appropriate technology to build an infrastructure. On the other hand, sellers want to enter a particular market and expect to do future business with it and with the surrounding countries' markets. Common and complementary objectives affect the negotiation process directly and positively, whereas conflicting objectives have negative effects. These effects, in turn, influence the atmosphere and the outcome. Opportunity for an agreement decreases as conflicting objectives dominate a relationship; it increases as common and complementary objectives dominate.

The *environment* refers to the political, social and structural factors relevant to both parties. Variation of the parties with respect to environment, in international negotiation, often hinders the process. There are greater chances of interaction interferences when unfamiliar parties, having different backgrounds, interact with one another. Some of the characteristics directly influence the process while others directly influence the atmosphere. Political and social aspects influence the process, and market structure influences the atmosphere. The parties' *market position* is an important factor influencing the negotiation process. The number of buyers and sellers in the market determines the number of alternatives available to each party, which, in turn, affects the amount of pressure imposed by its counterpart within the market. The process and bargaining position of the buyer or seller can be affected if either one has monopolistic power in the market place.

Most international business negotiations involve *third parties*, i.e., parties other than the buyer and seller, such as governments, agents, consultants and subcontractors. These parties may influence the negotiation process as they have different objectives. Often, governments are involved and influence the buyers towards complementary objectives, such as infrastructure, employment opportunities, foreign exchange considerations and any other prospective relationship between the countries involved.

Negotiators influence the negotiation process with their own experience and negotiating skills. Negotiators operate within two limits: firstly, they act to increase common interests and to expand cooperation among the parties; secondly, they act to maximize their own interests and to ensure an agreement valuable to themselves. The personality of the negotiators also plays a role, particularly when information about the other party is lacking and there is greater stress. A good personality is defined as an individual with the ability to make others understand his position, to approach strangers with ease and confidence and to appreciate the other person's position. However, the skills of negotiators are related to different objectives and motivations, pertaining to different people and professions. Negotiators with a technical background may place more emphasis on technical issues, while those with a business background might consider other issues to be more important.

Atmosphere

The relationship developed during the negotiation process between the parties is characterized by an atmosphere which is of fundamental importance to the process as a whole. The atmosphere and the process affect each other through interaction at each stage. Atmosphere is defined as the perceived "milieu" around the interaction, how the parties regard each other's behavior, and the properties of the process. It has to do with people's perception of reality. In other words, in negotiation it is the perception of reality which is more important than the reality itself. Some characteristics of the atmosphere are dominant at one stage; others at another stage. The pre-negotiation stage is dominated by cooperation rather than conflict, as parties look for mutual solutions. Different characteristics of the atmosphere dominate from process to process. These characteristics are conflict/cooperation, power/dependence and expectations.

The existence of both *conflict and cooperation* is a fundamental characteristic of the negotiation process. On one hand, parties have some common interests in finding a solution to the problem which fits both the parties. On the other hand, a conflict of interest may arise, as cost to one of them can mean income to the other. The magnitude of conflict or cooperation in the atmosphere depends upon the objectives of the negotiating parties. Some relationships are more complementary — and consequently less conflicting — than others. The degree of conflict or cooperation during different stages of the negotiation process is often a function of the issues being dealt with, while the degree of conflict or cooperation in the atmosphere is a function of how the parties handle various problems. Conflict is sometimes perceived, without the existence of real conflict, due to a misunderstanding of each other's behavior. The more unfamiliar the parties are with one another, the higher the risk of such perceived conflicts. Each process and even each stage of the process can be characterized somewhere on a scale with cooperation and conflict on opposite sides.

The *power/dependence* relation is another basic characteristic of all negotiation processes. It is closely related to the actual power relation, which is influenced by the value of the relationship to the parties and their available alternatives. Background factors — for example the market position — can influence the power/dependence relation. The ability to control a relationship is related to the perceived power of two parties, their relative expertise and access to information. This power is a property of the relationship and not an attribute of the actor; in fact, it is closely related to dependence. Therefore, the power relationship is in balance if both parties perceive equal power. The power relationship is unbalanced if one of the parties perceives more power, or if one party is dependent on the other.

The last aspect of atmosphere concerns two types of *expectations*. Firstly, there are long-term expectations regarding the possibilities and values of future business. The stronger these expectations are, the more inclined the negotiators are to agree on the present deal. Long-term expectations are related to primary objectives. Secondly, there are short-term expectations concerning prospects for the present deal. The parties' decision to enter negotiations and to continue after each stage implies expectations of a better outcome from participating than from not participating. This compels the parties to proceed from one stage to the next. Expectations develop and change in different stages of the process.

The negotiation process

The process of international business negotiation presented here is divided into three different stages. A stage of the process refers to a specific part of the process and includes all actions and communications by any party pertaining to negotiations made during that part. Parties communicate with each other to exchange information within each stage. A particular stage ends where parties decide to proceed further on to the next stage or decide to abandon the communication if they see no point in further negotiations. In the pre-negotiation stage, parties attempt to understand each other's needs and demands, which is done through information gathering and informal meetings. The negotiation stage refers to face-to-face negotiations and the post-negotiation stage refers to the stage when parties have agreed to most of the issues and are to agree on contract language and format and signing the contract.

In international business negotiations, the process has three dimensions. In addition to the three stages, it has a cultural dimension and a strategic dimension. These two dimensions are present in each of the three stages of the process. However, these can play different roles in different stages. This is illustrated by Figure 1.1.

FIGURE 1.1
The process of International Business Negotiations

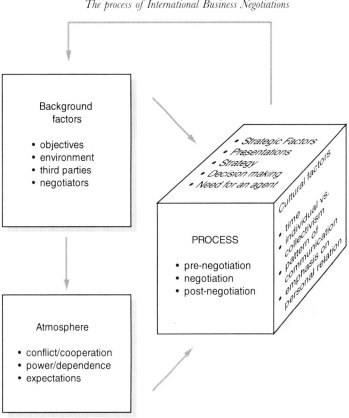

Source: Based on Ghauri (1986) and Cavusgil and Ghauri (1990)

Stage 1: Pre-negotiation

The pre-negotiation stage begins with the first contact between parties in which an interest in doing business with each other is shown. During this stage, some negotiations take place and tentative offers are made. The dynamism of the process can be observed at this early stage where parties begin to understand one another's needs and evaluate the benefits of entering into the process of negotiation.

The parties gather as much relevant information as possible on each other, the operating environment, the involvement of other third parties, influencers, competitors and the infrastructure. Parties need to be aware that their relative power relationship can be altered at any time by such events as the repositioning of competitors or movements in exchange rates. As we have defined this negotiation process as being of a problem-solving nature, the main issue here is to define the problem to be solved. It is important to define the problem jointly, as it will not only reflect each other's expectations but is also necessary to acquire commitment from both parties. The parties should, therefore, truly and openly discuss each other's objectives and expectations in order to achieve a positive problem-solving situation.

Informal meetings take place as the parties examine each other's position. Whether the parties continue to the next stage of the negotiation process depends on the perceived level of cooperation or conflict, of power or dependence and the expected benefits of the relationship. The process often ends in failure if excessive conflict is sensed or if a successful future relationship seems doubtful. The parties should truly see how they are going to cooperate, examine whether it is realistic to expect to achieve the objectives of both sides and to identify the obstacles that have to be overcome to achieve these objectives.

The pre-negotiation stage is often more important than the formal negotiations in an international business relationship. Social, informal relationships developed between negotiators at this stage can be of great help. Trust and confidence gained from these relationships increase the chances of agreement. One method of establishing such contacts is to invite individuals from the other side to visit your office/country in an attempt to develop trust. The prime objective here is to get to each other's priorities. The parties need to understand the interests and fears of the other party.

Parties also begin to formulate their strategy for face-to-face negotiation. By strategy we mean a complete plan regarding problems, the solutions available and preferred choices, relative to the other party's choices and preferences. Parties try to build up their relative power. They compare the alternatives available, make check lists and assign arguments for and against these alternatives. They also decide on possible points of concession and their extent.

Parties try to foresee and take precautions against predictable events. Remittance of funds, taxes and import duties and work permits are just some examples of the rules and regulations of the particular country that must be researched at this stage. An understanding of the infrastructure of the country and the company is also critical at this point. In some countries, especially when the public sector is the buyer, purchasing organizations issue a "letter of award" (also called letter of intent/acceptance) after the first stage. The negotiators from Western countries often perceive this letter of award as a grant of contract. However, this is an incorrect assumption, the letter merely indicates the other party's intention to negotiate further (Ghauri 1986 and Lewicki, R.J. *et al.* 1994).

Parties to international business negotiations should have an initial strategy, which is dependent on the information attained so far and the expectations. The negotiators should list the problems and issues, especially the conflicting issues and form strategies and choices for all possible solutions they or the other party could suggest. These solutions should be ranked in terms such as preferred, desired, expected and not acceptable. If not acceptable, a solution that could be acceptable to the other party should be suggested. It is, thus, important to have several solutions for each problem or issue (Mintzberg, H. 1991 and Cavusgil & Ghauri 1990).

Stage II: Face-to-face negotiation

The basic issue at this stage is that parties believe that they can work together to find a solution to a joint problem. The parties should also be aware that each side views the situation, the matter under discussion, in its own way. Not only that it has a different perception of the process but it has different expectations for the outcome. It is therefore, important to start face-to-face negotiation with an open mind and to have several alternatives. At this stage, as the process continues, the parties should evaluate the alternatives presented by the other party and select those that are compatible with their own expectations. The best way is to determine criteria for judging the alternatives and then rank order each alternative, one's own as well as those presented by the other party, against these criteria. Here the parties can even help each other in evaluating these alternatives and can discuss the criteria for judgement. The main issue is to explore the differences in preferences and expectations and to come closer to each other.

Experience shows that the negotiation process is controlled by the partner who arranges the agenda, since he can emphasize his own strengths and the other party's weaknesses, thus putting the other party on the defensive. However, the agenda may reveal the preparing party's position in advance and hence permit the other side to prepare its own counter-arguments on conflicting issues. Some negotiators prefer to start negotiations by discussing and agreeing on broad principles for the relationship. Another way to ensure success at this stage is to negotiate the contract step by step — discussing both conflicting issues and those of common interest. In particular, an initial discussion on items of common interest can create an atmosphere of cooperation between parties. The choice of strategy depends upon the customer or supplier with whom one is negotiating. It is helpful to anticipate the other party's strategy as early as possible and then to choose a strategy to match or complement it.

It is often suggested that the negotiator should not agree to a settlement at once, even if there is considerable overlap of his position with that of the other party. The negotiator may obtain further concessions by prolonging the negotiation process. A number of studies have revealed that negotiators who directly submit a "final offer" can be at a disadvantage. In view of the diverse cultural and business traditions prevailing in different countries, international negotiations inherently involve a discussion of differences. It is very difficult for parties to comprehend or adjust to each other's culture or traditions, but it is important to be aware of these differences. Social contacts developed between parties are far more significant than the technical and economic specifications in many emerging markets. Negotiators from these countries take their time and are very careful not to offend or use strong words; and the other party is expected to follow suit.

A balance between firmness and credibility is important in all types of negotiation. It is important to give and take signals of readiness to move from the initial stage without making concessions. Negotiators having prior dealings with each other can easily send and receive signals, but it is very difficult for those meeting for the first time. Negotiators often send conditional signals such as "We cannot accept your offer as it stands" or "We appreciate that your equipment is quite suitable for us but not at the price you mentioned".

It is also common that the party perceiving greater relative power makes fewer concessions and that the weaker party yields more, often to create a better atmosphere. Maintaining flexibility between parties and issues is of great importance in this stage. These usually occur after both parties have tested the level of commitment and have sent and received signals to move on. For example, the price can be reduced if the party offers better terms of payment. Other elements can be traded off but there may not be a way to evaluate them in accounting terms. For example, an entry into a huge protected market may be strategically more important than obtaining handsome profits on the present deal.

Stage III: Post-negotiation

At this stage, all the terms have been agreed upon. The contract is being drawn up and is ready to be signed. Experience has shown that writing the contract and the language used can be a negotiation process in itself, as meaning and values may differ between the two parties. In several cases involving Western firms and emerging-country parties, the language used and the recording of issues previously agreed upon took considerable time. This stage can lead to renewed face-to-face negotiation if there is negative feedback from background factors and atmosphere. Discussion should be summarized after neegotiationsto avoid unnecessary delays in the process. The terms agreed·upon should be read by both parties after concessions are exchanged and discussions held, by keeping minutes of meetings, for example. This will help test the understanding of the contract, as parties may have perceived issues or discussions differently. This not only applies to writing and signing the contract but also to its implementation. Trouble may arise later during the implementation of the contract if parties are too eager to reach an agreement and don't pay enough attention to details. The best way to solve this problem is to confirm that both sides thoroughly understand what they have agreed upon before leaving the negotiating table. A skilled negotiator will summarize and test understanding: "Do we understand correctly that if we agree to your terms of payment and repay the credit within three years from the date of the contract, you will reduce the price by 7 per cent?"

Cultural factors

As is apparent from the above discussion, cultural factors play an important role in international business negotiations. We have chosen to use the following factors that are most important in this respect:

Time

Time has different meaning and importance in different cultures. While "time is money" in the Western culture, it has no such value attached to it in many cultures in Asia, Latin America and Africa. This influences the pace of negotiations and the punctuality in meetings. For negotiators, it is important to have advance information on the opposite party's behavior regarding time. This will help them to plan their time as well as to have patience and not to get irritated during the process.

Individual vs. collective behavior

These are rather clear behavioral aspects in different cultures. As indicated by Hofstede's study of 69 countries, we can place different countries on different scales. Even countries in Western Europe have clear differences in this respect (Hofstede. G. 1980). In cases of negotiation, it is important to have knowledge of this cultural attribute, as it will help us to understand the behavior of the other party and to formulate an effective strategy. Knowing whether the opposite party is looking for a collective solution or an individual benefit will help in formulation of arguments and presentations.

Pattern of communication

Different cultures have different communication patterns as regards direct vs. indirect and explicit vs. implicit communication. These are related to culture as well as the contextual background of languages (Hall 1960). Some languages are traditionally vague and people from outside find it difficult to communicate with people with such language backgrounds. Indicators such as "maybe", "perhaps", "rather", "I'll consider it" and "inconvenient" are some examples of ambiguity in international communication and conversation. "Maybe" and "inconvenient" can mean impossible in some cultures. In some cultures even "yes" means "may be" and "perhaps" means "no". Some languages, for example some Arabic and some Asian languages, traditionally contain exaggerations, fantastic metaphors and repetition, which can be misleading for foreigners. It is, therefore, important to be aware of these aspects and read between the lines. This is even more important in non-verbal communication, the personal space, handshakes, ways of greeting each other, communication between males and females, signs of irritation, etc., are important aspects of communication patterns, and knowledge of these can improve the negotiation process and effectiveness.

Emphasis on personal relations

Different cultures give different importance to personal relations in negotiations. In many countries in the West, the negotiators are more concerned with the issue at hand and the future relationship between the organizations, irrespective of who is representing these firms, while in some cultures, the personality of the negotiator is more important than the organization he is representing or the importance of an issue. So the emphasis on personal relations can be different in different negotiations.

Strategic factors

While negotiating in an international setting, the parties have to prepare thoroughly with respect to how to present things, which type of strategy should be used and which type of decision-making process is followed by the other party. Whether or not they need an agent or an outside consultant is also a question of strategy.

Presentations

Negotiators have to know whether the presentations to be made are carried out in a formal or informal setting. Whether these are to be made to teams, as in China and Eastern Europe, or to individuals, as in India and the Middle East. The formal vs. informal presentation style is very distinct in many countries. If not prepared, the negotiators can make serious blunders at an early stage of negotiations. It is also important to know whether issues can be presented in groups or whether each issue should be handled individually, and whether presentations should be argumentative or informative, factual and to the point.

Strategy

There are several types of strategies in business negotiations. The most important are tough, soft or intermediate strategies. In tough strategy, a party starts with a very high initial offer and remains firm on its offer and expects the other party to make the first concession. In soft strategy, a party does not start with a very high initial offer and makes the first concession in the hope that the other party will reciprocate. In intermediate strategy, a party does not start with a very high initial offer and as soon as an offer is made which is within its realistic expectations, it accepts it. It is important to have information on the opposite party's strategy and to adapt one's own strategy to it and to have a counter-offer ready.

Decision-making

Some information on the other party's overall decision-making pattern is necessary before going into negotiations. Does the party use impulsive or rational decision-making? Who makes the decisions? Do the negotiators coming to the table have the power to make final decisions or not? These are issues which are important to know in advance. In many cultures in Asia, decision-making is highly influenced by the importance of face-saving and influences the timing of decisions made.

Need for an agent

It is part of strategy-formulation to realize whether or not the firm or negotiators can handle the particular negotiation on their own. What type of cost and benefits can be achieved by employing an agent for a particular negotiation process? In our opinion, the more unfamiliar or complicated the other party or the market is, the greater need for an agent or a consultant. These days, specialized agents and consultants are available for different geographic as well as technological areas. There are enormous efficiencies to be achieved by using their expertise.

Planning and managing negotiations

> Dozens of books have been written about negotiation, many of which I disagree with. I don't believe in negotiating through intimidation, fear, bluffing or dishonest tactics. A good negotiation concludes as a good deal for every one; negotiation starts with what you want to accomplish. Then the realities and, sometimes, the complexities enter the picture. Sometimes many points of view and many elements have to be considered, but the deal itself must always be kept in view. Your first step should be to rid yourself of an adversarial position. The reality is that you have a mutual problem, which you are going to solve to your mutual advantage. The intention must be to structure a deal that resolves the problem and gives each of you what you want. It's not always possible, of course. When it can't be done, you are better off making no deal than making a bad deal. A bad deal usually brings a future filled with enormous problems. Negotiating demands a recognition of reality on many levels. Only amateurs try to accomplish something that isn't real or possible; it is an attempt that inevitably leads to failure. Amateurs tend to dream; professionals consider the realities of a deal (Nadel 1987).

In the past, the ability to negotiate was considered innate or instinctive but it is now regarded as a technique which can be learned. Experimental studies, empirical observations and experience have made it possible to grasp the art of negotiation. This section provides some guidelines for planning and managing the negotiation process in three stages.

The pre-negotiation stage

The most important success factor in negotiation is preparation and planning. One may have excellent negotiating skills, persuasive and convincing communication style, a strong market position and relative power but all these cannot overcome the shortcomings caused by poor preparation. As mentioned in the previous section, the presence of cooperation as well as conflict and the relative power/dependence in international business negotiation demands careful preparation and planning. In the problem-solving approach, this becomes even more important as both parties do truly want to do business with each other. In spite of this cooperative behavior, negotiation involves trade-off between own and joint interests. A number of authors have stressed the importance of preparation and planning for negotiation, see, e.g., Kuhn (1988), Sperber (1983), Scott (1981) and Ghauri (1986).

Identify the contents of the deal

The initial points to consider are issues such as implications of the deal, the interests at stake, the "fit" with organizational objectives, and possible economic, political or other restrictions between parties. What will each gain or lose and how important is the deal for them? What alternatives does either side have? These issues must be considered in terms of tangible and intangible motives.

Comparison of one's own and the other party's strengths and weaknesses is quite important. In business negotiations, the other party does not only include the buyer or the party you are negotiating with, but also the competitors who also have an interest in the same business. In most cases, a party's arguments or preferences are influenced by the offers other competitors have made. Many negotiators use professional investigators for this task of getting information on the other parties and to find their weaknesses. According to one estimate, in the United States, $800 million is annually spent on industrial spying (Harrison and Saffer 1980). In our opinion, the information required to prepare and plan for negotiation need not include such rather unethical methods. It is quite easy to get a lot of information from the annual accounts of the firms and through talking to their executives, customers and suppliers.

In international business relations, buy-back arrangements are becoming more common, and in large international deals with emerging markets, buyers are demanding some sort of a buy-back. For more details on this issue, see, e.g., Rowe (1989). Emerging countries engage in countertrade deals to correct their trade deficits as well as to earn hard currency. It is important to calculate deals in monetary terms when conducting trade in this medium. The seller might end up with goods which cannot be easily marketed in the home country. The countertrade demand can be just a bluff, so that the seller who seeks to avoid the expenses of buy-back may offer a major price discount. The plant's output supplied under the particular contract is part of the payment in some cases. China uses its cheap labor and re-exports products from local plants to the seller's country. Another example is the iron-producing Carajas project in northern Brazil. Most of the production of this complex is exported to Japan to pay for project financing.

Create alternatives

To negotiate effectively, the marketer must gather information on the strengths and weaknesses not only of the opposite party, but also of the other related parties such as competitors. By considering the resources and behavior of competitors, marketers can develop their own alternatives on different issues. There are several strategies by which the seller can pre-empt competitors, for example, offering credit to the buyer, price reductions or long guarantee periods. Sellers must also allow for alternative solutions to conflicting issues. Question one's own position: "What if they do not accept this . . .?"

Quite often Western negotiators believe they have only three options: (i) persuasion; (ii) threat; or (iii) concession. In fact, there are many alternative solutions to a problem. Different issues can be combined to produce numerous alternatives. If the customer demands a 5 per cent concession on the price, the other party can ask the customer to pay cash instead of the one-year credit proposed. In one case, the buyer demanded a 5 per cent concession on the contract price after everything else had been agreed upon. The seller instead proposed that he was willing to give a 10 per cent rebate on all the spare parts to be bought by the buyer during the next three years. This offer was accepted gladly by the buyer. One way of creating alternatives is to judge each conflicting issue in the following scale: our ideal position–their ideal position. Here we should look for overlaps, is there any overlap of our and their position? If not, how can we create an overlap? What can be their minimum acceptable position? What is our minimum acceptable position? Can we move from there, perhaps give up on this issue and gain in another one which is not so sensitive to the other party, but equally important to us?

Put yourself in their shoes

For negotiations to be succesful, one party must understand the other party's position. This will help each side interpret and anticipate the other side's reactions to arguments. Anticipating and developing rational reactions to arguments allows each party to formulate new arguments and alternatives. This stimulates flexibility on different conflicting issues. Each party has to recognize the needs of the other, quite apart from gathering information and asking questions to check the other party's position. Being a patient listener will help improve negotiations. One can understand the meaning behind the words by listening attentively. One can create a positive and cooperative atmosphere in the negotiation process by showing the other party that he or she is well understood. However, be careful while listening — it is not what is said, but how it is said that is more important and one should read between the lines.

The harder a party tries to show understanding of the opposing viewpoint, the more open it will be to alternative solutions. A universal feeling exists that those who understand are intelligent and sympathetic. Parties feel obliged to reciprocate in these situations. The ability to look at the situation from the other's point of view is one of the most important skills in negotiations. It is important not only to see as the other party sees, but also to understand the other party's point of view and the power of its arguments.

Gauge the appropriateness of the message

The information exchanged must be adjusted for easier comprehension by the other party. Technical specifications and other material should be provided in the local language. Not only does this facilitate effective communication but it also demonstrates respect for the local language and environment.

The problems of perception and language barriers often cause difficulties in the negotiation process. This is frustrating and places an added burden on all parties involved in the negotiating process. Different cultures interpret messages differently. An octopus is said to have several arms in the United States. It is said to have several legs in Japan. In Sweden, "next Sunday" does not mean the coming Sunday but the Sunday after. In India "next Sunday" means the coming Sunday. "Nice weather" means sunshine in Europe. "Nice weather" means cloudy or rainy weather in Africa and many Asian countries. The exchange of gifts and terms of reciprocity are quite normal in Asia, yet considered close to a bribe in many Western countries. It is important that negotiators adopt appropriate behavior for each negotiation. The chosen arguments should be tailored to the particular customer. One standard argument cannot be used throughout the world. Barriers to communication also arise from real or perceived differences in expectations, which create conflict instead of cooperation between parties.

In cross-cultural negotiations, non-verbal communication, in particular in the expression of emotions and the attitude of a negotiator toward the other party, is sometimes more important than the spoken language. Non-verbal communication can be telling. Liking and disliking, tensions and appraisal of an argument are shown by numerous signs such as blushing, contraction of facial muscles, giggling, strained laughter or just silence. People, sitting down, lean forward when they like what you are saying or are interested in listening, or they sit back on their seat with crossed arms if they do not like the message. Nervousness can manifest itself through non-verbal behavior, and blinking can be related to feelings of guilt and fear. It is difficult to evaluate non-verbal communication, as it is connected to the subconscious and emotions. Effective communication and understanding of people will assist you in adjusting your arguments to the moods and expectations of the other party. Negotiators may continue to hold out, not because the proposal from the other side is unacceptable, but because they want to avoid feelings of surrender. Sometimes simple rephrasing of the proposal or a different approach to the presentation can alleviate the problem (Fisher and Ury 1991).

Build up relative power

Negotiators can determine who has the relative power advantage by gathering information about the other party, considering each party's position and developing different alternatives. They can try to build their own relative power by developing arguments against the elements of power and improving their own position. In the negotiation process, this kind of power may be increased by repeatedly mentioning the weak points of the other party. The uncertainty regarding infrastructure and exchange rates must be handled here. Parties can agree on adjustments in the event of exchange rate variations. The party with greater information automatically acquires more power. The negotiator may have to work as a detective to ascertain the buyer's needs, his strong and weak points, and the strong and weak points of competitors. By being active in the negotiation process an experienced negotiator can build up information in order to gain relative power. This can be done by asking the other party questions. It can also be done by giving conditional answers such as "*If* you agree to pay cash ... *then* we can consider looking at our price", or "*What if* we agree to pay cash *perhaps then* you can lower the price by 5 per cent".

The face-to-face negotiation stage

Who within the firm should negotiate?

A difficult question arises regarding who should conduct negotiations whenever a deal is to be made in a new market. Who is the most appropriate person to hammer out a particular deal? In fact, persons involved in international business negotiation can do more harm than good if they lack an integrated knowledge of their own firm and the objective of the deal. Whoever is selected for negotiations must have a good grasp of the deal's implications. This is especially true when long-term relationships are being discussed. One way to minimize this risk is to appoint a negotiation team, where the key members are selected from different departments.

Expendable person

It is important for management to realize that the selected person(s) should be expendable without creating organizational problems. When replacement is necessary, management must be able to escape deadlock. Sometimes negotiations end in an impasse and you may have to start with new players. It is also possible that the selected negotiators and the other party cannot reach a meeting of minds if there is a clash of personal chemistry. It may become necessary to change negotiators in such situations. This discussion gives rise to another question. From which level should the executives for the negotiations be chosen? In most countries, parties expect to negotiate with members of equal status. The managing director from one side expects to negotiate with his counterpart. It is advisable that firms match like with like.

Individuals vs. teams

Parties need to consider not only who should represent the company but also the number of negotiators, i.e., whether one goes for individual or team negotiations. Team negotiation affords marketers the opportunity to benefit from the advice and guidance of many participants. It is difficult for a single individual to be adept in all kinds of commercial, technical and legal issues. The best way however, is to conform to the opposite party. If the opposite side is coming with a team, we should also send a team.

What makes a good negotiator?

A number of studies identify characteristics of a good negotiator. Ikle defined a good negotiator as one having a "quick mind but unlimited patience, know how to dissemble without being a liar, inspire trust without trusting others, be modest but assertive, charm others without succumbing to their charm, and possess plenty of money and a beautiful wife while remaining indifferent to all temptations of riches and women" (Ikle 1964). A marketer's personality and social behavior are of equal importance to social contacts and formal negotiation in many emerging countries.

Depending upon their behavior, negotiators are often grouped into different categories, such as bullies, avoiders or acceptors. Bullies want to threaten, push, demand or attack. Avoiders like to avoid conflicting situations and hide in fear of making a wrong decision or being held responsible. They will normally refer to their superiors for a final decision, "I have to call my head office . . . ". Acceptors always give a very positive answer and say "Yes" to almost anything, which makes it difficult to realize which "Yes" is "Yes" and which "Yes" is "Maybe", and whether they will be able to deliver what they are promising or not. The best way to handle these behavior types is to first identify them and then confront them by drawing a limit, helping them feel safe and by asking them how and when they would be able to do what they are promising.

Patience

It is essential to know the negotiators' precise authority. In Eastern Europe and China, one team may negotiate one day, followed by a fresh team the next day. When this process is repeated a number of times, it becomes very difficult for negotiators to establish who is the negotiating party and who has the final authority. One of the characteristics of a good negotiator is the ability to discover the timetable of the other party and allow plenty of time for the negotiation process. It is usually not feasible to expect to fly to a distant country, wrap things up and be home again in a week. Nor is it reasonable to coerce a party that is not ready to reach a decision. Negotiations with emerging market customers take a long time! Patience and time are the greatest assets a negotiator can have while

19

negotiating with customers from these markets. Some negotiators take their time, discussing all issues and justifying their role through tough negotiations.

Negotiators must be in a position to change their strategies and arguments, as the process of negotiation is highly dynamic. They must be flexible. The other party will often ask questions, probing the seller's weaknesses, just to provoke and obtain more concessions. It is important to keep calm and find out first if the questions asked are relevant and justified. Negotiators can use this in their favor if questions are not justified and the buyer has wrong information. A good negotiator is not just a person who can conclude an apparently good contract for the company or one who can arrive at a contract in a short time. A good negotiator is one whose agreements lead to successful implementation.

The post-negotiation stage

What is a good outcome?

A good agreement is one which leads to successful implementation. There are many examples of firms getting into trouble because they could not implement the contract conditions of a particular deal. Therefore, in some cases, no agreement may be a better outcome for the firm. A good outcome benefits both parties and does not make either party feel that it has a less advantageous contract. Sometimes negotiators want to avoid specifying some issues and want to keep them ambiguous. It is important to understand that on the one hand, ambiguity can lead to reopening of the conflict later on, in the implementation stage, and on the other hand, if we want to specify such issues, it might prolong the negotiation process or prevent an agreement. Sometimes, this ambiguity is unintended, whereas, on other occasions, it is intentionally deployed to speed up the process or to give the impression that the particular issue needs to be re-negotiated (Ikle 1964).

It is normally considered that a good business deal is one which provides financial gains. But what were the objectives of the firm when it decided to enter into negotiations? Was it the present deal which was most important or was it future business? The outcome must be related to the firm's objectives. If the objectives have been met then it is a good outcome. A successful negotiation is not a question of "win–lose" but a problem-solving approach to a "win–win" outcome.

The main purpose of the contract is to avoid misunderstandings and trouble in the future. The agreement should foster relationship development and be flexible enough to deal with expected or unexpected future changes. The language and terminology used in the contract must be simple and clear. It must not be necessary to seek legal help every time the contract is consulted.

CHAPTER 2

How National Culture, Organizational Culture and Personality Impact Buyer-Seller Interactions

SUDHIR KALÉ

Introduction

The decade of the 1990s has witnessed more than its share of profound geopolitical changes. Ubiquitous loosening of trade barriers combined with the unprecedented zeal towards modernization exhibited by the developing countries has resulted in a global environment where nationalistic influences are dwindling in impact. Until recently, most international business phenomena could be largely explained on the basis of national culture, a dominant sculptor of consumer behavior and business practices. The universal weakening of nationalistic fervour and concomitant emergence of strong corporate and individual identities has necessitated that organizational culture and individual personality now be added to national culture to form the fundamental trinity of behavioral influences affecting international business interactions. This combination of national culture, organizational culture and individual personality is particularly relevant in appreciating cross-national sales interactions.

With the accelerated integration of world markets, the cosmopolitan salesperson has become a commonplace reality. However, scholarly work in the area of buyer–seller interactions has not incorporated this new reality in explaining the conduct and outcome of face-to-face selling. Most books on personal selling and sales management do not discuss the international context and many of the international marketing texts pay only scant attention to cross-national selling issues. As such, the art and science of cross-national selling remain under-researched and therefore difficult to fathom. Recent developments in market integration, particularly regarding the European Union, necessitate that the domain of cross-national selling be better comprehended. A crucial first step in this direction is to appreciate the factors that shape the behavior of actors in a dyadic cross-national selling encounter. This involves understanding how national culture, organizational culture, and individual personality combine to impact the personal selling transaction.

This chapter has three broad objectives: to explain the impact of national culture, organizational culture, and individual personality on dyadic sales encounters; to suggest an appropriate typology with which to evaluate, analyze, and measure each of these constructs; to offer suggestions on how this three-construct conceptual framework can help practitioners better comprehend cross-national sales interactions.

Cross-national Selling

The two main components of a personal selling transaction are content and style. Content refers to the substantive aspects of the interaction for which the buyer and seller come together. Sheth (1976) explains that the content of a personal selling interaction involves suggesting, offering, or negotiating a set of product-specific utilities and their expectations. Style refers to the rituals, format, mannerisms, and ground-rules that the buyer and the seller follow in their encounter (Sheth 1983). A satisfactory interaction between the buyer and the seller will be contingent upon buyer-seller compatibility with respect to both the content and style of communication (Weitz 1981). The level of dyadic compatibility in content and style will largely be determined by the national culture, organizational culture, and individual personality.

National culture

Culture has a profound impact on how people in the marketplace perceive and behave. The level of aggregation of this construct, however, has always been somewhat problematic. In the realm of international marketing, culture has been typically visualized at the national level. However, operationalization within the national context has been difficult because of a wide divergence of definitions, each reflecting different paradigms from varying disciplines (e.g., psychology, sociology, anthropology, etc.).

In this regard, Hofstede's four dimensions of culture appear most promising (Hofstede 1980). They are based on empirical research, and thus offer the advantage of quantifiability. Hofstede defines national culture as the "collective mental programming" of people in an environment. As such, it is not a characteristic of individuals, but of a large number of persons conditioned by similar background, education, and life experiences. Since this book was published, Hofstede has added a fifth dimension, however, conceptual and empirical support for this dimension is not very exhaustive (Hofstede 1991). Hofstede's dimensions of culture show meaningful relationships with important demographic, geographic, economic, and political national indicators (Triandis 1982). Uncertainty avoidance, individualism, masculinity, and power distance comprise the Hofstede framework.

Uncertainty avoidance (UAI) assesses the way in which societies react to the uncertainties and ambiguities inherent in daily living. At one extreme, weak UAI societies socialize members to accept and handle uncertainty without much discomfort. People in these societies tend to accept each day as it comes, take risks rather easily, and show a relatively greater tolerance for opinions and behaviors different from their own. The other extreme — strong UAI societies — feel threatened by ambiguity and uncertainty. Consequently, such societies emphasize the strong need to control environment, events, and situations. Based on Hofstede's research, Belgium, Japan, and France display strong uncertainty avoidance. Denmark, Sweden, and Hong Kong could be characterized as weak UAI societies; the United States is somewhat in the middle.

The dimension of individualism (IDV) describes the relationship between an individual and his or her fellow individuals, the collectivity which prevails in society. One extreme contains societies with very loose ties between individuals. Such societies allow a large degree of freedom, and everybody is expected to look after their own self-interest. At the other end are low-IDV societies, i.e., societies with very strong ties between individuals forming the in-group. People are expected to watch after the interests of their in-group and to hold only those opinions and beliefs sanctioned by the group. The United States, Great Britain, and the Netherlands display strong individualism, while countries such as Colombia, Pakistan, and Taiwan gravitate toward the other extreme.

Power distance (PDI) involves a society's solution to inequality. People possess unequal physical and intellectual capabilities, which some societies allow to grow into inequalities in power and wealth. Some other societies, those characterized by a small power distance, de-emphasize such inequalities and strive toward maintaining a relative equity in the distribution of power, status, and wealth. The Philippines, India, and France all display relatively large power distance. Austria, Israel, and Denmark depict relatively small PDI, while the United States lies in the mid-range of the PDI continuum.

Masculinity (MAS) pertains to the extent to which societies hold values traditionally regarded as predominantly masculine or feminine. Examples of "masculine" values include assertiveness, respect for the super-achiever, and the acquisition of money and material possessions. "Feminine" values include nurturing, concern for the environment, and championing the underdog. Japan, Austria, and Italy are examples of typically masculine societies, while Norway, Sweden, the Netherlands, and Denmark show strong feminine characteristics.

Organizational culture

Organizational culture encompasses the pattern of shared values and beliefs which enables people within the organization to understand its functioning, and furnishes them with behavioural norms (Apasu, Ichikawa, and Graham 1987; Deshpande and Webster 1989; Weitz, Sujan and Sujan 1986). The values inculcated by an organization along with the behaviors it prescribes have a discernible impact on a salesperson's (or buyer's) content and style of interaction (see Deshpande and Parasuraman 1986; Deshpande and Webster 1989; and Sathe 1984). Deshpande and Webster go so far as to assert that the marketing concept in itself is a manifestation of a firm's organizational culture (ibid.).

While extremely crucial in its import, the construct of organizational culture has been quite difficult to operationalize. Multiple definitions have caused the concept to remain fuzzy and elusive. Furthermore, until recently, empirical work in this area has been conspicuously lacking. A notable attempt to identify and operationalize the dimensions of organizational culture from a broad-based perspective was undertaken by Reynolds (1986).

Based on the premise that reliable procedures for the measurement of organizational culture are sorely needed, Reynolds identified 15 aspects of organizational culture derived from five earlier works (Ansoff 1979, Deal and Kennedy 1982, Harrison 1978, Hofstede 1980, and Peters and Waterman 1982). Table 2.1 provides brief definitions of each of these dimensions. From a marketing perspective, five of these aspects seem to be vital, particularly in understanding dyadic interactions: External vs. Internal Emphasis; Task vs. Social Focus; Conformity vs. Individuality; Safety vs. Risk; and Ad Hockery vs. Planning. These five aspects of organizational culture are logically and empirically independent.

An organization with an external emphasis underscores the task of satisfying customers, clients, or whoever. The other end of this dimension places a relatively greater accent on internal organizational activities such as committee meetings and reports. The outward orientation resulting from an external emphasis will make firms more market-driven as opposed to product-driven.

The dimension of task versus social focus contrasts the relative priorities of an organization between organizational work versus concern for the personal and social needs of its members. In recognition of the fact that an organization is a complex social system, firms with a social focus consciously try to accommodate the social needs of their members in terms of status, esteem, and belonging. Firms with a purely task-driven focus will strive toward robotic efficiency in the attainment of their financial and growth objectives. This acculturation for intra-organizational activities is expected to carry over to inter-organizational interactions as well.

The dimension of conformity versus individuality assesses an organization's degree of tolerance of distinctiveness and idiosyncrasy among its members. One extreme encourages homogeneity in work habits, dress, and even personal life while the other tolerates considerable within-group variation. Thus, firms emphasizing conformity portray a homogeneous organizational image and strive toward the perpetuation of the organizational stereotype. Firms which encourage individuality display an appreciation of diversity among their members, allowing a greater latitude in member lifestyles and behaviors.

An organization's response to risk is an important dimension of organizational culture, particularly in a fluid and rapidly changing business environment. One extreme depicts the tendency to be cautious and conservative in adopting new methods and practices while the other is a predisposition to change when

TABLE 2.1
Dimensions of organizational culture

1.	External vs. internal emphasis: Emphasis on satisfying customers, clients or whatever as opposed to focusing on internal organizational activities such as committee meetings and reports.
2.	Task vs. social focus: Focus on organizational "work" versus concern for personal and social needs of people.
3.	Safety vs risk: Relative openness to adopting new and different programs and procedures.
4.	Conformity vs. individuality: Extent to which organizations tolerate or encourage their members to be distinctive and idiosyncratic in work and social life.
5.	Individual vs. group rewards: Whether rewards are distributed to all members of a work unit or in response to individual contributions.
6.	Individual vs. collective decision-making: Whether decision-making reflects the inputs of one individual or the entire group.
7.	Centralized vs. decentralized decision-making: Whether decisions are made by those in key positions or by those affected by the decision.
8.	Ad hockery vs. planning: Whether *ad-hoc* response or elaborate plans are created in the face of changing circumstances.
9.	Stability vs. innovation: Relative tendency to search for novel and distinctive goods, services, and procedures.
10.	Cooperation vs. competition: Whether peers are considered as competitors for scarce resources or trusted colleagues in a common cause.
11.	Basis for commitment: Whether financial rewards, prestige, interesting/challenging work, opportunity for self-fulfilment/expression or satisfying personal relations constitutes the individual's involvement with the company.
12.	Simple vs. complex organization: Refers to the tendency of organizations to develop elaborate procedures and structures.
13.	Informal vs. formalized procedures: Whether extensive, detailed rules and procedures and elaborate forms and written documents are needed to justify actions.
14.	High vs. low loyalty: Extent to which members place their organization above competing groups such as family and professional colleagues.
15.	Ignorance vs. knowledge of organizational expectations: Degree to which individual members know what they are expected to do and how their efforts contribute to the accomplishment of organizational objectives.

confronted with new challenges and opportunities. Firms motivated by safety will typically be slow in decision-making, particularly when it comes to decisions involving the global marketplace. They are quite likely to curtail the level of autonomy of their members. Firms thriving on risk will typically want to be pioneers, be it in product development or in entering new markets. They will also allow their executives a fair degree of autonomy, and encourage learning through experimentation.

Ad hockery versus planning captures the tendency to anticipate and plan for change. Some organizations create *ad-hoc* responses to all changes, while others may opt for elaborate plans that anticipate most future scenarios. Planning-oriented firms will be typically drawn to elaborate forecasting, mathematical modelling, and economic analysis. Firms practicing ad hockery will rely less on forecasts and numbers, and more on intuition.

Personality factors

Dyadic communication takes place between individuals. Conditioned by the broader social environment at various levels (such as the family, school, and organization), people nevertheless exert their personality traits or individual preferences. The concept of personality has been called one of the "great" topics of behavioural sciences (Wilkie 1986). Drawing on commonality among hundreds of different definitions, personality can best be defined as an individual's consistency in behaviors and reactions to events.

Given the face-to-face nature of most buyer-seller encounters, personality will have a direct and discernible impact on such interactions. The most popular way to depict personality is the Myers-Briggs Type Indicator (MBTI). The theory of temperament as developed by Keirsey and Bates is a parsimonious depiction of the MBTI personality profile. Temperament denotes, "a moderation or unification of otherwise disparate forces, an overall coloration or tuning, kind of thematization of the whole, a uniformity of the diverse (Keirsey and Bates 1978, p. 27). Before proceeding to the characteristics of the four temperaments in the Keirsey and Bates framework, it would be useful to briefly discuss their underlying MBTI dimensions.

The MBTI describes valuable differences in the ways people see the world, make decisions, choose careers, and communicate with one another. It identifies sixteen different personality types based on four dichotomous dimensions: extroversion vs. introversion (E or I), sensing vs. intuition (S or N), thinking vs. feeling (T or F), and perceiving vs. judging (P or J).

Extroverts typically are oriented to the outer world of people and things, whereas introverts gravitate toward their inner world of ideas and feelings. Thus, while terms like sociability, interaction, and external focus would categorize an extrovert's life, apt descriptors for the lifestyle of an introvert would be territoriality, concentration, and internal focus.

A person with sensing-preference shows a marked predilection for facts whereas the intuitive person finds appeal in the metaphor and enjoys vivid imagery. Sensing types sniff out detail while intuitive people prefer to focus on the big picture. Words like sensible, down-to-earth, and practical would fit the sensing types. Intuitive types could be best described by words like imaginative, innovative, and ingenious.

The thinking–feeling dimension encompasses the basis for people's decision making in life. Thinkers want to decide things logically and objectively; feelers base their decisions on more subjective grounds. Words like objective, principled, and analysis-driven typify the decision making of thinkers, while the feeler's decision making could be described as subjective, value-based, and sympathetic.

Perceiving types tend to be flexible in life, always seeking more information. Persons who seek closure over open options are the judging types. Js fancy life to be settled, decided, and fixed; Ps opt for life to be in the pending, data gathering, and flexible mode. Judgers display a preference for organizing and controlling events of the outside world, whereas perceivers are primarily interested in observing and understanding such events. The four dimensions discussed here result in sixteen "types" of personality.

Keirsey and Bates collapse the sixteen possible MBTI types into four temperaments, thereby simplifying the MBTI framework while still preserving most of its substantive insights. These four temperaments have been metaphorically associated with four Greek Gods whom Zeus commissioned to make man more God-like: Dionysus, Epimetheus, Prometheus, and Apollo.

The Dionysian temperament (SP)

This temperament results from the combination of sensing (S) and perceiving (P) preferences. Focus on the SP temperament is joy. SPs prefer a life of freedom devoid of any responsibility. They tend to be impulsive and very expressive. SPs love to take risks and are always craving for adventure. "Action without constraints" typifies the SP lifestyle.

The Epimethean temperament (SJ)

Preferences of sensing (S) and judgement (J) fuse to form the SJ temperament. Unlike the thrill-seeking SPs, SJs exist primarily to be useful to the various social units they associate with. SJs feel the compulsion to belong, and they believe that belonging has to be earned. They have a very strong work ethic and they value hierarchy and order. SJs tend to be very attentive to details and can manipulate large amounts of data. The primary goal in life for an SJ is to maintain tradition and order in their environment. They live according to fairly rigid "shoulds" and "oughts".

The Promethean temperament (NT)

Intuition (N) combined with thinking (T) give rise to the NT temperament. This temperament values competence over everything. NTs dealings with others could be described as "coolly objective". They tend to be very critical of themselves and others. NTs tend to be very precise communicators and place little reliance on non-verbal qualifiers. They love to play with words, ideas, and models. They are very adept at planning but seldom care about the implementation of their plans.

Sudhir Kalé

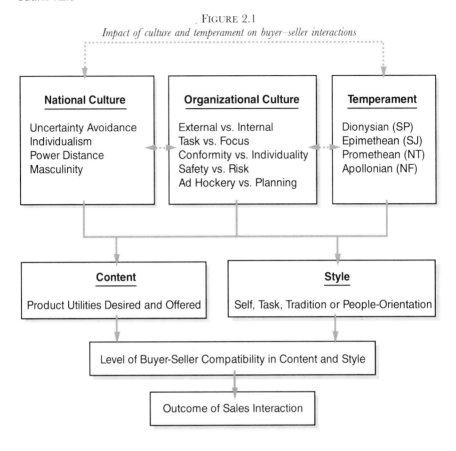

FIGURE 2.1

Impact of culture and temperament on buyer–seller interactions

The Apollonian temperament (NF)

This temperament results from the preferences of intuition (N) and feeling (F). NFs tend to be driven by authenticity. They value integrity and are easily put off by facades, masks, pretences, and shams. Their entire life revolves around people. They believe that the most important thing is to be in harmony with themselves and others. This temperament, more than any other, values relationships and desires to inspire and persuade others.

Interrelationships between constructs

Figure 2.1 depicts how national culture, organizational culture, and temperament (or personality) combine to produce a person's preferences in content and style of communication. It is important to note that the manifested impact of any one construct will be tempered or amplified by the other two constructs. For example, an actor nurtured in a national culture of high individualism may reduce his individualistic tendencies when functioning in a corporate environment characterized by strong conformity. Similarly, a Dionysian SP's impulsive behavior may be somewhat tempered by a planning-oriented organizational culture. Which behavioral characteristics are ultimately manifested in an interaction will ultimately depend upon the strength of national culture, the robustness of corporate acculturation, and the intensity of temperament.

Organizational culture of a firm and the model temperament of its members will be systematically related as people will tend to stay with organizations whose culture suits their own temperament. The bullish SPs will gravitate to a company characterized by ad hockery and risks, whereas the Epimethean SJs will tend to thrive in an organizational culture that emphasizes planning and safety. NFs will prefer companies with a social focus, whereas NTs will be drawn to companies emphasizing individuality.

There will be a strong relationship between national culture and individual personalities as well. National culture is, after all, shaped by the preferences and predispositions of its inhabitants (Clark 1990). A society characterized by strong uncertainty avoidance would probably have relatively more judging types, particularly SJs, in its population than it would perceivers. Correspondingly, a collective society will have more NFs in its population than an individualistic society. We will now take a closer look at how the three constructs in our framework affect the content and style in dyadic interactions.

Effect on sales interactions

National culture

The dimensions of uncertainty avoidance, individualism, power distance, and masculinity broadly shape certain aspects of content for each actor in the sales dyad. A buyer conditioned in a national culture of strong uncertainty avoidance should typically display a strong preference for security utility, i.e., the uncertainty-reducing attributes in a product offering. Facets such as established brand name, superior warranty, and money-back guarantee should figure prominently in the choice processes of strong UAI societies. By the same token, "environment-friendly" products such as biodegradable bags and recyclable packaging should find greater appeal in the relatively feminine Scandinavian countries than they would in masculine countries such as Venezuela and Italy.

Countries displaying high individualism (such as the United States) place a significantly greater emphasis on seeking variety and pleasure as compared to the relatively collectivist societies (such as Yugoslavia and Colombia). Sheth (1983) uses the term "epistemic value" to describe those product utilities that cater to the novelty, variety, and curiosity needs of people. Thus, product attributes designed to offer the epistemic utility will be more valued by American consumers than they would by Colombian customers. Social utility in a product results from

29

its association with a certain socio-economic group. It is this utility that endows certain products with "status". It is expected that large power distance societies such as Venezuela and Mexico would emphasize the status value of a particular product to a greater extent than would small power distance cultures such as Denmark and Austria.

The four dimensions of national culture should also shape the preferred style of communication. Hofstede (1984) observes that cultures displaying strong uncertainty avoidance also experience greater stress and anxiety when compared with weak UAI societies. Anxiety is often manifested into the level of aggressiveness displayed in social interactions. People nurtured in weak UAI cultures should evince greater receptivity to a soft-sell approach and non-aggressive sales techniques. Strong uncertainty avoidance societies, on the other hand, would show relatively greater preference and tolerance for the hard-sell approaches.

Graham *et al.* (1988) and his colleagues have investigated the use of the problem-solving approach (PSA) in sales negotiations. At one end of the PSA continuum are negotiation behaviors best characterized as cooperative and integrative. At the other end of the scale are negotiation behaviors described as competitive and individualistic. Collective societies aim at the welfare of everyone, individualistic societies focus on the relative maximization of self-interest. The use of PSA should therefore be more pronounced in low-IDV (or collective) societies than in high-IDV (or individualistic) cultures.

Power distance impacts style by way of the role of each negotiator in a sales transaction. Schmidt (1979) has observed that in a large PDI society like Japan, the seller has been considered "little more than a beggar". Sellers have to be respectful and subservient to their buyers in large PDI societies. Another manifestation of power distance is the willingness to trust other people. Large PDI societies typically view others as a threat and as a result show less inclination to trust others. People in small power distance societies, however, feel less threatened by others and consequently trust others more. Consequently, people in large power distance societies (e.g., the Arab countries) will discuss business only after developing trust in the salesperson. Thus, the no-nonsense "task oriented" style of interaction — motivated by the desire to expend a minimum amount of time, energy, and effort — may work well in the largely small PDI countries of Western Europe but would backfire in the Middle East.

Organizational culture

Culture control is increasingly used to replace rules-based control in an attempt to enhance the productivity of organizations (Lebas and Weigenstein 1986). Organizational culture of the buyer and the seller firms will not only affect intra-organizational conduct but should also impact the content and style of inter-organizational interactions.

An organization emphasizing an external orientation places singular emphasis on satisfying clients and customers. As opposed to a firm with internal emphasis, representatives of companies with external emphasis will use the problem solving approach to a greater degree. The external emphasis will also manifest into a relatively greater willingness on the part of the seller to modify the product offering in order to maximize a buyer's utility and convenience.

A task focus will drive a firm's employees toward the task-oriented style of interaction. A salesperson reared in such an environment will strive to conclude the sales transaction with utmost efficiency. The emphasis will be toward concluding the interaction with a minimum outgo of time, money, and effort. A culture emphasizing the social focus will show a relatively greater inclination for social chit-chat, personal rapport, and the socialization needs of each actor in the course of the sales transaction. A people-oriented preference in style will thus result. Also, the social and emotional utilities inherent in certain products will be valued higher by firms with a social focus as opposed to those with a task focus.

Persons conditioned by a culture of conformity should elicit a preference for standardized sales presentations or "canned approaches". Company policies and procedures will largely determine the scope of the concessions offered, terms of contract, and even the rituals of the transaction. Companies practicing relatively high individuality will allow their representatives a high level of autonomy in decision making during the sales negotiation process.

Self-oriented style of interaction is one where the individual is more concerned about his or her own needs than those of others and more interested in extrinsic as opposed to intrinsic rewards. This style will be manifested by representatives of firms bred in a climate of individuality especially when reinforced by the influences of a strongly individualistic national culture.

The dimension of safety vs. risk will determine the relative importance of attributes such as the reputation of the selling firm, the credit-worthiness of the buyer, the acceptable level of return privileges, and the desire for personal rapport between the buyer and the seller. A safety-oriented organizational culture may result in an emphasis on written contracts as opposed to oral agreements. Conversely, representatives of firms with greater risk tolerance will be more inclined to encourage new suppliers, trying out new and innovative products, and accepting a certain level of ambiguity in sales contracts. Safety-orientation may also translate into a tradition-oriented style of interaction, where the same ground rules of the transaction have been followed over the course of generations.

Finally, the content and style displayed in a sales transaction will also be impacted by the dimension of ad hockery vs. planning. Planning-orientation will emphasize the need for non-ambiguous communication in conveying product benefits, warranty features, and contingency clauses. Conversely, representatives of firms with a preference for ad hockery will tend to negotiate in a manner that encourages flexibility in the role stipulation, delivery, and other aspects of sales negotiation. The interaction style of such representatives will be somewhat informal, and less task-driven when compared to the style of representatives of firms inculcating a planning orientation.

Personality

Since a salesperson interacts with buyers spanning a whole spectrum of personalities, understanding how personality affects buyer preferences in content and style becomes crucial. Personality will determine the relative salience of various product utilities as well as the preferred format of the sales interaction.

The Epimethean (SJ) temperament values belonging to the various social units such as the church, school board, clubs, etc. Social-organizational utility results from the identification of a product with a selective set of demographic, socioeconomic, or organizational types, producing an imagery or stereotype (McIntyre and Kale 1988; Sheth 1983). It therefore follows that social-organizational utility (or disutility) would be more important to SJs than to any other temperament. Novelty or epistemic utility, on the other hand, will be most valued by the variety-seeking Dionysian SPs.

The people-driven NFs will prefer the people-oriented style of communication. They will elicit preference for establishing a personal bond with their dyadic counterpart prior to discussing business. Conservative SJs will probably prefer tradition-orientation in sales interactions.

SJs will also show a preference for quantifiable product performance data. They will be impressed by a factual presentation, full of charts, graphs, and statistics. Conversely, the Promethean NTs will be impressed by the use of metaphor and analogy.

While SJs will be swayed by reasoning and logic, NFs will be more comfortable with the use of emotional appeals such as love, loyalty, fear, and responsibility. Emotional utility (or disutility) — resulting from a product being associated with feelings such as anger, respect, love, and fear — will appeal more to NFs than to any other temperament.

SJs insist on being right and, consequently, may promote disagreements in a sales encounter. NFs, on the other hand, are more likely to be conversationalists. The discussion may go on and on, without any inclination for closure.

Managerial Implications

Conceptualizing buyer–seller interactions using the constructs of national culture, organizational culture, and temperament yields a wide array of managerial insights. It can help predict the outcome of a sales encounter. Based on the similarity hypothesis, the greatest level of success in buyer–seller interactions would occur where the buyer and seller are akin in their milieu of national culture, organizational culture, and individual personality (Evans 1963). Conversely, the most challenging scenario and the one with the least chance of success is denoted by a complete lack of congruence between the buyer and seller in the areas of national culture, organizational culture, and individual personality. In such a situation, should the seller fail to recognize this incongruence and take corrective action, a total mismatch in communication will occur resulting in virtual collapse of the transaction.

Bear in mind that the relative importance of the three dimensions in terms of their influence on a sales interaction will be situationally determined. For example, cross-cultural buyer–seller differences on the dimension of power distance may be potentially crippling in one situation (e.g., a U.S. vendor selling a fairly generic product to a powerful Japanese buyer), while in other cases they may not (e.g., an East Indian seller, who exhibits a large power distance, trying to sell a similar product to a U.S. buyer, whose national culture embodies smaller power distance). Similarly, consumer temperament will have little relevance if the seller is operating in a sellers' market (Frazier and Kale 1989; Kale 1986).

Situational factors aside, the importance of the three constructs discussed in this chapter has powerful implications in at least three areas: (i) choosing national markets for doing business; (ii) fine-tuning a firm's organizational culture; and (iii) recruiting and training salespeople for overseas business. This conceptional framework also leads to the development of a "selling sequence" to maximize the success rate of cross-national face-to-face selling transactions.

Choosing National Markets

National culture can be used as an important entry criterion along with such traditional criteria as population, per capita income, the existence of infrastructure, etc., with which to evaluate the attractiveness of various national markets (Root 1987). Economics and infrastructure alone do not adequately predict a firm's chances of success in a foreign market. For instance, although Britain and the United States have somewhat similar per capita income figures, most U.S. firms will not succeed in Bahrain unless they adapt their marketing practices to Bahrain's national culture. The U.S. firm will typically have an easier time selling to buyers in Australia (which also has a high per capita income) which is culturally closer to the U.S. along Hofstede's four dimensions of national culture.

Using Hofstede's cultural dimensions, major national markets of the world can be segmented into relatively homogeneous clusters (Kale 1985). A company choosing national markets with a national culture similar to its own (i.e., belonging to the same cluster) will have to undertake relatively little learning and acculturation to sell its products successfully within these markets. Conversely, if markets with radically dissimilar national cultures are chosen, a lot of investment in acculturation, recruitment, and training of personnel will be needed to sell a company's products successfully within these markets. Thus, if a firm has to choose between two markets with comparable levels of market potential, economic well-being, competition, and infrastructural facilities, it should first choose one with the smaller "cultural distance".

Fine-tuning Organizational Culture

If a firm is operating in a group of culturally homogeneous countries which have a national culture different from its own (such as a British trading company in

West Africa), it can consciously design its organizational culture to better reflect the national culture of its markets. This will enhance the skills of the firm's boundary personnel in dealing with buyers who share a different national culture. Hindustan Lever Limited, a subsidiary of the Anglo-Dutch conglomerate Unilever, has inculcated an organizational culture in its Indian subsidiary that takes into account the relatively low level of individualism, and the relatively large power distance within India. Similarly, Coca Cola in Japan has adopted the collective orientation of Japanese society (Wilson 1980).

Recruitment and training of salespeople

A cosmopolitan salesperson needs to possess a "flexible personality" (Simurda 1988). It has been suggested that the key attributes desired in a salesperson in a cross-cultural selling situation include openness and sensitivity to others, cultural appreciation and awareness, ability to relate across cultures, awareness of one's own culturally derived values, and a certain degree of resilience to bounce back after setbacks (Noer 1975). Using the Myers-Briggs insights into personality, the perceivers (especially SPs) are more likely to possess these attributes than are judgers. In their characterization of judgers and perceivers, Keirsey and Bates (1978) describe the judgers as "fixed" and the perceivers as "flexible". Furthermore, judgers, particularly SJs, like to plan their selling strategy a priori, whereas perceivers tend to follow an "adapt as you go" approach. Also, while the Epimethean SJs hunger for controlling the sales transaction, perceivers will try hard to observe, understand, and adapt. This adaptability gives perceivers an innate advantage in handling the various contingencies involved in cross-national selling (Weitz 1981).

Knowing the customer in international sales means more than comprehending the customer's product needs; it includes knowing the customer's culture. At broad levels, this culture is shaped by national culture and organizational culture. At the level of preferred ways of acting, an understanding of the customer's temperament becomes important. A cosmopolitan salesperson will become more adept at cross-national selling if given a thorough grounding in the constructs of national culture, organizational culture, and individual temperament.

The selling sequence

Figure 2.2 is a flowchart of cross-national selling transactions. This step-by-step approach can be utilized in training sales personnel.

A well-trained salesperson is aware of his or her own conditioning and personality. This awareness process has been portrayed in Figure 2.2 as self-appraisal. The aim of self-appraisal is to develop a frame of reference whereby one's own communication preferences with regard to content and style could be understood. Dimensions discussed in this paper under temperament, organizational culture, and national culture become convenient labels with which to generate self-awareness.

FIGURE 2.2

The cross-national selling sequence

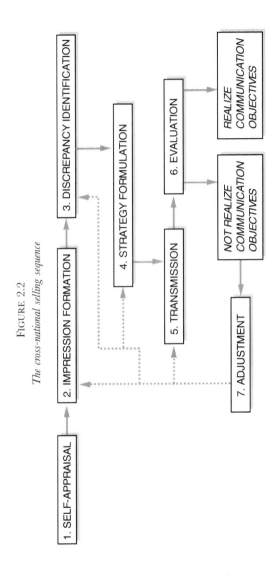

Impression formation involves understanding the buyer's position on the three constructs. Typically, national culture and organizational culture can be assessed even before the seller meets with the buyer. Hofstede (1983) provides scores and ranks for fifty countries on the basis of their positions on the four dimensions of national culture. The organizational culture of most large and medium sized companies can be gleaned from their press-releases, annual reports, and from popular literature (Deal and Kennedy 1982). A salesperson trained in type-watching can assess a buyer's temperament with a fair degree of accuracy in a relatively short period of interaction. An accurate impression of the buyer in terms of national culture, organizational culture, and temperament lays the foundation for relationship building, which is so critical to successful selling.

In the third step, the seller goes through the mental exercise of "discrepancy identification". This involves comparing the buyer's estimated position on the various dimensions of the three constructs with one's own. This alerts the seller to potential problem areas in communication arising out of differences in temperament and cultural conditioning.

Strategy formulation involves minimizing the impact of problem areas identified in the earlier step. For instance, if the buyer is a feeler, and the seller is a thinker, the seller needs to modify his persuasion style. While his preferred persuasion style is logical and impersonal, this may not fit well with the buyer. The appropriate style in this instance would be to appeal to the buyer's feelings and emotions, and to point out the people-benefits behind the seller's offering. Similar adjustments need to be made on other dimensions as well where discrepancies exist between the seller and the buyer.

Transmission involves implementation of the communication/persuasion strategy. During the course of transmission, the seller should be sensitive to the verbal and non-verbal feedback received from the buyer. If the seller has correctly identified the buyer's mind-set based on temperament and culture, the strategy should be on target, and the feedback received from the buyer will be encouraging.

Assessing the effect of the communication strategy constitutes the "evaluation" phase (Weitz 1978). If the seller's communication objectives are realized, then the encounter has been successful. If not, the seller goes through the "adjustment" process where buyer impressions, discrepancies, and strategy are re-evaluated, and the transmission modified. At the evaluation and adjustment phases, the seller always has the choice of cutting short the encounter, and trying again at a future point in time. Regardless of the outcome, every encounter adds to the seller's repertoire of experiences, skills, strategies, and alternative transmission approaches.

Summary

This paper provided a general framework to investigate cross-national personal selling transactions. Three levels of influences were identified: national culture, organizational culture and individual temperament. Buyer-seller positions along these constructs largely determine the overall compatibility in dyadic communication.

For each of the three constructs, there exist field-tested measurement instruments. Scholars in marketing and international business are urged to utilize these instruments in their studies of cross-national negotiation and marketing issues. From a managerial perspective, the practical applications and intuitive appeal of the proposed three-construct framework are indeed exciting. This conceptual schema should prove useful in the areas of selecting national markets, shaping an appropriate organizational culture, and the recruitment and training of cosmopolitan salespeople.

CHAPTER 3

A Model of the Negotiation Process with Different Strategies

CHRISTOPHE DUPONT

This volume is on international business negotiations. True, there are definite specificities in this type of negotiations distinguishing them both from domestic negotiations and from "non commercial" negotiations (such as labor, inter- or intra-organizational negotiations or diplomatic conferences). A major point however is that all negotiations exhibit some basic common features.

Negotiation research is often compared to the actual practice of negotiators. Practitioners are often sceptical about the applicability of present research results to actual negotiations whereas researchers — and to a large extent academics — regret that professionals do not invest more time and reflexion to what could help them to be more effective negotiators. Research contributions may really assist the negotiator on at least two grounds: first, by giving a global view of the process and perhaps of the determination of the outcomes; knowledge and understanding of certain relationships between key variables that theory has succeeded to identify could help the negotiator — even well groomed and efficient in the activity — to improve planning and implementation of the negotiation. Second, through a combined effort of researchers and practitioners, a more satisfactory (from a long-term or ethical view point) evolution of negotiations could gradually take place, or at least more clarity could be obtained in what are often ambiguous and too much self-centered behaviors of negotiators toward the search for optimal, balanced, mutually acceptable and durable solutions of conflicts, problems and projects.

Basic to the understanding of negotiations is the concept of "process". It is first necessary to explore the principal components underpinning this concept. This will be the theme of the first part of this chapter. These components may be translated in terms of variables and dealt with either quantitatively or qualitatively, and that corresponds to the elaboration of process models of negotiation, the theme of the second part. After exploring the main models available, the emphasis is placed on a model that is more applicable to IBN. Finally in commercial negotiations in particular the question may be raised on the need for and the availability of relevant strategies under the form of privileged "strategic choices". This aspect is the theme of the third part of this chapter.

Basic Elements of the Process

A number of reasons account for the fact that professional negotiators as well as theorists consider negotiation as an activity fraught with difficulties. To mention just a few: few negotiations replicate exactly a previous experience; the context may have changed, the opponent who acted "rationally" previously may appear somewhat "irrational" at present or his/her behavior is more erratic; there is a wide variety of negotiation situations according to the field observed which makes it difficult to generalize. To take an example, in the international sphere business negotiations differ in many respects from diplomatic conferences or domestic labor negotiations are different in many ways from commercial or organizational negotiations; efforts to reduce the negotiation process and the determination of outcomes to a small number of explanatory variables have proved extremely difficult; there are just too many variables intervening in the process and result. Two experienced researchers (Druckman in the United States and G.O. Faure in France) working together on this topic have inventoried more than one hundred such relevant and salient variables. The initial endeavor has been described in Druckman (1977). If some "tactics" may be regrouped into significant clusters so as to treat them as variables, the reality is that it is possible to differentiate some 200 of them, some major, others rather minor (or marginally used) see, for instance, Karrass (1970) and Audebert (1995). This somewhat discouraging picture is of more concern to the researcher (or academic) than to the professional more inclined to consider negotiation as an "art" — enhancing know-how, if not "knack", "feeling", experience and expertise — rather than a "science" (Raiffa 1982). Yet this does not undermine attempts to identify some elements of the process which combine the twofold quality of (observed) commonality in all negotiating situations and (proved) essentiality in the development of process and determination of outcomes. Later it will be seen that models embody such elements in their structure, in some form or another; the purpose is identification rather than structuration.

Although the following presentation anticipates somewhat the substance of later parts of this chapter, it will be used as a starting point for the exploration of the negotiation process. This approach has been the result of a joint effort by negotiation "experts" working in a network called PIN (Process of International Negotiations). The PIN group is multinational and consists of researchers, negotiation (University or Business School) professors and practitioners (including business executives and diplomats). For a few years the group has been "hosted" at IIASA (International Institute of Applied System Analysis) in Laxenburg (Austria). It now operates as a network deprived of an institutional framework. The presentation is explained and detailed in Kremenyuk, ed. (1991) and has served as a guide by the group to analyse certain aspects of various international negotiations (see for instance Rubin and Faure, eds, *Culture and Negotiation* (1993); Zartman, ed., *International Multilateral Negotiations* (1994). Negotiation is seen as a system consisting of a few interrelated blocks — in other terms major elements — representative of the process and of its outcome. Figure 3.1 is a diagrammatic representation of the PIN concept of negotiation.

As Figure 3.1 shows five major elements are identified, each one subject to further breakdowns ("sub-variables"). An important feature of the design is the interrelationships between these elements (and sub-elements). It is also necessary to see that this design represents only one facet of the process as it is replicated by a parallel system relating to the other party (or parties) to the negotiation. Negotiation is thus best defined as a confrontation (not necessarily conflictual) of divergent stakes and interests by parties who are also interdependent and for that reason seek together a joint solution to their differences (rather than trying to achieve their objectives either by sheer force or by some form of unilateral action). Thus when planning for a negotiation to come — or actually negotiating — it is essential not to forget this basic fact. Negotiation is never a unilateral exercise; the negotiator should never ignore the "reality" of the opponent(s).

The five major blocks relate to "actors" (i.e., negotiators acting individually or as delegations), "structure" (i.e., context, agenda, number of participants, site, moment, etc.), "strategy", "process" and "outcome". These three latter elements are best described and analyzed with the support of models as in the later parts of this chapter. In the present section the focus is mainly on actors — and secondarily on structure.

The emphasis put on actors is not arbitrary. It is because actor analysis — with the three components of stakes and interests, bargaining strength (i.e., power) and the climate (related to the type of relationships, behaviors and styles) — is the foundation of the whole process. These components constitute the forces or parameters (or in qualitative language the ingredients) of the dynamics that intervene in the negotiation.

Stakes and interests

Actors in a negotiation are faced by the pre-existence of a conflict (whatever the nature, the form and the intensity), a problem or a project. As already mentioned a given actor may either be unable or reluctant (rationally) to solve it by him/herself. This is obvious in the case of a conflict; in the case of a problem or a project there could be a possibility of acting alone but because of certain interdependencies the actor envisages the search for a solution on a joint rather than on an unilateral basis.

To reach an agreement when differences pre-exist (or are perceived as pre-existing) is not always easy. The problem is to bridge a gap between diverging interests or values. If these would be the same there would be no need to face each other to initiate a process of mutual information, influence or of some power to reconcile opposing points of views and differences. The process would then be a "pure" problem-solving exercise, not a negotiation. Negotiation implies a process allowing for ways (strategies, techniques, behaviors) to reconcile the divergences. These may range from confrontational ("distributive", "competitive") to cooperative ("integrative") as will be seen later; they are instruments or tools to transform the initial situation into a potential agreement.

The agreement is thus designed to make "opponents" satisfied (perhaps in an asymmetric measure) with regard to the attainment of the overarching objective of putting an end (perhaps only temporarily) to conflict, to allow the problem to be solved or the project to be launched. Thus the purpose of the agreement is to preserve or promote individual interests or values subject to the constraint that the solution also meets at least the minimal demands of the other party (parties).

This is why one of the best recent contributions to the negotiating literature calls "interests" the raw material of negotiations (Lax and Sebenius 1986). Interests may take many forms: economic such as profitability, volume, market share, etc., in a commercial negotiation but they may be more subtle and even intangible such as principles (a major factor in diplomatic negotiations), saving face (a major factor from a cultural view point in an international negotiation) or establishing/reinforcing a relationship (business or otherwise), defending or promoting an image, a reputation, etc. Negotiation analysis (planning, operating) starts with the problem of identifying interests (tangible or not) behind the issues (topics, themes) forming the agenda. In a commercial negotiation price is of course a major issue but the real point is how this topic is related to actor interests, in other terms preoccupations, expectations, constraints and risks; similarly how a given issue (e.g., price) may be (or not) related to other issues (e.g., volume, payment terms, deliveries, quality, viability, guarantees, etc.).

In an IBN, parties' interests are of a similar variety to domestic negotiations but in sharp contrast to the latter they are often complicated by cultural factors. An illustration is the negotiation which has taken place between the Walt Disney Company and the French government which resulted in the opening of the Euro Disney theme park near Paris in 1992. The interests of the two parties could be rather easily identified but an in-depth analysis shows that each party did not comprehend fully the interests (expectations, constraints and risks) of its partner, particularly regarding the sensitivity of the French actors (government, local communities, the media, interest groups) to the cultural issue (the Disneyland negotiations have been discussed in March 1995 by the PIN group at the IIASA on the basis of a report by Geoffrey D. Fink). Another illustration of the key importance of interest identification can be derived from the detailed description of the (failed) negotiations on the MFP project (massive fertilizer programme) in India (1963–65) between the Bechtel consortium and the Government of India (Kapoor 1970).

Where this analysis leads to is the relationship between interests (as manifestations — economic or principled — of concerns) and stakes of the negotiation. Every negotiation implies expectations (of interests safeguarded or enhanced) and risks (expectations not met). The stake of a negotiation is precisely the impact that the negotiation will bear on this twofold structure. In other terms it is the sanction that the process and its outcome will have on interests in a large sense; tangible elements as well as principles and values. Stakes may be high, perhaps vital, or they may be low. Obviously this will exert an important influence on strategies and behaviors. Stakes may be easy to decode (e.g., profitability or long-term relationship in a commercial negotiation) or difficult to uncover (e.g., in some cases, a desire of domination or of revenge). They may be an attribute of an individual negotiator or they may represent a collective factor (a firm's image, a State capability to exert influence, a specific cultural sensibility, etc.).

The negotiation process is also dependent on the "structure" of negotiation. This relates to conditions (which constitute the background framework of the negotiation) such as site, moment, number and status of participants, organization and procedures. By extension, it concerns also the antecedents of the negotiation episode that is going to take place as well as the present context (e.g., cyclical, social, political). It is debatable whether to place the issues ("points", "agenda", "items", etc.) within this concept of "structure". The agenda or the list of issues (points to be discussed) delineates the domain of the negotiations, hence it is part of the "structure" although the issues can also be examined from the point of views of "actors", thus being linked to stakes and interests. The same is true of procedures or the discussions relating to the order of the items on the agenda.

The number of issues in an IBN may, as in the case of domestic business negotiations, be limited (typically 10 to 20 items that are typical of "commercial" negotiations) or cover a vast number. In an international negotiation relative to the creation of a joint-venture the UNCTC (a unit of the European Commission for Europe of the UN, at Geneva, dealing with transnational trade) lists no less than 142 items for possible inclusion in the agenda. In the MFP negotiation referred to above Kapoor (1970) lists 72 items labelled as "major decision areas" subdivided in ten categories (the project, corporate entities, marketing, profitability, supply rights, guarantees, foreign exchange, government of India assurances, taxes and import duties and licenses).

When planning a negotiation it may be a recommended method to explore simultaneously — in a matrix form as in Table 3.1 — issues, interests/values and stakes to which may be added an item "implications" (e.g., positions, postures or strategies).

Power ("Bargaining Strength")

Parallel to "actors" and issues, another basic element of negotiation is relative power held by the participants. Power as a factor of negotiation has been widely discussed and opinions differ. To take the two extremes in the spectrum of approaches, one — defended by the "political school" — places power at the center of the negotiation process; the other considers that this concept is redundant and even tautological (since power can in the end be equated to result, i.e., a

TABLE 3.1

Planning matrix; an illustration for a commercial negotiation (seller's side)

Issues (selective)	Interests/Values	Stakes	Implications*
Price	• Profit • Resist competition • Increase market share	• Profit margin needed to be above 5% • Be price-leader in the market segment.	• Reservation price higher than $1000 per unit. • Link price negotiation to payment terms ("what if" technique)
Terms of payment	• Liquidity position • Cost of financing	• Impact of financing on total value of agreement	• Negotiate price and payments in a global "package deal"
Volume, etc.	. . .	. . .	. . .

*This may additionally refer to strategies, techniques or tactics, information (needed or handling), argumentation, etc.

superior negotiator obtains superior results in negotiations because superior results simply prove that he/she benefits from a more favorable power balance, or has more aptly controlled bargaining power). A middle-of-the-road position holds that power analysis in negotiation is both felt as a reality by professionals, and that power analysis is feasible and helpful in planning and conducting negotiations (see, for instance, Bacharach S. and Lawler L. 1980, Zartman 1988 and Zartman, ed. 1994).

Among the fundamental questions relating to power which are dealt with in depth in the literature are the following:

1. What is the basis of bargaining strength in a negotiation?
2. Is power stable, and to what extent?
3. What to do for a negotiator who does not enjoy bargaining power?
4. Can power be the basis of negotiation strategies?

These questions are relevant both for domestic and international negotiations. The use of power (in a "competitive" way in a first stage, more controlled subsequently) can be illustrated in the negotiating strategies of ATT.

ATT derived a strong power position because of its intellectual property rights and it used it according to an informed commentator "aggressively" until antitrust laws and deregulation led to a change in power utilization in the negotiations (for instance in entering into licensing agreements). As in the Disneyland case this was analyzed at IIASA (March 1994); the background report was by Robert E. Kerwin and Richard A. De Felice.

It is generally recognized that the bargaining strength of a negotiator may be derived from a number of sources. Some are tied to the negotiating situation, others are connected with the negotiator. Among the first category one may cite background factors such as:

1. The latitude of choice; for instance, the buyer may select the seller according to his/her own criteria. It may be the best bid on price but it may also concern more qualitative, subjective elements, e.g., the value given to a durable relationship. The latitude of choice may sometimes be more easily manipulated at the international than in the domestic sphere (e.g., *de facto* cartellization by producers of some materials, or restrictions on licensing).

2. The capacity to sanction either positively (benefits, rewards, compensations, etc.) or negatively (cost inflicted on the opponent). This capacity is sometimes used in international business negotiations through the channel of regulatory power.

3. The relative importance of the opponent in regard of the needs of the negotiator. For example, in a commercial negotiation a buyer often measures the share of the cost of contracts concluded with the seller compared with the share of other supplier sources (in other terms the market share of each supplier in the purchaser's market), or with total cost (or value added). A typical purchasing matrix shows on one of its axes this measure and on the other the relative "strategic" importance of the commodities or services for the buyer. This matrix sizes up the "weight" of the partner in relation to the strategic needs of the buyer and its application is relevant for domestic and IBN as well. Multinational enterprises may use imbalances of this kind when they deal with smaller firms (although the situation may be also the reverse when a small firm has a definitive specialized competitive advantage).

4. The latitude of the party in respect of time. If time (e.g., deadlines) is of little impact for one party while the opponent feels a sense of urgency for concluding the deal, the first negotiator benefits from a bargaining strength relative to the other.

In addition to these "objective" factors that are embodied in the situation (which does not mean however that the negotiator does not have any means to control them or that he/she cannot have any flexibility with regard to them) there are four other sources of strength that may be tied to the negotiator.

5. Skill. Negotiation is an art in which personal capacities, partly natural ("born negotiators") and partly acquired through experience, training, etc., play an important role. For instance, sound judgement, an agile mind, good psychological acuteness and sensitiveness in communication ability, a capacity to be both firm and flexible, character and sustained motivation, resistance to stress, and charisma are all obvious sources of bargaining strength. Conversely, failing to have these attributes may lead to vulnerabilities. However when it comes to "performing styles" — of which there are many, often described in terms of personality grids — one has to beware of simplistic assumptions about an overarching performing style. A "relational" negotiator, a "diplomat" may not have the punch characterizing the "competitive"

types of negotiators, yet he/she may be a good performer in negotiations requiring cultural sensitivity or designed to establish lasting relationships. In some negotiations the basic quality is to be creative, in other negotiations it is to be risk-prone. Skill diversity is thus complex and acquiring basic negotiating skills is a way to build strength in a negotiation. There have been examples that in IBN two top negotiators having different "styles" have performed equally well: the key to their efficiency is their capacity to adapt to the situation (and the cleverness of top management to assign them (or themselves) to countries or situations where their style is best adapted and accepted). Airbus is sometimes cited as a company that has succeeded in this duality of roles. Press articles have sometimes in the past compared the style of Arthur Howes who, as an article mentions, "sells planes like Hoover sells vacuum cleaners but unlike the brush salesman he sells deals too" using often a softer approach, to that of Bernard Lathiere (described as using often a hard-sell style of negotiating). These opposed types of negotiating have proved equally effective but in different environments and circumstances.

6. Credibility and reputation. Interpersonal confidence, capacity to be trusted ("my word is my bond"), reputation as being reliable and performing (e.g., apt to solve problems constructively, to find innovative solutions, etc.) are also strengths linked to the negotiation but extending also to the organization or business. This is particularly important in IBN. Contracts have been lost because documentation or behavior led the other party to doubt the credibility of the partner.

7. Close to the preceding categories is the capacity to influence: this should not be simply equated to the two preceding items: it covers a wider ground. To influence the other party (parties) in a negotiation requires a combination of skills (e.g., "persuasive power") and a will to use the means available to lead the opponent toward the satisfaction of one's own objectives subject to the constraint of making the proposed (advantageous) solution acceptable (at least minimally) for the other party.

There is a difference (and the point is very important for practitioners) between having access to sources of power (notably objective strengths such as items 1–4) and effectively using power toward goal achievement. A concept that has been elaborated to describe this possible gap is that of "propensity to use power". The propensity to use power may result from objective factors such as the need to enforce or defend strategic stakes or interests (or values) or from the expected impact of the transaction on the cost or profit structure (e.g., in a commercial negotiation the purchasing organization will be the more inclined to use power that savings can be obtained through rebates or be larger than those obtained by the competitors. Their position will be improved because rebates obtained are higher than those obtained by competitors in the case of "aggressive markets"). But it is also connected with personal traits (some people do not like to bargain only on price —

although they may be good negotiators when price is not the major element and that arbitrating between different elements or finding innovations is in fact the crucial variable).

8. Information is an important source of power (this item could be annexed to the influence factor just mentioned as a specific variety of influence). Information depends on a capacity of the individual and/or his/her organization to have access to relevant data; in part also it is a matter of mastering efficient communication techniques in pre-negotiation contacts and during the negotiation, especially in the first phases or sequences. Information power concerns also "touchy" matters such as espionage and spying (see for instance *The International Tribune*, 24 July 1995, p.1) a not altogether abstract issue.

Is it possible to elaborate a more synthetic view of power in the negotiation? Such an effort has been made by Bacharach and Lawler (1980) who have proposed to measure negotiating power by the degree of dependence with which the opponent is faced. The more dependent an actor is relative to opponent, the weaker the negotiating strength. This is to be combined with the weight given by each actor to the importance of the negotiation in respect of punctual, short-term or (better) overall, long-term stakes, interests or objectives (or expectations). According to these authors, "power" (of A) depends on the degree to which opponent (B) receives greater benefits from the relationship with A and B can get from alternatives (1980, pp. 149–50). Hence the power dimension can be broken down in four elements: A's benefits from alternatives; B's benefits from alternatives; value that A attributes to outcomes and value that B attributes to outcomes.

This approach leads to a formalization of power — first proposed by Fisher and Ury (1981) by using the concept of "BATNA": best alternative to a negotiated agreement. The strength of a negotiator is the greater, the number and the global value of his/her alternatives are larger and the number and global value of his/her opponent's alternatives are lower.

This inventory of power sources could be extended to include certain factors that are relevant for specific situations: for example, in organizational negotiations the status of an actor may be a crucial element of so-called "institutional" power; in group (conference) negotiations (e.g., the GATT negotiations) status and roles may also be important power factors. In such negotiations coalitions tend to be formed: "natural" leaders — on the basis of resources they command (votes of reliable allies, capacity to "reward" friendly followers, attractiveness of ideological proximities, etc.) — generally derive power from this leadership.[1] In the UN negotiations the privilege of having been given a veto power at the Security Council gives the five "permanent" members a large amount of effective power.

---

[1] For an analysis of coalitions as a source of power, refer to Zartman (1994). *International multilateral negotiation.* Jossey-Bass and Dupont C. (1996) 'Negotiation as coalition building' in *International Negotiation*, Vol. I, no. 1, pp. 47–64.

Exploring the basis (sources) of power is of key importance in planning a negotiation. Again it has to be recalled that such exploration has sense only if applied to all parties (even indirect ones such as third parties in a conflict): bargaining strength is not an absolute value but a net balance between strengths and vulnerabilities of actor A $(S_A - V_A)$ compared to actor B $(S_B - V_B)$; hence for A, $(S_A - V_B) - (V_A - V_B)$, i.e., the difference in strengths minus the difference in vulnerabilities. Skilled negotiators try to play on the four components: increase their own strengths (before, during and even after the negotiation) while trying to reduce the strengths of the opponent (e.g., for a buyer to threaten an opponent with the possibility of recourse to new suppliers or reducing the number of existing suppliers); similarly, decrease their own vulnerabilities (e.g., avoiding further dependence on a mono-source supply) while increasing opponent's vulnerabilities (e.g., demanding more innovative proposals from a supplier who has limited resources (*R&D*), etc. to innovate). An interesting analysis of the impact of power in IBN has been proposed by Fayerweather and Kapoor (1976) and by Cathelineau (1991) who illustrates the power factor by referring to actual negotiations either diplomatic or commercial and elaborates a model in which power plays a major role.

Apart from power identification several other questions are of interest. Of the four questions mentioned at the beginning of this section, the last two ("weak power", power strategies) may be best addressed in the section relating to strategies. The second item — stability — is a crucial element in the negotiation process. The reason is that two frequent mistakes of practical negotiators is to be wrong (over- under-value) the real relative power position and more frequently to deal and negotiate as if the power imbalance were a fixed (net) sum. Yet the power balance is liable to shifts (sometimes unexpected and brutal) during the negotiation. Failure to monitor continuing changes of the power balance may be detrimental to the effectiveness of the negotiator.

Relationships and climate

The third component of the concept of 'Actor' concerns the type of interpersonal relationships that are established during the negotiation, especially during the first sequences that are liable to structure the climate of the negotiation. Since Walton and McKersie (1965) it is traditional to differentiate cooperative ("integrative") and conflictual (confrontational or "distributive") relationships and behaviors. These behaviors can be described in detail. They manifest themselves in attitudes, actions and styles (see next section).

The interpersonal or group relationship has been given prominent attention (not surprisingly) by the "psychological school" of negotiation theory. This school has emphasized the role of certain personal characteristics (e.g., aggressiveness or openness, anxiety or calmness, risk-aversion or risk-proneness, evasiveness or frankness, etc.) that are treated as variables intervening in the process. Psychologists have focused on motivations (e.g., the threefold distinction between achievement (NACH), affectiveness (NAFF), and power (NEPO) orientations). Psychologists have stressed small group relationships (e.g., the role of a leader or of a "deviant", the development of small-size coalitions, etc.). Relatively recently methods or techniques have been devised to facilitate the acquisition of effective behaviors in negotiation; examples are transactional analysis or neuro-linguistic programming. Communication skills (the "art" of smart questioning, active listening, aptly reformulating, effectively dealing with objections, etc.) have been made part of basic negotiation training courses. Style grids either of a general application, e.g., the Thomas–Kilmann (1977) mode or of a more specific targeting (e.g., style grids of sellers or buyers) may also be used to get an improved knowledge of one's and other's behaviors in negotiation. Mastenbroek (1979) has also offered a style grid.

Structure of the Process

Negotiations are events that are dated, situated at given sites, regroup a given number of participants (size may be small such as in bilateral encounters or number more than one hundred in diplomatic conferences), respect (or not) certain formal procedures, etc. These events moreover cannot be separated from the past (precedents are not for instance a negligible factor in international negotiations); neither is the context (political, economic, social, etc. and in a general manner also logistical details) to be ignored in the negotiation process.

Mandates, the type, composition, status of delegations or negotiating teams, the role of constituencies, third parties or lobbies, are again variables or components of the structure of negotiation. These factors — some of them have sometimes been subsumed as "background factors", the others being rather "concomitant" with the process — are less important by themselves than through their (sometimes crucial) interaction with actors. For instance the moment and duration of negotiation episodes may definitely alter the balance of power or the attitudes of negotiators. They may also sometimes become themselves topics of the negotiation. A classical — although specific — example is the role that the number and shape of tables has played in the Paris negotiations ending the Vietnam War. Obviously what mattered for the negotiators was not the number or shape of the tables but the symbols (diplomatic status) attached to them. Yalta and Camp David are two contrasting illustrations of the use of situational elements to influence the climate of negotiation and perception of bargaining strength. Negotiation of the agenda may also be an important subject of the negotiation proper.

So far the basic elements in the negotiating process have been explored within the framework of a global view of the process (Figure 3.1). It has been underlined that — apart from issues (subject-matters, items, points) of the negotiation — the process is directly influenced by the interactions of stakes and interests, power and relationships of negotiators as well as by the structure of the episode. Acquiring a good knowledge of these elements is a prerequisite in successful planning and conduct of negotiations. The practice of negotiators has emphasized these factors under the form of recommendations, guiding principles or even "golden rules" (unfortunately sometimes put in rather simplistic ways). Research has endeavored to study in depth the various interactions between these elements. Generally based on empirical studies but also on qualitative analyses (case studies, content analysis of personal experiences of negotiators or of actual negotiations) research has developed a number of models of the process and outcomes. A panoramic view of these models is the purpose of what follows.

A Panoramic View of Negotiation Models

In this section the first part is designed to present a synthetic view of the various approaches behind the main models of negotiation that the literature has proposed. In the second part a summary description is given of a few models among those that are considered the best performing. A third section presents an adaptation of the model to IBN.

A synthetic view of models

A French sociologist and negotiation researcher G.O. Faure[2] has presented under the word "Negotiation" in the *Encyclopedia Universalis* a synthetic view of the main approaches of negotiation theories. The crucial question which these theories try to answer is the "why" and "how" of the development of the process and the determination of outcomes. Two principal tracks can be differentiated.

The first is based on the elaboration of models incorporating variables (or clusters of variables) intervening in the process and apt to explain process and outcomes. This line of approach has two basic characteristics, it is — in the words of Faure — "rational and artificial". The method is abstract and its rationality is derived from deductive logic. Two main streams can be distinguished, economic models of negotiation and application of game theories to negotiation. According to the former the key element in the process is the exchange of concessions based on economic calculus (benefits/costs analysis). Representatives of this approach are for example Zeuthen (1930), Pen (1952), Cross (1969), Bartos (1974), and Shakun (1988). Although the approach enlightens a clearly vital element of the negotiation dynamics (the Bartos model is particularly exemplary in this respect) its reliance on a meta-variable only and its non-explicitness of actors or structure components constitutes a severe limitation.

The second line is game theory as illustrated by such authors as Nash (1950), Harsanyi and Selten (1988), Ponssard (1977), Luce and Raiffa (1957). This approach to explain recent negotiations for the European Union, and the Uruguay

---

[2] G.O. Faure. "Negociation: de la théorie au réel". *Encyclopedia Universalis* (1991, pp. 245–8)

Round negotiations has been aptly used by Abrams (in Zartman, ed., 1994)[3]. *The art and science of negotiation* by Raiffa (1982) remains an indispensable reference to this approach (that however combines in a very nice way game theory and decision theory). Game theory applied to negotiations attempts to determine the optimal choice "strategies" faced by the negotiator to maximize his/her gains in a given situation (described by a matrix of potential results) account being taken of the choices (strategies) of the opponent. The explanatory power of this theory varies according to cases, its main limitations being the reliance on rather restrictive — somewhat artificial — assumptions, e.g., "pure" rationality of actors, quasi-perfect information, etc. The complexity of the process is not very well captured compared to the focus attributed to outcomes.

Compared with these "rational and artificial" models, Faure describes a second track which he encapsulates under the expression of "real but elusive". Reality is complex; it is necessary to simplify, i.e., to retain only essential factors but in this process, which is more qualitative than quantitative, the model, if it is closer to reality, captures only part of it; thus the explanation of the process and the determination of outcomes become "elusive". The approach is inductive. Many venues are open to the researcher: historical precedents of negotiations, case studies, content analysis of proceedings, empirical tests of hypotheses. Some of this methodology is purely qualitative, other is statistical. Many "disciplines" have included in their field negotiation as a subject matter. Sociologists (like Strauss or Axelrod), ethnologues (like Gulliver), politicologues (like Zartman), diplomats (like Talleyrand in the past or Kissinger or Plantey now), psychologists (like Walton and McKersie, Rubin and Brown, Touzard or Pruitt) are representatives of these approaches. To the list should be added the descriptions and advices of "practitioners" or "experts" (like Ury and Fisher) although their viewpoint is generally centered on a given domain of negotiation (e.g., labor, commercial or international negotiations — in the latter case; Fayerweather and Kapoor, Usunier), this being not the case with Fisher and Ury who claim that their model is of a general relevance.

A strong impression that results from this description is the variety of approaches and models. Faure remarks that efforts are being made now to bridge the gaps between these various trends. This has been the approach of the PIN group at IIASA (see Kremenyuk, ed., 1991 and Zartman, ed., 1994). Yet this is a real problem for negotiation research. The lack of a unitary paradigm is sorely felt; fortunately some progress is now under way and more synthetic approaches have emerged recently such as notably Lax and Sebenius (1986, see below) and Kremenyuk (1991). New approaches have also emerged such as the cognitive approach of negotiation in contributions by Jonsson (1991) or Bazerman and Neale (1992).

---

[3] See also Siebe's contribution on game theory in the synthetic book on negotiation: V. Kremenyuk, ed. (1991). Schelling (1960) is the author who helped formulate "mixed" strategies in the game theory.

Christophe Dupont

Selected models of negotiation

Here the main models of negotiation are presented; the inventory could have been more extensive but the five "models" that were selected may be considered as representative of theory in its evolution (the models of Walton and McKersie, and of Sawyer and Guetzkow date back some thirty years, yet they remain basic in the field) and in its present state (model of Lax and Sebenius). Another illustration is that of Fisher and Ury. The model proposed by Bartos is characterized by sophisticated statistical analysis of concessions. Another author who has distinguished himself in the study of concessions is Pruitt (1981). Finally mention has already been made of the PIN model (Figure 3.1).

Walton and McKersie (1965)

For these two authors the process of a negotiation is characterized by the dynamics generated by four distinct dimensions or "activities": integrative (non-conflictual goal achievement, leading to a search for solutions with joint gains), distributive (search for unilateral benefit as in a zero-sum game), attitude structuring, attitudes: motivational orientation, legitimacy of opponent, trust level and emotions, which lead to five types of such relationships (conflictual, resistance to aggression, accommodation, cooperation and collusion) and intra-group relationships (related to how the group functions and its relation to the constituencies in terms of expectations, authority and power).

The influence of this model on research, theory and even practice has been considerable: it is considered as the seminal work on negotiation, formulating concepts that have proved powerful such as the integrative/distributive dimensions, the use of "subjective utilities" to measure interests and priorities, and translating them in "positions" (resistance, target points, etc.). True, theory has been led to modify or attenuate certain propositions (e.g., bringing nuances in the dilemma between the cooperative and distributive dimensions) but the model remains a milestone in the history of negotiation theory. A review of the relevance of the model some twenty years after his publication has been the subject of an article by Walton and McKersie (1992).

Sawyer and Guetzkow (1965)

At the moment when Walton and McKersie presented their model two authors, Sawyer and Guetzkow, had approached negotiation from a different perspective. They have attempted to capture as large a number as possible of intervening variables regrouped in five clusters: goal factors (referring to the degree of convergence and to the specificity of goals of parties), "fundamental" factors (referring to a variety of variables such as personality, culture, intragroup relationships, attitudes) — both factors being "antecedent" to the episode of negotiation — "conditions" (regrouping of variables such as those mentioned in

FIGURE 3.1

A diagrammatic presentation of negotiations

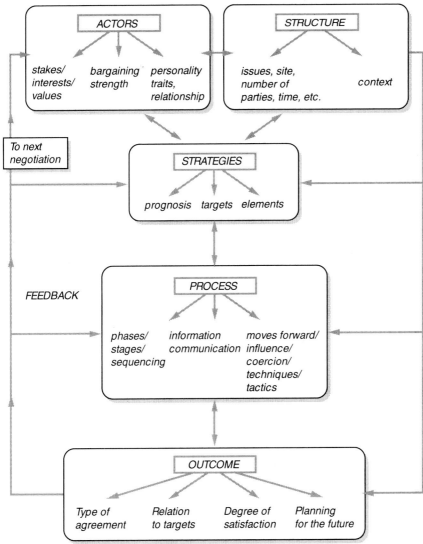

Source: Kremenyuk V. (1991) and Dupont (1994) p. 47

Figure 3.1 under "structure"), "process" (including the degree of planning by negotiators, "utilities", influence and coercion, search for solutions, etc.) — both factors being called "concomitant" to the negotiation episode — and "outcomes" (criteria, clarity, resilience to time, etc.). These five categories are seen as linked together in a causal way. Fundamental factors influence goals; they also influence — together with goals and "conditions" — the process; and

Christophe Dupont

outcomes are determined by process. One of the merits of this model is that it opens the way to identify individual variables, regroup them by nature and tries to explore their contribution to the dynamics of negotiation. The approach is being used by many researchers — such as Druckman — who attempt to inventory the various variables in negotiation and explore their links.

Bartos (1974)

Contrary to the previous authors — whose approch is global and mainly qualitative — Bartos has developed a mathematical model designed to explain the outcome by a limited number of variables. The core of the model is the study of the manner concessions depend on successive offers and demands. The model raises the problem of "hard" versus "soft" strategies and it provides an analysis of the relevance of normative, mathematically determined solutions (e.g., the "Nash" point) to a negotiation. For further developments on the contribution of Bartos see for instance Dupont (1994, pp. 208–212). Apart from this contribution on key problems of negotiation Bartos's approach is of great methodological interest.

Lax and Sebenius (1986)

Lax and Sebenius have elaborated a qualitative model of negotiation which constitutes at the present time one of the best explanations of process and outcome. The model comprises three major components. First the "raw material" of negotiation which include issues, stakes, interests, values and positions of the parties, these elements being the "units of measure" of negotiation. Second are the factors underpinning the process. It is in this analysis that Lax and Sebenius have brought originality and substance. The negotiation process develops through the constant confrontation of "value creating" and "value claiming" elements. While this presentation draws on Walton and McKersie, it proposes a new vocabulary leading the authors to deepen the analysis, orients it toward a strategic focus and reduce the polarization on one side only in the dilemma between cooperation and conflict. In addition their process analysis is accompanied by practical recommendations to negotiators. For example — apart from decoding properly and separating interests and stakes from "positions" (see Fisher and Ury below) — the skilled negotiator will focus on expanding the potential value and benefits of the negotiation options, look for fairness and sustainability and craft agreements that maximize the value that arises out of the differences among the parties as well as shared interests. These are integrative behaviors. Distributive behaviors will consist in trying to alter the opponent's perceptions of BATNAs and achieve one's objectives while avoiding impasses. This description is derived from the presentation by Lax and Sebenius of their seminars "Strategic negotiation. Maximizing the value of important agreements".

The third major component of the process refers to the limits that are imposed on negotiations as a result of their respective BATNAs (either initial or "transformed"[4] during the negotiation). This puts constraints on the margins each negotiator commands and explains the balance between integrative and conflictual forces needed to reach a "strategic outcome", i.e., the design and implementation of agreements that will endure over time.

Prescriptively Lax and Sebenius show their preferences for a predominantly cooperative type of negotiation.[5] They offer recommendations so that the "value creating" elements predominate over "claiming values" (see Lax and Sebenius, op. cit. pp. 164–82): part of the task is to facilitate the integrative factors (e.g., use complementarities, or differing value set by parties on time or risks, find innovative solutions, refer to norms, offer compensations, etc.); another part consists in unmasking and controlling conflictual elements or episodes (such as impasses). In this endeavor Pruitt (1981), and Pruitt and Rubin (1986) have made recommendations that practitioners may have interest to follow.

Fisher and Ury (1981, 1983)

These authors — whose contribution in 1981 *Getting to yes* has had worldwide success — have suggested that negotiators often miss the potential benefits of a negotiation because their focus is on "positions" rather than on what really matters, i.e., "interests". They present a condensed repertoire of four "principles": separate persons from problems; focus on "interests", not on "positions"; look for joint acceptable solutions through continuous un-biased search for new options and accept to adhere to certain mutually chosen criteria, rules and principles. Fisher and Ury's contribution is important (although its merits are more in formulation than in innovation) because it offers simple, clear and powerful concepts toward ideally good agreements. The limitation of the approach is that it tends to a large extent to merge descriptive and prescriptive approaches because it presupposes mutual agreement on "principles" and mutual good faith, and assumes that the situation itself makes a principled negotiation feasible.[6]

The "models" presented above are among the best known and performing in respect of negotiation effectiveness. They are not by any means the only ones.

---

[4] The concept of "transformation" is crucial in Zartman's analysis of negotiation. Although Zartman does not offer a model as such (except for the "formula-detail" decoding of a negotiation) his analysis of negotiation — is with Lax and Sebenius — at the forefront of negotiation theory. See Zartman (1976, 1977, 1994)

[5] In our analysis of Lax and Sebenius's contribution we have proposed not to discard the "old" Walton and McKersie dichotomy of integration–distribution but to attenuate it by observing that the real world shows both "predominantly" integrative and "predominantly" distributive dimensions (Dupont, 1994, pp. 49–54).

[6] For a discussion on this, see again Dupont, op. cit. pp. 134–7 based on McCarthy's analysis (1991).

Christophe Dupont

For instance, from a methodological viewpoint, Raiffa's book (1982) is a key contribution based mainly on decision and game theory. Axelrod's (1984) analysis of the cooperative dimension of negotiation based on an extended experimentation of the prisoner's dilemma is also of interest. Zartman's contributions and those of the PIN group (e.g., the Kremenyuk collective work) have already been mentioned.

The adaptation of the general models of negotiation to the specificity of international business negotiations

Although IBN do exhibit some unique features,[7] they share many of the characteristics of negotiations in general. For this reason the general models as described above have a large degree of relevance for them but they have to be adapted. In this section the approach is to explore how the "common elements" of the negotiation situation apply to IBN and what reconfiguration is needed.

Before presenting such a model, it is appropriate to mention that three sorts of particular difficulties confront this endeavor. First is the fact that under the term "IBN" a large number of categories are to be found. Typologically one would have to distinguish the various institutional contexts. In a matrix which would separate private from public actors on the one hand and characteristics of a country's structural social-economic types (e.g., market-oriented/developed; market-oriented/emergent; less industrialized; state-controlled; transitional from state-controlled to market-oriented) on the other the number of cells is impressive, yet the negotiating situations — due to context differences — may be sufficiently diverse to prevent undue generalization.

What is true of institutional/contextual differences is equally valid in respect of the variety of business dealings: are negotiations relative to standardized products (with probably some probability of repetition and simplified procedures) the same as negotiation for high-tech transactions, turn-key projects, joint-ventures, mergers or acquisitions, technology transfers or multi-media operational arrangements? A third limitation relates to the complex issue of the variety of cultural factors.[8]

A "generic" model of IBN should therefore show enough flexibility to account for this variety of situations: yet whatever the country institutional and cultural framework or the type of transactions all IBN have specific features of commonality as opposed to other negotiations: this is precisely what "a model for international business negotiations" should emphasize. One approach is to base the analysis

---

[7] Fayerweather (1976, p.31) notes for example that perhaps "the unique characteristic of international versus domestic business negotiations is that international negotiations are influenced by a wide variety of environments that determine the selection of appropriate tactics and strategies of negotiations to be adopted".

[8] This aspect is widely covered in this book.

on the major dimensions depicted in the general models and identify the necessary adaptations to be made. This approach has been used to elaborate the following Table 3.2. In the first column key dimensions (aspects, components) of negotiations have been listed. The contents of these dimensions and the references to the general models are detailed in the next columns. The remaining two columns identify the adaptations required and the specific particularly sensitive variables in IBN versus other types of negotiations.

The Negotiator's Different Strategies

The need for clarification

The concept of "strategy" in negotiations is not without certain ambiguities. Many authors — especially the "pragmatists" — use the word concurrently with "tactics" or "techniques". It must be recognized that there are semantic difficulties. While the concept clearly defines general orientations and a focus on the future — as opposed to punctual adjustments or initiatives due to circumstances, obstacles or opportunities — it is sometimes used to characterize goals and at other times to identify the means by which these goals could be reached. These two approaches can be merged. Negotiation strategies are then defined as the elaboration of the general principles which the negotiator — having set for him/herself the goals to be reached — intends to implement in the course of the negotiation to reach these objectives in face of the assumed reactions of the environment. Hence negotiation strategies are altogether a concept, a form of planning and a guide for implementation.

Definition is not the only difficulty. A real problem is the usefulness of strategic approaches in negotiations. Are not negotiations made up of continuous changes, necessary adaptations and improvisations — due to behavior volatilities and irrationalities as well as environmental transformations and uncertainties? Why, it is asked, plan a strategy (or more exactly several strategies) when the future is so uncertain? Rather than strategy would it not be better to emphasize flexibility? This is an opinion often defended in cultures showing a preference for adaptation to "facts" rather than attempts "to rationalize and plan".

However, there are merits in preparing and thinking strategy in the more important negotiations. "Thinking strategically" permits to better situate the negotiation (without concentrating on details), leads to the clarification of objectives, stimulates the search — and evaluation — of options, gives time to plan some major initiatives or actions, allows proper selection of delegates and forces negotiators to reflect on the appropriateness of behaviors according to plans.

The compromise between the two schools is to adapt the amount of resources and time allocated to strategic planning to the importance (stakes) of the negotiation. Routine negotiations, low-level stakes certainly do not call for detailed

TABLE 3.2
The adaptations required for IBN

(1) Key dimensions (elements of the "general models")	(2) The "general models"		(3) Adaptations required for IBN	(4) Sensitive variables in IBN
	Contents and focus	Typical references		
1 The "negotiating situation": (A) context and issues	– motivations to negotiate (why a negotiation is called for) – constituting elements of negotiation: interdependence and conflict – background factors – agenda	– Zartman – Walton and McKersie – Sawyer and Guetzkow – Lax and Sebenius – PIN: Kremenyuk and associates – PIN: Faure and Rubin and associates	– emphasize more the importance and the contents of the "wider context" (Fayerweather) – emphasize cultural variations – often: more complex issues – agenda may not reveal real prognosis of interdependence/ conflict may be more fuzzy – non-negotiability may be due to external factors (e.g., political)	– Antecedents and precedents – contextual and cultural differences – decision-making structure
2 The negotiating situation: (B) Actors ❶	– stakes and interests	– PIN (Kremenyuk) – Fisher and Ury – Dupont	– often: importance of "hidden" dimensions (real versus positional stakes and interests, including personal factors) – often: change of relative priorities over time	– complexity of criteria – hidden interests or stakes
❷	– negotiator's traits, styles and behaviors – types of interrelationship	– cultural models (Faure & Rubin, Weiss and Strip, Holstede, Hall, etc.)	– cultural factors as key dimension related uncertainties – particular importance of "atmosphere" and of personal relationships	– behavioural variables, including "emotional" ("face", pride) and cultural type variables (e.g., ethnocentrism, self-reference criteria, etc.; mono-versus polychronic approach, etc.; stereotypes; language

TABLE 3.2 (continued)

(1) Key dimensions (elements of the "general models")	(2) The "general models"		(3) Adaptations required for IBN	(4) Sensitive variables in IBN
	Contents and focus	Typical references		
❸	– power balance between actors (power factors), actor's constraints and limitations (e.g., legal barriers)	– Fayerweather – Kapoor – Bacharach and Lawler	– complexity of power factors (e.g. external interventions, lobbying, great pressures, change of power balance during negotiation, etc., role of status and real decision power)	– power trust relationships
3 The "negotiating situation": (C) Structure	– timing of meetings – number of meetings – site – teams (delegations, if any): form, organization, number of members (and roles), status – third (or indirect intervening) parties (e.g., government, bureaucracies, media, lobbies, consultants, etc.) – procedures (degree of formality, confidentiality, publicity)	– Sawyer and Guetzkow "concurrent variables"; see also "strategies" – Fayerweather – PIN : Kremenyuk – Raiffa (dyadic) multinational	– impact of cultural factors (including concept of negotiation) on structure – wide variety of designs (less standardized than in "general" negotiations)	– organizational variables – environmental variables – informational variables – cultural variables
4 Strategies	– formulation of negotiation as predominantly integrative or distributive – selection of objectives (goals) and relating priorities	– Walton and McKersic – Lax and Sebenius – Zartman (formula/details; "maturity") – Cathelineau/Dupont (strategic models)	– Differences in short versus long term expectation and goals (generally more pronounced than in other types) – need to distinguish essential from secondary issues and goals	– contextual, relational and power factors – complexity of real "utilities" (priorities, preference scales). Multiple criteria – BATNA's (and changes in)

TABLE 3.2 (continued)

(1) Key dimensions (elements of the "general models")	(2) The "general models"		(3) Adaptations required for IBN	(4) Sensitive variables in IBN
	Contents and focus	Typical references		
	– control on the "atmosphere" of the negotiation and monitoring transitions from one stage to the next – control of timing and duration – selective choice of strategic maneuvering (e.g., attack/defence; frontal/indirect; coalitions; selective use of techniques and tactics) – concessional strategy – analysis and use of resources within and without)	– Bartos/Pruitt (concessional strategy) – Fayerweather, Kapoor, Weiss (strategic sequencing and strategic analysis) – Ury and Fisher ("BATNA: Best Alternative To a Negotiated Agreement) – Axelrod: "tit for tat"	– need to control sequencing of stages more carefully – stronger need for flexibility and capacity to respond to (possibly) rapidly changing conditions and expectations – necessity to monitor frequent intervention of "external" forces or factors – possible (and sometimes unexpected) linkages with other negotiations, precedents or problems (both a threat and an opportunity)	– uncertainty and instability variables – expectations on future relationships.
5 Process	– Time structure (phases, episodes) and sequencing (transitions) – communication processes and argumentation – events, initiatives – techniques and tactics of negotiators – pressures (distributive) versus persuasion (cooperatives) (coercion versus influence)	– PIN (Kremenyuk) – Sawyer and Guetzkow (concurrent variables) – Lax and Sebenius (value-creating and value-claiming) – Fisher and Ury (getting to yes) – Bartos – Zartman (formula/details) – Faure and Rubin – S. Weiss	– Importance of rituals – often: large number of separate episodes over time – often: process, not linear (fuzzy rather than strict logic) – often: progress toward agreement somewhat erratic – concept of negotiation varies according to cultures (hence impacts on process)	– cultural variables (e.g., attitude toward time, language, concept of negotiation, etc.) – informational variables (include concept of "broad perspective") – power factors (multi-faceted, e.g., asymmetries, instability, coalitions, etc.) – negotiating skills in different contexts

TABLE 3.2 *(continued)*

(1) Key dimensions (elements of the "general models")	(2) The "general models"		(3) Adaptations required for IBN	(4) Sensitive variables in IBN
	Contents and focus	Typical references		
	– proposals and counterproposals – concessions and counterparts – stress – creativity	– Fayerweather, Kapoor		
6 Outcomes	– termination: agreement/ break-off/different – contents and legal form of agreement – feedback – re-negotiation(s)	– same as above plus law-oriented models	– key importance of how to conclude ("face") – differences in law and contract formulations and interpretations – need for special care relating to problem of guarantees (including arbitration, mediation, etc.) – increased need to prepare for future (re-negotiations, trust-building, perspectives of new business, etc.)	– assessment criteria – credibility trust and authority factors – legal dimensions

cost- and time-expensive strategic preparation. Crucial negotiations, especially those with content complexity or with expected extended length, need by contrast great care in strategic formulation.

The compromise calls also for flexible rather than rigid formulations. Contingency planning (ranging from best- to worst-case scenarii) is the way to reconcile the need for a guiding line and the necessity to take account of the unknown, the surprises and the possible (and probable) fragilities resulting from errors in framing assumptions and from judgemental errors shown by the cognitive school.

Planning a negotiation strategy

Flexibility addresses also the type of planning that is envisaged: as many concepts and even methods in negotiation should not be unduly generalized (in a given negotiation it is probably appropriate to provide the negotiator leeway in the manner he/she would like to plan the negotiation). However certain principles — based on practice and research — seem to hold. Planning a negotiation strategy implies several largely interrelated steps: diagnosis, goal-setting, determination of criteria and strategic choices and organization.

Diagnosis consists in exploring the elements which are bound to impact on goal-setting (a consideration of realism based on an analysis of constraints confronting the parties) and on strategic choices. Reference can be made to the model presented in Figure 3.1. Hence, diagnosis can be based on factors relating to the agenda (list of issues known or potential), actors (how the negotiation could affect stakes, interests and values, how it is influenced by precedents and context, how the power balance could impact on the process and potential result, and how the known or assumed behavior, personalities, experience and styles of negotiators could determine the type of interpersonal or intergroup relationships and the "atmosphere" that would result). Diagnosis is useful to the extent that it attempts to define (more or less accurately) the situational framework of the negotiation, helps to delineate the limits, risks and constraints present in the situation and offers a measure of "realism" within which to set objectives and apply strategic criteria to strategic choices to be made.

Target-setting is a necessary step in negotiation planning. It might be advisable to start from the facts that have been uncovered and analyzed in the diagnosis (this is a consequence of the saying that it is wise "to have the means of one's policies", i.e., to be realistic about aims given the situation and the resources available), but in certain circumstances target-setting may be more risk-prone, i.e., determining objectives beyond what the present situation seems to permit, such conduct implying a determined effort to change, rather than to adapt to, the environment. Target-setting may be formulated in different ways: some prefer rather fixed, detailed objectives others would rather content themselves with more flexible zones; however, it is advisable to define priorities (separating the "essential" from the "not-so-important", etc.) and set a clear bottom-line posture (see BATNA) which delimits the margin of action ("maneuvers"), and trading-off certain objectives against others. Some negotiators like to negotiate in a step-by-step (gradual) movement which implies achievement over time of certain partial goals leading in the end to the attainment of the overall objective.

Strategy presupposes a determination not only of priorities but of criteria. Criteria relate essentially to the contents of strategic choices and organization. Effectiveness of these choices is obviously the main factor to consider.

The problem of strategic contents: strategic choices

Strategy is intention and choice. Intention is a matter of will behind objective-setting. Choice is the solution of the most appropriate paths to attain these objectives. What are the main choices open to a negotiator; in other terms, what are the main different strategies available to the negotiator?

"Models" of different strategies

Contrary to "tactics" (punctual initiatives, tools and behaviors) and "techniques" (monitoring the various items of negotiations) which are manifold, there is only a limited number of strategic orientations for a negotiator (Dupont 1994). We shall explore first the main strategic modalities, then describe a few models used by some practitioners; while doing this we shall decode the criteria (variables) that underpin such models.

Modalities: "generic" strategies of negotiations

The same way as management theory and practice have developed "generic strategies", several main generic strategies for the negotiator may be differentiated.

The first, and probably the most important, is a choice between a predominantly cooperative and a predominantly conflictual ("competitive", confrontational, "distributive") orientation. The differences are many in terms of attitudes and behaviors, information exchange, concession handling, the role of problem solving and creativity, the types of pressure (persuasion versus distributive tactics such as threats, ultimatums, overbidding, machiavellianism, systematic bluff, destabilization, unilateral commitment of opponent, etc.), the type and stability of agreement, etc. Three remarks should be made regarding this first-basic-orientation.

First, selecting one of these orientations is not an entirely free choice: choice depends on the situation (agenda, stakes, interests, bargaining strength, perception of opponent behavior). True, it is often influenced by the negotiator personality, experience and competence (some negotiators are good performers in a soft style, other as "hard bargainers"). But certainly the major factor is the expectation and actual observation of opponent's choice. The Prisoner's dilemma paradigm has shown, especially after Axelrod (1984) that the worst choice a negotiator makes in a dyadic interaction is being soft in front of a hard bargainer, of being

Christophe Dupont

cooperative while the other is systematically distributive, of showing good faith when dealing with a machiavellian adversary. It is not necessary to consider long-past history; recent international conflicts are a present-time illustration. It is however necessary to be a little bit cautious in recommendation. Given certain — probably restricted — conditions, repeated cooperative attitudes may in the end be successful. That seems to be Fisher and Ury's advice (1991). Perhaps an appropriate strategy in these "mixed" situations is the "tit for tat" approach of Axelrod.

A second comment concerns the fact that strategies are now always "pure" strategies. As Lax and Sebenius (1986) have shown any negotiation embodies both cooperative ("value creating") and distributive ("value claiming") features. Hence a cooperative strategy will not be impasse-free: deadlocks and impasses might well emerge during some negotiation episodes. What will differentiate between the two types of negotiation is the way parties will undertake the problem-solving task. For a cooperative negotiation Pruitt (1981) has developed various procedures and actions to "break the impasse". He identifies not two but three main strategies in what he calls the "strategic choice model" (op. cit. p. 228): unilateral concession, competitive and coordinate behavior. One may perhaps also relate this first strategic orientation to Fisher and Ury's differentiation of "positional" versus "principled" negotiations.

A third comment is essential for practice. Strategy starts at the planning stage and this is elaborated on the bases of assumptions and expectations. Nothing guarantees that these hypothetical foundations are realistic. Hence the negotiator should be prepared to adapt strategy to reality. Flexibility (yet firmness about essential stakes and priorities) is called for. A wise negotiator should have fall-back strategies as a last resort.

Another basic strategy orientation differentiates offensive and defensive conducts and behaviors: in a commercial negotiation a seller will very often (but now always so) try to take the initiative while the buyer will respond (often but now always so) by a more defensive attitude. Different tactical actions are associated with each of these opposed choices.

Another important strategic orientation relates to time. The negotiator may choose to act so as to conclude rapidly or he/she may prefer a negotiation that develops over a series of long, perhaps delayed episodes.

The fourth orientation concerns the type of agreement sought: partial, comprehensive, conditional, broken into parts, etc.

Finally a fifth strategic choice model draws on Axelrod's concept of "tit for tat" responses. The dilemma is between trying to impose a scenario no matter what the opponent's reactions may be, or to be adaptative and flexible, changing scenarii as the negotiation develops and adapting one's behavior to that of the opponent.

These may be considered as the main strategic "generic" orientations. The list is indicative. For example one could also consider "generic" the choice between frontal (as in a chess game) or indirect (as in the gô game) approaches.

Also one could specifically refer to the diplomacy of small additive steps or step-by-step approaches although this could be analyzed as a variety of strategies relating to time. Some of them may be combined, others are mutually exclusive. In any case they are phrased in terms of general behaviors, initiatives and principles. It is required to translate them in concrete guiding lines once the issues and stakes are identified. This may look abstract but in fact the task is facilitated by experience, common sense and the concrete specifications of a given situation.

Planning for different strategies

Any given generic strategy as described above is associated with a number of different behaviors, initiatives and decisions. These concern techniques as well as tactics to be privileged. For example in a predominantly cooperative strategy a package-deal technique may be preferred to dealing issue-per-issue and warnings would be preferred to threats, etc. Some of these choices are rather well determined and constant, others have to be adapted or improvised according to circumstances.

Planning implementation of a "generic" strategy requires that certain elements have to be explored so as to ensure compatibility and cohesiveness. Various checklists are available. The elements to be explored may for instance be as follows (some of them are relevant only for certain situations):

- What scenarii (more or less detailed) are available for the negotiation? What is the degree of sure things to come? What may be generated by a negotiator so as to happen? What are the constraints, uncertainties, the risks? What "terrain" should be preferred? (facts, precedents, statistics, argumentative/legal approaches, norms, etc.)?
- What are the alternatives/options that are open or could be organized?
- What could be fall-back positions/strategies?
- How to deal with time (stages, pace of the negotiation)?
- What could be the preferential techniques (perhaps also tactics) to be used?
- What major initiatives/actions are to be resorted to, at what time, how? Should they be organized right now?
- How "positions" should be determined and presented? What is the likely zone of settlement? the BATNAs? the margins of maneuvering?
- What type of agreement (partial, comprehensive, differed) should be sought? Are these non-negotiable issues to be excluded from the agenda (and hence from the agreement)?
- How does the present negotiation deal with the future (short and long-term)? How does the present negotiation pave the way for the next one?

Different strategies: some practice-related models and associated criteria

As illustrations of practice-oriented models of negotiator's strategies two have been selected that are relevant in commercial negotiations.

A model based on "trust" and "strength" For Marc Cathelineau (1991), an author-practitioner, a model of strategic choice in complex negotiations may be based on two major variables: the balance of power and the level of trust. Combining these two dimensions which can be put graphically on two orthogonal axes) six major strategic choices are determined: a strategic choice intervenes in the phase of planning (then the choice is based on expectations and/or assumptions) or in conducting the negotiation (assumptions are then tested which may result in a changed strategic choice). This is a reminder that planning and above all implementing a strategy should never be based on unilateral preferences but on both preferences and anticipations or observation of opponent's behaviors and strategies.

Cathelineau's six categories are as follows:

- balance of power strongly favorable, trust level low; this calls for a coercive strategy
- balance of power indecisive, trust level low; this calls for an opportunistic strategy
- balance of power unfavorable, trust level low; this calls for a defensive strategy

These strategies are predominantly distributive (confrontational); the three other choices are by contrast mainly cooperative:

- balance of power strongly favorable, trust level high; this calls for a relation-oriented, long-term strategy
- balance of power undecisive, trust level high; the preferred choice should then be balanced cooperation (this case is — with the one mentioned above — the most likely to present itself in commercial dealings, including IBN)
- balance of power strongly unfavorable, trust level high; this corresponds to a "solution" strategy.

The author accompanies this differentiation by a list of practical recommendations on the use of certain tools (appropriate techniques and tactics).

A model based on relationship and market positioning Inspired by new ideas and concepts in industrial marketing or "Business to Business" (developed in particular by the IMP: The Industrial Marketing and Purchasing Project, a group of European academics and professionals) models have been developed which can be (and have been) adapted to commercial negotiations. One of these is proposed by Salle and Silvestre (1992), drawing on the previous research of McCall and Warrington (1986). Five strategic choices are identified by combining three sets of variables: the customer's "attractiveness" (strong or weak), the type of relationship (positive or negative) and the business-to-business perspectives (favorable or unfavorable). To take two extremes: strong attractiveness combined with positive (past and anticipated) relationships and favorable market perspectives would induce a relation-oriented, long-term strategy. The opposite positioning of each of the variables would induce a strategy based on withdrawal. Intermediate cases are defined as offensive, defensive and controlling. As for Cathelineau's model this one is also relevant for IBN.

A number of corporations and consultants have devised similar grids based on the specificities of the problems at hand. Most of them are inspired by "strategic grids", for example the initial BCG (Boston Consulting Group) matrix differentiating between "development", "consolidation" and "withdrawal". For international commercial negotiations Fayerweather and Kapoor (1976) have designed a model embodying in particular contextual and cultural factors.

Concluding Remarks

This chapter has focused on a panoramic exploration of several important dimensions of negotiation theory and practice. First the basic elements of the process have been examined, reference being made to issues; stakes, interests and values; bargaining strength; actors' relationships and the "structure" of the negotiation. The point has been made that in planning or conducting a negotiation the presence and "reality" of the opposite side should never be ignored.

Then a second key dimension has been explored based on the number and interrelations of a variety of variables. Research has been led to propose models of process, some of a quantitative, some of a qualitative type. A few illustrations have been given to show the guiding principles of these models. An application (implying adaptations of these models) to IBN has been presented.

A third dimension refers to the possibility for a negotiator to plan and implement strategies. The relevance of such approaches has been discussed as well as the main elements that can be embodied in a strategic choice. Two practice-oriented models have been used as illustrations and they can also be adapted to IBN.

Negotiation research is nowadays very active and even "fashionable". While there is as yet no unified paradigm to take account of the many facets of this activity, progress is constantly made as evidenced by the quality and innovativeness of recent contributions. Practice should also contribute to this development. All too often practitioners do not know the wealth of reflexion and general information that is available; they often rely on certain ready-made formulas, some of them very basic and clever, others rather simplistic in formulation and questionable in effectiveness. A bridge has to be built to gradually close the gap between research and practice. This is not only desirable but, equally important, feasible.

CHAPTER 4

Vis-a-vis International Business Negotiations

JOHN GRAHAM

> "All ya gotta do is act naturally ..."
> Ringo Starr

The Russian Kiss (Moscow)

What an adventure. It was 1989, and this was my last night in town after a two-week stay. The Mezh (Mezhdunarodnaya Hotel) had been comfortable for the first week. But I still wasn't over my jet lag by the time I got to the Sputnik Hotel for week two. There's an eleven-hour time difference between Irvine and Moscow. And nothing gets better at the Sputnik. The food, furniture, linens, laundry, electrical power and plumbing were all ... well, intermittent is the kindest adjective I can use. In the fifties I'm sure the Sputnik was a nice place. In fact, in the fifties, Moscow was probably a nice place. Now it isn't nice, but it is interesting.

Despite my personal problems with the business infrastructure in Moscow, my work had gone well and my host, Leonid, had dragged me out once again for a bit of a going-away party. This time it was the Russian equivalent of the Ed Sullivan Show, but staged in a huge smoke-filled, booze-guzzling restaurant. There were singers, dancers, jugglers, and fire-eaters. Most were scantily clad, but all were very talented in their specialties. Most impressive was the speed at which the big roller skater twirled his petite partner. They looked more like a NASA maximum-gravity experiment or perhaps a new cosmonaut launching system. Thankfully he didn't lose his grip.

Between the acts came the food, oceans of it including wave after wave of a greasy sliced salami and sliced cucumbers. Lots of cucumbers — obviously cucumbers ship well, even over Russian roads. And there was absolutely no reason to smoke at dinner. The concentration of Winston and Marlboro smoke floating free in the air was far greater than anyone could possibly suck out of the end of any one cigarette. And the alcohol — relentless toasting. Thick red

69

wine, volumes of vodka, and Moscow beer. Whatever you put your hand on first was fine. I had asked about the red-label Moscow beer the first time it was served to me in the Cosmos Hotel two weeks earlier, "Is this the most popular brand?" My hosts had all gotten a good laugh at my free-enterprise naivete — one replied, "Yes, it's not only the most popular, in fact it's the *only* brand!"

The two weeks had been a test of my physical stamina, a big change from decaf, cappuccinos and huevos rancheros in seaside patio cafes in California. I had entertained these same comrades in Newport Bearch and Disneyland, and now they were returning the favor. Good friends and colleagues, all wonderful people. Despite the partying or perhaps because of the partying, I was feeling quite at home, quite comfortable with these Russians. Remarkable. And then he kissed me. In saying good-bye to me at my hotel, Leonid wrapped his big arms around me, gave me a big hug, and planted his lips right on my cheek!

Now I know that Russian men kiss each other on the cheeks. I've seen *Doctor Zhivago* in the theaters and newspaper pictures of even Khrushchev or Gorbachev issuing kisses of greeting. The French do the same thing, although I assume there's a difference in technique. And after all, I teach and/or write about this "cultural difference stuff" every day. Manners of greeting vary from country to country.

And now my quandary? Do I kiss Leonid back? And if I do, how do I do it? After all, how hard you squeeze someone's hand says a lot in the United States. In Japan the intricacies of bowing properly are learned only after years of practice. Back in the States there are all kinds of kisses — pecks, smooches, wet ones, french ones, passionate and passionless, even "sucking face". This Russian kiss included much more lip than the typical touching of cheeks I had experienced in greeting women in Brazil, France and Spain. Would a peck be impersonal? But if I do it wrong, I can just picture Leonid getting into the cab, rubbing his cheek with his coat sleeve, and cursing those "sloppy Americans". Ringo's words, "All ya' gotta do is act naturally," simply didn't help me on that Moscow street in front of the Sputnik Hotel.

Marlin Fishing in Brazil (Rio de Janeiro)

Having a big fish on the end of the line can be quite exciting. It can also be a lot of work — back-breaking, muscle-cramping exasperation. The worst is when you've finally maneuvered that trophy close to the boat, and again your fishing reel begins to sing. There he goes again, down with your monofilament line playing out through the eyes of your arching pole to the dark blue depths. Once again, you'll have to begin the exhausting tedium of bringing him back to the boat.

I've seen this drama played out in a boat off Baja. I've also seen this drama played out in an office tower in Rio de Janeiro. In the latter case, the role of the fisherman was filled by a young vice-president of a major East Coast bank, and the role of the big fish was enacted by his Brazilian client.

It was a hot afternoon in February and all four of us were sweating because the air conditioning had gone out. Two representatives of the Bank of Boston were calling on the Brazilian financial manager of the local office of Solar Turbines (now a Division of Caterpillar Tractor Co.). I had been given permission by the top management at Solar to observe this meeting and several others in Brazil and other countries as part of my studies of international negotiation styles. Because I had previously worked at Solar, I was presented as an employee, which made it possible to observe unobtrusively.

The American bankers were in Brazil to present a new set of financial services developed specifically for branch offices of American companies in other countries. The junior Bank of Boston executive had been in Rio for more than two years. He spoke some Portuguese and had called on the client previously. Their relationship seemed quite positive. The vice-president, having recently been made responsible for the Rio de Janeiro branch, had come to Brazil for the first time to meet the people and to convey some of the particulars of the "new product options" to potential customers and his staff.

Because of the heat, the senior American refused the offered cup of coffee. Now I would be the first to agree that Brazilian coffee is a killer. More than one small espresso-sized cup and both your collar and shoes begin to feel too tight. In fact, the Brazilians who visit the US call our strongest, blackest brew "tea". But refusing the coffee was only the banker's first mistake. There would be others.

Introductions were made. The talk began with the usual "How do you like Rio?" questions — "have you been to Ipanema, Copacabana, Corcovado, ...?" We also talked about the flight down from New York, "Did you stop in Bahia?" After about five minutes of this chatting, the senior American quite conspicuously glanced at his watch, and then asked his client what he knew about the bank's new services.

"A little", responded the Brazilian. The senior American whipped a brochure out of his briefcase, opened it on the desk in front of the client, and began his sales pitch.

After about three minutes of "fewer forms, electronic transfers, and reducing accounts receivables," the Brazilian jumped back in, "Yes, that should make us more competitive ... and competition is important here in Brazil ... in fact, have you been following the World Cup futbol (soccer) matches recently, great games ..." And so the reel began to whir, paying out that monofilament, right there in that hot high-rise office.

Given a few minutes dissertation on the local futbol teams, Pele, and why futbol wasn't popular in the United States, the American started to try to crank the Brazilian back in. The first signal was the long look at his watch, then the interruption, "Perhaps we can get back to the new services we have to offer."

The Brazilian did get reeled back into the subject of the sale for a couple of minutes, but then the reel started to sing again. This time he went from efficient banking transactions to the nuances of the Brazilian financial system to the

Brazilian economy. Pretty soon we were all talking about the world economy and making predictions about the US presidential elections.

Another look at his Rolex, and the American started this little "sport fishing" ritual all over again. From my perspective (I wasn't investing time and money toward the success of this activity), this all seemed pretty funny. Every time the American VP looked at his watch during the next 45 minutes, I had to bite my cheeks to keep from laughing out loud. He never did get to page two of his brochure. The Brazilian just wasn't interested in talking business with someone he didn't know pretty well.

My guess is that the local American bank representative had told his boss that the best you can expect to accomplish in a first meeting with a Brazilian is to establish a good rapport. Maybe this can be done in five minutes in the States, but it takes much longer in most other countries, especially Brazil. The time it takes to sip that first canister of caffeine is the bare minimum. Then you should really forget about technical business talk at the first meeting.

Probably the VP actually heard the advice. Perhaps he really didn't comprehend its importance and he really didn't appreciate how rude this American "let's-get-down-to-business" attitude can appear to foreigners. Or more likely, even if he was trying to adapt to Brazilian customs, it's not so easy to *not* "act naturally". That's because much of our "acting" in such interpersonal situations is unconscious behavior.

That Brazilian never did get close to the boat, and it was not clear that the local rep could fix things after the VP returned to Boston. When the two of them left the Brazilian summed up the meeting, "Some of these Americans are unbelievable! At least most of the people I work with in this company know how things work outside the States."

Glimpses in an *Aisatsu* (Tokyo)

It is not so much that speaking only English is a disadvantage in international business. Instead, it's more that being bilingual is a huge advantage. My notes from sitting in on an *Aisatsu* (a meeting or formal greeting for high-level executives typical in Japan) involving the president of a large Japanese industrial distributor and the marketing vice-president of an American machinery manufacturer are instructive. The two companies were trying to reach an agreement on a long-term partnership in Japan.

Business cards were exchanged and formal introductions made. One of his three subordinates acted as an interpreter for the Japanese president, even though the president spoke and understood English. The president asked us to be seated. The interpreter sat on a stool between the two senior executives. The general attitude between the parties was friendly but polite. Tea and a Japanese orange drink were served.

The Japanese president controlled the interaction completely, asking questions of all of us Americans through the interpreter. Attention of all the participants was given to each speaker in turn. After this initial round of questions for all the Americans, the Japanese president focused on developing a conversation with the American vice-president. During this interaction an interesting pattern in nonverbal behaviors developed. The Japanese president would ask a question in Japanese. The interpreter then translated the question for the American vice president. While the interpreter spoke, the American's attention (gaze direction) was given to the interpreter. However, the Japanese president's gaze direction was at the American. Therefore, the Japanese president could carefully and unobtrusively observe the American's facial expressions and nonverbal responses. Additionally, when the American spoke, the Japanese president had twice the response time. Because he understood English, he could formulate his responses during the translation process.

What's this extra response time worth in a strategic conversation? What's it worth to be carefully able to observe the nonverbal responses of your top-level counterpart in a high-stakes business negotiation? Later in the article I'll talk more about some of the other strategic and tactical advantages of knowing more than one language. But for now, my point is a simple one — bilingualism is not a natural characteristic for Americans, and thereby we afford our competitors with greater language skills a natural advantage in international commerce.

The Importance of Culture (New Jersey)

A few years ago I attended a conference on international business alliances sponsored by the Rutgers and Wharton Business Schools. Now you New Yorkers probably see a Jersey joke coming (culture in New Jersey?) but the keynote speaker at the conference started out a bit differently.

"You've all heard the story about the invention of copper wire — two Dutchmen got a hold of a penny." This bit of anecdotage was served up during a dinner speech by the American president of a joint venture owned by AT&T and Philips. At one level the story is a friendly gibe, although the professor from the Netherlands sitting at our table didn't appreciate the American's remarks in general or the ethnic joke in particular. Indeed, at another level the story is stereotyping of the worst sort.

However, at an even deeper level there is an important lesson here for all managers of international commercial relationships. Culture can get in the way. The American president was in his "humorous" way attributing part of the friction between him and his Dutch associates to differences in cultural values. He might have blamed personality differences or clashing "corporate" cultures, but instead he identified national cultural barriers to be a major difficulty in managing his joint venture. And although I also did not appreciate his humour, I certainly agree that cultural differences between business partners can cause divisive, even decisive problems.

Kathryn Harrigan at Columbia University suggests that a crucial aspect of international commercial relationships is the negotiation of the original agreement.

The seeds of success or failure are often sown fact-to-face at the negotiating table, where not only are financial and legal details agreed but also, and perhaps more important, the ambience of cooperation is established. Indeed, as Harrigan indicates, the legal details and the structure of international business ventures are almost always modified over time, and usually through negotiations. But the atmosphere of cooperation established initially face-to-face at the negotiation table persists or the venture fails.

Plan for this chapter

"Okay, so Americans don't know how to return Russian kisses, we look at our watches too much, we just barely passed Spanish II in high school, and we tell bad jokes. So what?"

Although at this point it may seem so, this chapter is not about American bashing. You don't need me for that. There are more objective sources. I ran across this quote in *Expansion*, a Spanish business newspaper: "Los mejores negociadores son los japoneses, capaces de pasarse dias intentando conocer a su oponente. Los peores, los norteamericanos, que peinsan que las cosas funcionan igual que en su pais en todas partes" (29 November 1991, page 41). Roughly translated, this says, "The best negotiators are the Japanese because they will spend days trying to get to know their opponents. The worst are Americans because they think everything works in foreign countries as it does in the USA." Part of the reason I've included this quote is it balances out the aforementioned "penny stretching crack." That is, Samfrits Le Poole, the quoted author of *How to Negotiate with Success*, is Dutch. And I always listen to the Dutch guys. As a national group they have the best international skills. It ·seems they all speak about five languages and have lived in as many countries.

Certainly there are some Americans who are very effective in international business negotiations. And in some circumstances the best prescription might be something we call an American approach. However, in the pages to follow I must be critical at times, because a secondary purpose of this chapter is to get you to change your behavior. But usually meaningful changes in behavior take both time and many contacts with your foreign counterparts. In fact, the best way to learn to behave appropriately in a foreign country is by letting yourself unconsciously imitate those with whom you interact frequently. And a penchant for careful observation is also crucial. Hopefully, this article will help you sharpen your observation skills.

The primary purpose of this chapter is to make you aware of the multiple ways cultural differences in values and communication styles can cause serious misunderstandings between otherwise positively disposed business partners. And many of these problems manifest themselves in face-to-face meetings at the international negotiation table. For example, a silent Japanese doesn't necessarily mean reticence and a Spaniard's frequent interruptions shouldn't communicate rudeness to you. And if that aforementioned Japanese president spoke English, why didn't he use it? Was that Brazilian incompetent, a futbol freak, or what? And what does it mean to be kissed by your Russian business partner?

I cannot answer all of these questions here. Clearly, after you have finished the chapter, you'll still have more work to do. It will be your responsibility to deepen your understanding of cultural differences by asking your clients and partners directly about the strange things they do that weren't mentioned in Graham's article. Such informal interaction in a friendly place and in a friendly way will in the long run be far more important than any article, book or course on this subject, including mine!

Negotiation Styles in Other Countries

During the last 15 years, a group of colleagues[1] and I have systematically studied the negotiation styles of business people in 16 countries (18 cultures) — Japan, Korea, Taiwan, China (northern and southern), Hong Kong, the Philippines, Russia, Czechoslovakia, Germany, France, the United Kingdom, Spain, Brazil, Mexico, Canada (Anglophones and Francophones), and the United States. More than 1,000 business people have participated in our research. I chose these countries because they comprise America's most important present and future trading partners. I'd very much like to study negotiation styles in Tahiti, but, at the moment, we don't do much business there.

I have learned two important lessons by looking broadly across the several cultures. The first, I no longer generalize about regions. Had you asked me ten years ago, "Do Koreans and Japanese negotiate in the same way?", I would have responded, "I suppose so, they're both Oriental cultures." Anyone who has negotiated in both places knows the folly in that naivete. Indeed, the Japanese and Korean styles are quite similar in some ways, but, in other ways, they couldn't be more different. So now I talk about one country at a time, and even then the locals will always advocate within-country regional differences. For example, the Spaniards at my last seminar in Madrid told me the best negotiators in Spain

---

[1] Over the past 15 years, a group of colleagues and I have been gathering data for this research. The following institutions and people have provided crucial support for the research for this article: US Department of Education; Toyota Motor Sales USA, Inc.; Solar Turbines, International (a division of Caterpillar Tractors Co.); the Faculty Research and Innovation Fund and the International Business Educational Research (IBEAR) Program at the University of Southern California; Ford Motor Company; The Marketing Science Institute; Madrid Business School; and Professors Nancy J. Adler (McGill University), Nigel Campbell (Manchester Business School), A. Gabriel Esteban (University of Houston, Victoria), Leonid I. Evenko (Russian Academy of the National Economy), Richard H. Holton (University of California, Berkeley), Alain Jolibert (Université de Sciences de Grenoble), Dong Ki Kim (Korea University), C. Y. Lin (National Sun-Yat Sen University), Hans-Günther Meissner (Dortmund University), Alena Ockova (Czechoslovak Management Center), Sara Tang (Mass Transit Railway Corporation, Hong Kong), and Theodore Schwarz (Monterrey Institute of Technology).

are from Valencia, because of the persistent mercantile influence of the ancient Phoenicians. Now that's a stretch! But the point is, they see a difference between behaviors typical in Madrid and Valencia.

The second lesson from the list of countries is that Japan is a strange place. I don't mean that in a negative way. It's just that on almost every dimension of negotiation style we consider, the Japanese are on or near the end of the scale. Sometimes, we Americans are on the other end. Recall Le Poole's earlier comment. But, actually, most of the time we Americans are somewhere in the middle. You'll see this evinced in the data we present later in the article. The Japanese approach, however, is most distinct, even unique.

The methods of our studies include a combination of interviews with experienced executives from both sides of the table; field observations of business negotiations in most of the countries listed; behavioral science laboratory simulations. (See box 4.1 for details regarding the simulations.) The integration of these approaches allows a "triangulation" of our findings — that is, we can compare results across research methods. Indeed, we have found mostly consistency across methods, but we have also discovered discrepancies. For example, when we interviewed Americans who had negotiated with Japanese, their comments were consistent with those of Van Zandt (1970), "Negotiations take much longer." And, when in the behavioral science laboratory we match American negotiators with Japanese, the negotiations take longer (an average of about 25 minutes for Americans with Americans, 35 minutes for Americans with Japanese). So, in this respect, our findings are consistent for both interviews and laboratory observations. When we talk with Americans who have negotiated with Japanese, universally they describe them as being "poker-faced," or as displaying no facial expressions. However, in the laboratory simulations, we focused a camera on each person's face and recorded all facial expressions. We then counted them, finding no difference in the number of facial expressions (smiles and frowns). Apparently, Americans are unable to "read" Japanese expressions, and they wrongly describe Japanese as expressionless. Thus, discrepancies demonstrate the value of balancing and comparing research methods and results.

A Hierarchy of Problems

We find that cultural differences cause four kinds of problems in international business negotiations:

1. Language
2. Nonverbal behaviors
3. Values
4. Thinking and decision-making processes.

The order is important. As you go down the list, the problems are more serious because they are more subtle. Both negotiators notice immediately if one is speaking Japanese and the other German. The solution to the problem may be

76

> **Box 4.1** Behavioral science laboratory simulation
>
> The participants in the study included business people from 18 cultures. There were at least forty in each group. All have been members of executive education programs or graduate business classes, and all have at least two years' business experience in their respective countries. The average age of the 1,066 participants was 35.2 years, and the average work experience was 11.2 years.
>
> We asked participants to play the role of either a buyer or a seller in a negotiation simulation. In the case of the Japanese and Americans, three kinds of interactions were staged: Japanese/Japanese, American/American, and American/Japanese. In the other countries, only intracultural negotiations (that is, Koreans with Koreans, Brazilians with Brazilians, etc.) were conducted. The negotiation game involved bargaining over the prices of three commodities. The game was simple enough to be learned quickly but complex enough to provide usually one-half hour of face-to-face interaction (Kelley, 1966).
>
> Following the simulation, results were recorded and each participant was asked to fill out a questionnaire that included questions about each player's performance and strategies and his/her opponent's strategies. The profits attained by individuals in the negotiation exercise constituted the principal performance measure. We used a variety of statistical techniques to compose the results of the several kinds of interactions.
>
> Finally, we videotape-recorded some of the exercises for further analysis. Several trained observers then documented the persuasive tactics negotiators used, as well as a number of nonverbal behaviors (facial expressions, gaze direction, silent periods, etc.). Each of the Japanese and American participants was also asked to observe his/her own interaction and to interpret events and outcomes from his/her own point of view. Each participant's comments were tape-recorded and transcribed to form retrospective protocols of the interaction. Here, also, we employed a variety of statistical techniques in the analysis, as well as a more inductive, interpretive approach.

as simple as hiring an interpreter or talking in a common third language, or it may be as difficult as learning a language. But the problem is obvious.

Alternatively, cultural differences in nonverbal behaviors are almost always hidden below our awarenesses. That is, in a face-to-face negotiation, we nonverbally give off and take in a great deal of information, and some argue that such information is the more important exchanged. Almost all this signaling goes on below our levels of consciousness, and when the nonverbal signals from our foreign partners are different, we are most apt to misinterpret them without even being conscious of the mistake. When the French client consistently interrupts, we tend to feel uncomfortable without noticing exactly why. In this manner, interpersonal friction often colors business relationships, goes on undetected and, consequently, uncorrected. Differences in values and thinking processes are hidden even deeper and therefore are even harder to cure.

Problems at the level of language

I finally found a country worse at foreign languages than the United States. At a seminar in Melbourne, the Australians all agreed that they were worse. Being "so far" from everyone else, foreign languages were given little attention in their educational system. But even if we're not worse that the Aussies, we're clearly down at the bottom of the languages list along with them. I must add that recently American undergrads have begun to see the light and are flocking to language classes. Unfortunately, we don't have the teaching resources to satisfy the demand, so we'll stay behind for some time to come.

It's also fascinating to learn that the Czechs are now throwing away a hard-earned competitive advantage. Young Czechs won't take Russian anymore. It's easy to understand why, but the result will be a generation of Czechs who can't leverage their geographic advantage because they won't be able to speak to their neighbors to the East. However, even more appalling is my own university's contemplated elimination of the Russian language program. This is short-sightedness at its worst.

I've already mentioned the language problem in the *Aisatsu*. The most common complaint I hear from American managers, however, regards foreign clients and partners breaking into side conversations in their native languages. Americans hate it. At best, we see it as impolite, and, quite naturally, we are likely to attribute something sinister to the content of the foreign talk — they're plotting or telling secrets or . . .

This is our mistake. We've videotaped and translated many such conversations, and their usual purpose is to straighten out a translation problem. For instance, one Korean may lean over to another and ask, "What'd he say?" Or, the side conversation can regard a disagreement among the foreign team. Both circumstances should be seen as positive signs by Americans, because getting translations straight enhances the efficiency of the interactions and concessions often follow internal disagreements. But because most Americans speak only one language, we can't appreciate either circumstance. By the way, I always advise foreigners to give Americans a brief explanation of the content of their first few side conversations to assuage the sinister attributions.

Data from our simulated negotiations are also informative. Using the approach detailed in Graham (1985), we studied the verbal behaviors of negotiators in thirteen of the cultures (six negotiators in each of the ten groups were videotaped). The numbers in the body of Table 4.1 are the percentages of statements that were classified into each category. This is, 7 per cent of the statements made by Japanese negotiators were promises, 4 per cent were threats, 20 per cent were questions, and so on. The verbal bargaining behaviors used by the negotiators during the simulations proved to be surprisingly similar across cultures. Negotiations in all ten cultures studied were comprised primarily of information-exchange tactics — questions and self-disclosures. However, it should be noted that once again the Japanese appear on the end of the continuum of self-disclosures. Their 34 per cent (along with the Spaniards and the Anglophone Canadians) was the lowest across all thirteen groups, suggesting that they are the most reticent about giving information.

TABLE 4.1

Verbal negotiation tactics (the "what" of communications)

Bargaining Behaviors and Definitions (Anglemar and Stern, 1978)	Cultures (in each group, $n = 6$)													
	JPN	KOR	TWN	CHN*	RUSS	GRM	UK	FRN	SPN	BRZ	MEX	FCAN	ECAN	USA
Promise. A statement in which the source indicated his intention to provide the target with a reinforcing consequence which source anticipates target will evaluate as pleasant, positive, or rewarding	7†	4	9	6	5	7	11	5	11	3	7	8	6	8
Threat. Same as promise, except that the reinforcing consequences are thought to be noxious, unpleasant, or punishing	4	2	2	1	3	3	3	5	2	2	1	3	0	4
Recommendation. A statement in which the source predicts that a pleasant environmental consequence will occur to the target. Its occurrence is not under source's control	7	1	5	2	4	5	6	3	4	5	8	5	4	4
Warning. Same as recommendation, except that the consequences are thought to be unpleasant	2	0	3	1	0	1	1	3	1	1	2	5	0	1
Reward. A statement by the source that is thought to create pleasant consequences for the target	1	3	2	1	3	4	5	3	3	2	1	1	3	2
Punishment. Same as reward, except that the consequences are thought to be unpleasant	1	5	1	0	1	2	0	3	2	3	0	2	1	3

TABLE 4.1 (continued)

Verbal negotiation tactics (the "what" of communications)

Bargaining Behaviors and Definitions (Anglemar and Stern, 1978)	Cultures (in each group, $n = 6$)													
	JPN	KOR	TWN	CHN*	RUSS	GRM	UK	FRN	SPN	BRZ	MEX	FCAN	ECAN	USA
Positive normative appeal. A statement in which the source indicates that the target's past, present, or future behavior was or will be in conformity with social norms.	1	1	0	1	0	0	0	0	0	0	0	1	0	1
Negative normative appeal. Same as positive normative appeal except that the target's behavior is in violation of social norms.	3	2	1	0	0	1	1	0	1	1	1	2	1	1
Commitment. A statement by the source to the effect that its future bids will not go below or above a certain level.	15	13	9	10	11	9	13	10	9	8	9	8	14	13
Self-disclosure. A statement in which the source reveals information about itself.	34	36	42	36	40	47	39	42	34	39	38	42	34	36
Question. A statement in which the source asks the target to reveal information about itself.	20	21	14	34	27	11	15	18	17	22	27	19	26	20
Command. A statement in which the source suggests that the target perform a certain behavior.	8	13	11	7	7	12	9	9	17	14	7	5	10	6

*northern China (Tianjin and environs)

† Read "7% of the statements made by Japanese negotiators were promises."

Consider for a moment the complexity of this part of our work. Six business people in each culture played the same negotiation game in their native languages, we videotaped each negotiation, transcribed, translated, and classified each statement made into one of twelve categories, calculated percentages and averaged across the six negotiators. And look how similar are the verbal tactics used across the cultural groups!

Nonverbal behaviors

Reported in Table 4.2 are the analyses of some linguistic aspects and nonverbal behaviors for the thirteen videotaped groups, as in Graham (1985). While our efforts here merely scratch the surface of these kinds of behavioral analyses, they still provide indications of substantial cultural differences. Note that, once again, the Japanese are at or next to the end of almost every dimension of the behaviors listed in Table 4.2. Their facial gazing and touching are the least among the thirteen groups. Only the northern Chinese used the words "no" less frequently and only the Russians used more silent periods than did the Japanese.

A broader examination of the data in the Tables reveals a more meaningful conclusion. That is, the variation across cultures is greater when comparing linguistic aspects of language and nonverbal behaviors than when the verbal content of negotiations is considered. For example, notice the great differences between Japanese and Brazilians in Table 4.1 *vis-à-vis* Table 4.2.

Summary descriptions based upon the videotapes

Following are further descriptions of the distinctive aspects of each of the thirteen cultural groups we have videotaped. Certainly, we cannot draw conclusions about the individual cultures from an analysis of only six business people in each, but the suggested cultural differences are worthwhile to consider briefly:

- Japan.   Consistent with most descriptions of Japanese negotiation behavior in the literature, the results of this analysis suggest their style of interaction is among the least aggressive (or most polite). Threats, commands, and warnings appear to be de-emphasized in favor of the more positive promises, recommendations, and commitments. Particularly indicative of their polite conversational style was their infrequent use of "no" and "you" and facial gazing, as well as more frequent silent periods.
- Korea.   Perhaps one of the most interesting aspects of this study is the contrast of the Asian styles of negotiations. Non-Asians often generalize about the Orient. Our findings demonstrate that this is a mistake. Korean negotiators used considerably more punishments and commands than did the Japanese. Koreans used the word "no" and interrupted more than three times as frequently as the Japanese. Moreover, no silent periods occurred between Korean negotiators.
- China (northern).   The behaviors of the negotiators from northern China (i.e., in and around Tianjin) are most remarkable in the emphasis on asking

TABLE 4.2

Linguistic aspects of language and nonverbal behaviors ("how" things are said)

Bargaining Behaviors (per 30 minutes)	Cultures (in each group, $n = 6$)													
	JPN	KOR	TWN	CHN*	RUSS	GRM	UK	FRN	SPN	BRZ	MEX	FCAN	ECAN	USA
Structural Aspects														
"No's." The number of times the word "no" was used by each negotiator.	1.9	7.4	5.9	1.5	2.3	6.7	5.4	11.3	23.2	41.9	4.5	7.0	10.1	4.5
"You's." The number of times the word "you" was used by each negotiator.	31.5	34.2	36.6	26.8	23.6	39.7	54.8	70.2	73.3	90.4	56.3	72.4	64.4	54.1
Nonverbal Behaviors														
Silent Periods. The number of conversational gaps of 10 seconds or longer.	2.5	0	0	2.3	3.7	0	2.5	1.0	0	0	1.1	0.2	2.9	1.7
Conversational Overlaps. Number of interruptions.	6.2	22.0	12.3	17.1	13.3	20.8	5.3	20.7	28.0	14.3	10.6	24.0	17.0	5.1
Facial Gazing. Number of minutes negotiators spent looking at opponent's face.	3.9	9.9	19.7	11.1	8.7	10.2	9.0	16.0	13.7	15.6	14.7	18.8	10.4	10.0
Touching. Incidents of bargainers touching one another (not including handshaking)	0	0	0	0	0	0	0	0.1	0	4.7	0	0	0	0

*Northern China (Tianjin and environs)

questions at 34 per cent. Indeed, 70 per cent of the statements made by the Chinese negotiators were classified as information exchange tactics. Other aspects of their behavior were quite similar to the Japanese — the use of "no" and "you" and silent periods.

- Taiwan.   The behavior of the business people in Taiwan was quite different from that in China and Japan but similar to that in Korea. The Chinese on Taiwan were exceptional in the time of facial gazing, on the average almost 20 out of 30 minutes. They asked fewer questions and provided more information (self-disclosures) than did any of the other Asian groups.

- Russia.   The Russians' style was quite different from that of any other European group, and, indeed, was quite similar in many respects to the style of the Japanese. They used "no" and "you" infrequently and used the most silent periods of any group. Only the Japanese did less facial gazing, and only the Chinese asked a greater percentage of questions.

- Germany.   The behaviors of the western Germans are difficult to characterize because they fell toward the center of almost all the continua. However, the Germans were exceptional in the high percentage of self-disclosures at 47 per cent and the low percentage of questions at 11 per cent.

- United Kingdom.   The behaviors of the British negotiators are remarkably similar to those of the Americans in all respects.

- Spain.   "Diga" is perhaps a good metaphor for the Spanish approach to negotiations evinced in our data. When you make a phone call in Madrid, the usual greeting on the other end is not "hola" (hello) but is, instead, "diga" (speak). The Spaniards in our negotiations likewise used the highest percentage of commands (17 per cent) of any of the groups and gave comparatively little information (self-disclosures, 34 per cent). Moreover, they interrupted one another more frequently than any other group, and they used the terms "no" and "you" very frequently.

- France.   The style of the French negotiators is perhaps the most aggressive of all the groups. In particular, they used the highest percentage of threats and warnings (together, 8 per cent). They also used interruptions, facial gazing and "no" and "you" very frequently compared to the other groups, and one of the French negotiators touched his partner on the arm during the simulation.

- Brazil.   The Brazilian business people, like the French and Spanish, were quite aggressive. They used the highest percentage of commands of all the groups. On average, the Brazilians said the word "no" 42 times, "you" 90 times, and touched one another on the arm about 5 times during 30 minutes of negotiation. Facial gazing was also high.

- Mexico.   The patterns of Mexican behavior in our negotiations are good reminders of the dangers of regional or language-group generalizations. Both verbal and nonverbal behaviors are quite different than those of their Latin American (Brazilian) or continental (Spanish) cousins. Indeed Mexicans answer the telephone with the much less demanding "bueno." In many respects, the Mexican behavior is very similar to that of the negotiators from the United States.

- Francophone Canada. The French-speaking Canadians in our study behaved quite similarly to their continental cousins. Like the negotiators from France, they, too, used high percentages of threats and warnings, and even more interruptions and eye contact. Such an aggressive interaction style would not mix well with some of the more low-key styles of some of the Asian groups or with English speakers, including Anglophone Canadians.

- Anglophone Canada. The Canadians in our study who speak English as their first language used the lowest percentage of aggressive persuasive tactics (that is, threats, warnings and punishments totaled only 1 per cent) of all thirteen groups. Perhaps, as communications researchers suggest, such stylistic differences are the seeds of interethnic discord as witnessed in Canada over the years. With respect to international negotiations, the Anglophone Canadians used noticeably more interruptions and "no's" than negotiators from either of Canada's major trading partners, the United States and Japan.

- United States. Like the Germans and the British, the Americans fell in the middle of most continua. They did interrupt one another less frequently than all the others, but that was their sole distinction.

These differences across the cultures are quite complex. Specifically, you should not use this material *by itself* to predict the behaviors of your foreign counterparts. Please be very careful of the stereotypes. Rather, the key here is to be aware of *these kinds of differences* so you don't misinterpret the Japanese silence, the Brazilian "no, no, no ...," or the French threat.

Differences in values

It's true what Le Poole said earlier about we Americans presuming that everyone else in the world shares our values. After all, how could anyone *not* see the sense in objectivity, competitiveness, equity, and punctuality?

Objectivity

We Americans make decisions based upon the bottom line and on cold, hard facts. We don't play favorites. Economics and performance count, not people. Business is business.

Roger Fisher and Willian Ury have written the single most important book on the topic of negotiation, *Getting to Yes.* I highly recommend it to both American and foreign readers. The latter will learn not only about negotiations but, perhaps more important, about how Americans think about negotiations. Fisher and Ury are quite emphatic about "separating the people from the problem", and they state, "Every negotiator has two kinds of interests: in the substance and in the relationship" (p. 20). This advice is probably quite worthwhile in the United States or perhaps in Germany, but in most places in the world, their advice is nonsense. *In most places in the world, personalities and substance are not separate issues and can't be made so.*

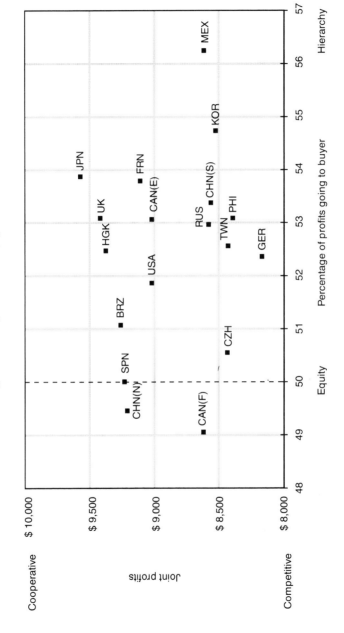

For example, look at how important nepotism is in Chinese or Hispanic cultures. John Kao (1993) tells us that businesses don't grow beyond the bounds and bonds of tight family control in the burgeoning "Chinese Commonwealth." Things work the same way in Spain, Mexico, and the Philippines *by nature*. And, just as naturally, negotiators from such countries not only will take things personally but will be personally affected by negotiation outcomes. What happens to them at the negotiation table will affect the business relationship regardless of the economics involved.

Competitiveness and equity

Our simulated negotiations can be viewed as a kind of experimental economics wherein the values of each cultural group are roughly reflected in the economic outcomes. The simple simulation we use well represents the essence of commercial negotiations — it has both competitive and cooperative aspects. That is, the "negotiation pie" can be made larger through cooperation before it is divided between the buyer and seller.

Our results are summarized in Figure 4.1. The Japanese are the champions at making the pie big. Their joint profits in the simulation were the highest (at $9,590) among the eighteen cultural groups. The American pie was more average-sized (at $9,030), but at least it was divided relatively equitably (51.8% of the profits went to the buyers). Alternatively, the Japanese (and others) split their pies in strange ways, with buyers making higher percentages of the profits (53.8%). The implications of our experimental economics are completely consistent with our own field work, the comments of other authors, and the adage that in Japan the buyer is "kinger." By nature, Americans have little understanding of the Japanese practice of giving complete deference to the needs and wishes of buyers. That's not the way things work in America. American sellers tend to treat American buyers more as equals. And the egalitarian values of American society support this behavior. Moreover, most Americans will, by nature, treat Japanese buyers more frequently as equals. Likewise, as suggested by Nakane (1970) and Graham (1981), American buyers will generally not "take care of" American sellers or Japanese sellers.

The American emphasis on competition and individualism represented in our findings is, in different ways, consistent with the work of both Geert Hofstede, the guru of international management, and J. Scott Armstrong of the Wharton School. Hofstede reports that Americans scored the highest among 40 other cultural groups on his individualism (versus collectivism) scale. Armstrong reports that "competition-oriented" objectives can have negative effects on profits. Of course, Adam Smith argued that competition ultimately serves society. However, in the context of the little society of our negotiation simulation, Smith's ideas don't appear to hold up. Perhaps the reason we hear so much about "win–win" negotiations here in the United States is because we really haven't learned the lesson well enough yet.

Finally, when we run the numbers on the Japanese and American results, not only do Japanese buyers achieve higher results than Americans do, but Japanese sellers ($4,430), compared to American sellers ($4,350), also get more of the commercial pie, as well. Interestingly, when I show these numbers to Americans in my executive seminars, the majority still prefer the American seller's role. That is, even though the American sellers make lower profits than the Japanese, the American managers prefer lower profits *if* those profits are yielded from an equitable split of the joint profits. Such an emphasis on equity is also echoed in a survey of American managers: "A recent Wall Street poll revealed this potentially destructive side of economic nationalism. Eighty-six per cent of those polled said they would rather have a policy of slower growth in both countries than a policy of faster growth in both countries if that meant allowing Japan to take the lead" (*Wall Street Journal*, 2 July, 1990, p. 1).

Punctuality

"Just make them wait." Everyone else in the world knows no negotiation tactic is more useful with Americans. Nobody places more value on time. Nobody has less patience when things slow down. Nobody looks at their wristwatch more than Americans. Recall our banker in Brazil. Edward T. Hall (1960) in his seminal writing is best at explaining how the passage of time is viewed differently across cultures and how these differences most often hurt Americans. But it is possible to put time to our own uses.

In the mid-1970s, my former company, Solar Turbines International (a division of Caterpillar), sold $34 million worth of industrial gas turbines and compressors to the Soviet Union for a natural gas pipeline application. It was agreed that final negotiations would be held in a neutral location, the south of France. In previous negotiations, the Soviets had been tough, but reasonable. But in Nice, the Soviets weren't nice. They became tougher and, in fact, completely unreasonable.

It took a couple of discouraging days before our people diagnosed the problem, but once they did, a crucial call was made back to headquarters in California. Why had the Soviet attitude turned so cold? Because they were enjoying the warm weather in Nice and weren't interested in making a quick deal and heading back to Moscow. The call to California was the key event in this negotiation. Our people in San Diego were sophisticated enough to allow our negotiators to take their time.

The routine of the negotiations changed to brief, 45-minute meetings in the mornings, with afternoons at the golf course, beach, or hotel, making calls and doing paperwork. Finally, during week four, the Soviets began to make concessions and to ask for longer meetings. Why? They couldn't go back to Moscow after four weeks on the Mediterranean *without a signed contract*. This strategic reversal of the time pressure yielded a wonderful contract for Solar.

Thinking and decision-making processes

When faced with a complex negotiation task, most Westerners (I will generalize here) divide the large task up into a series of smaller tasks. Issues such as prices, delivery, warranty and service contracts may be settled one issue at a time, with the final agreement being the sum of the sequence of smaller agreements. However, in Asia, a different approach is more often taken wherein all the issues are discussed at once, in no apparent order, and concessions are made on all issues at the end of the discussion. The Western sequential approach and the Eastern holistic approach do not mix well.

For example, American managers report great difficulties in measuring progress in Japan. After all, in America, you're half done when half the issues are settled. But in Japan, nothing seems to get settled. Then, surprise, you're done. Often, Americans make unnecessary concessions right before agreements are announced by the Japanese. For example, we know of an American retail goods buyer traveling to Japan to buy six different consumer products for a large chain of discount department stores. He told us that negotiations for his first purchase took an entire week. In the United States, such a purchase would be consummated in an afternoon. So, by his calculations, he expected to have to spend six weeks in Japan to complete his purchases. He considered raising his purchase prices to try to move things along faster. But before he was able to make such a concession, the Japanese quickly agreed on the other five products in just three days. This particular businessman was, by his own admission, lucky in his first encounter with Japanese bargainers.

This American businessman's near blunder reflects more than just a difference in decision-making style. To Americans, a business negotiation is a problem-solving activity, the best deal for both parties being the solution. To a Japanese businessperson, a business negotiation is a time to develop a business relationship with the goal of long-term mutual benefit. The economic issues are the *context*, not the *content*, of the talks. Thus, settling any one issue really isn't important. Such details will take care of themselves once a viable, harmonious business relationship is established. And, as happened in the case of our retail goods buyer, once the relationship was established — signaled by the first agreement — the other "details" were settled quickly.

American bargainers should anticipate such a holistic approach and be prepared to discuss all issues simultaneously and in an apparently haphazard order. Progress in the talks should not be measured by how many issues have been settled. Rather, Americans must try to gauge the quality of the business relationship. Important signals of progress will be:

- higher-level foreigners being included in the discussions
- their questions beginning to focus on specific areas of the deal
- a softening of their attitudes and position on some of the issues — "Let us take some time to study this issue"
- at the negotiation table, increased talk among themselves in their own language, which may often mean they're trying to decide something; and
- increased bargaining and use of the lower-level, informal and other channels of communication.

Implications for managers

Having read what I've written so far, it's a wonder that any international business gets done at all! Obviously, the economic imperatives of global trade make much of it happen despite the potential pitfalls but an appreciation of cultural differences can lead to even better international commercial transactions. It is not just business *deals* but highly profitable business *relationships* that are the goal here.

Another reason for our global business successes is the large number of skillful international negotiators. These are the managers who have lived in foreign countries and speak foreign languages. In many cases, they are immigrants to the United States or have been immersed in foreign cultures in other capacities. (Peace Corps volunteers and Mormon missionaries are common examples.) The Thunderbird School in Phoenix has long been a supplier of managers with international competencies. Thankfully, at more of our other business schools we are beginning to reemphasize language training and visits abroad. Indeed, it is interesting to note that the original Harvard Business School catalogue of 1908–09 listed German, French, and Spanish correspondence within its curriculum.

While I was teaching at the Madrid Business School in 1992, I was most encouraged to see as the February 10th, cover story of *Business Week*, "Ford and Mazda: The Partnership That Works." Although the article didn't credit directly the training program I helped design,[2] the interviews with Ford people throughout reflected lessons learned in their Executive Development Center programme on Japan. Ford does more business with Japanese companies than any other firm. They own 25 per cent of Mazda, they build a successful minivan with Nissan, and they buy and sell component parts and completed cars from and to Japanese companies. But perhaps the best measure of Ford's Japanese business is the 8,000 or so U.S.-Japan round-trip tickets the company buys annually!

Ford has made a large investment in training its managers with Japanese responsibilities. More than 1,500 of their executives have attended a three-day program on Japanese history and culture and the company's Japanese business strategies. More than 700 of their managers who work *vis-à-vis* with Japanese have attended a three-day program, "Managing Negotiations: Japan" (they call it MNJ), designed using many of the ideas in Yoshi Sano's and my book, *Smart Bargaining, Doing Business with the Japanese*. (Please see Box 1.2 for testimony regarding the latter program's effectiveness.) The program includes negotiation simulations with videotape feedback, lectures with cultural differences demonstrated via videotapes of Japanese/American interactions developed in our research, and rehearsals of upcoming negotiations. The company also conducts similar programs on Korea and the Peoples Republic of China.

---

[2] G. Richard Hartshorn, Antigone Kiriacopoulou, and Bruce Gibb were the other original design team members.

> **Box 4.2**
>
> Pro-active and direct is the approach Ford uses to develop competence in employees who interact with the Japanese. This occurs through a variety of practices, including programs which help Ford personnel better understand the Japanese culture and negotiating practices and by encouraging the study of the spoken language. By designing training which highlights both the pitfalls and the opportunities in negotiations, we increase the chance to "expand the negotiation pie".
>
> Back in 1988, the key personnel on our minivan team attended one of the first sessions of the Managing Negotiations: Japan Program at the Ford Executive Development Center. Our negotiations with the Nissan team improved immediately. But perhaps the best measure of the usefulness of the MNJ Program is the success of the Nissan joint-venture product itself. Reflected in the Villager/Quest are countless hours of effective face-to-face meetings with our Japanese partners.
>
> Not everyone negotiating outside the U.S. has the advantages of in-house training. However, many sources of information are available, books (particularly on Japan), periodicals, and colleagues with first-hand experience. To succeed, I believe negotiators have to be truly interested in and challenged by the international negotiating environment. Structuring negotiations to achieve win-win results AND building a long-term relationship takes thoughtful attention and commitment. Joe Gilmore is the Ford executive in charge of the minivan project with Nissan (marketed as the Mercury Villager and the Nissan Quest).

Despite my own pride in MNJ, I have to credit the broader Japan training efforts at Ford for their successes. Certainly, we see MNJ alumni exercising influence across and up the ranks regarding Japanese relationships. But the organizational awareness of the cultural dimensions of the Japanese business system was quickly raised by their broader, three-day program.

Please recall my story about the Soviets in Nice. There were two critical events. First, our negotiators diagnosed the problem. Second, and equally important, their California superiors appreciated the problem and approved the investments in time and money to outwait the Russians. So it is that the Ford programs have targeted not only the negotiators working directly with the Japanese but *also* their managers who spend most of their time in Detroit. Negotiators need information specific to the cultures in which they work. Their managers back in the United States need a basic awareness and appreciation for the importance of culture in international business so that they will be more apt to listen to the "odd" recommendations coming from their people in Moscow, Rio, or Tokyo.

Conclusions

In the almost twenty years I've been working in this area, things are getting better. The "innocents abroad" or cowboy stereotypes of American managers are becoming less accurate (see Graham and Herberger 1983). Likewise, we hope it is obvious that the stereotypes of the reticent Japanese or the pushy Brazilian evinced in our research may no longer hold so true. Experience levels are going up worldwide, and individual personalities are important. So you can find talkative Japanese, quiet Brazilians, and effective American negotiators. But culture still does, and always will, count. Hopefully, it is fast becoming the *natural* behavior of American managers to take it into account. Perhaps Ringo Starr may yet be right!

Part II

CHAPTER 5

Cultural Aspects of International Business Negotiations

JEAN-CLAUDE USUNIER

When negotiating internationally, one needs cultural knowledge and skills in intercultural communication. Many agreements have to be negotiated, drafted, signed and finally implemented: sales contracts, licensing agreements, joint ventures and various kinds of partnerships, agency and distribution agreements, turnkey contracts, etc. Negotiation is not only based on legal and business matters, hard facts which are often emphasized as being the sole important facts, but also on the quality of human and social relations, "soft facts" which become of the utmost importance in an intercultural encounter. Goldman (1994) emphasizes for instance, the importance to the Japanese of *ningensei* which, literally translated, means an all-encompassing and overriding concern and prioritizing of "humanity" or *human beingness* (see Box 5.1). According to Japanese specialists in international marketing negotiations:

> The North American and UK negotiators failed to communicate *ningensei* at the first table meeting. Rushing into bottom lines and demanding quick decisions on the pending contract, they also overlooked the crucial need for *ningensei* in developing good-will ... Hard business facts alone are not enough ... *Ningensei* is critical in getting Japanese to comply or in persuading Japanese negotiating partners. (Nippon Inc. Consultation, quoted in Goldman, 1994, p. 31)

There are various kinds of "distances" between the potential partners: physical distance certainly, but also economic, educational and cultural distance, which tend to inflate the cost of negotiating internationally. Difficulties in interacting, negotiating, planning common ventures, working them out and achieving them together are deeply rooted in the cultural, human and social background of business people. They are not related to a superficial variance of business customs, and simple "empathy" is not enough for the avoidance of misunderstandings. In fact, people with different cultural backgrounds often do not share the same basic assumptions (see below) and this has an influence at several levels of international business negotiations: the behavioral predispositions of the parties;

their concept of what is negotiation and what would be an appropriate negotiation strategy; their attitudes during the negotiation process which may lead to cultural misunderstandings and undermine trust between the parties; differences in outcome orientation. This chapter is the introductory text to Part II: it makes a summary of the topic, especially through Table 5.1, and it indicates where particular aspects of the influence of culture on international business negotiations are treated at greater length in other chapters.

Culture Defined

Culture as learned and forgotten norms and behavioral patterns

Sometimes culture has a reputation for being rather vague, for being a somewhat "blurred" concept. The Swedish writer Selma Lagerlöf defines culture as "what remains when that which has been learned is entirely forgotten". Depicted thus, culture may appear to be a "rubbish bin" concept. Its main use would be as a "synthesis variable"; serving when more precise concepts or theories have either proved unsuccessful or need to be linked together. It would also serve as an explanatory variable for residuals, when other more operative explanations have proved unsuccessful. Nevertheless, Selma Lagerlöf's definition does have the important merit of identifying two basic elements of cultural dynamics (at the individual level):

1. It is learned.
2. It is forgotten, in the sense that we cease to be conscious (if we ever have been) of its existence as learned behavior.

For example, if one has been told during childhood that modest and self-effacing behavior is suitable when addressing other people, especially at first contact — which is the case in most Asian cultures — one forgets about this and is easily shocked by the assertive, apparently boastful, behavior which may appear in other cultures. Although largely forgotten, culture permeates our daily individual and collective actions. It is entirely oriented towards our adaptation to reality (both as constraints and opportunities). Since culture is "forgotten", it is mostly unconsciously embedded in individual and collective behavior. Individuals find, in their cultural group, pre-set and agreed-upon solutions which indicate to them how to articulate properly their behavior and actions with members of the same cultural group.

Basic definitions of culture

Culture has been defined extensively, precisely because it is somewhat all-encompassing. After having assessed its nature as learned and forgotten, we need to provide some additional definitions of culture. Ralph Linton (1945, p. 21), for instance, stresses that it is *shared* and *transmitted*: "A culture is the configuration of learned behavior and results of behavior whose component elements are shared and transmitted by the members of a particular society." However, we should not go too far in considering the individual as simply *programmed* by culture. At a previous point in his prominent book, *The Cultural Background of Personality*, Linton had clearly indicated the limits of the cultural programming which a society can impose on an individual:

> No matter how carefully the individual has been trained or how successful his conditioning has been, he remains a distinct organism with his own needs and with capacities for independent thought, feeling and action. Moreover he retains a considerable degree of individuality (1945, p. 14–15).

If individuals have some leeway, then what use is culture to them? According to Goodenough (1971), culture is a set of beliefs or standards, shared by a group of people, which help the individual decide what is, what can be, how one feels about it, what to do and how to go about doing it. On the basis of this operational definition of culture, there is no longer any reason why culture should be equated with the whole of one particular society. It may be more related to activities that are shared by a definite group of people. Consequently, individuals may share different cultures with several different groups, a corporate culture with colleagues at work, an educational culture with other MBA graduates, an ethnic culture with people of the same ethnic origin. When in a particular situation, they will switch into the culture that is operational. The term "operational", in this context, implies that a culture must be shared with those with whom there must be co-operation, and that it must be suitable for the task.

Goodenough's concept of "operating culture" assumes that the individual is able to choose the culture within which to interact at a given moment and in a given situation. This is, of course, subject to the overriding condition that this culture has been correctly internalized during past experience, that *it is so well-learned that it can be forgotten*. Although the concept of operating culture is somewhat debatable, it does have the advantage of clearly highlighting the multicultural nature of many individuals in today's societies, including binationals, multilingual people and people who have an international professional culture or are influenced as employees by the corporate culture of a multinational company.

Significant components of culture

The following are some significant elements of culture that have an impact on international business negotiations, illustrated by examples in this chapter and other chapters of Part II.

Language and communication

The way in which people communicate (that is both emit and receive messages) and the extent to which their native language frames their world-views and attitudes directly affects international business negotiations. These require a dialogue, although partners may have different native languages, writing contracts in a foreign language (at least foreign to one side), using interpreters, trying to express ideas, concepts which may be unique to a particular language etc.

Institutional and legal systems

Differences in legal systems, contractual formalism and recourse to litigation, express contrasts in how societies are organized in terms of rules and decision-making systems. The level of formality in addressing public and private issues has to be considered in any kind of negotiated partnership, including the discussion of joint-venture contracts, the registration of subsidiaries and the addressing of sensitive issues with the public authorities of the host country.

Value systems

The prevailing values in a particular society, and the extent to which they are respected in the everyday behavior of individuals, are important because they affect the willingness to take risks, the leadership style and the superior-subordinate relationships. This is true for the relationships between negotiators within a particular team, antagonistic negotiation teams and the negotiators on both sides and those from whom they have received the mandate for negotiating.

Time orientations

Attitudes towards time and how it shapes the way people structure their actions have a pervasive yet mostly invisible influence. Differences in punctuality, reflected in everyday negotiation behavior, may probably appear as the most visible consequence, but differences in time orientations, especially toward the future, are more important as they affect long-range issues such as the strategic framework of decisions made when negotiating.

Mindsets

Whether called "Mindsets" (Fisher 1988) or "intellectual styles" (Galtung, 1981), another major difference concerns the way people reflect on issues. Do they prefer to rely on data, ideas or speech, and which combination of these? How does this influence the way they relate words and actions? Mindsets influence ways of addressing issues, of collecting information, of choosing the relevant pieces of information and of assessing their "truthfulness", so that finally they influence the negotiation process and the resulting decisions.

Relationships

These concern how the individual relates to the group(s); what the dominant family and kinship patterns are; and how relationships are framed (individualism/collectivism; patronage relationships). These patterns affect international business negotiations through the style of interaction between people, their decision-making process, and the way in which they mix human relationships and business matters.

The Influence of Culture on some Important Aspects of Business Negotiations

Culture and negotiation: the academic literature

A large part of the academic literature on the influence of culture on international business negotiations uses a comparative and cross-cultural setting (see for instance Graham, 1985). A laboratory experiment (the negotiation simulation by Kelley, 1966) helps in the comparison of negotiations between people of various nationalities. Nationality is used as a proxy and summary variable for culture. A basic description is made of the cultural traits of a specific nationality in negotiations, which is then contrasted with one or more different national groups. It is the basis for hypotheses on either the process or the outcome of these negotiations, where the membership of a specific national group is one of the main explanatory variables.

It is advisable to be prudent before directly transposing data, on the behavior or negotiation strategies of people from a particular country which have been collected during negotiations with their compatriots. Some traits may not recur when people are negotiating with partners of other nationalities. For instance, when Italians negotiate together or with the French, they may not adopt exactly the same behavior and strategies as they do when negotiating with Americans. Adler and Graham (1989) address the issue of whether these simple international comparisons are fallacies, when and if researchers are trying to describe cross-cultural interactions accurately. They demonstrate that negotiators tend to adapt their behavior in intercultural negotiation. They do not behave as predicted by that which has been observed in intracultural negotiations. Therefore, their behavior as observed in intracultural negotiations can only serve as a partial basis for the prediction of their style and strategies when negotiating with people belonging to different cultures. Graham and Adler, for instance, show that French-speaking Canadians are more problem-solving oriented when negotiating with English-speaking Canadians than they normally are among themselves.

Hence, the word "intercultural" in this text directly relates to the study of interaction between people with different cultural backgrounds. The word "cross-cultural" relates to a research design that is generally comparative but may also be centered on the encounter/interaction.

Jean-Claude Usunier

General influence of culture on business negotiations

Culture has mostly an indirect influence on the outcome of negotiations (see, for instance, the models of McCall and Warrington, 1990, and Graham and Sano, 1990). It works through two basic groups of mediating variables: the situational aspects of the negotiation (time and time pressure, power and exercise of power, number of participants, location etc.); and the characteristics of the negotiators (especially personality variables and cultural variables). These two groups of factors, in turn, influence the negotiation process, which ultimately determines the outcome (Jolibert, 1988). However, it is my contention that culture also has an influence on the outcome orientation: certain cultures are more deal/contract-oriented whereas others favor relationship development. This is further developed later in this chapter and in Chapters 8 and 9. A census of the impact of culture on international business negotiations is given in Table 5.1. It indicates the positions in other chapters where these topics are treated in more detail.

TABLE 5.1
The impact of cultural differences on international marketing negotiations

1. Behavioral predispositions of the parties	
Concept of the self	Impact on credibility (in the awareness and exploration phases)
Interpersonal orientation	Individualism versus collectivism/relationship versus deal orientation
In-group orientation	Similarity/"Limited good concept"
Power orientation	Power distance (Chap. 6)/Roles in negotiation teams/Negotiators' leeway
Willingness to take risks	Uncertainty avoidance (Chap. 5)/Degree of self-reliance of negotiators
2. Underlying concept of negotiation/Negotiation strategies	
Distributive strategy	Related to in-group orientation/Power distance/Individualism/Strong past orientation (Chapters 5 and 6)
Integrative strategy	Related to problem-solving approach and future orientation (Chapter 8)
Role of the negotiator	Buyer and seller's respective position of strength (Chapters 4 and 17)
Strategic time frame	Continuous versus discontinuous/Temporal orientations (Chapter 8)
3. Negotiation process	
Agenda setting/Scheduling the negotiation process	Linear-separable time/Economicity of time/Monochronism/Negotiating globally versus negotiating clauses (Chapter 8)
Information processing	Ideologism versus pragmatism/Intellectual styles (Chapter 5)
Communication	Communication styles (Chapter 7)/Degree of formality and informality.
Negotiation tactics	Type and frequency of tactics/Mix of business with affectivity (Chapter 7)
Relationship development	The role of "Atmosphere" as bearing the history of the relationship and facilitating transition (Chapter 9)
4. Outcome orientations	
Partnership as outcome	Making a new in-group "marriage" as metaphoric outcome
Deal/Contract as outcome	Contract rules being the law of the parties (litigation orientation)
Profit as outcome	Accounting profit orientation (economicity)
Winning over the other party	Distributive orientation
Time line of negotiation	Continuous versus discontinuous view of negotiation (Chapter 8)

Behavioral Predispositions of the Parties

Who is seen as a credible partner?

Triandis (1983, p. 147) has emphasized three dimensions of the self-concept which may have a strong influence on the cultural coding/decoding process of credibility:

1. self-esteem: the extent to which people think of themselves as very good or not too good;
2. perceived potency: the extent to which people view themselves as powerful, able to accomplish almost any task; and
3. perceived activity: the person sees him/herself as a doer, an active shaper of the world.

Since people generally live in homogeneous cultural settings (i.e., countries or regions within countries with one language, a dominant religion and shared values), they use the same cultural codes. But when people do not share the same codes, this may create problems for establishing credibility/trust. For example, a credible person may be considered by the emitter (coder) to be somebody showing a low self-concept profile (modes, patiently listening to partners, speaking little and cautiously etc.); if, conversely, the receiver (decoder) considers a credible person as somebody with a high self-concept profile (showing self-confidence, speaking arrogantly, not paying much attention to what the other is saying etc.), there will be a credibility misunderstanding.

A classic example is the misinterpretation by the Soviet leader Khrushchev of the credibility of the American president, John F. Kennedy. It was one of the main reasons for the seriousness of the Cuban missile crisis at the beginning of the 1960s. Kennedy and Khrushchev had held talks in Vienna, after the unsuccessful invasion by US soldiers resulting in defeat at the Bay of Pigs. During their meeting, the young President Kennedy recognized that this attack had been a military and political mistake, which he regretted. Khrushchev saw this confession of error as a testimony of Kennedy's frank naivety and lack of character. He therefore inferred that it was possible to gain advantage by installing nuclear missiles in Cuba, which would have been targeted at the United States. This led the world to the brink of nuclear war between the superpowers. The events which followed showed that Khrushchev had been wrong in evaluating Kennedy's credibility. Ultimately, Kennedy showed great firmness and negotiation skill.

Khrushchev's mistake may be explained by differences in cultural coding of credibility. Whereas in the United States, reaching a high position while still young is positively perceived, Soviet people associate age with the ability to carry responsibilities. Moreover, the admission of a mistake or a misjudgement is also positively perceived in the United States. US ethics value frankness and honesty. There is the belief that individuals may improve their behavior and decisions by taking into account the lessons of experience. On the other hand, in the Soviet Union, admission of errors was rare. It generally implied the very weak position of people subjected to the enforced confessions of the Stalinist trials.

Signs of credibility

Personal credibility is decoded through the filter of numerous physical traits, which are not often actively taken into consideration as they seem to be only appearances, or because we tend to use these reference points unconsciously (Lee, 1966). Being tall may, for instance, be perceived as a sign of strength and character. Stoutness may be considered a positive sign for a partner in societies where starvation is still a recent memory. Where malnutrition is a reality for a section of the population, it is better to be fat, that is, well-nourished and therefore rich- and powerful-looking. Naturally, these signs have a relative value. Weight, height, age and sex cannot be considered as adequate criteria for selecting negotiators. Furthermore, people may, in fact, be largely aware of the cultural code of the partner.

Each of these basic signs plays a role in the initial building of a credibility profile: age, sex, height, stoutness, face, tone and strength of the voice, self-esteem, perceived potency, perceived activity, etc. The profile is a priori because it only influences credibility in early contacts, that is, in the phase of awareness and at the beginning of the exploration phase (Scanzoni, 1979).

Interpersonal orientation

The reproach made to Western business people by the Japanese, quoted in the introduction of this chapter, illustrates differences in interpersonal orientation. The concept of *ningensei*, presented at the beginning of this chapter, has to do with the Confucian ethic which favors smooth interactions, underplaying conflict to the benefit of social harmony. For instance, the interpersonal sensitivity of Japanese people and their sincere interest in foreign cultures and people may make them friendly hosts at business lunches or dinners. As emphasized by Hawrysh and Zaichkowsky (1990, p. 42): "Before entering serious negotiations, Japanese business men will spend considerable time and money entertaining foreign negotiating teams, in order to get to know their negotiating partners and establish with them a rapport built on friendship and trust." But it should never be forgotten that Japanese negotiators remain down-to-earth: they are strongly aware of what their basic interests are. *Ningensei* is, in fact, typical of collectivist values of interpersonal relationships, see Box 5.1. A basic divide in the interpersonal orientation is the individualism/collectivism divide. Its relevance for international business negotiations is examined in the following chapter.

Box 5.1

Ningensei exemplifies four interrelated principles of Confucian philosophy: *jen*, *shu*, *i* and *li*.

1. Based on active listening, *Jen* is a form of humanism that translates into empathetic interaction and caring for the feelings of negotiating associates, and seeking out the other's views, sentiments and true intentions.

2. *Shu* emphasizes the importance of reciprocity in establishing human relationships and the cultivation of "like-heartedness"; in Matsumoto's (1988) words it is "belly communication", a means of coding messages within negotiating, social and corporate channels that is highly contingent upon affective, intuitive and non verbal channels.

3. *i*, also termed *amae*, is the dimension which is concerned with the welfare of the collectivity, directing human relationships to the betterment of the common good. "The *i* component of *ningensei* surfaces in Japanese negotiators' commitment to the organization, group agendas and a reciprocity (*shu*) and humanism (*jen*) that is long-term, consistent and looks beyond personal motivation."

4. *Li* refers to the codes, corresponding to precise and formal manners, which facilitate the outer manifestation and social expression of *jen*, *shu* and *i*. The Japanese *meishi* ritual of exchanging business cards is typical of *li* coded etiquette.

Source: adapted from Goldman, 1994, pp. 32–3.

In-group orientation

Equal concern for the other party's outcome is not necessarily to be found across all cultures. Cultures place a stronger or weaker emphasis on group membership (the other party is/is not a member of the in-group) as a prerequisite for being considered a trustworthy partner. In cultures where there is a clear-cut distinction between the in-group and the out-group (according to age, sex, race or kinship criteria), people tend to perceive the interests of both groups as diametrically opposed. This is related to what has been called the concept of "limited good" (Foster, 1965).

According to the concept of "limited good", if something positive happens in favor of the out-group, the wealth and well-being of the in-group will be threatened. Such reactions are largely based on culture-based collective subjectivity: they stem from the conservative idea that goods and riches are by their very nature restricted. If one yields to the other party even the tiniest concession, this is perceived as directly reducing what is left for in-group members. The concept of "limited good" induces negotiators to adopt very territorial and distributive strategies. It is a view which clearly favors the idea of the zero sum game, where "I will lose whatever you may win" and vice versa. In Mediterranean and Middle Eastern societies where the in-group is highly valued (clan, tribe, extended family), the concept of "limited good" is often to be found; it slows the adoption of a problem-solving orientation, since co-operative opportunities are simply difficult to envisage.

Power orientation

One must distinguish between the formal power orientation on the one hand and the real power/decision-making orientation on the other. The first has to do with the display of status and how it may enhance credibility, especially in high perceived-potency societies. This involves the kind of meetings, societies, clubs, alumni organizations which assemble potentially powerful people. Belonging to such circles gives an opportunity for socializing and getting to know each other. The simple fact of being there and being a member of a certain club is the main credibility message. The signs of formal power orientation differ across cultures; they may range from education and titles (English public schools, French *Grandes Ecoles*, *Herr Doktor*, etc.) to belonging to a particular social class or caste.

Real power orientation is a somewhat different issue. As illustrated in Box 5.2 with an African example, there may be wide differences between formal and actual influence on the decision-making process. When making contacts, in a cross-cultural perspective, people should be aware of the following:

- status is not shown in the same way according to culture
- influential persons are not the same and individual influence is not exerted in the same way and
- the decision-making process differs.

Box 5.2

The story takes place in the corridor to the office of the Minister of Industry of the Popular Republic of Guinea in the beginning of the 80s. Whether you had an appointment or you came to request a meeting, you had to be let in by the door-keeper. Besides, the door was locked and he had the key. He was a little man, looking tired and wearing worn-out clothes; his appearance led foreign visitors to treat him as negligible and to pay little attention to him. When visitors had a lengthy wait while seeing other people being given quick access to the minister, they often spoke unreservedly to the old man who seemed to have only limited language proficiency. In fact, the door-keeper spoke perfect French and was the uncle of the minister, which gave him power over his nephew according to the African tradition. It was well-known that the Minister placed high confidence in his uncle's recommendations. Thus, some foreign contractors never understood why they did not clinch the deal although they had developed winning arguments with the minister himself. *Source*: reported by Prof. Gérard Verna, Université Laval, Quebec. Reproduced with permission.

Hofstede (1989), in an article about the cultural predictors of negotiation styles, hypothesizes that larger power distance will lead to a more centralized control and decision-making structure because key negotiations have to be concluded by the top authority (see Chapter 6 in this book, which examines how Hofstede's four-dimension framework may be applied to aspects of international business negotiations). And, in fact, Fisher (1980) notes that in the case of Mexico, a typically high-power distance country (score of 81 on Hofstede's scale; see the following chapter), one finds a relatively centralized decision-making, based on individuals who have extended responsibility at the top of the organization. They become frustrated when confronted by the Americans who tend to have several negotiators in charge of compartmentalized issues:

> In another mismatch of the systems, the Americans find it hard to determine how much Mexican decision-making authority goes with which designated authority. There, as in many of the more traditional systems, authority tends to reside somewhat more in the person than in the position, and an organization chart does little to tell the outsider just what leverage (*palanca*) the incumbent has (Fisher 1980, p. 29).

Willingness to take risks

A high level of uncertainty-avoidance is noted by Hofstede (1980) as being associated with a more bureaucratic functioning and a lower tendency for individuals to take risks. This may be a problem for business negotiators when they have received a mandate from top management. For instance, the bureaucratic orientation in ex-communist countries has imposed strong government control on industry. As a consequence, Chinese negotiators, for instance, tend not to be capable of individual decision-making. Before any agreement is reached, official government approval must be sought by Chinese negotiators (Eiteman, 1990). The same has been noted by Beliaev *et al.* (1985, p. 110) in the case of Russian negotiators: "Throughout the process, a series of ministries are involved ... Such a process also limits the degree of risk taking that is possible ... the American who does see it from (the Soviet) perspective may well interpret it as being slow, lacking in initiative and unproductive." Tse *et al.* (1994) confirm this tendency in the case of Chinese executives who tend to consult their superior significantly more than Canadian executives who belong to a low uncertainty-avoidance society.

Underlying Concepts of Negotiation and Negotiation Strategies

Integrative orientation versus distribution orientation

In business negotiations, the purchaser (or team of purchasers) and the vendor (or group of vendors) are mutually interdependent, and their individual interests clash. The ability to choose effective negotiation largely explains the individual performance of each party on the one hand, and the joint outcome on the other. In pitting themselves against each other, the parties may develop opposing points of view towards the negotiation strategy which they intend to adopt: distributive or integrative. In the distributive strategy (or orientation), the negotiation process is seen as leading to the division of a specific "cake" which the parties feel they cannot enlarge even if they were willing to do so. This orientation is also termed "competitive negotiation" or "zero sum game". It leads to a perception of

103

negotiation as a war of positions — territorial in essence. These are negotiations of the "win–lose" type: "anything that isn't yours is mine" and vice versa.

The negotiators hold attitudes and objectives that are quasi-conflictive. Interdependence is minimized whereas opposition is emphasized. At the opposite end of the spectrum is the integrative orientation (Walton and McKersie, 1965). The central assumption is that the size of the "cake", the joint outcome of the negotiations, can be increased if the parties adopt a co-operative attitude. This idea is directly linked to problem-solving orientation (Pruitt, 1983). Negotiators may not be concerned purely with their own objectives, but may also be interested in the other party's aspirations and results, seeing them as almost equally important. Integrative orientation has been termed "co-operative" or "collaborative". It results in negotiation being seen as an attempt to maximize the joint outcome. The division of this outcome is to a certain extent secondary or is at least perceived as an important but later issue. Here negotiation is a "positive sum game" where the joint outcome is greater than zero.

In practice, effective negotiation combines distributive and integrative orientations simultaneously, or at different stages in the negotiation process (Pruitt, 1981). The "dual concern model" (Pruitt, 1983) explains negotiation strategies according to two basic variables: concern for one's own outcome (horizontal axis) and concern for the other party's outcome (vertical axis). This leads to four possible strategies (see Table 5.2). According to this model, the ability to envisage the other party's outcome is a prerequisite for the adoption of an integrative strategy.

TABLE 5.2
The dual concern model

Concern for one's own outcomes ⇒ Concern for the other party's outcomes ⇓	Low	High
High	Yielding	Integrative strategy
Low	Inaction	Contending

Problem-solving orientation can be defined as an overall negotiating behavior that is co-operative, integrative and oriented towards the exchange of information (Campbell *et al.*, 1988). Fair communication and the exchange of information between negotiators are important. "Problem solvers" exchange representative information, that is, honest and objective data. There is no desire to manipulate the partner, as in instrumental communication (Angelmar and Stern, 1978). Exchanging representative information is considered a basic element in problem-solving orientation. Empirical studies (experimental negotiation stimulation) have shown that this orientation positively influences the common results of negotiation (Pruitt, 1983). Rubin and Carter (1990), for instance, demonstrate the general superiority of co-operative negotiation by developing a model whereby a new, more co-operative contract provides both the buyer and the seller with cost reduction, compared to a previous adversarial contract.

There are, however, some conditions; the first is the availability of cost-related data, the second is the release of this data to the other party during negotiation. The sharing of data is obviously conditioned by culture, language and communication-related issues. The adoption of an integrative strategy is facilitated by the following:

- a high level of aspiration on both sides (Pruitt and Lewis, 1975)
- the ability to envisage the future (see Chapter 9)
- the existence of sufficient "perceived common ground", that is, enough overlap between the interests of the two parties (Pruitt, 1983).

Cultural dispositions to being integrative

Even though one may accept the superior effectiveness of integrative strategies, in as far as they aim to maximize the joint outcome, the problem of how this joint outcome is divided between the two sides remains largely unaddressed. When integrating the cultural dimension, three questions merit consideration:

1. Do the parties tend to perceive negotiations as being easier, and do they tend to adopt an integrative orientation more readily, when they both share the same culture?
2. Do negotiators originating from particular cultures tend towards an integrative or distributive orientation? Furthermore, do negotiators originating from cultures which favor a problem-solving orientation risk seeing their personal results heavily diminished by a distributive partner who cynically exploits their good will?
3. Do cultural differences and intercultural negotiation reduce the likelihood of integrative strategy?

Difficulties in being integrative in an intercultural negotiation situation

Generally, speaking, it seems more difficult to pursue an integrative strategy in an intercultural than intracultural setting. Nationalistic feelings are easily aroused by conflicts of interest and the partner may easily be subjectively perceived as an "adversary", occupying a different and rival territory. These negative feelings are often reinforced by an alleged atmosphere of "economic war" which, for instance, results in "Japan bashing" in the United States where the Japanese are considered to be unfair competitors. According to this view, a potential partner belonging to another country-culture would also be perceived as a global adversary.

There is general agreement in the existing literature that the results of negotiation are less favorable when the negotiation is intercultural as opposed to intracultural, all other things being equal (Sawyer and Guetzkow, 1965). Van Zandt (1970) suggests that the negotiations between Americans and the Japanese are six times as long and three times as difficult as those exclusively between Americans. This increases the costs of the transaction for the American firms in Japan owing to the relative inefficiency of communication. The subjective satisfaction of the negotiators (measured by a questionnaire) in their result tends to be inferior for intercultural negotiation compared to intracultural negotiation (Weitz, 1979; Graham, 1985).

Problem-solving depends on a collaborative attitude which is easier with a partner from the same culture. The similarity, according to Rubin and Brown (1975), leads to more trust and an enhanced level of interpersonal attraction. As a result of similarity, each side tends to consider communication from the other as more representative, more honest and truthful: in other words, one party perceives that it transmits fairly objective information and does not try to unduly influence the other party, as is the case with instrumental communication (in the sense of Angelmar and Stern, 1978). The hypothesis that the similarity of the parties leads to a more favorable outcome was proposed by Evans (1963). Similarity facilitates awareness and exploration between parties. In fact, it is more a question of perceived similarity which leads to more co-operative behavior in negotiation (Matthews et al., 1972). If this similarity is perceived but not based on strictly objective indications (such as shared nationality, language or educational backgrounds), a dissymmetric view of similarity may arise between the buyer and seller. For instance, many business people in the Middle East have a good command of either the English or French language and culture. Middle Eastern business people are often perceived by their American or European counterparts as being similar, whereas they may perceive their Western counterparts as different.

The role adopted in negotiation, buyer or seller, combines with perceived similarity: if sellers perceive a greater similarity, this can lead to a stronger problem-solving orientation on their part. Although appealing, similarity-based hypotheses have been poorly validated by the empirical study carried out by Campbell et al., (1988). No significant relationship was found among American and British buyer/seller pairs: similarity did not favor problem-solving orientation. In the case of the French and the Germans, the perceived similarity only led to a stronger problem-solving orientation on the part of the seller. However, in Campbell et al. (1988), the actual dissimilarity between negotiations was strongly reduced by the fact that all the simulated negotiations were intracultural.

In intercultural terms, there is the possibility of a misunderstanding arising from a perception of similarity which is not shared by both parties. For example, one can imagine a situation where a seller (American, for instance) perceives the buyer as similar (an Arab buyer who is very Westernized in appearance, who has a superficial but misleading cultural outlook because of his cultural borrowing).

However, the reverse situation does not occur: the Arab buyer is aware that the American seller knows little about the Arabic culture. In this case the seller will have a tendency to take a problem-solving orientation, because of fallacious perceived similarity, whereas the buyer may exploit the seller without feeling obliged to reciprocate, and ultimately maximize his personal outcome by adopting a distributive strategy. However, the dynamics of similarity (showing the other side that one understands, and thus laying the foundation for an integrative attitude on both sides) can be reversed, more positively. Harris and Moran (1987, p. 472) cite the case of a US banker from the Midwest invited by an Arab sheik for a meeting in London. The banker demonstrates unusual patience and deep awareness of the other party's power.

> The banker arrives in London and waits to meet the sheik. After two days he is told to fly to Riyadh in Saudi Arabia, which he does. He waits. After three days in Riyadh, he meets the sheik and the beginning of what was to become a very beneficial business relationship between the two persons and their organizations began.

National orientations favoring the integrative strategy

The second question concerns the adoption of integrative strategies by some nationalities more than others. Studies tend to show that American business people show trust more willingly and more spontaneously than other cultural groups, and have a stronger tendency towards a problem-solving and integrative orientation (Druckman et al., 1976; Harnett and Cummings, 1980; Campbell et al., 1988). The level of their profits as sellers depends on the buyer responding positively by also adopting a problem-solving approach (Campbell et al., 1988). American negotiators have a stronger tendency to exchange representative communication, making clear and explicit messages a priority. This is in line with the American appreciation of frankness and directness and their explicit communication style according to Hall (1976). This is what Graham and Herberger (1983) call the "John Wayne Style". They often meet certain difficulties with cultures who take more time in the preliminaries: getting to know each other, that is, talking generally and only actually getting down to business later. As a result, Americans may not foster feelings of trust in negotiators from other cultural groups who feel it necessary to get to know the person they are dealing with (Hall 1976). Graham and Meissner (1986) have shown, in a study comparing five countries, that the most integrative strategies are adopted by the Brazilians, followed by the Japanese. On the other hand, the Americans, the Germans and the Koreans choose intermediate strategies that are more distributive. This is consistent in the case of the Germans who, according to Cateora (1993), use the hard-sell approach, where the seller is fairly pushy and adopts an instrumental communication and a distributive strategy (Campbell et al. 1988).

The concept of integrative strategy is strongly culturally influenced by the American tradition of experimental research in social psychology applied to commercial negotiation. It is also based on a "master of destiny" orientation which feeds attitudes of problem resolution. As noted recently by Graham *et al.* (1994), the problem-solving approach appears to make sense to the American negotiators, but this framework may not work in all cases when applied to foreign negotiators. Americans tend to see the world as consisting of problems to be solved whereas Arabs, for instance, see it more as a creation of God. However, to our knowledge, there is no empirical study that has shown, for example, that the Arabs from the Middle East have a tendency to be more distributive and or less problem-solving oriented than the Americans.

Box 5.3

Americans, more than any other national group, value informality and equality in human relations. The emphasis on first names is only the beginning. We go out of our way to make our clients feel comfortable by playing down status distinctions such as clients and by eliminating "unnecessary" formalities such as lengthy introductions. All too often, however, we succeed only in making ourselves feel comfortable while our clients become uneasy or even annoyed. For example, in Japanese society interpersonal relationships are vertical; in almost all two-person relationships a difference in status exists. The basis for such distinction may be one or several factors: age, sex, university attended, position in an organization, and even one's particular firm or company. Each Japanese is very much aware of his or her own position relative to others with whom he or she deals ... The roles of the higher status position and the lower status position are quite different, even to the extent that Japanese use different words to express the same idea depending on which person makes the statement. For example a buyer would say *otaku* (your company), while a seller would say *on sha* (your great company). Status relations dictate not only what is said but also how it is said. (*Source*: Graham and Herberger, 1983, p. 162. Reproduced with permission.)

Ignorance of the other party's culture as an obstacle to the implementation of an integrative strategy in negotiation

One of the most important obstacles to effective international business negotiation is the ignorance of all or at least the basics of the other party's culture. This is intellectually obvious, but is often forgotten by international negotiators. It refers not only to the cognitive ignorance of the main traits of the other party's culture, but also to the unconscious prejudice that differences are minor (that is, ignorance as absence of awareness). This favors the natural tendency to refer implicitly to one's own cultural norms, especially for the coding/decoding process of communication (the self reference criterion of Lee (1966). Lucian Pye (1982, 1986) and Eiteman (1990) in the case of business negotiations between American and Chinese people, and Tung (1984) and Hawrish and Zaichkowsky (1990) with US-Japanese business negotiations, note the lack of prior knowledge of the American negotiators about their partner's culture. Before coming to the negotiation table, Americans do not generally read books, nor do they train themselves for the foreign communication style, nor learn about the potential traps which could lead to misunderstandings. As Carlos Fuentes states (in a rather harsh aphorism): "What the US does best is understand itself. What it does worst is understand others" (Fuentes 1986). French negotiators also tend to be underprepared in terms of cultural knowledge (Burt 1984), whereas the Japanese seemingly try to learn a lot more than the French or the Americans about the other party's culture before negotiation takes place.

The negotiation and implementation (which often means ongoing negotiations) of a joint venture may last for several years. In this case, national cultures tend to disappear as the two teams partly merge their values and behavior in a common "venture culture". In order to improve intercultural negotiation effectiveness, it is advisable to build this common culture between the partners/adversaries right from the start of the negotiations. It means establishing common rules, communication codes, finding people on each side who will act as go-betweens and trying to agree on a common interpretation of issues, facts, solutions and decision-making. This must not be considered as a formal process; it is informal and built on implicit communications. Furthermore, it relies heavily on those individuals who have been involved in the joint venture over a long period of time and who get on well together.

Cultural Misunderstandings during the Negotiation Process

If future partners do not share common "mental schemes", it could be difficult for them to solve problems together. Buyer and seller should share some joint views of the world, especially on the questions: What is the relevant information? How should this information be sought, evaluated and fed into the decision-making process?

An important distinction in the field of cross-cultural psychology opposes ideologism to pragmatism (Glenn, 1981; Triandis, 1983). As indicated by Triandis (1983, p. 148): "Ideologism versus pragmatism, which corresponds to Glenn's universalism versus particularism, refers to the extent to which the information extracted from the environment is transmitted within a broad framework, such as a religion or a political ideology, or a relatively narrow framework." This dimension refers to a way of thinking, an important element of the "mindset."

Ways of processing information: is there a common rationality between partners?

People differ in their ways of relating thinking to action: whereas the ideologists tend to think broadly and relate to general principles, the pragmatist orientation concentrates on focusing on detailed issues that are to be solved one by one. Pragmatists will prefer to negotiate specific clauses, in sequential manner. Conversely, ideologists see arguments in favor of their "global way of thinking", when negotiating a large contract such as a nuclear plant or a television satellite for instance: it is a unitary production, it is a complex multi-partner business, it often involves government financing and also has far-reaching social, economic and political consequences. Pragmatists will also find many arguments in favor of their way of thinking: the technicalities of the plant and its desired performance require an achievement and deadline orientation (pragmatist values).

Triandis hypothesizes that complex traditional societies will tend to be ideologist ones, whereas pluralistic societies or cultures experiencing rapid social change, will tend to be pragmatist. This distinction may also be traced back to the difference between the legal systems of *common law* (mainly English and American) and the legal system of *code law*. Whereas the former one favors legal precedents set by the courts and past rulings (cases), the latter favors laws and general texts. These general provisions are intended to build an all-inclusive system of written rules of law (code). Codes aim to formulate general principles so as to embody the entire set of particular cases.

The ideologist orientation, which is to be found mostly in Southern and Eastern Europe, leads the negotiators to try and set principles before any detailed discussion of specific clauses of the contract. Ideologists have a tendency to prefer and promote globalized negotiations in which all the issues are gathered in a "package deal". The pragmatist attitude corresponds more to attitudes found in Northern Europe and the United States. It entails defining limited scope problems, then solving them one after the other. Pragmatists concentrate their thinking on factual aspects (deeds, not words; evidence, not opinions; figures, not value judgements). They are willing to reach real world decisions, even if they have to be down to earth ones.

Ideologists will use a wide body of ideas which provide them with a formal and coherent description of the world, Marxism or Liberalism for instance. Every event is supposed to carry meaning when it is seen through this ideologist framework. On the other hand, the pragmatist attitude first considers the extreme diversity of real world situations, and then derives its principles inductively. Reality will be seen as a series of rather independent and concrete problems to be solved ("issues"). These issues will make complete sense when related to practical, precise, and even down-to-earth decisions. Typically, ideologists will *take* decisions (*prendre des décisions*), that is, pick a solution from a range of possible decisions (which are located outside the decision maker). Conversely, pragmatists will *make* decisions, that is, both decide and implement: decisions will be enacted, not selected. Box 5.4 illustrates how the pragmatist Americans can resent the ideologist French in international negotiations.

Communication may be difficult when partners do not share the same mindset. The most unlikely situation for success is an ideology-oriented contractor/supplier who tries to sell to a pragmatism-oriented owner/buyer. The ideologist will see the pragmatist as being too interested in trivial details, too practical, too down-to-earth, too much data-oriented (Galtung, 1981) and incapable of looking at issues from a higher standpoint. Pragmatists will resent ideologists for being

Box 5.4

Rather imprecisely defined, the idea is that one reasons from a starting point based on what is known, and then pays careful attention to the logical way in which one point leads to the next, and finally reaches a conclusion regarding the issue at hand. The French also assign greater priority than Americans do to establishing the principles on which the reasoning process should be based. Once this reasoning process is under way, it becomes relatively difficult to introduce new evidence or facts, most especially during a negotiation. Hence the appearance of French inflexibility, and the need to introduce new information and considerations early in the game. All this reflects the tradition of French education and becomes the status mark of the educated person. In an earlier era, observers made such sweeping generalizations as: "The French always place a school of thought, a formula, convention, a priori arguments, abstraction and artificiality above reality; they prefer clarity to truth, words to things, rhetoric to science ..." *Source*: Fisher 1980, Zeldin 1977.

too theoretical, lacking practical sense, concerned with issues that are too broad to lead to implementable decisions. In the first steps of the negotiation process, differences between ideologists and pragmatists may create communication misunderstandings which will be difficult to overcome during subsequent phases. Indeed, developing common norms will be fairly difficult, although it is necessary if partners want to be able to predict the other party's behavior. A frequent comment in such situations will be: "One never knows what these people have in mind; their behavior is largely unpredictable." An American (pragmatism-oriented) describes negotiations with the French (more ideology-oriented) in the following terms (Burt, 1984, p. 6): "The French are extremely difficult to negotiate with. Often they will not accept facts, no matter how convincing they may be."

Argument in negotiation: data, theory, speech and virtue

Galtung (1981) contrasts what he calls the "intellectual styles" of four important cultural groups: the "Gallic" (prototype: the French), the "Teutonic" (prototype: the Germans), the "Saxonic" (prototype: the English and the Americans) and the "Nipponic" intellectual style (prototype: the Japanese). Saxons prefer to look for facts and evidence which results in factual accuracy and abundance. They are interested in "hard facts" and proofs, and do not like what they call "unsupported statements". As Galtung states (1981, pp. 827–8) when he describes the intellectual style of Anglo-Americans: "... data unite, theories divide. There are clear, relatively explicit canons for establishing what constitutes a valid fact and what does not; the corresponding canons in connection with theories are more vague ... One might now complete the picture of the Saxonic intellectual style by emphasizing its weak point: not very strong on theory formation, and not on paradigm awareness."

Galtung contrasts the Saxonic style with the Teutonic and Gallic styles, which place theoretical arguments at the center of their intellectual process. Data and facts are there to illustrate what is said rather than to demonstrate it. "Discrepancy between theory and data would be handled at the expense of data: they may either be seen as atypical or wholly erroneous, or more significantly as not really pertinent to the theory. And here the distinction between empirical and potential reality comes in: to the Teutonic and Gallic intellectual, potential reality may be not so much the reality to be even more avoided or even more pursued than the empirical one but rather a *more real reality*, free from the noise and impurities of empirical reality." (p. 828). However, Teutonic and Gallic intellectual styles do differ in the role that is assigned to words and discourse. The Teutonic ideal is that of the ineluctability of true reasoning *Gedankennotwendigkeit*, that is, perfection of concepts and the indisputability of their mental articulation. The Gallic style is less preoccupied with deduction and intellectual construction. It is directed more towards the use of the persuasive strength of words and speeches in an aesthetically perfect way (*élégance*). Words have an inherent power to convince. They may create *potential reality*, thus probably the often-noted Latin love of words.

Finally the Nipponic intellectual style, imbued with Hindu, Buddhist and Taoist philosophies, favors a more modest, global and provisional approach. Thinking and knowledge are conceived of as being in a temporary state, open to alteration. The Japanese "rarely pronounce absolute, categorical statements in daily discourse; they prefer vagueness even about trivial matters ... because clear statements have a ring of immodesty, of being judgements of reality" (Galtung 1981, p. 833).

Communication

Needless to remark that the cross-cultural communication processes are a key component of the influence of culture on international marketing negotiations. For instance, the role of high context versus low context communication (Hall, 1960, 1976) is to be noted. When messages are exchanged, the degree to which they should be interpreted has to be taken into account. For instance, silence is a full form of communication for the Japanese, and Graham (1985) reports twice as much silence in Japanese interaction than in American. Westerners often have the impression that they "do all the talking". In fact, the capacity to cope with very different communication styles is the key to successful international business negotiation. This is especially true for non-verbal communication. For instance, a lack of eye contact for the Americans is a signal that something is amiss and "American executives reported that the lack of eye contact was not only disconcerting but reduced their bargaining performance." (Hawrysh and Zaichkowsky, 1990, p. 34).

Negotiators must be ready to hear true as well as false information, discourse based on facts as well as on wishful thinking or pure obedience to superiors. Frankness and sincerity are culturally relative values: they can be interpreted as mere naivety, a lack of realism, or a lack of self-control in speaking one's own mind. Furthermore, waiting for reciprocation when disclosing useful information for the other party, makes little sense in an intercultural context. Frankness and directness in communication are of substantial value to the Americans and to a lesser extent to the French, but not to Mexicans in formal encounters, nor to Japanese at any time (Fisher, 1980).

The issue of formality versus informality is a difficult one. Frequently, a contrast is made between cultures which value informality (e.g., American) and those which are more formal (most cultures which have long historical roots and high power distance). "Informality" may be simply another kind of formalism, and the "icebreaking" at the beginning of any typical US meeting between unknown people is generally an expected ritual. It is more important to try and understand what kind of formality is required in which circumstances with which people. Outside of formal negotiation sessions, people belonging to apparently quite formal cultures can become much more informal. In Chapter 7 Camilla Schuster and Michael Copeland give a detailed account of the influence of patterns of communication on negotiations.

Negotiation tactics

Graham (1993) studied the negotiation tactics used in eight cultures, using videotaped negotiations in which statements were classified into twelve categories using the framework of Angelmar and Stern (1978). His results show very similar negotiation tactics across cultures, most of them using a majority of tactics based on an exchange of information, either by self-disclosure or questions (more than 50 per cent in all cases). The Chinese score the highest in posing questions, which is consistent with Pye's comments about them: "Once negotiations begin the Chinese seem passive. They simply ask questions, probe for information, and conceal any eagerness they may feel." (1986, p. 78). On the other hand, the Spaniards score the highest in making promises. The proportion of "negative" tactics, including threats, warnings, punishment and negative normative appeal (a statement in which the source indicates that the target's behavior is in violation of social norms) is fairly low in all cases, never exceeding 10 per cent of the information exchange. Finally, cross-national differences are not great at the level of the type of tactics used, nor at the level of their frequency, but are more signficant at the level of how they are implemented.

The use of theatricality, withdrawal threats and tactics based on time, such as waiting for the last moment to obtain further concessions by making new demands, are based on national styles of negotiations. Tactics are also related to the ambiguous atmosphere of business negotiations when implied warm human relations are supposed to be mixed with business. This relates to the divide between affective and neutral cultures (Trompenaars, 1993). Negotiations are always interspersed with friendship and enmity, based on personal as well as cultural reasons. *Atmosphere* can be considered as a central issue in the negotiation process: Ghauri and Johanson (1979) posit atmosphere as being of basic importance to the development of the negotiation process. Atmosphere has a double role, as a bearer of the history of the relationship and as main factor explaining the transition from one stage to the next. Atmosphere is characterized in a number of respects, namely the dynamics of conflict and cooperation, reducing or overcoming the distance between the partners, the power/dependence relation and, lastly, the expectations of the parties concerning future deals. Chapter 9 examines in detail the role of atmosphere in international business negotiations.

Differences in Outcome Orientation: Oral versus Written Agreements

It would be naive to believe that profits, especially future accounting profits for each party, are the only possible outcome of the negotiation process. Other possible outcomes are listed in Table 5.1. The main reason for profits not being the sole possible outcome is that they are not really foreseeable. Basic differences in outcome orientation are generally hidden from the negotiation partners, generating increased misunderstandings. Another reason is that many cultures are relationship- rather than deal-oriented: as is described by Oh (1984) in the case of the Japanese, and Pye (1986) in the case of the Chinese, they prefer a gentleman's agreement, a loosely-worded statement expressing mutual co-operation and trust between the parties, to a formal Western-style contract.

Asymmetry in the perceived degree of agreement

Agreements are generally considered as being mostly written. They are achieved by negotiation and by the signing of written contracts, which are often considered "the law of the parties". This is unfortunately not always true. Keegan (1984) points out that for some cultures "my word is my bond" and trust is a personal matter, which he contrasts with the "get-it-in-writing" mentality where trust is more impersonal. The former is typical of the Middle East, whereas the latter is to be found in the United States where hundreds of thousands of lawyers help people negotiate written agreements and litigate within the framework of these written agreements. This has to be interpreted: it does not mean that people rely *entirely* on either an oral base (oaths, confidence between people, membership of a common group where perjury is considered a crime) or a written base. Exploring, maintaining and checking the bases for trust is a more complex process (Usunier, 1989). It entails various possibilities:

1. An agreement may be non-symmetrical. A agrees with B, but B does not agree with A. Various reasons may explain this situation: either B wishes to conceal the disagreement or there is some sort of misunderstanding, usually language-based.
2. People agree, but on different bases, and they do not perceive the divergence. They have, for instance, quite different interpretations of a clause or some kind of non-written agreement. Although much may be written down, some

things will always remain unwritten. What is unwritten may, to one party, seem obviously in line with a written clause, but not to the other. Moreover, if there is no opportunity to confront their interpretations, they cannot be aware of their divergent nature.

3. The agreement is not understood by both parties as having the same degree of influence on:
   - the stability;
   - the precision and explicitness of the exchange relation.

Written documents as a basis for mutual trust between the parties

There is a fundamental *dialectic* in written agreements between *distrust* and *confidence*. At the beginning there is distrust. It is implicitly assumed that such distrust is natural. This has to be reduced in order to establish confidence. Trust is not achieved on a global and personal basis but only by breaking down potential distrust in concrete situations where it may hamper common action. Trust is built step by step, with a view towards the future. Therefore *real trust* is achieved only gradually. Trust is deprived of its personal aspects. Thanks to the written agreement, the parties may trust each other in business, although they do not trust each other as people. Trust is taken to its highest point when the parties sign a written agreement.

On the other hand, cultures that favor oral agreements tend not to hypothesize that trust is constructed by the negotiation process. They see trust more as a prerequisite to the negotiation of written agreements. Naturally, they do not expect this prerequisite to be met in every case. Trust tends to be mostly personal. Establishing trust requires that people know each other. That is probably why many Far Eastern cultures (Chinese, Pye, 1982; Japanese, Graham and Sano, 1990; Tung, 1984; de Mente, 1987) need to make informal contacts, discuss general topics and spend time together before they get to the point, even though all this may not appear task-related.

Subsequently, the negotiation process will be lengthy because another dialectic is at work. Since people are supposed to trust each other, the negotiation process should not damage or destroy the basic asset of their exchange relationship — trust. They will avoid direct confrontation on a specific clause, and therefore globalize the negotiation process. Global friends may be local foes, provided trust as the basic asset of the negotiation process is not lost.

The ambiguity of the cultural status of written materials

That one should always "get-it-in-writing" is not self-evident. The contrary idea may even impose itself ("if they want it written down, it means that they don't trust me"). Regina Traoré Sérié (1986, quoted in Ollivier and De Maricourt, 1990) explains, for instance, the respective roles of oral communication (spoken, transmitted through personal and concrete communication, passed through generations by storytellers) and written materials (read, industrially printed, impersonally transmitted, with no concrete communication) in the African culture.

> Reading is an individual act, which does not easily incorporate itself into African culture. Written documents are presented as either irrelevant to everyday social practices, or as an anti-social practice. This is because someone who reads, is also isolating himself, which is resented by the other members of the community. But at the same time, people find books attractive, because they are the symbol of access to a certain kind of power. By reading, people appropriate foreign culture, they get to know "the paper of the whites". As a consequence, reading is coded as a positive activity in the collective ideal of Ivory Coast society, since it is a synonym for social success. This contradiction between "alien" and "fetish" written documents encapsulates the ambiguity of the status of books in African society.

Do written contracts and the intervention of lawyers produce irreversible commitments?

In cultures where relationships are very personalized, confidence cannot be separated from the person in whom the confidence is placed. The basis for mutual trust is no longer the detailed written contractual documents, but a man's word, which is his bond. It is not "just any word", but a special kind of word, which is heavily imbued with cultural codes (Hall 1959, 1976). These words as bonds cannot easily be transferred from one culture to another. Adler (1980) describes the case of an Egyptian executive who, after entertaining his Canadian guest, offered him joint partnership in a business venture. The Canadian was very keen to enter this venture with the Egyptian businessman. He therefore suggested that they meet again the next morning with their respective lawyers to fill in the details. The Egyptians never arrived. The Canadian businessman wondered whether this was caused by the lack of punctuality of the Egyptians, or by the Egyptian expecting a counteroffer, or even the absence of available lawyers in Cairo. Adler (1980, p. 178), explains:

> None of these explanations was true, although the Canadian executive suggested all of them. At issue was the perceived meaning of inviting lawyers. The Canadian saw the lawyer's presence as facilitating the successful completion of the negotiation; the Egyptian interpreted it as signaling the Canadian's mistrust of his verbal commitment. Canadians often use the impersonal formality of a lawyer's services to finalize an agreement. Egyptians more frequently depend on a personal relationship developed between bargaining partners for the same purposes.

If agreements are mostly person-based, then their written base may be less important. Thus the demand for renegotiation of clauses by a Middle Eastern buyer in a contract already negotiated and signed, should not be seen as astonishing. It should not necessarily lead to litigation. Behind the demand for renegotiation is the assumption that, if people really trust each other, they should go much further than simple and literal implementation of their written agreements. This leads to the following question; to what extent should the contract signature date be considered as a time line which signals the end of the negotiation? (See Chapter 8).

Different attitudes towards litigation

It is easy to understand that the function of litigation will be different for both sides. Recourse to litigation will be fairly easily made by those favoring written-based agreements as the ultimate means of resolving breaches of contract. The oral and personal tradition is less susceptible to recourse to litigation, because litigation has major drawbacks.

1. It breaks the implicit assumption of trust.
2. It breaches the required state of social harmony, especially in the Far Eastern countries, and may therefore be quite threatening to the community as a whole.

As David (1987, p. 89, author's translation) states:

> ... in Far Eastern countries, as well as in Black Africa and Madagascar ... subject to the Westernization process which has been attempted, one does not find, as in Hinduism or Islam, a body of legal rules whose influence may be weakened by the recognized influence of other factors; it is the very notion of legal rules which is challenged. Despite authorities having sometimes established legal codes, it is well known and seems obvious that the prescriptions of these codes are not designed to be implemented literally. They should only be considered as simple patterns. The judge will be able to moderate their strictness and, moreover, it is hoped that this will not be necessary. The "good judge", whether Chinese, Japanese or Vietnamese, is not concerned with making a good decision. The "good judge" is the one who succeeds in not making any award, because he has been skillful enough to lead the opponents to reconciliation. Any dispute, as it is a threat to social harmony, has to be solved by a settlement through conciliation. The individual only has "duties" towards the society. Recognition of "subjective rights" in his favor is out of the question. Law as it is conceived in the West is seen as good for barbarians, and the occupation of lawyer, in the limited extent that it exists, is regarded with contempt by the society.

These remarks by a specialist in comparative law give a good idea of the differences of litigious tradition between the Far East and the West. In the field of contracts, the Western saying "the contract is the law of the parties" dominates the practices of international trade. But this is, in part, window-dressing. When negotiating internationally, a set of written contracts is always signed. This is not to say that people choose either oral or written agreements as a basis for trust. The real question is rather: how should the mix of written and oral bases for trust, as they are perceived by the parties, be interpreted? People do not deal with conflicts in the same way. Negotiating together requires a capacity to envisage different ways of managing disputes. Not only differences in rationality and mental programs, but also differences in time representations, may lead to a partner "who thinks differently" being considered a partner "who thinks wrongly".

Jean-Claude Usunier

The utmost caution is recommended when interpreting the bases of trust, whether written documents or oral and personal bonds. Even in the Anglo-Saxon world, where it is preferred to "get-it-in-writing", a number of business deals, sometimes large ones — in the area of finance, for instance — are based on a simple telex or fax, or the simple agreement between two key decision-makers. It would be a mistake to believe that personal relationships do not exist in places where written contracts are generally required. Moreover, in cultures where "my word is my bond", it should never be forgotten that it is difficult to trust somebody who is not a member of the in-group, whether on a written or spoken basis. Therefore, trust has to be established (and monitored) on both bases, while at the same time keeping in mind a clear awareness of the limits of each.

CHAPTER 6

Hofstede's Dimensions of Culture and their Influence on International Business Negotiations

GEERT HOFSTEDE AND JEAN-CLAUDE USUNIER

National, Professional, and Organizational Cultures in International Negotiations

Negotiators in international negotiations, by definition, have different national cultural backgrounds. "Cultural" is used here in a sense of "collective programming of the mind which distinguishes the members of one category of people from another". National culture is that component of our mental programming which we share with more of our compatriots as opposed to most other world citizens. Besides our national component, our cultural programs contain components associated with our profession, regional background, sex, age group, and the organizations to which we belong. National cultural programming leads to patterns of thinking, feeling and acting that may differ from one party to another in an international negotiation.

The most fundamental component of our national culture consists of values. Values are broad preferences for one state of affairs above others. Values are acquired in the family during the first years of our lives, further developed and confirmed at school, and reinforced in work organizations and in daily life within a national cultural environment. Values determine what we consider to be good and evil, beautiful and ugly, natural and unnatural, rational and irrational, normal and abnormal. Values are partly unconscious and because of their normative character, hardly discussible. We cannot convince someone else that his/her

---

NOTE: The first part of this chapter originally appeared as Hofstede, G., "Cultural predictors of national negotiating styles" in Frances Mautner-Markhof (ed.), *Processes of International Negotiations*, Westview Press and the International Institute for Applied Systems Analysis, 1989, pp. 193–201, and is reproduced by kind permission of the author and publishers.

values are wrong. It is essential that negotiators share the national culture and values of the country they represent, because otherwise they will not be trusted by their own side.

Other components of national culture are more superficial — that is, visible, conscious, and easy to learn, even by adults. They include symbols: words, gestures, and objects that carry a specific meaning in a given culture. The entire field of language consists of symbols; and a culture group's language can be learned by outsiders. Besides symbols, a culture has its collective habits or rituals, ways of behavior that serve to communicate feelings more than information; these, too, can be learned by outsiders, although not as easily.

Those involved in international negotiations will have developed a professional negotiation culture, which considerably facilitates the negotiation process. This professional culture, however, is more superficial than their national cultures: it consists of commonly understood symbols and commonly learned habits more than of shared values. Different types of negotiators will have their own kind of professional cultures: diplomats, bureaucrats, politicians, business people, lawyers, engineers etc. Negotiations are easier with people from other countries sharing the same professional culture than with those who do not.

Finally, organizations, too, develop their own cultures. In the field of international negotiations, international bodies, such as the International Institute for Applied Systems Analysis (IIASA), the IAEA and the various other United Nations (UN) agencies, can play an important role because their internal culture facilitates communication. Again, and even more than in the case of professional cultures, these organization cultures are superficial — that is, they reside on the level of the easily acquired common symbols and habits. Organizational cultures are not always an asset; they can develop into liabilities, too, by blocking communication instead of facilitating it. The behavior of negotiators in international negotiations will thus be influenced by at least three levels of culture: national, professional and organizational, besides the contribution of their own personal skills and character.

Dimensions of Differences in National Cultures

The remainder of this chapter will be devoted to national culture differences and their supposed impact on negotiation styles, because it is on this area that the author's research has mostly been focused. National culture differences, as we argued, reside to a large extent in values acquired in early life, and are therefore quite deep-seated, often unconscious and hardly discussible.

National cultural value systems are quite stable over time; the element of national culture can survive amazingly long, being carried forward from generation to generation. For example, countries that were once part of the Roman empire still share some common value elements today, as opposed to countries without a Roman cultural heritage.

National cultural value systems have been measured in international comparative research projects. Such projects use samples of people from different countries as respondents on value questions. These samples should be carefully matched — that is, composed of similar people from one country to another, similar in all respects except nationality (same age, sex, profession, etc.). They need not be representative of the entire population of a country, although if this is possible, it makes the sample even more attractive. Two such international comparative value research projects were carried out by this author (Hofstede, 1980, 1983) and by Bond (1987), respectively.

The Hofstede IBM study

The Hofstede research used a data bank containing 116,000 questionnaires on the values of employees of the IBM multinational business organization in 72 countries, collected between 1967 and 1973. These employees represent extremely well-matched subjects of each country's population, because they do the same jobs with the same technology in the same kind of organization, have the same education levels, and can be matched by age and sex. Initially, data from 40 countries were analyzed; later on, this number was extended to 50, and data from 14 more countries were grouped into three geographic regions — East Africa, West Africa and the Arab speaking countries — bringing the total number of cultures covered up to 53. As the data were collected inside a capitalist enterprise, the socialist countries are not covered in this research project. However, matched data from a Yugoslavian organization selling and servicing IBM equipment are included. The IBM project revealed that the 53 countries covered differed mainly along four dimensions:

1. *Power distance*, that is, the extent to which the less powerful members of organizations and institutions (like the family) accept and expect that power is distributed unequally. This represents inequality (more versus less), but defined from below, not from above. It suggests that a society's level of inequality resides in the followers as much as in the leaders. Power and inequality, of course, are extremely fundamental facts of any society, and anybody with some international experience will be aware that "all societies are unequal, but some are more unequal than others"

2. *Individualism* on the one side versus its opposite, *Collectivism*. This describes the degree to which the individuals are integrated into groups. On the individualist side, we find societies in which the ties between individuals are loose: everyone is expected to look after him/herself and his/her family. On the collectivist side, we find societies in which people from birth onward are integrated into strong, cohesive ingroups; often their extended families (with uncles, aunts and grandparents) continue protecting them in exchange for unquestioning loyalty. The word "collectivism" in this sense has no political meaning: it refers to the group, not to the state. Again, the issue addressed by this dimension is an extremely fundamental one, relevant to all societies in the world.

121

3. *Masculinity* versus its opposite *Femininity*. The distribution of roles between the sexes is another fundamental issue for any society, involving a whole range of solutions. The analysis of the IBM data revealed that (a) women's values differ less between societies than men's values; (b) if we restrict ourselves to men's values (which vary more from one country to another), we find that they contain a dimension ranging from very assertive and competitive and maximally different from women's values on the one hand, to modest and caring and similar to women's values on the other. We have called the assertive pole "masculine" and the modest, caring pole "feminine". The women in the feminine countries have the same modest, caring values as the men; in the masculine countries they are somewhat assertive and competitive, but not as much as the men, so that these countries show a gap between men's values and women's values.

The three dimensions described so far all refer to expected social behavior: toward people higher or lower in rank (Power Distance), toward the group (Individualism/Collectivism), and as a function of one's sex (Masculinity/Femininity). It is obvious that the values corresponding to these cultural choices are bred in the family: Power Distance by the degree to which children are expected to have a will of their own, Individualism/Collectivism by the cohesion of the family versus other people, and Masculinity/Femininity by the role models that parents and older children present to the younger child.

4. A fourth dimension found in the IBM studies does not refer to social behavior, but to man's search for truth. We called it "Uncertainty Avoidance": it indicates the extent to which a culture programs its members to feel either uncomfortable or comfortable in unstructured situations. "Unstructured situations" are novel, unknown, surprising, different from the usual. Uncertainty-avoiding cultures try to prevent such situations by strict laws and rules, safety and security and, on the philosophical and religious level, by a belief in absolute truth: "There can only be one Truth and we have it". People in uncertainty-avoiding countries are also more emotional, and are motivated by inner nervous energy. The opposite type, uncertainty-accepting cultures, are more tolerant of behavior and opinions different from those they are used to; they try to have as few rules as possible and, on the philosophical and religious level, they are relativist and allow many currents to flow side by side. People within these cultures are more phlegmatic and contemplative, and are not expected by their environment to express emotions.

Table 6.1 lists scores for the 53 cultures in the IBM research, which allows one to position them in each of the four dimensions (plus a fifth, which we shall describe in the next section). These scores are relative: we have chosen our scales so that the distance between the lowest- and the highest-scoring country is about 100 points.

TABLE 6.1

Scores on five dimensions for 50 countries and 3 regions. Rank numbers: 1 = lowest; 53 = highest (for CFD: 22 = highest)

Country	Power distance Index (PDI)	Rank	Individualism Index (IDV)	Rank	Masculinity Index (MAS)	Rank	Uncertainty avoidance Index (UAI)	Rank	Confucian dynamism Index (CFD)	Rank
Argentina	49	18–19	46	31–2	56	33–4	86	39–44	–	–
Australia	36	13	90	52	61	38	51	17	31	9–10
Austria	11	1	55	36	79	52	70	29–30	–	–
Belgium	65	34	75	46	54	32	94	48–9	–	–
Brazil	69	40	38	27–8	49	27	76	32–3	65	18
Canada	39	15	80	49–50	52	30	48	12–13	23	4
Chile	63	29–30	23	16	28	8	86	39–44	–	–
Colombia	67	37	13	5	64	42–3	80	34	–	–
Costa Rica	35	10–12	15	8	21	5–6	86	39–44	–	–
Denmark	18	3	74	45	16	4	23	3	–	–
Ecuador	78	45–6	8	2	63	40–1	67	26	–	–
Finland	33	8	63	37	26	7	59	22–3	–	–
France	68	38–9	71	43–4	43	18–19	86	39–44	–	–
Germany, F.R.	35	10–12	67	39	66	44–5	35	6–7	25	5–6
Great Britain	35	10–12	89	51	66	44–5	35	6–7	25	5–6
Greece	60	26–7	35	24	57	35–6	112	53	–	–
Guatemala	95	51–2	6	1	37	11	101	51	–	–
Hong Kong	68	38–9	25	17	57	35–6	29	4–5	96	22
Indonesia	78	45–6	14	6–7	46	23–4	48	12–13	–	–
India	77	43–4	48	33	56	33–4	40	9	61	17
Iran	58	24–5	41	30	43	18–19	59	22–3	–	–
Ireland	28	5	70	42	68	46–7	35	6–7	–	–
Israel	13	2	54	35	47	25	81	35	–	–
Italy	50	20	76	47	70	49–50	75	31	–	–
Jamaica	45	17	39	29	68	46–7	13	2	–	–
Japan	54	21	46	31–2	95	53	92	47	80	20
Korea, Rep. of	60	26–7	18	11	39	13	35	37–8	75	19
Malaysia	104	53	26	18	50	28–9	36	8	–	–
Mexico	81	48–9	30	22	69	48	82	36	–	–
Netherlands	38	14	80	49–50	14	3	53	19	44	14
Norway	31	6–7	69	41	8	2	50	16	–	–
New Zealand	22	4	79	48	58	37	49	14–15	30	8
Pakistan	55	22	14	6–7	50	28–9	70	29–30	0	1
Panama	95	51–2	11	3	44	20	86	39–44	–	–
Peru	64	31–3	16	9	42	16–17	37	45	–	–
Philippines	94	50	32	23	64	42–3	44	10	19	3
Portugal	63	29–30	27	19–21	31	9	104	52	–	–
South Africa	49	18–19	65	38	63	40–91	49	14–15	–	–
Salvador	66	35–6	19	12	40	14	94	48–9	–	–
Singapore	74	41	20	13–15	48	26	8	1	48	15
Spain	57	23	51	34	42	16–17	36	39–44	–	–
Sweden	31	6–7	71	43–4	5	1	29	4–5	33	12
Switzerland	34	9	68	40	70	49–50	58	21	–	–
Taiwan	58	24–5	17	10	45	21–2	69	28	87	21
Thailand	64	31–3	20	13–15	34	10	64	24	56	16
Turkey	66	35–6	37	26	45	21–2	35	37–8	–	–
Uruguay	61	28	36	25	38	12	100	50	–	–
USA	40	16	91	53	62	39	46	11	29	7
Venezuela	81	48–9	12	4	73	51	76	32–3	–	–
Yugoslavia	76	42	27	19–21	21	5–6	88	46	–	–
Regions:										
East Africa	64	31–3	27	19–21	41	15	52	18	25	5–6
West Africa	77	43–4	20	13–15	46	23–4	54	20	16	2
Arab Countries	80	47	38	27–8	53	31	68	27	–	–
Bangladesh	–	–	–	–			–	–	40	13
Poland	–	–	–	–			–	–	32	11

123

Geert Hofstede and Jean-Claude Usunier

The Bond Study

The other comparative value research project relevant to our topic was carried out by Michael Bond of the Chinese University of Hong Kong. He asked a number of Chinese social scientists to prepare a list of basic values for Chinese people. After discussion and elimination of redundancies, this led to a 40-item Chinese questionnaire, which was subsequently translated into English. Through an international network of colleagues, this Chinese Value Survey was administered to 1000 students in a variety of disciplines (500 male, 500 female) in each of the 22 countries from all five continents; the only socialist country covered was Poland. Wherever possible, translations into the local language were made directly from the Chinese. To a Western mind, some of the items such as, "filial piety" look exotic — so exotic that it was explained as "obedience to parents, respect for parents, honoring of ancestors, financial support of parents". Of course, to the Chinese mind, some of the items on the IBM questionnaire, designed by Western social scientists, may have looked equally exotic.

A statistical analysis of the 22-country Chinese Value Survey (CVS) results, based on the relative importance attached, in a country to each value versus the other values, again yielded four dimensions. Twenty out of 22 countries were covered earlier in the IBM studies. Thus, we could compare the country scores on each CVS dimension to those of the IBM dimensions. One Individualism–Collectivism (most of the Chinese value being associated with the collective pole), and one to Masculinity–Femininity. This in spite of the completely different questions, different populations, different moments in time, and different mix of countries. One dimension from the IBM studies, however, is missing in the CVS data. We did not find a CVS dimension related to Uncertainty Avoidance. We previously associated this dimension with man's search for truth; it seems to the Chinese mind that this is not an essential issue. However, we did find another quite clearly marked dimension. It is made up of the following values:

On the positive side:

- persistence (perseverance)
- ordering relationships by status and observing this order
- thrift
- having a sense of shame

On the negative side:

- personal steadiness and stability
- protecting one's "face"
- respect for tradition
- reciprocation of greetings, favors and gifts

For some countries, the values on the positive side are relatively more important; for others, those on the negative side. All of them are to be found in the teachings of Confucius, dating from 500 BC. However, the values on the positive side are more oriented toward the future (especially perseverance and thrift), those on the negative side toward the past and present. Bond has, therefore, called this dimension Confucian Dynamism. Country scores on Confucian Dynamism for the countries surveyed with the CVS are listed in the last column in Table 1, raising the total number of relevant dimensions to five. Interestingly, Individualism (in both the Hofstede and the Bond study) is strongly correlated ($r = 0.84$) with a country's wealth (per capita GNP), and we can prove with diachronic data that the causality goes from wealth to individualism. Confucian Dynamism is strongly correlated ($r = 0.70$) with a country's economic growth over the past 25 years (increase in per capita GNP), with a likely causality from Confucian Dynamism to economic growth.

National Cultures and International Negotiations

Negotiations, whether international or not, share some universal characteristics:

- two or more parties with (partly) conflicting interests
- a common need for agreement because of an expected gain from such agreement
- an initially undefined outcome
- a means of communication between parties
- a control and decision-making structure on either side by which either side's negotiator(s) is/are linked to his/their superiors.

However, in international negotiations, the following characteristics vary according to the national negotiation styles of either side:

- the nature of the control and decision-making structure on either side
- reasons for trusting or distrusting the behavior of the other side (a certain amount of trust is an indispensable ingredient for successful negotiation)
- tolerance of ambiguity during the negotiation process
- emotional needs of negotiators, e.g., ego-boosting or ego-effacement.

If one knows the approximate position of a country's national cultural value system on the various cultural dimensions listed in Table 6.1, one can predict aspects of the negotiation style of its negotiators.

1. Larger Power Distance will lead to a more centralized control and decision-making structure (key negotiations have to be concluded by the top authority).
2. Collectivism will lead to a need for stable relationships, so that negotiations can be carried out among persons who have become familiar with each other over a long time (often several years). Every replacement of one person by another is a serious disturbance to the relationship, which has to be reestablished from scratch.

In collectivist cultures, mediators or go-betweens have a more important role in negotiations than in individual cultures. Formal Harmony is very important in a collectivist setting; overt conflict is taboo. Mediators are able to raise sensitive issues with either party within an atmosphere of confidence, and to avoid confrontation.

3.   Masculinity leads to ego-boosting behavior and sympathy for the strong on the part of negotiators and their superiors. Masculine cultures tend to resolve conflicts by fighting rather than compromising. Femininity leads to ego-effacing behavior and sympathy for the weak. Negotiations between two masculine cultures are more difficult than if at least one of the cultures is more feminine. A historical comparison that can be cited in this respect is the difference between the solution of the Aland Island crisis between Finland and Sweden in 1921, and the Falkland Island crisis between Argentina and Great Britain in 1983; the first was resolved peacefully through a plebiscite, the second is still unresolved despite a bloody war. In our research, both Finland and Sweden are found on the feminine side of the scale; both Argentina and Britain on the masculine side.
4.   Uncertainty Avoidance leads to a low tolerance of ambiguity and distrust of opponents who show unfamiliar behavior; negotiators from uncertainty-avoiding cultures prefer highly structured, ritualistic procedures during negotiations.
5.   Confucian Dynamism leads to perseverance for achieving desired ends even at the cost of sacrifices.

Obviously, such predictions should be checked in empirical research.

Conclusion

For success in international negotiations, it is important for parties to acquire an insight into the range of cultural values they are going to meet in the negotiations. This includes an insight into their own cultural values and the extent to which these deviate from those of the other side(s). Such insight will allow them to interpret more accurately the meaning of the behavior of the other side(s).

In addition to insight, cultural differences in international negotiations demand specific skills:

•   For communicating the desired information and emotions to the other party by the spoken word, the written word and nonverbal behavior.
•   For preparing, planning and arranging negotiations: making an appropriate use of go-betweens, choosing places and times for meeting, setting up the proper social gatherings etc.

It is important that cultural differences in international negotiations be recognized as a legitimate phenomenon, worthy of study, and as a liability which skilled and well-trained negotiators can turn into an asset.

A comment on the use of Hofstede's cultural dimensions in the academic literature on international business negotiations

JEAN-CLAUDE USUNIER

A number of authors have referred to Hofstede's cultural dimensions as potential explanatory variables of the processes and outcomes of international business negotiations, either in general (Adler *et al.*, 1987; Elgström, 1990; Kale and Barnes, 1992; Weiss, 1993 and 1994) or in the case of negotiations with the Chinese (Shenkar and Ronen, 1987; Kirkbride *et al.*, 1991; Adler *et al.*, 1992; Tse *et al.*, 1994) or with the Japanese (Hawrysh and Zaichkowski, 1990; Goldman, 1994). In Chapter 2 of this book Sudhir Kalé has outlined some of the consequences of these cultural dimensions on negotiation behavior, in combination with personality traits and organizational variables.

Graham *et al.* (1994) are the only researchers to have empirically tested the relevance of Hofstede's dimensions for international business negotiations. They did it by comparing negotiation behavior across eleven cultures (United States, Canada (Francophone), Canada (Anglophone), Mexico, United Kingdom, France, Germany, former USSR, Taiwan, China and Korea). A number of negotiation variables (profits, satisfaction, problem-solving approach (PSA), attractiveness of the other party) and relationships between these variables have been tested for correlation with the scores of these countries on Power Distance, Individualism, Masculinity and Long-Term Orientation (LTO), using Pearson correlation coefficients.

On the basis of Hofstede's concept of power distance, which is deeply ingrained in social life and takes its roots in early socialization, Graham *et al.* expect that cultures with higher PDI will place more emphasis on the importance of role relations, that is, buyer-seller. Indeed, Power Distance is significantly correlated with the hypothesis that buyers achieve higher individual profits than do sellers (0.75 with $p < 0.05$).

In line with point 2 of Hofstede's view on the influence of collectivism on negotiator's attitudes, Graham *et al.* expect negotiators from individualistic cultures to behave more individualistically, being competitive and antagonistic rather than problem-solving oriented, and achieving higher profits when they behave individualistically. The correlation coefficients confirm these findings (IDV scores with profits: 0.67; IDV scores with PSA: 0.83; IDV scores with the relationship linking PSA to profits: 0.64; all $p < 0.05$). This confirms the strong preference of collectivist cultures for the maintenance of formal harmony and the avoidance of overt conflict, which is often a direct consequence of individualistic and competitive values.

Concerning the two last dimensions (masculinity and LTO), Graham *et al.* (1994) do not find significant links. In line with the third point of Hofstede (see "Conclusion"), Graham *et al.* expect higher masculinity to lead to less nurturing attitudes and to lower satisfaction levels; the contrary result appears: masculinity leads to significantly higher satisfaction levels (0.68, $p < 0.05$) signalling that, probably, the influence of the masculine/feminine dimension on international negotiation behavior should be interpreted cautiously. The sample of 700 experienced business people in 11 countries, used by Graham *et al.*, was probably composed of predominantly male national subsamples (their demographics do not describe distribution by sex); it is not a problem if the various samples have similar gender distributions. But, the test of the influence of the masculinity/femininity dimension on negotiation variables may be biased if the gender repartition of the national subsamples is not similar.

Graham *et al.* expect higher LTO to lead to a stronger influence of the role relations (buyer-seller) on profits. They cite Hofstede arguing that LTO should reflect "ordering relationships by status and observing this order" (Hofstede, 1991, p. 165). However, this is not supported by their empirical findings. The expectation that the traditional Confucian, hierarchical society would lead the buyer to dominate was also disconfirmed by Adler *et al.* (1992), in the case of PRC Chinese negotiators. They explain that the prevailing economic conditions in present-day PRC still make it a seller's market, thus probably offsetting the dominance of the buyer's role which, on the contrary, can be found clearly in Japan (Hawrish and Zaichkowski, 1990), with an affluent economy which allows the traditional strength of the buyer's role in Asian societies to emerge.

Similarly, it was expected by Graham *et al.* that negotiators from lower LTO cultures would behave on the basis of reciprocation, a series of closely tabulated favors on each side within a relatively short time period, thus calling for a stronger reciprocal relationship between PSA on each side. This is not confirmed. However, their study brings an unexpected result which seems quite consistent with the prediction of Hofstede that "Confucian Dynamism (LTO) leads to perseverance for achieving desired ends even at the cost of sacrifices" (1989, p. 200). In fact, PSA, problem solving approach, is strongly correlated with Long-Term Orientation (0.89, $p < 0.05$).

A dimension which has not been examined by Graham *et al.* (1994) is uncertainty avoidance (UA). However in their study of US–USSR trade negotiations, Beliaev *et al.* (1985) find support for the fact that negotiators coming from higher UA countries are somewhat unwilling to take risks, and prefer, as emphasized by Hofstede, "highly structured, ritualistic procedures during negotiations" (1989, p. 200). These comments must be considered with some caution: the Ex-USSR or Russia were not included in Hofstede's study since there was no IBM subsidiary there. However, a less remote country in terms of geography, language, and political regime, Yugoslavia, scored quite high on uncertainty avoidance (p. 88). Beliaev *et al.* describe in the following terms the typical Soviet negotiator: "well trained in Party discipline; obedient, with a well-developed sense of hierarchy; hard working and trained but with narrow horizons; loyal to the state and fearful of making mistakes because of the risk of falling to the level of the average Soviet citizen; cautious, tough, inflexible because of the strictness of their instruction" (1985, p. 105). This portrait of a highly risk-averse Russian negotiator, is confirmed by Graham *et al.* (1992), even after the Soviet regime has been abolished.

Some of the hypothesized influence of cultural dimensions on international business negotiations still remain to be tested, especially the influence of high power distance on a more centralized control exerted over negotiators, final decisions having to be made by the top authority. However, the relevance of Hofstede's cultural dimensions for international business negotiations seems now clearly established.

CHAPTER 7

Cross-Cultural Communication: Issues and Implications

CAMILLE SCHUSTER AND MICHAEL COPELAND

Regardless of industry or country, business transactions take place between individuals. Even when companies share data, systems, and processes electronically, the original steps of establishing the electronic interchange take place between individuals. The ability of those individuals to connect with one another, trust one another, understand one another and develop a common purpose determines their success in establishing the business arrangement. Therefore, the communication process is critical to successful negotiation.

When representatives from two businesses engage in a formal business transaction, their ability to communicate effectively will, in large measure, determine their success. This process is extremely demanding because it is imprecise and fraught with considerable potential for misunderstanding. Language is symbolic, meaning that words are interpreted by individuals and do not have specific, inherent referents. Nonverbal messages may enhance, contradict, or confuse the verbal message being sent. The circumstances of the business transaction often place severe constraints on what may or may not be said and what may or may not be understood. The level of trust between the individuals or companies will affect the meaning of what is stated by the other partner. Distractions during the process may interrupt a train of thought or flow of conversation and important points may be missed, misunderstood, or forgotten, as a result.

Depending upon one's background, education, training, and environment, the verbal and non-verbal symbols chosen by one person to express an idea may not transmit the information accurately because the other person may interpret the words and gestures to mean something different than was intended. Successful communication, even between two individuals from the same country or within the same industry, can be difficult, because no two people use the same context to distil the words to their specific meanings (Downs *et al.* 1977). The more overlap that occurs between the participants' backgrounds, contexts or perceptual filters, the greater the possibility of successful communication.

Communicating across cultures is even more demanding than working at effectively communicating in a single culture, because the participants' references, experiences or filters have less overlap. The native language of the two individuals is not the same; therefore, interpretations of specific words used are less likely to be identical. When a translator is used, the process is even more imprecise because a third, and sometimes a fourth, person's interpretation is added to the process. In addition, the same meanings are not necessarily attributed to nonverbal symbols. The political and economic environment is often different, creating a mismatch between goals and objectives. The process of decision-making within organizations may differ significantly resulting in a more tentative and less decisive style of communication during the interaction by one partner. Since each element of culture shapes the filters used for interpretation, cultural differences can significantly affect the process of successful communication.

The purpose of this chapter is to examine the nature of differences across cultures and their implications for the process of communication. The first section provides a context for examining the process of communication. The second section describes a Cultural Classification Model which categorizes the major cultural groups in the world using the dimensions of time, task, and relationship. The final section describes the Communication Implications Matrix which catalogues differences in communication style.

Process of Communication

Words and actions are symbols selected by individuals to transmit images, concepts, ideas, and perceptions from themselves to others. As such, both the sender and receiver play an active role in the transmission and reception of messages, (see Figure 7.1). The transactional nature of communication implies that both participants share in the encoding and decoding process and affect one another (Berko *et al.* 1980, Bradley *et al.* 1980). An important characteristic of this perspective is that the success of the process depends upon "mutual reciprocal exchanges of feelings, meanings, ideas, and responses" (Bradley and Baird 1980).

The overlap between the Fields of Experiences of senders and receivers establishes how easy or difficult the communication process is likely to be. If there is little common experience or culture, successful communication will be very difficult (Schramm 1980). For instance, understanding a lecture about quantum physics or genetic engineering will likely be difficult for a layperson. Similarly, understanding the desire for, and the amount of time spent, negotiating over the details of a contract is difficult for a business partner to perceive, when the legal system in that country is not well-established and functions unpredictably by the foreign partner's norms or expectations.

Striving to understand the other person's Field of Experience is a necessary step for facilitating a more successful communication process. The more each partner understands the other's situation, perspective and culture, the easier it is to create verbal and nonverbal symbols that will be encoded and decoded

FIGURE 7.1
Model of communication

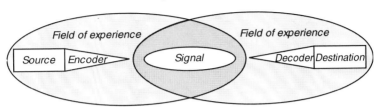

Source: Schramm, W. (1980)

similarly by both sides (Downs *et al.* 1980). It is incumbent upon each partner to learn about the other side's perspective and practices. Therefore, specifying and understanding cultural differences is critical for successful communication in any intercultural negotiation process.

Culture Classification Model

Assumptions regarding the use of time, the approach to the task at hand, and the role of relationships in making decisions vary throughout the world and have significant implications for the way people communicate in business situations (Ghauri 1986, Joy 1989, Lee 1966, Mortenson 1992, Perkins 1993, Salacuse 1991, Schuster *et al.* 1993, Wasnak 1986). Inspired by Tucker's (1982) lecture and presentation, Copeland (1987) and Schuster and Copeland (1996) developed a Culture Classification Model that is anchored by elements fundamental to business decision-making across the world for use in training and development work with international colleagues and students (see Figure 7.2). This section briefly describes the model. A more detailed description and justification is also found in Schuster and Copeland (1996).

In the late twentieth century, time has become even more important to individuals than ever before. The advent of information technologies, real-time interactive communication systems and global access to the same information and sources has made speed and reaction time a competitive factor to those who can access and leverage them. For people engaged in global business, the 24 hours in the day have to be managed like a commodity, carefully allocated, parceled out or saved. At the same time, cultures hold core values that do not respond to technological change quickly. These values are shared by people from these cultures and are manifest in the way individuals behave, typically.

The same 24-hour day includes time for eating, sleeping, working, interacting with people, accomplishing tasks and relaxing. Although time is a constant, people around the world use it differently. The amount of time spent on each activity varies. Often, the more time spent on an activity, the more that culture values that activity, often describing it in terms of "higher quality" or as "sacred." Those cultures on the left hand side of the model focus on completing tasks

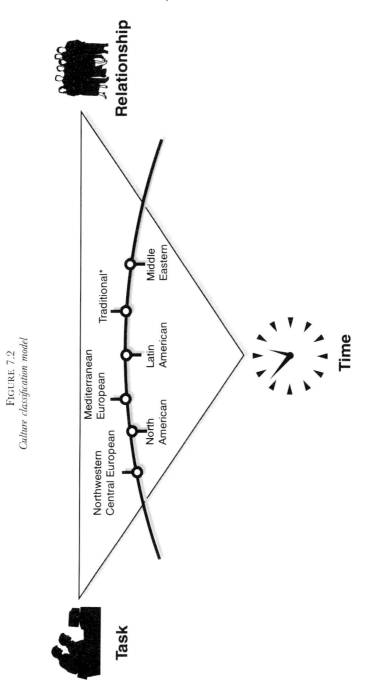

FIGURE 7.2
Culture classification model

*Traditional cultures include the Asian, centrally-planned and formerly centrally-planned countries.

efficiently and effectively within agreed deadlines, so time is spent getting the job done. Those cultures on the right hand side of the model focus on knowing their business partners well and a significant amount of time is spent ensuring the continuance of good relationships. Depending upon how time is used, cultural groups are placed in different locations along the continuum. Each group will be described briefly.

The model presented here typifies cultural groups based upon three characteristics, but several caveats need to be mentioned. Although it is convenient to think of national cultural norms, cultures have subtle, yet distinctive differences across their different regions. For example, if a traveler to the United States were to venture from New England in the northeast, through New York City, through the Middle Atlantic states, through the Deep South, into the Midwestern states, across the Rocky Mountains, through the Southwest and up the Pacific Coast, at least eight different sub-cultures could easily be experienced. Most present nation-states have similar diversity, given sufficient geography to have had relatively isolated segments of their population in their history.

The concentration of people at the location of production, in most cases far away from their ancestral roots, has caused a sense of anomie that is one of the underlying causes of the resurgence of local chauvinism and may lead to the further disintegration of nation-states, as ethnic groups break away to form new entities. As this phenomenon occurs, generalizations such as this model will need to be updated, always with a tendency to move toward the relationship side of the model. The reaction of people to the impersonal nature of central governments is to find familiarity in similarities at the local level, using language and culture as the basis for common communication. For the time being, the intercultural communicator needs to be constantly aware of these dynamics and be ready to adapt accordingly. Individuals will deviate from the model presented here depending upon how much that person adheres to the norms of the major cultural group in that country or the degree of multi-culturalism the individual exhibits.

North American and Northwestern and Central European

North American and Northwestern and Central European cultural groups are deceptively similar in their orientation toward Time, Task, and Relationships. The primary focus of these interactions is on getting to the task at hand and accomplishing it to get results as efficiently and quickly as possible. Typically, the relationships between individuals are less important than task completion. Time is an important component in these cultures and using it efficiently is a critical goal and admired measure of skill. Time dominates how meetings are planned, phone calls are made, meals are scheduled and what success really looks like to participants. This concept is so strong that it characterizes the differences that occur between these groups.

Generally, the Northwestern and Central Europeans use time to structure interactions to a greater extent than do North Americans. In the UK, Germany, and Scandinavia, business people tend to view starting and ending times of meetings as fixed. Foreigners who do not respect this time orientation are viewed as less professional or less sophisticated than those who do. If meetings or meals are scheduled at specific times, the local nationals expect these events to begin and end on time.

The structure of an interaction is also likely to be more formal in Europe. For instance, in Germany, agendas are agreed upon and adhered to, often with times noted for different topics, and are used as a measurement tool to evaluate both the effectiveness of the meeting and the professionalism of the participants. If the meetings have not been brought to closure, time will be rescheduled for subsequent meetings or the business will be conducted by correspondence. Going beyond the scheduled time is normally not allowed. To enforce adherence to the agenda, a "gatekeeper" role is commonly used. During a meeting, a participant in this role keeps agenda topics in focus and free from tangential discussions.

Anglophones in America and Australia tend to be more casual and less formal, outwardly, in general, than their European counterparts. In many cases, in an Anglophone setting, complete names are exchanged and the first names of each participant will be used in meetings or during the conduct of business. Northwestern and Central Europeans, as a rule, use titles, such as Mister or Miss, educational levels or job-related rank, with given names throughout the business interactions. In addition, greetings and small talk in North America will be more informal and persistent. Northwestern and Central Europeans usually limit these discussions to prior to the beginning of meetings or during meals.

Generally, communication styles developed in North America or Northwestern and Central Europe are relatively transferable and individuals will be successful when communicating with one another. While surface behaviors may be recognizable or even similar, fundamental values and beliefs of the culture are distinct. For instance, people in Canada, Australia, and the US typically have a more optimistic view of projects and proposals resulting in a greater tendency to take risks or attempt large scale projects than is typically done in Europe (Miller 1987). Assuming a common orientation toward task accomplishment can be problematic with such fundamental differences in play. By clarifying expectations and trying to identify how differences in perception can be addressed, each side can learn to accept and understand the other, resulting in a greater likelihood for successful communication, the basis for successful intercultural negotiation.

Mediterranean Europeans

The Mediterranean European cultures include French, Iberian, Italian, and Greek cultures. Paris is more aligned with Northwestern and Central Europe in its business dynamics so Parisians are very comfortable being task and time oriented with Northwestern and Central Europeans. However, within France, Parisians are quite comfortable using their Mediterranean style. Likewise, the people in the Mediterranean regions are entirely capable of interacting with representatives from North America and Northwestern and Central Europe, using the task orientation with facility and skill. However, a concept of "extended tribe" begins here. If an individual is considered to be part of the same clan, tribe, country, or cultural group, some effort during an interaction will need to focus on developing a connection between members by establishing a common bond, individually, one-to-one.

The recognized nation-states of this region generally describe the extended tribal boundaries. Italians, while quite diverse within Italy, will attempt to establish some degree of commonality between/among themselves if two or more Italians are present during an interaction. This will happen in advance, during breaks, or during the interaction itself. In doing so, the subtleties of culture come into play including quality of language, slang, educational experience, work experience or personal connections, all playing important parts in determining the individual relationship and its value to the participants as well as discovering what overlap exists between the participants' Fields of Experience. Similarly, Spaniards, French (outside Paris), Greeks, and Portuguese will put forth some effort toward finding a common bond with one another, based on common language and culture. However, this bond does not generally exist across country boundaries in this area of the world.

For non-natives of a given country, extending the opportunity to develop an individual or personal relationship is a powerful way to change communication dynamics. By expressing a similarity of attitude or opinion or simply an interest in the people or subject at hand, identifying shared family roots, comparing similar experiences, identifying similar connections or having facility or competence with the language being spoken, the foreign partner becomes more approachable. For example, having traveled to the country previously, having worked with people from the region, or having common familial ties or traditions can build bridges. Once the link is established or reinforced, attention can be turned to the task at hand.

Another difference from other cultural groups is the polychronic attitude toward time. While the task is still held to be important, time in Mediterranean Europe is more flexible than in North America or Northwestern and Central Europe. Time will be used first for important tasks, which may mean attending to personal or a seemingly unimportant business problem until it can be resolved, at the expense of being late for another meeting, not completing another job on time, or even delaying delivery of a product or service. This is considered an acceptable trade-off in this part of the world when the reasons are communicated clearly and in a timely fashion to the individuals concerned.

The tasks agreed to be most important by the key decision-maker must be given adequate time. Each important task, in its time, will be given ample focus and attention. As a result, the timing of the communication process, the sequence of solving issues and the intensity of the approach to the task taken by the foreigner, may be very different from the accepted approach in Mediterranean Europe and include other non-task items, such as socializing. In addition to longer lunches and/or later dinners, appointments may be delayed or rescheduled frequently. Thus, the foreigner must demonstrate patience, maturity and tolerance to be considered a worthy partner in this region.

Latin Americans

In the Latin American cultural groups the importance of relationships increases and the previously mentioned notion of extended tribe broadens to include any other Latin, Spanish-speaking country, and, in some cases, other Romance-language countries. The cross-boundary kinship is a result of both common colonial and independence movement experiences, similar political and economic histories, as well as linguistic and religious commonalties. Members of this cultural group are entirely capable of doing business using North American or North-western and Central European assumptions, but this is clearly *not* their preferred method and represents a bi-cultural understanding that will affect their partici-pation in the communication process.

With the increased importance of relationship, business people from the North American or Northwestern and Central European tradition find that the rules of communication have changed: persuasion and influence are directly related to the quality of the relationship between the two parties, and the nature of relationships is quite different than in their native country.

Relationship is the development of a personal connection with another individual, over time, and includes certain implied obligations and duties. It requires that meetings with a Latin partner take place for more than simply conducting business, include meals with other local people, or involve discussions of general business conditions so participants can begin to know and appreciate each other as individuals. By showing genuine interest in the host culture, history, language, business, cuisine, arts, religion, or politics, the Latin partner shares information related to personal perceptions and is able to demonstrate national pride. As a result, participants begin to know one another, not as business associates, but on a deeper, personal level. This provides a richer and more meaningful context for the relationship to develop with multiple dimensions from which to draw as the business dynamic of the relationship develops.

By making deposits in the "emotional bank account" of the business partner over repeated interactions, the "local" Latin American develops a sense of whether or not a potential business partner is trustworthy and the kind of person with whom he/she would like to do business. Addressing the task is still important with the Latin cultural group, but the importance of relationship changes the role of the persuasion process. Time is spent determining whether or not the other side is trustworthy, honorable, and compatible. By developing a partner relationship with the other person, questions of trust, honor, integrity, compati-bility and comfort will be answered prior to the completion of the task.

Traditional Cultures

The Traditional Cultures include the Japanese, Chinese, centrally planned and formerly centrally planned economies. While tremendous diversity exists across these groups, a fundamental similarity in the way of life across these groups binds them together. Countries within this classification have a strong agrarian tradition, whereby the means of making a living and daily activities are inherently part of the fabric of life in the local community, creating strong reliance on a network of contacts to accomplish tasks. As these countries move to an industrial or information-based economy, the structures of economic and legal institutions begin to take a new form. The countries within this classification are at different points in the process of moving away from an agrarian tradition to more formal structures. However, the agrarian tradition, which has established interdependence and collaboration is still dominant and is the primary means to obtain results.

Relationship has the same meaning as that presented in the Latin American section, but plays a larger and more important role, in that members of the Traditional cultural groups prefer not to do business with anyone unless a relationship is established first. Relationship is similar to a gateway which needs to be passed through prior to arriving in the inner sanctum where activities take place. It is the necessary way to get to the point of the business. Relationship does not come from rank, position or hierarchical titles, but from individual sincerity and respect.

In all of these groups, the sense of "clan," as an identifying factor, is extremely important. Entry into the group provides identity, protection, and unconscious and conscious preference while, at the same time, requiring adherence to emerging group norms. "Clan" can be defined by ethnicity, education, language, or some other common characteristic that can be used to differentiate individuals from others who do not share this trait, behavior or skill. Communicating with members of this group is extremely difficult for someone who is not part of the group or does not have a product or service that is in great demand and unavailable elsewhere. As these countries evolve from their agrarian-based roots to an industrial or information-based economy, their orientation toward business also changes, with laws, rules and formal procedures regulating exchanges between people who may not necessarily know one another well.

Many of the cultural groups in this classification, especially the Asian groups, also operate within a High Context (Hall 1983) language environment, in which words and direct communication are not as important as in those countries, like Germany, the UK, or the US, which operate in a Low Context language environment. Linguistically, Hall placed countries on a continuum which classifies a country's language based upon the importance of words and situational elements. Using this criterion, language in High Context countries may be secondary to relationships. For example, when talking with another person with whom a strong relationships exists, a question such as "Could you check into this matter?" is not a request, but rather a statement of expectations regarding the task. On the other hand, language in low context countries is specific and legalistic. For example, defining who is responsible for exactly which tasks, by which date, under threat of what penalty, is necessary. Therefore, individuals from High and Low Context countries use different methods of presentation, styles of communication, and influence strategies.

Exceptions to this guideline are when one partner has a unique product or service needed by the other partner. In this situation, cultural sensibilities are normally subordinated. Recognize that initial success may well evaporate, if and when a competitor appears who *has* developed a relationship that is sustaining in nature. Once the competitor has an "equitable" product or service *and* has trust and relationship developed, the contract or agreement is transferred as soon as possible to the relationship-based competitor. Often, the original individual/organization never understands why the business was lost. In fact, the temporary competitive advantage of technology or process is easily duplicated in the late 20th century; the advantage of a long-term, personal relationship, based on trust, comfort and familiarity, is very difficult for an "outsider" to replicate, understand or be willing to undertake.

Middle Eastern

People from Middle Eastern countries also operate from within a paradigm that puts relationships first. However, a significant difference from the Traditional cultures is that blood relationships are distinctly more significant than other relationships. Deriving partly from the "clan" concept and partly from the religious tenet that emphasizes the importance of being responsible for and taking care of family members and others of the same faith, family relationships are a fundamental element of doing business. Communication will be more productive if conducted between family members or if a family relation is part of the negotiating team for the foreign company.

When products or services, not available from family members, are needed, members of the Middle Eastern cultural group can and do negotiate with people outside their family members. However, as with the Traditional cultural group members, establishing a personal relationship is essential *before* attending to business. Introductions by relatives or trusted friends carry great significance and imply opportunity to do business. Often "middlemen" act as intermediaries between people who need to do business but have no common basis for doing so. The "middleman" reduces the perceived risk to either side and acts to find a common basis, both formally and informally. After a solid trust relationship is established and appropriately maintained, it is necessary to discuss the constraints and parameters of the situation. If the objective is mutually agreeable, the other side will, of course, grant the favor, go along with the deal, or give permission to the project, *to help a friend*. "Western" standards of conflict of interest, nepotism, and integrity cause confusion and harsh judgments between the two parties when fundamental issues and values conflict.

In this environment, learning how to establish and maintain relationships, how to become part of an appropriate family network, and how to present a position acceptably are absolutely critical parts of a negotiation. The North American and Northwestern and Central European perspective, where focusing on the task in the least amount of time is ideal, is considered rude, disrespectful and insensitive. This behavior is inappropriate in the Middle East where an introduction from a family member or trusted friend is normally necessary before time is taken to develop a relationship, which is the gateway to be traversed before business can begin.

But remember: while the Culture Classification Model organizes groups using the time, task, and relationships dimensions, several caveats need to be kept in mind.

- **First**, cultures are dynamic and in a constant state of evolution. The fundamental culture of a country will change slowly with behavioral or linguistic changes occurring naturally over time, or in response to specific national traumatic events. Therefore, a static assessment of a culture will never be completely accurate. Sometimes behaviors are quickly adapted that seem to be comfortable for foreign visitors; however, underlying values do not change quickly. The foreign negotiator needs to be alert for nuance and ready to adapt, but must always remain conscious of the fundamentals of the visited culture.
- **Second**, every country exhibits a range of cultures. Assuming that all members of the country will be operating from the same cultural norms is problematic. Each region, major city, and/or ethnic group will have its own set of cultural assumptions that are related to the country's overall culture, but not necessarily identical. The foreigner must identify the paradigms of the local culture and be prepared to adapt appropriately.
- **Third**, each person's past socialization and development will also affect their cultural assumptions. Since business negotiations and sales are conducted on a person-to-person basis, it is essential to remember that a general set of cultural assumptions may or may not be appropriate for the *individual* with whom you are to meet and do business.
- **Fourth**, if a foreigner tried to develop a relationship but was unprepared to deliver on the relationship over time, the trust lost will likely never be recovered. Trust in relationships must first be delivered unreciprocated, then reinforced, before a sound basis for the relationship is established. If there is no sincere intention to be a part of a relationship long term, it is better, strategically, to remain within one's own cultural norms and work across cultural boundaries within the limitations of common commercial interests with no inherent long term expectations.

Implications of Communication Style Differences for Negotiation

The Culture Classification Model distinguishes task and relationship differences between groups and signifies that time is used differently by each group. An

FIGURE 7.3
Communication implications matrix

Assumptions	NA	N W&CE	ME	LA	TR	ME*
People vs. Task	T	T	T/P	P/T	P/T	P
Formal vs. Extended Hospitality	F	F	F/E	E	E	E
Disclosure vs. Social Topics	S/P	S	S/P	P	P/S	P/S
Words vs. Actions	W	W	W/A	A	A	A
Business vs. Personal Commitment	B	B	B/P	P	P	P
Inductive vs. Deductive vs. Circular reasoning	I/D	I/D	D	D/I	C	C
Direct vs. Indirect Style	D	D/I	I/D	I	I	I
Specific vs. Ambiguous Agreements	S	S	S/A	A	A	A
On-Going vs. Sporadic Contact	S	S	S/C	C	C	C
Individual vs. Hierarchy Empowerment	I	H/I	H/I	H	H	H

Notes:NA North America and Australia, NW&CE = Northwestern and Central Europe, ME = Mediterranean Europe, LA = Latin America, T = Traditional Cultures including developing, centrally-planned and formerly centrally-planned economies, ME = Middle East

important implication of this model is that the further away from each other on the task-relationship dimension the cultural groups are, the more different the Fields of Experience will be for members of each group, thereby making successful communication more difficult.

With varying orientations toward people, time and tasks, members of each cultural group have a unique set of assumptions regarding the process of communication. These assumptions govern the choice of content, appropriateness of topics, type of reasoning, importance of verbal and non-verbal communication, as well as the frequency of communication and determine the Fields of Experience used to interpret verbal and nonverbal symbols. Figure 7.3 displays the communication implications of the cultural differences presented in the previous section. Each pair of assumptions will now be discussed.

People vs. task

The North American and Northwestern and Central European groups are more likely to focus their discussions on the task rather than on the individuals themselves. Small talk is kept to a minimum. Time spent talking about concerts or sports events attended, restaurants visited, travel experiences or hobbies is only considered necessary for building initial rapport and is thought to be non-productive if carried on too long. If lengthy discussions occur, time is seen as being wasted, cutting into the productivity of the individuals involved. Diversions and tangential conversations are often cut short or interrupted to bring the participants back to the issue at hand.

People in Mediterranean Europe often find it necessary to make a personal connection with individuals and will generally spend time getting acquainted or reacquainted with one another before meetings, at the beginning of meetings or at the first reasonable opportunity during breaks or meals. They can operate effectively in a situation requiring initial concentration on the task without interruptions for personal discussions, but do not prefer that style of communication.

In Latin America, Traditional Cultures and the Middle East, spending time becoming acquainted with the other individuals involved in the meeting is essential prior to starting on task accomplishment. Normally business will not proceed until this step is successfully completed. Making a personal connection by having extended conversations involving sports or cultural events, personal hobbies, the company's history, making complimentary remarks about individuals known to both sides or recalling past meetings or common experiences is an important step in developing a relationship. During the course of any business conversation, interruptions regarding individual interests, plans for social activities, other meetings, or personal requests are acceptable in the ordinary flow of a meeting and do not result in judgments being made about the professionalism or value of the person who initiates these kinds of discussions.

The content of the conversation at the beginning of meetings, the amount of time devoted to small talk, the kind of interruptions expected, tolerated or enjoyed, the flow of topics and the number of meetings required to accomplish a task will vary from one group to another. The closer together the groups are on the continuum, the more similar will be their expectations regarding whether task or people related issues will dominate the conversation.

The farther apart on the continuum, the more different the expectations of both partners will be. This set of expectations affects the amount of time spent socializing before the substance of the negotiation is addressed, the pace of negotiations, and type of interruptions considered appropriate during the negotiation process. Different expectations can generate conflict and frustration from the very beginning of the process if conscious efforts at adaptation are not made, especially by the foreign negotiator.

Regardless of the proximity of groups on the Culture Classification Model, on some level, "foreign" is different to a host or potential business partner. Awareness of differences, successful adaptation to cultural nuance and the facility with local language and content do not make the foreigner a "local" in the eyes of the host. Maintaining a respectful distance is the recommended strategy for the foreigner until the host initiates more familiarity and willingness to invite the foreign visitor "inside" the professional or social circle. Attempting too much familiarity or assuming acceptance by a host can result in serious setbacks in the negotiation dynamic. It is always better to ask for permission, rather than to act and then need to apologize in a negotiation.

Formal vs. extended hospitality

Depending upon the assumptions related to the nature of local hospitality, norms and practices, participants will form expectations about what type of social activity is appropriate, whether business is to be discussed during these social events, how much time is to be spent on social activities and how important appropriate behavior and conversation are during social events. Determining whether the social activities are an integral part of the business process or are viewed as necessary, but non-essential events provides an initial context for these activities.

In Mediterranean Europe, Latin America, Traditional Cultures and the Middle East, getting to know the people involved as individuals is important, and social activities are often an integral part of the business process. Generally, business is not the focus of discussion during these events. The purpose of the conversation and activity is to learn about the other people as individuals, their interests, their thinking, what is important to them, and how they like to spend their time. Scheduled social activities such as dinners, concerts, tours, luncheons, receptions or sports events, all provide occasions for general conversation about events, circumstances, problems and general topics which reveal an individual's view of the world, values, habits, flexibility, interest, and patience.

On the other extreme, people in North America, Northwestern and Central Europe, and Mediterranean Europe see social events as a way to relax from the formal business protocol, talk in a more informal atmosphere and pass time between scheduled meetings. Social activities are planned to show off the local area to visitors, to entertain individuals during their free time or to provide an opportunity for business conversation in a less formal atmosphere. Business conversation is often part of these social events, thereby making them a continuation of the task orientation, but with less formality.

Expectations regarding the role of social events as part of the process of doing business, the kinds of topics that are appropriate during social events and the purpose of conversation during these events varies across cultural groups creating different Fields of Experience. Partners who do not share similar expectations may perceive business associates as rude when they talk about business at dinner or other social activities and may find that comments made while relaxing during informal social events have a significant effect on the outcome of the negotiation. Further, the foreigners may perceive their associates to be stalling the negotiation with all the social activities or may jeopardize their success by refusing to participate in social activities. Appropriate expectations regarding the role of hospitality and the behavior required during social events are essential for successful intercultural negotiations.

Disclosure vs. social topics

When the conversation focuses on the people, choosing appropriate topics depends upon the expectations of the participants. Northwestern and Central Europeans tend to be more formal and are much less likely than any of the other groups to discuss personal issues. The importance placed on the value of privacy, combined with a strong task emphasis, leaves little inclination for conversations about personal matters. However, that does not mean there is no interest in anything non-task related. Discussions of the arts, fine cuisine, architecture, or politics can be lively, entertaining, and lengthy. Foreign participants are expected to have sufficient knowledge to be part of these conversations and to add their perspective to the observations of the locals.

Latin Americans, on the other hand, are likely to be very interested in other people's hobbies, interests, activities, family members, travels and cultural interests. Non-Latins are sometimes surprised by questions about personal matters or inquiries about relatives. However, families in Latin America are close and it is considered important to know the people with whom one is talking. Within economic and social strata there are relatively few secrets in such close-knit communities. However, even in reasonably open atmospheres like this, some topics, such as salaries, are considered "private" and not openly discussed outside one's family.

Generally, the visitor needs to let the host lead the level of disclosure. There is no need to be "too open," disclosing topics or experiences that are embarrassing or too personal. Many experienced Canadians and Mediterranean Europeans have been cited by their local partners as being especially adroit at moving into or out of disclosure, with few topics "out of bounds."

People from the Traditional Cultures and the Middle East have two distinct styles of communication: one for the inner circle of family, network, clan, or tribe members and one for anyone else in the outer circle. Conversation with members of the outer circle remains more social and little is revealed about one's own personal views of the world. Only within the inner circle is more personal information exchanged. Both styles of communication exist and are used regularly. However, the relationship between the individuals involved will determine the expectations for which set of topics will be considered appropriate.

While conversation with members of some cultural groups focuses more on the relationships between people than on the task at hand, not all topics are equally suitable for these non-task discussions. Focusing on people or relationships does not necessarily mean that participants want to discuss personal issues. Depending upon the nature of the relationship, the formality of the culture and the desire for privacy within a cultural group, social topics, such as art, cuisine, sports, or architecture, may be more appropriate than personal ones, such as activities of family members or someone's health. Within any cultural group, some topics are regarded as private and discussed only with certain individuals.

Determining what topics of conversation are appropriate for which situations, with which people, is an important element of successful communication.

Becoming too personal or disclosing private information about one's self is very difficult for foreign business people to deal with and, as a rule, is something to avoid.

Words vs. actions

Hall classifies linguistic groups along a continuum of High Context to Low Context. The Low Context groups rely upon words to convey precise meanings; whereas, the High Context groups rely upon the context of a situation, the relationship between individuals, the purpose of the conversation and the nonverbal activity, in addition to the words actually used to convey ambiguous meanings open to individual interpretation.

The Middle Eastern, Traditional, Latin American, and Mediterranean cultural groups use more High Context languages. Words convey a sentiment, direction, intention or desired state of affairs. However, circumstances, issues and pressures change. Therefore, precise statements are not always possible or desirable. However, individuals are expected to honor their promises. In these cultures, determining a person's reliability, credibility or veracity is judged more by what people do, than by what is said.

In the Low Context cultures of North America, Australia, Northwestern and Central Europe, words are significant in and of themselves. What someone says or promises, establishes a set of expectations about future activity. After finishing a conversation, participants will leave with a specific expectation of what will be done, by whom, within what timeframe and to an agreed standard. Parties that cannot meet the expectations are often accused of talking in "bad faith." Waiting to see whether actions conform to the words should not be necessary; of course, the expectation in Low Context culture is that the actions *will* conform to the words.

The linguistic heritage of particular cultural groups establishes different sets of expectations regarding the way words are used when communicating with one another. At one extreme, the words are a flexible part of a larger context of information that is being processed; at the other extreme, the words themselves are the critical part of the interaction.

Business vs. personal commitment

The statement, "I will do my best to make it work," conveys a very different type of commitment depending upon the Field of Experiences created within cultural groups. In more formal, task-oriented cultures, the above statement invokes a business commitment, albeit an ambiguous one. In effect, people from these groups would mean that to support their own or their company's credibility, they, or someone within their organization, will do what is possible within the confines of job constraints, resources, time and ability to accomplish the task. The expectation is that the organization is making the commitment and that, whether or not that specific individual is assigned to the final project, the company will stand behind the agreement.

In the more relationship-oriented and people-oriented cultures, people making the above statement are making a personal, individual commitment that, to the very best of their ability, they will ensure, personally, that the project is accomplished. Regardless of organizational support or constraints, regardless of other time pressures, the individual will see that the agreement is honored, if at all possible. The individual's credibility and reliability is attached to the statement and the outcomes of the project.

An important caveat is that many of the Middle Eastern and Traditional Cultures have a philosophy that accepts a level of predetermination and fate. Therefore, individuals promising to "do their best" make that statement within the context of assuming that while they will do their best, success depends upon whether it has been ordained or whether God has willed it so. While people from each group are promising to do their best, the Field of Experiences from each cultural group interprets that statement to have a different meaning for the individual commitment implied. Therefore, the same statement made by individuals from different cultural groups implies a different level of commitment. What one partner perceives as a guarantee of personal involvement to make an agreement work, the other partner perceives as a commitment to do what is possible within the constraints of the system. Personal credibility can be damaged, which can result in a harsh evaluation of an individual's efforts when partners have divergent expectations regarding the probability of accomplishing the agreement. These differences can, and do, affect organizations attempting to develop long term relationships across cultures.

Inductive vs. deductive vs. circular reasoning

Presentation of specific information and forms of arguments differs across cultural groups. For instance, scientists, engineers, and mathematicians in North America, Australia, and Northwestern and Central Europe use formal, deductive forms of logic when presenting proofs for their work. These arguments are often technical and highly persuasive with specific supporting documentation to present conclusions in as persuasive a manner as possible. In conversation, however, people do not often use formal, deductive syllogisms. Rather, examples are often used to illustrate points when engaged in persuasive forms of communication. As a result, even though both deductive and inductive forms of logic are used for persuasion by these groups, inductive forms of logic are preferred in conversation between individuals.

However, the Cartesian logic of Mediterranean Europe, also represented in Latin America, involves the use of deductive reasoning in ordinary conversation and argumentation, which can cause misunderstanding when communicating across cultural groups. What one side may accept as a specific instance, the other side is presenting and accepting as a formal proposition from which conclusions will be drawn. For instance, the statement that "Company A is often late with deliveries" could either be an example of a type of situation to be guarded against or the initial premise of an argument (Company A from Country X is often late with deliveries. Company B is from Country X. Therefore, Company B will often be late with deliveries.) that could result in the conclusion that Company B's delivery dates can not be considered firm commitments or that Company B is an unreliable business partner. The way in which premises are offered, accepted, and used in persuasive arguments depends, in large part, upon the Fields of Experience normally accepted within a particular cultural group. This certainly affects the presentation and acceptance of persuasive arguments across groups.

The Traditional and Middle Eastern groups share a different perspective partly as a result of their strong tradition as agrarian societies which emphasize the cyclical nature of seasons. As a result, people think of time as a series of recurring events at regular intervals. This assumption permeates the pattern of conversation and persuasion. The ambiguous nature of High Context languages used in combination with a circular or cyclical form of presentation is not easily recognizable as either an inductive or deductive pattern of logic. Indirect forms of communication, touching on issues tangentially, assessing reactions, backing off, making other tentative overtures, assessing reactions and backing off to reevaluate and reposition a response are more typical. Business partners from outside these groups often find conversations disjointed and difficult to follow. Neither side is very effective offering persuasive arguments from their own perspective to foreign partners. The conversation often results in frustration with a mismatch of ideas, proposals, rationale and goals.

As a result, the way in which arguments and evidence are presented, interpreted, and accepted varies significantly across cultural groups. Knowing which information or evidence will be most persuasive, when it is best to present it, in what form, to which groups, are critical pieces of information for successful communication when engaged in intercultural negotiations.

Direct vs. indirect

In North America, especially in the United States, there are strong values regarding independence, freedom and individual equality, resulting in an emphasis on frank discussions among peers. The idea is that people working together on a task should be candid in their communication with one another so that the problem can be addressed more efficiently and productively. Emotions may not always be addressed directly, but are certainly a factor in the process. To address the issue of hard feelings, people are cautioned to try to be tactful while pointing out someone's mistakes, to offer positive comments as well as criticism or to make negative comments in private and positive comments in public. While people's feelings may sometimes be hurt or people may be offended at times, that is an unfortunate by-product of being hardworking and successful.

In Northwestern and Central European countries, people are generally less direct and more tactful in their comments with one another when conflict or differing points of view are irreconcilable. While disagreements do exist and can be discussed directly, people are more adroit at using a conversational style that is both reserved and tactful while still being direct. Emotion is always held in check and should not be allowed to be part of the process.

In the Mediterranean European countries, emotions are more readily and openly expressed. Tact is essential and personal attacks are inappropriate and always avoided, since these inevitably jeopardize relationships. At the same time, arguments can be loud and lengthy because neither side gives in or compromises willingly. The object of the emotion and energy is the task, not the individual.

In the other cultural groups, personal slights and loss of face are critical issues, and care must be taken in conversations to avoid negative comments or even the suggestion of criticism. Learning appropriate ways of letting disapproval or disagreement be known in a subtle manner is an important and valued skill. Learning how and when pressure can be applied successfully takes a great deal of tact and facility with indirect communication. Direct and obvious criticism will result in loss of face not only for the person receiving the negative comments but also for the person making them and loss of face is a serious issue affecting a person's ability to engage in business successfully. Since loss of face is not to be taken lightly, learning when and how to express a negative point of view or disagreement is critical for success in these cultures.

Successful negotiation depends upon knowing how to address and reconcile different points of view. When the preferred communication style of one group regarding how to address differences is not compatible with another group's communication style, successful completion of the negotiation is in jeopardy. Directly confronting a business partner, who is comfortable with an indirect, ambiguous conversation, regarding a point of disagreement puts both sides in an awkward position, damages the relationship and does nothing to resolve the issue. Knowing the generally accepted style of communication used by a business partner and adapting to that style allows both sides the opportunity to focus on the issue at hand, thereby increasing the likelihood of a successful negotiation.

Specific vs. ambiguous agreements

In those cultural groups placing primary importance on task accomplishment and using a low context language, agreements and contracts are the goal of any business dealings. Using words to specify who does what, when, within what parameters, under threat of what penalties, with the possibility of what bonuses, within what specifications is the goal of any business deal. Direct communication, spending as little time as is necessary on the relationship or people part of the interaction, is the preferred way to arrive at a contract that is so clear that little or no interpretation is needed. This contract will then establish the expectations for all future behavior regardless of what kind of communication patterns are used to maintain the contract.

On the other hand, cultural groups emphasizing relationships, people and flexibility over a task-only orientation and using a high context language are more likely to view agreements and contracts as ambiguous. Since the environment has and can change rapidly, as has been the case in the face of natural disasters or revolutions, a paper document that cannot adapt to changing circumstances is not practical. Contracts are very useful as tools for articulating guidelines and goals, but not for establishing specific legally-mandated, accountable requirements.

The goal, process, and approach to contracts is very different philosophically, legally, and culturally, creating conflicting Fields of Experience across cultural groups. With varying expectations regarding the role of a contract, members of different cultural groups approach the task of negotiating a contract with divergent assumptions. The goal of writing a contract, the length of time it takes to write a contract, the specificity of language in a contract and the binding nature of a contract are assumptions that vary across cultural groups creating many different perspectives regarding the purpose of negotiation as well as the role of a contract as the conclusion of the negotiation process. These perspectives and expectations must be brought into some type of alignment or be addressed in some fashion for intercultural negotiations to be successful.

On-going vs. sporadic contact

In those cultural groups relying upon signed contracts to establish the expectations, specific behaviors, and results for agreed upon activities, regular contact is not necessary. The contract is not ambiguous; all specifications are clearly articulated in the contract; everyone knows what is expected and each party can do its job without interference. Questions of clarification or new issues might need to be discussed, thereby necessitating some continued contact. However, on-going contact is not scheduled regularly; it occurs when needed.

Those cultural groups emphasizing relationships and personal contact need continued, regular interactions between participants. Communication is not a one-time event, but a regular dialog between mutual friends who like one another, who want to know what is going on in the other person's life and who want to reaffirm their relationship. In addition, continued communication is especially necessary with people from High Context linguistic groups. Words are not seen as precise; therefore, the words in a contract do not convey a specific set of expectations. The signed contract means that the parties *intend* to *work together* toward achieving this ideal. However, everyone knows that specific circumstances often make it impossible for a single contract to cover every contingency. Therefore, partners need regular communication to understand what is happening, what progress has been made, what difficulties are being encountered, what is being done to deal with the difficulties and what new options have arisen, for the contract to be implemented effectively. Communication needs, processes and skill requirements are significantly different from one cultural group to another requiring an on-going negotiation process in many cultures rather than a negotiation process with a discrete ending point.

Individual vs. hierarchy empowerment

In the task-oriented cultures of North America and Australia, the sense of personal freedom is very strong. Individuals are not necessarily constrained to a particular social class, location or even socio-economic group by birth. As a result, individuals strive to achieve personal goals, seek personal autonomy and often prefer to act as individuals rather than as a member of a group. As the business culture changes to facilitate greater competitiveness, to produce higher quality goods and services and to encompass the efficiencies of the information age, individuals are being empowered as decision-makers for their departments, divisions and companies. As a result, their communication pattern tends to be present-oriented, self-oriented and action-oriented.

In the European countries, the legacy of the aristocracy, guilds and traditional landowners results in a more ordered and less flexible socio-economic arrangement. Therefore, an individual's family, education, location of residence and occupation play a role in the position in society open to that person. Within these parameters, individual effort, decisions and accomplishment determine an individual's success. While a person's effort does result in personal success, decision-making within organizations continues to follow a structured, centralized model of hierarchy.

The Latin American, Traditional, and Middle Eastern cultural groups place more emphasis on hierarchy, whether positions are achieved by title, family, election, group ability or individual merit. However, in these countries, some citizens are more equal because of age, birth, education, success, seniority or power. Individuals are expected to follow the orders of their superiors and the superiors are expected to make decisions in the interests of their followers. Therefore, communication patterns by individuals other than the central decision-making figure are less decisive, less action-oriented, less risk-taking, and more other-oriented. Decisions are not likely to be made at one meeting because other people, not in attendance, need to be consulted, other people may be the actual decision makers and decisions will be made after much thought, research, and consultation.

The communication style, actions desired and decision-making orientation differs significantly across cultural groups. The differences in Fields of Experience establish different expectations regarding the role and decision making responsibilities for positions within the hierarchy. These expectations affect the success of the communication process when two parties are trying to come to agreement over a course of future action during negotiation. The assumptions of each cultural group determine how the process evolves, how much power the negotiators have, and who makes the final decision, thereby affecting the dynamics of the intercultural negotiation process.

151

Camille Schuster and Michael Copeland

Conclusion

Communication is more likely to be successful when the Field of Experiences of participants significantly overlap. However, even when participants share the same general culture, company culture, education and have similar personalities, the overlap of experiences is not identical, making successful communication problematic. With some overlap, participants will share similar expectations of a situation, the decisions to be made, the implications of those decisions, will understand the style and pattern of communication to be used, will plan to discuss similar topics, and may choose to use similar forms of communication.

The Culture Classification Model categorizes major cultural groups in the world using the dimensions of time, task and relationship. Given these assumptions, the implications for the process of communication not only demonstrate differences in the Fields of Experience, but also the difficulty of cross-cultural communication.

The Communications Implications Matrix categorizes the position of each cultural group on a set of ten concepts, thereby illustrating the areas in which the Fields of Experience are likely to be different from one group to the next. In general, the greater the difference between groups on the Culture Classification Model, the greater the differences in experience, expectations, and communication style.

An important reminder is that every individual in each cultural group may not demonstrate these norms or behave in a similar way, especially in communication style. Differences exist within regions in countries, across companies and between individuals. The purpose of the model and matrix are to provide a general context to look at the issues, identifying areas of potential similarity and difference to facilitate planning for adaptation and increase the likelihood of successful communication in intercultural negotiation situations.

Using the model and matrix to prepare a set of guidelines, questions and tactics, individuals can expand their Fields of Experience so that more overlap is possible between participants. As the overlap increases, so does the ability to adapt to different Fields of Experience, thereby increasing the possibility of successful cross-cultural communication. Each successful encounter can be used to foster future success and expanded effectiveness in the global environment.

CHAPTER 8

The Role of Time in International Business Negotiations

JEAN-CLAUDE USUNIER

Introduction

Herb Cohen recounts a negotiation with Japanese partners in the following terms: "Instead of beginning negotiations right away, they first had me experience Japanese hospitality and culture. For more than a week I toured the country from the Imperial Palace to the shrines of Kyoto. They even enrolled me in an English-language course in Zen to study their religion. Every evening for four and a half hours, they had me sit on a cushion on a hardwood floor for a traditional dinner and entertainment. Can you imagine what it's like sitting on a hardwood floor for all those hours? If I didn't get hemorrhoids as a result, I'll probably never get them. Whenever I inquired about the start of the negotiations, they'd murmur, "Plenty of time! Plenty of time!" (Cohen, 1980, p. 94).

Time-based misunderstandings in international business is a classic topic which has drawn much attention and given rise to a lot of anecdotes, most of them relating to appointments, punctuality, and the diverse concepts of time-related courtesy across cultures. Synchronization is always difficult; even when the basic time codes seem to be shared by people or by organizations, there still may be some significant variations related to the particular time systems of individuals, or the specific temporal cultures of organisations. Complex negotiation, such as in the case of international turnkey operations, requires a synchronization process which is heavily loaded with precise, linear time; meeting the dates is strongly emphasized and delay penalties are assigned to lateness in the realization phase.

Among all the dimensions of culture which have a significant but almost invisible impact on business negotiations, time patterns are probably the strongest. It illustrates the invisible nature of culture particularly well: business negotiators wear watches, use a planner, and agree that it is standard practice to fix dates and deadlines. Yet, beyond this apparent uniformity, they behave quite differently

Jean-Claude Usunier

in terms of planning and scheduling tasks. In fact, time permeates the whole of business negotiation, both the starting phase and the process, and finally also the outcome of the negotiation, at least in terms of durability of the business relationship. Taking time explictly into account in international business negotiations makes all the more sense when one realises that there are differences in the representation of time and how the patterning of time consistently differs across cultures. As the example of Cohen shows, there are substantial differences in the very beginnning of business negotiations, and that is why use of time in the starting phase is dealt with: getting to know each other, scheduling the process and making appointments. The negotiation process itself involves a series of tasks that are either directly time-related (planning tasks for instance) or are embedded in time, such as time pressure in the bargaining process which may result in one party unnecessarily yielding for reasons of perceived time pressure. When discussing substantive clauses dealing with plant construction or common operations, the partners plan, define dates and deadlines, and possibly set delay penalties. How this common planning process is often flawed by the uneven temporal cultures of the partners is explained, sometimes making the negotiation of common planning an illusion rather than a reality. Time is viewed as an outcome of the negotiation; interpretations vary as to the extent to which the signing of a contract is seen as actually concluding the negotiation process. Finally, advice is offered for using time shrewdly in international business negotiations. Although examples in this chapter are taken from a great many countries and cultures, the major contrast is between Western temporal models (linear, economic time), mostly that of Americans and Northern Europeans, and Eastern Asian time patterns (cyclical-integrated time), especially Chinese and Japanese, as East Asian nations are now obvious challengers to the Westerners in terms of business efficacy, given their rise in world trade.

The influence of Time on International Business Negotiations

An isolated round of negotiation for selling aircraft can take place over some months (the negotiation time itself); several such "rounds" may be necessary for signing a particular contract between an airline and a plane manufacturer that will extend over the next five years, including maintenance and possible change for a new version of the plane (venture time). These two time frames are generally embedded in a much longer relationship between the airline and the aircraft company, which may have been continuous over the last twenty-five years (time frame of the exchange relationship). Time aspects of negotiation have their initial basis in the actors: How long will they negotiate, from start to finish? Will they participate up to implementation? What is their own cultural background as fas a time is concerned? How does the negotiation fit with their personal agenda, as individuals and as members of organizations, with their degree of occupation and the possible scarcity of their individual time? Time is related to *the structure of negotiation*: parties may set a common agenda, plan and organize negotiation on the base of precise time schedules or, on the contrary, they may prefer an informal style of negotiation in which time is seen as a constraint rather than a key resource. Time may also influence *negotiation strategies* in as much as future orientation seems a necessary prerequisite for developing an integrative strategy. Time works also as a *process variable*, influencing negotiation phases, the appointments between the parties, and the rhythm of negotiation, its pace, speed, and its rituals. Finally, time is embedded in the kind of outcomes sought by the parties, whether a deal, with strict time boundaries, or a relationship which is hoped to extend into the long term. Table 8.1 presents the different aspects of time which must be considered in international business negotiations when they involve people from different cultural backgrounds.

TABLE 8.1
Time in international business negotiations

Starting the negotiation	• Time for preliminaries (getting to know each other) • Setting the agenda/scheduling the negotiation process
Time in the negotiation process	• Making appointments and setting deadlines • Managing temporal clash in IBNs • Temporal clashes between negotiating organizations • Time pressure in the bargaining process • Timing of concessions
Relationship time frame	• Long-term orientation favouring an integrative orientation • Making plans together: planning construction and resources; dealing with deadlines and delays • Discrepancies in the partners' temporal cultures
Time as an outcome variable	• Relationship versus deal: continuous versus discontinuous view of time • Written agreements as a time-line for negotiation

Cross-cultural Differences in the Patterning of Time

Most business concepts are time-based: actualization, investment choice, product life-cycle, sales forecasting or the planning of new product launches, to name but a few. Normative time in marketing and management seems indisputable, and its very nature is rarely questioned: it is perceived as linear, continuous and economic. However, time, in a cross-cultural perspective, is probably the area where differences are both the largest and the most difficult to pinpoint, because assumptions are very deep-seated and formally, we adopt a common model of time. People's relationship with time changes with respect to periods of history and the level of human development, according to the technology available for measuring time, to the emphasis given to natural and social rhythms, and to the prevailing metaphysical views. Each vision of time (*Zeitanschauung*) corresponds to a vision of the real world, its origins and destiny (*Weltanschauung*). Time manifests itself prominently through its social functions in that it allows people to have a

155

common organization of activities and helps to synchronize individual human behaviour. Encyclopaedic approaches to the concept of time (Attali, 1982) show that never has one time pattern eliminated another previous one. Each new time pattern superimposes itself on the one that previously prevailed. As a consequence, individual time perceptions may result from adding or mixing different basic patterns of time. Most of the literature in cultural anthropology considers time perceptions as cultural artifacts. As Gurevitch states (1976, p. 229): "Time occupies a prominent place in the 'model of the world' characterizing a given culture."

Dimensions of time orientation

Table 8.2 shows time-related cultural assumptions, which correspond to four common problems:

TABLE 8.2
Time-related cultural differences

Basic problem/Cultural orientation	Contrasts across cultures
Is time money? (a) Economicity of time	Time is regarded as a scarce resource or, conversely, as plentiful and indefinitely available.
How to schedule tasks (b) Monochronism versus polychronism.	Only one task is undertaken at any (preset) time, following a schedule ("agenda society"), versus dealing simultaneously with different tasks, actions and/or communications (polychronism) for convenience, pleasure and efficiency.
Is time a continuous line? (c) Linearity (L) versus cyclicity (C) of time	Time is seen as linear-separable, cut in slices (L) versus the daily, yearly and seasonal cycles which are emphasized (C).
How should we emphasize past, present and future? (d) Temporal orientations	
(i) towards the past	People with high past orientation consider that the past is important, that resources must be spent on teaching history and building museums, referring to oral and written traditions and past works. Their basic assumption is that their roots are implanted in the past and no plant can survive without its roots. Conversely for low past orientation.
(ii) towards the present	People with high present orientation consider that they basically live "here and now". Although not always enjoyable, the present must be accepted for what it is: the only *true* reality we live in.
(iii) towards the future.	People easily and precisely envisage and plan their future. They are project-oriented, prepare for the long-term, appreciate the achievements of science, and so on. For them the future is inevitably "bigger and better"? Conversely for low future orientation.

1. To what extent should time be regarded as a tangible commodity (economicity of time)?
2. How should tasks and time be combined? (Monochronic versus polychronic use of time.)
3. Should time be seen as a single continuous line or as combining multiple cyclical episodes? (Linearity versus cyclicity of time)
4. What are the appropriate temporal orientations: towards the past, the present and the future?

As the reader will see, there is some overlap between the prevailing solutions to these four questions. However, I have noted all four basic time assumptions because they need to be considered in order to acquire a substantive view of what is a cultural model of time, which is exemplified at the end of this section by the Japanese *Makimono* time.

Economicity of time

Time may be seen as external to us and, as such, be treated like a tangible commodity. The concept of economic time is based on accurate time reckoning, dependent on precise dating and defined duration. It results in people trying to use their time as wisely as possible, scheduling, establishing timetables and deadlines. Measurement of parking meter time in units of 7.5 minutes or sport performance in hundredths of a second is typical of economic time being precisely measured and bearing direct and explicit financial consequences. Many European countries as well as the United States, are emblematic of the "time-is-money" culture, where time is an economic good. Since time is a scarce resource, or at least perceived as such, people should try to achieve its optimal allocation between the competing ways of using it. Norms tend to be very strict regarding time schedules, appointments and the precise setting of dates and durations in a society where time is strongly felt as economic. Needless to say, attitudes towards money and the money-value of time are inseparable from marketing (Jacoby *et al.*, 1976). Economicity of time has a general impact on buyer–seller interaction: "undue" waiting is experienced as a waste of scarce resource and the time spent negotiating together is always balanced by the potential return on the deal.

Monochronic versus polychronic use of time

Hall (1983) has described two extreme types of behaviour in task scheduling, which he calls monochronism (M-time) and polychronism (P-time). Individuals working under M-time do one thing at a time and tend to adhere to preset schedules. When confronted by a dilemma (e.g., a discussion with someone that lasts longer than planned), M-time people will politely stop the conversation, in order to keep to their schedule. In M-time societies, not only the start of a meeting but also its finish will be planned. P-time, on the other hand, stresses the involvement of people

157

who do several things at the same moment, easily modify preset schedules and seldom experience time as "wasted". P-time may seem quite hectic to M-time people: "There is no recognized order as to who is to be served next, no queue or numbers indicating who has been waiting the longest" (Hall, 1983, p. 47). P-time people are more committed to persons than to schedules. When confronted with a conflict such as the one described above, they prefer to go on talking or working after the preset hours and break their schedule, if they have one.

The PERT (programme evaluation and review technique) programming method is an example of a typical "agenda-culture", where M-time is the central assumption. PERT is based on graph theory, and has an appealing US "management science" look: the technique is based on the starting and finishing dates of each individual task and the constraints across tasks (especially those which need to be finished before other tasks can be started). The algorithm calculates the "critical path", that is, the succession of particular tasks which have to be realized without delay if the total completion time is to be minimized. It explicitly aims to reduce a universe of polychronic tasks (they really take place simultaneously, which is part of the problem) to a monochronic solution (the critical path). Management methods, basically originating in the United States and Europe, favour pure monochronic organization. They clearly push aside polychronic attitudes, which tend to make plans and schedules rather hectic. When it comes to delays and being "on time", precise monochronic systems give priority to meeting dates and commitment to schedules.

To illustrate sources of tension between people who have internalized different time systems, Hall (1983, pp. 53–4) takes the example of a monochronic woman who has a polychronic hairdresser. The woman, who has a regular appointment at a specific time each week, feels frustrated and angry when she is kept waiting. At the same time, the hairdresser also feels frustrated. He inevitably feels compelled to "squeeze people in", particularly his friends and acquaintances. The schedule is reserved for impersonal people such as this woman, but since he does not know them personally, keeping to the schedule is not important to him. The distinction between M and P-time is important for business negotiations, in as much as the parties will have to discuss issues, write down clauses, schedule their meetings.

Linearity versus cyclicity of time

It is easy to guess that a strongly economic view of time, when it is combined with monochronism, emphasizes the linearity of time. Time is viewed as being a line with a point at the centre, the present. Each portion of the line can be cut into slices, which are supposed to have a certain money value. Basic religious beliefs play a key role in supporting this linear view of time: Christianity has a one-shot interpretation of worldly life, and people do not live twice (as in the James Bond film title). People wait until the final judgement to enjoy reincarnation. On the contrary, Asian religions, including Hinduism and Buddhism, assume that, on the death of the body, the soul is born again in another body. The belief in regular reincarnation, until a pure soul is allowed to escape the cycle and go to *nirvana*, radically changes the nature of time in a specific life: it is not all the time I have got, it is simply one of my "times" across several lives. For most Asians, cyclicity is central to their pattern of time: the *nirvana* is the final release from the cycle of reincarnation, attained by extinction of all desires and individual existence, culminating (in Buddhism) in absolute blessedness, or (in Hinduism) in absorption into Brahman. Naturally, patience is on the side of the people believing in cyclical reincarnation of the soul. For the Christians, it is more urgent to achieve, because their souls are given only one worldly chance. But, as the New Testament puts it clearly, those who do right, even at the very last moment, will be considered favourably.

Another element which favours a cyclical view of time is the degree of emphasis put on the natural rhythms of years and seasons, the sun and the moon. So-called "modern" societies are then largely opposed to "traditional" ones, in as much as modern means technology, mastering nature and, to a certain extent, the loss of nature-related reference points. The Japanese are known for having maintained a strong orientation towards nature, even in a highly developed society. Their floral art of *Ikebana* or the emphasis on maintaining a contact with nature, even in highly urban environments, is a testimony to their attachment to the natural rythms of nature. Even within a country, the relationship to nature influences the model of time adopted by urban people in contrast to rural people.

Elements of cyclicity are mostly based on metaphysical assumptions or on astronomical observations, but they also include some arbitrary divisions, which are more social than natural. The example of the duration of the week is a good example of the social origins of the reckoning of time cycles. In a classical article, Sorokin and Merton (1937) give the following illustrations of the variability in the number of days of the week, through anthropological observation:

> Our system of weekly division into quantitatively equal periods is a perfect type of conventionally determined time-reckoning. The Khasi week almost universally consists of eight days because the markets are usually held every eighth day. A reflection of the fact that the Khasi week had a social, rather than a "natural", origin is found in the names of the days of the week which are not those of planets (a late and arbitrary development) but of places where the principal markets are held. In a similar fashion, the Roman week was marked by *nundinae* which recurred every eighth day and upon which the agriculturists came into the city to sell their produce. The Muysca in Bogota had a three-day week; many East African tribes a four-day week; in Central America, the East Indian Archipelago, old Assyria (and now in Soviet Russia), there is found a five-day week ... and the Incas had a ten-day week. The constant feature of virtually all these weeks of varying length is that they were always found to have been originally in association with the market.

Elements of cyclicity of time have therefore three main origins: religious assumptions about reincarnation of the soul; natural rhythms of years, seasons and days; the social division of time periods which is more arbitrary, less natural and "given", than we assume. Time is naturally both linear and cyclical, and culture has complex time patterns which combine both views, as shown below by the example of Japanese *makimono* time. It is important for business negotiations that linear time emphasizes *discontinuity*: a point on the time-line such as the signing of a contract or the start-up of a plant is perceived as opening a totally new period of time. Conversely, cyclical time favours a more integrative picture of the universe, a stronger sense of the *continuity* of events.

Temporal orientations: past, present, future

The perception of time also tends to be related to temporal orientations *vis-à-vis* the arrow of time. As stated by Kluckhohn and Strodtbeck (1961, pp. 13–15):

> The possible cultural interpretations of temporal focus of human life break easily into the three-point range of past, present and future ... Spanish-Americans, who have been described as taking the view that man is a victim of natural forces, are also a people who place the present time alternative in first position ... Many modern European countries ... have strong leanings to a past orientation ... Americans, more strongly than most people of the world, place an emphasis upon the future — a future which is anticipated to be " bigger and better".

Being past-oriented means that people emphasize the role of the past in the explanation of where we are now. Europeans are typical of this assumption, as are some Asian people. They will tend to restore old buildings, invest in museums, teach history at school etc. It does not mean that temporal orientation to the past is only based on cultural assumptions. It also depends on individual psychological traits (Usunier and Valette-Florence, 1994). Futhermore, in societies undergoing a rapid process of economic change, past orientation is often provisionally underplayed.

Present orientation is the most logical assumption, in terms of quality of life at least. It means that people favour the "here and now", believing that the past is over and the future is uncertain, theoretical and difficult to imagine. Religion may play an important role in pushing people towards present orientation, if it emphasizes that only God decides about the future. In terms of temporal orientation, the Arabic-Muslim character has been described as fatalistic, rather short-term oriented, and not future oriented (Ferraro, 1990). As stated by Harris and Moran (1987, p. 474): "Who controls time? A Western belief is that one controls his own time. Arabs believe that their time is controlled, to a certain extent, by an outside force — namely Allah — therefore the Arabs become very fatalistic in their view of time ... most Arabs are not clock watchers, nor are they planners of time."

Future orientation is naturally related to the view that people can master nature, but also to the view that the future can in some way be predicted or at least significantly influenced; future orientation is reflected in languages. In societies where future orientation is strong, it is backed by the educational system and by an "imagination of the future" supported by reports on scientific breakthroughs and technological developments.

Box 8.1

Time vocabulary tells a lot about the linkage between language and cultural representations. For those who have doubts about the existence of differences in cultural representations of time which are revealed, conveyed and reproduced by language, the example of the English/US word "deadline" is very illustrative. A quick translation in French would give "échéance [temporelle]" or "délai de rigueur" (Langenscheidt, 1989) but would not render the intensity of this word. Taken literally, it seems to suggest something like "beyond this (temporal) line, you will (there is a danger of) die (dying)." It therefore gives a genuine notion of urgency to what was originally a very abstract notion (a point which has been agreed upon on a line of time). The word deadline is used in French by many businesspeople as such (un deadline), even though it is not in the official dictionary, because it conveys a typically Anglo-American sense of urgency that French people do not find in their own language.

Language also reflects (and pre-shapes) how people envisage the future. In some African languages (Kamba and Kikuyu), there are three future tenses which express (i) action in two to six months; (ii) action that will take place immediately; (iii) action "in the foreseeable future, after this or that event." Commenting on the uses of these African tenses, M'biti demonstrates how coherence and sophistication in the accurate use of the near future, are important to people. "You have these tenses before you: just try to imagine the tense into which you would translate passages of the New Testament concerning the Parousia of Our Lord Jesus Christ, or how you would teach eschatology ... If you use tense no. 1, you are speaking about something that will take place in the next two to six months, or in any case within two years at most. If you use no. 2, you are referring to something that will take place in the immediate future, and if it does not take place you are exposed as a liar in people's eyes. Should you use no. 3 you are telling people that the event concerned will definitely take place, but when something else has happened first. In all these tenses, the event must be very near to the present moment: if, however, it lies in the far distant future — beyond the two-year limit — you are neither understood nor taken seriously." (M'biti, 1968, p. 10.)

Combined cultural models of time: the Japanese *makimono* time

Economic time usually goes with linear time, monochronism and future orientation, and it is our "modern" time, near to R. J. Graham"s (1981, p. 335) concept of the "European-American (Anglo) perception that allows time to have a past, present and future, and to be sliced into discrete units and then allocated for specific tasks." From this view, time can be saved, spent, wasted or even bought, just like money. Graham has tried to represent a synthesis of time perception dimensions, not only as a set of different perceptual dimensions, but also as complete temporal systems. He contrasts "Anglo" time, which he describes as being "linear-separable", with the "circular-traditional" time of most Latin-American countries. This perception arises from traditional cultures where action and everyday life were not regulated by the clock, but rather by the natural cycles of the moon, sun and seasons. Graham proposes a third model, "procedural-traditional", in which the amount of time spent on the activity is irrelevant, since activities are procedure-driven rather than time-driven. This system is typical of the American Indians, and to a large extent it also typifies the African time. Graham's "procedural-traditional" time is hardly a "time", in the Western sense.

But it is not that simple: some people may share different cultures and move from one time model to another, depending on the other people involved and the particular situation, using different types of "operating cultures" (Goodenough, 1971). As Hall states (1983, p. 58) "The Japanese are polychronic when looking and working inward, toward themselves. When dealing with the outside world . . . they shift to the monochronic mode. . . . The French are monochronic intellectually, but polychronic in behaviour."

A naive view of Japanese temporal orientation would lead one to assume that the Japanese are simply future oriented. In fact, a specialist in Japanese business, Robert Ballon, argues that the Japanese are neither future nor past oriented. To him, the Japanese are present oriented and focused on the here and now (in Hayashi, 1988). Hayashi explains the difficult attempt at finding cross-culturally equivalent terms by asserting that: "Many kinds of Japanese behaviour are extratemporaneous" (p. 2), meaning that they are not time-based. Hayashi explains further what he calls the *Makimono* time. In their model of time, the Japanese tend to posit the future as a natural extension of the present. Japanese are basically people working with a cyclical view of time, based on their Buddhist background which believes that souls of dead people transmigrate to newly-born human beings, in an eternal cycle. As Hayashi states (1988, p. 10) "In Japanese cultural time, the past flows continuously toward the present and also the present is firmly linked to the future. In philosophical terms, we might say the past and the future exist simultaneously in the present".

Therefore, the linear-separable model of time, found in Western cultures, does not predominate in Japan. The notion of continuity is central to Japanese time, just as the notion of discontinuity is central to Western models of time. A Japanese definition would say "the present is a temporal period that links the region of the past with the world of the future" (Hayashi, 1988, p. 18). Both the notion of continuity and the arrow of the future targeted *towards* the present are central in the *Makimono* time pattern (Figure 8.1). Coming back to Cohen's experience cited at the beginning of this chapter, the Japanese concern to have him learn what they are reflects a preoccupation with continuity; if he is to make deals with them he has to understand their past.

Starting the Negotiation

Time for preliminaries

The role of spending time on establishing personal relationships, especially in Asia and South America, is noted by many authors (Hall, 1983, Pye, 1986, Graham and Sano, 1990; Hawrysh and Zaichkowski, 1990). There is a series of reasons why a personal relationship is needed: establishing the context of communication

FIGURE 8.1
Japanese Makimono *time pattern*

Source: Hayashi (1988) p. 9

(Hall, 1976), acquaintance with the other persons being part of the necessary context; a less strict separation between personal and professional spheres than in the West; the importance of personal status that creates the need to spend time in exploring who is who with some discretion, in order not to offend partners. This is all summed up in Burt's comments (1984, p. 7) that an American negotiator will be well advised to develop personal relations away from the negotiation room: "The usual intense and rather dry approach to doing business must be supplemented with a social relationship. The Japanese are accustomed to the use of entertainment as a means of becoming better acquainted and of developing goodwill."

The cultural time concept of Americans, strongly economic, partly explains why spending time to build personal relations is implicitly seen as bad. Time being seen as a resource not to be wasted, spending time on non-business matters, on non-task related issues, is experienced as a violation of their cultural norms. What Graham (in Graham and Lin, 1987) calls "non-task sounding", that is, establishing rapport and getting to know each other, the first phase in his four-phase process of business negotiations, not only needs a relaxed sense of economic time but also some past orientation: seeing Japanese shrines, learning the basics about Zen or Ikebana, the Japanese floral art. The Japanese feel that an understanding of their past is necessary for understanding them as negotiation partners today.

Setting the agenda and scheduling the negotiation process

These tasks are considered by most of the negotiation literature as necessary for the second step in Graham's four-stage model: task-related exchange of information. An agenda is a schedule and list of items to be discussed during the negotiation process. In many cultures, the very notion of "agenda setting" is unheard of: cutting the process into pieces in advance and allocating time lots to each "task" is, at best, theoretical. Hall's differences between monochronic and polychronic is highly relevant for the scheduling of negotiation. An agenda-oriented negotiation team, basically monochronic, tends to try to negotiate clauses sequentially, whereas the other party, polychronic, may skip from one issue to another, coming back to points which had apparently been already settled, because they tend to negotiate globally. Graham and Herberger (1983) call it "One thing at a time": Americans

Jean-Claude Usunier

usually attack a complex negotiation task sequentially, that is, they separate the issues and settle them one at a time.

Time in the Negotiation Process

Making appointments and setting deadlines: managing temporal clash in intercultural business negotiations

Partners from different cultures may be working together to develop a low-cost operation, or a new R & D project, or distribution and sales facilities, depending on the objective of the joint venture. In such settings, issues to do with time will inevitably arise, both at an everyday level, simply in order to meet at the same time, and at a deeper level, that of assigning a common time frame to business operations. The fictitious case in Box 8.2 is an excerpt from Fons Trompenaars, it recounts a story which is stereotypical and illustrates the clash of temporal cultures, both at the individual and at organizational levels, when negotiating.

Box 8.2

Young Mr Johnson, a US (or English) executive, is organising an international meeting: "At 1.50 p.m. most participants returned to the meeting room. At 2.05 Johnson started pacing restlessly up and down. Munoz and Gialli were still down the hall making telephone calls. They came in at 2.20 p.m. Johnson said, 'Now, gentlemen, can we finally start the meeting.' The Singaporean and African representatives looked puzzled. They thought the meeting had already started. The first point on the agenda was the time intervals determining bonuses and merits. All except the American, Dutch and other north-west European representatives complained that these were far too frequent. To Johnson and his Dutch and Scandinavian colleagues the frequency was obviously right: 'Rewards must closely follow the behaviour they are intended to reinforce, otherwise you lose the connection.' The manager from Singapore said: 'Possibly, but this go-for-the-quick-buck philosophy has been losing us customers. They don't like the pressure we put on at the end of the quarter. They want our representatives to serve them, not to have private agendas. We need to keep our customers long-term, not push them into buying so that one sales person can beat a rival.'" (*Source*: Trompenaars 1993, p. 115.)

Different time perspectives, be they organizational or cultural, result in temporal clashes. The conflicts that result from the inability to merge different ways of dealing with time may be located at an individual level, that of business people interacting with foreign partners and negotiating with them. Temporal clash at the level of individual interaction results from differing answers given to the following questions: how is somebody treated when he or she arrives half an hour late for a negotiation session? Do sessions have a finishing time in addition to their starting time? Is time also structured during the meeting by setting an agenda and a definite time limit for discussion on each point?

164

To illustrate the synchronisation problem at work, let us take the example of a French business meeting versus a meeting in the United States (a fairly polychronic versus a fairly monochronic culture). In France, some people come a quarter of an hour late, and some half an hour. Not only does the meeting not start on time, but those people who were on time have to wait for those who are late. Rarely do people who are late apologize. Some, not all, simply explain why they were late. It is not rare that, when somebody arrives quite late, most other people stop their discussion and spend five or ten minutes explaining to the latecomers what has been said up to now (fortunately, the content of French meetings is generally easy to summarise!). Moreover, contrary to the US meetings, French meetings are almost never assigned a finishing time. This means that quite often, if there are several successive meetings, the reason why some people arrive late is that the previous meeting was late and finished one or two hours after the (more or less vaguely and implicitly) agreed finishing time.

Temporal clashes between negotiating organizations

Temporal clash in negotiation may also be based at an organizational level, that of companies trying to design some sort of common venture, through a merger, an acquisition or a joint venture. There are many instances where the failure of an international alliance has been attributed to lack of cultural fit, or conflict between the two cultures; temporal clash based on culturally different time patterns is also a cultural clash. Knittel and Stefanini (1993) recount the case of a French-Indian joint venture which they call IJV (Indian Joint Venture). The French partner, a world leader in specialized equipment goods with one plant in France and two in the United states, was willing to enter the Indian market with a 5–6 year time horizon for pay-back. India limits foreign ownership to 40 per cent and sets strong red-tape on foreign partners' route to JV formation. Finally, it was decided to invest in two stages. In the first stage, IJV was supposed only to assemble imported parts. In a second stage, it was due to increase local manufacturing. But, in fact, communication misunderstandings added to delays in some governmental authorizations and, finally, financial difficulties related to expected large orders that did not come led the two partners to a typical temporal clash. The Indian partner interpreted the situation as a lack of long-term commitment on the French side and asked for a direct progression to the second stage. Having a much shorter horizon than that which needed to overcome the problem, the French company refused. Finally, IJV slowly came to a halt because neither of the two partners wanted to take the responsibility for officially discontinuing the venture.

Time-based tactical moves: exerting time pressures in the bargaining process

The place where the negotiation takes place has an obvious influence on time-scarcity. Those who are "at home" can monitor their regular business tasks while participating in the negotiations. Those who have left their home country to negotiate at their partner's location can for many reasons, both professional and personal, be impatient to go back. The pressure of "wasted time" can be easily used against those who have both an economic pattern of time and are far from their home base.

As such, the expression "to waste time" has little meaning for many cultures, especially for most African cultures (Usunier, 1996). One may lose something tangible, like a ring or a pencil. But in order to waste and lose time, time should be a thing or, at least, it would be necessary to be able to separate time from the events with which it is inextricably bound up, making it difficult to equate abstract time with a monetary unit of measurement. For instance, within their culture, the Bantu people of the Southern part of Africa know nothing comparable to a linear Newtonian time, in which events take place. There are events, and each one of these events carries its own desire and its own time. Time cannot be wasted or lost, because time has simply to be lived or experienced, whatever may be the way to experience it. No one can steal time, not even death.

The same tranquillity in the face of time may be seen in the Orient, compared to the Occidental anguish and guilt about time that might be wasted or lost. Several authors in the field of international business negotiations note that time pressure is strongly felt by American negotiators, whether they negotiate with the Chinese (Pye, 1982) or with the Japanese (Graham, 1981; Graham and Sano, 1990; Tung, 1984a,b). American negotiators are eventually forced to yield by their representation of time, potentially wasted or lost if it is not optimally allocated. When this logic is pushed to its extreme, it may result in total inefficiency. People spend their whole time thinking of possible alternative uses of their time and calculating which of these alternatives offers the best marginal return. As noted by Adler (1986, p. 162):

> Americans' sense of urgency disadvantages them with respect to less hurried bargaining partners. Negotiators from other countries recognize Americans' time consciousness, achievement orientation, and impatience. They know that Americans will make concessions close to their deadline (time consciousness) in order to get a signed contract (achievement orientation).

Pressure can be exerted on economic-time-minded negotiators by postponing the beginning of the negotiation, delaying meetings, keeping the end of the negotiations a secret etc. Cohen gives a classical example of how the Japanese manipulate their Western partner's excessive time consciousness. The Japanese ask him when he is arriving at Tokyo airport :

> "Are you concerned about getting back to your plane on time?" (Up to that moment I had not been concerned.) "We can schedule this limousine to transport you back to the airport." I thought in myself, "how considerate." Reaching my pocket, I handed them my return flight ticket, so the limousine would know when to get me. I didn't realize it then, but they knew my deadline, whereas I didn't know theirs. (Cohen, 1980, p. 94).

Timing of concessions

The pattern of timing of concessions tends to differ whether people tend to settle one issue and proceed to the next or whether they negotiate more globally. Certain cultures, like the Chinese and the Japanese, tend to make fewer concessions through the earlier stages of the negotiation process, because they have a much longer non-task sounding phase, needing more time to establish the relationship and obtain information. US executives tend to offer concessions throughout the negotiation process, seeing the "give and take" process as having to start early and to lead to reciprocal and balanced concessions. The difference in the appropriate view of what are "timely concessions" (continuous versus last moment, "cherry-on-the-cake" concessions) can lead to misunderstandings between the partners.

As noted above, time pressure can be seen as a legitimate tool to be used for extracting last-minute concessions from the other party. Exploitation of time pressure can be resented by the party which is taken advantage of. However, this party should probably have prepared some minor but noteworthy concession to be offered in such a case.

It has been noted that, in highly bureaucratic contexts, negotiators will use argument of the complexity of their organizational process and the consequent necessity to refer to various bodies in order to delay concessions (see for instance Eiteman, 1990). However, negotiators from such countries also need to bring back something to their superiors, and as noted in Chapter 4 by John Graham, the timing of concessions can be inverted when these negotiators come close to their deadline. They run short of time and, if they are negotiating in a costly place, their organisation will not allow them to stay longer and, ultimately, they risk being blamed by their superiors if they go back empty-handed. This leads them to concede.

The Time Frame of Relationship between the Negotiation Partners

Negotiation strategies: long term orientation as favouring an integrative strategy

The strategic time frame depends on temporal orientation (Hay and Usunier, 1993): the lack of future orientation, for instance, may be a serious impediment to the true involvement of a party. In business negotiations, the purchaser and the vendor organizations are mutually interdependent and their interests clash. In order for the parties to adopt an integrative orientation, they must assume that the size of the "cake" can be increased if they cooperate. Going on with the same metaphor, this needs time for deciding about a common recipe, preparing the ingredients, mixing the whole appropriately and, finally, cooking it. This "cooking metaphor" highlights that the more extended the time frame of the relationship between the partners is (that is particularly, the longer they have been accustomed to be in interdependence) the more likely they are to adopt an integrative orientation to negotiation. The history of the partnership will be important as well as the future time horizon which is considered by both parties as appropriate for the expected outcomes to come.

Some types of IBN agreements are by their very nature not conducive to cooperative bargaining because their frame is quite short; for instance, a spot sales contract between as yet unknown partners who have no expectations concerning continuity of business in the future. At the other extreme, a joint venture which is largely turned towards the future has a high potential for developing common interests, while a distributorship agreement lies somewhere in the middle. A special case occurs when the time horizon of one of the negotiating teams is curtailed by some key event. This may be a change of top management due to occur in a few weeks or a new regulation about to be adopted wich could change the whole economy of the project. This will dramatically reduce this party's capacity to envisage integrative solutions.

The adoption of an integrative strategy is facilitated, *inter alia*, by the ability to envisage the future; this permits the discovery or "invention" of new solutions, which enables both partners to overcome the problem of the fixed size of the "territorial cake". Its size is limited in the very short term and it is only by envisaging what the future between the negotiation partners could be does it become feasible to adopt a more expansive view of the "common cake". The nature of international transactions often imposes it: business is fairly continuous over several years, and therefore implies a very strong buyer-seller interdependence. The performance level depends largely on the extent and the quality of the collaboration between the partners.

This is often better understood by the Asians for whom a new fifth dimension has been added to Hofstede's four dimensions (Hofstede, 1980). Michael Bond, a researcher based in Hong Kong, has designed a questionnaire called CVS, Chinese Value Survey, which has been administered in 23 countries (Chinese Culture Connection, 1987). It is based on basic values as seen by native Chinese social scientists. A new dimension was discovered through the CVS. Bond coined the term "Confucian dynamism", to emphasize the importance of Confucius' practical ethics, based on the development of long term relationships, and valuing (i) the stability of society based on unequal relationships, expressing mutual and complementary obligations; (ii) the family as the prototype of all social organizations; individuality; (iii) virtuous behaviour towards others consists of not treating others as one would not like to be treated oneself; (iv) virtue, with regard to one's tasks in life consists of trying to work hard and being patient and persevering.

Pye (1986) notes the role played by differences of attitude relating to the concept of "friendship", in terms of time-span and expectations from the other side. Thus, it seems that whereas the Americans view friendship in terms of a feeling which rests on a natural mutual exchange within definite time limits, in other words on a principle of reciprocity, the Chinese view friendship in terms of loyalty. The idea is that of a long-lasting obligation: "What the Chinese neglect in terms of reciprocity they more than match in loyalty. They not only keep their commitments, but they also assume that any positive relationship can be permanent. A good example of this is the number of Chinese who have tried to establish pre-1949 ties with US companies and individuals — as though nothing had happened in the intervening time." (Pye 1986, p. 79).

Making plans together: co-ordinating and planning the common venture

In many international negotiations planning a common venture, the steps of construction of a turnkey plant, or the implementation phases of a joint venture or licence agreement, need explicit reference to dates, deadlines, and the sequencing of interdependent tasks, that is, planning. Planning is such a basic function of management that it is extremely difficult to admit that there are other models of time than those on which it implicitly rests. Naturally, it would be naive to consider that business people have purely traditional time patterns, such as those described earlier. In fact, complex patterns of time-related behaviour may be used by people sharing several cultural backgrounds, one of them being the original in-depth background, the other(s) being much more superficial. Furthermore, the native cultural background may be undervalued because it is supposed to be "inefficient" or it is unknown to foreigners. Accordingly, people belonging to non-linear/economic time cultures often have a tendency to imitate the cultural way of life that they tend to regard as the "best". It might result in buying a superb watch as an item of jewellery or a diary because it is fashionable. But the functional behaviour which is in line with the watch or the diary will not be adopted. After these objects have been bought, they lose their cultural value as practical tools of the economic/monochronic/linear/separable time pattern. People involved in this type of cultural borrowing might prove unable to take any appointment seriously. They will probably experience difficulties in following any preset schedule.

Ideal and actual temporal behaviour

Ideal patterns of time and actual temporal behaviour may differ widely for negotiators who apparently use their partners' time culture rather than their own. The idea of possible discrepancies between ideal patterns and actual behaviour was expressed by Linton (1945, pp. 52–4): "All cultures include a certain number of what may be called ideal patterns. ... They represent the consensus of opinion on the part of the society's members as to how people should behave in particular situations ... comparison of narratives usually reveals the presence of a real culture pattern with a recognizable mode of variation ... it [the ideal pattern] represents a desideratum, a value, which has always been more honoured in the breach than in the observance."

Bista (1990), in the case of Nepal, highlights the conflict between time-based behaviour related to foreign education and the traditional influence of fatalistic beliefs on the lack of future orientation and sense of planning:

Jean-Claude Usunier

> Planning involves the detailing of the connections between resources, objects and events, and the determination of an efficient course of action to attain desired results ... Control is placed in the hands of the planner. But fatalism does not allow this kind of control, and is inherently antithetical to pragmatic thought ... Over the past few decades, many Nepali students have travelled abroad to study in other countries, and have returned with advanced degrees in various professional capacities ... Upon their return many are placed in positions of authority, as they represent the cream of Nepal's manpower resources. Though they may be initially inspired by a high degree of idealism, the new values that they bring back with them immediately confront fatalism and are typically defeated by it ... After forty years of planning and an accumulation of foreign trained graduates, Nepal, then, still has little manpower to effectively bridge the disparities between the culture of the foreign aid donors and that of their own (137–8).

Hidden language of time: the fallacies of borrowed time patterns in negotiation

In everyday management behaviour (appointments, scheduling, meetings), it is quite probable that we face a high level of cultural borrowing: actual time behaviour of economically successful countries like the United States or countries of northern Europe have been imported by other nations as ideal patterns (Usunier 1991). It is, for instance, very clear that in Latin-European countries, the PERT technique, which is designed for the scheduling of interrelated tasks, has been implemented mostly for its intellectual appeal. In France, where many managers and top executives have been trained as engineers, there has been a great interest in this scientific management technique. Real project planning in France and Latin-European countries very often works with high discrepancies relative to PERT dates: French people tend to be intellectually monochronic but actually behave in a polychronic manner (Hall, 1983).

Sometimes people even use two completely different systems in parallel. This somewhat schizophrenic situation is most easily recognized by looking at the construction of some turnkey projects in developing countries (CNUCED 1978; Tiano 1981, Bista 1990). At the beginning, during the negotiation process and on signature of the contract, everybody seemingly (and also sincerely) agrees about using economic time/monochronic pattern. In fact, the partners share the same belief, but it is an ideal pattern on one side and the actual behaviour on the other. There may not even be discussion about it: obviously it is the right way to proceed. But afterwards, extreme confusion appears when the project is being implemented.

Time as an Outcome Variable

Relationship versus deal: A continuous versus discontinuous view of time

Many Western negotiators consider that a signed contract places a clear-cut temporal limit upon the negotiation process. It is stopped and the implementation phase starts, based on the precise contractual outcomes: time-based clauses and agreements. As noted by Ghauri (1994, p. 9) in the Chinese case:

> ... the real problems begin after the formal negotiations, at the time of the signing of the contract and quite often during the implementation of the agreement. The Chinese want to agree on broad principles and general policies in formal negotiations and want to keep the detail rather ambiguous. This policy creates problems at the time of writing out and signing the contract, when foreign firms want to specify and make responsibilities clear.

Cultures which have a cyclical and integrative view of time, described in section 8.2, have an underlying concept of negotiation in which it is only one round of a recurrent relational process, with little sequencing compared with people holding a linear/separable view of time. This is to be found also in the outcome orientation, where the time line of negotiation is less important to people with a cyclical/integrative view of time: to them, a signed contract is no real reason not to pursue the negotiation process further. Eiteman (1990, p.62), reporting on American executives' perceptions of negotiating joint ventures with PRC managers, notes the comments of a negotiatior for a major US firm that: "the bargaining (with the Chinese) never stopped after the original agreement was signed and business actually started" and the president of this firm, located in Beijing, remarks that "production operations were nothing more than a continuation of the frustrations of the original negotiating sessions, with previously agreed upon points always changed by the Chinese."

Written agreements as a time line for negotiations

Following what has been explained in Chapter 6, there are two different ways to look at the influence and function of the written agreement on the time span of the exchange relationship. Those favouring written-based trust-building tend to see a written agreement as a very definite break in the exchange relationship, embedded in "written" time, based on dates, deadlines and delay penalties, all of them task-centred rather than relationship-centred. It completes a phase during which potential relations have been carefully discussed and explored. It establishes a strict contractual code, which then has to be implemented with punctuality and timeliness. Written words, sentences and formulas have to be strictly observed. If a party feels free to depart from what has been written down, the Damoclean sword of litigation will hang over the parties.

Those favouring oral-based, personal trust consider the signing of a written agreement as an important step, but only one of many in a continuous negotiation process. The negotiation process was active before signature and will be active afterwards. A continuous negotiation process, where the contract is only one step, is seen as the best basis for maintaining trust.

As stated by Edward Hall (1960, p. 94):

Americans consider that negotiations have more or less ceased when the contract is signed. With the Greeks, on the other hand, the contract is seen as a sort of way station on the route to negotiation, that will cease only when the work is completed. The contract is nothing more than a charter for serious negotiations. In the Arab world, once a man's word is given in a particular kind of way, it is just as binding, if not more so, than most of our written contracts. The written contract therefore violates the Moslem's sensitivities and reflects on his honour. Unfortunately, the situation is now so hopelessly confused that neither system can be counted on to prevail consistently.

Using Time shrewdly in International Business Negotiations

In short, the international business negotiator, should follow some basic rules:

1. Take time for adequate preliminaries: getting to know the other party is most often crucial. More time is needed than in domestic business negotiations, since cultural as well as personal knowledge has to be acquired.
2. Control your time: do not get trapped by your own cultural time model; that is, try to be aware of it. If needed, be prepared to renounce a negotiation, because the stakes are too low, or send lower level, less expensive executives. If possible, negotiate at home where you have a competitive advantage over your foreign partner in terms of time control.
3. Never tell the other side when you are leaving because this gives them control over your time.
4. Allow yourself plenty of time, and even more: patience is an asset for negotiation and it is destroyed by time prèssure. In the US–Vietnamese peace talks in Paris, the Vietnamese were at a time advantage because they had rented a villa with a two and a half years lease, whereas the Americans rented hotel rooms on a week-to-week basis.
5. Do not get fooled by the other party seemingly sharing your time pattern: try to set realistic dates and deadlines and, if needed, plan softly, introducing time slack, allowing for delays to be absorbed without ruining the economy of the whole venture. Remember: better plan modestly and realistically than go into enormous delays that ruin the credibility of the whole planning process.
6. Accept temporal clash to the extent possible. Before participating in a negotiation, learn the basics about the behavioural norms in your partner's culture concerning appointments, punctuality and planning.
7. Wait for the negotiation process to extend beyond the signature of the deal. For most cultures there is no clear time-line defined by the signing of a contract, the most important time frame is that of the relationship, not that of a particular deal.

CHAPTER 9

The Role of Atmosphere in Negotiations

PERVEZ GHAURI

> An Indian company, Hindustan Paper Corporation (HPC) approached the Swedish
> company Defibrator and asked for a quotation for a pulp mill. The quotation was
> sent eighteen months later. Two competitors of Defibrator also gave quotations for
> the project. A number of meetings were held between the parties, before and after
> the quotation, and the quotation was revised. Later there were two intensive, formal
> negotiation sessions before the contract was signed some four years after the first
> enquiry.

Introduction

The above-mentioned type of business transactions are becoming increasingly
frequent in international business. The opening up of several centrally planned
economies in Europe and Asia will, in the coming decades, further encourage such
business transactions. This type of negotiation between parties with no previous
experience of each other and coming from entirely different environments is thus
quite typical in today's international business relationships. Initially, the parties are
unfamiliar with each other's environment and a rather long and complex
negotiation process has to be carried out before the agreement is reached.

The delay and complexity is mainly caused by unfamiliarity and the parties'
perceptions of the other's country, company and individuals. The purpose of this
chapter is to shed some light on the impact of the "ambience" around the
negotiation and on the process itself. This "milieu" has been defined as
"Atmosphere" in our model of international business negotiations (see Chapter 1)
and includes perceptions of parties on each other's behaviour. It includes issues
such as: cooperation and conflict, power and dependence and expectations. For
the sake of this chapter, we shall also refer to the "Atmosphere" of the formal
session as including items such as: seating arrangements and nonverbal communication.[1] In our opinion these factors add to the perceptions of the parties about
each other's behaviour. A process can be more conflict oriented if the seating
arrangement and settings are not properly taken care of. On the other hand, a

---

[1] This chapter is based on: Ghauri and Johanson (1979) and Ghauri (1986).

process can acquire a positive (cooperative) atmosphere if the seating arrangements and settings are pleasant and thoroughly considered: the same is true for nonverbal communication, which can send positive or negative signals, thereby creating a certain atmosphere.

A fundamental characteristic of these negotiations is the existence of conflict as well as cooperation in the relationship. To some extent, especially in "win–win" negotiation, the two parties have a common interest in finding a solution which is optimal and suitable with regard to the supplier's ability and the user's requirements. Basically, the two parties complement each other. At the same time, however, there is a conflict of interest — costs to one of them are income to the other. The degree of conflict or cooperation in the atmosphere is also a matter of how the parties handle various problems. Atmosphere is thus a subjective and perceived view of the process and is related to the objective situation in the negotiation process. In a way, negotiation skill is the ability to let the cooperative aspects dominate the negotiation process. Unless there is some degree of cooperation, it is not worthwhile to continue negotiating. One function of the negotiation process is to reduce or even to overcome the distance between the parties. It is particularly important in international deals where parties have no earlier experience of one another or possibility to develop a relationship gradually by demonstrating in practice what they mean and can.

Conflict and Cooperation

In the context of negotiation, the conflict can best be defined as "the perceived divergence of interests, or a belief that the parties' current aspirations cannot be achieved simultaneously". (Pruitt and Rubin, 1986, p. 4.) Or as, "the interaction of interdependent people who perceive incompatible goals and interference from each other in achieving those goals". (Hocker and Wilmot, 1985.) For this purpose we refer to interpersonal or intergroup conflict perceived by interacting parties to a negotiation process. As we have explained above, conflict not only has a negative connotation but also negatively influences the process as a whole. In reality however, the parties may not be in conflict, as both of them want the transaction to take place. Moreover, as conflict intensifies, perceptions become distorted and people interpret everything according to their own perspective. In extreme cases, people endorse and accept proposals coming from people they perceive as being cooperative and reject outright the proposals or opinions of those they perceive as being conflicting. The perceptions and feelings become emotionally charged as parties become irritated, annoyed or frustrated. Moreover, as the perceived conflict escalates, parties become more and more irrational (Lewicki et al. 1994).

There is a universal feeling that we increase our communication with those people we perceive as being cooperative and agreeable and we decrease our communication with those whom we find antagonistic. As a result, parties get locked into their position and the negotiation process is seriously and negatively affected. There is hardly any negotiation process where there is no conflict, so conflict in a negotiation process is almost unavoidable. The issue at hand is how to handle this conflict and how to perceive, and let the other party perceive, more cooperation than conflict. The more the parties perceive cooperation the more the conflict appears to disappear. Moreover, the more problem solving orientation the parties have the more they will perceive cooperation in the process.

Power/Dependence

One function of the negotiation process is to bring about unanimity in the perception of the power/dependence relationship. Generally, it is assumed that the buyer from an emerging market has less power than other buyers (for example, from the domestic market of the seller). On the other hand, it is assumed that a buyer of a one-shot deal has no commitment to the supplier as regards an earlier relationship etc., which makes it less dependent or more powerful. If there is a big difference between two parties' perceptions of the power situation, there will be no deal. Furthermore, a deal can only be made if this situation is acceptable to both parties. The parties cannot become independent of each other as they are interdependent, or dependent on each other to find a solution to the problem. That is why they are in negotiation with each other. However, in our negotiation setting, the interdependence is one of a "win–win" nature and not that of "win–lose". Mutually dependent relationships are normally very complex. Thus, the behaviour in such relationships is very calculated behaviour. It is therefore evident that the more information parties have on each other, the more easily they will understand each other's behaviour.

As interdependence is a fundamental issue in these negotiations, it is of the utmost importance to realize how the perceptions of this interdependence influence the negotiation process. It is widely accepted that the perception of these interdependencies may influence the process in a number of ways, as their perceptions can have important influence on the judgements one party makes about; (i) the other party; (ii) itself; (iii) utilities of both parties; (iv) offers and counter-offers; (v) negotiation outcomes; and (vi) the negotiation process.

One side of this issue is that if one of the parties perceives more dependence, the other party is most likely to perceive more power. Most negotiators thus actively seek power, as it gives them an advantage over the more dependent party. The powerful party can control and guide the process to secure a desired outcome. Power has been defined in different ways by different authors (see, for example, Salancik and Pfeffer, (1977) and Emerson, (1962).) For our purpose however, the following definition is most appropriate:

> ... an actor ... has power in a given situation (situational power) to the degree that he can satisfy the purposes (goals, desires or wants) that he is attempting to fulfil in that situation. Power is a relational concept; it does not reside in the individual but rather in the relationship between persons to his/her environment. Thus, the power of an actor is in a given situation determined by the characteristics of the situation as well as by his/her own characteristics.(Deutsch, (1973) pp. 84–5.)

It is clear that power is not an attribute of the actor but of the particular relationship, in our case, the negotiation process. There are several sources of power in such a process. Some of these sources are listed in Table 9.1.

TABLE 9.1
Sources of power

1.	Information power
	• information on the other party
	• information on the situation
2.	Expert power
	• superior technology
	• superior know-how
3.	Legitimate power
	• authority
	• performance
4.	Location in structure
	• centrality
	• criticality
5.	Personal power
	• attractiveness and friendliness
	• integrity

Source: Based on Lewicki *et al.* (1994), p. 298

In negotiation, information is the most important power source. The party that wants to be powerful must gather information on the other party, its capabilities, its limitations and its financial position. Information on organisational as well as individual level is important. This information can then be used in the negotiation process to support the position the party wants to take. This information can also be used to counterbalance the other party's power. The information on the situation refers to the information on environments and other factors related to the particular deal: the rules and regulations of one's own and other party's government/country, the competitors involved, the third parties such as consultants, and their role in the process. All this information will help the party to handle the process efficiently and smoothly. This will also help to check the counter-offers and bluffs by the other party and will help one to prepare counteroffers to the expected demands of the other party. The information is gathered before hand, even during the process, by being extra observant about what is exchanged. What we do in negotiation is, in fact, exchange information on each other. Expert power is often exercised by Western MNE's while negotiating with emerging markets.

Expert power refers to the power that has clearly been achieved by the other party. A particular firm can be accepted as having achieved a certain expertise in a certain technology. Defibrator, the Swedish producer of pulp plants, has, over the years, achieved this type of expert power as a supplier of pulp plants. A particular party can, if it feels that it lacks such expert power, hire specialist consultants. This will demonstrate that it does have expert power, even if it does not possess it itself. A certain university/professional degree can also provide one with this expert power (e.g., lawyers and accountants). Finally, a negotiator can let the other party perceive him as an expert, just by acting like one and by demonstrating that he has the required knowhow.

Legitimate power refers to a formal job title, office or hierarchy in the organisation. For example, by sending the CEO or managing director to a negotiation process, one gives the impression that he has all the power to make concessions and close the deal. One can also establish legitimacy through proven performance.

Location in structure refers to the position of the individuals of this particular project in the overall organisational and strategic perspective of the respective organisation. How central is that position? Is he in a position to get all the support from his organisation or not? Also, how critical is this project for each organisation? In recession periods, the suppliers of heavy machinery might be willing to sign the contract just to be able to keep their employees busy, or to find a reference project. The criticality of different issues in a particular negotiation process may also influence this power source.

Personal power refers to the personal characteristics of the negotiators. Can he be trusted or not? Is he perceived as being friendly or not? Can he demonstrate integrity or not? Being a good listener and demonstrating empathy and sensitivity are some of the characteristics that enhance trustworthiness in a person. To show interest in the other party's comments and points of view is an important aspect of a good negotiator. On one hand, one has to understand and show sympathy for the other party's point of view, on the other hand, one has to be firm on one's own point of view and position. Finding the right balance between the two is showing integrity. It is also closely related to trust, that people believe that if an agreement has been made with someone, they will get what is promised (Lewicki et al., 1994).

Expectations

One of the characteristic features of the atmosphere is the expectations each party has from the negotiation process and from each session of the negotiation process. When entering a negotiation process, both parties have some idea of what they want to achieve as a whole, as well as what they want to achieve on most crucial issues, such as price. It is also called minimum vs. maximum position of the parties. Once the parties know what they expect to achieve, they can easily decide about their limits. For a negotiation process to progress, both parties need to perceive some overlap in their minimum vs. maximum expectations. If a party perceives that it cannot achieve an outcome that will fulfil its minimum expectations, a negative atmosphere prevails. The same happens when a party perceives that the other party is demanding something beyond its maximum limit; in that case, it will see no point in continuing negotiations. Besides these short-term expectations, parties may also have long-term expectations that go beyond the scope of a particular session or process. For example, a company might be looking for a reference project or may want to penetrate a lucrative market, in which case the profits on the particular deal are less important. The parties need to have a clear picture of their short-term as well as long-term expectations. These expectations should not be based on wishful thinking but on realistic ambitions and possibilities. This demands an understanding of one's own as well as the other party's position and limitations. The realistic expectations create a positive atmosphere, while unjustified demands or objectives create a negative atmosphere.

In face-to-face negotiation, the longer the parties debate on a particular issue, the more the parties perceive that they will not be able to achieve their expected outcome, at least on that issue, and the parties perceive a negative atmosphere. The atmosphere during the negotiation process is dynamic and constantly changing. Each session and each argument may influence the expectations of the parties. Moreover, different dimensions of atmosphere also influence each other. For example, if the parties perceive a lot of conflict or cooperation, the expectations are influenced accordingly. The way the negotiations are run and the rules by which negotiations are conducted have great impact on the atmosphere. The site, the agenda, the participants, the seating arrangement and the manner in which the information is exchanged (e.g., threatening vs. persuasive) all work together to create a positive or negative atmosphere. It is thus up to the negotiators to take the above into consideration and create a positive atmosphere around and in the negotiation process.

The parties may have different expectations about the value of a deal. Consider the case of a singer negotiating with the owner of a concert hall over the payment for a proposed concert. They could not agree over the size of fee, with the singer's demand exceeding owner's maximum limit. The fixed amount demanded by the singer was based on the assumption that the house would be full while the owner's expectations were based on half-capacity. In fact, this difference in their expected value was the key to the deadlock. They reached an agreement where the singer received a modest fee plus a percentage of ticket receipts. As the singer expected a full house, he perceived it as a very valuable outcome. The hall owner was happy with the agreement as he only had to pay a very moderate fee (Lax and Sebenius 1986, pp. 30–1).

Non-verbal communication

One of the important issues that influence the atmosphere in face-to-face negotiations is non-verbal communication. Language can be a barrier in international business negotiation. What may not be readily recognised is that non-verbal communication (also called "silent language" or "body language") can interfere in cross-cultural interactions. Non-verbal communication includes the values 'attached to time, space, material possessions as well as body movements, eye contact, hand gestures, friendship and simple nods of agreement (Cavusgil and Ghauri 1990).

In non-verbal communication, our sense-organs pick up predominant clues (e.g., the firmness in the handshake, eye contact, etc.) and we give meaning to these non-verbal symbols through our filter of knowledge, viewpoints and emotions. We also respond to non-verbal communication in the same manner (e.g. through a smile, eye contact, grip of the handshake or by stepping back). We select one or more of these gestures which is right for the situation, just as we would construct a spoken message. The difference is that quite often the messages received and sent through non-verbal communication are unconsciously done (Lesikar and Pettit 1989).

In negotiations, we should carefully observe the body language in order to grasp the full message. For example, someone leaning on the table and listening attentively suggests that he/she wants to hear more and appreciates our point of view. The movement of an eyebrow can also reflect his/her acceptance or rejection. Coughing or swallowing of saliva often indicates that the other person is nervous or rejects the idea. Moving restlessly on the chair or looking at the wristwatch also shows that the person does not approve of our comments and that he/she does not want to hear any more. Eye contact has different meanings in some cultures. For example, in many Asian countries such as Japan and Thailand, people of low rank (subordinates) normally do not look into the eyes of superiors. In crucial negotiation, the seating arrangements are often such that the parties do not sit directly facing each other, especially not at a small table. This is done to avoid the feeling of confrontation. All these aspects influence the atmosphere through its different dimensions: power/dependence, cooperation/conflict and expectations.

The rules of negotiating differ from country to country. Some of these rules are spelled out while others are based on implicit customs and practices. While Westerners rely more on written rules, in many countries of Asia and the Middle East people rely more on implicit practices. Therefore it is advisable to be briefed on crucial characteristics of the culture of the country in which the negotiations are to be held. All cultures resent certain gestures or actions. For example, in some countries it is not considered polite to point at people or to cross legs in a manner that the soles of your feet are pointing towards the other person. Ignorance of these non-verbal or implicit aspects of face-to-face interactions may create a negative atmosphere and thereby disturb the negotiation process.

The case study[2]

Defibrator is a Swedish company which designs, manufactures, and markets a whole line of machines for pulp processes. In its special field — thermo-mechanical processes — it is considered a world leader; it has developed the technique and it has supplied half of the plants in the world. The competitors have, however, followed suit and the technical lead is diminishing. Organisationally, the company is divided in three units: development, manufacturing and marketing. The marketing unit is further divided into four departments, sales, project, service and marketing services. The sales department has a sales manager and there are sales

---

[2] The case study is based on interviews in Sweden and India, and studies of correspondence between the companies and other documents.

engineers, each one being responsible for a part of the world. The project department designs the plants and for each project a project group is formed, which consists of a project manager and a number of technical specialists. The company has a number of agents abroad. Their main functions are market contacts and service. All negotiations, technical as well as commercial, are carried out by the Swedish sales department. The agent in India is a well-established subsidiary of an old Swedish trading firm. Hindustan Paper Corporation (HPC) is state-owned. It was formed in 1971 and given control over several Indian pulp and paper mills. It has a board of directors, which is responsible to the Department of Industry. There are some limits to its decision-making power, so that it has to get approval from the Department of Industry. It has also to follow a number of government rules and policies. Thus, when buying equipment it has to ask for quotations from all prospective vendors and there must be at least three comparable quotations.

The Indian government planned to use a West German government loan to finance the project. One condition of this loan was that the project had to be evaluated by a reputable foreign consultant. As it was a new process with a new raw material, of which HPC had no previous experience, HPC also considered it necessary to have a consultant. Sandwell & Co from the USA was selected.

The negotiation process

The following seven stages of the negotiation process were distinguished:

- the first offer
- informal negotiations
- the final offer
- planning for the formal negotiation
- the first formal negotiation session
- internal meetings
- the second formal negotiation session.

The first offer

HPC contacted Defibrator and asked for a quotation for the project. After some time, a project group was formed within Defibrator with the sales manager as the project leader. But it took about one and a half years until Defibrator produced the quotation. According to the project manager, the reason for the delay was that Defibrator did not have the necessary information about the customer and about the availability of chemicals and raw materials. Defibrator also had to receive quotations from the subcontractors. Besides, their opinion was "in deals with unfamiliar customers it always pays to wait and see, and let the idea of the project mature". In other words, they were not sure about the seriousness of the buyer.

Before giving the quotation, Defibrator asked for a meeting and HPC's technical staff visited Sweden. In those meetings, mostly technical issues were discussed. But

HPC also informed that they intended to pay cash and that there would not be any foreign exchange problems in India. By the time Defibrator gave the quotation three other companies had also given quotations, one Indian supplier, one from Finland — Enso — and one from Austria — Voith. Quite naturally, during this stage, the atmosphere was mainly characterized by distance, a distance which was dependent on the physical distance between the countries and the lack of experience of each other's country. As a consequence, with regard to the dimensions of the atmosphere, the situation was very vague. The strong influence of the distance is illustrated by the project manager's view that "with a Swedish or otherwise familiar customer this kind of quotation would only take one month".

Informal negotiations

After Defibrator's submission of the quotation, a period of informal negotiations followed, which lasted about two years. The parties met each other several times, mostly to discuss technical matters. HPC's representatives visited Sweden a number of times and Defibrator's engineers were in India twice. HPC's consultants and Defibrator's agent took an active part in some of those meetings. A group of HPC board members studied the quotations and prepared a report in which they rejected the Indian quotation and strongly recommended Defibrator's machines. The consultants, Sandwell & Co examined the quotations and supported the views of the board members. HPC decided, after consulting Sandwell, that the capacity of the plant should be enhanced and that laboratory tests should be made on Defibrator's and Enso's machines, as the raw material — eucalyptus — to be used was quite new. The laboratory test was performed and that was important because the test and the meetings around it gave Defibrator information about the raw material and other chemicals to be used in the plant. Finally, after similar informal meetings with Enso, the technical staff of HPC and the consultants prepared another report, in which they strongly advocated that Defibrator's machines were the only ones suitable for the project. However, both foreign vendors were asked to give their final quotations for the project with the enhanced capacity. This was in accordance with the rules of the Indian government.

During this stage, the atmosphere cleared in several ways. Firstly, the distance decreased and the parties learned more about each other. "In the beginning it was very difficult for us to understand the objectives of the buyer and what he really wanted. During this stage, we met the buyer again and again, the situation became much clearer to us and we could perceive what was to be delivered." HPC became seriously interested in cooperating with Defibrator. Defibrator also got some ideas about the Indian firm's way of doing business. They received copies of a contract draft that HPC had concluded with a German firm for another project, and they got copies of standard terms and conditions, which the Indian government requires of such projects. Defibrator also realized HPC's strong financial situation and thus, during this stage, expectations of a future deal really evolved. Defibrator also learnt that HPC's engineers and consultants strongly supported their machines, which clarified and strengthened Defibrator's sense of power in the relation.

The final offer

Although Defibrator spent many more resources on the final quotation than on the first, it was delivered after a month only. The parties knew that this was the final quotation, which was to serve as a base for the contract. Thus, almost all issues had been considered. The technical problems had already been solved, now terms and conditions and financial matters took most of the time; in particular, the price was crucial. The margin for bargaining was difficult to reach. The atmosphere did not change very much during this stage; it was mainly characterized by growing expectations of a future deal.

Planning for the formal negotiation

About one month after the submission of the offer, the formal negotiation started in India after more than three years from the first contact. Defibrator nominated a negotiation team with a senior sales engineer as leader. He had some experience of negotiating deals with less developed countries. The company lawyer was a member of the team. A number of meetings were held and they tried to get some information on the behaviour of the buyer through the Indian agent. However, they had to accept that they did not have nearly enough knowledge. With the help of HPC's terms and conditions they worked out a contract draft, which they sent to HPC and demanded that it should serve as an agenda in the forthcoming negotiations. At HPC, the board of directors was to act as the negotiation team and they had to follow the previously determined terms and conditions of the government. Their preparation was mainly to examine how, and with regard to which issues, Defibrator's offer and contract draft differed from the government regulations. They also tried to get final quotations from the competitors who, however, did not respond.

Both parties had rather high expectations of a deal at the time. They felt inclined to cooperate with each other. Defibrator had spent so many resources on the offer stage and HPC wanted the machines. The power situation had become even more advantageous for Defibrator as HPC could not get final quotations from the competitors.

The first formal negotiation session

The session lasted two weeks and a number of meetings were held. During these two weeks the parties met twice a day, once in the morning and once in the afternoon. The buyer's consultant took part in the meetings and Defibrator's agent was present without playing an active role. Almost all issues were discussed but most of the time was spent on terms and conditions and real issues. On the whole, the technical problems had already been solved. Defibrator's contract draft was discussed but not accepted. There was disagreement on most of the issues. Whenever a conflict arose, the session was disrupted and the parties went into their chambers and worked separately. In the next meeting, they came with proposals for the disputed paragraph. The following issues were under conflict right from the beginning:

- infringements of patent
- governing law of the contract
- technical documents
- sales conditions
- arbitration
- technical documents
- working hours of Swedish engineers
- price.

The atmosphere was characterized by HPC's realization that they were strongly dependent on Defibrator and by the efforts to make the Department of Industry accept this situation.

Internal meetings

Both parties started working on contract drafts. A number of contacts were also made through the Indian agent and through correspondence. Defibrator prepared a revised contract draft. HPC also had a number of internal meetings and also, in particular, with the Department of Industry. After many discussions, the Department of Industry approved most of the clauses of Defibrator's contract draft with the exception of

- governing law
- arbitration
- technical documents
- working hours of Swedish engineers
- price.

The second formal negotiation session

Some four years after HPC asked for the first quotation, Defibrator's negotiation team visited India for the second negotiation session. The team brought the new contract draft, which HPC refused to consider, as the previous one had by now been accepted by the government, except for the disputed clauses. This time they could agree on all issues except that of price which remained the single source of disagreement. The price discussion ended when HPC announced that "if you give 7 per cent discount, the order is yours". Defibrator's team leader said that it was such a big discount that he had to phone his head office for advice. In the telephone

Pervez Ghauri

discussion, the sales director and even the managing director took part and gave their approval.

It seems that both parties were definitely determined to complete the deal during this session. There were some critical points but, on the whole, they moved forward in an atmosphere characterized by cooperation. HPC's consultant played an important role in this respect and made a number of suggestions. The atmosphere was quite clear with regard to power/dependence, and the formal obstacles to an agreement related to the power relation had been removed. The parties were strongly committed to a deal.

Concluding Remarks

It seems appropriate to describe and analyse the negotiation process as an interaction in which the atmosphere gradually, as the distance between the parties slowly diminishes, gets differentiated with regard to conflict/cooperation, power/dependence and expectations. The above-mentioned case study is a good illustration of the impact atmosphere can have on the negotiation process. As the case revealed, with a few interruptions, the expectations of a future deal were raised and the parties eventually committed themselves to the deal. The main — and perhaps critical — interruption had to do with the power relation. It seems as if the parties had a similar perception of their relative power but that one of the parties had no authority to act in accordance with its perception of the situation.

The perceptions of the parties influenced the cooperation/conflict situation, which resulted in a deadlock and then one more formal session. In particular, the rules of the Indian government were a critical factor. Perhaps it is important for suppliers from industrial countries to acquire a better understanding of the relations between the state and the industrial companies in a particular country. The consultant also played an important role in this process. He had a mediating role, contributed actively to the decrease in distance and to the cooperative atmosphere during the final stage. The Indian agent of the supplier, on the other hand, seems to have played a surprisingly passive role.

Finally, it seems as if the resources of the parties were the dominating factor behind the power/dependence relation. The lack of competitors probably decisively affected the whole process as well as the outcome. Thus, we can conclude that, whereas the power/dependence perceptions of the parties had an influence on the negotiation process, it seems that the perceived power relation had a greater impact on the outcome of the negotiations.

Part III

CHAPTER 10

Negotiating Sales, Export Transactions and Agency Agreements

J. B. McCALL

Introduction

The principal export transactions are those which involve sales direct to users and to resellers in open marketing channels, to distributors in an established channel of distribution and through agents. They are characterised by a mutual dependence which can be transitory or enduring and regulated by the agreements which legitimise them. The parties seeking to enter these agreements do so because they have simultaneously a reason to cooperate and, because their expectations differ, a reason to be in competition. Competition begets conflict, and bargaining and negotiation take place to help resolve the conflict. Negotiation outcomes depend on how the parties interact with, and on, each other and these hang on the behavioural predispositions of the negotiators, the situational and environmental influences on them and the influence strategies and skills they use (McCall and Cousins 1990, pp. 104–13).

Characteristics of export sales and distributorship/agency agreements

Export sales agreements and distributorship/agency agreements differ in a number of respects. Thousands of sales agreements are negotiated every day whereas distributorship/agency agreements are made (and terminated) much less frequently. The agreement of sale is characterised by its capacity to create profit or meet other objectives of the selling organisation while that of distributorship/agency provides the basis under which profit may be created in the future and is normally seen as long term in its strategic view. A sale can be a one-off episode or linked with others which precede or follow it; distributorship/agency is an on-going relationship subject to the pressures of change in the context in which it is played out. This chapter addresses the fully negotiated sales/purchase transaction which subsumes other and more limited kinds of sales transaction. Issues to be negotiated in sales contracts range from contract scope, delivery, terms of payment, performance, specification, service and arbitration to simple reduction in price or minor revision in terms; in distributorship/agency contracts, negotiations are dominated by issues such as exclusivity, extent of territory, supplier support, terms of payment, commission and commitment to the relationship in terms of investing in it. The process is one in which confrontation is more likely to occur in the actions of people brought up in certain cultures and is also more likely to happen in sales negotiations than in distributorship/agency ones.

Agreements of Sale

The bargaining framework

Sellers will normally know their costs and will have established a minimum price below which they are not prepared to go while buyers will have determined a maximum amount over which they cannot or will not pay. The range within which they will settle will lie between that figure and the price of asking/offer. Where these ranges overlap is the area of negotiation. Karrass (1974) makes the point that the settlement range is "the buyer's estimate of the seller's minimum and the seller's estimate of the buyer's maximum". The heart of the negotiation process is the information the parties can extract from each other and use for mutual influence. This can change the seller's and buyer's perceptions of what the other will pay or receive and is the strategic function of the face-to-face situation.

A seller's level of first offer will be affected by factors such as need to cover fixed costs, maintain cost/profit/volume advantages, long term aspirations, contractual risk, contingency amounts and the relationship between the parties. A Norwegian, coming from a country with a low power distance and a consensus tradition will expect the offer to be close to the final price. In Brazil, a high power distance country with high uncertainty avoidance, there is evidence that the readiness of Brazilians to make concessions leads to the perception that prices are inflated. The dilemma confronting the seller is to pitch the offer at a level that takes these factors into account but will not shut out the business. A buyer has to consider his level of first offer in relation to time costs as any delay brought about by extended negotiation times may result in higher costs or cause delay in completion. The relative power residing with the buying/selling parties will bear on levels of first offer and hence on outcomes. This can change over time and can be affected by environmental factors such as changing market structures, alterations in consumer preferences and varying exchange rates; and also situational factors like the degree of the seller's need for the work and the buyer's need for the product or service. Power can often be built into a situation by the collection, analysis and use of all relevant information, e.g., data on tariff reductions on the occasion of the accession of Austria to the European Union.

Face to face

If the selling organisation has a good reputation in the buyer country and/or has put forward a quotation based on prior contact with the buying organisation to establish what it really wants and has supported this with appropriate selling and influence activities, then the invitation to enter negotiations is a foregone conclusion. Even at this early stage there are differences in what constitute appropriate influences. Attempts to go over the head of the person responsible for negotiations may be quite acceptable in low power distance places like Israel or Scandinavia but unacceptable in places where hierarchy is strong as in France or relationships vertical as in Japan. A seller, in advocating his product, may sell its consideration by stressing its innovativeness in the USA or France where technical advances are welcomed, its assistance to performance in Germany where dependability is valued highly or what it will do for the buyer's or influencer's standing in England where image is an important attribute in establishing an individual's power base.

The agenda

The negotiation agenda can itself be negotiated and can be used to strengthen the position of one or other of the parties. For example, if the sellers have discovered in pre-negotiation contact that the potential buyer puts a premium on performance guarantees and wants to use this leverage on performance to draw out a better price, then they can ask to have performance guarantees put ahead of price on the agenda and put up strong resistance when guarantees come up for discussion. After this has gone on for some time to no avail, the suggestion can be made that it might be better to return to the issue after price has been discussed, the implication being that if the customer gives on price, they might be prepared to give on performance guarantees (MacMillan 1978). But not everyone likes to negotiate an agenda. Many Swedish businessmen consider it honest and efficient to prepare an agenda in advance and keep to it and see such activity as sharp practice (Philipps-Martinsson 1981).

Finding the negotiation range

At the opening stage of discussions, negotiators seek to explore the entire area covered by negotiations through the taking up of extreme positions which include their hopes for outcome plus the concession factors built in to their levels of first offer. The kinds of question asked and statements made will be conditioned by attitudes created by prior knowledge the participants have of each other and experience of prior negotiations with their organisations. If a quotation or offer has been made, this will form the starting point for the dialogue. The language used at this juncture will, certainly for Europeans and Americans, be forthright and uncompromising : "Do you mean to say that you cannot supply for less than ...?" "We couldn't possibly agree to such a low price — you don't appear to appreciate the quality built into our product." The problem for negotiators in these skirmishes is to identify if there is a gap between what the other says and is prepared to do. If the other's language is strong and simple, there is a presumption that the commitment is considerable. The less ambiguity there is in their statements, the greater can the other's commitment be taken to be. Where there is an overlap in the bargaining zone, the negotiator should be able to identify all the individual issues which comprise the negotiating area. Where there is no overlap, the lowering of aspirations is of critical importance. If either of the parties is convinced that the degree of movement needed can be achieved, this they may do by negotiating with their own management or team for a revision of authority or seeking to get the other party to obtain revised authority.

Such confrontational means of determining the negotiation range sit uncomfortably in an East Asian setting. Confrontation threatens face and other means are employed to establish the issues that separate the participants in the negotiation. Similarly, the Latin American or Arab buyer often bases his buying decision on the personality of the salesman and not on the quality of the product (Muna 1980, p. 30). It is the salesman's ability to strike chords in him that makes the buyer decide and confrontation is not the way to the relationship that aids this decision. In these circumstances, the opportunity should be provided to start in a more cooperative or relationship inducing mode. People of other nationalities adopt similar behaviour if they have had a good relationship and shared satisfactory recent transactions. When the people involved in the negotiation take up their positions strongly and reinforce them with harsh and unyielding repetitions of their basic position or variations on the same theme, the situation can rapidly deteriorate into what has been called "attack/defend spirals" from which it can be difficult to escape although technically agreement is still possible.

Escaping impasse

Playing the strong negotiator can be overdone. If a negotiator is compelled to withdraw from a position of extreme firmness in the face of an opponent's pressure, the loss of image will be carried over to other issues and subsequent negotiations. A buyer or seller has to strike a balance between firmness and credibility. If on the other hand they have got themselves into an attack/defend spiral , then to escape this dilemma they have to signal a willingness to move from initial stances they have taken up. It is encapsulated in the phrase "to convey without commitment" e.g., "If you were prepared to accept a later delivery, we might consider a reduction in price". A suitable reply might be "We might consider such a step should you find it possible to ...". The possibility of agreement has been created without the parties committing themselves. Not only the words spoken but the pitch and stress used and signalling action such as that shown in negotiating the agenda, are indications of a willingness to move.

When one of the parties is of a very different culture, the time taken is likely to be longer and cues are likely to be more specific: "This is what we did in the case of ..." Where a practical demonstration is required as a signal of intention, this can often be given by conceding a "straw issue".

Identifying common ground

When movement has been initiated, the negotiators can test the assumptions they have made concerning the commitment of the other side to the issues on which they appear to be adamant and can ensure that the commitment to the issues that matter most to themselves is maintained. The example below is of further probing behaviour into the other's commitment to the issues taken to be important at the stage of exploring the negotiation range.

"How reliable are your new drive motors in high ambient temperatures?" Here the buyer is asking an apparently innocuous question. If the reply is a general one about the high quality, a supplementary question might be asked: "Have you had any problems with them in installations similar to the ones we are considering?" The question is now more specific. "If the questioner possesses information about problems at such installations, then the question is loaded. It is designed to force an admission. A wise seller would assume knowledge by the buyer and perhaps turn it to advantage by demonstrating a cooperative and open attitude: "We did have problems at the plant of X Company. That was a fabrication problem which we have now overcome". He might go on to emphasise the lengths to which his company had gone to resolve the problems, so demonstrating commitment to the customer's interest. "The problem was one of breaking rotor bars that tore the windings of the stators. What we did was to re-check our designs and ask an independent engineering laboratory to perform a similar exercise in parallel. Having confirmed there was no design fault, we then checked our construction methods and found that a new machine being used to fit the rotor bars to the rings was leaving a certain play in operation which led to breakdown. Our current methods positively preclude this". The seller's position may have been slightly weakened but nothing like the extent to which it would have been had he denied the existence of a problem.

"In that case the buyer might have come back: "Do you deny that you have had problems at X Company?" The question is now a pointed one, framed in a way that requires a simple "Yes" or "No" as an answer. These are perhaps the words which best show how great the commitment is. The buyer was reasonably sure, or should have been, before putting the question in that way, of the answer he was going to receive. From a position in which he was seeking information, he has moved to a position where he has forced an admission, and is now poised to extract a concession. "In our business down-time of any equipment is revenue lost. You are asking us to pay these prices for machinery which we would have to take largely on trust?"

If the seller in the above exchanges denies that a problem exists or has existed until recently, he loses credibility as a negotiator on this and any other issues in conflict. He has been caught out because of the information held by the buyer and his bargaining position has been weakened (McCall and Warrington 1989, p. 198).

The negotiation seeks progressively to sort out those issues on which the parties are obdurate and those on which they are ready to concede provided there is an equivalent concession in the overall package eventually agreed.

It may not be possible to find concessions of equal worth on individual issues. It is more likely that equitability is obtained by relating the issues to the overall agreement. For this reason good negotiators do not seek to obtain a fair exchange of resources on individual items. They reserve their positions until they know what the extent of all the issues is and achieve perceived equitability in the overall package agreed.

In Western Europe and the USA in particular, the more precisely a position is defined, the stronger is the definer's commitment likely to be. If an Arab speaks like a person from one of these parts of the world, he is either attuned to Western culture or his commitment is not great. Because his language, built as it is on the beautiful style of the Koran, is not perfectly suited to the demands of modern commerce, he has to exaggerate and elaborate on it to create meaning (Shouby 1951). The Chinese do not seek to identify where common ground exists by confrontational means. To avoid possible loss of face they set about obtaining information by an apparently endless string of questions to build up a picture they feel will be acceptable to both parties. It tests to the full the cultural sensitivity of the foreign negotiator.

In all these exchanges it is important to create the climate of understanding by communicating as far as possible in a way in which the utterance of one party has a true reflection in the felt meaning of the other. Even in places as geographically close as some European countries, there can be wide difference in business thinking (Laurent 1983) and in the wider national perspectives (Hofstede 1991, Hampden-Turner and Trompenaars 1994). The skill is to match what is being said to what is understood.

In support of a commitment and in defence of any attack made on it, a negotiator can plead limited authority. One of the weaknesses of high level negotiators is that, while they can exercise more discretionary judgement, they are less able to appeal to limited authority as a source of negotiation power. A buyer who cannot approve an order over a certain value, or a salesman who does not have the authority to vary terms, is more difficult to deal with than someone who has. Restrictions on authority like budget limits, credit limits, cash discount limits, house rules against divulging costs, fair trading laws, specification changes, all give their user negotiation strength. Like any strength, if played too hard it may result in no bargain. Used with judgement, authority limits provide a negotiator with a face-saving way of testing the firmness of an opponent's stance and providing him with a face-saving way of giving in. Officials in the Republic of China, because of their bureaucratic need to diffuse responsibility, use such behaviors widely. Businessmen in countries with non-convertible currencies often use it deliberately to exert pressure for price concessions because of the need to conserve hard currency earnings as far as possible.

If the other party is perceived to be making unfair demands on the negotiator, then the latter may appeal to some form of legitimate power or moral rules related to social norms of equity, equality, need, opportunities, equal concessions and historical precedent (Magenau and Pruitt 1979). Such appeals are emotional and may be successful if the parties share a culture where people express their positions through appeals and emotions e.g., in most Latin American and African countries. A Mexican, for example, may find it hard going to convince someone from a Germanic or Anglo-Saxon culture whose style of persuasion is more influenced by hard facts or expert opinion. A person with an action or process dominant style may find it difficult to interact with someone having a people style (Casse 1994) unless aware of it.

Trading-off

The very fact of identifying common ground isolates those areas where there is no common ground and there is conflict to be resolved. Once commitments have been demonstrated and tested the participants can proceed to the bargaining process in order to bring the two sides closer together. A seller might agree to an earlier delivery provided the information allowing him to proceed could be produced within a stipulated period. A buyer might agree to a reduced penalty for late delivery if the seller would requote and accept payment in the buyer's country currency. A negotiator from a Muslim country might insist on disputes being taken to local courts, but may be less resistant than a Western counterpart on issues of warranty. By such means the gap separating the parties is narrowed until they see the possibility of the ultimate bargain.

To come to an ultimate bargain, a negotiator has to assess what constitutes a fair outcome. If all issues are to be part of an overall package, then a judgement has to be made on the spot. This hangs on earlier preparation, both in relation to the costs of possible trade-offs and the communication arrangements between negotiators and the team that they are representing for quick handling of queries on such things as specification amendment and delivery. If a potential purchaser is required by his central bank in Chile to pay no more than 6 per cent interest on an extended payment contract, and the supplier has a going rate of 10 per cent in his offer under negotiation, then the supplier's negotiator has to be able to recalculate the offer including the unwanted 4 per cent in the capital sum and showing an interest rate of 6 per cent to meet the customer's needs. He is expected to have the authority of the company to do this and the capacity to do so without hesitation.

Some elements which are traded off are worth less than, or more than, any figure determined by an accounting convention. If a seller is less interested in immediate profit than in a long range goal like obtaining a foothold in a growing market, then he may be prepared to trade it off for a value much less than cost. If a buyer in Poland is prepared to pay up to ten times the value of an essential part because that was the cost of the loss of a week's production, a seller might just take advantage of this and charge above the going rate.

The problem of setting a value on concessions is made more difficult by the fact that some aspects of a concession are not measurable in money terms. With penalty clauses in contracts, for example, these "should bite into the profits of the seller" to encourage the seller to maintain promised delivery or performance. But if the rates normally used are 3 per cent up to 10 per cent per month or more, and what is asked is well in excess of what is normal, then this combined with the probability of a penalty being incurred, may raise the monetary equivalent value.

Neither buyer nor seller knows exactly how far he can maximise his advantages. A negotiator can only make assumptions about an opponent's preferences, expectations and goals. It is the testing of these assumptions that is a prime function of negotiation and the interpretation made will vary with the experience of the tester.

In testing assumptions negotiators are careful to mitigate the extent of any apparent disagreement by revealing, or appearing to reveal, what is going on in their minds, as in "I am very concerned that we seem to be so far apart on …". There are two forces at work on the seller and buyer. One is the esteem motivation that drives them to strike the best possible bargains and provide the satisfaction of a job well done, perhaps establishing a precedent for future negotiations. The other is the security motivation to settle when a reasonable bargain is identified, rather than seek a more advantageous outcome at the possible risk of not reaching agreement.

It is against this background that buyers and sellers convey to each other, by the moves and counter-moves they make, how they see a resolution of their differences. This is the time when they have to bring together all those items they have promised to "consider", "bear in mind", "take account of" — and all the other phrases used when waiting to establish the full negotiating range before making a commitment on issues — and put forward a package for the consideration of the other party.

In Western cultures the negotiator may look his opponent straight in the eye and speak with a tone of complete finality supported by corresponding non-verbal language like sitting back with arms folded and putting papers in order. The language is terse and to the point, confirming the finality. Sometimes, perhaps during a break, the negotiator may have signalled intentions by treating the opponent with a greater degree of familiarity, using cordial expressions and similar manifestations of intimacy. Phrases like "I have done as much as I can. Now it's up to you".

In Eastern cultures signals may not be so apparent. It has been reported by Pye (1982) that Chinese negotiators never telegraph their next move through a show of emotions. The level of friendliness or impersonality remains the same whether negotiations are approaching agreement or failure. To Western eyes a sudden move to agreement following the seemingly endless quest for information comes as a considerable element of surprise.

Making the agreement

The position has now been reached where the area of conflict has been reduced to a point at which the negotiators are in a position to assess the possibilities of early agreement. One or the other will put forward his proposal for the final bargain. This will normally be in the form of a package because issues have been kept linked while matters in conflict have been addressed. In major sales agreements characterised by some complexity, more than one package may be proposed.

To bring a negotiation to a conclusion many negotiators find that summarising the steps through which they have proceeded is a convincing way of getting agreement. This may be a repetition of the concessions that have been exchanged and proposals made which a weaker party may accept entirely: "Let me summarise what I think we have agreed". Often, agreement is achieved by a final concession. It has to be big enough that it is not considered trivial, but small enough to convince an opponent that there are no more concessions to be had. The opponent may also wish something in return. The opponent may try to conclude by posing some such question as "Do we understand that if we do what you ask us you will reduce your price by . . .?" An agreement is about to be made. In the process the participants will have, knowingly or not, tried to resolved the negotiator's eternal dilemma of whether to go for the best possible deal or settle for an acceptable but not optimal outcome. East Asians have less feeling for the drama of agreement than Europeans and Americans and view it as the beginning of a relationship rather than the culmination of a commercial process.

"Memorandum of agreement" is a term commonly used for the recorded bargain. It emphasises intent rather than the language of lawyers. A simplified form summarises what has been agreed under heads of agreement. This makes it less threatening for Chinese negotiators than an agreement put in the framework of a legal contract.

Agreements with governments and government sponsored agencies

Despite galloping privatisation of the public sector, there will always remain a substantial government market for suppliers. Negotiations with government departments go through a similar process to that described above but they are played out to a different set of rules and assumptions. The differences are set out in Table 10.1.

The law and the negotiation of sales agreements

The eventual contract which seals the agreement is the conclusion of a legal process in which the export sales negotiation has been embedded. Because it may affect eventual outcomes, the knowledge of the law under which an agreement is made is essential for international negotiators. It is within the framework of national, supranational and international laws that businessmen make their agreements. So knowledge of the commercial law of one's own country is not enough. Required knowledge covers the UN Convention on Contracts for the International Sale of Goods which a purchaser might wish to regulate the contract, the law of the country under which a contract is agreed, and the custom of the merchants which has been a successful source of the harmonisation of international trade law and is embodied in "INCOTERMS 1990" (International Chamber of Commerce 1990) which forms part of a contract of sale if so agreed.

TABLE 10.1

Negotiating international sales agreements in the private and public sectors. (Table does not apply to contracts of relatively low value.)

	Private sector	Public sector
Philosophy	Market forces determine outcomes; best deal in the circumstances	Fair and reasonable price; value for money in the circumstances
Scope of supply	Arm's length or special relationship; often open to all suppliers to try for business	Approved list of suppliers; selective tendering in certain circumstances; open procurement for large public contracts in EU
Original contact	Direct approach to suppliers often as result of selling activity; invitation to tender	Open call for tender; direct approach to selected suppliers
Basis of negotiation	seller's offer/quotation or large buyer's standard conditions of purchase based on known seller price	Standard form of contract based on tendered selling price
Transaction constraints	Varying national practices; extent of negotiators' authority	Procedures, methods, rules; extent of negotiators' authority
Nature of compensation	Price based on bargaining process	Price based on lowest offer; price based on cost plus management fee often including element of negotiation
Price criteria	Structure of buyer's costs or unique advantages of seller's product; investment appraisal	Investment appraisal as mediated by policy factors; lowest prices
Selection criteria	Cost; degree of differentiation	Policy dictated choice
Level of first offer	Reasonable to high; profit objective leaving room for trade-off	Reasonable to meet the needs of competitive tendering
Issue emphasis	Specification, price, delivery, service level	Specification and cost; formula for profit
Mode of negotiation	Cooperative to competitive; often confrontational at early stages; effort frequently required to escape impasse; information seeking for mutual influence; often need for closing concession	Cooperative; confrontation unlikely to be important; easy transition to identifying common ground; open exchange of information; little need for closing concession
Legal framework	Almost invariably contract law; not highly developed in some countries	Contract law in different stages of development; in certain jurisdictions there are administrative contracts/special rules

The minimum knowledge required is the process of offer and acceptance and how it varies in different jurisdictions and how offer and acceptance are usually excluded in formal contractual documents; the performance of contracts especially as it refers to delivery, the passing of property and the passing of risk and how arbitration rules and practices change to meet the cultural needs of different countries.

In most circumstances good practice in addressing the legal environment of contracts of international sale will not be measurable. Should however the contingencies they are intended to cover come to pass, then the negotiator who has taken the appropriate steps will have left his organisation in a strong position should litigation ensue.

Distributorship/Agency Agreements

The relationship

Companies attempt to enjoy the benefits of specialisation whenever and however possible. When they have been involved in a regular course of dealing which has been marked by a series of sales agreements and acknowledge that it is in their mutual interest to perpetuate what is a dependence relationship, this is generally viewed as an indication that a channel of distribution has emerged. The parties are committed to a cooperative arrangement which takes the form of fulfilling a negotiated role in the channel. The arrangement is regulated by the distributorship agreement.

The relationship is more likely to be characterised by unequal rather than by equal power. One party to the relationship will therefore enjoy a relative power advantage. Under conditions of unequal power, the party possessing the greater relative power tends to behave exploitatively while the less powerful tends to behave submissively. For the supplier in distributorship negotiations the temptation to exercise that power has to be held in check. The supplier seeking to develop a market through a distributor depends on the performance of that distributor for the success of company plans. If, from a position of strength, he arbitrarily sets targets at an unattainable level, his actions will be against his own interests.

Because organisations wish to work with others to achieve goals, cooperation is the most commonly observed behaviour in channels of distribution. It exists either on a voluntary basis or as a result of conflict resolution by the channel leader through the exercise of power that he holds. If cooperative behaviour is necessary between organisations, it is equally so between the individuals who represent their organisations. Mutual goodwill is a prerequisite to the establishment of lasting relationships.

Agency agreements similarly depend on relationships. In this case the agent is an arm of the principal promoting sales of the principal's products in return for payment by commission or retainer plus commission.

Negotiating original agreements

The agreements made in distribution channels provide the foundation for channel management. The purpose of original agreements is to define the terms of operation and the ground rules by which conflict may be resolved. The legal issues involved have been examined and frameworks around which different agreements may be drawn up have been provided (Ezer 1993).

The negotiation of an original agreement begins with the necessary preparation for a satisfactory outcome. It presupposes the choice of distributor or agent has been made. It starts with identification of where the power lies. Where alternative intermediaries are in short supply, the apparently weaker has a strong negotiating base. This will be strengthened further if it is established during the course of negotiation that the distributor or agent has a special relationship with key customers. A supplier's or principal's hand will be strengthened if his product is covered by patent, trademark or copyright.

The negotiation

There is not the same degree of extreme position posturing and hard language or bluffing as in many sales/purchase agreements since the supplier/distributor relationship is normally perceived as one of trust arising from agreement on roles and rewards for joint marketing performance. Nevertheless, the cooperative nature of relationships does not mean there cannot be a competitive element to the negotiation. What might be seen to be an outrageously demanding proposal in a mature channel can be viewed much more tolerantly when the people are meeting for the first time. To that extent there is scope for settlement within a bargaining area perceived to be reasonable and for varying the bargaining area by reducing the other party's aspirations.

Areas of potential dispute can relate to factors like the stake the distributor or agent will hold in the joint activity. A manufacturer of consumer durables might see an investment in specialist staff an immediate necessity to service the product(s) while the distributor/agent might see that as an imposition until a large enough customer base has been built up to justify the expense. A distributor of branded consumer goods might be interested in price and discounts, payment terms, the stocks to be carried, exclusivity in a defined area, how far the supplier will assist in advertising, tight conditions under which an agreement may be terminated and protection under the law and arbitration in the event of unresolved conflict. On the other hand, the supplier may be interested in agreeing quotas, feedback on market conditions, promotion plans of the distributor and in getting the distributor's agreement to his standard contract of distributorship. The outcome may eventually be agreement based on a variation of the standard contract in return for a higher quota for the first year than originally envisaged by the distributor and perhaps an undertaking to provide information according to the supplier's format in exchange for some concession on levels of discount for different quantities and contribution to advertising in the overall settlement.

An agent, like a distributor, is interested in the area covered, exclusivity, products handled, duration of agreement, conditions of termination and the law under which it will be interpreted. He will, in addition, be concerned with his own remuneration by way of commission, the basis of its calculation and the terms of its payment and any other duties and expenses to which he will be committed.

In practice, the distinction between agent and distributor is not quite so clear cut. An agent may act as such for his principal's products but as a distributor for spares and consumables. A distributor may act as such for his supplier but may be paid commission when required to service accounts of competitive distributors being supplied by the same manufacturer.

Negotiating the continuity of agreements

The distributorship/agency agreement is not a one-off transaction. It can be viewed as a continuing series of episodes, the original agreement holding good only for that moment in time in which it was made. The relationship moves on and clouds the original objectivity. It can be put under stress by a variety of factors requiring the agreement or specific aspects of it to be reviewed.

Economic changes, like a change in the exchange rates (as with the volatility of the US dollar and the Japanese yen in the mid-nineties, which varied between 80 and 130 yen to the dollar necessitated new arrangements to accommodate for example the fall of the distributor's/agent's country currency in relation to the supplier's. Revised arrangements need to be put in place to counter the loss of competitiveness in relation to domestic and other country suppliers whose currencies have not moved to the same extent.

Political and legal changes can also affect the relationship and require the agreement to be modified in some way as when countries joining the European Union in 1995 needed to ensure their agreements complied with the competition laws whose principles were set in the Treaty of Rome and are clarified in different situations by decisions of the EU Commission and judgments of the European Court of Justice.

Changes in the perceived strengths of the parties as a result of working together can enrich a relationship and produce a mutual regard and dependence arising from the more effective use of mutual resources and may sometimes change the nature of the power relationship between them. A Latin American agent had close contacts with *financieros* or development banks and was able to obtain for his customers finance for large projects not normally available. As a result he made the supplier more dependent on his services and could ask more in return which was likely to be reflected in any revised agreement. Agreements should have a relatively short term put on them to ensure they meet current conditions but should be long enough in the first instance to encourage a new distributor/agent to invest in the relationship.

Negotiations arising within agreements

Once the parties have experience of operating an agreement, they are able to establish whether the objectives of the parties really coincide. The supplier may be seeking to exploit the market through a distributorship or agency. If either chooses to have a spread of distributorships or agencies rather than develop a core of related ones, then there may be something to be negotiated which could well end in termination if there is no evidence of changed behaviour.

Most of the issues to be negotiated during the course of a mature agreement are associated with the marketing mix. Modifications to product, packaging or service level may need to be made to meet the requirements of the distributor or agent. Channels may have to be revised or extended to accommodate new strategies derived from changes in the environment, and new communication arrangements made.

When product modifications are made, discount structures are adjusted, terms of payment changed, or amended distribution and communication arrangements introduced, price is rightly seen as the value placed on these changes.

Termination of distributorship and agency agreements

Even long-standing agreements can be brought to an early end by changes in circumstances which no longer support the common objectives on which the original agreement was founded or they can be terminated by a specific act of one of the parties, usually the supplier, for failure to perform.

There are problems to be resolved by negotiation in dissolving an agreement. If a distributor or agent holding stocks has his agreement terminated, he should not have to be left with stocks to dispose of as he can. A good agreement will have made provision for this, e.g., by stating that in the event of termination by the supplier, they will be bought back at the price paid plus any charges of carriage if quoted in the supplier's standard catalogue. But this does not resolve everything. An intermediary may be carrying stocks that are obsolete but held as a service to customers using old equipment and may wish this goodwill element to be recovered in the termination arrangement.

As in the approach to new and revised agreements, information bearing on the negotiation is crucial. If the agent or distributor has consistently failed to meet agreed targets written into the contract, that has to be established. If the supplier terminates but has himself failed to meet the terms, such as failing to deliver outstanding orders, his position has been weakened. A critical aim is to terminate in such a way that the outgoing agent or distributor assists in the transfer, for example, of stocks, customer enquiries and information on customers and markets. It is often necessary to concede on things like buying back stock to obtain this continuity.

The law and the negotiation of distributorship/agency agreements

Agency and especially distribution are embedded in a web of national and transnational laws. Competition policy varies from country to country and laws vary accordingly. It is therefore in the interest of anyone making one of these agreements to know the appropriate law. This allows, when circumstances permit, for this knowledge to be used as a negotiation counter.

In the USA contracts are surrounded by a complexity of laws stemming from the Sherman Act which prohibits contracts in restraint of foreign trade and monopoly. Agreements the sole effect of which are to restrict competition, are void. The granting exclusively to a distributor of a territory or product/brand is increasingly seen as violation of the law irrespective of its competitive effects.

In most Arab countries there are commercial codes in which provision is made for disputes to be taken before local courts but it is normal for disputes to be referred to arbitration for quick settlement. This can either be at the International Court of Arbitration in Paris or locally. The local court has discretion to set aside arbitration according to certain rules.

Under EU law agents are exempt from a general prohibition on agreements likely to affect trade between states. Distributors are only exempt from such prohibition where they have a market share below a certain percentage and combined turnover of under a given value of ecus. Equally, under the concept of parallel imports, there are certain restrictions on what may not be included in an agreement, e.g., forbidding a distributor to re-export his products to another EU country.

Where an agreement is not considered to affect trade between countries, then the law that is relied on in the event of dispute is the law agreed between the parties. In the United Kingdom the law of agency is weak; in France, Germany the Netherlands and some other countries, the law presumes the agent the weaker of the parties and provides for compensation if an agent's services are dispensed with. It is therefore to the interest of a British agent to have an agreement with a French supplier under French law; for the French supplier English or Scots law provides an advantage should that supplier wish to terminate the agreement. If a French supplier can establish that an English agent is unaware of this then he can trade off to his advantage an apparent concession to agree to English law in return for a substantial one. In Belgium there is a law specific to distributorship which provides for compensation under specific rules for the goodwill which the distributor is assumed to have built up for the supplier.

Conclusion

Export sales agreements and distributorship/agency agreements are subject to similar processes and depend for their effectiveness on how well the agreements are made. They do, however, differ in a number of respects.

Power, usually asymmetric, exists in both cases, but the nature of the power tends to differ between the two. In major sales negotiations there is considerable power in the system and the party exercising the greater power usually has the advantage whether or not the latent power which exists is exercised. In distributorship/agency negotiations there is not the same power as these negotiations usually take place in a context of a relatively low level of investment of resources. As a result there can be, in distributorship/agency negotiations, much less of the hard and confrontational bargaining necessary in large sales contracts to ensure all details of the proposals of the parties are exposed. The cooperative mode is more likely to be met in distributorship/agency negotiations which presume a long relationship than in one-off sales negotiations. In either case assumptions have to be tested. In the case of sales we do not know whether our assumptions are correct as these are based on a judgement derived largely from an on-the-spot assessment of the other side's use of language in the negotiation. The objective is to get the best possible outcome in the circumstances. In distributorship/agency negotiations the objective is to establish firstly goal congruence which is to a considerable extent dependent on what the would-be distributor/agent says and which is only testable in the light of future operation of the agreement.

Sales and distributorship/agency negotiations take place within a legal framework on the basis in most cases of contract, but where the applicable law differs considerably. Sound agreements are made within a legal framework by salesmen and buyers, suppliers and distributors and principals and agents by businessmen acting in these capacities. Sound agreements for these form the basis of good working relationships. It has been said that arbitration is better than litigation, conciliation better than arbitration and prevention of legal disputes better than conciliation. Such prevention is the responsibility of executives negotiating and drafting the relevant agreements.

CHAPTER 11

Negotiating Licensing Agreements

VERNON PARKER

Introduction

Licensing has, as its aim, establishing in a receptive business enterprise ("the licensee") a technical capability presently lacking and which is denied to it for want of enabling knowledge or necessary permissions which another enterprise ("the licensor") can supply.

The prospective technical capability might be

- making a new or improved product (for use or sale)
- making an existing product in a new or improved way
- providing a new or improved technical service.

This is not an exhaustive classification and within each category there are numerous different types. But in every case the licensee acquires an enhanced technical competence, based on transferred knowledge or on legally recognised permissions under what are called intellectual property rights or, very often, on a combination of both. We shall need to amplify this statement in the course of this chapter but the reader may care at this stage to read the brief descriptions of relevant intellectual property rights that appear in the appendix to this chapter.

By far the most significant IP Right in technology licensing is the patent right. In summary, a patent is an exclusive right, recognised and enforceable under National Statutes, which grants to the patent owner for a period the sole right to allow others to work within a defined technical area. The technical area must embody a unified technical advance ("an invention") which is new, non-obvious and industrially applicable. The patent documentation must fully and sufficiently describe the advance such that at the end of the exclusion period (up to 20 years, if designated National fees are paid) the public may freely enjoy the benefit of the advance. The bargain with the state is, therefore, a temporary "monopoly" in return for a full disclosure of the invention in enabling and scope-defining language. A person who is allowed to work the patented invention during the exclusion period is truly a licensee. Strictly, a person who is supplied with confidential technical knowhow (also commonly referred to as proprietary technical information and trade secrets) for his commercial use is not a licensee (although the misnomer is too well established and too convenient to be changed now). This is because there is, in law, no property right in information as such, as is further explained in the appendix. Essentially, in the case of licensed technology, the licensee is prevented from disclosing or making any use he chooses of information received only by the terms of the contract he accepts as the preconditions for the disclosure of that information to him. The distinction between the right to use published but patented information (only as licensed by the patent owner) and the right to use confidential but unpatented knowhow (unrestricted except to the extent agreed otherwise) is fundamental in licensing and it shapes the relationship between licensor and licensee, their mutual obligations and rights, and the process they go through to arrive at an agreed licence position. So, to repeat, the aim of the licensing agreement is to make it possible for the licensee to acquire a new technical capability through supplied knowledge and/or IP licences.

The issues confronting a technology licensor and his licensee find echoes in the world of real estate. An architect and his client will agree the general shape and form of a building which the architect will design. The design must meet the client's purposes for the building, will draw on the proven experience and competence of the architect, and will take account of environmental circumstances, all necessary planning permissions and building regulations. The detailed design which is ultimately presented to the builder will be an aggregation of component elements. It will specify materials of construction and unit designs that are well-established as suitable for their role in the overall design. It will reflect the architect's and client's agreement on details and their personal preferences. It will conform to the requirements of the various regulatory authorities. Aside from the design and the legal/regulatory framework, there are other aspects of the relationship between architect and client that have counterparts in a licensing agreement between licensor and licensee. Thus, the architect will be paid a fee for his services which will reflect the quality and value of his product. The licence agreement will similarly specify what the licensor is to be paid both for his services and for the value to the licensee of the transferred technology and rights in the form of licence fees or royalties. The architect will accept responsibility and liability (at least to an extent) if his product is not fit for the agreed purposes, does not meet regulatory requirements, or infringes the rights of third parties. This would also be expected from a licensor.

The building of a house is a step-wise process over a substantial period of time. The performance of a licensing agreement can also be in planned stages, particularly in the case of a technology licence for a new plant, and in such case the licensing agreement must deal with needs for checks, reviews, possible break points, contracting with others, project management responsibilities just as for a building project.

In broad summary, a licensing agreement must specify: What the licensor is to do and permit the licensee to do, what the licensee has to do, how and when they are to do these things, and how costs, expenses, licence fees (or royalties proportional to the extent of use of the licensed technology) are calculated and borne. Especially it must define the scope of licence grants under IP Rights and regulate disclosure and use of the licensor's "proprietary" information. It must deal with what may happen if performance of the licence agreement, or ultimate exploitaton of the licensed technology, does not turn out as intended, for a variety of innocent or culpable reasons.

What we have considered so far is the ultimate objective of a process of focused business activity comprising a sequence of stages which the prospective licensor and licensee must go through, separately and jointly, before they arrive at a consensual conclusion. It is this process we shall now discuss, keeping in mind, as we must, the point and purpose of it. For those readers wishing to have a deeper appreciation of what technology and patent licensing entails, of the business motivators and implications for licensors and licensees of offering and seeking technology/patent licences, of pre-licence corporate technology evaluation and assessment, of the common types of licence agreements and of the typical content, structure and wording of licence agreements with annotated examples, they may usefully refer to *Licensing Technology and Patents* by V. Parker, published by the Institution of Chemical Engineers (UK). (ISBN 085295 277 5) and derive added perspective in the context of international, cross-border, licensing from *Introduction to International Licensing* by G. W. D. Karnell and E. M. Andersson, published by Intellectual Property Publicity Ltd (UK) (ISBN 1870497 02 3).

Box 11.1

Contract negotiations were well advanced in the former Soviet Union between an International Contractor and the FSU Authorities on a proposal to supply and install a TV-tube factory. As usual in such cases, the processes for technology selection and contract negotiation were lengthy and detailed. The factory was to be located some 250 miles from Moscow on a rail terminus, and the principal market was the Moscow region. At a late-stage pre-contract award, the Contractor casually enquired where the necessary suitable packaging material would be supplied from. That need had been overlooked. The TV-tube project was aborted.

The lesson from this is to consider at the earliest stage the industrial and social infrastructure into which the licensed technology is going.

Types of Licence

The range of possible licence subject matter is enormously varied in type and complexity. At one extreme it may be a simple non-exclusive patent/design/ software licence. At the other it may be a major production technology licence envisaging multi-national investment, global sales, and design, engineering, and training services. Realistically, this presentation must select a few representative types of licence as the object of the preliminary phases and the eventual negotiations towards the licence. We shall, therefore, select as our ultimate targets:

1. A patents-only licence, as an example of an IP Rights licence
2. A knowhow-only licence
3. A combined patents/knowhow licence to the extent the combination introduces new factors in the negotiation process beyond those inherent in 1 and 2 above.

These selections will nevertheless provide us with a framework within which to relate the core issues that are common to all technology licences of these types to strategies for negotiation of more general application.

Within each section, we shall consider the various things prospective licensors and licensees must do before openly declaring to each other an interest in pursuing particular licensing opportunities, meaning to offer licences or to seek licences as applicable. The quality of this preparation will ensure that both parties go in to preliminary enquiries and evaluations with eyes open, alert to the business impact, especially the competitive consequences, of what is being envisaged. Additionally, when the negotiating forum becomes a window on each organisation's competence and professionalism, a showing of thorough preparation by the negotiators will reflect well on those they represent. Early questions in the mind of negotiators are always, Are these people serious? Are they people we can do effective business with?

We shall then consider the enquiry and assessment stages when the prospective licensor and licensee are in direct dealings, and are answering the question, Is there a realistic basis for the parties to agree a licence in both their interests? It must always be fixed in the minds of representatives of the parties that no licence will result unless both parties wish it to and they are able to agree a basis for doing so. In these stages, the potential licensee's requirements and the prospective licensor's capacity to license confront each other.

Patent licences

General

Patents are a spin-off from R&D activities undertaken for reasons other than to generate or license patents. The patent owner ("patentee") may be a University, Research Institute, or Corporate body, even an individual. Patentees who are not in the business of manufacture and sales of goods (or a service industry) will have embarked on the patenting route in the expectation that licence revenue will accrue. At the outset, they must devise a patent acquisition strategy that balances financial risk (the cost of patenting) with realistic prospects of interesting potential licensee enterprises. Seldom will they have the resources and financial backing (or the product market knowledge) to be able to take the patented technology to the point of demonstrated market relevance. Statistically, the chances of this happening are in any case low. Very few inventions reach the market place or the factory. Therefore, such parties are well-advised to seek a development partner from commercial enterprises already in the relevant field and at the earliest realistic time. Early market research is imperative. Such parties would be advised to initiate the patent acquisition process by filing a priority application which can provide the basis for a follow-up process of appropriate international filings. Prospective licensee companies are loath to receive unsolicited invention disclosures before a priority filing has been made. They fear embarrassment if they are engaged in similar investigations through unintentional contamination of their ongoing research and exposure to charges of bad faith. An initial enquiry on such companies might request permission to submit an outline confidential disclosure (having indicated the general field in which the invention falls) making it clear that a priority patent filing has been made. Leaders in a particular industry sector are not renowned for receptivity to externally generated inventions although their curiosity will often lead them to entertain an outline submission on a non-confidential basis or on the basis of short-term confidentiality, meaning that period (1 to 2 years) within which the patenting process would lead to publication of the patent specification describing the invention. The aims of such submissions are to attract an optimum commercial partner (or more than one where the global market is regionalised and not truly international), to grant it (or them) rights in the invention, including most importantly the right to seek international or regional patenting at their cost and expense as they see fit, and to receive in return a lump sum fee or royalties measured on extent of exploitation or, better, a combination of these. Periodic royalty returns enable the inventor entity to monitor the extent of exploitation and can be a determinant of whether or not to trigger a right (which should be provided for) to cancel any exclusivity granted, or require reversion of control of the patents, or invoke independent sublicensing rights. The inventor entity should ensure it maintains an up-to-date schedule of the patent portfolio for the invention. In this way, it can ensure patents are being kept alive by annuity payments. Once a patent in a country has been allowed to lapse it is difficult and expensive or, if long delayed, impossible to recover it. The commercial partner's interest will usually be to keep control over the patent portfolio and use it, or not, as it sees fit to serve its business interests. Acquisition of all rights in an invention that is a genuine threat to a vested interest in order then to suppress it is sadly a known strategy. Bona fide abandonment of a development programme because the invention cannot satisfy a practical need or deliver a profit or cost savings is very common.

In contrast to the above class of patentee, a company in the business of manufacture, sales or services on a regional basis, but which is not well placed itself to exploit all major market opportunities, will have a quite different patent licensing strategy which may be offensive or defensive or just opportunistic. The difference in this corporate setting is that the licensor knows the relevant product/service field, at least within its market sector. The patents he will be seeking to license will be relevant to today's business activity — not possibly of value in some years' time if all goes well! The patent portfolio will be in place and not further extendable. It will already be of several years' standing. It commonly takes a minimum of 5 to 8 years to achieve proven commercialisation of an invention that is one of the blessed few ($< 1\%$) that survive the rigours of development and market testing.

Licensing strategies; enquiries; responses

An offensive patent licensing strategy is one that confronts a perception (even conviction) that other companies in the same industry sector, whether direct competitors or not (e.g., companies in remoter market regions whose products and services do not directly compete) are infringing one's patents.

The first step that must be taken is to confirm that patents in the relevant territories are in force (i.e., annuities have been paid). It is very embarrassing to seek to assert a patent that has been allowed to lapse, perhaps during an earlier phase of corporate cost-saving. The next step is to take advice on the enforceable scope of each such patent. What does this mean? It means, for example, that patents in different countries often have differing definitions of the exclusion field reserved to the patentee. This is not a reflection of nuances of translation but arises because of the different standards of challenge applied to patent applications by National Patent Offices on behalf of the public interest. Some do not consider the merits of the invention or the scope of monopoly sought, but leave that to the industry to sort out for itself. Others, like the European Patent Office, are rigorous in defending the public interest in not having patents granted for subject matter which is in fact already available to the public in some retrievable form, or is obvious in the light of what is known. In some countries, the semantic limits of the patent language are not necessarily applied strictly when assessing an alleged infringement. In some countries, there will be presumptions that a distinctive product has been made by a patented process, so reversing the burden of proof. The advice that has to be sought is whether the patent can be enforced in the present form, whether in any case it may usefully be asserted in its present form, or whether remedial steps should first be taken, including the prospects of success.

Remedies for patent infringement are solely civil remedies (almost everywhere) and significantly include an injunction as well as the expected award of damages. It is this possibility that induces infringers to trade for a licence and provides leverage to a patentee in his efforts to get fair recompense. Most patent infringement actions end in settlement, even if they do not usually start out with that intention. It is an important consideration for patentees contemplating "a vigorous defence of their patents" to estimate realistically what the alleged infringer could afford to pay in royalties for a licence. They should also consider and evaluate the benefit to them of obtaining, as part of a settlement, access to any improvements the infringers have made or may well make later as licensees. It should not be presumed that infringers are always knowingly so; often they are not. Patent infringement can be like trespass on what you believe to be public land but which would be shown not to be if proper enquiries had been made. By contrast, for copyright infringement there must be copying.

The recommended first approach to the assumed infringer is a letter drawing the attention of the alleged infringer to the existence of the patent and expressing a willingness to discuss any issues it may raise. Threats of legal action are to be avoided (and may be actionable). However, if the patent owner is willing to consider licensing on some reasonable basis, he would indicate this in his letter. This approach does not guarantee the maximum in damages for past infringement which the law might award but it is still considered wiser than more aggressive alternative strategies and is more conducive to achieving agreement for licensing, cross-licensing, or other mutually beneficial arrangements.

The alleged infringer before responding to the patentee's letter will set in hand an enquiry as to the status and validity of the patent and assemble for use in negotiations any arguments for invalidity/non-infringement. He will also assess the cost and effort and necessary time it would take to "design around the patent" (i.e., secure a realistic technical evasion) in order to see what his fall-back position is. He is not likely to wish to simply withdraw from the patented field.

A defensive patent licensing strategy is one that responds to a perceived threat to one's product/services/production base from another's alternative technology known to be under serious consideration for development or which is actually being developed. There have been many cases in the chemical industry where the leading technology has been made technologically obsolescent 'overnight'. Indeed, in some cases, the old could not compete against the new despite written-off production plant. Knowledge of potential new technologies is provided by the early publication that flows from the patenting process. Many companies routinely evaluate new ideas and proposals revealed by an international patent-watch service, which covers most of the industrialised world's patent literature as it issues.

An offer of a licence under these circumstances can seem like an admission of vulnerability. But properly planned and presented it need not. The target company might welcome a licence. It might give it an immediate position in the market; it might remove the need for, or at least the urgency for, developing its new technology; it might open up avenues for technology cooperation, say, in the embryonic new technology to the parties' mutual advantage. The target company may not have any sound understanding of the competitive resilience of the current technology nor of the market barriers that any new product or differently made product may face. This is especially the case for effect materials, such as films, fibres and pharmaceuticals, and for products which downstream industry is tooled up to use in its operations and knows well.

Defensive patent licensing can also secure clear divisions of product markets because a licensee is less inclined to risk infringement when he has agreed a limited territorial licence and benefits from home market protection. Additionally the granting and taking of a licence adds stature to a patent and can dissuade other would-be infringers.

Opportunistic, revenue-generating patent licensing by companies only makes sense when a thorough assessment of the competitive impact of such licensing is undertaken and it is shown to be non-threatening. It is a feature of mature industries and markets. Licensing revenue is mostly extra profit; licence fees paid buy in to the fruits of creative R&D at a price usually much less than the true cost of developing equivalents. The patent owner would ordinarily indicate his terms for a licence, as a basis for negotiation. They will, of course, be optimistic but they should not be utterly unrealistic.

Scope issues

In any patent licensing the issue arises whether the licence should be exclusive (i.e., even of the patent owner), in respect of manufacture or both manufacture and sales; whether it should be sole (i.e., no other licensee to be appointed); or whether it should be non-exclusive (i.e., the patentee can license others as he wishes). There are many conceivable variants and combinations, especially as between manufacturing licences (e.g., local, exclusive at least for a period) and sales licences (e.g., international, non-exclusive). Prior to negotiations in earnest for a licence, the parties must assess their needs, their preferences and what they could accept. A patent owner may need to realise that any licence to a major player in a market may be in effect exclusive even if legally non-exclusive because that licence exhausts the opportunity to license, and export sales or direct entry into that market by him will confront insuperable barriers and economic resistance. Typical contents of patent licence agreements are discussed in detail in Parker op. cit. above.

The post-negotiation period

Once the negotiations are successfully completed, execution copies of the licence agreement will be prepared and duly signed by the parties in such manner as their corporate statutes or the relevant laws prescribe. The agreement may become binding at that time or it may first need to be approved or "taken on record" by the relevant authorities or central banks. The agreement will anticipate such conditions precedent and will usually set a time limit for achieving them. It may further specify that the licence grants will only be perfected when a down-payment is made. Given competent planning and preparation, these conditions precedent need not be a problem.

The agreement may have specified that the licensee will wish to register his licence to establish precedence in law over others who may claim a right under the patent. In that case the licensor will have agreed to cooperate as may be necessary for that purpose.

Unless a fully-paid up licence is bought by a lump-sum payment (or phased instalment), the agreement will have specified the licensee's obligations to report extent of working of the licensed patent and pay stipulated royalties, and perhaps to pay at least certain annual sums to keep the licence, or any special concession such as exclusivity, alive.

Other common post-agreement issues will relate to future grants of rights (or cross-licences) under so-called improvement patents, and what is to be done if the licence grant is "devalued" by unabated infringement of the licensed patent by third parties. These matters cannot be left for "agreement on the day". The agreement made must anticipate needs and must moderate unreasonable expectations. Provisions on future improvements call for knowledgeable definition if the parties are not to be disappointed. The importance of considering improvement patents derives from the reality that the patent system rewards the first to make and patent a new discovery. It is a "first past the post" system. The licensor and licensee are both in the race; the possibility of both discovering the same advances independently is real. Provisions to deal effectively with abating infringement are especially difficult to draw up. Indeed, they are always an uneasy compromise because the parties approach the issue from totally incompatible (but subjectively quite reasonable) positions. The licensee wants the licensor to stop all infringements by all necessary action at his cost and, meantime, the licensee would wish to be relieved of his royalty obligation (this is the level playing field rationale). The licensor wants to remain free to take such steps as he alone thinks fit in the circumstances. In the case of an exclusive licensee, there may be a statutory right to pursue an infringer. Any licensee can by agreement be empowered to challenge an infringer, usually by the patentee "lending his name" to the action. This is one common compromise arrangement.

Finally, another necessary agreement provision will be one setting out respective rights of termination of the licence unilaterally either from choice or for specified cause such as an uncured breach of a condition of the licence.

Box 11.2

A company made and sold a specialist plastic material. The company had developed and patented a particular coating application for that material and had a separate patent licensing arm that was profitably licensing the patent in different markets exclusively to selected coaters. An unlicensed coater had been buying the specialist plastic material from the company and sought assistance from the sales staff to help him make best use of the plastics material in his proposed coating application. Help was given until the patent licensing arm was asked by the local exclusive coating licensee to explain what was happening. There was much embarrassment and ill will.

The lesson here is ensure consistent policies are established and fully understood for sales of products, customer technical support, and licensing of product applications.

Vernon Parker

Knowhow licences

General

We have seen that, in the case of patent licences, the preparative enquiries are objective; factual as to the status of the relevant patents and with the patent documentation there for all to see. The issues of patent validity and enforceability, though demanding the services of expert advisers and being rarely totally unequivocal, are nevertheless ones capable of determination sufficient to shape negotiating strategy. There is no need to involve the patentee in this, nor would it be helpful to do so. Additionally, patents announce to the relevant industry sector, "Here we are", and by implication, "What are you going to do in response?" They advertise themselves.

The position is quite the opposite for knowhow. It is hidden within a product; it is confined within factory walls; it is held in confidence by company employees under their employment contracts; it is recorded in company reports to which access is controlled. The presence of leading edge knowhow is merely suggested to other companies in the same industry sector by the quality of the owning company's products, their competitiveness and other indicia of a particularly successful company or business. Individual items of knowhow can seem small and insignificant, but if you put a lot together and make them cooperate you have a powerful technology force.

There are no statistics but trading in knowhow is likely to come about as a result of enquiry from a company in the same industry sector, if not the same market region. Unless an exchange of knowhow were proposed the enquirer would not be expected to be a direct competitor of the company perceived to have desirable knowhow. In an exchange of knowhow (cross-licensing) there might be exchange of research and development information as well as applied operating information but in a one-way supply of knowhow it will surely be for applied information of proven utility in products, processes and services. The benefit to an acquirer of such knowhow is the economic impact of it on his business less the price paid (i.e., its utility value) or it is the saving in cost, effort and time which would have otherwise had to be expended in order to generate equivalent information independently (i.e., its investment saving).

Pre-enquiry

A factor in any consideration of whether to seek acquisition of knowhow (or for that matter a patent licence) is the added time element implicit in alternative strategies. This is the great uncertainty. R&D is unpredictable; success cannot be assured. The company is in what the Americans call "catch up mode" and inexorably the market moves on while the company is about it.

Another consideration for any company seeking to acquire technology-enhancing knowhow for privileged use in its market regions will be the impact of anti-competition laws if there should be restrictive conditions attaching to the licence (or effects ensuing from it) such as might distort or foreclose market competition. It is possible to relinquish a patent licence and you will know exactly where you stand, but you cannot unlearn confidential knowhow. You might box it in and abandon it, perhaps, if either you have a well-documented record of your pre-licence technology position or you have an opportunity to make a sideways or forwards leap in your technology portfolio as a result of distinct R&D, or business acquisition, or even another licence from an independent source. We shall revert to this later.

The enquiry phase

During the preparative and enquiry stages the suitor company cannot know what the target information in fact consists of. Since the best way to keep something secret is not to tell anyone, the owner company will be at pains not to reveal the nature of the information he possesses. A strategy has therefore to be devised which can bring the parties confidently to a deal, trusting it is the right thing to do, or alternatively before the position of either is compromised to call a halt to negotiations at any stage, and part on good terms. A word of caution is appropriate here. There is a compulsive desire amongst the technical and engineering fraternity to know details of how things are done. This commendable inquisitiveness must be curbed during negotiations towards a knowhow licence.

When an initial indication of interest in its knowhow has been received the target company will first satisfy itself that the enquiry concerns knowhow which it is prepared to licence and, further, that it is willing, in principle, to license this suitor company. The next step will be to put in place a non-disclosure agreement which will have two purposes: first, to structure and control the information flow so that it meets (and not more than that) the information needs of the companies to answer the question "Is there a fit between the knowhow that can be offered and the realistic needs of the enquiring company?" and, secondly, to stipulate the confidentiality obligations regulating disclosure, dissemination, copying and use of received information which must be accepted as a condition of its disclosure by the owner company.

The evaluation/assessment phase to which the non-disclosure agreement applies may involve a two-way flow of confidential information, or at least of information neither would wish to see broadcast, cost bases, efficiencies, scale of production, effluents and emissions, etc. The company possessing the targeted knowhow will strive to accomplish the evaluation/assessment without revealing too much of what its knowhow is while being forthright about what its knowhow could achieve for the enquirer, albeit without guarantee. It will not wish to be contaminated with any information about the technology base of the enquirer than that necessary to satisfy itself that the type of facilities, resources and skills possessed by the enquirer company are suitable for absorbing its knowhow (duly packaged).

The enquirer company must, at the very latest when the terms of the non-disclosure agreement and any enquiry questionnaires are being settled, ensure that its present knowledge is suitably fully recorded in a provable form as of a date prior to receipt of confidential information from the target company. This knowledge comprises that which is being used commercially, that which has been used on occasion as demand required, that which is in R&D reports, and that which describes plans, targets, approaches and methodology for R&D programmes in progress and intended to be implemented when space and funds allow. This is a major exercise but vital, since it is possible that the target knowhow will be found not to be significantly different as such but that what has made the difference in the perception of relative technology competence has been attention to detail, quality standards and controls, a skilful and experienced production team, and other such factors outside the technology "tool kit". A recommended practice is to deposit a sealed and dated package of the significant already possessed knowledge with a reputable outside body (a bank, or a leading firm of lawyers) with instructions that it is to be released only on the written request of the company solicitor or secretary, or corporate counsel.

No matter how close or far apart the technology "tool kits" of the two companies are, this provable record will be relevant to the effect of the confidentiality obligations accepted by the enquiry company both at the enquiry stage and more importantly (since then useful specific technical information is received) after the knowhow package has been purchased under licence.

The assessment/evaluation agreement

The reader will find in Parker op. cit. (above) a detailed review of the contents and effects of technical non-disclosure ("confidentiality") agreements but a brief outline is appropriate here of what a typical assessment/evaluation agreement would say.

Sometimes the agreement merely recognises that the prospective licensor will be supplying information of a certain class, without legally obliging him to do so. More usually, the prospective licensor undertakes to supply information of a certain class but only that which, in his sole judgement, will be sufficient to enable the recipient party to make a preliminary assessment of the technology and to determine his interest in acquiring a right to practise the technology. In some cases, the agreement will define by type, category, and depth of treatment, as well as form of presentation, the information to be supplied.

Even when the information to be supplied will have no practical utility but will be relevant only to a decision-making process the prospective licensee's non-disclosure obligations will consist of an undertaking not to disclose to other persons (individuals or companies) any received information and, perhaps additionally, the fact that the technology is being evaluated. There may be an obligation to confine received information to those regular employees, officers and directors who reasonably need to have it for the purpose of the evaluation.

Occasionally, individual recipients are required to countersign a copy of the agreement to acknowledge their understanding of their responsibilities. Sometimes, but not often, licensors insist on knowing who these individuals are. There is merit, in suitable cases, in limiting confidentiality to information supplied in written form, or promptly confirmed in writing.

The non-disclosure obligations should expressly not apply to, or should cease to apply to, information corresponding in substance to

1. Information already in the public domain by publications or otherwise (e.g., discernible by study or analysis or dismantling of things publicly available).
2. Information subsequently coming into the public domain except by default on the part of the recipient, his servants or agents.
3. Information which the recipient can show was in the recipient's possession at the time of receipt of the evaluation/assessment data, being information which is at the recipient's free disposal.
4. Information lawfully acquired by the recipient from a third party and which the recipient is no longer required to keep secret under the terms of acquisition from the third party. (Sometimes it is stated that the third party shall not have himself acquired the information directly or indirectly from the licensor).

One further exclusion should always be considered at the technology assessment stage. It is information which has been developed within the recipient's organisation after receipt of the received information, or alternatively, by persons who did not use or materially rely on received confidential information in the planning and execution of the development that generated that information. This provision is a shield not a sword to use against the licensor. What it does do is seek to exempt from restriction information acquired by duplication that has no causal connection with received information. If development of similar technology on similar lines is going on in the recipient company, but lagging behind perhaps in some or many aspects, the prospects for eventual honest duplication are real, certainly within the life of many confidentiality agreements. It ought to be possible for evaluating companies to avoid undue prejudice by some such provision backed up with tight administrative segregation of information and security practices. It involves 'proving a negative', but the evaluator should give himself a clear chance, in good faith, to answer effectively the charge that, but for receipt of the licensor's information, he would not have pursued this or that line of development or made this or that development. This added provision is particularly important when restrictions of use obligations are considered. These are always present and ordinarily consist of a straightgforward undertaking to use the information for the purposes of the evaluation and not otherwise. Again there must be exclusion of independently available information in categories 1 and 2 above and, if possible, independent developments should be excluded. Two further exclusions are needed.

First, a recipient should not be denied by contract the right to use as he pleases information already in his possession which was developed by him, however similar it may be to information he receives from the licensor.

Secondly, a recipient should not be denied the right to use information acquired by him at any time from a third party in whatever ways his arrangements with that third party allow. Sometimes, it is stated that the third party information should not have been obtained by the third party directly or indirectly from the licensor. This rider, which was also mentioned under non-disclosure obligations, will ensure that disclosures by contractors or other licensees in the course of discussions of previous experience of the licensor's technology will not defeat the letter of the secrecy agreement.

The agreement will have additional general provisions. These may deal with allowed disclosures to consultants/contractors and government agencies, and the terms governing such disclosures. The right, on terms, to pass the information to the licensee's parent or to subsidiaries may be conceded. A release to make disclosures required by a court in legal proceedings may be given. They may also deal with procedural matters such as the return of information after decision or after a set time period or even on demand, express limitations on copying, the right in any event to retain one copy of record in corporate confidential records, and reporting back the results of the evaluation. They often stipulate ("for avoidance of doubt") that no right or licence under any patent or patent application is implied or granted by the evaluation agreement.

The parties should always consider placing a time limit (a back-stop date) on "non-disclosure" and "restriction of use" undertakings. Perpetual obligations are a legal and administrative nuisance. The shortest time that reasonably protects the licensor from prejudicial use or disclosure of his confidential information is the minimum period; say 5 years for economic assessment data. A reasonable period in most cases, bearing in mind that technologies keep advancing or get replaced, and recognising the limited practical utility of information supplied to the potential licensee at the assessment stage is 10 years, exceptionally 15.

External constraints

It has been presumed in this section that licensor's patents are not relevant. We shall see later how the eventual licence agreement may deal with such matters, as a precaution. However, there is a need, at the evaluation/assessment stage, for the parties to feel comfortable that third-party patents will not be a problem. From the discussion on patents earlier it will be recalled that patents are national. National bodies of patents differ from one country to another, as different patentees have different patenting policies, some choosing to patent process technologies, others preferring to rely on secrecy and a local "right to work". This local "right to work" is not licensable or transferable, except with transfer of an entire business. So, the potential licensor should assure himself that the territory in to which his knowhow may pass for commercial use is indeed as patent-free as presumably his own is. Additionally he should expect to give an appropriate assurance to the prospective licensee at the evaluation stage because the prospective licensee is in no position then to assess the situation himself (because, as we have noted, he will not be given details of what the technology is). The prospective licensee may have done a general patent search and may seek specific assurances, but this is not a substitute for a clear general assurance from the prospective licensor based on his detailed search and enquiry in the clear knowledge of what knowhow is under consideration.

National governments subject exports of technology to controls of varying degrees of severity. Usually, the severity of control depends on the field of the technology and will vary from no controls (or a general licence) to notification and consent necessary. In some cases, a distinction will be made on the basis of the country to which the technology is being exported. But some national governments also control the import of technology and will seek to determine the terms on which technology is acquired. (This also applies to patent licences.) It should be noted that unapproved agreements may be void or unenforceable

---

Box 11.3

A technology owner decided to license technology to a foreign company through its own wholly owned subsidiary in the same country as the licensee. Agreements were drawn up and signed, which then had to be submitted to the Authorities for approval. The local subsidiary was essentially a promotional and sales-brokering company; its people knew nothing of technology licensing. The Authorities gave their approval subject to a reduction in the specified daily rates for technical/engineering services. The MD of the local subsidiary company agreed without reference back to his principals and the licence agreement took effect. As a result, services performed in support of the licence were rewarded at less than actual cost, seriously eroding the profit on the licence.

The lesson is of course to set proper controls in place if the technology owner who will perform the licence services is not the licensor.

Box 11.4

A small Central American company sought a technology licence from a European company in order to up-grade its production technology to higher safety standards. It was a minor matter for the European company, which produced and submitted a simple licence agreement specifying US dollar payments to a US bank account and its preferred choice of law of contract. The agreement language was accepted, after perfunctory changes, but almost as an afterthought before signature the European company sent the proposed licence document to reputable Central American lawyers only to be advised that the agreement would be void unless approved by sundry government departments and the reserve bank and that it would have been an illegal act for the licensee to execute the agreement and make payments under it.

There are two principal lessons. Firstly, do not assume the local licensee knows the laws and regulations surrounding licensing, which for him may be a rare occurrence. Secondly, when licensing to an unfamiliar environment take local independent advice and do not assume the norms of the industrialised world apply.

(even occasionally illegal). Accordingly at the evaluation/assessment stage the parties need to satisfy themselves that the contemplated transaction will be allowed by their national governments and they must identify any approval processes that may have to be gone through with the relevant authorities and any controls there may be on the eventual transfer of licence fees and royalties.

Payment and tax issues

At the assessment/evaluation stage it may be helpful if the parties give consideration to the tax regimes they are subject to for an international transaction. Certainly, during the purchase negotiations these issues will need to be clear and provided for. A detailed discussion of the tax treatment of patent licences, payment for documentary information supply, service fees, and licence fees for use of knowhow in different countries is beyond the scope of this work but an outline of the common treatment is given later in this chapter. It will be possible at the assessment/evaluation stage for the prospective licensor to indicate the fee he would seek to charge for assembling and transferring a defined package of information. This fee would include compensation for the effort involved in assembling the package (with a profit element usually) and, importantly, would reward the disclosure of useful knowhow to another with an option (or licence) to use it. It would not reward the value of the knowhow package to a prospective licensee. That value is difficult to quantify at this stage and must be left to the detailed licence negotiation stage when an objective (or at least a sensible pragmatic) basis of determination will emerge as the relative capabilities of the two technology positions can be economically compared.

A possible distorting influence on the negotiation of licence fees arises when the prospective licensor has already licensed essentially the same technology or IP rights to another on terms such that, if more favourable terms should be offered to a later licensee in equivalent circumstances, those more favourable terms must be offered to the existing licensee.

The licence agreement and beyond

When the negotiation process has reached a satisfactory consensual conclusion, the agreement capturing in binding contractual form the parties' undertakings and promises will be put in place, much as described above. Space does not permit a discussion of the typical full contents of such an agreement, but again details may be found in Parker op. cit. Two points of difference from patent licences deserve mention, however. First, the scope of the licence, as between the parties, might be as discussed earlier in this chapter but the critical factor here is that there can be no exclusivity against an independent possessor of similar knowhow. Secondly, the licensee will be concerned if he finds his freedom to use the acquired knowhow in the intended way is prevented or hampered by third party patents. The licence agreement must address this issue in some acceptable, but inevitably compromise fashion.

Combined patents/knowhow licences

General

It is indeed possible to envisage a knowhow only licence as being the entire licence basis of a major business venture by a company in an industry sector which is entirely new to it. Such is the diversity of industry and the maturity of sectors within it. Additionally, the world is not a single market; there are regional markets existing alongside each other at different stages of technology and product development and with different customer needs and preferences. The barriers to entry confronting a company in one region that has an eye to doing business in another can be insuperable. Technology can cross the barriers where companies may not.

It is likewise possible for combined knowhow and patent licences to have as their primary aim to supplement and enhance existing capabilities. In this treatment, however, we shall focus on a total technology licence comprising a structured, investment focused package of knowhow and patent rights the object for which is to establish a production capability with technology entirely new to the prospective licensee. We shall assume the product is either also new to the licensee's business or is in material respects significantly different from its current counterpart in the licensee's business. We shall assume there are to be export sales.

The matters already discussed above are relevant but what adds a new dimension of depth and complexity to the assessment and evaluation stages in this instance are the substantial financial and market risks on not getting the choice of technology right, not enjoying the rights and opportunities that were expected, not establishing the production facility properly and on time, and not being able effectively to market the products. The assessment and evaluation stages must anticipate all these issues even though it will be the ultimately negotiated licence agreement that will enshrine the contractual and legal provisions designed to assure, so far as practicable, that desired outcome. Licensees need success, but licensors desire success too — and not merely to avoid legal disputes and liabilities.

A major investment in new production technology forces early decisions on

- What kind of technology to use?
- Whose version of it to acquire?
- What scale and location for a first plant?
- Are suitable raw materials/feedstocks, utilities and services available?
- What by-products, effluents and wastes have to disposed of?
- How new to the licensee are the component unit operations?
- Are skilled operators available?
- Is there a certain market for the principal product(s)?
- Does the existing customer base need to be weaned onto the new/different product(s)? and of course,
- Does the prospective initial investment outlay make financial sense?

Vernon Parker

Pre-negotiation planning and enquiry

A company seeking to license in technology will seek to shortlist types and sources of appropriate technologies from which a choice is to be made. This will involve enquiries on the major international engineering contractors who offer their own technologies or provide conduits for operating companies' technologies where those companies do not have the resources, or inclination, to be involved directly in licensing. It will involve enquiries on operating companies who do license their technologies direct. It should further involve enquiries on leaders in the relevant technology in other market regions who may not, so far, have considered licensing their technologies. This is a resource-consuming activity and consideration should be given to engaging a consultant firm to make these enquiries on the prospective licensee's behalf. This may be more efficient and effective and has the further advantage that it may be possible to preserve licensee anonymity during the general enquiry phase.

A licensor company that is itself in the product business may seek through its licensing policy to dissuade particular prospective licensors from investment because of a perceived threat to its product business. However, if it becomes convinced that the prospective licensee is determined to invest it may prefer to license its technology rather than see another's technology used. This is not just about possible earnings. A licensor inevitably knows the scale and technology basis of his licensee's plant. He controls the extent to which the licensed technology may be used for expansions or additional plants, and where those may be located. He may also impose a feedback (or exchange) of operational improvements, even R&D advances in the field, made by his licensee. All these benefits impact on relative competitiveness.

An advantage of having the basic design of the licensed production plant supplied directly or indirectly by an operating company licensor (even if detailed engineering procurement and construction are contracted out) is that the technology is likely to work as intended and the investment and unit product cost will be reasonably predictable. If the prospective licensor is not itself an operating company, even though it may have apparently successfully licensed its technology, there are significant risks to a potential licensee. First, the licensor's knowledge of precisely what his licensees have done, for example to solve problems inherent in the technology supplied to them, may be limited. Secondly, such licensors use new licensees as test beds for technology- or design variants which have not been proven at the commercial scale. Licensees may have little contractual redress and may not have the knowledge and skills to solve encountered problems.

If the proposed licence is a one-plant licence, from licensee choice or because that is all that is offered, there will be a tendency to go for a larger plant size. Indeed, the relationship between investment capital and plant capacity is usually favourable to increasing size. However the so-called "break even" occupacity of a production plant may be high, say $>60\%$ even $>80\%$. So, the licensee needs to be confident in his market projections for product sales and needs to consider the impact of having to shut down older capacity.

Evaluation

A strategy which should always be considered by a prospective licensee is to purchase from a preferred potential licensor a package comprising a basic process- and outline engineering design together with a clear licence option in which all the essential provisions are spelled out. (This option is the fall-back position of the licensee; it can be renegotiated when the technology has been fully evaluated). Of course, the package will be supplied only on strict confidentiality terms and will cost money. But, what it does is: enable the licensee himself to evaluate and cost the technology; to have an informed debate with the licensor and consider alternatives; to assess the patent position thoroughly; to visit other licensees and see how the technology has been implemented by them; to confirm that the licensor can transfer the technology effectively; to confirm capital cost estimates; to confirm suitability of other sources of raw materials; to confirm that the product will sell; to establish effluent and emissions standards. This process is enormously confidence building.

Of course, if the prospective licensee decides after such a detailed evaluation not to proceed with the offered technology and later elects to proceed with another's technology for his investment, he is exposed to challenge from the disappointed licensor that there has been mis-use of the knowledge provided by that licensor. It is therefore vital that a prospective licensee has well-understood control policies in place so that such a challenge can be rebutted and further that he secure an assurance that the ultimately chosen licensor will cooperate in the defence of any such challenge, e.g., by agreeing to an independent arbitrator or expert being engaged to determine or advise on the dispute and even, if unavoidable, cooperating in a court defence.

It was mentioned earlier that a remedy available to a patentee for infringement is an injunction. Indeed if there is a prima-facie showing of infringement, an interim injunction may be granted by a court before there has been any serious consideration of the merits of the patent. A major investment must not be exposed to such risks. Most licensors will make bland comfort statements during the evaluation phase but responsible licensors know they must do more. It is fairly straightforward to deal in the eventual licence agreement with the licensor's own patent portfolio, by express licences and so-called hold-harmless undertakings related to use of classes of information or defined kinds of activity. Opportunity should also be taken to discuss with an operating company licensor whether licences or cross-licences might be granted for significant patented downstream uses of products such that the licensee may use products in these ways or may sublicense his customers to do so. A hold-harmless undertaking is a contractual promise not to sue under any patents that may cover the use of defined information in defined ways for defined purposes or against defined acts (e.g., product sales or downstream uses). A pure knowhow licence may include such an undertaking for the licensee's peace of mind.

Box 11.5

A technology consultant had, by report, successfully licensed new production technology for a special industrial solvent. A company negotiated to buy a basic design package on strict confidentiality terms together with a licence option which could be brought into force within an allowed review period. On review and as confirmed by a visit to an existing licencee the technology was shown to suffer from significant unsolved problems. The company proceeded with a combination of its own technology and technology acquired under licence from another operating company. The rejected licensor sued for mis-use of his confidential information. He was unsuccessful but the publicity was unwelcome and the defence costly in lawyer's bills and technical assessors' fees.

The lesson here is to ensure the technology record is clear and complete. Be especially diligent in recording your own technology position before receiving evaluation packages from others. Lawsuits are a fact of business life, so make sure you can defend yourself effectively.

Scope issues

During the enquiry phase the prospective licensor and potential licensee will have discussed the extent to which the licensed production technology might be used to establish further production plant and where these might be located. (Obviously, expansions of the first plant must be accommodated.) Likewise, the potential licensee will have clarified where export sales of product will be allowed. This subject has a number of distinct aspects to consider. First, a right to use knowhow supplied as a design package of a first plant for the design of further plants is an empty right if the licensee does not have the competence to design such plants. So, a potential licensee should ensure that he will acquire from the licensor not merely an instruction kit to engineer, build and operate a particular plant but also an insight into the basis of its design. Additionally, he may seek assurances that the licensor will provide design services for a new plant. The eventual licence agreement will have to clarify and define this service and, in particular, address the question of whether the new design will embody licensee's and licensor's improvements subsequently developed and on what terms. A licensee would be expected to implement R&D — and production process support — programmes for any technology underpinning a core business activity. Secondly, licensors may seek to prevent, by imposing contractual undertakings, product sales in given territories or outside a defined licensed distribution area. The legality and enforceability of such impositions will need to be researched before they can be agreed. However, it is legitimate for licensors to reserve the right to enforce their patents in territories where they wish to prevent, so far as the law permits and their patents allow, imports of licensee's products. These patents might be for production processes/operations or for products possessing certain distinguishing characteristics. Major consumer uses of the products may also be under the licensor's control through their patents in export territories. A clear understanding of all these proposed restrictions, impositions and limitations (and their legal effectiveness) needs to emerge from the enquiry and evaluation stages.

As a further assurance to a prospective licensor and the potential licensee, it may be agreed that the prospective licensor or one of his existing licensees should process raw materials or feedstocks of the sorts intended by the licensee for the licensed plant to ensure they will be suitable. Likewise, it may be agreed that the potential licensee will purchase products from the prospective licensor or one of his licensees to ensure that the products will be suitable for the intended market or downstream consuming units. This might be part of an assisted market development strategy.

Box 11.6

A company in the Far East made and sold chemicals of the kind known as plasticizers. It used a classical production technology. A European company had devised a new, more economic technology that also produced a different quality product. The Far East company sought a basis for design ("design package") for a "greenfield" plant of nominal 15000 tes/yr capacity. It explained it would use the information to design and build a plant capable of using both the new technology and the classical technology, in campaigns, as product demand required. It was agreed to license the Far East company, but on a clear legal basis that the licensor would not be responsible for the outcome. The new plant did not work well and the licensee complained to the licensor's Chief Executive that the information supplied had been inadequate. For business reasons, the licensor chose, at its cost and expense, to send specialists to the Far East to assist, successfully, in resolving the problem. Fortunately, the licensor was very familiar with both technologies.

The lesson here is that, as a legal matter, you may have a contract that shields you from all responsibility and liability but in the wider context it may avail you nothing. There is probably another lesson. Be very circumspect about licensing technology for other than the specific purpose the design was produced for.

Financial Issues

The financial provisions of a licence agreement will receive much attention during the negotiation process. The magnitude of service fees (including the payment for an information package) and of licence payments on a present worth (DCF) basis will be set by finally reaching congruence between what the respective parties felt they could impose or afford in the particular circumstances facing them. External influences may have constrained free choice, such as Government intervention in the approvals process and any prior undertakings to other licensees ("equal treatment clauses"). The sums that the licensee has to pay for exploitation of his licence may be certain in amount and timing (licence fees) or be periodic payments based on the measured extent of use (royalties). The tax impact and the risk will be different in the two cases. The method of calculation of sums due to the licensor, how they are paid (how frequently, what currency and by what route) and how tax withholdings are treated will be specified in detail. Of concern to the licensor will be the levels of withholding taxes applied to payments by the licensee for information packages prepared and delivered in the licensor's home country, for services performed in the licensor's home country (design reviews, operator training), for services performed in the licensee's country (construction reviews, commissioning, operations support) and for the exploitation of the licensed technology and patents. The existence of a Double Taxation Treaty or legislation granting credit unilaterally will be significant. Additionally, for tax reasons or because of the particular contributions made to the value of the licence by patents and knowhow respectively, it may be important to either party to deal with the financial provisions of the patent licence separately from those for the knowhow licence. Any payment consequences of the future supply by one party to the other of improvements to the licensed technology (patented or not) will be agreed.

Box 11.7

A licence was granted to an Asian company through an international contractor who was given a right to licence by the technology owner and who had a contract with the technology owner for necessary technical and process engineering services. The contractor would collect the licence fees and would transfer them to the technology owner under the back-to-back arrangements. There would be a 30 per cent withholding tax on licence fee payments by the Asian company. The contractor became concerned, after contracts had come into force, that its trading position might result in it not being able to use all the certified tax withholding as a credit against its domestic tax liability. The technology owner stood to make a budget loss because the contractor was only obliged to pass on benefit received. A new set of agreements had to be put in place urgently to replace the contractor by the technology owner as the licensor of the rights. Fortunately, all parties and the Asian Government authorities cooperated to achieve this promptly. Subsequently it was discovered that wrong assumptions had been made as to the effective levels of tax withholdings on payments for information packages produced abroad and on payments for certain types of services. Under the agreement's payment clauses this gave rise to a budget loss to the Contractor and an unforeseen bonus to the licensee.

The lesson is that the parties need to give thorough attention to the peculiar tax regimes that can apply to technology licences and services, and to ensure the benefits of tax credits for tax withholdings can be taken.

The Legal Significance of the Negotiation Process

It is critical that neither party to the negotiations give undertakings or make promises that are legally enforceable except in those specific agreed respects which are necessary for the parties to determine whether a basis for an effective licence of technology or IP Rights exists. There should be no warranties or guarantees given during the negotiations. What is to be supplied/granted, its scope, form, restrictions, limitation and timing are determined by the ultimately executed agreement, as are the financial terms for services, options, and exploitation of licence grants. Responsibilities and liabilities for performance and non-performance, including excuses and capping, are also set by the executed licence agreement, nowhere else so far as understandings between the parties are concerned. Indeed, it is a common provision in licence agreements to declare and agree that the licence agreements and their schedules contain the entire understanding and agreement between the parties, excepting for an earlier confidentiality agreement which may not be wholly superseded by the licence agreement. All that preceded will be declared of no relevance or effect.

Prior to negotiations, the parties should make it clear in a written memorandum or exchange of letters that they intend to negotiate in good faith but that nothing of legal effect will arise unless recorded in a duly signed memorandum expressed to create legally enforceable obligations.

Too cynical a view of this practice should not be taken. It is legally necessary (because some legal systems will otherwise impute legal obligations before a party is consciously ready to accept them) and it is practically useful because it frees up the negotiations and allows the parties to work through proposals in some detail on a "what if" basis.

Each party to the negotiations will wish to be assured that those who act for the other party have capacity and authority to negotiate in good faith. This can be achieved at a suitable initial face-to-face meeting of the parties when a senior corporate or business general manager is present for each side. The negotiating team would typically comprise a Project Manager or Licensing Manager, as the case may be, who will have a technical and business background, and they may be supported by technical, engineering, legal and IP specialists as appropriate to the demands of the negotiations.

The negotiations should be periodically face-to-face to ensure that misunderstandings are aired openly and to maintain the momentum. In parallel, there will be written communications conveying information, and making considered proposals for discussion by the parties. In particular, at an appropriate stage the prospective licensor (usually) will table a pro-forma outline licence agreement for consideration. This will be an indication of one party's view of the matters on which there needs to be ultimate agreement, neither a check-list nor an offer. Indeed specific essential matters will be left blank. Depending on progress in the negotiations this outline draft licence agreement will be worked up by both parties, usually by their legal/IP specialists at Head Office, and drafts exchanged. These drafts will both reflect "agreed" matters and progressively become an agenda for the hard-nosed debate to fix the bargain in a legal and contractual format. They will also deal with uncontentious issues that must be specified but need not occupy the attentions of the principal negotiators e.g. reporting and payment routings for fees and royalties, currency exchange calculations, tax withholdings and certificates, the effective date of the agreement, any necessary government or central bank procedures and approvals, and what the Americans delightfully call "the boiler plate": *Force Majeure*; choice of law of contract; Assignment; Termination for Default; right of independent audit of royalty-relevant facts; dispute resolutions. A discussion of the typical full contents of different types of licence agreement and of the different ways in which essential matters may be expressed as well as of the different contractual and legal effects of different language is beyond the scope of this work. Again the reader is recommended to refer to Parker (op. cit.) for a more detailed exposition.

Culture Traits

A discussion of the manner and style of the negotiation process cannot conclude without brief reference to cultural impediments to smooth progress. Cultural impediments can be corporate as well as national. A US Attorney once blurted out in a meeting with the writer, "There is   morality in business". This certainly set the tone for subsequent meetings since there is much in the performance of licensing agreements which, though couched as a legal obligation, cannot be ordered to be done by a court, the only remedy being damages if provable. Damages are not equivalent to performance, if performance is what you must have. Generally, it might be inferred, perhaps wrongly by Europeans, that in the USA lawyers have a greater role and influence in business dealings than their value would justify. Certainly, the USA is a litigious country and the burden and expense of litigation in the USA is daunting, so much so that US laywers are prone to use this as leverage for opportunistic settlements of disputes. More importantly, a US company sees a licence agreement as an entirety. Nothing is agreed until all is agreed. Their negotiators will readily revisit earlier seemingly settled points whereas the British tend to be embarrassed to do so without some clear reason that can now be seen to necessitate it. A bad trait found in British companies is for a senior executive to "agree" with his opposite number "the deal" without proper consideration of the full implications and to delegate it to "the lawyers to work out the details" — like a master artist or composer might let his prodigies fill in his canvas or manuscript. In other cultures (and the writer has met this in France and Japan) a senior executive who does evidently have the power to commit his company will insist on leading negotiations for his company. His team cannot allow him to lose "face" and neither may they negotiate independently to facilitate progress. The importance of "face" in some Eastern countries is always emphasised to western negotiators. A recommended practice is to engage as translators and facilitators persons who have lived and worked in both relevant cultures, and to do serious negotiations of contentious points by exchange of documents.

Appendix IP Rights

Patents

1. A statutory monopoly for creativity in applied science and engineering. Patents for new products and industrially applicable techniques/processes are granted, country by country, on application. A block European Application designating chosen countries is possible. The Patent Cooperation Treaty (PCT) also offers a valuable procedural option for multinational protection.

2. The term of monopoly is set by National Statutes but is now mostly 20 years from the application date (if fees paid).

3. There must be an invention step (i.e., not obvious) over "prior art". The challenge in the patenting process is to conceive of and define a generic class of thing or method/process, all embodiments of which (and not just those you have tried) would be reasonably expected to show the demonstrated new, non-obvious inventive quality. It is this definition which determines the scope of the monopoly granted. To achieve its purpose it must not make a free gift to the world of easily devised equivalents to what has been shown to work by using language that is too restrictive, but at the other extreme it must not be covetous and, say, seek to monopolise all solutions to a problem.

4. "Prior art" means all public knowledge at date of application for patent (not at date of making invention). US rules still treat invention date as controlling if patenting is not too long delayed.

5. Own non-confidential disclosure will destroy patentability, if before date of priority application, except for USA patents if applied for within one year of first disclosure or commercial public use.

6. A patent is infringed by working within the claimed monopoly, including importation of product made abroad by a process covered by the patent. Relief includes an injunction, damages or an account of profits.

7. A patent does not give the patentee the right to work his invention. Other earlier local patents of third parties could prevent working, e.g., where the later patent is for an inventive improvement on an earlier patented system.

8. A patentee does not (unless local statutory conditions on inexcusable non-working/inadequate working are met) have to license his patent.

9. Secret commercial use by a third party gives him a personal right to continue use in the EEC and in some countries will even invalidate the patent.

In the USA, if the prior use is not such as to defeat the patent, the prior user has no rights under the patent.

10. Patenting is expensive — say up to £2000 per country for an initial 5 years cover. (Includes agent's fees, translations, official fees.)

Registered designs/design rights

1. A monopoly for aesthetic designs applied to articles of manufacture and granted, country by country, on application.

2. The term of the monopoly is broadly similar to that for patents, again if maintenance fees are paid — but this is not an expensive form of protection.

3. To be registrable, the design must be new as judged by its appeal to the eye. Function is irrelevant and purely functional designs are not registrable.

4. Newness (whether in form, shape, ornament or pattern) at date of application is essential.

5. Rights are infringed by making or producing articles to that design (or moulds or patterns) without consent. No requirement to prove copying. Relief is as for patents.

6. Design copyright can be important for articles that are artistic works and may give similar automatic rights without formality, if there has been direct or indirect copying of the design.

7. Additionally, design right protection may be available for purely functional designs and designs devoid of aesthetic appeal. Must fit/must match designs will probably be excluded. The UK Design Right period of protection is 10 years from date first applied industrially. Design must be original but need not be new.

Registered trade marks

1. Effectively a perpetual national monopoly (if fees paid), but an honest concurrent user is protected. In Europe, the new Community Trade Mark has been introduced — a single registration of effect throughout the Community.

2. A registrable trade mark is any invented word, any pictorial device, symbol or logo, any name written in a distinctive way (e.g., a signature) or any other distinctive mark.

3. Prior use — no bar. Indeed helpful.

4. Purpose of trade mark to indicate a connection in the course of trade between particular goods and the owner of the trade mark.

5. Registration is for classes of goods.

6. Use of the mark by others without consent (if used as a trade mark on goods within the class or classes for which it is registered) is an infringement actionable by the owner.

7. Not too expensive to get.

Copyright in literary works

1. Copyright in literary works exists automatically when the work is fixed in some form.

2. It is an internationally recognised right of authors and those who commission such works.

3. It is free.

4. It is a long term right to prevent copying of the work (or any substantial part of it) for public or commercial purposes.

5. Licence documentation is copyright.

6. Significantly, computer programs/software are increasingly being granted copyright on the same basis as for classical literary works.

The protection of confidential information

None of the above statutory intellectual property rights directly gives protection for confidential, secret and proprietary technical knowledge either against prejudicial disclosure or publication (since design and copyright concerns form of expression not intellectual content) or against prejudicial use (except to the extent a field of use is dominated by patents still in force). Were there not such protection available, or were it of application only to higher orders of information such as uniquely held trade secrets, licensing would not be the major international activity that it is.

When information is acquired as a result of confidential dealings, or through the performance of a contract, and it was implicit in the relationship or expressly or implicitly agreed that the information was supplied only for a specific purpose and was not to be used for other purposes and was to be held in confidence, legal obligations are created not to disclose or use the information except in approved ways and these will be enforceable under contract law or, as the case may be, through an action under "fair dealing" laws where there has been prejudice to supplier of the information.

This is the legal basis for the protection of a licensor's confidential and secret information. The protection rests solely on the true construction of the licensee's self-restricting obligations, normally as determined by express contractual under-takings but sometimes by a necessary implication the law reads into the relationship and the nature of the transaction. There is not a property right in knowledge. Thus, another person may possess the same information independently. He can publish, use, license or sell it as he sees fit. Independent publication would ordinarily cancel a licensee's duty not to disclose (or not to use in unlicensed ways) that information. Even a licensee may find he already possesses some of what the licensor has disclosed to him and ordinarily he would not be further constrained by the licence agreement on to what he may do with it.

CHAPTER 12

Negotiating International Joint Ventures

SABINE URBAN

Introduction

Joint ventures (JV) represent an operational framework for merging and integrating businesses. When they become international, they take part in a process of multinationalization of protagonist corporations and are part of the vast movement of globalization that the world economy has known since the 1980s; this explains the importance of the JV phenomenon we have witnessed in recent years.

Contrary to the purely contractual partnership agreements, joint ventures are characterized by the creation of a new corporate identity, whose equity is owned by several existing companies. That is, JVs account for only a part of the range of strategic alliances, as clearly illustrated by Figure 12.1 taken from Yoshino and Rangan (1995). In exchange, these founding companies create an autonomous structure which corresponds to a relatively precise and predetermined operational framework. This underscores the importance of negotiating this frame of reference.

The problem presented is not simple because it not only encompasses the procedures involved in creating a new company but also touches on its very foundations, that is on its *raison d'être*. Here negotiation aims to develop an agreement among several companies that have decided to act jointly in operational areas such as research, production, or the marketing of goods or services. At least two different countries are involved: the context of the negotiation will be therefore more of less complex because of the need to accommodate different cultures and distinct operational styles (socio-economic, political, psychological, regulatory, technical). However, the parties involved in the joint venture desire to embark on a common venture. "Joint" signifies that the companies which agree to become linked have common expectations based on identical or complementary goals. These goals will only be achieved if the participating parties (the JV shareholders) behave with a sense of fair play in a climate of reciprocal trust. Nonetheless, potential conflicts are not excluded. The term "venture" inevitably includes an element of risk and should be expected as early as the

FIGURE 12.1
Range of inter-firm links

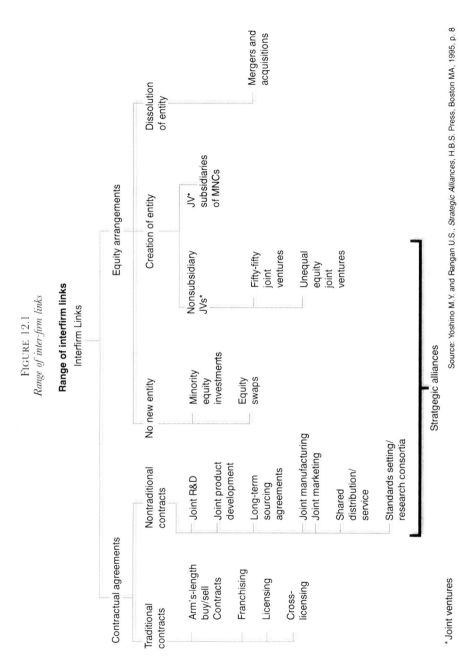

Source: Yoshino M.Y. and Rangan U.S., *Strategic Alliances*, H.B.S. Press, Boston MA, 1995, p. 8

negotiation process, with solutions envisioned from the onset: adequate organization, methods of conflict resolution, and a control system.

In the beginning, each of the partners in the joint venture has specific interests. Are these interests clearly expressed or partially hidden? What are they? Are they coherent and compatible with the interests of the other partners? Can they be balanced against the interests of the other parties concerned in the IJV? We will attempt to shed light on these questions, and the responses we propose appear below under "The Participants".

We move then to the identity of the collaborative creation: the IJV, its objectives, and its architecture — results of the negotiations ("The Organization of Coexistence within the IJV").

Finally, we will address problems linked with "Negotiating the evolution of and withdrawal from an IJV".

The Participants

Negotiations are animated in the early stages by actors who are seeking to optimize their individual interests. The expectations of each of the parties participating in this process form the background of the negotiations.

Once these individual interests are brought to light and consciously assimilated into the negotiator's minds, they are debated among future partner-shareholders in the IJV in order to bring them together toward a joint organization.

Individual expectations, the basis of negotiations

Negotiations begin once each company involved has analyzed its particular situation in terms of its resources and its strengths and weaknesses, has compared them to needs and demands required by its development strategy, and has arrived at the conclusion that a joint commitment appears more promising than an independent project.

The quality of the motivations specific to each company constitute therefore a first element in the negotiations (A). The nature and the strength of these motivations are, in fact, largely dependent on the environment framework (industry segment, country) in which the companies are evolving (B). It is appropriate also to reflect upon the strategic context of each of the future partner-shareholders because it will likely affect their reactions during the course of the negotiation process (C).

A. Initial motivations of participating companies

It is clear that at the inception of an IJV, each party seeks to defend its individual interests, expressed by the development of its added value and an increase in profitability.

233

Sabine Urban

Concerns relating to access

- to technological competencies already mastered by the partner or to be developed jointly (new pharmaceutical molecule or space technology, for example)
- to raw materials which are more or less strategic or rare
- to products controlled by an oligopolistic structure: "Euroglas" was created in Alsace (France) by two glass processing companies, German and Swiss, in order to insure that the two founding companies would have control over their supply
- to complex fields of activity (telecommunications, information technology, aviation)
- to regulated or protected markets: thanks to an IJV created in 1988 between McDonald's and the city of Moscow, the world's largest McDonald's was inaugurated in Moscow in 1990 (Garrette & Dussauge 1995, p. 115)
- to cultural competencies and the relational network of local partners.

These objectives of access are relatively radical in character because, in the absence of IJV, the development orientations mentioned above would be extremely difficult, if not impossible. Less categorical, but just as important, are the objectives of the second category.

Objectives of improving competitiveness We can regroup the keys to international competitiveness by distinguishing three categories of factors: those which are quantifiable in monetary terms (price), those focused on the qualitative characteristics of the products produced, and those linked to the organizational competencies or the mastery of cultural elements (Urban 1993).

In order to clarify the presentation of these arguments, we assume a matrix structure of the firm (Figure 12.2).

Any IJV in the negotiation phase may refer to one of three levels of corporate responsibility:

- functional efficiency: agreements for manufacturing, sales, research development, etc. The desired effects are economy of scale, cost sharing according to the specific competencies of each player, qualitative improvement of services, re-engineering, "lean management", etc., i.e., optimal management of the supply side, including opportunities created by relocating activities taking into account comparative costs from country to country and monetary parities
- competitive dynamics of activities: effects of synergism, strategies for access to new markets or innovation systems, good adaptation to demand and to change
- potential for corporate development: effects on the corporate image, negotiating power, risk-taking, financial performance, organizational efficiency.

FIGURE 12.2
A matrix structure of the firm

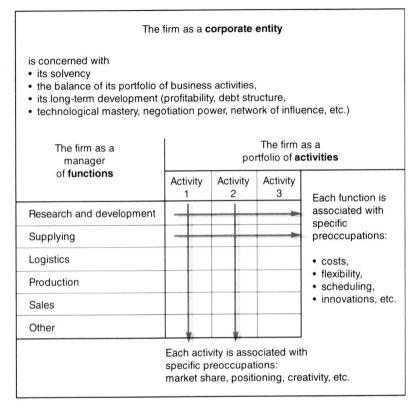

The firm as a corporate entity

is concerned with
• its solvency
• the balance of its portfolio of business activities,
• its long-term development (profitability, debt structure,
• technological mastery, negotiation power, network of influence, etc.)

The firm as a manager of **functions**	The firm as a portfolio of **activities**			
	Activity 1	Activity 2	Activity 3	Each function is associated with specific preoccupations:
Research and development				
Supplying				• costs,
Logistics				• flexibility,
Production				• scheduling,
Sales				• innovations, etc.
Other				

Each activity is associated with specific preoccupations: market share, positioning, creativity, etc.

At each level of responsibility, an IJV can prove especially useful — if not indispensable — in certain sectors for benefiting from the heterogeneity of the global environment in terms of size, costs, compared resources, and monetary parities. By crossing the variables of competitiveness factors with the motives of the founding IJV companies, we arrive at the following Table 12.1.

B. The motives of IJV partners depend on the context in which they evolve

Because these aspects are discussed in detail in Part IV of this book, we will only point out here that in a given industry the conditions for success and the rules for competition are determined by competitive forces. The model proposed by Porter (1985) regroups five determining forces of the competitive structure:

• rivalry among firms within the industry
• the power of negotiating with clients

Sabine Urban

TABLE 12.1
IJV and the competitiveness of partners

Competitiveness factors	Motives of IJV partners
1. Costs, price	• cost savings from resource sharing • economies of scale through overcoming entry barriers to international markets; search for critical size • risk-sharing • reduction of transaction costs • reduction of tax burden and environmental costs • lengthening of the product life cycle (phase 3, maturity, being the most profitable)
2. Qualitative factors	• pooling of rare resources • skill or technology transfer • good adaptation to demand and to local norms • enlargement of product range • stimulation of creativity by integrating diversity • creation of new competencies • contribution to vertical integration along the production and distribution chain • exit from traditional business core activity of the partners • improvement of the strategic position of the partners by a rapid entry onto the market (time management, shortened product life cycles) • creation and utilization of economic ratchet factors
3. Organizational factors	• improved bargaining power • organizational learning • transformation of competitors into allies with whom to face common competitors • improved coverage of the world market • better local acceptance (by bringing resources, foreign currencies, employment, revenues) • collaboration leading to one-time or occasional projects

- the power of negotiating with suppliers
- the threat of newcomers in the industry
- the threat of substitute products or services.

It is with respect to these forces that each partner of the future IJV will model its strategy for negotiation, according to information that it possesses regarding the above aspects and on the positions or support of the other partner(s) (Reix 1995).

Each type of business generates its own constraints; each company has its own efficiency perspective and its strategic vision.

C. The companies's negotiation and strategic vision

The goal of the negotiation process will depend on the competitive position of each of the parties and on its major strategic objectives as shown in the following Table 12.2.

236

TABLE 12.2
Relative importance of strategic objectives in alliances

Alliance type	Strategic objectives[a]			
	Flexibility	Core protection	Learning	Value adding
Precompetitive	****	***	**	*
Competitive	*	****	***	**
Noncompetitive	**	*	****	***
Procompetitive	***	**	*	****

[a] Number of asterisks indicates relative importance in each alliance type.
Source: Yoshino M.Y. and Rangan U.S., *Strategic Alliances*, H.B.S. Press, Boston MA, 1995, p. 22.

Each field of business results in a more or less strong environmental pressure which gives a more or less comfortable position at the negotiation table.

In the process of globalization (Urban 1992) the contribution of the JV becomes more and more important (Hyder and Ghauri 1993). Several reasons for this trend are suggested:

- negotiating power has eroded for multinational corporations in less developed zones (because of their desire to secure their expertise) (Connolly, 1984)
- multinational companies discovered the potential contributions of local partners (specific skills, costs, local relations …) (Hall 1984)
- corporate and national development policies are becoming more and more interdependent; one cannot exist without the other (Contractor and Lorange 1988; Porter 1990); a structured platform for dialogue (IJV) is thus required.

From a theoretical point of view, these considerations are consistent with the Swedish model of internationalization: the model of Uppsala (Mattson and Johanson 1993) which describes the process of internationalization as an increasing commitment to international sales and production as part of growth and experimental learning processes. In this model, internationalization is described as a sequential learning process by which a company goes through stages of increased commitment to foreign markets: from exportation or licensing to international direct investment and IJV. In this way, a new system of international relations is developed, one that is more united, under the form of interconnected networks. These networks imply, of course, the negotiation of new procedures for coordinating and balancing power (Thorelli 1990).

The negotiation process

The process of negotiation should normally lead to the creation of the new joint venture (IJV) supposing that no misunderstandings between the partners occurred to stop the process with disagreements that are too difficult to be solved. The creation of an IJV is an arduous and risky process, as attest the high number of failures of new IJV (Contractor & Lorange 1988; Zahra & Elhagrasen 1994).

The primary difficulty resides in the choice of partners; agreeing on the methods for running the negotiations, and on the methodical organization of the steps involved in the negotiations.

Box 12.1 IJV without illusions, in China

"As foreigners, we are courted here as long as the Chinese need us." The choice of an industrial and commercial partner is essential, the hiring and training of quality personnel is also decisive. But over all interpersonal trust should be favored because the Chinese are in the habit of considering a signed contract as only a starting point for discussion, which can be reconsidered. In order to establish oneself in China, one cannot be naïve!

The comments are made and illustrated by directors in China of Chinese–German JVs: Lufthansa, Wella, Bayer, BASF, Hoechst, Krupp, Siemens, Henkel, Volkswagen. (*Source: Manager Magazine,* April 1995)

Finding the right partner

Very often industrial partners know one another before entering into negotiations targeting an IJV. Professional meetings and systems of technological and commercial scanning are sufficiently numerous to offer good possibilities for contact (Lindsey 1989). In other cases, it is third parties who are responsible for interfacing (consultants, trade associations, BCNet, publications, etc).

Corporate joint ventures are generally instituted by two active partners; the presence of a third or fourth active partner (that is, no "silent" or "sleeping" partners) seriously complicates the mechanisms.

The choice of a good partner is clearly a delicate operation, but considerations employing good sense and a common desire to succeed can orient this decision. Brouthers & Wilkinson (1955) summarize these points by stating that chances for success of an IJV are strong when:

- complementary skills are offered by the partners
- cooperative cultures exist between the firms
- the firms have compatible goals
- commensurate levels of risk are involved.

These components are not mutually exclusive; rather they are all necessary. We may add here to these four aspects taking into account the reputation of a potential partner, the confidence that it suggests, its international experience or past experience in JVs, and possibly its financial performance and the solidity of its organizational structures.

Negotiation management

The initial contact among potential future partners can be formal or informal; it can take place among members of the various corporate headquarters or may come from lower in the hierarchy, notably when potential partners belong to the same business sector. In high-tech fields (electronics, telecommunications, information technology, pharmaceuticals), the actors are used to meeting regularly to discuss professional norms or to adapt product offerings (for example, in the area of disease management).

Negotiations begin by an exchange of information, rarely of a confidential nature at this stage in the process. The negotiations aiming at the creation of an IJV necessarily cover the varied aspects of the activity concerned (production, marketing, finance, human resource management, etc.); therefore, it is usually a multi-disciplinary team that is responsible for these negotiations. It is this team that will set the tone for the remainder of the negotiations. From the beginning, the ambience can be more conciliatory and smooth, more "fair's fair" based on strict reciprocity (Axelrod 1992), or of a more fighting nature, with the stronger trying to impose the rules and thus sowing the seeds of a future imbalance (taking more than giving). The style of the negotiation is of course linked to the temperament of the individual negotiators but also depends to a great extent on national business practices (Japanese, Germans, Americans and Italians do not behave in the same manner!).

The idea of negotiation must be conceptualized on three levels. It is in fact a concept with three steps which can be presented as follows from general to specific: (i) negotiation takes place in a given environment and thus has a pre-established structure, at least in the short term; (ii) then comes a process through which divergent interests and directed activities oppose the different players; (iii) finally, the individual negotiators go through the real interactions. As the attention moves from one level to the next, the cognitive domain where precise knowledge may be acquired, accumulated, and transmitted didactically becomes increasingly less important than the domain of knowhow, intuition, custom, or past encounters with similar situations which replace the knowledge of the apprenticeship (Rojot 1994, p. 3).

Operational content, individual behavior, and social psychology meet in the negotiating melting pot. The negotiators are admittedly rational, but we also know that this rationality is limited (Simon 1965; Crozier & Friedberg 1977) and that the power of negotiation is, in part, subjective.

The steps to negotiation

Managing the negotiation process is not just a matter of following fixed rules. Every negotiation is special; there are, however, certain generic phases to the negotiation process that are common (see also Figure 12.3).

Sabine Urban

FIGURE 12.3
The A, B, C, D, E negotiation process

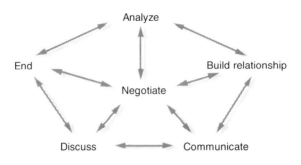

Note: Negotiation is far from a linear process. You may move from A to B and into C and then find you need to return to A before moving back into C. You should always contain elements of B in C, D, and E.

Source: T. Brake, D.M. Walker and T. Walker, *Doing Business Internationally, The Guide to Cross-Cultural Success*, Irwin, Burr Ridge Ill., 1995, p. 199.

- 1st step: Analysis of relevant qualitative elements (the company's core values, plans, positions, arguments) and quantitative elements.
- 2nd step: Development of a constructive and trusting relationship in a climate of mutual respect. Determination of responsibilities and of the hierarchical level of the participants in the negotiations.
- 3rd step: Communication. During the process, aim at identifying the elements of agreement and disagreement, setting the chronological steps for the future, and identifying the respective positions.
- 4th step: Discussion of possible alternatives and solutions. Examination of the management methods which could be applied to the new IJV including the integration of cultural differences and the choice of management indicators (according to accounting and tax laws, deductions, etc.). The choice of management tools is to be made by paying particular attention to the information systems of the partners.
- 5th step: Conclusion. Precise determination of the IJVs organization methods, the country of implantation, the recources committed by each of the parties, the selected performance criteria, the guidelines for reporting to the parent company, leadership during a possible transition period, the schedule for beginning initial operations, and the targeted return on investment.

The Organization of Coexistence within the IJV

We saw earlier (Figure 12.1) that the decision to develop a strategic alliance in the form of a joint venture supposes the creation of a new legal entity. For the parties concerned, this raises the problem of choosing a legal status for the shared organization.

The decision to create a new entity supposes that the partners involved have previously rejected the simpler — but more uncertain — formula of a *contractual agreement* which generates the often delicate problems of execution or of interpretation. The *corporation* is characterized by rules of functioning which are relatively constrictive; it offers more legal security to the joined parties.

The involvement of the partners in an IJV is not simple because the interested parties are trying to achieve, in fact, two objectives: on the one hand, they want to mobilize means to pursue shared goals; on the other, they want to preserve their own interests, similar yet distinct.

The creation of an alliance in the form of a *corporation* has the advantage of conceiving an *affectio societatis*, that is a form of collaboration among associates on equal footing in order to strive for the aim of the newly created legal entity. This concept is expressed in German law by the term "Treuepflicht" or obligation of fidelity, or of loyalty. The interests of the corporation *per se* have the right to be defended in priority in relation to the individual interests of the shareholders or partners. This leads to the recognition of a certain balance among the partners, and this balance is destined to sustain confidence, an indispensable element to the success of a JV.

The international character of a JV, however, makes it all the more fragile because in the absence of an *international* corporation with an appropriate and recognized corporate status (such as a limited liability company or European "SARL", for example) the new IJV will necessarily be created under "national" law giving an indirect advantage to one or another of the partners (well-known, familiar laws and legal precedents). The choice of the legal status does not then resolve all of the functioning problems of an IJV; the negotiations must then reach beyond the formalities of specifying the general framework to touch on more specific aspects of the management.

Legal status

The needs which must be satisfied by the IJV's structure can vary according to the nature and the purpose of the IJV. It is nonetheless possible to isolate certain constant necessities, such as the existence of a forum for discussion or sufficient flexibility in terms of leaving the legal entity. Beyond national legal particularities, it is also possible to identify categories of companies presenting common characteristics. Two types of corporations may be judged appropriate, two others to a much lesser extent. Among the latter:

- **Companies with unlimited liability**: the French "société en nom collectif", the English "unlimited partnership", the German "Offene Handelsgesellschaft (OHG)", the Italian "Società in nome collectivo", etc.

The absense of an organ for discussion within this category of companies — and the very principle of undefined joint and united responsibility among its associates — make it difficult to use in the case of a joint venture.

In exceptional cases this form of corporation is, however, sometimes retained in the case of common subsidiaries for which the partners know that they will generate significant losses in the short term. These losses can then be deducted from the profits of the parent companies and, therefore, reduce their tax burdens. Later, when the joint venture becomes profitable, it will be made into a joint stock company.

- **Limited partnerships**: French "société en commandite", English "limited partnership", Italian "Società in accomandità italienne", German "Kommanditgesellschaft", etc.

The formal separation between decision power and capital in this type of partnership, make it a well-liked tool in the war against takeover bids. However, the principle of non-interference of the silent partners in the management of the company is poorly adapted to the needs of joint ventures where financial management and industrial and commercial policies are usually tightly linked.

The formulas which are most commonly adopted are:

- **Private limited liability companies**: French "SARL", German "GmbH", Italian "Srl", Belgian "SPRL", Dutch "BV"...

This refers to a private partnership status, based on the concept of *intuitu personae*, giving a dominant role to the manager ("gérant") and not offering a body for discussion open to all the different partners in the common partnership. The shares of a private limited liability partnership are not freely transferable; they preserve then the interests of the partners who created the JV and who do not need to fear the unwanted arrival of a third party who might appropriate cheaply the advantages acquired by or built within the joint partnership. Moreover, the private limited liability partnership enables associates to allow for significant freedom in establishing the rules governing the organization of the partnership, which is extremely valuable in an international, heterogeneous context.

- **Limited liability companies**: French, Belgian, Luxembourg, Swiss or Spanish "SA", Italian "SpA", German "AG", English "Limited Liability Company", Dutch "NV", Danish "A/S", Swedish "AB", etc.

In most cases, this type of company will be selected.

Limited liability companies present in fact the advantage of having a forum (similar to the French "conseil d'administration" or board of directors) in which the policies of the common corporation can be debated; furthermore, they generally offer the authors of the statutes the possibility of establishing rules of a qualified majority for the most important decisions within the board of directors; the authors can also define, at least internally, limitations of powers (generally very broad) for the directors, who will be required to submit the most important decisions for the prior agreement to the board of directors.[1]

Formal agreements and statutes for IJV operations

In many JVs, cooperation rests on the principle of 50/50 equality between two partners; decisions must then be made by mutual agreement. When the partners are active in similar or competing fields, the risk of confrontation of interests is reinforced. Consequently, the resolution of conflicts, the modes of transformation and of adaptation of the JV as well as the means of withdrawing from the JV, must be anticipated from the start, from the time of the negotiation of the company's statutes. In this area of supplementary agreements, it is necessary to avoid two extreme pitfalls: that of "whatiffing" ("what if?, what if?") which attempts to anticipate all the possible situations that might occur in the future (American tendency) leading to a dense set of texts or the inverse pitfall which consists of imposing upon the partners the fewest constraints possible at the beginning in order to keep a maximum of flexibility to resolve conflicts according to the current circumstances. Nonetheless, the absence of precise clauses can lead to regrettable disagreements. Two types of agreements are generally negotiated: "memorandum of agreement" also called "shareholders' agreement", or "joint venture agreement" and "satellite agreements".

The "Shareholders' Agreement" or "Joint-Venture Agreement"

This constitutes both a prerequisite and adjustment to the statutes of the future joint venture company. It includes particularly the following points.

- Capital structure: the shareholders' agreement determines whether the partners of the joint venture will participate equally or unequally. Equity capital is most often represented by shares in the company. However, in order to account for the wide variety of situations which may occur, more complex shares are often used in joint ventures.

  Several categories of shares can be created, each with its specific rights: double-vote shares, non-voting preference shares, non-voting shares (in public sector enterprises), equity warrant shares. It will be important to verify whether it is possible to issue the shares at the time of the company's creation, what is the total amount authorized, the deadline for payment in full of capital, etc.

---

[1] Comments by Jacques Salès, Attorney, at the seminar of the Institute for International Research, Paris, December 2–3, 1991.

Rules for increases in capital following the constitution of the joint venture can also be planned for, as well as the major policies concerning the distribution of dividends.

- Distribution of the corporate executive positions throughout the IJV: it is possible to negotiate, for example, an arrangement where the president and top managers are appointed according to a system of rotation in order to maintain a trustful relationship and a balance of power.

It is important, however, not to confuse the concept of share holding (the responsibility of the parent companies) and management (the responsibility of the head office). Moreover, it is important to recognize and to not interfere with the general manager's autonomy (given regular and formal evaluation of his performance: budget, plans, audits) and to permit each upper-level manager to develop a feeling of belonging to the IJV (in respect to the fundamental values of each partner).

- Determination of a list of decisions requiring approval of the board of directors.
- Provisions for exiting the IJV by transmitting shares representing the company's equity.
- Rights of minority shareholders: particular care should be taken to preserve the rights of potential minority shareholders. It may be planned in the written agreement that, should a particularly important decision be made despite opposition from a minority shareholder, this minority shareholder be entitled to oblige one or several of the majority shareholders to buy back his shares.

"Satellite agreements"

These specific agreements generally concern the methods of executing the agreement such as:

- trademark licences or patents: these contracts define the legal, technical, and financial conditions linking the joint venture to one or several of the parent companies transferring or granting a trademark license or patent. Also included are arrangements relating to the fate of licenses should the transferring company withdraw from the joint venture, to confidentiality, to conciliatory procedures, etc.;
- contracts for technical assistance and licenses pertaining to technical skills;
- supply contracts with the parent companies;
- contracts between the IJV and the parent companies relating to commercial representation and sales or distribution assistance for the products manufactured by the IJV.

In each of these cases determining the transfer price is clearly of utmost importance (in terms of costs, profitability, taxation, etc.).

Conflict resolution

This "satellite" agreement merits particular attention given the high failure rate of IJVs.

Two major categories of conflict among partners in a joint venture can be identified: those that relate to management decisions, and those that relate to the rights and duties of the participating companies, that is, to the interpretation of the joint venture agreement.

It is not possible to predict in advance all of the possible areas of disagreement among the joint venture partners. Conflicts relating to the management of the joint venture can be avoided by adopting a collegial structure for decision-making in which the rights of minority shareholders and the need for efficiency can be reconciled. When disagreements do arise, it is necessary to have recourse to specific methods of conflict resolution.

Creation of a steering committee

Composed of a limited number of representatives of the IJV partners, this steering committee is responsible for decisions that the statutory collegial organ directing the IJV is not allowed to make. It is possible to distinguish during the initial negotiations the different situations, for example:

- decisions requiring a unanimous vote by the steering committee (admission of new partners, acquisition or transfer of major assets, withdrawal from an activity, contracts between the IJV and a participating company)
- decisions requiring a majority vote (policies relating to pricing for the products manufactured)
- day-to-day management decisions delegated to a designated manager.

Despite these precautions, it is possible that a disagreement may persist among the partners. In this case, it is the provisions for conflict resolution ("deadlock" clauses) which may appear in the shareholder's agreement which will come into play.

"Deadlock" clauses: methods for conflict resolution

The classic choice is that of attributing competence for conflict resolution to an internal court or to an arbitrator. But "alternative" methods (Alternative Dispute Resolution methods or ADR) exist, and they offer the advantages of more rapid and less expensive proceedings. The ADR methods which are most commonly used are:

- Conciliation: requires the intervention of a third party to improve dialogue among the parties. The conciliator does not have the power to make a decision.
- Mediation: the mediator is, in addition to his role as conciliator, obliged to submit his conclusions to the involved parties in writing.

- The "mini-trial": this involves a type of structure negotiation which requires representatives of each of the parties in question to present their case, and is presided by an objective third party. The goal of these debates is to arrive at a "business agreement", i.e., an economically satisfactory solution.
- The Disputes Review Board (DRB): the characteristic trait of the DRB (most commonly used in the United States) resides in the fact that it is put in place at the creation of the IJV. The members of the board are selected according to their technical competencies and thus benefit from the partners' trust from the outset. The DRB meets several times per year at the site of the IJV. The DRB makes suggestions in writing; their suggestions are generally followed by the parties concerned based on the recognized authority of the members of the DRB.

Negotiating the Evolution of and Withdrawal from an IJV

The basics

New corporate theories demonstrate that a company has no reason to be stable, and this notion proves particularly true for IJVs where multiple influences from diverse horizons and related to politics, the economy, law, the psycho-sociology of organizations — in other words, to the player's culture — are interlaced (Coriat and Weinstein, 1995). Since Williamson and Simon, we know that individual cognitive capacity is limited. The primary consequence of this limited rationality is the *lack of fulfillment of contracts*. It is, hence, agreed that the agents cannot predict all of the possible eventualities which will affect the results of their transactions; therefore, procedures of adaptation "ex post" — that might lead to radical decisions such as the dissolution of the IJV — must be anticipated.

Tensions within an IJV are largely attributable to *cultural differences* which can be experienced at three levels: individual, organizational, and contextual. At each level, a series of "heritages" as defined by Bartlett and Ghoshal (1989), intervene.

Past experience also proves that *opportunistic behaviors* greatly disturb the game — when one of the partners of the IJV (or both) seeks to become more of a "winner" than the other; that is, seeks to acquire a larger share in the positive sum game planned from the beginning. An opportunistic behavior consists of watching out for one's own interest, or that of one's own group, with recourse to trickery or to different types of deceit (distorted or incomplete information, hidden intentions, commitments which are only partially fulfilled, etc.). According to Williamson, this leads to the necessity of a dynamic analysis of contractual relations, which means emphasizing the interest of a post-contractual opportunism.

Another aspect which deserves consideration in IJVs is that of the *exchange of property rights*, the transfer of knowledge and know-how (training procedures in place). Privately owned tangible or intangible assets become shared property with the creation of the IJV. The use of this shared property can clearly give substance to discussions. This type of difficulty has been analyzed in the context of *agency relationships* (Jensen & Meckling, 1976) where several people (in this case the founders) entrust a third party, "the agent" (i.e., the newly constituted entity, or IJV) with the execution of the contract by delegation of power. This "agent" may not prove to be completely fair-play and make the venture of the IJV impossible due to the unequal appropriation of the results. Instead of becoming an organization aimed at creating wealth, the IJV becomes then a center for conflicts of interest, unprofitable or dangerous in the long term. The incompatibility of uncooperative behaviors (poorly tested in the first stage of negotiation between the future partners) then becomes a source of rupture.

Adapting to change

In a rapidly evolving environment, an efficient IJV structure requires the capacity for adaptation to change. This is necessary and justified for several reasons:

1. It is widely known that every product is characterized by an individual life cycle; each stage in the cycle corresponds to a determined international method of management.
2. Each joint venture also has a life cycle which brings about a necessary need for adaptation.
3. Every organization evolves; from alliances to international joint ventures, to networks delimiting new fields of competition which are, themselves, evolving.
4. IJVs can be exploited by partners beyond their initial objective: they are a favored tool for restructuring.

Box 12.2 IJV: a successful learning process

Bosch, a German car supplier and electronic company, maintains five JVs in Japan. Bosch has begun to pursue the goal of internalizing the knowledge resource of its joint ventures in Japan. The content of this strategy is to consciously transfer the acquired knowledge to the German or other European production sites. In order to achieve this goal Bosch established so-called strategy meetings focusing on directing the regional flow of knowledge, e.g., meetings aiming to coordinate Bosch activities on Asian markets. Superordinated to the local meetings, global strategy meetings developed the joint ventures into a worldwide internationalization strategy.

On the operational level, Bosch promotes an intense exchange of technicians to establish a worldwide "Bosch standard". Representatives of the joint ventures are trained at German production facilities to become familiar with technologies and production processes. Bosch sends German technicians to the Japanese joint ventures to guarantee an effective transfer of technology and of company internal quality standards. A further incentive is to get in-depth insights and information on culture-based knowledge created in the joint ventures and to transfer that experience to the German headquarters.

The resulting knowledge benefits all members of the Bosch group trying to get access to worldwide operating clients like Japanese production sites in the US or UK. (*Source: Long Range Planning*, Vol. 28, June 1995, p. 43.)

Sabine Urban

IJVs and product life cycle

It was stated above that it is important in the initial negotiation to define precisely the objectives of the project and its positioning as it relates to the global strategy of each partner. This requirement is illustrated in Figure 12.4.

During growth and concentration stages of the life cycle of the product, the IJV is a structure which is well adapted for access to new geographic markets and for enlarging the customer base. This way, partner companies can acquire resources that aren't for sale such as the expertise of local managers or access to a distribution network.

Later, merger can be the solution which is best adapted to the problems of maturity and decline stages of a product's life cycle: it can also be a means of disinvestment valued by one of the shareholders of the IJV.

The life cycle of joint ventures

This idea was developed by Kogut (1988, p. 169). "Joint ventures, like any form of organization, undergo a cycle of creation, institutionalization, and, with high probability, termination. . . . The competitive conditions that motivate the creation of a JV may also be responsible for its termination." The principal reasons for this evolution can be perceived across three theoretical frames of reference: transaction cost economics, strategic behavior, and organizational behavior.

Environmental and strategic changes over time may shift the relative bargaining power among the partners and cause IJV instability. In fact JV stability/instability is influenced jointly by competitive incentives among the partners and competitive changes in industry structure. Whereas ventures located in growing industries are more likely to survive, those located in industries that are becoming more concentrated and to which both partners belong, are more likely to terminate (op. cit. p. 180). IJVs are troubled by the enduring influence of competitive rivalry on stability.

IJVs play, however, another role outside of resolving or effecting competitive factors: IJVs are vehicles by which knowledge is transferred and by which firms learn from each other. Imitation is frequently the goal of an IJV, and when imitation is complete, the sign of success is termination.

From JV to network

Globalization of the economy leads inevitably to the development of strategic alliances and to the increased creation of IJVs. Beyond this phenomenon, the same rationale leads to the development of global network corporations (Yoshino & Rangan 1995, pp. 196–206). This trend will result in the mutation of many IJVs into more flexible operational frameworks, integrating the multiplicity of technologies, management systems, markets, and entrepreneurial cultures. This new combination of knowledge and skills will burst the traditional corporate

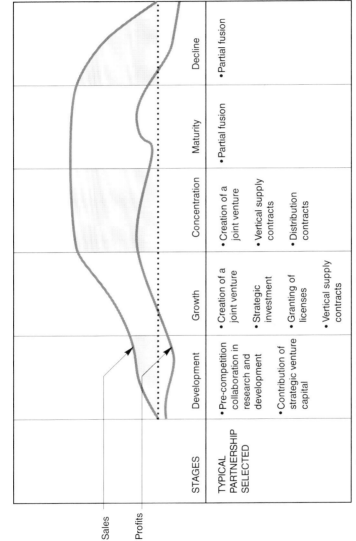

FIGURE 12.4
Life cycle of products/markets and joint ventures

STAGES	Development	Growth	Concentration	Maturity	Decline
TYPICAL PARTNERSHIP SELECTED	• Pre-competition collaboration in research and development • Contribution of strategic venture capital	• Creation of a joint venture • Strategic investment • Granting of licenses • Vertical supply contracts	• Creation of a joint venture • Vertical supply contracts • Distribution contracts	• Partial fusion	• Partial fusion

Sales

Profits

•••••••• Strong potential for major changes in the competitive situation.
Source: Coopers & Lybrand (1995), *Guide pour une joint-venture réussie*, Paris, Ed. interne, 1995, p. 28)

boundaries, including those of IJVs. We are approaching a time of "boundaryless" management. Perhaps the key challenge in the new global environment is the management of both internal and external networks, of various common understandings. Networks of mixed-motive relationships are probably going to be a permanent feature of the competitive landscape of the future. IJVs used to be seen as a way of filling well-defined competence gaps through learning and restructuring. They are becoming a basic building block of global network companies.

IJV tools for corporate restructuring

Increasingly, demonstrated adaptation skills are becoming a key factor to international competitiveness. Here, too, IJVs have their role to play (Nanda & Williamson 1995). Accordingly, from the time of the negotiations of the joint venture agreement, the participants must be aware of this to define the rules for buying back and transferring shares among partners.

The separation: withdrawal from the IJV

This action — about which empirical studies do not agree on the frequency — will ratify a situation with unmanaged difficulties; the nature of the difficulties encountered is, on the other hand, quite stable. With regard only to the recent studies published in 1995 (Brake, Walker & Walker; Beamish & Inkpen, Coopers & Lybrand), it appears that the principal difficulties are, in decreasing order of importance, as follows:

- adaptation to the local culture
- lack of real integration
- divergence of strategic objectives
- incompatible corporate cultures
- too large an imbalance among the partners
- inappropriateness and complexity of decision-making processes
- differences in financial objectives
- poor evaluation of or changes in the marketplace
- climate of mistrust among the partners.

These factors are also underlined by Eisele (1995).

Given these potential difficulties, it is important to specify during the negotiating process which conditions will trigger the withdrawal mechanisms. The choice of a method will be influenced by national law.

First method: dissolution and liquidation of the IJV

French law provides for the legal dissolution of a company upon the request of one of the partners for "just cause" (obvious non-fulfillment of a partner's obligations, misunderstanding among the partners paralyzing the company's operations). The possibility of dissolution also exists in most national laws governing companies.

Methods for withdrawal without dissolving the IJV

These can refer to different clauses, notably,

- clauses relating to withdrawal due to a change in control;
- the "right to be carried along" which enables one of the partners to require another partner to arrange for a potential buyer for his shares to simultaneously purchase both sets of shares at the same time under the same conditions
- the "buy-sell" clause: this clause (if it is inserted in the written agreement) enables one of the partners of the IJV to either make an offer to buy the shares of another or to offer to sell its own shares. In either case, the party taking advantage of the "buy-sell" clause sets the price at which the transaction will take place. The other party is, of course, free to refuse.

Box 12.3 Value destruction is common

Through linkage influence, the corporate parent seeks to create value by fostering cooperation and synergy between different businesses. But the search for synergies often leads to "anergy" problems. (*Source:* Guy Jillings, Head of Shell International Petroleum, quoted in *California Management Review*, Vol. 38, no. 1, Fall 1995, p. 81.)

Negotiations among parties in the case of disagreement

Withdrawal from an IJV by the sale of one of the partners' shares can be illusory. When the joint venture was created between a "local" company and a foreign company for reasons directly or indirectly linked to obtaining or executing a procurement contact, the withdrawal of the "local" company can compromise the purpose of the joint venture and destroy its value. It is the same when a joint venture is created to use a network of customers who are loyal to one of the partners; the more or less "fair-play" withdrawal of one of the partners places the other in a completely disadvantageous position.

In such a case, withdrawal generally involves difficult negotiations, possibly combined with penalties for the premature termination of the agreement or for not respecting the IJVs configuration (purpose, methods of joint control, sharing of benefits of cooperation, resources committed, expected results, behavior by one of the partners outside the alliance of the partnership).

CHAPTER 13

Project Negotiations: An Episode in the Relationship

BERNARD COVA, FLORENCE NAZET AND ROBERT SALLE

Project Negotiation and Relationship Discontinuity

A "project" is understood here to mean "a complex transaction covering a discrete package of products, services and other actions designed specifically to create unique capital assets that produce benefits for the buyer over an extended period of time" (Cova and Holstius, 1993, p. 107). For example, a building, a "turnkey" factory, a power station, a limited series of undercarriage assemblies or setting up a complex system to manage power distribution.

The first, and principal, characteristic of projects from the seller's standpoint is the uniqueness of each transaction (Ahmed, 1993). A project requires the mobilisation of both internal resources and the organisation's network of external partners to deliver a specified scope of work.

A second important characteristic of projects is the high degree of complexity associated with each transaction (Günter, 1986). The number of organisations and individuals which may be involved is equally significant from both buyer and seller standpoints: the many economic and non-economic (public authorities, local associations, etc.) parties who may be implicated, the prevailing multi-cultural dimension, as much in terms of languages and countries as in sectoral overlaps: the cost of the transaction is very high, requiring complex financial engineering: the duration of the transaction process may be several months and execution may take place over many years.

A third characteristic is the high degree of discontinuity in the economic relationship between the buyer and seller. For example, the buyer of a power station may only need to develop such a facility every five or ten years. Hence, it is not possible to talk of establishing "partner" type relationships through frequent economic exchanges as is the case in industry relations based upon frequent product or service purchases (Håkansson, 1982).

This last point is fundamental to an appreciation of the dynamic conditions within which project negotiations take place. The main marketing strategy

253

adopted by sellers when faced with particularly irregular purchasing patterns among their clients is to try to overcome the effects of economic discontinuity by developing strong social and relational bonds. When viewed from the outside, this may sometimes give rise to an impression of collusion and a lack of transparency in the project negotiations (Usunier, 1992). However, a company stands little chance of securing a project award if it only becomes aware of the opportunity at the point when "Request for Proposal" (RFP) documents are issued. The approach to marketing project business[1] must therefore be based upon maintaining relations, either directly with the customer organisation or, indirectly, by gaining support among the various socio-economic parties which may become involved in projects with the customer and possess the necessary information. Such relations essentially permit the company to anticipate projects (from information in advance of an RFP) and adapt to the opportunity (using information and influence following receipt of the RFP). Project negotiations are therefore rarely an isolated commercial event, conducted on a strictly professional basis following proposal submission but, in most instances, represent an episode in the development of a socioeconomic relationship between the Project Development Manager (PDM), and other members of the company, with one (or several) of the parties in contact with the buyer or the buying centre. In this context, the prelude to all negotiations is an analysis of the relational components of the socio-economic environment within which the buyer operates and, more precisely, an analysis of the parties involved (organisations and individuals) including their respective roles, possible influence on the project and inter-relationships (Hoskins, 1996).

The first part of this chapter sets out a general framework for analysing and mapping these relational environments in order to gain a network position (Mattson, 1985) and also discusses the main foundations of a project relationship (from interest to friendship).

Subsequently, it would seem useful to illustrate the project negotiation process in several stages so as to distinguish between the face-to-face bargaining encounter and the wider aspects of the relationship, both within and outside a specific project situation. A second part will therefore introduce a model of the distinct phases of the project negotiating process developed by the Scandinavian Industrial Marketing and Purchasing School (Ghauri, 1981, 1982 and 1986; Ghauri and

---

[1] The reader will find an exhaustive reference list of material on project marketing and project negotiations (in German, English and French) at the end of the article "Towards Flexible Anticipation: The Challenge of Project Marketing" by Cova, B., Mazet, F. and Salle, R., published 1993 as chapter 17 in the book *Perspectives on Marketing Management* Volume 3 edited by Michael J. Baker (John Wiley & Sons). This list includes, in particular, most of the work carried out by members of the European Network on Project Marketing and Systems Selling. See also the forthcoming issue of the *International Business Review* dedicated to Project Marketing and Systems Selling.

Johansson, 1979) and up-dated by the results of the EAP–IRE[2] pan-European research programme on project marketing (Cova, Mazet and Salle, 1993, 1994 and 1995).

Then, negotiating practise will be considered, not so much from the standpoint of the specific techniques, but the means by which a seller might differentiate a proposal from competitor offers on the basis of his network position. In the third section, we will put forward the four main dimensions of a project proposal (technical, financial, political and societal) and the possibility of achieving competitive differentiation by manipulating either the overall mix or individual dimensions. Particular attention will be given to the "risk approach" (Salle and Silvestre, 1992), as adapted to the specificities of project business, in promoting the seller's expertise through the construction of demand.

The final part concentrates on the organisation of a negotiating team. In particular its member profiles; the PDM, once the odd-job man, is now the conductor of the orchestra who mobilises the selling effort, both within the company and among the various external partners. Additionally, the "part-time marketer" role of engineers, finance specialists and its repercussions will be discussed.

On the other hand, it is not the intention within this chapter to deal with the necessary qualities of project negotiators. The combined arguments developed here are based upon reflection from a socio-economic as opposed to a psychological perspective. Hence, for a more detailed examination of the abilities and profile of an effective international project negotiator, as well as inter-cultural management (Usunier, 1992), rituals and face-to-face negotiating agenda (Groupe Ecully, 1996), reference to other chapters would be recommended.

Investing in Relationships

Milieu positioning

Due to the dispersed structure of the buying and selling centers in project marketing, integrating other actors than just the customer and the supplier (consultants, financial backers, agents, engineering companies, subcontractors), companies try to indirectly anticipate customer's projects through links with central actors within the socio-economic environment concerned. Similarly to the marketing discipline in general, project marketing has become increasingly relational with a growing account for the social dimension. In this type of marketing, it is as important to have a good "linkage mix" as a good "package

---

[2] The EAP–IRE research program is a joint program, extending over several years between the European School of Management (Paris/Oxford/Berlin/Madrid) and the Institut de Recherche de l'Enterprise of the Lyon Graduate School of Business, the aim of which is to develop knowledge on project marketing. It enjoys the support of companies representing the following sectors of activity: construction, electrical engineering, nuclear energy, power and telecommunications.

mix" (Jansson, 1989). This linkage mix corresponds to a relational position in the network of both business and non-business actors forming the social context embedding the project. It's a necessary prerequisite for project business in order to create trust and gain information.

Many of the actors are integrated in local networks and even contribute in some cases to a local socio-economic system in which the project only appears as a disturbance, an event, an episode within all relationships existing between the various actors of the system. Thus, the company need for increased anticipation calls for the integration of all projects in the perspective of a kind of territorial network, what practitioners call a *milieu* (Cova, Mazet and Salle, 1995).[3] Project marketing then focuses on the firm's relational investment in a milieu outside of a given project opportunity. In this approach, the relational logic is paramount, exchanges are more of a social nature than of a technico-economic nature and are concerned with other actors than just business actors, i.e., so-called "institutional actors" (Hadjikhani and Håkansson, 1995).

To reinforce this analysis, we have chosen to begin with a relevant case study from which to draw upon compelling theoretical conclusions (Cova, Mazet and Salle, 1995). In 1986, the construction group BTP covers the entire French territory through local subsidiaries. These local subsidiaries were not created by BTP but were the result of buying local firms. In order to preserve the local character of its subsidiaries in local markets in which it represents an important competitive advantage, BTP kept the original name of each subsidiary. In the Loiret department (central region of France), the subsidiary is called Antolini. Antolini presently specializes in local public markets but is also interested in industrial markets, i.e., in the construction of premises for foreign industrial firms willing to develop in the Loiret department. Economically, if we adopt a traditional marketing approach, this market is formed by all the firms looking for industrial premises in the Loiret. This demand stems from all the companies in the world that may settle in the Loiret, and from those French and local industries willing to extend their factories or to transfer their premises to the Loiret. This means that it is impossible to circumscribe and to anticipate the demand as it may stem from any part of the globe. To do so, Antolini would need a world scanning system of relocation projects. Actually, Antolini cannot wait for a foreign company

---

[3] A milieu can be defined as a socio-spatial configuration that can be characterized by four elements:

- a territory,
- a network of heterogeneous actors related to each other on this territory,
- a representation constructed and shared by these actors,
- a set of rules and norms ("the law of the milieu") regulating the interactions between these actors.

What distinguishes the milieu from a simple localized network of industrial actors is its collective linkage to the territory developed by practices of all types. The actors share, both in their life and in their imagination, the community of some elementary structures.

to decide the details of its settlement in the Loiret; it would then have no chance to win the order as another company would presumably have the construction contract in hand already. As a reminder, the construction of industrial premises is a private purchase which escapes the advertisement rules of public markets. In general, a call for tender is issued and sent by the foreign company to some construction and engineering firms — often suppliers of the customer country — selected for their reputation or their relational proximity to the buyer. In fact, we observe that Antolini's marketing practice takes into account a local network having its own rules and in which each actor shares certain representations and values. Antolini's marketing manager and his team of sales engineers share the idea that there is a geographically circumscribed entity gathering all "business" and "non business" actors, and conditioning industrial setting-up in the Loiret. It is through the relations with some of these actors and through an on-going learning process enriched with each project, that they developed this shared representation. The local network formed in this way is called the "milieu" of industrial setting-up in the Loiret. The knowledge of the milieu developed through relation investments enables Antolini to anticipate projects and obtain support on its offers. We can even consider that Antolini has and develops an invaluable informational and prescriptive resource that can be translated into a competitive advantage. Effectively, any foreign company willing to set-up in the Loiret must actually go through the milieu and some of its actors.

In general, the company nets the milieu of demand through social interaction with those actors having a large number of contacts with others in a given milieu (Jansson, 1989; Björkman and Kock, 1995). These so-called central actors permit the company to keep in touch with all opportunities related to its activities without necessarily making direct contact with all potential clients. In so doing, they enable information gathering activity to be focused and sometimes serve to promote the company, facilitating a reduction in the number of direct investments. A wide variety of such actors might be described as constituting "poles of continuity". This can be illustrated by the different public sector and political organisations which might be concerned, directly or indirectly, with company activities (ministries and regional authorities in both the home country and in target territories) also, experts in a particular area of activity are likely to be consulted on a particular project (consultants, etc.), lending institutions involved in project finance (World Bank, Asian Development Bank, etc.), together with Unions and even "Old Boy" networks (schools, universities etc.). The investment in relations with these poles of continuity will also serve project specific marketing efforts by enabling the company to gain access to, improve or confirm information at all stages of negotiations; they may even be able to provide valuable support.

As an example, Björkman and Kock (1995, p. 523) give detailed account of a Chinese business network consisting of the actors involved in a project with a Finnish company: "the project in question consisted of a few million US dollar delivery by the Finnish company Infratech to a relatively large city in China. The project was financed through a foreign soft loan which had been channeled to a Chinese ministry. The ministry's FTC (Foreign Trade Corporation) was responsible for handling the process. A research and design institute belonging to the same ministry was involved in testing the products that were supplied. The actual contract was signed by Infratech's Hong Kong subsidiary and the US office of the Chinese FTC. Most contacts were directly between representatives of the end user and a Chinese employee in Infratech's Beijing office. The Chinese employee also maintained close contacts with the focal Chinese research and design institute. The relations between the key employee and representatives of the end user and the research and design institute had existed for several years prior to the initiation of the sale process. Engineers from the production unit in Finland were involved in the presentation of the product that was offered, while the director of the Hong Kong subsidiary played a significant role in the formal contact negotiations".

Certain companies have recently been tempted to develop formal systems for analysing and mapping milieus and networks. The relational investment therefore becomes part of an intelligence system for project based companies (Cova, Mazet and Salle, 1994), that is to say, a continuous, operational system aimed at the early detection of project opportunities and their relational criteria (Fletcher and Wheeler, 1989; Jansson, 1989). Such a system integrates the general relational factors (institutions and their personnel, the culture and profiles of each party, connections between parties) and power structures (roles and influence of each party, the nature of cooperation or conflict between parties) within each milieu. This intelligence can operate at two levels:

- at a general level: enabling the company to detect project opportunities at the earliest possible stage, which may be of interest within priority milieus;
- at a project level: enabling the company to gather as much information as possible on influential parties, budgetary constraints, the ability or otherwise to modify the specifications, etc., and thereby increase the chances of success.

If we look closely at the way in which market intelligence systems function in project-based industries, it is readily apparent that intelligence gathering is principally aligned with the relations that have been created, developed and maintained by members of the supplier organisation among a group of socio-economic actors operating within the buyer organisation's circle of contacts. Responsibility for maintaining these external relationships rests with managers, functional representatives and indeed, all members of the organisation, not simply the sales department. Hence, the role of such "part-time marketers" should be considered a fundamental element of the total marketing process. We might even refer to the families and friends of personnel as an extension of the company's intelligence system.

Building social links?

It is in this context that discrepancies arising from the use of relational investments in specific milieus, come to light. The use of relationships between individuals in the wider interests of the organisation contradicts the idea of "managing" the network, since their strength is often related to the absence of any disciplined planning or management activity. In other words, they can be effective precisely because they are not organised to achieve the specific practical goals (intelligence gathering, influence, etc.) for which they may be intended.

The study of personal networks in major international corporations puts to light different basis for relationship from self-interest to pure gift (Belk and Coon, 1993; Godbout and Caillé, 1992). We can, in effect, see that relationships between professional individuals are less guided by opportunism, based upon short-term selfish motives, than by the development of trust based upon shared long-term interests: that the basis of a long-term business relationship between two people is less inclined towards reciprocity — getting something in return — than in achieving an equal share of the rewards arising from a joint effort — distribution of benefits — i.e., establishing a mutuality of interest. In this instance (as is also the case with opportunism), the social ties between two parties reinforce the economic rationale behind their initial introduction.

However, to consider only this issue would be to ignore the numerous situations in the business world where the economic link reinforces the social link. The classic example, which occurs in everyday life, might be jointly conceiving a plan as much for the opportunity to get together with friends as for the prospect of achieving a business purpose. And, outside of a designed activity, how much information is exchanged every day simply in order to maintain the social links? We might thus speak more in terms of compatibity than purpose. The episodes in such a relationship consist less of equal exchanges than gifts. This is the case with countless daily service and consideration given to those we like and with whom we would wish to maintain a social tie. These small gifts, or favours, serve to nourish the debt which perpetuates between two individuals, in both directions, to the extent they might wish it to develop. This is the phenomenon known as "mutual debt" (Godbout et Caillé, 1992), which contrasts with gift-giving reciprocity, in the sense that the debt must not be settled. If one of the parties settles the debt and puts the relationship back on a reciprocal footing, it is probably because that same party wishes to reduce, or even cancel, the social link.

Thus, we can draw a continuum of business relationship types between individuals based upon the balance between purpose and compatibility: from the one-off transaction to mutual debt, punctuated by reciprocity and mutuality of interest. Furthermore, we can observe that, in addition to pure typologies, purpose and compatibility are often closely linked and dependent upon each other. A business relationship based upon reciprocity can develop into one based upon mutual debt in as much as mutual debt can be replaced by a mutuality of interest. A friendly business relationship can alternate between episodes guided by purpose and others by compatibility. Relationships governed more by mutual debt than interest, and apparently not geared towards the achievement of a specific purpose, can sometimes deliver major contracts and brilliant successes for companies with an interest in using them to develop advantageous positions

Bernard Cova, Florence Mazet and Robert Salle

within a milieu. In this vein, Björkman and Kock (1995) give numerous examples of cases in China where old Chinese friends had helped people secure deals. To reinforce this argument, we will look at a case study from the European aerospace industry to show how the concept of mutual debt can give a different complexion to exchanges between individuals involved in a project negotiation.

A German supplier was in competition with his British rival for the supply of an important component associated with a new aircraft project being undertaken by an Italian constructor. Shortly before the Farnborough Air Show, the marketing department of the German supplier learned from the purchasing department of the Italian constructor that the British supplier would be awarded the contract on the basis of having submitted a more advantageous offer. Following this announcement, the German marketing department resigned to its failure. However, during the inaugural dinner of the Air Show, the head of the German supplier had the occasion to dine with the head of the Italian constructor whom he had known for a long time. In essence, the Italian constructor was part of the European consortium, Europaero, within which the German manager has held a position of some importance prior to changing companies. Furthermore, the Italian constructor was able to join the consortium because (ten years earlier) the German manager had fought within the consortium for its acceptance alongside German, British and French organisations. That evening, the head of the Italian constructor slipped some information to his German friend, who had made no such request: "*here is the price you need to submit to undercut and beat the British*". The next day, stunned by the news, the German marketing department submitted a revised offer in panic and, before the end of the Air Show, a contract was signed ceremoniously between the German supplier and the Italian constructor.

Two opposite insights can be drawn from this case:

- A first insight, from a utilitarian point of view, shows how the Italian manager, ten years later, settled his debt with his German colleague. We thus have a good illustration of delayed reciprocity between two individuals who have confidence in each other. Some will equally see this in terms of a kind of corruption. In fact, bribery and corruption are the dark side of relational investments and milieu positioning in project business (Usunier, 1992). In any case, the social link appears to be a means to support the economic transaction.
- A second, from a non-utilitarian point of view, shows how the Italian manager having less opportunity than in the past to meet his German friend, due to a job change (from Europaero to a component supplier), seized the opportunity of a long-term economic relationship (a project to supply a short series of major components for his new aircraft) to reestablish the social link. Contrary to a desire to settle his debt, he was looking to revive a mutual debt arrangement which would support more frequent social encounters with his friend. In this perspective, the awarding of the contract is not an end, but just an economic means to support the social link.

The five stages of the negotiation process

It will be apparent that negotiations are key to the gradual process of adapting the supplier's anticipation (anticipation of financial and technical capabilities, anticipation of relationships in the offer milieu, anticipation of social and political arelationships in the milieu of demand) to a specific project. Negotiations are therefore not an isolated event, without a history or a future, but an episode in the company's relationship with the milieu of demand and thereby the individual relations built, developed and maintained by company personnel with those parties we have referred to as poles of continuity. This process begins with the first contact related to the project and concludes with agreement on the terms of contract and final signature.

Firstly, negotiations allow the supplier to continually adapt a proposal to the customer's demand criteria which, on complex projects, are rarely fixed from the outset but evolve under the influence of the numerous actors in the milieu. Negotiations also enable the supplier to modify the demand criteria towards a more favorable solution and, in extreme cases, participate at an early stage in the construction of all or part of the RFP documents. At the beginning of the process of project negotiations nothing — the demand and the offer — is "given" or fixed, everything has to be constructed. Thus, the project is a social construction of the actors (Sahlin-Andersson, 1992).

The process of project negotiations can be divided into five phases (Ghauri, 1996; Cova and Holstius, 1993):

1. *Proposal preparation* begins at the first specific contact related to the project and concludes at the time of submission. It can finish earlier if the supplier is not invited to submit an offer (selection on the "bidding list");
2. Following submission, *Informal meetings* take place between the customer and each bidder in order to clarify, in detail, any areas of confusion or misunderstanding regarding both the offer and the requirements. In certain cases, such as public sector enquiries in North America, these meetings can take place in more formal, collective surrondings ("bidders conference") before or after the invitation to tender.
3. *Formulation of the negotiating strategy* can begin once the customer has received all the proposals, together with the necessary clarification, and is in a position to make an effective comparison. This phase may be the final one for a supplier who is not selected for face-to-face negotiations (selection on the "short list")
4. *Face-to-face discussions* enable the parties to develop a more subtle appreciation of the match between the buyer requirements and the respective offers (usually two or three). It represents an opportunity to test the existence (or not) of an air of cooperation between the respective parties. We usually feel this to be the most important phase of the decision making process although, in reality, the decision has all but been made beforehand.

5. *The outcome of negotiations* is set out in an agreement between the parties ("Memorandum of Understanding") confirming the appointment of the supplier subject to the drafting of detailed terms and conditions prior to contract signature.

Progress through the five phases is strongly related to both the project specific context (the atmosphere created in the interaction between the buying and selling centres) and the environmental context (the milieu of both offer and demand) within which the negotiations take place. The key success factors (in addition to the intrinsic qualities of the proposal), which facilitate the passage between phases, are based largely upon the anticipatory work carried out within the milieux and correspond to the attitude adopted by a client from active support to complete rejection of any pro-active approach by the supplier (the Anglo-Saxon attitude which maintains the distance between the parties versus the Latin attitude, which is oriented more towards cooperating with the supplier).

They can be summarised, in phase specific terms, from the suppliers standpoint as follows:

- *Phase 1 — proposal preparation*: requires the ability to become involved at an early stage in the process through effective intelligence gathering within the milieu/mapping the project specific relational criteria/rapidly mobilise a project team to follow the emerging opportunity/use either the support of a pole of continuity to facilitate direct customer contact (some customers reject supplier involvement at this stage of the process) or, a third party to generate customer awareness/establish a two way dialogue in order to build or influence the contents of the tender document/be aware of competitor actions.
- *Phase 2 — informal meetings*: use the strength of a relational position to set up an informal discusson/build a climate of collaboration and confidence within which to reinforce relationships between individuals/bring together a team capable of responding to the full range of questions which may be asked/eventually, in an expert capacity, explain the reasons behind suggested alternatives without revealing one's hand completely/gain as much competitive intelligence as possible concerning competitor proposals.
- *Phase 3 — development of a negotiating strategy*: complete the project relationship map/understand the role the customer wishes the supplier to play (partner or instruction taker)/activate and maintain as many informal contacts as possible within the client organisation (if a culture of openness exists) so as to pick up any weak signals/predict proposal amendments which may be called for (local remuneration, financing of the local part, risk-sharing etc.)/ encourage the active involvement of those parties in the milieu able to positively influence the customer during the selection process/prepare to de-construct the demand.
- *Phase 4 — face-to-face bargaining*: be prepared to make a new offer after the first round of negotiations (don't stick to the first proposal in an evolving

competitive situation)/be prepared to change one of the offer partners for someone who may have a closer relationship with the customer/maintain an atmosphere of collaboration/be able to participate in a two way dialogue within the limits of the role the customer intends to assign to the supplier/ be prepared to re-construct the demand at the right time.

- *Phase 5 — conclusion of negotiations*: be ready to send in a legal advisor, sometimes to the other side of the world for an indefinite period/include the proposed project manager in the sales team and in face-to-face discussions/plan a return to normal relations with those parties in the milieu who were used to assist in negotiations (the return to a social as opposed to economic link)/ be ready to eventually negotiate additional work (both that required by the customer and that initiated by the supplier).

Face-to-face with the buyer

The four dimensions of the offer

Negotiations, despite being an integral part of the relationship, only exist because there is a tangible offer to be discussed. The offer is therefore the tangible element in negotiations, even if other aspects have an impact on the parties: power, dependency, upholding social links, personal ambition and interest, etc.

Traditionally, project-based companies have broken down the offer into two key dimensions in accordance with the technical, commercial and general parameters of the tender documents:

- the technical/functional offer;
- the commercial offer, which addresses the financial and contractual conditions imposed by the customer.

Specialists attach great importance to a third offer dimension, which is often hidden or ignored, the political offer: "while playing an important role, it is often difficult to describe" (Balenbois, 1981). In effect, it rarely corresponds with something expressly mentioned by the customer (except where certain compensation issues or technology transfer is involved) and is not documented. Although implicit, it is readily identified by the customer when reading between the lines of a proposal. It describes the position of the company in the demand milieu and, in particular, within the network of quasi-political figures. For example, in the Spanish building industry, there exists a complex network of relationships between contractors and decision makers, at all levels, be they appointed or elected. This huge, informal network operates in accordance with un-written rules. It has its habits and its customs, as in all societies, but the goals sought by its members, more often, differ widely: public welfare, profit.

It should be noted that today, most organisations are vicitms of political myopia: in identifying politics (*polis* = city in Ancient Greece), too readily, with politicians many don't give sufficient consideration to society as a whole. With the increasing illegitimacy of politicians, their parties, and the rising numbers of associations and other spontaneous, non-political groups, companies also have great difficulty in putting together a proposal which might bear scrutiny from a societal perspective having taken into account those parties which do not belong to the traditional sphere of politics. The global deterioration of standards in public life and those of elected officials has been to the benefit of emerging local, and primarily non-political, bodies whose "hands are clean" (the Italian *mane pulite*) and who are now able to play an influential role on projects. As a result, it is now prudent to distinguish between four offer dimensions:

1. the technical/functional offer, including products, services (technical assistance, after sales, training) work, etc.
2. the financial/contractual offer, including financial terms (price, conditions of payment, revision formulae), conditions of contract (warranties, hardship clauses) and also, details of any financial (barter, counter-trade, buy back) and contractual arrangements (BOOT, joint ventures);
3. the political offer, including both formal and informal accords between local partners, details of local investments and, generally speaking, all investments made by the supplier within the customer's milieu to improve his political position;
4. the societal offer, including all action taken by the supplier to improve his position with civilian groups having an interest in, or against, the project (associations, users, inhabitants).

The international competition for the huge waste treatment concession for the town of Marseille, as summarised below, provides a good example of the integration of political and societal dimensions within the offer. Three groups were selected to participate in the final round of negotiations: Générale des Eaux and Lyonnaise-Dumez in consortium, EdF (Electricité de France) was represented by its joint-subsidiary (with the Caisse des Dépôts), Pronergies. As for the huge American corporation, Waste Management, it was relying on its alliance with SAE and the establishment of a joint venture company, Auxiwaste, to make significant inroads in France. The other groups, having generally weak positions in the Marseille milieu, were thrown out including, among others, Bouygues and its SAUR subsidiary, which had never managed to become established in the south of France. The three groups had been refining their technical and financial proposals over several months. However, it appeared that the social and political dimensions would be more important in the decision making process and both were inextricably linked. The Mayor of Marseille was hanging on for some practical assistance from the bidders in his efforts to satisfy the voters. SAE demonstrated a keenness to make a political investment in Marseille, particularly in the Grand Prado property development or, in the Prado-Carénage tunnel. Waste guaranteed an environmentally friendly solution for the Entressen discharge. Générale des Eaux offered to provide a substantial push to enable property development around the Porte d'Aix to get off the ground, albeit on a reduced scale. *Cité de la Biotique*, the future centre for biotechnologies in the town was at last beginning to see the light of day thanks to some help from the property division of Générale des Eaux and negotiations for the renovation of the Palais de Congrès were at the point of succeeding. Elsewhere, the two giants of the water industry offered to create a research centre on the environment at the Marseille College of Engineering and the *Institut Universitaire des Sciences et Techniques de l'ingénieur*. Finally, EdF tried to give itself a green, socially conscious perspective by contributing towards the protection of the *calanques* — a twenty mile stretch of particularly attractive coastline — which is close to the heart of all the inhabitants of the area. Such pledges, although voluntary, would certainly not come for free and must be considered a fundamental element of the negotiation.

Companies must today manage each of the offer dimensions in order to differentiate themselves and their proposals from the competition. Based upon the habits and customs in both the milieux of offer and demand and an assessment of the various actors within the milieu of demand, one mode of differentiating a proposal is to concentrate on a single dimension given relatively less attention by competitors. In the case of the Marseille waste treatment contract, while its competitors were prepared to compete on the political dimension, EdF appeared to prefer playing the societal card in the hope of mobilising those elements of Marseille society who felt it was more important to conserve the charm of the *calanques* than to develop more buildings or a *Cité de la Biotique*. Furthermore, it is not uncommon for companies to compensate with local jobs for gaining the contract during times of crisis or actual unemployment. All these are effective mechanisms for achieving a differential advantage and a better alignment with emergent parties in the milieu. Some companies may even not hesitate to mobilise public opinion against a competing project which is either environmentally unfriendly or in-aesthetic to give the impression of being a white knight which will solve the problems of society and those of the politicians grappling with the same public.

The risk approach

The differentiation of the offer remains the principal problem for project negotiators. In an effort to find a solution the early eighties were marked by an adherence (too quickly!) to the marketing credo "listen to your customers". It was not until later that they realised this credo bore little relevance for them. Why? Because, unlike companies working in the area of consumer goods or standard industrial products, project-based companies do not need to carry out market research to ascertain customer needs. The customer's needs are imposed through the tender documents and specifications, which can sometimes run into several thousand pages. In fact, project organisations are never in a position to anticipate demand in the same manner as consumer goods suppliers but must react to customer requirements. It goes without saying that the demand criteria are not always stated or clearly expressed in the tender documents and it is important to be able to clarify certain requirements. However, to rely too much on this approach, will ensure all competitors have access to the same information (even to the extent of being aware of the customer's budget) and accordingly, submit similar, totally banal, offers. Listening to the customer is therefore not sufficient to achieve a differential advantage and the negotiations must not be restricted to this one line of enquiry. To the contrary, we increasingly observe what might be termed a constructive dialogue with the customer. That is to say, a dialogue which leads to a better understanding and, at the same time, an opportunity to influence the customer's needs. Project negotiation is not a question of adopting a neutral stance in relation to client requirements, neither is it a case of going to the extreme of attempting to impose a ready prepared solution or be so convinced as to the worthiness of one's proposal that little effort is made to understand the problems of the customer and his partners. It requires the seller to establish his credibility as an expert in the client's problem and thus be in a position to build or influence the customer's perception of the risk associated with the various options under consideration.

Under these circumstances we might use the risk approach (Salle and Silvestre, 1992), which is based upon the assumption that all purchase decisions involve acceptance of risk, to a greater or lesser extent, by the organisations and/or individuals concerned. Similarly, the perceived risks will greatly influence the buying centre's behaviour. The importance attached to such risks (the level and nature of the perceived risk) depends, firstly, on their project related impact (costs, completion times, performance characteristics, importance to the customer, positioning within its context) and, secondly, on the individuals involved (the personal stakes, their zest for innovation, culture, personality characteristics, power structures). The attitude to risk can be ascertained by the behaviour of figures in the buying centre (what they say, or do) as negotiations progress, which reflects a desire to reduce such risk from their point of view.

It is important to stress that perceived risks in the buying centre can differ from any evaluation of risk made by the negotiator, based upon an assessment of the stakes at play for the customer (which we will refer to as incurred risks). In effect, the amount of information and its subsequent dissemination, together with the consideration and importance attached to certain issues may differ between the buying and selling parties to the negotiation. Furthermore, the supplier is confronted by interpretations of two kinds. In the first instance, those emanating from customer behaviour during specific project negotiations (arising from perceived risks) with all the attendant possibilities during this phase and, secondly, those derived from the project characteristics (interpreted as incurred risks) which he has accumulated, to a greater or lesser extent, from relational investments within the milieu, both generally and in terms of the project in question. The difference between incurred risk and perceived risk can become a window of opportunity during negotiations once the gap has been clearly identified. Given his expertise in the field, the negotiator is able to re-phrase the customer's problem in a more distinctive manner which may encourage a change in attitude towards the acceptance of particular variations which are better aligned with the specific competencies of the supplier: a kind of de-construction and re-construction of the demand.

Guided by the customer and the characteristics of his proposal, the negotiator has a number of options available to him:

- Minimise the customer's perceived risk on the project he wishes to carry through to a successful conclusion. In this case, the negotiator restricts his attention to the client's requirements, as expressed in the RFP documents and, in such circumstances, the negotiating agenda is invariably set by the customer. Contractors competing for work on the Eurodisney theme park were faced with this type of negotiation. There is no possibility of putting forward alternatives for consideration and risk reduction, as perceived by the client, focuses on two of the four offer dimensions: the technical/functional and financial/contractual elements.
- Re-evaluate the priority attached to perceived risks in such a way as to minimise the inherent risk associated with an offer by increasing the importance of those risks associated with competitor proposals or those which are minimised by one's own approach. In this case the aim of the negotiator is to modify the hierarchy of customer expectations.
- Impress upon the customer those risks judged to be important but which may not have been perceived in such terms. For example, the risk of wear in one of the project components, specific issues affecting project viability, the risk of some residents employing blocking tactics to delay the project. In these instances, the negotiator must be able to put forward risk reduction measures.

It is therefore possible to use each of the offer dimensions. The Marseille waste treatment project illustrates well the different manner in which the three groups concerned set out to look for incurred risk. We can almost say that in particular cases the interaction between the parties during negotiations can influence, or even create, the structure of the buying centre by identifying a given risk which may be attributed to one of the figures in the buying centre. Finally, the aim of the negotiator must be to build a comprehensive solution which reduces the combined risks as perceived by the customer.

If, during the course of face-to-face negotiations, the negotiator decides to adopt the risk approach, great care must be taken as to the timing. However, it is out of the question to identify an area of risk, as yet not perceived by the customer, and immediately propose a sweeping remedy. The customer must be allowed to appreciate the risk, blend it with his representations and begin to redefine the problem in the light of this new information before being able to contemplate the embryo of a solution. The negotiator must therefore encourage the gradual evolution of a negotiating climate which will allow a possible solution, which is oriented towards the supplier's distinctive competencies, to be put forward. In such circumstances, the offer becomes truly differentiated since it is related to a re-definition of the problem in conjunction with, and by, the customer himself. It's a kind of real-time marketing as stated recently by McKenna (1995). On the other hand there are many examples of differentiation gimmicks whereby the introduction of new elements or alternatives has little impact (other than a seductive one) because the customer does not have the mind set, an awareness of the issues, the time to take them on board or understand their originality (if there is any) and utility potential.

The Project Development Manager: Broker of Internal and External Resources

If intelligence gathering and, consequently, relationship development outside a particular project environment, are the responsibility of all personnel within the company, the co-ordination of project negotiations and thus, the integration of all relational investments within a project, would appear to be the responsibility of the Project Development Manager (PDM).

In fact, rather than being the "odd-job" man, the PDM is increasingly required to play the conductor's role. The days have gone when the PDM arrived alone to negotiate each element of the project: technical specifications, the financial package, after sales service, contractual conditions, etc. Then, he was the connection, for life, between the company and customer organisation without always being in control of what was signed. To highlight the end of this era, a tale which is told in different forms, is well known in project based companies. It tells how, in the early 1980s, a South-European PDM was visiting a Scandinavian client and found himself defenceless in front of ten people, that is to say the customer's complete buying team: the Purchasing Director, Chief Buyer, Production Director, Design Engineer, Commissioning Manager, After-Sales Manager, Financial Director, the client's banker, the PDM of one of the customer's major sub-contractors and a Marketing Manager. Each person had well prepared questions and expected precise answers. Our engineer, fully understanding his limitations, could only note the questions and pass them on, by telex, to his headquarters somewhere in the South of Europe.

It is interesting to see how things have changed over the last decade by comparing two articles dedicated to the PDM by the same publication, *l'Usine Nouvelle*, only ten years apart.

1980. "Ingénieurs d'affaires: maîtriser un projet dans toutes ses dimensions". (Project Development Manager: controlling all dimensions of a project). (Nicolas Perris, *l'Usine Nouvelle*, May 1980, pp. 104–9):

> Whatever the product sold and the phase of intervention, the PDM must be in control of each dimension of the project and be able, at any time, to effect a compromise between the commercial, technical, contractual and managerial

requirements. The commercial aspects of his role generally give rise to passionate and contradictory relationships. Without always admitting it, many still think, that for an engineer to get involved in commercial activities, is something akin to relinquishing the prestige of his profession and wasting his training. A good PDM can be a mediocre prospector (a role fulfilled by the sales department). On the other hand, he dare not be ineffective during commercial negotiations, calling for firm control of all of the strings. He must understand, in particular, the financial and contractual issues, which are an area of deficiency among many PDM's, few of whom are aware that a price depends upon the conditions of payment. Furthermore, he must understand how to use these variables to his advantage during negotiations: to fight on a price variation formula or a warranty clause [. . .] The complexity of the solutions to be evaluated within strict deadlines often give rise to a failure on the part of the PDM to appreciate that the context within which he operates is not a purely technical one.

1990. "Ingénieur d'affaires: ce nouveau négociateur" (Project Development Manager: this new negotiator) (Philippe Andréani, *l'Usine Nouvelle*, no. 2285. 4 October 1990. (pp. 74–5):

> This technician, increasingly a marketing man, orchestrates, supervises and co-ordinates the multiple contributors and participants involved in the definition and selling of project business. He has an aptitude for negotiations, an acute awareness of human relations, he is rigorous and enquiring, has sound technical knowledge, financial and contractual competence and usually speaks two languages. However, the PDM is not a "wonder of the world", and even less the fruit of a capricious recruiting agent's imagination. Whatever his level of intervention within the project process, the PDM's responsibility relates principally to his skill as a communicator: on the one hand with his client and, on the other, with the functional disciplines in his own organisation and other parties with an interest in the project. Hence, the PDM can be compared with a turntable around which revolve a multitude of contributors, each with multiple and often contradictory expectations. His role is to integrate this diversity, all the more so on international projects.

In fact, our man is less an engineer and more an "intrapreneur", that is to say, a person able to motivate a project team charged with responsibility for preparing a proposal and carrying out negotiations to the point of contract signature. Henceforth, he rarely travels alone, being flanked by his partners in the selling team: either members of the organisation (technicians, lawyers, financial experts, etc.) or external contributors (allies, subcontractors, friendly institutions).

Outside the confines of a particular project, the PDM encourages his/her colleagues to net the "offer milieu" throughout poles of resources: core external parties within the company's network of resources (sources of skills, competencies and capacity) which the project group can mobilise, if need be, in a particular situation. The offer milieu includes not only a diversity of organisations which are able to undertake specific project packages (sub-contractors, joint venture partners, etc.), but also competitors who participate on joint research and development projects or, figures which may play an intermediary role between the supplier and the customer and who are simultaneously represented in both the offer and demand milieux (architects, consultants, etc.). The particular responsibility of the PDM is to encourage the mobilisation and adaptation of both internal and external resources to meet the specific requirements of each project: which partner, what level of responsibility (technical, economic, political), what level of influence in the project.

This introduces questions regarding the mode of entry into the project system: alone, in joint venture, as a main contractor or as a sub-contractor? The company may not always be the principal respondent if it has been introduced to the project by another party. In certain circumstances a degree of flexibility may exist by which to alter both the status and roles of parties within the milieu: the hierarchical relationship between management and sub-contractors need not necessarily be fixed once and for all and each party can, in turn, agree to become the final client. The mobilisation and adaptation of resources is equally relevant in terms of internal strengths and capacity constraints which may be influenced by a heavy workload within the company or in one of the affiliates it relies upon to provide particular skills. In such cases the negotiating talents of the PDM may be put to the test in order to achieve a proper balance between internal and external resources commitments.

Should we still be referring to the engineer when more and more companies are using business school graduates or even lawyers and accountants completing a postgraduate degree to play this intrapreneurial role? Of course, this trend has not reached all companies, far from it. However, the pre-eminent image of engineers has been badly shaken. Many see the future of this role as being open to any individual capable of motivating a project group and specialised in at least one of the project dimensions, whether it be technical, financial, legal or logistic; someone with a systems orientation supported by a project team of part time marketers, each of whom has a relationship with actors in the milieu of demand. According to the nature of the relationship to be developed (technical, financial, political) and also the attributes of a leadership style focusing upon communication, the PDM would encourage and stimulate the interactive role played by certain members of the project team within the demand environment.

Conclusion

In summary, project negotiations appear to place less emphasis upon the capabilities we generally associate with salesmen (tenacity, persistence, etc.) and reflect to a much greater extent relationship skills together with the expertise of the negotiator and his project team. The ability to animate and combine the respective strengths of the buying centre and its satellites, together with the selling centre and its partners, in order to re-evaluate and resolve the customer's predicament is central to project negotiations. This ability is dependent upon relational investments made by company personnel in the offer and demand milieus which allow the organisation to anticipate projects and their negotiations.

We have come a long way from the time when project negotiations appeared essentially to revolve around discussions concerning price following a call for tenders. Today, we are facing more complexity: a negotiating process divided into five phases, an offer composed of four dimensions, a PDM supported by a project team, a customer circulating in a milieu with poles of continuity, a supplier developing submissions in conjunction with poles of resources from his offer milieu, etc. Each of these developments can give the company a different perspective of project negotiations: the only permanency lies in the fact that, in all cases, project negotiations are simply an episode in the relationship. This must not be seen as being unique to project negotiations: major account sales progress in a similar manner. In a wider context, we can even say that it is the pre-eminent feature of all business to business negotiations.

CHAPTER 14

Preparing Mergers and Acquisitions in the European Union: The Asset of Cooperative Negotiation*

VIVIANE DE BEAUFORT AND ALAIN LEMPEREUR

Introduction

If two people want their marriage to succeed, they often need to know each other well, *before* the wedding, disclosing enough information to each other about their real qualities and "the rest". Cooperation at this preparation stage will help both partners to strengthen qualities and to overcome weaknesses during their life together.

Drawing further on the preparation-to-marriage metaphor, we will analyze its relevance to the *intercorporate* level for making European mergers and acquisitions more efficient. We will assert in the first part that many failures of M&A may well be caused by the lack of fruitful contacts between the two sides at various stages. This is particularly true for hostile takeovers, where contacts are minimal and often tense. Many opportunities to know each other better are lost in the absence of cooperative negotiation.

The remainder parts of this chapter focuses on the content of this required mutual knowledge, whatever strategy is chosen. In a preparation for a M&A in the European Union, there are many elements to learn about one's own company, and even more to learn about oneself and the other when the M&A is cross-cultural. There is also much to learn about the other company as such, through audit. We hope to prove that, under many circumstances, this multi-faceted knowledge — the possession or the refinement of which often depends on the other — will condition an efficient implementation of the M&A. These multiple elements aim at reinforcing our thesis that a successful M&A may strongly rely on early cooperative negotiation.

---

*The authors are grateful to Raymond Gianno, Christian Koenig, and Jane Salk, who have been kind enough to review this chapter in an early version. Remaining mistakes should not be attributed to them, but only to the authors' inability to deal with their perceptive comments.

Viviane de Beaufort and Alain Lempereur

Toward a Better Strategy: Hostile or Negotiated M&A?

This first part may seem provocative, for we argue that faced with the alternative of selecting a hostile takeover or a negotiated M&A, though hostile takeovers are often available, managers have strong incentives to opt for negotiated options. Hostile takeovers and tender offers are exposed with their respective advantages and drawbacks. When tender offers are dealt with, some essential keys to their successful negotiation are also briefly presented.

Hostile takeovers

The major advantage of a hostile takeover is that, if it succeeds, it may grant the purchasers a broader control to do what they wish in the target company. They did not have to negotiate and do not have to negotiate at a later stage. Accomplishing a *coup* in secrecy, without disclosing anything about their own intentions, can also be gratifying. However, beyond any momentary enjoyment, a hostile takeover often produces three types of counter-effects, linked with three lost opportunities of negotiation: before, during and after the operation itself.

First lost opportunity of negotiation: before the takeover bid

In order to keep the whole initiative discreet and to maintain the effect of surprise, prospective bidders need to keep their distance from the target, limiting contacts to a minimum. In doing so, they lose a chance to have access to information that they could have obtained, had they initiated some pre-negotiations. Their knowledge is limited to what is diffused to the public, i.e., in reality to what is known from professional outsiders. As we will show later, the audit of the target should be thorough to be efficient, and integrate many dimensions: financial, commercial, legal, social. Many gaps appear for each of these elements in a hostile bid, as investigating them would uncover the raider's intentions that by definition are to remain secret. The audit of the target remains general, since most often it does not benefit from these insiders' data.

Getting such restricted information and refusing to negotiate create an "ivory tower effect", that frequently persists in following steps of the takeover. Bidders claim to know how a target is good for them and what is good for the target. These presumptions are unchallenged, as target managers do not participate in any review process — that would likely happen otherwise — and therefore do not have the possibility to provide reality checks, or to refine any conclusion or strategy that they conceive of for the target.

In that context, bidders' self-examination is often limited. With no prospective negotiating partner in mind, potential acquirers tend not to fully incorporate the target interests in their own vision or strategy, which can be sketched in too narrow ways. As none is to be persuaded, there is no real incentive for acquirers to really challenge their own views of the acquisition, even formally, and no need to ever change their convictions. Hostile takeovers are then often started as a fight, without much testing of the accuracy of one's strategy and of one's information about the target. As in the prisoner's dilemma (Axlerod 1984), the hope, in being the first to defect, to strike, is to appropriate some competitive advantage without giving the other any time to retaliate.

Second lost opportunity of negotiation: during the takeover

When the takeover is launched, more or less overtly, things do not necessarily follow the course bidders had predicted. Bidders may have underestimated the will of the target managers to defend their company and their capacity to resist. The battle may cost much to both sides. This can prove even more ominous if other possible contestants, beside the bidders and the target managers, enter the scene.

In theory, understanding the risks of successive, mutual defections and aggressions, detrimental to both companies, prospective buyers may still decide to turn to negotiation, in order to explain their strategy of acquisition. They can also use communication channels — documents to shareholders, to the press. This strategic change towards cooperation can prevent much trouble and waste of energy. Yet, it needs to be reciprocated by the target.

In reality, once a relationship has been played from the beginning in the mode of a power struggle, it is rare that either side of the contest will easily shift to, and engage into cooperative negotiation. Each group of managers will likely refuse a shift until they can justify it by some obvious advantage for their side. The target managers, frustrated by what they perceive as a first aggressive move, may want to suspend all operations of the acquirers, and by some one-sided move, may then defect too, returning in kind what may have been taken away from their control. As will be shown, they have several means to stop the raider's acquisition. As for the managers in charge of the interests of the acquiring company, they will probably want to keep the competitive advantage of the first move of surprise and not cancel it. Consequently, this second moment of possible negotiation often corresponds with one more lost opportunity of establishing productive contacts between parties. It rather gives rise to what has been called in M&A literature "takeover defenses". Let us recall some means specifically provided for by legislation or regulations and which can be brought in Europe before different authorities (see Table 14. 1.).

Some of these defenses may have been introduced by legislators to limit hostile takeovers, the legality of which may also be interpreted restrictively by courts. The target may also lobby its national concentration or merger authority to prevent the operation on the basis of abusive dominating position. In Sweden (Beaufort 1995b), for example, the case may be brought before the *Konkurrensverket*, which first, will try to negotiate the case first with its *Konkurrentsombudsmannen* and later, if conciliation fails, will ask the Tribunal of first resort of Stockholm

TABLE 14.1
Legal battle against hostile takeovers

Means	Issues	Examples	Outcome
• Referral to concentration or merger control national or EU authorities	• Offeree/counter bidder tries to have bid blocked on competition grounds (national or EU level)	• Gold Fields • Irish Distillers (Ireland) • MBB (West Germany) • Rowntree (UK)	‡ ‡ † *
• Referral to courts: commercial or others	• Unfair trading/insider trading cases referred by stock exchange authorities investigations	• BAM (Italy) • Bénédictine (France) • Compagnie du Midi (France) • Epéda (France) • Irish Distillers (Ireland) • Télémécanique (France)	* ‡ * ‡‡ * ‡‡† *
• Referral to stock exchange authorities	• Offeree/counter bidder tries to have bid blocked on unfair trading/insider trading/ shareholders equal treatment grounds	• Assubel (Belgium) • Banesto (Spain) • Epéda (France) • Télémécanique (France)	† ‡‡ ‡‡† *
• Referral to foreign direct investment control authority/ specific control authorities	• Have the offer blocked/ delayed on foreign investment control or sector control grounds	• Assubel (Belgium) • Britoil (UK) • Compagnie du Midi (France) • Grupo 16 (Spain) • MBB (West Germany)	† * * † †
• Referral to authorities outside the EU	• Appeal to foreign legislation when possible (i.e. subsidiaries in foreign countries, intern. laws)	• Gold Fields (UK)	‡

Source: Booz-Allen Acquisitions Services (1989), 19.
* Lost battle (acquired by contested bidder)
† Delayed/pending result or partially acquired by first/second bidder or totally acquired by second bidder
‡ Won battle/remained independent or partially owned by white knight

(Stockholms Tingsärtt) to decide the case. If some thresholds[1] are reached, the European Commission (DG IV), may also intervene, and decide if the proposed M&A affects competition in the European market.

Next to these regulatory defenses, others may have been introduced preventively by the shareholders in the Articles of Association: pre-emption rights, voting rights, however some of these clauses are forbidden for French quoted companies, for example. Other board and management protections, usually named "golden parachutes",[2] can make it very costly for a prospective purchaser to get rid of current managers. Finally, on the spot, the imagination of target managers can be inexhaustible. Several scenarios of defense can be played (Booz-Allen 1989):

- The capital increase defense: Though a simple decision by the board of directors can sometimes be authorized in advance provided, e.g., it is reconfirmed every five years, this operation must normally receive the agreement of an extraordinary general meeting. Sometimes this tactic consists in debt conversion into capital, so that the raider's shares become diluted.
- The pac man defense: here, the board members themselves launch a takeover bid against their raider. This is a version of tit-for-tat strategy (Axelrod 1984), that aims at making the other give up a competitive behavior while adopting the same behavior.
- The fat man defense: by simplified takeovers, the target acquires the assets of its subsidiaries in order to become more difficult to swallow (cf. Time Warner).
- The crown jewels defense: this tactic consists for the target to get rid of its most coveted element. The would-be raider needs to decide whether to become the owner of an empty shell. Redoubtable, this defense is rarely used in Europe as often corporate law prohibits selling of essential assets, once a takeover operation has started. It violates the principle of day-to-day matters left to managers and requires prior shareholders' acceptance. It failed when the Agnelli, Perrier owners, tried to use it to prevent Nestlé from a takeover.
- The white knight defense: The board looks for a savior, with whom it will be possible to negotiate a better deal. The white knight may assist with the escalation of the bid itself or participate in reserved capital increase (cf. Société Générale de Belgique and Suez).

---

[1] Three thresholds must be crossed for the European Commission to intervene: the companies involved in the M&A must (i) have a world-wide turnover of more than 5 billion ECU; (ii) a EU turnover of more than 250 million ECU for the two parties at least, and (iii) realize at least one-third of their turnover in more than one member state (Regulation 4064/89 (JOCE L. 291, December 21, 1989)).

[2] Normally, managers can be dismissed *ad lib* by owners. Yet, in some countries, like the United Kingdom or Germany, managers' mandates may be linked with a labor contract with high severance premiums. See Booz-Allen (1989).

The bidders may have to face one or several of these barriers that the law or target managers are able to raise. The consequence of this struggle is often unpredictable (Booz-Allen 1989, pp. 17–19). Neither the potential acquirer nor the target can predict where maneuvers and counter-maneuvers will lead. Even an apparent victory can be deceiving: the acquisition may finally be realized at a higher price than expected for the bidder, or prevented only at a high cost for the target (Mnookin & Wilson 1989; Mnookin & Ross 1995a, pp. 4, 20–1). Again the refusal to negotiate is often detrimental to both companies.

Third lost opportunity of negotiation: after the takeover

If the bidders overcome all these obstacles at their advantage, they are controlling alone the highly coveted company, or at least sitting at the board with a strong majority. Yet, their hardest time may still lie ahead, particularly if they refuse to negotiate now. They may view the implementation of their post-M&A strategy as their private business, without caring so much about whom it applies to. Indeed, weighing how much easier it seems for them to simply give orders, why would they bargain, especially if much energy has already been drained by previous fights?

Yet, this third refusal to negotiate may imply consequences which are as equally unpleasant for the acquirers as they were before in prior refusals. What frequently happens at this post-acquisition stage is a covert confrontation of the acquirer with a coalition built around the different defeated forces of the target. This coalition, which is often tacit, gathers minority shareholders, old managers and workers. Minority shareholders may fear for their profits. Managers and workers may fear for their jobs. This coalition of discontent, that is ready to corner the new acquirers, raises the "principal/agent problem" (Pratt & Zeckhauser 1985; Mnookin & Ross 1995a, pp. 20–1; Mnookin, Peppet & Tulumello 1995b, Chapter 3), i.e., a possible conflict of interests between the owners (the principals) and those supposed to manage or to work for the company (the agents). In this context, within the company, agents may be tempted to optimize their personal interest rather than the company's interest. The results may be catastrophic, for the working atmosphere, as well as for the profits.[3]

Various strategies are available to quickly limit the effects of the principal/agent tension. From the beginning, what seems the most essential is that, before even the M&A occurs, the acquirer has a CEO available for the target company, who will unmistakably act in the interest of the acquiring company.[4] Immediately after taking control, acquirers (with the help of trustworthy managers) may need

---

[3] Beckers (1989), 444 sq. Studying post-M & A consequences, the author has shown that bidding companies could even be worse off in the long run than target themselves, especially if the raiders have not reached the hoped-for majority.

[4] Anslinger & Copeland (1996), pp. 130–1. Often protections of corporate interest exist to prevent this new manager from abuse of corporate assets.

to replace some of the present personnel who may not satisfy their needs. Yet, if some of the target managers cannot be easily removed, acquirers may need to resort to negotiation. They can offer them "golden handcuffs", i.e., strong incentives to remain on board and to work for, rather than against, the M&A. These incentives can be high salaries, but also profit shares or compensations that are contingent upon reaching some financial objectives (Anslinger & Copeland 1996, pp. 130–1.)

After this catalogue of possible advantages and drawbacks of hostile takeovers, it may be clearer *a contrario* why negotiations may offer many advantages for M&A. Dangers of hostile takeovers have appeared at a pre-contractual stage with the deficit of information, and have been confirmed during the bid or after, during implementation, where insufficient attention has been paid to the "reception" by the target of the bidder's strategy.

Negotiation of tender offers or mergers

Advantages and inconveniences of this option are very often directly opposite to those of hostile takeovers. First, in tender offers, there are higher risks issuing from information disclosure. Second, there is no way of being a winner alone. The potential offeree — and its managers in priority — must be convinced of the possible gains to derive from the M&A. In order to do so, the target counterparts must be involved in the M&A and considered as partners as soon as possible, from the auditing stage if managers so decide.

Getting information about the target through "pre-negotiation"

Through an initial stage of self-scrutiny and general investigation about potential offerees' culture, that we examine in detail in the two following parts of the chapter, managers have prepared themselves for this "pre-negotiation". The analytical tools that they have applied to themselves to discover their objectives and constraints, and to expand their cultural references and evaluations, can now be applied to the audit process of the other company. If they initiate contacts with the target managers and explain why they are interested in knowing more about their company, suggesting that some close collaboration is envisioned for the future, they may be able to have access to data which complete the limited public data that they were able to screen.

Progressively, as information is collected, prospective acquirers can refine the content they gave *a priori* to all their preparatory negotiation tools. Was the objective of having the target market the acquirer's own products such a feasible idea, when this complementary audit reveals that the target marketing department is overloaded? How must this previously unknown constraint in the target company change the acquirer's strategy? Does it mean that they should abandon this objective, or think of expanding the department? What kind of option should be discussed later at a negotiation stage to solve this problem? Who will pay for it? Should they think of another target already?

Getting an agreement of M&A : the actual negotiation

At best, after completing this audit and reviewing the content of their negotiation tools, which now apply to both sides, managers conclude that it is in the interest of their company to collaborate with such target in view of a M&A. It is time for them to transform preliminary contacts into actual negotiation, with the hope to reach a satisfactory agreement for both parties. They need to tell the CEO of the target, for instance, that even if they still consider different options, like joint-ventures or alliances, they would really appreciate to discuss with his or her delegates the possibility of a M&A.

By a thorough preparation, that we develop in the last three parts, and by first signs of opening, the prospective acquirers have empowered themselves as negotiators. Yet they have not made up their mind about the type of agreement that would satisfy their needs; they have simply investigated their strengths and weaknesses. They have made every effort to also be informed about their future partners. Now they will extend these preparatory tools in a joint problem-solving context. They will negotiate with the target managers or directly with the owner. Legally only the owner needs to be contacted, though practically target managers may be involved for the sake of future management. At this time, the potential seller of the target must also be aware of the possible conflict of interests that his or her own managers may face, knowing that they may have a personal interest in favoring the future owners, with whom they are going to work, at the expense of the present owner.

How should this negotiation be framed to be more efficient? Even if M&A are not joint ventures or strategic alliances, owners and managers of both companies have a strong interest in working together in order to render the negotiation as balanced as possible, and to build a relationship with each other. Beyond the deal with the target owner, the representatives of the acquirer will be better off involving early on in the process of M&A the target managers. The latter must view the success of the M&A as their success and continue to explain its legitimacy to their CEO, the shareholders, and the workers, i.e., all the people whose support is either required or beneficial. It can often be an error for the acquirers to come with a pre-cooked plan and to present some take-it-or-leave-it offer to the target owners and managers. It may be the best way to make the latter perceive a tender offer as a hostile bid, and to have them raise these defenses which were exposed in the previous section.

How can the managers of the acquiring company make sure that managers from the two companies work in joint problem-solving? They must establish procedures where each negotiation team is allowed to be questioner and answerer in turn. Each must have the opportunity to enrich their preparatory tools; the target managers must have time to prepare themselves, as the acquirer did. Each must be able to raise questions about the other company and to get answers. On the one hand, they must be able to investigate, and learn, about the objectives and constraints of the other in order to discover how they can be helpful. On the other hand, they must accept to expose and be questioned about their own objectives and constraints, in order to get appropriate aid. The idea is to make the process a two-way questioning and answering, to avoid the impression that the managers of one company have all the questions and answers. Offerer and offeree will not be afraid of uncovering their strengths and weaknesses.

Whenever it is necessary, managers of the offerer should also find imaginative ways of bypassing the principal/agent problem, reinforcing the responsibilities of the target managers whenever it is possible. As a rule of thumb, managers of the offerer should practise the principle of reciprocity, proposing to learn from their counterparts, before even asking them to learn from them. This way everyone can get acquainted to the other's methods of accounting, practices of production or distribution, etc.

During the negotiation, managers of both companies will be confronted with objectives and interests which may not be easy to reconcile. This will require sessions of brain-storming, to generate creative options. At the end of this process of invention, hopefully, some solutions will appear more susceptible to meet both parties' interests. These integrative solutions create value for both (Fisher, Ury & Patton 1991, pp. 56–80; Lax & Sebenius 1986, pp. 88–116; Haspeslagh & Jemison 1991). Some appropriate techniques may also need to be developed to solve smoothly distributive issues, like the determination of the price. Rather than being preoccupied only by guarantees of liabilities, legal or contractual, the options will have a broader scope, encompassing all these categories that matter in the life of corporations and that are envisioned in the multi-dimensional auditing that is explained in the last part of the chapter. Though the past matters, it is mainly in this sense that it helps focus on the future, on a common strategy to be followed after the agreement is signed. The talks need to determine which degree of autonomy should be maintained, which changes should be operated, which systems of decision making and of communication should be carried out (Rostand 1993, p. 58; Tanneau 1993, p. 64).

Above all, while they are working on producing satisfactory options for both, managers of the two companies should feel committed to forecast, as much as possible, the problems that may be raised at each integration stage of their companies. They should focus on their respective assets, and how each company can benefit from them, seeing the third identity of their relationship as expanding their own identity: in the interest of both entities, they can merge or federate some of their directions, and keep some others entirely separate (Salk 1994). Managers, when possible, should also fix clear strategic objectives and demand quick financial results.

They also should not hesitate to talk about changes to cope with weaknesses. Otherwise, "antisynergies" will work their way through, where only synergies were expected (Frank 1989 p. 99). Weaknesses can be worked on through exchange of personnel, methods and technologies, rather than through cash flow poured by the acquiring company. If restructuring is seen as necessary, it should be looked at from all the relevant dimensions; not only in commercial and financial terms, but also in human terms. Communication matters with all relevant agents. How will a restructuring plan be explained to, and accepted by, the personnel? How can workers be associated in this reflection?

The key of success of M&A can be linked with the degree of care with which integration has been prepared prior to the agreement, as much in terms of strengths and weaknesses (Beckers 1989, p. 448; Rostand 1993, p. 56). Agents drafting contracts (Reed 1989, p. 541; Newman 1989, p. 285; Fabre & Marois 1992, pp. 176–8; Poulain de Saint-Père 1995, p. 538) could nearly use the four rules of Cartesian methods: accepting to question or raise doubts about everything, oneself or the other ("rule of doubt"); going from the most complex to the simplest aspects, units, dealing with them carefully as auditing ("rule of analysis"); recomposing all these elements of the puzzle together as a consistent whole ("rule of synthesis"); and checking that no element has been forgotten ("rule of enumeration"). The rest of this chapter investigates the different elements of this puzzle which need to be put together, whatever M&A is concerned.

When some options have received full support from both negotiating teams, it is time for the relevant agents to report the results of the negotiation process to their respective principals, as the options must be translated into the reality of a future agreement. A good advice is to keep the channels of communication widely open between agents and principals during the whole process, from letters of intent, memorandum of understanding, and preparatory convention, to the final agreement (Reed 1989, pp. 530–86). It helps clarify the mandates of the respective negotiation teams. In mergers, it also avoids a last minute grandiose flop, when CEOs disapprove of the ready-to-be-signed contract.

Getting the negotiation profit: post-M&A implementation

Negotiators who have cooperated during previous stages, have accumulated a capital of trust, that will serve the M&A implementation. Integration will be present before the M&A even starts. Through early joint problem-solving and information disclosure, managers from both sides have built a working relationship. Thanks to this asset, though all the following hypotheses should be checked by further empirical studies, we may guess not only that success is more likely to occur for the M&A, but also that there will be a better capacity to adapt to future conflicts and needs for changes. If a problem arises in the execution of the integration program, negotiation methods may just be called for again, and used to solve it. Channels of communication will fully carry on the dialectic of questioning and answering we evoked, and that none will hesitate to apply to themselves or the other. Integration will just follow its course.

Through the contrast between hostile takeovers and negotiated offers, we have shown how negotiation can be viewed *a priori* as an asset for a more satisfactory strategy of M&A. Now we need to explore internally how negotiation itself can be made more efficient in order to create as much value as possible for both partners before the M&A even occurs, initiating as early as possible the process of integration that is proved to be essential for post-M&A success (Haspeslagh

& Jemison 1991). It raises the issue of accurate preparation, where different dimensions must be examined integratively too. Questions need to be asked about one's own company *and* the prospect, and about the cultural context of their present and future collaboration. These preparatory dimensions are not only relevant to negotiated M&A, but also to hostile takeovers too, though in this case, as we will continue to prove, collected answers may not be as outstanding and thorough as they should.

Self-examination as a Prospective Partner: Building M&A Tools

Self-examination, even on a specific question, is not an easy task in a company. Knowing how difficult it is within the same company, for each of its members, we foresee how difficult it may be at the actual negotiation stage of M&A to open oneself to potential prospects and to spontaneously disclose information to them. In general, managers do not want their company to look weak at all, or to uncover with precision its strength to a potential competitor who could use this information to his or her relative advantage.

Yet, however painful, during the preparation of a transaction, self-auditing has advantages for those who carry it on soon. The more quickly, as agents of your corporation, you screen the relevant-to-M&A aspects of your company, the easier it may be later for you to welcome some questioning from representatives of the target, for it will likely be directed towards data of your own review. If your screening precedes that of others and, if it brings you some insights, it is also probable that you will be better able to present them to the target managers, if you choose to, in a more acceptable light. You may even have explored means and actions in order to correct some imperfections you noticed, before you are even questioned about them by the other side.

For the scope of self-audit[5] in a European M&A context, early on, managers may distinguish whether the potential M&A will be cross-cultural. In most cases,

---

[5] Self-audit, which would go beyond what compulsory audit legally requires, is not such a frequent reflex in Europe, unfortunately. If it was, it would be highly desirable in M&A contexts, not only for potential acquirers as it is described in this section, but for potential targets or partners who aggree to play the game. Indeed voluntary self-audit would avoid many inconveniences, which can be observed when the acquirer (or, even worse, several acquirers with their respective audits) is (or are) screening a similar target. When these audits are realized by acquirers before the M&A, there is often some retention of information by the target managers and some subsequent errors of evaluations. When a complementary audit takes place after the decision of acquisition, it may uncover some detrimental elements which could have influenced the price and for which appropriate action, when possible, could have been undertaken (Cf. Beckers, 448). Self-audit by the target is sometimes practised in England however, where a company can be viewed without scruple as a product to sell. It can be done before the M&A happens, without retention of information and without waste of time for the acquirer(s). The risk is sometimes the disclosure of information about the company as such.

if managers intend to do business with a company of the same nation, self-examination may not be as explicit and as thorough. Managers on both sides share some similar national background. Yet, this difference between national and cross-border M&A may not be as clear-cut as it appears, as there may be deep cultural contrasts among corporations of the same nation. Therefore "cross-cultural" M&A would nearly be the rule (Frank 1989). Differences between corporate and national cultures would not be more than a question of degree.

The test would then be for managers to examine to which extent the corporate culture, where they are about to set up operations, practices elements they are familiar with: language; conventions of politeness; techniques of decision-making, of accounting, of management; assumptions about good services; behaviors towards the state, towards workers' participation; solutions from the legal system, etc. The closer managers feel to this culture; the more easily they will be able to work with the representatives of potential prospects; the more they will be able to focus on the transaction itself and find answers to a first range of questions, which are dealt with in this part and which are indispensable for any sort of M&A. The further managers are, the more homework they will have to do. They will have to add further questions, which are addressed in the following part and which deepen the self-audit and initiate the other-centered audit.

What are the underlying objectives of M&A for my company?

There can be many answers to this question, probably as many as M&A. They relate to the underlying interests that drive a company board to suggest M&A in the first place (Fabre & Marois 1992, pp. 24–8). The main interest is generally expansion, but if one digs deeper, M&A are realized for many more motivations, the possible combination of which often requires a well-crafted strategy: investing cash flow productively, reinforcing one's position on a market, gaining access to new markets, benefiting from complementary skills, restructuring, diversifying activities and risks, integrating up- or down-stream, controlling the costs of production or the prices of distribution, etc.[6] Knowing better one's objectives, one may already determine key factors of success and possible impediments. The multiple objectives of a company often require a multidimensional synergy for future departments to work together with compatible goals and methods, with comparable instruments of evaluation, etc. Yet, especially when financial buyers are involved, "unsynergistic" strategies can also be developed (Salk 1994, Anslinger & Copeland 1996).

In order to determine what objectives are beyond the surface of simple expansion, managers need to clarify them early on and to continue to do so as

---

[6] Next to, and often complementary to, these positive respectable goals that satisfy various corporate needs, some can be perceived as more negative: an industry may just want to eliminate a competitor, sometimes anticipating a takeover by the coveted target.

the process evolves. Yet, clarification of purpose does not exclude flexibility. Strategic objectives must leave room for decentralized maneuvering: agents must be free to invent satisfactory solutions during intermediary stages of the M&A operation, avoiding deadlocks, but also during later stages of implementation, avoiding obsolete answers. Questioning continues in order to solve new problems in the most pertinent way.

However, this flexibility to invent solutions at multiple stages may need to be contingent upon reaching precise financial objectives. Negotiators or, later, managers of the target may be assigned precise results, determining a satisfactory outcome of the M&A transaction or of its implementation, according to "reasonable" standards (Tanneau 1993, p. 67). For example, when the M&A has occurred, the criterion of financial success can be measured by the return on investment that the company or its competitors get for similar activities. Fixing such financial targets avoids easy contentment with narrow margins, and opens the way to other more successful decision-makers or policies, if necessary. It also adds incentives for agents to be more inventive, all the more so if a substantial part of their commission or salary depends on reaching these financial targets (Anslinger & Copeland 1996, p. 131).

Which constraints affect the strategy of my company?

Many aspects may restrain managers' capability to develop a M&A. They rest on the situation of a company, both internally and on the market. As illustrations of internal constraints that limit expansion, suffice it to quote the lack of funds to finance the operation, or knowledge about the targeted market, or know-how in the target activity, or skilled personnel to supervise the post-M&A stage in the future target. All these elements require a relevant report that evaluates their impact on the planned M&A and prevents them from becoming the causes of failure. This report must also determine if these constraints may or may not be tackled within the company by appropriate measures.

Managers of a company must strive to progressively overcome these constraints. If extra funds are needed to finance a M&A, could alternative ways of paying for the operation be imagined? Can a share of the benefits be used as cash? Can your bank participate? Because of the liberation of capital and of financial services within the European internal market, could local banks help better, or a subsidiary your company would create? Are there European structural funds or state subsidies available? Is cross-ownership an option? (Fauquet 1995.)

Creative ways of coping with internal conditions of financing for instance could also depend on external constraints, over which acquirers have a limited influence or no influence at all. If the M&A is to take place in Belgium or Spain, cross-holdings are legal; they are not in the United Kingdom or in Germany. For any option, there may thus be an "in-out" loop: solutions to internal constraints can sometimes be found through a careful study of the external conditions of a market that imposes in return its own limits on our imagination.

These "limits-opportunities" will even be more obvious and interesting to consider, when preparing cross-cultural M&A.

The most prominent external constraint, one that reduces or even suppresses freedom of action for M&A in the European Union, refers to the present position of a corporation on the market, be it national or European. Henceforth, a M&A is submitted to European or national concentration authorities. Thresholds determine if the M&A is to be examined by the Commission (cf. *supra* footnote 1), or by national anti-trust authorities, like the British Monopolies and Mergers Commission, the German *Bundeskartelamt*, the Swedish *Konkurrentsverket*, etc. Managers, preparing for a M&A involving a EU company, need to inquire about its probable impact on competition, checking that their future position on the market, as a likely result of the M&A, does not imply market distortions. Whatever mode of growth is chosen, negotiations may be compulsory with the national anti-trust authority or with the European Commission, that will need to be convinced that the M&A is congruent with legal criteria.[7]

Is a M&A an appropriate strategy?

Before managers engage into any M&A program, they need to investigate very carefully possible alternatives to M&A (Newman 1989, pp. 282–5). For any negotiation to proceed, it must be clear to decision-makers that there is no better alternative. We do not only mean (i) a negotiation of M&A with another target, but (ii) maybe a negotiation with this or another potential partner about another way of reaching more surely one's objectives (for example, through strategic alliances or joint-ventures), or (iii) no negotiation at all by creating oneself a branch or a subsidiary.

Why, in the European Union, has the ratio M&A/creation of subsidiaries grown two to one during the last ten years? The realization of the EU internal market has provoked a fast decompartmentalization of European economies. A context of emergency caused swift external growth. In this context, though M&A can prove costly operations, they often appear as better, quicker options, than creating subsidiaries for example. Indeed who knows, for example, how to market a product in Spain better than existing Spanish companies? Acquiring one of them often turns out to be more efficient than creating a subsidiary which always takes time, and involves the typical operational risks in a foreign maze.

Nonetheless the question of choosing an adequate strategy, possibly apart from M&A, should not be underestimated. It aims at discovering what has been called

---

[7] If a hostile takeover is envisioned, one may well expect the target company to be the opponent in legal argument, whereas if negotiated offers are preferred, the prospective partner is expected to be cooperative, and to provide his or her help to overcome this barrier. It is one more reason to favor the second mode.

the "best alternative" in negotiation literature.[8] Whatever happens at a later stage of the process, costs and predictable outcomes of the M&A must be measured according to this best alternative, that should always be kept in mind. If the total pay off of the operation remains higher than the best alternative, it makes sense to stick to the M&A and not to resort to the latter. If it does not, the best alternative must be preferred; there is no reason to remain attached to some specific negotiation strategy or target, when a more attractive solution is available.

Extended Self- and Other-Examination: Tools for Cross-Cultural M&A

If previous dimensions of preparation are requirements for any M&A, they must be complemented — in Europe as in anywhere in the world — by some close attention to other aspects when the operation is foreseen in a different culture, corporate or national (Frank 1989; Foster 1992; Faure & Rubin 1993; Véry 1995) Managers must focus on some further learning, in view of coping with a potential *double ignorance*:

- Managers dealing outside of their culture have to learn more deeply what they often ignore: the *underlying elements of another culture*, in terms of conventions or rules of accounting, organizations, labor relationships, etc. They need to go beyond ready-at-hand caricatures of the other's general and corporate culture, and to make an effort to empathize with elements that they may not be familiar with, as difficult as it may be. This trip outside of themselves will help them understand any target counterpart better, and also make it easier for this other person to understand them, as they will have tried to fill a possible gap that separates them.
- Cross-national managers also have to learn more about the *underlying elements of their own culture*, with its routines, legal habits, favored operations, etc. Beyond the superficial level, they need to reflect on what is so much part of their identity that they do not see it, and that they would not even waste time talking about, with one of the colleagues of their firm. They need to make more explicit much of what they have internalized as obvious, without reflection, under the impression of having always done it. This helps them understand and even adopt a foreign perspective about themselves and their culture, but more importantly, it can help them make a foreign person understand them better, as they already know what it is for them to be foreign to their own culture.

---

[8] Fisher, Ury & Patton (1991), 99–106, 164-5. They speak of BATNA, or "best alternative to a negotiated agreement". Applied to our chapter that favors cooperative M&A, the BATNA, the best alternative to a negotiated M&A, may be a hostile takeover; it may also be something else, like a joint-venture, a strategic alliance or the establishment of a subsidiary.

In a word, managers bridge the gap between the other and themselves: they reduce the difference between the other and them, by knowing more about the other's culture, and they distance themselves from their own culture. It means opening ourselves to others — opening ourselves and opening to others, making a trip inside and outside ourselves, adopting what Dean Allen Foster (1992) calls a "global mindset". This double work is first and foremost for managers to put their assumptions to the test, questioning the answers that they hold about others and themselves, what goes without saying, for example, in their company, in their national corporate law, in their taxation system; what they would have hastily assumed to exist elsewhere as such.

How to prepare for different cultural references?

What does global mindset mean concretely? How can it contribute to strategy? It helps turn assumptions into doubts, doubts into inquiries, inquiries into checked information, this information into strategy. It helps find differences where only the existence of similarities was presumed. However insignificant some information can look at first sight, it may prove later useful in a strategy. For example, from a legal viewpoint, efforts of European harmonization have been made. In Community law, Directives have established some coordination (Coopers and Lybrand 1989, Vol. 1., Appendix D1) (Those with an asterisk have *not yet* come into force.)

> First Directive (March 9, 1968). : On safeguards required by all companies, i.e. basic requirements for registered private companies, including the publication of the Articles of Association, with director names, and share capital information.
>
> Second Directive (December 13, 1976): On safeguards for the formation of public limited liability companies, including conditions for their maintenance, increase and reduction of capital, in view of a minimum protection of shareholders and creditors.
>
> Third Directive (October 9, 1978): On mergers of public limited liability companies, which oblige managers to prepare and publish drafts of mergers.
>
> Fourth Directive (July 25, 1978): On annual accounts of some companies, which defines evaluation rules, a specific content, auditing and publication of annual accounts for public and private companies.
>
> *Fifth Directive (proposed on September 9, 1983): On the structure of public limited companies and the powers and obligations of directors, of shareholders, of supervisory boards, of employees.
>
> Sixth Directive (December 17, 1982): On the de-mergers of public limited companies, and the special risks for shareholders and creditors.
>
> Seventh Directive (June 13, 1983): On consolidated accounts, especially important for the financial transparency of groups of companies.
>
> Eighth Directive (April 10, 1984): On the approval of auditors.
>
> *Tenth Directive (proposed on January 25, 1983): On cross-border mergers of public limited companies.
>
> Eleventh Directive (December 21, 1989): On the disclosure requirements of branches in another Member State.
>
> Twelfth Directive (December 21, 1989): On single member private limited companies.

* Thirteenth Directive (proposed February 16, 1989): On takeovers and other general bids.

Yet, despite these Directives, major differences remain and will remain, from one legal system to another (Beaufort 1994). Managers need to adapt to these situations, and learn for example that legal conditions for limited companies still vary in the member states, despite the common rules of First and Second Directives (Table 14.2.). Minimum capital investment range from ECU 2500 ($3200) in Finland to ECU 127,000 ($160,000) in Italy; minimum number of shareholders from one to seven; Articles of Association need to be notarized in some countries only. More importantly, management structures may be *monist*, with only a board of directors ruling the company, like in the UK or in France, or *dualist*, where it shares the power with a supervisory board, involving workers' participation, like in Germany or Sweden. Indeed the Fifth Directive, which is supposed to introduce some harmonization in that field, has not been adopted yet. Only to mention this last difference of monist or dualist structure, it bears consequences for negotiation strategy. By lack of attention paid to the supervisory board and to its indispensable support, a M&A may fail, as the merger between Renault/Volvo did in 1993 (Fusions & Acquisitions (Dec. 1993), 11.)

From one angle, the existence of such legal differences makes the preparation longer and more exhausting. From another angle, it opens windows of opportunity. If well-prepared, some managers may become aware of what others may miss, and therefore benefit from a competitive advantage. We can illustrate this hypothesis with the following example. Let us assume that a French company wants to buy a small Belgian company. The two companies are labeled SA (*société anonyme*) in each of their respective countries. Let us also assume that the representatives of the French company ignore that contrary to French Law, for Belgian limited companies, auditors (*commissaires aux comptes*) are not required in all cases, but only beyond a certain threshold, one that the Belgian target company does not cross. The French representatives may not verify the accounts of the firm with the same attention as they would have, had they known books do not have to be reviewed independently in Belgium in such a case.

Other windows of opportunity can be offered, for instance, by a good knowledge of the taxation system attached to acquisitions (Poulain de Saint-Père (1995), pp. 539–43). In France, rather than purchasing an entire business (*fonds de commerce*) and having to pay up to 11.4 per cent of registration taxes beyond 700,000 FF, it may be preferable to acquire the property of a majority of assets with an act of transfer (4.8 per cent, or slightly over 1 per cent if it is a *Société anonyme*) or even better without any act of transfer, or to operate a merger which, though not easy across borders, benefits from tax exemption.[9] In order to find the least costly option, managers need to ask their services to check the various tax modes

---

[9] Directive 90/434 (JOCE, July 23, 1990); See also Beaufort (1994).

TABLE 14.2

Comparative approach to public limited companies in the EU

	Denomination	Minimum number of shareholders	Minimum authorized capital	Paying up capital	Independent author	Articles of Association
Austria	A.G. Aktien-Gesellschaft	2 at creation; 1 afterwards	1 000 000 ATS	25 % at creation	Obligatory	Notarized
Belgium	S.A./N.V. Société Anonyme Naamloze Vennootschap	2	1 250 000 BEF	25 % at creation with minimum 1 250 000 BEF	Obligatory after a threshold	Notarized
Denmark	A.S. Aktieselskab	3 founding members plus 1 shareholder	300 000 DKK	50 % at creation with minimum 300 000 DKK	Obligatory	Notarized or under private agreement
Finland	O.Y. Osakeyhtiö	7	15 000 FM	50 % at creation	Obligatory after a threshold	Notarized
France	S.A. Société Anonyme	7	250 000 FF (1 250 000 FF if public call for capital)	50 % at creation	Obligatory	Notarized or under private agreement
Germany	A.G. Aktien-Gesellschaft	5 founding members plus 1 shareholder	100 000 DEM	25 % at creation	Obligatory	Notarized
Greece	A.E. Anonymos Eteria	2	5 000 000 GRD	25 % at creation with minimum 5 million GRD	Obligatory	Notarized
Ireland	P.L.C. Public Limited Company	7	30 000 IEP	25 % at creation	Obligatory	Notarized or under private agreement

TABLE 14.2 (continued)

	Denomination	Minimum number of shareholders	Minimum authorized capital	Paying up capital	Independent author	Articles of Association
Italy	S.P.A. Società per Azioni	2	2 000 000 000 ITL	30% at creation	Obligatory	Notarized or under private agreement
Luxembourg	S.A. Société Anonyme	2	1 250 000 LUF	25% at creation	Obligatory	Notarized
Netherlands	N.V. Naamloze Vennootschap	1	100 000 NLG	25% at creation with minimum 100 000 NLG	Obligatory after a threshold	Notarized
Portugal	S.A. Sociedad Anonima	5	5 000 000 PTE	30% at creation	Obligatory	Notarized
Spain	S.A. Sociedad Anonima	3	10 000 000 ESP	25% at creation	Obligatory after a threshold	Notarized
Sweden	Publik AB Akitebolag	1	500 000 SEK	Total	Obligatory	Notarized
United Kingdom	P.L.C. Public Limited Company	2	50 000 GBP	25% at creation	Obligatory	Notarized or under private agreement

Source: Beaufort (1994).

TABLE 14.3
Comparative approach to tax rates in the EU

	Tax rate on EU Company profits	Average allocation of social charges (% of gross salary)	Current rates of valued added tax: reduced/normal/increased	Taxation rate in the sale/auction of real estate
Austria	34%	37%	10% – 20% – 32%	3.5%
Belgium	28% up to 41%	46%	6% – 20.5% – 25 + 8%	12.5%
Denmark	34%	Included in income taxes	25%	1.2%
Finland	25%	30.4%	12/17% – 22%	1.2% (28% on capital gain)
France	33.33%	50% to 70%	5.5% – 20.6%	18.585%
Germany	36% on allotted profits; 50% on reinvested profits	35%	7% – 15%	2%
Greece	35% up to 46%	36%	3.6% – 18% – 36%	11%
Ireland	40% (with 10% for some activities)	23%	0/12.5% – 23%	0.5%
Italy	16.2% (ILOR) + 36% (IRPEG) Overall Tax = 47.8%	50%	4/9% – 19% – 38%	4%
Luxembourg	20% up to 400 000 LUF; 33% from 1 312 001 LUF	28% to 32%	3/6% – 15%	6%
Netherlands	40% up to 250 000 NLG 35% from 250 001 NLG	53% to 60%	6% – 17.5%	6%
Portugal	36% (+ maximum 3.6% local tax)	36%	5% – 17% – 30%	10%
Spain	35%	50% to 70%	6% – 16% – 33%	6%
Sweden	28%	35.35%	18% – 25%	30% on capital gain
United Kingdom	25% up to 250 000 GBP; 33% from 250 001 GBP with 1/40 difference between profit & ceiling of 1 250 000 GBP; 33% from 1 250 000 GBP	19.45%	7.5%	1%

Source: Beaufort (1994).

attached to the multiple ways of acquiring or sharing company control in the different legal systems.

Major disparities for other taxes, VAT and contributions, are also striking within the European Union. Corporation tax on benefits varies from 25 per cent in Finland to 47.8 per cent in Italy. Tax on the purchase of non-rural real estate stretches from 0.5 per cent in Ireland or 1 per cent in the United Kingdom to 18.585 per cent in France. VAT rates range from 3 to 12 per cent in Luxembourg, and from 4 to 38 per cent in Italy. In the same vein, welfare contributions represent between 19.45 per cent in England and 70 per cent in France or Spain of gross salary. According to the foreseeable type of activities and to the need for personnel, some knowledge of all these references can make managers minimize their costs in the European Union, and opt for an acquisition in a particular country (cf. Table 14.3.).

How to prepare for different reference assessments

Even if some references, like legal structures, are similar from one culture to another, they can still be submitted to different assessments. Two people, sharing the same reference, may not attribute the same value to it. Some structures tend to be more practised in some countries. For instance, the United Kingdom or the Netherlands have a tradition of listing companies that is not as developed in other countries, in particular in Germany. If the managers of a British corporation hope to extend their activities in Germany and limit their search to companies on the stock market, they may miss the right partner that a German bank, very often quite involved in corporate controls and well informed about corporations, could have easily quoted.

On top of legal structures and of their uses which frame many aspects of a company life, there is another set of assumptions that managers may hold about corporate functioning and operations: about how shareholders monitor a company, about who they are, about the role of institutional actors, about the role of trade unions, about what is considered fair trade practices, or reasonable flows of capital, or fair and true review of accounts. Such a descriptive set has the tendency to become quickly normative in the minds of those who hold it: what *we* usually do in our corporate or national culture is what we, and others, *ought* to do. Yet, what should be done here to be successful may not be shared in other cultures as keys of success. Managers need to check the validity of their descriptive set, before any automatic transposition to another context. This prudence reduces the risks of erroneous strategy, resistance and backfire.

For instance, in the United Kingdom, some favored structure, like company listing, can be in close correlation with some specific operations, like takeovers. In a context of quicker flow of capitals, many British managers may not have as much difficulty in accepting and practising takeovers at home, even hostile. They can simply view them as acts of good management, with consequent restructuring and laying off. These managers can be tempted to export some of these techniques

Viviane de Beaufort and Alain Lempereur

as such, and to lobby their government to denounce barriers to takeovers in other member states. However, some of these "barriers" that the British Department of Trade and Industry may inquire about[10], and complain about in Brussels, in the name of freedom of commerce, may be seen as legitimate "protections" in other member states with strong economies. In Germany, high stability of capital and long term mandate for managers are viewed as conditions for economic growth, while takeovers, with purchaser's possible swift disinvestment, are often considered as unproductive.[11]

In pursuance thereof, at least two views of takeovers can coexist in European corporate cultures, both asking for more integration, but in different directions (Booz-Allen 1989, pp. 53 *et sq.*) Partisans of the Anglo-American model will look at takeovers more from the acquirers' viewpoint, promoting quick competition and restructuring, fighting protectionism, inefficiency and labor impediments. Partisans of the German-Japanese model will rather adopt the offeree's viewpoint, promoting shared cooperation, business relationships and labor participation, fighting aggressive raiders and social carelessness. Wherever their heart lies, future acquirers must guess what their future business counterparts likely believe in that respect. Informed of the repulsion against hostile takeovers that prevails in the target culture, acquirers may even have stronger incentives to prefer negotiated offers. In addition to cultural sensitivity, acquirers will rarely be wrong to expect that their counterparts, as potential targets, may naturally feel more empathy with tender offers.

For this example, as for many others, working towards a European model will probably mean to accommodate many tendencies, understanding their perspectives integratively (*Idem.*) This is the hope of the Thirteenth European Directive on takeovers and other general public bids, that has not been adopted for obvious reasons. The challenge for a manager preparing a M&A is to precede European law, and for better success, on this topic or another, to embody the qualities of a European manager, who regardless of his or her origin, (i) integrates as many perspectives as possible, (ii) with careful respect for the perspective of his or her actual counterpart, that cannot be assumed to be known for sure without check, (iii) in creative tension with a deepened open knowledge of his or her own perspective.

---

[10] One of the most exhaustive studies in the field of barriers to takeovers has been produced by Coopers & Lybrand (1989) for the British Department of Trade and Industry.

[11] The difference between these two assessments of hostile takeovers is coherent with how corporation is viewed in each country. In the United Kingdom, a company is seen as a transmissible good. The shareholder prevails, sanctioning the good or bad health of a corporation by selling or not. Financial information is accurate. The flow of shares, which are in many hands, is fluid and ample. The role of the banks is limited. In Germany, a company is rather seen as a close group, with some financial lack of transparency, a slow pace of share flow, and fewer shareholders. Managers as well as banks are key players.

How to prepare for strategic uses of perspectives

Integration of references and evaluations of one's counterpart is not simply a matter of knowledge or even of acknowledgement; but of genuine acceptance, sharing and also strategic use. In the best case, this wide capacity involves a deep empathy with another culture, with a willingness to learn more about it, and to confess ignorance at times. The reality offers many occasions to put this capacity to the test, for spontaneous reflex of rejection and dismissal has to be fought.

The capacity for perspective-taking may be highly helpful in transactions. At a stage of preparation of an offer, it enables managers to reframe their strategies, in terms which are likely to be better understood by prospective negotiating partners. It is a ground rule from ancient rhetoric to contemporary marketing: any argument or speech must fit its audience. This other-centered behavior goes beyond language; it applies to all the elements of an environment.

Managers can learn, for instance, from the simple observation that in "Latin" regions of Europe, meeting people informally outside the office, and building personal relationships through the "old-boy network" are often more appreciated than exchanging precise, unemotional faxes through anonymous channels (Newman 1989, p. 280). More unusual times and places to negotiate can be discovered, which would have been dismissed otherwise with impatience to "get back to business". Managers, who are conscious of cultural differences, take seriously what may influence unexpectedly the success of negotiation itself: they do not simply focus on the formal technical discussions at the office, but incorporate meals and pauses, smiles and leisures in what becomes a wider vision of what negotiation is all about: building relationships and trust. Wide knowledge becomes a tool for awareness of oneself and of the other; it maintains alertness to a multi-faceted environment and encourages more appropriate action.

If such knowledge helps confirm (or adopt) a course of action, it may also prevent from continuing (or considering) one. In some European regions, where the power of notables and ruling families is recognized with formality, a higher respect for hierarchical authority is expected.[12] It can be expressed through the use of titles, the places at the table, etc. Managers, who make these apparent details part of their negotiated strategy of M&A, will not take long to discover the key players to focus on and to pay tribute to. They will keep on looking for their approval, asking for their advice; they will not forget to report to them, at a crucial stage of the process. In permanence, they will remain attentive to how their arguments are received by these authorities. Whenever skilful managers observe that one of their recent moves has provoked some unforeseen tension or rejection, they will redirect their argument accordingly, apologize for not having explained their point clearly, propose to restate it in another way, making explicit one more time that they are engaged in a friendly, and not hostile, acquisition. Rather than sticking to a particular formulation, they will always promote their interests through alternatives which increase their persuasive power.

[12] See the concept of "power distance" in Hofstede 1980 and Véry 1995.

When cultural references and their evaluations as positive or negative warnings are integrated in a personal equation like a "second nature", they contribute simultaneously to improve understanding and arguments, lowering the risk of miscommunication. They help us as listeners, for they decrease the noises that we would otherwise perceive in a foreign culture. They help us as speakers, for they increase the harmony of our own sounds. Listening and speaking are involved in a virtuous circle of communication, where heightened empathy becomes a tool for persuasive assertiveness. (See Sanchez 1994, and Mnookin, Peppet & Tulumello 1995, Chapter 2.)

To summarize: auditing oneself and expanding toward the other involve a complex program. It requires an investigation into the objectives and constraints of one's company, but also, when cross-cultural M&A are considered, into one's own possible limited knowledge about somebody else's culture, references and evaluations. All of these elements can be gathered by managers, before even collecting particular information about a specific target. Managers understand better what the interests of their company can be *in particular*, and how they can be worked on, having learnt more about the culture of their counterparts in general. The next task is for the managers to inquire about who the targets are *in particular* and behave *actually*. This is the topic of the last part of this chapter.

Examination of the Prospective Partner through Extensive Audit

In prior stages, managers had to face many questions relating to the M&A. If they really strove, they could answer them through self-help. At most, they had to resort to publications from the ministry of foreign trade or some chambers of commerce, or to consultants' reports. All of this could remain private preparation. In this first act, the prospect had not officially entered the scene yet.

Now, for the concrete audit of the prospect(s)[13], managers are close to the

---

[13] The word "prospects" could indeed be kept in the plural at this stage. For the process of auditing to dispose of comparative data, it often needs to apply to more than one potential offeree, even if in many cases, there may not be more than one in a specific market. Even if managers consider that one of them would be a more attractive target, they need to determine with precision what makes this company so relevant to their needs. Managers are led to check their intuitions, by comparing this company with its competitors, as to already define its strengths and weaknesses, its objectives and constraints, its corporate structures and habits, in contrast with these alternative targets. Another reason to audit the prospective target with other possible targets is to be provided with possible back-up target companies in case the negotiation or the takeover with the prospective target lasts too long, or fails. It may sometimes be judicious to associate with a so-called "second best", who is a cooperative challenger and has a potential and a will to grow, rather than with a current "first choice", which could be ultra-protectionist, and frightened by changes. Contacting this back-up company and even discussing an offer with it may also be part of a strategy to improve one's BATNA (see note) with the "first choice" target. Preliminary side-contacts with the "second best", i.e., with a competitor, may often be sufficient to make the "first choice" target lower its expectations, or think twice before rejecting an offer. Note however that, in countries like Germany, negotiating with different prospects can be considered as negotiating in bad faith, which may lead to financial compensation. See also Reed (1989), 534–5.

moment of intercorporate contacts, which they can delay or undertake at once. We suggested before why undertaking early contacts cooperatively, instead of abstaining from them, could be an asset to usefully carry out an audit. Potential offerers, with their short list of possible prospects, need to scrutinize them as closely as possible. Accurate, complete information is not easy to collect; its quality and quantity often depends precisely on the type of strategy and relationship that the future acquirer chooses to establish with prospective targets. The more open and cooperative it is, the more disclosure and accuracy can be expected.

A careful approach to the prospect, possibly secret, may discover what kind of general strategy — conservative or audacious — the possible partner has followed during the last few years, what kind of external communication policy has been adopted, in terms of public image, of transparency of information, of labor management, etc. It is a first opportunity for managers to confront the general cultural image that they have formed, with actual practices of this particular company, and of its managers.

Yet, managers may need more than this unrefined view of the prospect to prepare an efficient post-M&A integration plan. They may want to go beyond public data. Then, preliminary careful contacts — careful in order not to uncover all their objectives — become nearly imperative. Progressively, as a working relationship is founded, offerers will likely have access to many more elements of the prospect than otherwise, and mainly they will examine them in comparison with these respective elements in their company. The goal is to distinguish areas in which the fit would work probably better, and other areas where further work is required. Through negotiations, managers will therefore gather sharper information that directly relates to the post-M&A context and addresses problems that could have been ignored. They can also involve managers of the prospect in early joint problem-solving.

It may be difficult for potential acquirers to get some information. Patience is required. However, knowing how challenging it may be for them to speak about their company among themselves and in front of others may help them acknowledge in less judgmental ways how uneasy it may be for the managers of the prospect to give all the requested information, especially if the managers of the potential acquirer are not ready to return the favor. Finally, cultural norms can differ in that respect too. For example, in Germany, target managers or owners are not likely to disclose any information, before potential buyers sign a letter of intent, i.e. a clear commitment to purchase the target.

Accounting and financial audit

Cross-border, more than national M&A give rise to difficult evaluation of prospects (Perez 1995). Accounting transparency is supposed to have been established by various European directives,[14] through compulsory schemes for annual reports,

---

[14] Fourth Directive no. 78/660; Seventh Directive no. 83/349; both complemented by Directives 90/604 & 90/605 (*JOCE*, L 317, 16 November 1990); Eighth Directive no. 84/253.

profit and loss accounts, and annexes, including also rules of accreditation for auditors, and a requirement of harmonizing rules of disclosure for holdings.

Again the reality is blurred. In different countries, multiple methods of evaluation and of write-offs survive, which lead to serious discrepancies here and there. A striking study, realized in 1990, showed that by application of the accounting rules of five EU countries (plus the United States) to a hypothetical company, you could get six different statements of accounts: the "same" company would turn a profit in France, while having less profit in the Netherlands and in Belgium; it would be slightly in deficit in the United Kingdom, while having a higher deficit in the United States, and the highest deficit in Germany (Kerdellant 1990). This is one more warning against hasty judgment. More or less freedom in accounting explains this spectrum, that one must keep in mind as a prospective buyer while evaluating the target from a financial viewpoint. It is important for a buyer to be aware of some unusual accounting methods.

The same study also insists on not rushing to conclusions, i.e., attributing more or less laxity to such or such country. Indeed, with different hypothetical companies and figures, the results could have been the opposite. However that may be, it obliges managers to pay extreme attention to the particulars of such or such target accounts, translating nearly step by step what it means into their financial schemes. For example, in France and the Netherlands, research and development costs can be listed in fixed assets, whereas they can appear as expenses in the United Kingdom or in Germany (Perez 1995, p. 553). An awareness of these possible differences at an early stage, before the M&A is signed, will add one more challenge for managers; they may want to set up a harmonization plan of accounting structures, which will be quickly implemented after the M&A. Such a plan may also serve as an obvious technique to later verify more easily that financial objectives are reached.

Commercial audit

The analysis of current turnovers must be complemented with a dynamic view of the target business. How have past contracts been implemented and honored? Which prospective clients and growth can be hoped for? Who are the creditors? And the debtors? Are the latter dependable? What is the state of the stock? In some sectors, like mass marketing, taking over a stock also means being liable for defective products for a period of ten years.[15] It is better for acquirers to know what they can become responsible for. Again, this information may not be grasped by only examining compulsory accounts. Opting for an early cooperative behavior, prospective buyers may want to disclose some relevant information about their firm and interests, in order to also learn elements from a prospective target that are essential to their assessment, namely such aspects of liability for defective products.

---

[15] This non-fault liability stems from the Directive 85/375, (*JOCE*, L 525, 25 July, 1985). See Beaufort (1995a), pp. 525–6.

If offerers intend to operate in European countries where the tradition of fair and true review is very recent, like Portugal and Greece, there are even more incentives to favor a cooperative approach in that field (Perez 1995, p. 552; Coopers and Lybrand 1989, Volume 3). Moreover, through an extensive commercial audit, friendly offerers may also develop better arguments to justify their will to buy or to be associated with the company in question; they may find for instance "objective" opportunities for complementary productions or skills, and therefore attach a *commercial* or *industrial* flavor to the M&A, which otherwise could have seemed purely *speculative*.

Legal audit

Legal audit in a broad sense can encompass some of the previous aspects of auditing, as well as social audit which follows. The following examples will focus on a narrower conception of legal audit, involving more precisely corporate law. Whatever form corporations adopt — limited company or not, listed company or not — as suggested above, there can be many variations in legal requirements from one country to another and therefore in legal latitudes. The Articles of Association of the target may reveal the intent to use these latitudes in several fields. This point can be evidenced by statutory clauses which are allowed for example in Swedish corporate law, and which may be included to protect all or some current shareholders. These clauses may hinder or even stop some takeovers which are protected by Swedish law:[16]

- Pre-emption clauses: shareholders have a preemptive right to repurchase shares sold to a third party. For public limited companies, shareholders can even agree to forbid themselves to sell their shares to a third party, before other shareholders agree to it.
- Voting rights clauses: some "A" shares may have up to 10 votes, whereas "B" shares may only have one. Hence, one shareholder with 10 per cent of the shares could control an entire company.
- Clauses for preferential subscription rights: some shareholders are authorized to be granted preferential rights of subscription, by a board of directors who wish to increase the corporation capital. This clause can prevent "A" shareholders from being threatened by "B" shareholders.

Managers auditing a company must therefore pay close attention to the Articles of Association. They want to make sure that they will be able to control effectively their acquisition. They must also examine the conditions of other major contracts, like commercial leases, loans, franchising.

---

[16] Beaufort (1995b), p. 22 *et sq*. Statutory defenses are also very common in the Netherlands, for example.

Social audit

Target evaluation should also include human resources and labor relationships. It is important to identify some of its main elements, like labor requirements, pension plans, internal disruptions, etc. What is the content of labor contracts? Which principles regulate the salary: seniority, productivity, etc.? Which benefits are included? Do workers participate in the firm's profits? What is the age pyramid, the ratio between young and old employees? What are their qualifications? How are retirement pensions calculated and funded? If personnel are to be laid off, which procedure and compensation are required? In Italy, for instance, severance compensations can be very high. What is the ratio between executives and non-executives? How are workers involved in the management of the company? What is the role of trade unions? How does collective bargaining work? What kind of labor conflicts has the firm known? How were they solved? How frequent were strikes?

Answers to these questions evaluate how labor contracts and work forces may be assets for growth, or costly obstacles. Again, offerers must avoid a priori negative judgments, namely about the lack or the excess of participation or workers' rights in the target company. Indeed these judgments can be rooted in their own cultural references and assessments. A company involving much workers' participation and sharing of firm's profits may well be so well-off *thanks to* these features. In an environment where these characteristics are prerequisites that are legitimized by results, deciding to curtail them may well increase owners' profits for a while, but prove to be disastrous in the long run.

On the other hand, in some settings, well-known conservative trade unions may have a deeply embedded strategy of confrontation with the management, escalate demands despite the difficulties of a company, refuse any change to *droits acquis*, repeatedly go on strike, and be real impediments to productivity by their deficient liability. The company managers may play the same game, considering confrontations and hierarchical authority as the only solution to all problems, also refusing to engage in serious collective bargaining. Resting upon the social audit of this company, acquirers may already diagnose the need for substantial changes in the human resources department. They may plan to remove some of its managers, replacing them with more skilful negotiators who can improve the relationship and communication between management and the workforce. A new "social contract" can also be offered to trade unions to restore a sense of responsibility on all sides.

After this multi-dimensional preliminary audit, managers may determine more accurately some *price range* for the operation. It is an estimate based primarily on the financial audit and on the potential for growth that the commercial audit assessed. Legal and social audits help qualify the price, rectifying it according to how much, for example, the shareholders' structure or the workforce can be trumps to manage the society. Managers may now proceed knowingly with a partner as was suggested in the first part of this chapter, choosing either hostile takeovers or tender offers. Through a three-fold examination perspective, managers have learnt to master many dimensions that will be most helpful during the M&A and its implementation.

After careful preparation, the M&A operation can actually proceed — through negotiation or public takeover. Whatever mode is selected, auditing which is applied to oneself and the other continues. It is complemented as the other, partner or target, reacts to the various moves of M&A, disclosing analytical information that may not be public. Offerers go on processing relevant data in order to correct their views of the target in permanence, rather than sticking to a prior, even well-prepared, assessment. So do the offerees with respect to their potential acquirers. As offerers work with or against the target, their major objective is to remain focused on the requirements of post-M&A integration.

In view of achieving this goal of integration, does anything seem more coherent, and probably more successful than cooperative negotiation itself? It aims at creating value for both partners and not simply at claiming it for one, at reconciling present methods of joint problem-solving with future expectations of mutual gains. In brief, it makes integrative ends and means coincide the most up-stream.

Part IV

CHAPTER 15

The IBM–Mexico Microcomputer Investment Negotiations

STEPHEN WEISS

In July 1985, the Government of Mexico approved an IBM Corporation proposal to assemble personal computers in a wholly owned plant near Guadalajara. President Miguel de la Madrid praised the plan as an "expression of faith" in the country's economic progress and a "most significant milestone on Mexico's road to self-sufficiency in electronic technology" (MEU 1986). Approval had come after seventeen months of negotiation reported in news headlines such as "IBM threatens Miguel de la Madrid's Government" (Martines 1984) and "Mexico Rejects IBM Control For New Plant" (Meislin 1985b) and after widespread debate over whether Mexico's review of the IBM proposal constituted a "test case" or "special case" of its treatment of foreign investors (*Economist* 1985a, p. 62; Orme 1984b).

Such observations raise questions about the process of the negotiation and the determinants of the final outcome. How did the parties interact? Why did they agree upon those terms? These queries apply to most cases of negotiation, but they are reinforced here by the prominence of the parties and the publicity that attended their talks.

There is additional impetus for studying this case. The issue of its generalizability aside, the case offers researchers and managers a vehicle for insights into multinational enterprise (MNE)-government relations, international corporate strategy, contemporary government attitudes toward national computer industries and the bilateral, US–Mexico relationship. More directly, the literature on international business negotiation to date comprises large-scale, statistical studies

NOTE: This chapter was originally published as "The long path to the IBM-Mexico Agreement: an analysis of the microcomputer investment negotiations, 1983–86" in *Journal of International Business Studies*, 21(4), 1990, pp. 565–96, and is reproduced by kind permission of the publishers. The author also gratefully acknowledges the assistance of the IBM Corporation, Tim Berry, anonymous interviewees, *JIBS* referees and researchers Naveen Seth and Chris DeMarco.

of MNEs' capabilities and achievements *vis-à-vis* governments (e.g., Fagre & Wells 1982; Kobrin 1987) that do not evidence the intricacies and dynamism of such negotiation; strategic analyses focusing on organizations as units (e.g., de la Torre 1981; Lecraw 1984) that neglect aspects of individual negotiator's behaviors (e.g., Graham 1983; Tung 1982), and vice versa; and a few case studies (e.g., Stoever 1979; Young & Hood 1977) whose dissimilar or unspecified analytic frameworks hinder cross-case comparisons. This article attempts to complement and extend this literature as well as deepen understanding of the IBM-Mexico negotiation itself.

Existing Literature

Research on international business negotiation includes studies on three areas pertinent here: MNE bargaining power, governmental review of foreign invest-ments, and cultural aspects of negotiation.

The "bargaining school" of MNE-host government relationships (see Grieco 1982) asserts that terms of these relationships, at point of market entry and over time, are negotiable. Often these researchers examine MNE bargaining power. For example, in their study of US-based MNEs in Latin America, Fagre and Wells (1982) found that an MNE's percentage ownership of foreign subsidiaries (a proxy for overall outcome of negotiation) positively, albeit weakly, correlated with the MNE's level of technology, product differentiation, product diversity, and access to foreign markets. For subsidiaries in Mexico specifically, these variables combined with size of the MNE's investment, which carried a negative but not significant value, explained 25 per cent of the variation in actual foreign ownership.

Lecraw (1984) modified Fagre and Wells' approach, obtained consistent results and demonstrated further that the relationship between percentage MNE ownership of a subsidiary and subsidiary success (or effective control) is J-shaped, not linear. Thus he advised MNEs and governments to consider joint ventures that do not evenly split ownership. Discussions of international corporate strategies, such as the worldwide integration strategy (Doz 1980), bear upon these findings and suggest additional MNE bargaining objectives and sources of power (see also Holt 1978).

De la Torre (1981) stands out from the aforementioned studies, while still remaining within the bargaining school, by exploring entry negotiations from both sides — for governments and MNEs. In his view, an MNE that perceives high market attractiveness (or great fit with corporate strategy) and a good investment climate should commit maximum resources and pursue establishment of a wholly owned affiliate. For governments, de la Torre recommends explicit statement of national development objectives, social cost-benefit analysis, and contralization of foreign investment decisionmaking. (For another bilateral view, see Grosse and Aramburu 1989).

Studies in the second major area have emphasized government perspectives and behavior. Among four Southeast Asian countries, Encarnation and Wells (1985) found four organizational structures for foreign investment review "coordinated" (one interministerial body), "abstention" from negotiation (straightforward application of rules), "diffused" (serial negotiations), and "delegated" (to one ministry). Internal politics influenced the effectiveness of all of them in one way or another. Further, contrary to the defensive, empowering rationale offered by several writers (e.g., de la Torre 1981), the two researchers found that governments adopted centralization (coordinated or delegated structures) in order to smooth the way for foreign investors.

Details of experiences especially relevant to the IBM-Mexico case have appeared in at least two studies. Grieco (1982) describes the Indian government's negotiations with MNEs from 1960-80 as it sought to develop the country's computer industry. With respect to IBM, the government advised the company in 1966, 1968 and 1973–74, to share ownership of its local subsidiary with Indian nationals. Instead, in the mid-70s, IBM offered increased manufacturing operations and technical assistance, a trade-off that the government rejected. IBM chose to leave the country by June 1978. By then, however, the industry seemed well established, and Grieco concluded that "assertive, upper-tier developing countries" like Mexico might also achieve India's "bargaining success".

Mexico's experiences negotiating with MNEs during the early development of its auto industry (1960–64) have been analyzed by Bennett and Sharpe (1979). They argue persuasively that actual bargaining power is not easily discerned because potential power tends to be constrained or augmented by various contextual factors and relationships. With auto MNEs, the bilateral US–Mexico relationship limited Mexico's power, as did Mexico's intragovernmental disputes (see also Story 1982). Nevertheless, neither the Bennett and Sharpe (1979) nor the Grieco (1982) study treats its subject as a case of negotiation, with process and outcome, from start to finish (cf., Bennett & Sharpe's later work (1985) pp. 80–93).

Third and lastly, a small body of literature has described cultural aspects of Mexican negotiation. Weiss and Stripp (1985, pp. 31–5) highlighted the significance of status and formality, relationship concerns, an open orientation toward time, and centralized decisionmaking. A recent comparative investigation based on experiments (Adler, Graham & Gehrke 1987) demonstrated that Mexicans place greater emphasis than Americans do on the quality of relationships between negotiators. (For characteristics of Mexican diplomatic negotiations, see Fisher 1980; Grayson 1987.)

These studies reflect the thrusts of the embryonic literature on international business negotiation. They provide a background for considering IBM and Mexico's strategies, relationships, and behavior. At the same time, they reveal the need for and value of a detailed, integrative case study. A case study can suggest confirmation or modification of some "ideas and stereotypes prevalent in current theory," generate hypotheses, and indicate "interconnections between various relevant factors" (see Gulliver 1979, p. 64; see also Yin 1984, pp. 15–23).

Stephen Weiss

Analytic Approach

The following account of IBM and Mexico's negotiation draws on a framework for analysis of complex negotiations. It was designed to organize rich description of parties' interactions and to stimulate formulation of broad-based explanations of negotiation outcomes. The framework thus highlights primary parties' relationships, behaviors, and relevant conditions, and various facets and levels of analysis within each of those elements (for a full exposition, see Weiss 1988).

This case study follows a form derived from the framework and previously applied to the GM-Toyota talks of 1982–84 (Weiss 1987). It begins with the factors that motivated IBM and Mexico to negotiate (including the conditions that shaped their respective "interests" (Lax & Sebenius 1986) and possible courses of action). Then the analysis explores the issues arising from the parties' relationships, pre-negotiation preparations, the negotiations (that is, issues, players, conditions, process and outcome for each round), and the post-negotiation period.

Besides organizing the discussion below, these categories provided foci for gathering and selecting relevant information about the case. The varied sources used included author-conducted interviews of negotiation participants and knowledgeable observers,[1] proprietary industry studies, news articles and other periodicals, and a few academic writings on the case (e.g., Cline 1987; Miller 1986; Whiting & Shank 1986). In line with the recommendations of Lincoln and Guba (1985, p. 268) and Yin (1984, p. 137), the author asked interviewees to review a draft of the case study and incorporated their feedback in what follows.

Figure 15.1 guides the discussion by identifying significant actors. The primary organizations involved, Mexico's Secretariat of Commerce and Industrial Development (in Spanish, SECOFI) and National Commission on Foreign Investment (CNIE), and IBM Corporation's wholly owned subsidiary, IBM World Trade Americas/Far East (A/FE), and specifically A/FE's Latin American Division (LAD) and IBM de Mexico, S.A., appear at the center of the diagram in the center of activity. Other orgnaizations, whose actions conditioned the talks, are listed according to their degree of involvement (Rings 1a–3a). In addition to treating these organizations as wholes (Level a), Figure 15.1 recognizes two other types of actors: groups (b) and invididuals (c).[2] Almost every organization's activities could be described on each of the three levels, but for clarity, the figure specifies only the most active representatives of IBM and SECOFI (Boxes 1b,c).

---

[1] Those interviewed in primarily open-ended formats include fifteen individuals from the American Chamber of Commerce in Mexico City, IBM organizations, industry analysts, the Mexican business community, the U.S. Commerce and State Departments, and the U.S. Trade Representative's office. Mexican government negotiators did not respond to requests for interviews, but some general documents were provided to the author. Unless otherwise stated, however, the author takes responsibility for views in the text.

[2] As subsequent text shows, the negotiators did not pair off in as clear an IBM team-Mexico team format as Figure 15.1 may convey. But the figure systematically highlights key organizations and can be readily compared with the figure used for the GM-Toyota talks (Weiss 1987).

FIGURE 15.1

Actors and audiences in the IBM–Mexico negotiations

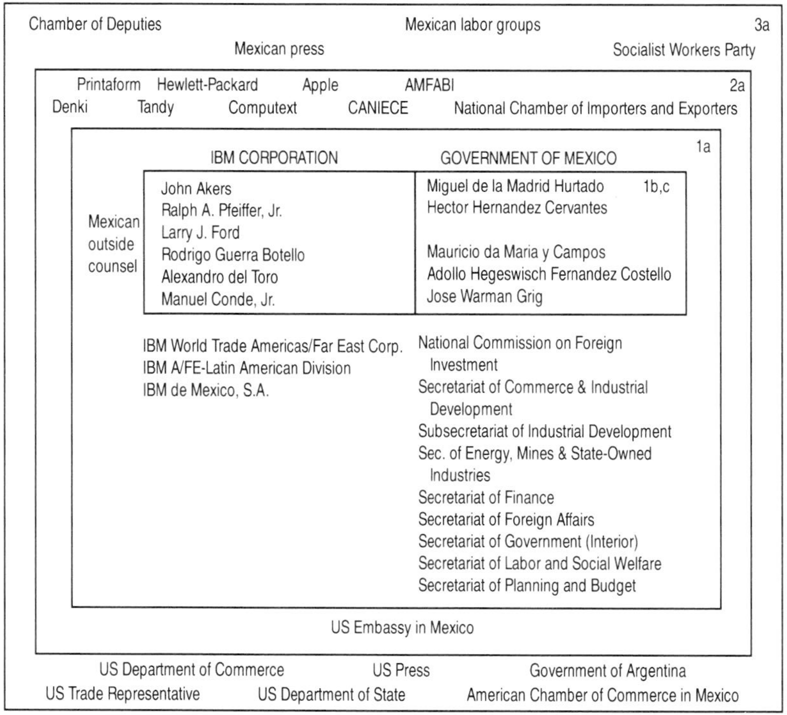

Chamber of Deputies   Mexican labor groups   Socialist Workers Party   3a

Mexican press   AMFABI   National Chamber of Importers and Exporters   2a

Printaform   Hewlett-Packard   Apple   CANIECE

Denki   Tandy   Computext

IBM CORPORATION

GOVERNMENT OF MEXICO   1a

John Akers
Ralph A. Pfeiffer, Jr.
Larry J. Ford
Rodrigo Guerra Botello
Alexandro del Toro
Manuel Conde, Jr.

Mexican outside counsel

IBM World Trade Americas/Far East Corp.
IBM A/FE-Latin American Division
IBM de Mexico, S.A.

Miguel de la Madrid Hurtado   1b,c
Hector Hernandez Cervantes

Mauricio da Maria y Campos
Adollo Hegeswisch Fernandez Costello
Jose Warman Grig

National Commission on Foreign
   Investment
Secretariat of Commerce & Industrial
   Development
Subsecretariat of Industrial Development
Sec. of Energy, Mines & State-Owned
   Industries
Secretariat of Finance
Secretariat of Foreign Affairs
Secretariat of Government (Interior)
Secretariat of Labor and Social Welfare
Secretariat of Planning and Budget

US Embassy in Mexico

US Department of Commerce   US Press   Government of Argentina

US Trade Representative   US Department of State   American Chamber of Commerce in Mexico

Notes: Larger rectangles (rings) represent diminishing degrees of involvement: 1-primary actors; 2-secondary parties to the negotiations; 3-interested, not directly involved audiences. Letters designate levels of behavioral analysis: a-organizations; b-groups; c-individuals. Except for Akers and de la Madrid, Boxes 1b,c contain negotiating teams as well as primary individual players.

Stephen Weiss

Motivating Factors

The negotiations that began in March 1984 followed important steps taken by both IBM and the Government of Mexico in late 1981. On August 12, IBM introduced its first personal computer (PC); in September, the Mexican Bureau of Industries issued a set of regulations and incentives that because known as the "Computer Decree." These actions — and the parties' subsequent negotiations and agreement — were motivated by noteworthy, underlying interests and organizational and environmental conditions.

The global computer market

By 1980, the computer market had increased five-fold since 1970 to $53.5 billion, and industry analysts in the US expected it to "explode" to $145 billion by 1985 (*Business Week* 1981). The microcomputer segment (a stand-alone computer whose central processing unit consists of a single microprocessor), which Apple Computer, Inc. opened in 1978, looked particularly promising. From 1980–83, its worldwide value more than doubled each year. In 1983, worldwide shipments exceeded 11 million units for an if-sold value, according to Dataquest, of nearly $15 billion.[3]

IBM performance

Although IBM had long dominated the computer industry (its 1984 total revenues exceeded those of its closest competitor, DEC, by 7.4 times), it delayed entry into microcomputers. Then the company made up ground quickly. At the end of 1983, only the second full year of its microcomputer production, unit shipments hit 572,000 (a 266 per cent increase over 1982) for revenues of $2.6 billion (420 per cent greater than in 1982). IBM held 8.2 per cent of the US market (in terms of unit shipments) and 5.1 per cent of the world market. In 1984, demand for its PCs would continue rising at that pace — even as those geographical markets' growth rates slowed.

Mexico's computer industry and market

In 1981, Mexico had a computer market estimated at $600 million (Miller 1986, p. 176) and an import market for computers and office equipment ranked second to Brazil's in Latin America and twentieth in the world (Sauvant 1986, p. 24). Analysts expected the computer market to grow 25 per cent annually into the

[3] Statistics on computer markets vary by source and sometimes for the same source, by date (see Table 15.1, Notes e,f). Some statistical differences stem from specified and unspecified definitional differences. Some market researchers count as microcomputers only single-user systems, while others also include low-end home computers and high-end multi-user systems. This article relies on respected sources and notes discrepancies.

310

TABLE 15.1

The microcomputer industry: corporate and market profiles, 1981–86

Corporate Net Sales/Net Income (US$ mn.)

	IBM (Net Sales)	IBM (Net Income)	Apple (Net Sales)	Apple (Net Income)	Mexico	US Total	World Total
1981	29,070[a]	3,610	334.8	39.4	—	—	—
1982	34,364	4,409	583.1	61.3	—	—	—
1983	40,180	5,485	982.8	76.7	—	—	—
1984*	45,937	6,582	1,515.9	64.1	—	—	—
1985*	50,056	6,555	1,918.3	61.2	—	—	—
1986	51,250	4,789	1,901.9	154.0	—	—	—

Microcomputer Revenues[2] (US$ mn., % change)

	IBM	IBM (% change)	Apple	Apple (% change)	Mexico	US Total — Shipments' If-Sold Value (US$ mn.)	US Total (%)	World Total — Shipments' If-Sold Value (US$ mn.)	World Total (%)
1981	...[b]	...	401.0[d]	143.0	...	1,633.4	...	2,674.1	...
1982	500.0[c]	—	664.0	65.6	31	3,757.7	130	6,623.1	148
1983	2,600.0	420.0	1,064.7	63.4	30	8,680	131	14,721	122
1984*	4,000.0	53.8	1,897.9	75.0	34	14,273	64	24,710	68
1985*	5,500.0	37.5	1,603.0	−15.4	43	16,005	12	30,414	23
1986	5,650.0	2.7	1,781.0	11.1	91[e]	16,183	1	30,685	1

Microcomputer Shipments[3] (units)

	IBM (units)	IBM (% world share)	Apple (units)	Apple (% world share)	Mexico (units)	US Total (units)	World Total (units)
1981	17,500	1.0	210,000	13.0	...	750,500	1,612,120
1982	156,000	3.0	323,000	7.0	10,270[g]	2,545,000	4,863,200
1983	572,000	5.1	745,000	6.7	...	6,199,000	11,123,000
1984*	1,881,000	12.5	1,397,000	9.3	27,780	7,768,000	15,044,000
1985*	2,052,000	14.0	1,272,000	8.6	36,700	6,072,000	14,705,000
1986	1,854,000	12.3	1,177,000	7.8	92,156[h]	6,814,000	15,064,000

TABLE 15.1 (continued)

	IBM	Apple	Mexico		US Total	World Total
			(units)	(US$ mn.)		
Microcomputer Production[4]						
1981	—	—	0	...	...	—
1982	—	—	...	26		—
1983	—	—	...	34		—
1984*	—	—	...	51		—
1985*	—	—	27,600	66		—
1986	—	—	...	128		—
Microcomputer Imports[5] (US$ mn., % change)						
1981	—	—	...		...	—
1982	—	—	7[i]		−16.7	—
1983	—	—	6		0	—
1984*	—	—	6		66.7	—
1985*	—	—	10		−20.0	—
1986	—	—	8			—

Sources:

1 IBM, Apple annual reports. For IBM: consolidated figures, year end Dec. 31. For Apple: consolidated figures, year end between Sept. 27–28 for years above.

2 Datamation (June 1, 1984, June 1, 1985 and June 1–5, 1987 Issues). For Mexico, see Source 4. For shipments' If-sold value, see Source 3.

3 Dataquest's Personal Computer service binders (April 1988). Dataquest defines micros as systems priced up to $10,000. For Mexico, 1982 and 1984. W.R. Cline, Informatics and Development (Washington, DC: 1987), pp. 88–9; for 1985–86, U.S. Department of Commerce, Market Research Summary for Mexico (4/87).

4,5 Wallace y Asociados, Profile of Mini and Micro Computer Systems Market (Mexico City, June 1988). For units, Informatics and Development.

Notes:

– Irrelevant or not meaningful.

... Unavailable data.

a IBM's column figures represent gross revenues rather than net sales.

b IBM introduced its first microcomputer (the "PC") on August 12, 1981.

c For IBM's 1982 revenues, cf. estimates of $566 (Dataquest), $1500 (Data Dialogues), and $1800 (Gartner Group).

d Apple's column figures, which are for calendar year, are compiled from quarterly reports by same source (Wallace y Asociados).

e Cf. $140 million for 1986 and $74 million for 1984 in 1985 report by same source (Wallace y Asociados).

f Cf. estimates of $5,391 (International Data Corp.) and $3,447 (Data Dialogues) in HBS Note (1984).

g Cf. estimates for 1982 or 2,245 and for 1984 of 11,410 (Infotext).

h Sales (not shipment) figure.

i Cf. estimate of $26 million (Informatics and Development, p. 88).

*Indicates main years of negotiation between IBM and Mexican government

TABLE 15.2

The economy of Mexico: internal and external indicators

Internal

	GDP (US$ bn.) nominal	GDP (% growth real[b])	Government Budget Balance (US$ bn.)	Central Bank Reserve (US$ bn.) For. Exch.	Central Bank Reserve (US$ bn.) Total	Inflation (CPI) (1980 = 100)	Unemployment[1] (%)
1980	186.34[a]	—	-5.82[a,c]	2.69	3.81	100	...
1981	239.58	7.7	-15.99	3.71	4.93	127.9	...
1982	171.25	-0.6	-26.43	.83	1.66	203.3	13.0
1983	142.73	-5.4	-11.35	3.80	4.74	410.2	14.0[d]
1984	171.33	3.6	-12.48	7.27	7.99	679.0	14.0
1985	177.46	2.8	-15.49	4.91	...	1,071.2	15.6
1986	127.13	-3.8	...	5.66	...	1,994.9	...

External

	Current Account (US$ bn.)	Petroleum Exports (US$ bn.)	Foreign Debt[2] (US$ bn.)	Foreign Direct Investment (US$ bn.)	Exchange Rate (Pesos per US$)
1980	-8.16	9.83[a]	57.5[e]	2.19	22.95[f]
1981	-13.90	13.80	78.3	2.54	24.52
1982	-6.22	17.13	86.1	1.66	54.99
1983	5.42	15.17	93.0	.46	120.1
1984	4.24	16.41	96.4	.39	167.8
1985	1.24	14.79	97.1	.49	256.9
1986	-1.27	6.37	101.7	.91	611.8

Sources:

For all except 1 and 2. *International Financial Statistics.* 1983 and 1987 Yearbooks, and May 1988 edition.

[1]*World Political Risk Services, Fact Sheet: United Mexican States* (Frost & Sullivan). 10/1/1986 edition.

[2]*World Debt Tables* (World Bank). 1987–88 edition.

Notes:

— Irrelevant or not meaningful

... Unavailable data.

[a]Converted from pesos using the appropriate exchange rates within this table.

[b]Base year is 1980.

[c]Column figures are year end, December 31.

[d]This year carried the highest rate of urban unemployment (in Mexico City, Guadalajara, and Monterrey) for 1980–86: 6.8%. Source: *Yearbook of Labour Statistics* (International Labor Organization). 1987.

[e]Column figures represent total disbursed external debt, including IMF debt.

[f]Column figures represent IMF rf series (Par Rate/Market Rate).

313

mid-1980s (Rout 1982). Imports had tripled from 1979–80 (Cline 1987, p. 78), with the US supplying 70 per cent of them (Jacobsen 1983, p. 1172). According to the US Department of Commerce (USDoC 1981), Mexico itself produced no computers or peripherals.

In response, in 1981, the Mexican government created the "Development Program for the Manufacturing of Electronic Computer Systems, Their Main Modules, and Peripheral Equipment." Not officially published, it was nevertheless implemented and has been informally referred to as the "Computer Decree" or "Warman Plan," after its main architect, Natan Warman. The Decree set broad goals for national technological development as well as specific ones such as locally supplying 70 per cent of the country's computer needs within five years (Cline 1986; Jacobsen 1983). Import shares permitted to distributors dropped over time and rose for manufacturers. Mini- and microcomputer makers faced performance requirements for research and development, local content, and exports and were offered incentives such as tax credits and preferential treatment in government procurement.[4]

Microcomputers drew special attention from the government. Introduced to Mexico in the late 1970s, their importation had "surged" (Cline 1987, p. 78). Apple and Tandy held 40 per cent and 30 per cent shares respectively of a market estimated at 8,000–20,000 units per year (Gardner 1984; Whiting and Shank 1986). Further, because of import duties, Mexicans were paying two-to-three times the US price of microcomputers (*Business Week* 1983). Some writers (Junco 1985) estimated that 50 per cent of Mexico's installed base had been smuggled across the US–Mexico border.

Two years later, at the end of 1983, several former Mexican distributors (e.g., Micron, Computadoras y Asesoramiento) and one US–Mexican joint venture, Computext (minority-owned by Franklin) were assembling microcomputers in Mexico (Infotext 1985). Computext was making 300–400 microcomputers a month, according to one interviewee. Imports had dropped, local production reached $34 million, and market revenues amounted to $30 million (see Table 15.1).[5] At the same time, from 1981–82, Mexican exports of peripheral equipment to the US sank from $4.67 million to $8,000 and from 1981–83, annual exports of all types of computers to the US (breakdowns are not available) doubled, then plummeted to $281,000 (USDoC telephone interview; cf. USDoC 1981).

In June 1983, Apple, IBM's chief microcomputer competitor in Latin America at the time, filed with the Mexican government a plan to begin locally assembling its model IIe (*Business Week* 1983). Six months later, the company announced the establishment of its minority-owned joint venture, Apple de Mexico.

---

[4] The first foreign plans for local computer production, from Hewlett-Packard for its HP3000 minicomputer, were approved in March 1982. By May, over forty other US companies had applied for such permission.
[5] In their market report for the US Department of Commerce, however, Wallace y Asociados (1988, 10) caution that "There are no official statistics covering the production and sale of computers and peripheral equipment in Mexico."

The State of Mexico's economy

Mexico's economy in 1983 was in dire straits. Heavily dependent on exports of oil, the price of which had collapsed in 1981, unable to make the late 1982 payments on its foreign debt, and now bound to an IMF-sponsored austerity program, the country saw its gross domestic product shrink 5.4 per cent. That had not happened since the Crash of 1929 (de la Madrid 1984, p. 66). Inflation was running four times the 1980 level, and 1983 payments on its $93 billion foreign debt had reached $13 billion (Bartlett 1989). During the year, new foreign direct investment dropped 72 per cent.

Computer industry shakeout

In late 1983, competition among microcomputer makers stiffened. IBM had set a standard — PC compatibility — but even IBM had to slash prices. The PC's initial 1981 price dropped 39 per cent by March 1983 to $3,339, not counting upgrades (*Business Week* 1985). Apple's share of US shipments went from 28 per cent in 1981 to 9.4 per cent in 1983; in September, Osborne Computer went bankrupt; and in October 1983, Texas Instruments withdrew from the market. During the next year, even IBM would face slower growth in its microcomputer revenues — despite the dramatic climb of unit shipments.

IBM's interests

In light of the foregoing conditions, in early 1984 the IBM organization as a whole had several basic interests:

- surviving — even profiting from — the microcomputer shakeout,
- meeting demand for PCs,
- maintaining the integrity and efficacy of its worldwide integration strategy,
- establishing a PC presence in "every country in the world"
- countering negative publicity about its predominance, and with respect to Mexico and Latin America,
- pursuing new business opportunities, and
- maintaining its relationship with the Mexican government and its already established Mexican operations.

The first interest dovetailed with a company-wide emphasis for the 1980s on low-cost production, which was reflected in an $11 billion investment in new plant and equipment from 1979-83 (*Business Week* 1981, p. 85; IBM Corp. 1983, p. 31; Marbach *et al.* 1983, p. 40). In 1984, four plants in Florida, Texas, Scotland and Australia produced the PC. There were customers and competitors (Apple, Hewlett-Packard) to respond to in Latin America, Canada, and Asia as well as the US. Coincidentally, IBM undoubtedly desired to maintain its well-known integration strategy, whose economic and managerial benefits have been discussed in depth elsewhere (Doz 1980).

IBM also wanted to join in virtually every government's national efforts to computerize (Meislin 1985a). In 1983, it operated in 131 countries. Yet the company was portrayed negatively in prominent news articles (see Pollack 1982; later, *Economist* 1985b; Pollack 1985), sued on antitrust grounds by the US Department of Justice (1969–82), and under investigation since 1977 by the Commission of the European Community for abusing its market position (de Jonquieres 1984).

Finally, the growing Mexican market and some provisions of the Computer Decree presented IBM with new opportunities. The company entered Mexico in 1927, enjoyed dominant market shares in mainframes and minicomputers (many of them purchased by the government and public enterprises), and was already assembling minicomputers and typewriters in its Guadalajara, Jalisco plant. Wholly owned IBM de Mexico, S.A. was exporting to up to 30 countries and reportedly had sales of $245 million in 1984 (Sanchez 1984).

Additional, specific interests could be enumerated for other organizations affiliated with IBM Corporation (i.e., IBM de Mexico, IBM World Trade A/FE Corporation, and A/FE's Latin American Division) and for the numerous groups and individuals within each of them (recall Figure 15.1). Such interests are too sensitive to detail here. Still, one could reasonably assume the existence of certain interests for each of these parties and of some typical differences and similarities between them, e.g., control by headquarters, autonomy for the subsidiary (see Egelhoff 1984; Prahalad and Doz 1981) and career advancement for individuals (Walton and McKersie 1965, p. 281ff).

The Government of Mexico's interests

The Government also had decipherable basic interests. They included:

- generally strengthening the economy (e.g., increasing GNP),
- expanding exports to improve the balance of payments,
- increasing employment,
- maintaining control over key sectors, meeting commitments to foreign lenders and the IMF, and with respect to the computer industry in particular,
- developing capacity to supply 70 per cent of local needs within five years,
- acquiring leading-edge technology, and diversifying investment.

Economic concerns and goals were publicly expressed by President de la Madrid (de la Madrid 1984; *Business Week* 1984b, p. 78). They derived from and would affect domestic politics, social conditions, and foreign relations. The Computer Decree signaled computer-specific interests (Jacobsen 1983). What linked the two areas, according to an American interviewee, was the Government's belief that the nation's falling behind technologically would weaken all sectors of the economy.

Not every individual or organization within the Government assessed or ranked the interests similarly. Differences arose within and between secretariats because of functions, jurisdictions, and the ideologies evidenced in an intense debate during this period over the extent to liberalize the Mexican economy (see below). At the same time, this picture was complicated by ubiquitous family and other personal ties between government officials (e.g., brothers Natan and Jose Warman), and between officials and constituents.

Mexico's strategic options

On a broad plane, the potential bargaining power with which IBM and the Government could pursue their respective interests in joint talks depended partly upon the number and desirability of their options (Bennett and Sharpe 1979; Holt 1978). Mexico had traditionally followed import substitution policies, but President de la Madrid, without entirely rejecting those policies, called for export promotion, especially of non-oil products. He upheld government control of certain sectors as stipulated in the Constitution and the 1973 Law to Promote Mexican Investment and to Regulate Foreign Investment, but sought foreign investment as a "complement" to national investment (*Business Week* 1984b, p. 79). Upon entering office in 1982, he reportedly instructed bureaucrats to apply the foreign investment guidelines "flexibly" (*Economist* 1985a, p. 61).

That directive, coupled with the status of the Computer Decree (see below), gave the Government at least three options for directing computer industry development and evaluating investment proposals:

- formally establishing the Decree and adhering strictly to its terms,
- modifying the Decree or allowing for major exceptions, and
- developing an entirely new computer policy.

Consistent with the 1973 Foreign Investment Law, the Decree restricted foreign mini- and microcomputer manufacturers to minority ownership in local ventures. On the other hand, in 1984, the Decree had still not been published in the Diario Official, which led some observers to believe that its terms were not legally binding (cf., Jacobsen 1983, p. 1172).

IBM's strategic options

From an outsider's perspective, IBM also appears to have had more than one possible course by which to pursue its global and Latin America interests. The conceivable options included:

- expanding capacity at existing PC assembly plants,
- building a new PC plant outside Mexico (e.g., in Argentina or South Korea),
- building a new plant in Mexico as a wholly owned operation,
- with a minority- or split-ownership position, forming a joint venture to produce PCs, and

- influencing Mexico's computer policy via operations based on other product lines (e.g., minicomputers).

The exact capacities of IBM's four existing PC plants have not been publicly reported, but the annual output of such plants, which are highly automated, ranges from 240,000–1,000,000 units.[6] Thus the four plants seem to have had the capacity to meet worldwide demand for IBM PCs, and their continued use would have been consistent with a global, low-cost strategy. And yet, Mexico held considerable appeal as host to an additional plant.

Choosing to propose a wholly owned plant in Mexico

According to IBM interviewees, the company decided to pursue a microcomputer plant investment in Mexico because of the country's strategic position as a major Latin American market and the not-yet solidified status of its computer policy. At this point, IBM was producing mainframes in Brazil, printers in Argentina, and minicomputers in Mexico, so establishing a PC plant in Latin America that would give the company the capability to produce its full product line locally. Mexico, in particular, represented the largest, quasi-open microcomputer market (Argentina's domestic market was only one-fourth of Mexico's size (Cline 1987, p. 121)), and as a member of the Latin American Integration Association, it also promised preferential tariff treatment within the region.[7]

Further, Brazil had already expressly embargoed computer imports, excluded foreign firms from local production (IBM's mainframe plant notwithstanding), and specifically rejected previous IBM investment proposals (Cline 1987, p. 36). IBM sought an opportunity to demonstrate to governments the benefits of its participation (see also Akers quoted in Meislin 1985a). On February 17, 1984, SECOFI Secretary Hernandez announced that "priority industrial activities" including computing equipment would be open to 100 per cent foreign ownership. This receptiveness in Mexico, as opposed to other sites, could also enable IBM to maintain its longstanding policy of 100 per cent ownership.[8]

Issues

IBM and the Mexican government would face numerous interorganizational issues, from business topics (e.g., type of venture, ownership and control, level

---

[6] In 1988, Apple's Fremont, California plant, working on one shift, made one million Macs (Kindel and Teitelman 1988, p. 28). In 1986, IBM's fully automated Austin, Texas plant made one PC Convertible every two minutes (Saporito 1986). On the assumption that two lines work one 8-hour shift a day, 250 days a year, the plant could produce 240,000 PCs.

[7] Mexico's renowned low-cost labor was not a major plus, given the high level of automation in microcomputer assembly operations.

[8] At this time, IBM reportedly had only seven joint ventures worldwide (Jeffrey 1984, p. 17). Moreover, an IBM interviewee stated the corporation simply would not consider a joint venture with a main line product.

of investment) to economic concerns (e.g., export markets, foreign exchange), and interpersonal and procedural matters as well. The parties' underlying interests and provisions of the Computer Decree suggested issues such as the technological sophistication of products, production volume and site (in order to decentralize industry, the Government had set priority development zones), employment levels and government procurement. There were also sourcing and local content issues, which called for discussion of microcomputer components ranging from high-value semiconductors and disk drives to low-value items like cables and cabinets.

Pre-negotiation Preparations

IBM

IBM began studying the Computer Decree in January 1982 and sounded out the de la Madrid government shortly after its formation. A proposal for local production of the System /34 minicomputer followed. It was approved, and production got under way in late 1982. Then in early 1984, to prepare for formal submission of a microcomputer proposal to the CNIE, the body charged with review of foreign investment applications, IBM hired Mexican attorneys, consulted other local experts such as the American Chamber of Commerce and the US Embassy, and met several times with CNIE representatives. (For more on this process generally, see Miller 1986; Radway 1980.)

At the time, according to an IBM interviewee, there was little information on the Mexican microcomputer market. (Statistics in Table 15.1 have appeared since then.) IBM's deliberations undoubtedly touched on the company's sources of bargaining power, e.g., its level of technology, differentiated product, and access to foreign markets (recall the literature review above). IBM expected Mexico's key concern to be export volumes.

Mexico

Within the government, officials and staff who prepared for the IBM proposal resided in the CNIE and within SECOFI's Directorate of the Electronics Industry and Industrial Coordination. An American analyst interviewed by the author said the latter studied the computer industry intensively during the early 1980s, starting from a position of little familiarity. These officials attended to local needs and capabilities. Other officials and bureaucrats viewed the upcoming IBM proposal in the context of Mexico's overall trade and foreign investment.

The Negotiations

In March 1984, IBM President John Akers presented to Secretary of Government Manuel Bartlett, a personal representative of President de la Madrid and member of the CNIE, a proposal to expand IBM's Guadalajara plant with a wholly owned

319

operation for PC assembly. Despite the CNIE's ostensible authority simply to grant approval or deny it, negotiations ensued. This went on for some seventeen months and another six thereafter. This period divides into four rounds: March–July 19, 1984; July 20, 1984–January 19, 1985; January 20–July 23, 1985; August 1985–January 1986. The negotiations usually took place not in formal sessions in conference rooms, but by letter and telephone and in spontaneous meetings. Specific actions during the four rounds are outlined in Table 15.3. It serves as a companion reference to Figure 15.1 for accounts that delve into issues, players, conditions, the negotiation process and the outcome of each round.

Round One: March–July 19, 1984

The first round of negotiation extended from the top level, Akers-Bartlett meeting to the CNIE's first, formal rejection of IBM's proposal.

Issues

At the outset, all of the issues described above lay before IBM and Mexico.

Players

On the part of the Mexican government, the interministerial CNIE carried responsibility for the government's decision concerning IBM. Each of the seven member secretariats' representatives (see Figure 15.1) had to sign off on the company's proposal. Within SECOFI, which provided the staff support for CNIE, the individual officials most actively involved in the review process were: the Secretary himself (Hernandez), the Executive Secretary of the CNIE (Hegewisch), who served concurrently as Undersecretary of Foreign Investment and Regulation of Technology Transfer; and the Undersecretary of Industrial Development (Maria y Campos). Under him, the chief of the Electronics Directorate (J. Warman), which included a Computer Section, also played a role. Each of these officials and Secretary of Government Bartlett could speak English fluently. President de la Madrid generally listened to his American interlocutors in top-level meetings in English but responded through an interpreter. CNIE and Industrial Development staffs carried out day-to-day activities.

IBM was represented by IBM de Mexico. Although the subsidiary pursued plans previously agreed upon with A/FE's Latin American Division and IBM Corporation, its role also reflects A/FE's confidence in the effectiveness of representatives who shared with their counterparts a cultural affinity and familiarity with local conditions. The individuals most involved were IBM de Mexico's President (Guerra) and other executives (del Toro, Conde) and LAD's President (Ford). Beyond them, the senior IBM executive responsible was A/FE's Chairman and CEO (Pfeiffer). Ford, Pfeiffer and IBM President Akers were not fluent in Spanish.

TABLE 15.3
Chronology of the IBM–Mexico negotiations

Pre-negotiation 1983	
	Pursuant to Computer Decree (Sept. 1981). IBM sounds out Mexican government on a possible investment
March 8	IBM introduces PC XT in the US
June	Apple Computer, Inc. begins investment task with Secretarial of Commerce & Industrial Development (SECOFI)
1984	
Jan.	IBM Introduces PCjr in the US
Jan.	Apple establishes minority-owned joint venture (Apple de Mexico) with Grupo Manzana to produce model IIe
Feb. 17	SECOFI issues revised guidelines for foreign investment
Round One	
March	Akers meets with Bartlett in Mexico and presents specific IBM proposal to assemble PCs locally
April	National Commission on Foreign Investment (CNIE) leaning against proposal but agrees to postpone decision
June 30	Deadline set by IBM for reply from SECOFI
July 9	Trade groups AMFABI and CANIECE publish letters opposing policy exceptions in *Excelsior*, *Novededes*, and *Heraldo*
July 19	CNIE rejects IBM's initial proposal
Round Two	
August	IBM extends its June deadline for a final settlement but threatens to approach Argentina with its proposal
August 10	Apple de Mexico produces its first Mexican IIe in Nanicalpan and projects annual production of 7,000 units
August 14	IBM introduced PC AT in the US
Oct.	IBM submits revised proposal, raising local content and financial and technical aid to local computer industry
Oct. 25	Tentative agreement on several issues announced by government
Nov. 26	*New York Times* City Edition reports rejection of IBM's proposal based on report from Socialist Deputy Gobela
Nov. 28	Mexican officials deny reported rejection and declare that formal approval will be made the following week
Nov. 29	IBM begins contacting Mexican ad agencies for campaigns to promote its PCs
1985	
Jan.	Argentina announces Resolution 44 to protect and stimulate small computer and peripherals industry
Jan. 19	Mexico officially rejects IBM's latest terms but invites another IBM proposal; IBM intends to continue dialogue
Round Three	
Feb. 9	Hegewisch reportedly threatened to resign because of the rejection of IBM
March 11	Conde announces IBM is improving offers on level of investment, jobs, exports and technology
March (mid)	Pfeiffer meets with de la Madrid; Akers meets with Argentina's Alfonsin to discuss IBM Investments.
July 23	CNIE announces approval of IBM's investment plan
Round Four	
1986	
Jan.	Details of agreement finalized
Feb. 3	Guerra publicly announces IBM's program in Mexico City; de la Madrid publicly applauds it the next day
May	IBM begins production of PC XT in El Salto, Jalisco (Mexico's "Silicon Valley", near Guadalajara)

Stephen Weiss

Conditions

The setting for talks during the spring of 1984 differed notably from pre-negotiation conditions. On Mexico's economic front, between the first and second quarters, inflation rose 13 per cent and the current account surplus dropped by almost half — despite devaluation of the peso. In January, Ford Motor Company announced plans to build a $500-million plant to assemble cars, but foreign direct investment generally continued to decline. In February, the Government issued a decree restricting the role of foreign MNEs and urging self-sufficiency in pharmaceuticals. (There had also been an Auto Decree in April 1983.) This decree, separate negotiations over a bilateral subsidies pact, Mexico's entry to GATT, and multi-year debt rescheduling (July 16-September 8, 1984), and long-running issues such as immigration policies all appeared on the bilateral, Mexican-US agenda. When US pharmaceutical companies and government representatives complained, many Mexicans no doubt felt anew their historical resentment and suspiciousness toward their northern neighbor (Grayson 1987).

In the Mexican computer industry, in April, Hewlett-Packard linked up with the Mexican conglomerate Grupo DESC to assemble microcomputers. They produced their first HP150 on July 17. Other assemblers (e.g., Printaform, Denki, and soon, Apple de Mexico) were also operating and adding to local capacity.

IBM continued numerous activities worldwide and initiated others while negotiating with Mexico, but two are particularly noteworthy. First, IBM began a publicity drive in Brazil, whose small-computer market was eighth in the world and expected to grow to fifth, to counter the government's hardening of its restrictive informatics policy. According to one report (Michaels 1984), the company approached twelve Brazilian companies about possible joint ventures and licensing agreements. Then, in April 1984, the company engaged the Hyundai Group in South Korea in talks concerning joint production of a small, high-performance computer (Schiffman 1984).

One more aspect of context deserves mention: internal decision making of the two primary parties. In the Mexican government, the president had traditionally wielded tremendous power by virtue of his office and his role as chief representative of the long dominant political party, the PRI. Indeed, that power ultimately came to bear on this negotiation. At the same time, administration was handled by a formidable, not always unified bureaucracy (Frazier 1984a) and constituencies and interest groups (e.g., the private sector) had been able to influence presidential actions (see Story 1982).

In the IBM case, conflict and negotiation occurred between departments close to local companies and those not, among officials, between officials and staff, and within Congress (Orme 1984a). Industrial chambers, which have semi-official status as designated representatives of the private sector before the Government (without being controlled by the PRI), also became involved and wielded considerable influence. According to one interviewee, however, Mexican businessmen in the computer industry were not united. A split developed between low-technology component producers and young, foreign-educated Mexicans who wanted access to new technology. Government and industry representatives thus debated among themselves and with each other, and Mexican and US mass media coverage sustained them.

IBM's decision making involved IBM de Mexico, A/FE's Latin American Division, A/FE executives, and the parent IBM Corporation. Each of them contributed to planning for external negotiations. IBM Corporation itself was guided by some nineteen members of a Corporate Management Board, one third of whom constituted a "management committee" that made decisions about mergers and acquisitions, financing, new sites, capital investment, and product introductions. As a member of this board and an IBM Corporation Senior Vice-President, A/FE Chairman Pfeiffer personally linked these organizations.[9]

In the talks with Mexico, the heaviest internal negotiations occurred within A/FE. LAD had primary decision making responsibility and worked closely with IBM de Mexico before conveying plans for Mexico to IBM headquarters. As negotiations with the Government intensified, so, too, did the movement of LAD officials to Mexico and of IBM de Mexico officials to LAD headquarters near New York City.

That was the context for Round One.

The negotiation process

After preliminary meetings with government officials in March 1984, IBM submitted to the CNIE for approval a written proposal prepared by IBM de Mexico. The plan included:

- $6.6 million expansion of IBM's El Salto plant;
- wholly owned operation to produce 603,000 PCs over five years;
- exporting 88–89 per cent of production (leading to export revenues of $528 million over five years);
- balance of payments surplus estimated at $103 million;
- local content levels of 35 per cent for Year 1, 50 per cent for Year 4 (in terms of pure content, i.e., $35 for each $100); and
- jobs; 80 direct; 800 indirect (Business International 1985a; IBM interview; Montes 1985).

Such an application usually contains descriptions of the company and its technology, financial analyses and import/export projections in order to persuade officials of the justification for the terms of the proposed investment. With this submission, the Government's formal review process got under way.

Ensuing talks went on in various arenas. IBM de Mexico representatives met separately with representatives of the CNIE, the Department of Technology

---

[9] The top PC executive at IBM Corporation, Entry Level Systems President Philip D. Estridge, also had to approve LAD's PC plans.

Development, Patents and Trademarks, the Industrial Development Subsecretariat and then the industrial chambers. Besides SECOFI, other CNIE-member secretariats such as Finance each met with IBM (all of which suggests some "diffusion" rather than a straightforwardly "coordinated" review process (Encarnation and Wells, 1985). At this stage, IBM took the lead in trying to justify its proposal.

In this approach, according to an IBM interviewee, the company's representatives were following recommendations of top-level government officials who had assured them, at the outset, that IBM's investment would be approved. They had said the process would take time. On the other hand, a leading Mexican businessman interviewed by the author felt the Government's final decision was far from a foregone conclusion.

In April, existence of the proposal was reported in the Mexican press. Those opposing "special treatment" for IBM — opposition that would build in subsequent months — included the National Chamber of Electronic Industry and Electric Communications (CANIECE), which represented most of the twenty-two foreign and Mexican firms authorized to make microcomputers in Mexico, and the Mexican Association of Manufacturers of Computer Products (AMFABI) established by Apple and Hewlett-Packard.

Within the Government, a number of bureaucrats responsible for industries, especially electronics and computers, enunciated longstanding concerns about local producers' displacement by MNEs and asserted, moreover, that Mexico only needed local firms to build the computer industry. The 11–12 per cent of IBM's proposed annual production set aside for local consumption represented over 65 per cent of the largest estimate of Mexico's microcomputer market. Further, in comparison to IBM's offer, Apple de Mexico had committed to 54 per cent local content (cf. pure content and Mexico's GIN formula[10]) by the end of its first year of production (Clark 1985).

On the other hand, officials favoring IBM's proposal could point to Apple Computer, Inc.'s mere $600,000 initial investment, the joint venture's production of 7,000 units per year and its use of dated technology (the IIe debuted in 1977). IBM underscored its proposed export levels and the consistency of the plan with SECOFI's February 1984 annoucement on foreign investment and later (July), with the National Development Program for Promotion of Industry and Foreign Trade. The company also reportedly augmented its original proposal at least once by offering to donate $20 million in computers to Mexico's educational system (Oster 1984). In the late spring, three months after submitting their proposal, IBM representatives thought they had completed negotiations.

No decision was announced, however. In June, an IBM executive was quoted saying a decision could be made "tomorrow, days, or weeks away" (Business

---

[10] The GIN formula, which stands for Degree of National Integration and is stipulated in the Computer Decree, can differ from the actual ratio of domestic to total physical inputs by more than half (Cline 1987, p. 83).

Week 1984a). The company gave SECOFI a June 30 deadline for a reply. By that summer, according to one market analyst who was interviewed, government planners for the computer industry were "euphoric" about having weathered the low early years and witnessing now the rising capabilities of local assemblers. On July 12, 1984, CANIECE and AMFABI sent letters to President de la Madrid and three newspapers underscoring the contributions and progress of local manufacturers to date and reminding the Government of its prior request that CANIECE help to implement the Computer Decree.

These proceedings apparently ran counter to both parties' expectations and preferences. Some Mexican observers felt IBM was "squeezing concessions" from the Government (Gardner 1984). On the other hand, an American participant observed that government representatives did not present their views with the level of detail and information to which American negotiators were accustomed. Like their compatriots in other international negotiations (see Weiss 1987), American IBM representatives also appear to have viewed time as much more pressing than their counterparts did.

The outcome

On July 19, the CNIE rejected IBM's plan. The reasons cited vary with the observers and account. Some interviewees pointed to internal politics (e.g., the degree of dissent, the amount of decision making done by staffs); others pointed to the economics of the proposal. Mexican officials communicated to IBM a desire for much broader plans, plans that entailed more than PC production.

Round Two: July 20, 1984–January 19, 1985

Despite the formal rejection, the Government made clear to IBM its interest in new proposals. Thus the July 19, 1984 rejection doubly ended Round One and initiated Round Two. This round, which would also end in a government rejection, lasted six months, until January 19, 1985.

Issues

The parties' agenda went beyond export levels to include local content levels, specific PC models and other issues concerning technology transfer (e.g., developing local capacity to design logic boards). Limiting IBM's share of the Mexican microcomputer market and price ceilings on PCs came up in the talks. So did job creation.

Players

In this round, Mexico's economic ministers and other members of the President's economic cabinet, aided by their direct subordinates, became more active.

Stephen Weiss

Hegewisch and Maria y Campos played prominent albeit opposing roles. IBM continued to be represented by IBM de Mexico executives and LAD President Ford and in high level meetings by A/FE Chairman Pfeiffer. In addition, US Commerce and State Department officers, particularly those posted to the US Embassy in Mexico, and US Ambassador John Gavin became involved. Some of these individual players' personal relationships bridged the two sides (e.g., IBM's Conde is related to Finance Secretary Jesus Silva Herzog).

Conditions

As IBM and Mexico negotiated during this round, significant features of the context shifted. The Mexican economy made some gains over its 1983 performance. For 1984, real GDP growth hit 3.6 per cent. But the trade surplus shriveled between the second and third quarters, and inflation continued to rise. At year end, inflowing foreign direct investment was even lower than in 1983 (see Table 15.2).

President de la Madrid, long in favor of Mexico's accession to GATT, took greater strides toward trade liberalization. This view developed momentum against the strictly statist position assumed by some officials within the Government. In the same vein, the President voiced concern in the fall about the US's "growing protectionism" toward Mexico (de la Madrid 1984).

With respect to the Mexican computer industry, Apple produced its first Mexican microcomputer on August 10, 1984. By then, the Government had approved some thirty companies' plans to assemble microcomputers in Mexico and was still receiving new ones (e.g., Tandy's). During 1984, demand for low-end home computers rose dramatically with the high-volume strategies and promotions of Mexican companies like Sigma/Commodore (Infotext 1985).

Worldwide, the pace of microcomputer revenue growth dropped by half compared to 1983, although demand continued to climb. In 1984, IBM cornered 20.1 per cent of the US market, up from 1983's 8 per cent. The second half of the year — Round Two of the talks — brought two other developments for IBM, both in August: its introduction of the PC AT in the US, and an agreement with the Commission of the EEC that ended its seven-year long antitrust investigation of IBM.

Lastly, the IBM-Mexico talks were monitored and assessed by secondary parties and others not directly involved in the proceedings. Beyond CANIECE's efforts, local computer companies such as Apple individually took the position that "[IBM should] play by the same rules" (Frazier 1984b; Meislin 1984). Mexican businessman Richard Hojel, the Chairman of Apple de Mexico, was prominent in such efforts. News editorials also appeared, foreseeing threats to national sovereignty (see *New York Times* 1984b; Martinex 1984). The national debate over IBM's plan and foreign investors' concerns about government decision making intensified when shortly after the rejection of IBM, the Government approved an investment plan by McDonalds restaurants.

326

The negotiation process

IBM representatives met with CNIE and Industrial Development counterparts during this round. They also saw Ambassador Gavin several times, and he as well as other US government officials pressed Mexican counterparts to give IBM a "fair hearing". A US/government interviewee said even President Reagan's cabinet members raised this point when they met with their Mexican counterparts. And yet, according to two interviewees, IBM itself had decided by this stage to pull back from active advocacy to a quiet strategy and to take cues from government officials.

Some among them urged the company to produce the new PC AT in Mexico (Meislin 1984) and to limit its share of the Mexican micro market to 25 per cent (Cline 1987, p. 84; Orme 1985). In a published interview not specific to the IBM case in September, CNIE Executive Secretary Hegewisch, who favored the IBM proposal, set forth his criteria for approving foreign investment: export potential, furthering technological development, and a high level of investment per employee (Wall Street Journal 1984). Two weeks later, IBM de Mexico issued a press release underscoring the contributions of its El Salto plant to date (e.g., export earnings of $50 million, parts purchases of $12 million between 1982–84 from some 120 local vendors) and potential benefits to Mexico from its microcomputer plan, benefits including business for local firms representing 80 per cent of the national computer industry (IBM Mexico 1984).

By the fall of 1984, the US and Mexican press had become part of the negotiation process. They not only covered the parties' actions but were used by the parties to bolster their own commitments and to signal or float new views. But the press also confused the participants, their constituencies, and audiences with misinformation — whatever its source. In October, one US newspaper article reported that IBM would invest "more than $300 million" (Meislin 1984); another stated that IBM agreed to use 65 per cent local content in Year 1, rising to 95 per cent in Year 4 (recall note 10), and to produce three models, the PC AT, PCjr and PC (Frazier 1984b).

Tensions rose. As early as August, IBM representatives had told SECOFI Secretary Hernandez that the company was running out of time and would have to consider Argentina as an alternative site. To Mexicans, that came across as a threat (Junco 1985; Orme 1984a). As one Mexican legislator said: "Welcoming IBM's project 'would weaken Mexico's negotiating position with big companies that will see us as a vacillating, not-very-serious adversary susceptible to giving in to pressure and willing to turn its back on national investment' (Orme 1984b). By this stage, however, IBM was also receiving invitations from other national presidents to invest in their countries.

Still, by late October, IBM had augmented its offers and reports circulated of agreement in principle on many aspects of the project (Frazier 1984a). These points included 100 per cent ownership, 50 per cent local content in Year 1, exporting 92 per cent of production, and $40 million of funds to develop local supplies. Opponents expected imminent approval, and IBM reportedly began contacting advertising agencies (Orme 1984a). (See Table 15.3).

On November 28, the New York Times City Edition (1984a) reported government rejection of the latest IBM plan. In contrast, an edition of the paper later that day (New York Times 1984b) stated a 100 per cent owned plant would be permitted if IBM met "certain rules". The first report cited as a source an advance copy of a recommendation from SECOFI; the second, "top government officials." Hegewisch had formally proposed approval (Orme, 1985). Apparently, the rift within the Government continued, sharpened by reactions to the government positions having been announced in the US before they appeared in Mexican press.

To some Americans monitoring the talks, the Government appeared unpredictable. As one interviewee stated, it kept changing — escalating — its demands. That image may have stemmed in part from intragovernmental differences. Another interviewee felt that IBM and its supporters did not clearly see the Government's key concerns. A number of Mexicans continued criticizing IBM tactics such as threatening to go to Argentina and appealing to the US government. These attitudes and reactions, coupled with the nature of the media coverage, complicated the negotiations considerably.

The outcome

On January 19, 1985 some ten months after IBM's initial submission and exactly six months after its rejection, the CNIE formally rejected IBM's latest proposal. The CNIE cited the inconsistency of the plan "with the central government's economic objectives" and concern about the displacement of "national capital" (Orme 1985; Business International 1985b, p. 42). Some observers pointed specifically to the low level of IBM's offer on local content and to the nature of its lobbying (Business International 1985b; Economist 1985a).

Round Three: January 20–July 23, 1985

Just after the CNIE announced its decision, a spokesman stated "The door isn't closed" (Orme 1985). At the same time, IBM issued a statement that its officers would "continue . . . [their] dialogue with the Mexican government . . ." (Frazier 1985a). So began Round Three, which would last six months.

Issues

CNIE Executive Secretary Hegewisch revealed some outstanding issues to the public in February, saying, "If IBM comes back here tomorrow with more to offer in the way of research and development, domestic content, and exports, they will be welcome" (Economist 1985a, 62).

Players

After the January rejection, Hegewisch offered to resign but did stay on for Round Three (Economist 1985a). Undersecretary Maria y Campos also continued to play a role. More importantly, President de la Madrid directly reentered the process and guided decision making.

On the IBM side, in addition to IBM de Mexico negotiators, there were A/FE Chairman Pfeiffer, LAD President Ford, and to a small extent, John Akers, now Chairman of IBM Corporation. US government officials remained in the picture.

Conditions

During this round, Mexico's GDP grew, though not at its 1984 rate. Furthermore, by the end of 1985, inflation increased 58 per cent over its 1984 level and the government deficit increased 25 per cent. Most dramatically, from the first to second quarters of 1985, Mexico's current account changed 200 per cent, dropping to $-\$424$ million.

Mexico's negotiations with the US concerning a subsidies agreement, which had been forestalled by US reaction to the 1984 Pharmaceutical Decree, concluded with an agreement in April. The US Trade Representative's press release announcing the agreement also included a statement of the two governments' intent to pursue a bilateral framework for general principles of trade. Thus the Mexican government abolished its incentive program for foreign computer makers and in July, announced a substantial trade liberalization policy (Miller 1986, p. 193).[11]

Relevant events and conditions in the Mexican computer industry during this time included Sperry and Tandy's entering into separate joint ventures to produce microcomputers in May. By this point, all MNEs in Mexico sourced printers locally; some used local monitors. Even some 3.5-inch disk drives were being made in Mexico (Infotext 1985, p. 4). Mexican demand for micros rose 32 per cent over the 1984 level (see Table 15.1); the business segment was booming (Infotext 1985, p. 50). Apple led vendors of single-user systems with a market share, in units, estimated at 35.9 per cent. Further, Mexico's exports of all types of computers to the US during 1985 increased more than ten times, to $2.82 million.

Elsewhere, however, microcomputer markets contracted. World total revenues continued to grow, but at a much slower rate (see Table 15.1). From 1984–85, Apple's micro revenues slipped 15.4 per cent; Hewlett-Packard's dropped 21.6 per cent. By the end of 1985, unit shipments in the US dropped 22 per cent from their 1984 volumes. Still, IBM managed to ship more units and to increase its US and world market shares.

---

[11] In November 1985, the Mexican government announced its intention to join GATT (which it finally did in September 1986).

Stephen Weiss

After the January 1985 rejection, the intensity of public debate in Mexico and the role of the press faded. During the next six months, only one news article (Frazier 1985b) and one op-ed piece written by a Mexican newspaper editor (Junco 1985) appeared in major US newspapers.

The negotiation process

Top-level meetings took place during this round. A/FE Chairman Pfeiffer met with President de la Madrid in Mexico. IBM officials realized that exports was, in one interviewee's words, the "hot *economic* issue" but not the "hot *political* issue," which was jobs.

In March, IBM de Mexico Director General Conde told an American reporter (Frazier 1985b) that IBM was increasing levels of investment, jobs and exports, and improving offers on technology. He even mentioned IBM's considering a smaller, minority-owned joint venture as a "last option," a statement which subsequently surprised a LAD interviewee (see also note 8).

The company's representatives still faced some government and public resistance to their plans and negotiating efforts. The latter included a reported meeting in mid-March between IBM Chairman Akers and Argentinian President Alfonsin (Junco 1985). But opposition was less vociferous.

Overall, the process led participants who were interviewed to emphasize the impact of individuals' status and personal contacts in negotiations in Mexico (recall Adler, Graham and Gehrke 1987; Weiss and Stripp 1985). Interviewees also cited the Mexican president's power (Grayson 1987). Indeed, when IBM formally resubmitted a revised plan that summer, President de la Madrid himself acted on it.

The outcome

On July 23, 1985, CNIE announced approval of the following IBM plan:

- wholly owned operation to produce 603,000 PCs over five years;
- jobs — 240 direct; 1,460 indirect;
- local content levels of 51 per cent for Year 1, 82 per cent for Year 4;
- exporting 92 per cent of production (leading to export revenues of $620 million over five years);
- balance of payments surplus of $280 million;
- introducing new products within six months of their US debut;
- limiting differences between US and Mexican computer prices to 10–15 per cent; and
- total investment of $91.1 million, consisting of (in millions):
  - $6.6 for fixed assets,
  - $35 to local research and development,
  - $20 to develop local suppliers,

   −$12.9 for national dealer and international distribution networks,
   −$11.5 for a new, government-run Semiconductor Technology Center, and
   −$5.1 for a Spanish-speaking software center, university partnerships, and a packing system (Business International 1985a; Montes 1985).

Negotiatons had not yet ended, however.

Round Four: August 1985–January 1986

It took several more months for IBM and government negotiators to finalize details. Under markedly quieter conditions than before, they worked on a delimited agenda comprising the items of the July plan. According to an interviewee at the IBM LAD, the final agreement reached in January 1986 entails:

- wholly owned operation to produce 603,000 PCs over five years;
- 240 direct jobs;
- increasing local content levels, going from 51 per cent up to 71 per cent;
- export revenues of $620 million over five years;
- balance of payments surplus of $200 million;
- introduction of new technology within six months of its US debut;
- limiting differences between the PC's list price in the US and Mexican prices to 10–15 per cent; and
- total investment of $91.1 million, consisting of (in millions):
   −$14.5 international procurement/software/distribution,
   −$11.5 semiconductor technology center,
   −$1.0 MLT-SMT card technology,
   −$22.5 vendor development program,
   −$22.0 academic partnership (human resource development), and
   −$19.6 manufacturing plant.

Note the major differences between the January and July accords: indirect jobs, percentage export of production, and dollar amounts for balance of payments, academic partnerships, and the manufacturing plant. Final agreement was publicly announced by IBM de Mexico President Guerra on February 3, 1986 and by Mexican President de la Madrid on February 4th (MEU 1986).

Post-negotiation

Only the implementation of the IBM plan will enable the parties to assess the real individual and joint gains and the degree to which the agreed terms satisfy respective, original motivations and evolving interests. IBM de Mexico began production of the PC XT in May 1986. By mid-1988, the facility had switched to assembly of the PS/2 and accounted for 10 per cent of IBM's worldwide PC production.

Stephen Weiss

The Mexican government has had to continue wrestling with broad economic problems and attraction of foreign investors.[12] After July 1985, Apple, Hewlett-Packard and UNISYS all applied to the CNIE for 100 per cent ownership of their Mexican ventures and received approval. Apple later withdrew from Mexico altogether, but computer industry statistics putting 1987 microcomputer production at $210 million, market revenues at $154 million (Wallace y Asociados 1988) and 1986 exports to the US high above 1985's (USDoC, tel. interview) indicate significant developmental gains.

Conclusions

Motivated by questions about negotiation process and outcomes, this article traced in detail the March 1984–January 1986 talks between the IBM Corporation and the Government of Mexico. The account bears upon existing international business negotiation literature and goes beyond it by hinting at topics for future research. Thus both case-specific observations and implications for negotiation research deserve reconsideration here.

The case study

With respect to IBM and the Government's interactions, this study has most strikingly shown their complexity. "IBM" and "the Government" served as shorthand labels, for numerous actors were involved, and they ranged in type from individuals and groups to departments, organizations and "constellations" of organizations (Allison 1971). Both sides went through significant internal negotiations. In their negotiations with each other, different representatives played prominent roles at different stages.

They negotiated via consultations and informal communications as well as proposals and responses, and for a long period of twenty-three months — through two publicized rejections. They educated each other about computer technology and local conditions, respectively, but also used tough tactics like threats and unyielding postures. Secondary parties and the media took actions that further complicated the proceedings.

That IBM and the Government reached an agreement is not surprising, though, given the fit between their underlying interests, the options, and the stakes involved by July 1985. Mexico was a valuable, strategic market within Latin America for IBM. Besides IBM's intrinsic qualities, top-level Mexican decision makers who had favored the initial investment plan and by this point reentered the review process, could base their approval on the Government's responsiveness to local interests in past months, the additional commitments from IBM, the importance of foreign investors' impressions, and pressures from the US government.

---

[12] In May 1990, SECOFI announced major liberalization of foreign investment regulations and streamlining of review procedures.

The particular terms of the agreement, however, are more difficult for an outside analyst to explain. In the US, industry observers found the extent of IBM concessions reported in July "surprising" (Sanger 1985). Indeed, the ostensible cost of the final investment plan to IBM exceeded by fourteen times the $6.6 million of the original plan. But then $91.1 million looks quite different relative to IBM's corporate resources and to projected earnings of the venture itself.[13]

On Mexico's part, some of the augmented and added items (e.g., jobs and human resources development, the semiconductor center and date of technology, price ceilings) clearly correspond with the interests of groups inside and outside of government concerned with local industry. Increased figures for exports, balance of payments and local content had to appeal to officials responsible for trade and investment who had favored even the original IBM proposal. In short, the last proposal held the promise of widespread and substantial benefits for the Mexican computer industry and economy.

More generally, as mentioned at the outset, this case study has illustrated facets of MNE-host government relationships, the contemporary, strategic concern of developing countries for their domestic computer industries, and the intricacies of bilateral ties. It relates to literature on the power of the Mexican president, cultural differences in negotiating styles, and MNE bargaining power and ownership of foreign subsidiaries.[14] The case also elucidates the process of foreign investment review and substantiates Encarnation and Wells' (1985, p. 62ff, p. 75) assertion that salient investment plans elicit diffused organizational review even when an interministerial body exists. Conclusions specific to foreign investment in Mexico that stem from this case have been drawn by other observers (e.g., Business International 1985a).

Future Negotiation Research

At least as importantly, this study raises questions for the budding research literature on international business negotiations. Thus far, that research has flowed in two separate streams: the macro-strategic, which treats organizations as units and addresses static variables such as MNE bargaining power (e.g., Fagre and Wells 1982); and the micro-behavioral, which focuses on tactics of individuals not situated within organizations (e.g., Graham 1983). This analysis of the

---

[13] Assuming production of 120,600 units per year, a unit price of $2000 and a conservative gross profit margin of 40 per cent, IBM's PC venture in Mexico would yield an annual gross profit of $96.48 million.

[14] The bargaining school (e.g., Fagre and Wells 1982; Grosse and Aramburu 1989) informed the identification in this analysis of resources held by IBM and the Mexican government. This perspective is generally used to explain the relative amounts gained on an item (e.g., ownership position) of an already concluded agreement, rather than the occurence or non-occurence of agreement itself. For the latter, this analysis showed the value of additional considerations such as players, interests and conditions, coupled with a basic assumption of rational self-interest.

Stephen Weiss

IBM-Mexico negotiations drew on both streams and propounds their confluence in order to better understand such negotiation. Richer understanding may also come from future research in four areas.

Complexity of party behavior

As the IBM-Mexico case suggests, large, organizational parties may not be internally unified. How can cohesiveness be systematically described, and what is the nature and extent of its effect on interparty negotiations? An interviewee for this case suggested, for instance, that disunity allowed the Government to use competing demands and hard-soft tactics against IBM. Unpublicized intermediaries are often involved in such cases, and their influence deserves more attention. More generally, the various actors and multiple levels of behavior call for the development of methods by which to identify, describe and evaluate parties to these negotiations.

Audiences

One participant estimated that publicity and media coverage protracted the IBM-Mexico negotiations by six months (26 per cent). When can and should publicity be minimized? Similarly, the influence of secondary parties like home governments on allied and opposing primary parties deserves study.

Conditions of negotiations

Interorganizational negotiations, like most behavior, occur within contexts. How do parties and their representatives evaluate markets, economies, and intergovernmental relations and use those results in negotiations? Conditions directly affecting negotiators' relationships also need to be explored in systematic ways.

Dynamics and the long term of negotiators' relationships

Conditions, like other factors, usually change over time, as the worldwide microcomputer market and the Mexican computer industry did in this case. When do such factors alter parties' original motivations and their ongoing relationship? More broadly, the parties' relationship may be more usefully viewed across periods before, during and after negotiation. Then researchers can study the effect of negotiation behavior on the implementation of an agreement in the post-negotiation period.

Other substantive areas and theoretical concerns such as model development also deserve attention in the future. There is ample opportunity and need for more extensive and varied research on international business negotiation. It is the detail of a substantively rich, systematically organized study of a case like the long IBM-Mexico negotiations that brings these points to light.

CHAPTER 16

Negotiating with Eastern and Central Europe

PERVEZ GHAURI AND JEAN-CLAUDE USUNIER

The end of the cold war and the liberalization of Eastern and Central Europe are perhaps the most dynamic and exciting events of recent years. The introduction of Perestroika in 1985 and the fall of the Berlin Wall in 1989 have created enormous opportunities for the world economy and for Western firms. However, more than half a century of communist regimes has left its mark on these societies, so that Western standards for doing business cannot fully apply. This chapter first reviews the economic transition in Eastern and Central Europe, the gaps between Western and Eastern economies and the necessity of a long-term commitment. The next section is devoted to the negotiation aspects, presenting key issues to be considered when negotiating, and the common features of Eastern and Central Europeans when working out business deals, such as the pace of negotiations, the strategic orientation and the decision-making process. The final two sections of the chapter focus on specific countries: Russia, Poland, Hungary and the Czech Republic.

The economic transition in Eastern and Central Europe

The importance of Eastern and Central Europe, with a population of 429 million people, cannot be questioned. This is 30 per cent more than the European Community (EC) and almost double that of the United States. The new situation has enhanced the importance of entire Europe, now it has a population of 720 million people (Buckley and Ghauri 1994).

Today, in most of East European countries, there are democratically elected governments which are committed to establishing market economies based on free competition. Most of the countries are desperately trying to attract foreign companies in order to establish technology transfer and trading links. There are some apparent leaders; Poland, Hungary and the Czech Republic now have free pricing, convertible currencies and a considerable amount of foreign investments.

Pervez Ghauri and Jean-Claude Usunier

These countries have clear goals and objectives to achieve Western style market economies and have taken rigorous measures to achieve these.

Although most countries of Eastern Europe are committed to improving their economies, there are still too many inter-related obstacles in the path of growth which have to be dealt with. Issues such as trade barriers, the development of banking and loan systems, pricing mechanisms, property and contract law all need immediate attention. Privatization is considered to be a solution to achieve market economies and growth, but there is no easy way to achieve privatization in Eastern Europe. Over-optimistic estimates are now being revised and people have started realizing that it might take a decade or two before a privatized market economy can be achieved.

Due to the above reasons, reactions from Western companies have been rather cautious. However, in spite of this reluctance, most multinationals have entered these markets. Companies such as McDonald's, Pepsi Cola, Coca Cola, Statoil, Ericsson, Ikea, Fiat, Nokia, Volkswagen, Estée Lauder, Philip Morris, almost all pharmaceutical firms and several small and medium-sized companies have already established operations in these markets. The governments are providing a number of incentives to foreign companies to invest in their countries (Tietz 1994).

In spite of the reluctance of Western companies to invest, there has been a considerable increase in registered Joint Ventures. By March 1992, there were 34,121 registered Joint Ventures between Western Companies and organizations from Eastern Europe. This figure had been 12,512 in 1989, and it increased to 106,295 in 1994. The Joint Ventures registered in different East European countries during the period 1989, 1992 and 1994 are illustrated by Table 16.1.

TABLE 16.1
Registered joint ventures in selected countries

Country	Registered JVs 1989	1992	1994
Bulgaria	35	239	2,185
Czech & Slovak Republics	50	3,000	10,700
Hungary	600	11,000	15,205
Poland	400	5,286	17,577
Romania	9,327	9,327	30,441
Russia (CIS)	1,000	2,600	30,187
Former Yugoslavia	1,100	2,669	n.a.
Total	12,512	34,121	106,295

Source: Based on Van Berendonk, Oosterveer and Associates (1992), ECE, East-West Joint Ventures, No. 31989 and ECE, East-West Investment News, No. 3/4/4, 1994.

A major part of these Joint Ventures is, however, still non-operative, as the Western companies are sitting still and waiting for these economies to stabilize. With the exception of the three market leaders, Hungary, Poland and the Czech

336

Republic, there are a number of problems that have to be solved before a proper marketing involvement can be expected from Western companies.

Factors Influencing Business Transactions in Eastern Europe

The left-overs of communism in Eastern Europe

Communism meant collective ownership of production means. In most countries, except Poland, a large part of agriculture was state-owned and managed. The same was true for foreign trade, which was the monopoly of sectoral agencies. Administered trade was the rule in the Comecon, where both production and trade were centrally organized. Ikarus buses were made in Hungary for the whole of Eastern Europe, just as Balkancar forklifts were made by the Bulgarians. As emphasized by Naor in the case of Romania (Naor 1986), distribution was urged to be as cost-efficient as possible, that is, direct distribution from producer to retailers was advocated to the greatest possible extent. But distribution was very poor and parallel, informal distribution often replaced state-run retail outlets where people had to wait a long time to obtain the few products available. Although the concept of marketing had been known for a good number of years in countries such as Hungary and Poland, there was an absence of real marketing infrastructure, such as market research consultants, panels, advertising agencies etc. Communism, although a political system rather than a full culture, has left its mark after forty to seventy years, depending on the country in question. Consumers have been used to facing systematic undersupply moderated by queues rather than prices. In Bulgaria, for instance, people had to wait several years to obtain a car for which they finally paid a price so low that it could not be compared with a market price elsewhere. Managers had to take into account political and ideological rather than management criteria, when taking initiative.

In recent years, since 1989–1991, with the de-communization of Eastern European countries (Domanski 1992), marketing infrastructures have been established, the same being true to a lesser extent for Russia (Holden 1995). However, such a process is a lengthy one. A fundamental condition for the development of markets and marketing is the change in ownership structure. In 1992, 83 per cent of the Polish production assets were still state or cooperative property (Dietl 1992). Privatization programmes have, therefore, been a major challenge for the governments, with major problems related to their implementation, such as valuing companies, establishing a stock exchange, creating notaries and specialized intermediaries for real estate. One of the trickiest problems was to find local shareholders in countries where capitalism had long been associated with exploitation. Private ownership presupposes rules and institutions such as contract law, bankruptcy law, or courts where business disputes can be dealt with. The absence of such "infrastructure" created massive opportunism, as in the case of the ex-Soviet Asian republics.

Box 16.1

In April 1994, a commodity trader discusses the purchase of raw cotton in ex-Soviet Asia (mainly Uzbekistan, Turkmenistan and Tadjikistan): "The last two years, the market for raw cotton has been tense, mainly for the following three reasons: (i) climatic hazards in certain producing regions which thus became net importers instead of net exporters, especially China; (ii) reduction of cultivated zones in Uzbekistan; (iii) to this, you must add the fact that sales people break their word in ex-Soviet Asia. Last year, the Uzbeks sold their crops twice or thrice; this year, they seem to be a little more serious; but the worst is to be experienced in Turkmenistan. Last year, I signed several contracts for 20,000 metric tons (MT), one of them for 4,000 MT, with an official export license, a ministerial approval and a shipment certificate; I have never received anything!" This appears all the more striking when one takes into account that, in world-wide cotton trading, it is a well-established custom that the professional who does not respect a contract not only must pay damages but also is blacklisted by the whole trading community. (*Source:* M.O. Ancel, commodity trader at Louis Dreyfus & Co., Paris, 1994.)

"Gaps" between Western and Eastern economies

There are vast opportunities for Western firms to market their products and technologies in Eastern Europe, but we must realize that the marketing situation is quite different from that in Western countries. It is not as simple as selecting a market and applying one of the existing market entry strategies. There is a new set of problems and situations to be dealt with in these markets. These countries are moving quickly towards a market economy, starting from a situation where people have little or even no idea of what a contract, a price or delivery times actually mean. Holden, for instance, comments about the two Russian marketing textbooks (Holden, 1995, pp. 36–7):

> The one text *Contemporary Marketing* by Khrutskogo (1991), which stresses the importance of modern marketing knowledge to Russia, introduces marketing in ideological terms, citing both Marx and Engels. The second book, *Marketing — The Success Formula* by Zayavlov and Demidov (1991) focuses on marketing squarely in terms of "how to operate effectively in foreign markets". The differing orientation of these books sheds useful light on the Russian approach to marketing knowledge. The Khrutskogo book emphasizes a preference for presenting marketing knowledge in relatively intellectual terms, using discredited, yet still very familiar concepts for explaining the market. His approach reveals a Russian penchant for searching for laws that govern social and economic behavior. The contribution of Zavyalov and Demidov reinforces the conviction that marketing knowledge is held by many Russians to be mainly applicable to foreign business interactions and not so much to home-market activities.

Free-market economy tends to be confused with mere business opportunities, as illustrated above by an earlier example. The absence of rules, which is even stronger in the ex-USSR than in other Eastern European countries, helps further the development of corrupt behavior in business. However, this is only a transitory situation. A big comparative advantage of ex-communist countries is their good level of general education. Some authors characterize these problems as "gaps", such as a marketing gap, technology gap, capital gap, management gap and motivation gap, which exist between Western and Eastern economies (See, for example, Kraljic 1990 and Ghauri, 1995.)

In addition to these gaps, there are some fundamental differences between marketing to the West and to the East. In Eastern Europe, despite the fact that most countries have democratically elected governments and that there is a high degree of privatization, government still plays a major role in the business sector. This role is even greater when a foreign company is involved. The most important difference between the West and Eastern Europe is the fact that there is a gap of at least two or three generations in terms of productivity and infrastructure. In the more advanced countries, Hungary, Poland and the Czech Republic, some progress has been made in maintaining property rights and removing some market imperfections, but this progress lags far behind the West.

The problem is that, before 1990–91, the economies of Eastern Europe were overestimated, partly because there were no statistics available and partly because of political reasons. According to the CIA (Central Intelligence Agency), the GNP of the Soviet Union was about half of that in the US. This gave Western companies an exaggerated and over- optimistic picture. After 1990, due to recent devaluations of the ruble, the estimated GNP of the former Soviet Union is about one tenth that of the US, with a per capita income that is only 14 per cent of that of the United States. This is apparently an underestimated figure. Consequently, many companies are reluctant to enter these markets (Pear 1990).

Going East: a long term commitment

Even if we assume a doubling of the standards of living and completion of some major privatization schemes by the year 2000, Eastern Europe would require an investment of $100 billion (Dunning 1994). There are thus numerous examples of successful entries, such as: Siemens (Germany), Alcatel (France), ABB (Sweden/Switzerland), General Electrics (USA), McDonald's (USA), Coca Cola and Pepsi Cola (USA), VW (Germany), Fiat (Italy), Statoil (Norway). Only VW has come up with huge investments, $3 billion in the Czech Republic and $1.5 billion in Eastern Germany. These are only a few examples, so there are great opportunities and companies should not be reluctant to enter due to some transitional problems.

To be successful in these markets, the companies should demonstrate *long-term commitment and seriousness*. It is not possible to appear at these markets occasionally and expect to establish successful business operations. It is important for companies to have a long-term representative in these markets. The managers involved in marketing should stay there for longer periods in order to understand the market and culture of the respective countries. We have already discussed the fact that there are differences in the development and commitment levels of different countries of Eastern Europe and it is not advisable to treat all countries in the same manner. The companies, therefore, have to have innovative approaches.

As far as doing business in Eastern Europe is concerned, one has to choose the *right alternative for the right reason*. The first step is to be clear about why we want to enter that market. There are two basic alternatives: do we want to enter the market in order to simply market our products, or do we wish to utilize the low cost of labor and raw materials. In the first case, one can use the traditional entry strategy analysis to determine whether to trade (manufacture in one's own country and sell in these markets through export agents or distributors), or to produce in the respective market/country with or without a local partner. Some companies, however, believe that they can manage the entry on their own and do not need a local partner. They also believe that they need to be in a market to understand it and need to understand the market properly before they can profitably adapt their products to local tastes. IKEA is one example of this type of company. When exporting to these countries, there are enormous opportunities, due to the excessive demand for all types of Western products, especially consumer goods. However, there are some problems in using export as a strategy, due to the lack of distribution channels and lack of convertible currencies. Some companies have established their own retailing outlets in the market where they are selling products in local currency as well as in hard currencies. Companies such as IKEA (Sweden) and Statoil (Norway) are good examples.

Box 16.2

McDonald's is a good example of a company that developed its own infrastructure to manage its business in Eastern Europe. McDonald's chose Moscow City Council as a partner, (51 per cent Moscow City Council, 49 per cent McDonald's, as, at the time of contract, this was maximum a foreign company could own). McDonald's considered the infrastructure, especially for supply procurement, to be a major problem. This problem is faced by most foreign companies and is due to the rigid bureaucratic system, shortage in supplies (due to production, distribution), and the quality of the supplies. The company had to be sure that it would get sufficient supplies of different raw materials such as sugar, flour, meat, mustard etc. Moreover, some of the supplies, such as iceberg lettuce, pickled cucumber and special type of potatoes, were not available in Russia. To handle these problems, McDonald's trained its suppliers and built a US $40 million food-processing center close to its restaurant. To deal with the distribution problems, it provided its own trucks to carry the supplies. As a result, today McDonald's has its most successful restaurant in Russia, serving on average 50,000 customers a day. (*Source:* Daniels, J.D. and Radebaugh, L.H. (1995), *International Business: Environments and Operations*, 7th edn, Reading Mass. Addison & Wesley, pp. 117–19.)

As mentioned in the previous section of this chapter, foreign companies, as well as local organizations, have been very keen to register and start joint ventures. In this case, the evaluation of the local partner's contribution is the most difficult aspect. Sometimes the local government is the local partner, which leads to contradictory objectives between partners. Quite often, a local partner wants to come up with a contribution in the form of technology or know-how which is obsolete or of no value to the new operations. Nevertheless, although many East European countries allow wholly owned subsidiaries, foreign companies are more interested in joint ventures. The companies have realized the synergetic benefits of these cooperative agreements. When entering these countries, a company should consider the following step-by-step approach:

1. Checking priorities: learning about the priorities of the government and business sectors to determine whether the goods or projects at hand are among the priorities of the market.
2. Checking regulations: what rules and regulations apply to the import of goods? Are import licenses or other documents necessary? In the case of a joint venture, check all applicable rules and regulations. Is it allowed to have a majority-owned joint venture, property rights etc?
3. Checking the local agent/partner: is it difficult to check the validity of the claims made by the local partner or agent? If the claims are valid, how can they be evaluated?
4. Checking the competition: it is very important to establish who your competitors are. Are these local government or another foreign company? It is important to check the potential competitors and what your position would be in the long term. Would you have the same competitive advantage five years from now?
5. Check the financial implications: check to see whether you would be forced to participate in counter-purchasing or bartering. This should be checked at an early stage in order to avoid surprises. In this case, you should also check the financial position of your counterparts to determine whether they would be able to fulfil their financial obligations.
6. Negotiations: it is very important to determine whether the objectives of both parties are complementary. If you can see that the other party has totally different objectives, then you should analyze that situation and determine whether or not it is acceptable to you. In this case, you should also evaluate whether or not you would be able to achieve your objectives and commit yourself accordingly. This issue is also discussed separately.
7. Implementations: it is very important to carry out the project whole-heartedly and think in the long term. The potentials and opportunities should be evaluated at every step or implementation and matched with the company's objectives.

Many of these countries have a simple supply of raw material, cheap labor, government incentives and other resources that can provide Western companies with global competitive advantages (Hertzfeld 1991 and Jain and Tucker 1994). In this type of business activity, a foreign company must be aware of the pitfalls and crucial factors that may influence the success or failure of such a venture.

Firstly, due to an excessive demand, the price mechanisms may not be functioning at this moment, which could lead to overestimated profit expectations. In the long run, when the gap between supply and demand is filled, market pricing will start functioning automatically. The same applies to labor, raw materials and component pricing. Secondly, these markets are not, in the long run, typically low labor cost economies. The standards of living are improving fast and there is a great chance that, within a couple of decades, the standards will come quite close to those of Western Europe. Finally, sectors that may appear attractive at this moment may not survive in the long run.

That means that, in spite of an excessive demand at this moment, some sectors might not survive the transition period. Consequently, it would no longer be beneficial to produce certain products in Eastern Europe and sell them to Western markets. A long-term analysis and strategy is, therefore, of great importance. There are, of course, differences among the countries of Eastern Europe. Some countries offer excellent opportunities for export-oriented investments while others do not.

To summarize, the process of doing business in Eastern Europe differs to a great extent from a traditional market entry process in a foreign market. In a normal market entry, a foreign firm faces a lot of problems in the early stages of the entry process, as they need to establish contacts at a macro level, which is quite difficult. They have to have middle men to get access to government officials and departments. In Eastern Europe, however, it is very easy to get access to government officials at most highest levels, in the early stages of the entry process. This aspect often leads to over-expectations on the part of a foreign firm, as the real problems start in the later stages of the process (Ghauri and Holstius 1996).

Negotiating in Eastern and Central Europe

In reality, it is not possible to provide some standard conditions and guidelines for negotiation with customers/parties from Eastern Europe. The conditions have been rather volatile in most of these countries. Rules and regulations have been changing. Though every transaction involves a different type of negotiation process and factors, some degree of uniformity in the process and the factors influencing this is possible.

Price adjustments due to *inflation* is one such factor. In almost all these countries, there has been rocketing inflation. Even in countries such as Poland and Hungary, relatively the most advanced markets, inflation hovers around 30 per cent. In Russia, the biggest market, the inflation has been 15 per cent per month in recent months. Exchange rate variations is another factor which should be kept in mind while negotiating business deals with these countries. Table 16.2 illustrates the exchange rate of rubles to one US dollar, since liberalization.

Although the ruble is an extreme example and many of the currencies have stabilized against Western currencies, this is one of the major factors causing hindrances in negotiation processes among parties from the West and the East.

TABLE 16.2
Ruble exchange rate against the dollar, 1989–95

1989	0.6
1990	1.7
1991 (Jan)	37.6
1991 (Dec)	60.0
1992 (Jan)	110.0
1992 (Dec)	398.0
1993 (Jan)	417.0
1993 (Dec)	1,100.0
1994 (Jan)	1,400.0
1994 (Dec)	3,800.0
1995 (Jan)	4,500.0
1995 (May)	5,088.0
1995 (Dec)	4,523.0
1996 (June)	4,999,0

Source: Buckley & Ghauri (1994: 25), *The Economist*, January 21st (1995: 32), *Guide for TACIS Experts*, August 1995 and *Business Central Europe*. The Economist Group, June 1996.

In most cases, a foreign firm requires a distribution channel to sell its products within these newly available markets. In these cases, a local partner is essential to represent the foreign party and to engage in marketing and customer service functions. In this relationship, a mutual dependence exists. The parties have to go through a negotiation process to agree on the mutual dependence and the contribution to be made by each party. *Finding the right partner* and evaluating each other's contribution is, thus, a crucial issue in this process. Establishment of this relationship is difficult and time-consuming, but it is even more difficult to terminate or modify the relationship. As the process of negotiation should foresee the future complexities of a relationship, this is typically an issue which must be efficiently handled in a negotiation process. The power/dependence aspect of the atmosphere discussed earlier is most relevant here. Power or dependence perceived by one of the parties may have long-term influence on the relationship, with one party always demanding a better performance from the other. In short, it is difficult to enter these markets, but it can be even more difficult to depart from one particular relationship. For example, the company may want to enhance its involvement, start manufacturing or gain more control over its operations.

The firms entering these markets should have *clear objectives*, both in the short term and in the long term. The information on present legal criteria and any relevant changes expected in the future is very important, and should be matched with the objectives mentioned above. In most of these countries, the *rules* regarding foreign ownership (minority, majority or wholly owned foreign operations), remittance of profits, property rights and tax exemption are still changing. The foreign firm should, therefore, keep this in mind. One way is to build in a renegotiation of contract after regular intervals, or after changes in the above or other important rules and factors.

Sometimes these negotiations are only undertaken for a single transaction. This is particularly true in case of project marketing. A project sales negotiation is apparently different from a process where a long-term relationship is being negotiated. In project-based negotiation, a foreign firm should be very specific about what it can and cannot do. In case an agent or a local third party is involved, his role should be properly defined and related to one particular deal.

So far, joint ventures have been the most popular entry mode in these markets. In this type of entry mode, the evaluation of a joint venture partner's contribution is considered to be the most complex issue. Facilities and resources, such as market position, personnel, premises and local capital to be offered by the local partners, are difficult to evaluate. The distribution of tasks and responsibilities between the parties should be clearly specified. Otherwise this can be a major source of conflict in the future. The parties should be open to each other and the agenda for negotiations should be mutually prepared. The negotiation process for a joint venture with Eastern Europe should have *built-in flexibility* and allow renegotiations due to changes in circumstances outside the relationship. Table 16.3 sums up the main aspects of negotiations with Eastern Europeans.

TABLE 16.3
Nature of negotiation in Eastern Europe

Negotiation factors	Comments
1. Pace of Negotiation	Slow
• Value of time	Moderate & punctual
2. Negotiation Strategy	
• Offer vs. agreement	High initial demand
• Presentation of issues	Group issues may be presented
• Presentations	Quite formal
• Discussions	Argumentative
• Communication	Rather direct, little small talk
• Interpreters	Necessary
3. Emphasis on personal relationship	Very low
4. Influence of third parties	High
5. Distance	Personal space shorter
6. Decision making	
• Overall	Somewhat impulsive
• Emphasize	Logic & long-term benefit
• Hierarchy	Top down decision-making
• Collective vs. individual behavior	Emphasis on group & team work
7. Administrative Factors	
• Need for agent or local partner	Average
• Degree of details	Moderate specificity
• Degree of bureaucracy	High
• Need for agenda	High
8. Emotional Aspects	
• Degree of rationality	Rather high
• Sensitivity	Low

In the following two sections, we present a brief analysis of the most attractive emerging markets of this region: Russia, Poland, Hungary and the Czech Republic.

Negotiating Business with Russia

Russia, with a population of more than 200 million, is the most important market of the former Soviet Union. After the collapse of the Soviet Union and the communist party, Russia has become more democratic. Different members of the government, the army, regional politicians and industrialists are all fighting openly for power. Although it has brought enormous political instability for the time being, the change is expected to lead Russia towards normalization. A new constitution was adopted by referendum in December 1993. Prices have been liberalized, large and medium-sized manufacturers are being privatized, lavish government subsidies to inefficient producers have been cut and the companies are paying normal or positive interest rates, i.e. above the rate of inflation. All these changes are forcing a massive restructuring of Russian industry. At the end of 1993 unemployment amounted to 1.1 million or 1.5 per cent of the work

---

Box 16.3

Design Talo is a small firm making wooden houses for private clients in the northern city of Kemi in Finland. The company was a typical victim of Finnish depression as the Finnish market for private housing fell from 10,000 houses to 2000 houses per annum. Design Talo, a company with 300 employees building 500 houses a year, was badly hit. At this point Mr Kurkela, the owner and manager, started looking for other markets. In 1993, he heard from a consultant company that local authorities in Russian city of Cherepovits, 600 km north of Moscow, were looking for a company to supply municipal guest houses. He travelled with Mr Erkki Hurtig, the consultant, to Cherepovits. In the words of Mr Hurtig, "We took a car and drove 14 hours to Cherepovits, through the snow and cold. The radiator froze and it was a terrible journey. But we got there, met the municipality and the building engineer, and looked at the site". At this point, Mr Kurkela decided to prepare a bid to build two houses. Drawing up the details, negotiating and reaching a deal took several months. The deal included all the supplies as well as labor from Finland. Kurkela wanted payment in advance in Finnish Markka, which was agreed. But things went very slowly, several faxes were sent and received. There were no signs of payment and Kurkela insisted on advance payment. "Finally the Russians said the problem was that they didn't have any Finnish Markka, only dollars. We laughed and said just send us the dollars", says Mr Hurtig. The money came and the houses were built. The local authorities were pleased and they ordered four more houses. Mr Kurkela wants to expand further in Russia, but it is not an easy task for a small firm. In the second contract, Mr Kurkela managed to agree on a proportion of labor to come from Russia. The material is still to be imported from Finland to ensure the quality, making the houses very expensive. Payment is still a problem as Finnish banks are reluctant to accept guarantees from Russian banks. Selling to private, newly-rich customers is even more difficult, as they are not willing to pay in advance and banks are not willing to give guarantees. Accordingly, Design Talo and the consultant have problems in expanding in Russia. As stated by Mr Hurtig: "It is too hard. What we would prefer to do is to sell our know-how to them, rather than carrying out the whole building project. That is what they need in Russia." (*Source:* Financial Times, *Exporter 8*, April 18, 1995, p. 8.)

force (*The Economist* 1994). The major problem for Russia, however, is instability. "If you could remove uncertainty, there would be a major investment boom in 1995, leading to sustained and rapid growth to the end of the century." (Laynard 1995, p. 32.)

Some elements of the Russian style in business negotiations

In addition to the above mentioned issues, the following points should be noted:

- As a consequence of more than 70 years of communist regime, the Soviet system has left some deep imprints on Russian society. As emphasized above, this has resulted in a lack of understanding of basic economic concepts, such as that of a free-market price, company valuation or a balance sheet. The lack of knowledge of the free-market mechanisms is being progressively redressed by management education.
- The low level of individual initiative and the strong aversion to risk-taking are explained by Beliaev *et al.* in the following terms. – Each negotiator will be well trained in the party discipline; obedient, with a well-developed sense of hierarchy; hard-working and trained for stress, but with narrow horizons; loyal to the state and fearful of mistakes because of the risk of falling to the level of the average Soviet citizen; cautious, tough, and inflexible because of the strictness of their instructions; and willing to subordinate personal life to the demand of the position (Beliaev *et al.* 1985, p. 105.)
- As a result the Soviet style, a part of the Russian style, even after the fall of the Communist regime, can still be described as fairly tough and unilateral. Negotiators tended to make extreme initial demands, to view adversary concessions as weakness, to be stingy in concessions, and to ignore deadlines. On the other hand, the Soviet-style Russians were good payers and did respect contracts which were drafted in a very detailed way (Cohen 1980).
- Graham *et al.* note the consensus of description of the ex-Soviet negotiators as "competitive" and "uncompromising". They show in a laboratory experiment, that Russian negotiators tend to prefer a distributive strategy, and one with minimal negative effects on their (Russian) partner's satisfaction, which tends to suggest that such competitive behavior is considered locally as standard practice (Graham *et al.* 1992).
- The ethical system of Russians widely differs from that of Americans according to Lefebvre: "Something that an American considers normative positive behavior (for example, negotiating and reaching a compromise with an enemy, and even any deal with another individual), a Russian man perceives as showing Philistine cowardice, weakness, as something unworthy (the word 'deal' itself has a strong negative connotation in contemporary Russian)." (Lefebvre, 1983 p. 396.)
- Communist centralized planning, based on five-year detailed plans, has not infused the Soviets with a sense of economic time, which they lack. Given

the complexity of co-ordination between government bodies, the Soviet had renounced meeting exact schedules. This logically, in present-day Russia, results in a highly immediate and short-term oriented society.

- Russia is now in a deep transition. The bureaucratic controls have been progressively relaxed, giving birth to a new society with deep contrasts. New entrepreneurs almost Western-style, full of initiative but lacking professionalism and reliability, may seem very far from the Soviet-style described above. However, what has been gained in terms of flexibility is largely compensated by the lack of reliability, with opportunistic behavior and the confusion between business and wild capitalism being largely the rule. Payments incidents and negotiated contracts which are never enforced are now frequent. Many new Russian entrepreneurs do not feel bound by normal business norms and contracts because either they ignore them or they view them as foreign and therefore inapplicable to their context.

A word of caution

Even if people in ex-communist countries progressively build marketing infrastructures, an international marketer there still has to live a very adventurous life (Quelch *et al.*, 1991). Anecdotally, West European business people coming with their own cars are told to take the wipers with them each time they park their car so that they will not be stolen. If they have to take a taxi, some precautions must be taken.

Box 16.4

A Belgian engineer, with no particular knowledge of 1994 Russia, was due to go to a construction site in Siberia for the German contractor he worked for. Arriving in Russia, he was transferred, in Moscow, from the international to the national airport by a chauffeur of the German company. After working on the site in Siberia, which was much quieter than Moscow, he decided to come back home on his own, earlier than initially planned, because the job had been done quicker. When in Moscow, he took a taxi to the local office of the German company. Taking the first available car, he negotiated the drive for $50. At first, all seemed to be normal, but after a while, the taxi stopped in a fairly remote, deserted and unfriendly area. The driver then explained that he needed an additional $50 to continue to transport him. He paid without discussion and reached the company office with no problem. He was lucky: it could have been much worse... (*Source:* M.O. Ancel, commodity trader at Louis Dreyfus & Co., Paris, 1994.)

Moreover, Russia has a body of contradictory, overlapping and rapidly changing laws and rules which lead to an unpredictable approach in doing business. Independent or impartial resolution of dispute is quite difficult to obtain. The courts are not familiar with dealing with commercial and international matters. There have been some cases of dispute with Western firms. For example, in one of the cases, an American partner ceased participation in its joint venture citing: "A pattern of harassment, physical threats, attempted extortion and misinformation by the Russian partner, aimed at forcing (us) out". In this case, the Moscow city government supported liquidation of the venture and declared that continued operation of the venture was illegal. According to the American partner, both the city and the Russian partner felt that they could make more money without the American partner, and therefore decided to get rid of him. In such cases it is difficult to achieve justice in the local judicial system. The only way out is to sell your share and get out of the venture.

Doing business in Poland, Hungary and the Czech Republic

The Eastern European countries comprise two groups; the Northern part has built an alliance called the Visegrad group (Hungary, Czech Republic, Slovakia and Poland). The group of Southern Balkan states is traditionally less developed and more fragmented. National identity is privileged above co-operation in an area where ethnic and religious diversity has always been quite strong. The following sections center on the three main countries of the Visegrad group.

Poland

Poland was one of the early adopters of reforms and after five years it is showing results. In 1994, GDP rose by 5 per cent, the third growth year in a row. The Warsaw stock exchange was re-opened in April 1991 after having been closed for almost fifty years. In the same year, new foreign investment law was introduced to make investment conditions more attractive. The aim was that, within five years, 80 per cent of the state-run economy would have been privatized. To attract foreign investment, the finance ministry may exempt a company from income tax if the foreign partner's contribution exceeds ECU 2 million. Poland has received generous help from the West to develop an efficient infrastructure.

Remittance of profits in foreign currency is permitted and private land or property can be purchased or leased on long term (up to 99 years), after permission from the Home Office. Most of the investments are coming from Western Europe, especially Germany. Fiat invested US $2 billion and some $5 billion have been invested in the oil and petroleum sector by different countries. Firms and government from the United States have been very active in Poland. Since 1991, US trade with Poland has been increasing by more than 100 per cent per year. In 1993, it rose to $916 million and in 1994 to more than $1 billion. The trade started with agriculture but now also consists of manufactured goods, machinery, computers, telecommunication equipment, automobiles and even aircraft. US firms are among Poland's top 10 largest import partners. However, Germany, Russia, UK, Italy and France are still at the top. Thus, Poland is considered to have managed the transition period quite efficiently.

Poland is seriously trying to join the EU (European Union), which is considered by the US and many European countries to be very likely. Therefore Poland is making a lot of progress to become compatible with European Union rules and regulations. The new law on copyrights is one such example. Reduction in tax rates, providing new tax exemptions and controlling inflation are also steps taken in this direction. In 1994, the Polish parliament adopted a budget with a deficit of 1.4 per cent of GDP and got a favorable debt-rescheduling with the London Club of Commercial banks, which will reduce Poland's $13 billion commercial debt by almost half. The balance of payment is still at a deficit but is structured in a way that affords positive interpretation. The main deficit post is merchandise trade, where imports are running about 10 per cent higher than exports. The Net inflow of capital is, however, very positive, showing a surplus of more than $3 billion.

The investment climate is quite suitable for foreign investors. The privatization plans include foreign investors and, in fact, in most privatized industries, foreign investors are involved. A number of smaller Western firms are involved in these investments. Capital brought into Poland by foreign investors may be withdrawn freely. Moreover, full repatriation of profits and dividends is allowed without any prior permission. The Foreign Investment Act of 1991 guarantees availability of foreign currency for these purposes. The legal system is based on German and French laws and is quite efficient in handling commercial conflicts and disputes.

Hungary

Hungary has been implementing economic reforms since 1968, but since 1989 these reforms are more directed towards replacing the system of central allocation of resources by market allocation, and towards the creation of equal legal conditions for local as well as foreign capital and enterprises. The aim is also to increase the share of foreign enterprise in the economy as a whole. Attracting foreign capital has therefore been one of the prime objectives of Hungarian reforms. Hungary is the only market where the USA has invested more than any other single country. However, if we put all European countries together and look at EU vs US investments, European investments are more than double. The largest investments are by Hunslet (UK), General Electric, General Motors, Ford and Suzuki (40 per cent stake in a $10 billion venture).

Hungary started off with a rather difficult position. In 1990, it had accumulated a debt of $20 billion and it had a foreign exchange reserve of only $700 million. The government was unable to stop the outflow of foreign exchange arising from private imports, and it failed to meet the conditions of the last stand-by credit by IMF. However, by the end of 1992, Hungary had a current account surplus of $600 million and a hard currency reserve of $5 billion, which represented enormous progress since 1990. In spite of this difficult start, Hungary has accounted for about half of all Foreign Direct Investment in Eastern Europe since 1989. At present, about half of the GDP originates in the private sector.

In 1993, it carried out the largest privatization yet in Eastern Europe. The largest growth sectors include: telecommunication, pharmaceuticals, cosmetics, oil and gas, electric power systems, the plastics industry, chemicals, computers and software and food-processing machinery (*The World Factbook*, 1994).

The investment climate has been very favorable for foreign companies. Hungarian enterprises with a foreign partner pay 20 per cent less tax on profit than a locally owned company, if the foreign capital represents more than 20 per cent of the total capital of at least 5 million forints. Foreigners are allowed free transfer of funds in foreign exchange, whether the enterprise runs at a profit or not. Hungary is in advance of most other Eastern European countries, as its legal and institutional framework for foreign investments is developed, adequate and, most of all functioning. Hungary's transition towards a free market economy is not without blemish. Its current-account deficit of $3.7 billion and an overall foreign debt of $28 billion are dangerous for such a small economy.

Foreign investors are allowed to enter in any way they want, they may have a joint venture or a wholly own subsidiary. They may also buy state companies or just make portfolio investment. There are no restrictions. The exceptions include the defence industry, the media and acquisition of land. In some cases, foreigners may acquire land with prior permission of the government. These restrictions however, do not apply to companies corporately based in Hungary, even if 100 per cent foreign-owned. There are also some tax exemptions available for some priority industries, firms with a certain level of foreign investment and firms achieving a certain level of revenues related to their gross investment. Duty-free imports are also allowed for goods needed to establish a joint venture. Some concessional loans are also available for firms involving at least 30 per cent foreign capital with a minimum of $50,000. Foreign investors are allowed to keep and maintain accounts in foreign currency. The companies can use these funds for travelling, advertising, import of duty-free goods and investment goods.

The Czech Republic

Czechoslovakia has traditionally had an advanced industrial base and its technology and products have been comparable with those of the West. Before the Second World War, Czechoslovakia ranked as one of the most highly industrialized nations in Europe. Until about the mid-1960s, it was on a par with Austria as regards GDP per capita, while at the time of dissolution, its per capita income was about 30 per cent lower than that of Austria. As mentioned earlier, Czechoslovakia, along with Hungary and Poland, was considered to be a leader and had made great progress towards a Western-style market economy. The dissolution of Czechoslovakia into two independent nation states, the Czech Republic and Slovakia, on 1 January 1993, has complicated the task of moving towards a more open market economy. The Republic is facing problems such as ageing capital plants, lagging technology and a deficiency in energy and many raw materials.

Since the dissolution, thousands of businesses in the Czech Republic have been privatized, leased out and some have even been returned to their original owners. In general, the Czech Republic has been quite successful in attracting foreign firms, and huge investments are being made by Western firms, such as a \$3 billion investment by VW and most of the renowned consumer goods companies. More than 100,000 small and medium-sized trading and services firms were auctioned. There have been several well-publicized cases of both Japanese and Western manufactures switching the location of their new investments from the Iberian peninsula and Greece to countries such as the Czech Republic (Dunning 1994). More than half of the country's trade is with neighboring European countries: Germany, Austria, Slovakia and Poland. It is a common opinion that the Czech Republic is the most advanced emerging market of the former Eastern Bloc. It has a stable currency, low unemployment (in fact lower than most countries of EU), low national debt and huge foreign currency reserves. The main problem is that the market lacks marketing and financial expertise.

Foreign firms doing business in the country operate as Czech firms and are allowed to repatriate profits and withdraw their investments without any restrictions. These firms are also protected from expropriation under both international and Czech law. There is a bilateral tax treaty between the Czech and the US government, which has been in operation since December 1993. Development of the basic infrastructure and privatization have been the priority issues for the government. Other priority areas include the acquisition and organization of equipment for: pollution control equipment, telecommunication, medical equipment, building equipment, machine tools, electric power systems, computers and software and food processing and packaging equipment.

A relatively small-size, homogeneous population in favor of reforms and tight monetary and fiscal policies has helped its government to quickly overcome the transition period and the division of the country without any political or economic crisis. The Czech Republic trade relations with Germany and Austria are very useful. Almost 30 per cent of its exports consist of heavy machinery and equipment and another 30 per cent of semi-manufactured goods. The products exported from the Czech Republic include: steel, cement, timber, building stones, sand, leather, glass and ceramics. With regard to imports, almost 40 per cent consists of machinery and transportation equipment. Automobiles, computers and service machines make up another 20 per cent, while consumer products represent only 25 per cent of the total goods brought into the country. At present, more than 70 per cent of the total output comes from the private sector.

All sectors of the economy are open to foreign investors — sectors such as: defence, industry, national and cultural monuments, salt production and distillation of pure alcohol are the only exemptions. In all other sectors 100 per cent foreign ownership is possible. The country adheres to international copyright conventions and the government ensures the protection of intellectual property rights in the line with the EU.

Box 16.5

Budejovicky Budvar, which makes the original Budweiser lager beer, is perhaps the most well-known Czech company. Its most famous brand, Budweiser Budvar, is exported to 30 countries. More than 50 per cent of its production is sold outside the country. The production has risen from 490,000 hectoliters in 1991 to 755,000 hectoliters in 1994 and to 1 million hectoliters in 1995. The demand abroad is paralleled by the local demand. As a result the demand is always higher than the supply.

Budvar is a small brewery, even according to Czech standards. The industry is dominated by three other breweries. A bottle of beer is cheaper than a bottle of mineral water or Coca Cola. Budvar's biggest problem is, however, its dispute with Anheuser-Busch, the giant US brewery which also makes Budweiser. The decades-old dispute about who has the right to use the brandname, Budweiser, is keeping Budvar from expansion into North American markets.

The Budvar is still state-owned and is in no hurry to privatize the company. It is said that it first wants to solve the brandname dispute with the American company. At present, the parties are trying to reach an agreement but the Czech side does not seem to be in a hurry. The company is expanding in Europe and has a very sound position. (*Source*: Financial Times, *Exporter 8*, 18 April 1995.)

Conclusion

Changes in the economic and social environment of the Eastern and Central European countries have to be monitored carefully: Poland, Hungary and the Czech Republic could join the European Union shortly after the year 2000. On the other hand, Russia and many of the former republics of the ex-USSR are experiencing a more difficult move out of the state-run economy towards a free market economy. The turmoil is not only economic, it is social and political as well. This imposes special constraints on the attitudes of international business negotiators in five areas:

1. Only a long-term commitment makes sense in such environments.
2. Extreme precautions have to be taken in selecting partners: written agreements cannot be solely relied upon.
3. The pace of change in these transitory economies may further increase when they have brought into force the basic regulations for a free-market.
4. When negotiating, the influence of the local government or other third parties must be properly evaluated.
5. The contract should allow renegotiation in case of drastic changes.

CHAPTER 17

Business negotiations between Japanese and Americans

JOHN GRAHAM AND YOSHIHIRO SANO

More than 35 years ago, anthropologist E. T. Hall (1960: 87) warned, "When the American executive travels abroad to do business, he is frequently shocked to discover to what extent the many variables of foreign behavior and custom complicate his efforts." Despite Hall's comments, little attention has been paid to the "typically ethnocentric American" sitting across the table from "inscrutable Japanese customers," trying to negotiate an acceptable business contract. This chapter attempts to shed light on this circumstance. The topic is most worthy of consideration since business negotiations with Japanese often fail for seemingly inexplicable reasons and because most others have ignored such questions.

Conceptual Framework: A Framework for Understanding Negotiation Processes

The most difficult aspect of international business negotiations is the actual conduct of the face-to-face meeting. Assuming that the best representatives have been chosen, and assuming those representatives are well-prepared, and that situational factors have been manipulated in one's favor, things can still go sour at the negotiation table.

Obviously, if these other preliminaries haven't been managed properly, things *will* go wrong during the meetings. Even with great care and attention to preliminary details, managing the dynamics of the negotiation process is almost always the greatest challenge facing Americans seeking to do business with Japanese.

Going into a business negotiation, most people have expectations about the "proper" or normal process of such a meeting. Based on these expectations, progress is measured and appropriate bargaining strategies are selected. That is, things may be done differently in the latter stages of a negotiation than they were in the earlier. Higher risk strategies may be employed to conclude the talks — as in the final two minutes of a close football game. But all such decisions about strategy are made relative to perceptions of progress through an expected course of events.

Differences in the expectations held by parties from different cultures are one of the major difficulties in any cross-cultural business negotiation. Before we discuss differences between the processes of business negotiations in Japan and the United States, however, it is important to point out similarities. In both countries, business negotiations proceed through four stages: (i) non-task sounding; (ii) task-related exchange of information; (iii) persuasion; and (iv) concessions and agreement.

The first stage, non-task sounding, includes all those activities which might be described as establishing a rapport or getting to know one another, but it does not include information related to the "business" of the meeting.

The information exchanged in the second stage of business negotiations regards the parties' needs and preferences, or, stated more precisely, the parties' subjective expected utilities of the various alternatives open to the interactants.

The third stage, persuasion, involves the parties' attempts to modify one another's subjective expected utilities through the use of various persuasive tactics. The final stage of business negotiations involves the consummation of an agreement which often is the summation of a series of concessions or smaller agreements.

Despite the consistency of this process across cultures, the content and duration of the four stages differ substantially between the two cultural groups (see Table 17.1). Compared to Japanese, Americans spend little time establishing a relationship.[1]

The typical Japanese negotiation may involve a series of non-task interactions and even ceremonial gift giving. Witness the media attention given to the very large *kosai-hi* (literally, entertainment expenses) that once were typical of business dealings in Japan: "While the Japanese defense budget is 0.9 per cent of the country's GNP, corporate wining and dining accounts for 1.5 per cent of the total national output" (*Time* 1981). In the 1990s, since the steep decline in the Japanese economy, Japanese executives have cut back on the "excesses" of the 1980s. Even so, a greater emphasis on business entertainment by the Japanese will be noticeable. To the American critic, this may seem a waste. However, the Japanese make a great effort in the beginning to establish a harmonious relationship.

In America, the second stage (exchanging task-related information) is relatively direct, with clear statements of needs and preferences. For the Japanese, this exchange of information is the main part of the negotiation. A "complete"

---

[1] It is imperative that we avoid stereotyping the behavior of Japanese and American managers. In Graham and Sano (1989), we discuss how norms in Japan vary across age groups and industries. Moreover, personalities may be even more important than cultural norms, particularly in business negotiations. Even so, an understanding of norms, particularly when there are major differences, should help negotiators on both sides of the table be more patient.

TABLE 17.1

Four stages of business negotiations

	Japan	United States
1. Non-task sounding	Considerable time and expense devoted to such efforts is the practice in Japan.	Relatively shorter periods are typical.
2. Task-related exchange of information	This is the most important step — high first offers with long explanations and in-depth clarification.	Information is given briefly and directly. "Fair" first offers are more typical.
3. Persuasion	Persuasion is accomplished primarily behind the scenes. Vertical status relations dictate bargaining outcomes.	The most important step, minds are changed at the negotiation table and aggressive persuasive tactics used.
4. Concessions and agreement	Concessions are made only toward the end of negotiations — a holistic approach to decision making. Progress is difficult to measure for Americans.	Concessions and commitments are made throughout — a sequential approach to decision making.

understanding is imperative. The Japanese are reported to ask "endless" questions while offering little information and ambiguous responses. Japanese negotiators spend much more time trying to understand the situation and associated details of one another's bargaining position.

Americans tend to spend the most time in the third stage of negotiation–persuasion. Americans openly disagree and use aggressive persuasive tactics such as threats and warnings. Alternatively, Japanese take the time to understand one another during the first two stages of the negotiation, so little persuasion is necessary, and they avoid confrontations and respond to threats by a change of subject, a silent period, or withdrawal. For Japanese, it is more important to maintain the relationship than to be frank and open.

Regarding the fourth and final stage of business negotiations, Americans tend to make concessions throughout, settling one issue, then proceeding to the next. Thus, the final agreement is a sequence of several smaller concessions, and progress is easy to measure. The Japanese tend to make concessions at the end of the negotiation, and agreements are concluded rather abruptly from the American point of view. Such differences are a major point of procedural conflict for trans-Pacific negotiations.

The following presentation of recommendations regarding face-to-face meetings with Japanese clients is ordered according to the four stages typical in most business negotiations. First comes non-task sounding.

Non-Task Sounding

Americans always discuss topics other than business at the negotiations table (e.g., the weather, family, sports, politics, business conditions in general), but not for long. Usually, the discussion is moved to the specific business at hand after 5 to 10 minutes. Such preliminary talk is much more than just being friendly or polite. Before getting to the "business" at hand, it is important to learn how the other side feels *this particular day*. One can determine during non-task sounding if a client's attention is focused on business or distracted by other matters, personal or professional.

Learning about a client's background and interests also provides important cues about appropriate communication styles. To the extent that people's backgrounds are similar, communication can be more efficient. Engineers can use technical jargon when talking to other engineers. Golfers can use golfing analogies — "the deal is 'in the rough'" — with other golfers. Those with children can compare the cash drain of "putting a kid through college," and so on.

During these initial stages of conversation, judgments, too, are made about the "kind" of person(s) with whom one is dealing: Can this person be trusted? Will he be reliable? How much power does she have in her organization? All such judgments are made before business discussions even begin.

So there is a definite purpose to these preliminary non-task discussions. Although most people often are unaware of it, such time almost always is used to size up (or "sound", in the nautical sense) one's clients. Depending on the results of this sounding process, proposals and arguments are formed using different jargon and analogies. Or it may be decided not to discuss business at all if clients are distracted by other personal matters or if the other person seems untrustworthy. All this sounds like a lot to accomplish in 5 or 10 minutes, but that's how long it usually takes in the United States. This is not the case in Japan; the goals of the non-task sounding are identical, but the time spent is much longer.

In the United States, firms resort to lawyers when they've made a bad deal because of a mistake in sizing up a client or vendor. In Japan, lawyers are not used for such purposes. Instead, Japanese executives spend substantial time and effort in non-task sounding so that problems do not develop later. Japanese clients and suppliers will want to spend much more time in non-task sounding than Americans will want, and Americans must reconsider, from the Japanese perspective, the importance of this stage of bargaining if negotiations with Japanese are to be successful.

Negotiations with Japanese firms often include three levels of executives — top executives, middle managers, and operational staff. Depending on the level of the negotiations, the process of non-task sounding is somewhat different, so we will first discuss recommendations for non-task sounding among top executives, and then we will discuss the processes among middle managers and operational staff.

Non-task sounding for top executives

The role of the top executive in Japanese negotiations usually is ceremonial in nature. Ordinarily, top executives are brought into negotiations only to sign the agreement, and this only after all issues have been settled and agreed upon by lower-level executives. On occasion, top executives are included earlier to communicate commitment and importance. In either case, the main activity of top executives is non-task sounding.

The ceremony, formality and apparent triviality will seem very out of place for American executives, because to most Americans it will seem "unnatural" to avoid discussing specific business and to leave the persuasion to others. They need, however, a very clear understanding of their role in the negotiation, though getting them to make adjustments in their behavior may be difficult. It could be helpful to supply a long list of "non-task sounding" questions for them to ask during such sessions. It is important, too, that American executives understand that *what* is said is not so important, from a Japanese perspective, as *how* things are said.

The Japanese top executive is making gut-level judgments about the integrity, reliability, commitment and humility of his American counterpart (particularly if the Japanese is considerably older or if his company is more powerful). The non-task sounding provides a context or vehicle for making such judgments. To the Americans, the "content" of early conversations — words and verbal information — may seem inane, but the Japanese regard as critical the non-verbal messages and feelings — the *wa* (interpersonal harmony) and *shinyo* (trust) such talk conveys.

Non-task sounding for middle-level executives

Establishing business relationships in the United States typically involves certain procedures, such as a letter of introduction, followed by a phone call for an appointment, then a meeting at the client's office (including 5 to 10 minutes of non-task sounding followed by the business proposal), and perhaps lunch, with more business talk. Almost always, after 5 or 10 minutes of non-task sounding, an American client will ask, "Well, what can I do for you?"

In Tokyo, the typical routine goes something like this: The initial appointment will be set up and attended by a *shokai-sha* (third-party introducer), and the Japanese client will invite the American party, including the *shokai-sha*, for a late afternoon (approximately 4 p.m.) meeting at the Japanese firm's offices. There, the Americans will meet the concerned operational-level personnel for a "chat," not to include business talk or proposals. At around 6 p.m., the Japanese suggest dinner. Ordinarily, they will pick the restaurant and pick up the tab. Americans will not have a chance to "fight" for the bill because they will never see one. At this point, business talk still is inappropriate. After dinner, the Japanese will suggest a few drinks, and conversation with the bar hostesses will be the bill of fare. The sessions ordinarily go on past 11 p.m. and end with the scheduling of future meetings. While the 1990s have witnessed cutbacks in the lavish expenditures of the 1980s, the need for more informal non-task time in Japan persists.

John Graham and Yoshihiro Sano

Throughout the introductions, the business of the meeting, the purposes of the visit, are not discussed. Again, vague and indirect references to a future relationship may be made, but only in response to similar comments by the Japanese. The Japanese will be looking for integrity, sincerity, a cooperative attitude – *shinyo* and *wa*. Economics will come later.

Task-related Exchange of Information

Only when the non-task sounding is complete, when *wa* has been established, should business be introduced. American executives are advised to let the Japanese side decide when such substantive discussions should begin. Typically, the Japanese will signal their readiness for an exchange of task-related information, after tea or coffee has been served, by remarks such as, "Can you tell me more about your company?" or "Tell me, what has brought you to Japan?"

A task-related *exchange* of information implies a *two-way* communication process. However, observations suggest that when Americans meet Japanese across a negotiating table, the information flow is unidirectional — from Americans to Japanese. The Japanese appear (i) to ask "thousands" of questions and (ii) to give little feedback. The first severely tests American negotiators' patience, and the latter causes them great anxiety. Both can add up to much longer stays in Japan (compared to negotiating in other countries), which means higher travel expenses.

Giving information

The most obvious problem associated with providing information to Japanese clients will be doing so in another language. It is true that there are many more Japanese executives who understand and speak English than there are Americans who understand and speak Japanese, thus meetings on both sides of the Pacific usually can be handled in English. Americans should be careful, however, of misunderstandings that can arise from the Japanese side's limited knowledge of English. Often, confusion can result because Japanese executives are too polite to indicate they do not understand. When doubt exists, Americans should use visual media (slides, brochures, videos, etc.), and should provide copies of written support materials.

American negotiators should provide an interpreter, if the Japanese side has not, and even then there may be critical stages when an interpreter should be included on the American negotiation team as well. Even with the best of interpreters, language problems still can be sources of misunderstandings. Sullivan and Kameda (1982: 72–3) suggest that

> Americans and Japanese have different conceptualizations of the word *profit* and that these differences lead to what general semanticists call *bypassing*. Bypassing occurs when two people use the same word. Japanese and American negotiators,

358

usually communicating in English, initially may think they are in agreement regarding profit and profitability discussions when in fact they are not. This false agreement can lead to bewilderment, confusion, frustration, and perhaps failure in future negotiations.

Once comfortable with the language, attention can be turned to more subtle aspects of giving information to the Japanese. The first of these has to do with the order of presentation. In the United Stages, negotiators tend to say what they want and explain the reasons behind the request only if necessary. That's why the task-related exchange of information goes quickly in America.

Things don't work this way in Japan. Very long explanations come first, then the request/proposal. Accordingly, it is not surprising to hear the American executives' complaints about the "1000 questions." The Japanese expect long explanations.

American negotiators should be prepared with detailed information to back up their proposals and should *include appropriate technical experts on negotiation teams*, as their contribution will be required. Finally, we recommend the Japanese style of presentation, with background and explanations presented first and the actual request/proposal made only toward the end. While such an approach will take longer, with Japanese clients it will obtain better results.

Another reason for the "1000 questions" has to do with the consensus decision making style of Japanese organizations. Several people on their side may ask for the same information or explanation. Most Americans find this repetitive questioning irritating and even insulting. "Didn't they believe me the first time?" Such tactics should be viewed in light of the Japanese consensus decision making style when everyone must be convinced, not just the key decision maker. To some degree this questioning may be a tactic to make sure explanations hold up under close scrutiny. A degree of patience with this process is recommended, along with the kind of detailed preparations necessary to prevent inconsistent answers.

Americans tend to make initial offers they consider "fair" or near what they expect the eventual agreement to be, while Japanese executives expect to spend time in bargaining and tend to ask for more initially. Thus, Americans dealing with Japanese clients should *present second best offers first.*

The same can be anticipated from them. They initially may ask for more than appears reasonable, but they will move from that position, albeit with reluctance. After each party has supported its "second best offer" with detailed explanations, the Japanese consider it "fair" behavior to move — however reluctantly — from their initial position. American bargainers should guard against their own tendency to make concessions during the exchange of information. Often they are impatient with the process and make concessions before they have determined what the Japanese negotiators' interests and position are. Americans need to constrain their natural urge to get on to stage three, persuasion, via making concessions in the hope that the Japanese will reciprocate.

John Graham and Yoshihiro Sano

Getting information

Hopefully Japanese clients will be the ones seeking American business, because in such situations the Japanese will be the ones making the proposals and supplying more information than appears necessary. In situations where Amerian firms initiate contact or try to make sales, they experience great difficulty in getting feedback on their proposals. For example, if they ask a group of Japanese executives what they think of an American firm's price quote, the Japanese will often say, "Oh, it looks fine," even if they think the quote is totally unacceptable. Americans need to consider, for a moment, the Japanese reasons for such "strange" behavior.

In the first place, no Japanese, *especially not the boss*, will venture to speak for the entire group until a consensus has been reached. Second, the Japanese executives wish to maintain the *wa*, and, from their point of view, a negative (albeit honest) answer during the negotiation may disrupt the harmony already established. Finally, even the most experienced American negotiator may not be able to read the subtle, nonverbal, negative cues that another Japanese executive would read (via tone of voice, body movements, pauses in speech, looks of surprise, etc.) along with the politely offered phrase, "Oh, it looks fine."

Besides their language differences, the non-verbal behaviors of Japanese and American executives differ. The Japanese conversational style in both simulated and real business negotiations includes much less eye contact than the American style. This difference seems to cause problems for both sides. The Japanese report discomfort at the "aggressive staring" of the Americans. Americans suggest that "something must be wrong" because the Japanese won't look them in the eye. Eye contact and movements, ordinarily a source of information about the other person's feelings, don't communicate across cultural barriers.

Most people process such information as the facial expression of a client reacting to a proposal, etc., but in the United States such processing often is subconscious. Attention should always be paid to this channel of information, however. Many American executives report great frustration in trying to read Japanese negotiators' "poker faces." In our studies of videotapes of simulated business negotiations involving Japanese we found little difference in the quantity of facial expression. Rather, the inscrutability has more to do with the timing and cultural rules for facial expressions. This, then, is the reason we hear very experienced Americans say, "I make deals all over the world. Everywhere I go I can pretty much tell where I stand with my clients — everywhere, that is, except Japan." How, then, are Americans ever to get at the *honne*, or true mind, of Japanese negotiators?

At the negotiation table, the *tatemae* (truthful, official stance) often isn't very helpful. An informal channel of communication, which can be established only between and through the lower levels of the negotiation teams, is the only way Americans can become privy to the *honne*. This, then, is the primary reason for including lower-level executives on negotiation teams. Besides, it would be too difficult, without some division of efforts, to handle both formal communications at the negotiating table and informal communications after hours.

Management of the informal channel of communications is critical for efficient and successful negotiations, as it can be a delicate undertaking. During the non-task sounding activities, lower-level members of the American team should be assigned the task of establishing rapport with the operational level managers on the Japanese side. Then, throughout the task-related exchange of information and the rest of the negotiations, they should invest in after-hours nurturing such relationships. They can begin by simply asking the selected and/or indicated Japanese executive(s) out for a drink "to solve our companies' problems." The Japanese will be looking to open such a channel of communication, and the Americans should be alert for such overtures.

Once this informal channel has been opened, it will be used for aggressive persuasive tactics (discussed later) and to learn how the Japanese really feel about proposals and the associated arguments. After hours, such information is communicated in restaurants, over drinks, and at bath houses. It emanates from and is transmitted to all members of the Japanese negotiation team. While everyone knows about this informal channel of communication, it is critical that it remain "under the table," and any reference to such a channel (e.g., "Suzuki-san told Mr Smith last night that ...") will lead to elimination of the "leak" by immediate dismissal of Mr Suzuki from the negotiations.

The following illustrates the importance of this informal channel. A large American firm sought to acquire a smaller Japanese firm. Talks between executives of the two companies had not been fruitful. Although the Japanese executives showed initial interest in the deal and the American firm had a final proposal ready, the Japanese seemed to be hesitant. The American side decided on a wait-and-see strategy, and nothing happened for almost six months. Then, a lower-level manager of the American firm received a call from an acquaintance (they had played golf and had a drinks together a few times) asking if they could have drinks. When they met, the Japanese explained the delays: "I have something to tell you that just couldn't be talked about by my boss to your boss. ...' He went on to explain the primary problems, from the Japanese point of view, which were with the acquisition price and the renaming of the company. Once these were out in "the open" (the informal "gut spilling" by these lower-level players was never discussed), the companies were able to deal with both issues. The Japanese side simply felt it inappropriate to voice such objections to a higher-status buyer and potential owner at the negotiation table, using a formal communication channel.

Persuasion

In Japan, a clear separation does not exist between task-related exchange of information and persuasion. The two stages tend to blend together as each side defines and refines its needs and preferences. Much time is spent in the task-related exchange of information, leaving little to "argue" about during the persuasion stage. Indeed, Robert March (1982: 97) reports that Japanese negotiators tend

John Graham and Yoshihiro Sano

to prepare for negotiations in a way that differs greatly from how Americans prepare:

> They [Japanese negotiators] developed defensive arguments with no consideration of persuading or selling or converting the other side. Nor did they consider what the other side might be thinking or offering, nor of anticipated strategies, nor of any concession strategies.
>
> A strong consensus was reached based on the arguments supporting their position after the leader had reviewed these and everyone had noted them down. There was strong group cohesion.

TABLE 17.2

Bargaining tactics, definitions, and examples (Angelmar and Stern 1978)

POSITIVE INFLUENCE TACTICS

Promise. A statement in which the source indicates his intention to provide the target with a reinforcing consequence which source anticipates target will evaluate as pleasant, positive, or rewarding. "If you can deliver the equipment by 1 June, we will make another order right away."

Recommendation. A statement in which the source predicts that a pleasant environmental consequence will occur to the target. Its occurrence is not under the source's control. "If you keep the company name after the acquisition, then your present customers will stay with the company."

Reward. A statement by the source that is thought to create pleasant consequences for the target. "This negotiation is progressing smoothly because you have prepared well."

Positive normative appeal. A statement in which the source indicates that the target's past, present, or future behavior was or will be in conformity with social norms. "Lowering your price in light of the new information will demonstrate your interest in good principles of business."

AGGRESSIVE INFLUENCE TACTICS

Threat. Same as promise, except that the reinforcing consequences are thought to be noxious, unpleasant, or punishing. "If you insist on those terms we will have to find another suitor for our company."

Warning. Same as recommendation, except that the consequences are thought to be noxious, unpleasant, or punishing. "If we can't get together at this stage, few other companies will be interested in your proposal."

Punishment. Same as reward, except that the consequences are thought to be unpleasant. "You can't possibly mean that. Only a fool would ask for such a high price."

Negative normative appeal. Same as positive normative appeal, except that the target's behavior is in violation of social norms. "No one else we deal with requires that kind of guarantee."

Command. A statement in which the source suggests that the target perform a certain behavior. "It's your turn to make a counter offer."

INFORMATION EXCHANGE TACTICS

Commitment. A statement by the source to the effect that its future bids will not go below or above a certain level. "We will deliver the equipment within three months, and at the price we originally quoted."

Self-Disclosure. A statement in which the source reveals information about itself. "My company now requires an ROI of at least 15% during the first year."

Question. A statement in which the source asks the target to reveal information about itself. "Why are you asking for such a high royalty payment?"

However, from the American perspective, persuasion is the heart of a negotiation. Once it is determined what each side wants, then "the fun" begins — trying to change the other side's mind and bring them closer to one's own side's proposal. Many persuasive tactics can be applied, and often are, to change clients' minds. Researchers at the Kellogg School of Business Administration at Northwestern University have come up with a list of such persuasive tactics (Table 17.2). We have observed Americans using all such persuasive tactics.

Table 17.3 is a list of persuasive tactics considered appropriate in Japan. One of the primary differences between American and Japanese bargaining styles has to do with the importance of the role or power position of the bargainer.

Relationships in Japan, whether personal or business, are vertical in nature. A simple analogy demonstrates this: bargaining in Japan is like an interaction between father and son, while in America it is like that of two brothers. The point is, the repertoire of persuasive tactics available to bargainers in Japan is prescribed by status/power relations. Buyers, playing the role of "father," can say things to sellers that sellers would not even consider saying to buyers. Alternatively, buyers and sellers in the United States are on much more of an equal footing (although still not completely equal).

TABLE 17.3

Persuasive tactics appropriate for negotiations with Japanese

At the Negotiation Table	Informal Channels and Buyers Only
1. Questions 2. Self-disclosures 3. Positive influence tactics 4. Silence 5. Change subject 6. Recess and delays 7. Concessions and commitments	1. Aggressive influence tactics

Another important factor in Japan is *where* specific tactics are used. That is, at the negotiation table, bargainers are limited to the use of questions, self-disclosures, and other positive tactics that influence behaviors. Aggressive influence tactics, which can be used only by negotiators in high power/status positions, should be communicated through the low-level, informal communication channel. Even there, threats, commands, etc., are subtle and indirect. This makes establishing an informal channel of communication doubly important to the American side, because it not only can provide a "reading" of Japanese clients but will allow them to employ persuasive tactics that would be completely inappropriate (from the Japanese perspective) at the formal talks.

To sum up, if an impasse is reached with Japanese clients, rather than trying to persuade them in the usual American manner, it is appropriate to use the following nine persuasive tactics, in order and in the specified circumstances:

John Graham and Yoshihiro Sano

1. Ask more *questions*. The single most important consideration is the use of questions as a persuasive tactic. This is true not only in Japan but anywhere in the world, including the United States. Chester Karrass (1970) in his book, *The Negotiation Game*, suggests that sometimes it is "smart to be a little bit dumb" in business negotiations. Ask the same questions more than once; for example, "I didn't completely understand what you meant — can you please explain that again?" If clients or potential business partners have good answers, then perhaps it is best to compromise on the issue. Often, however, under close and repeated scrutiny their answers are not very good. When their weak position has been exposed, they will be obligated to concede. Questions can elicit key information, being powerful yet passive persuasive devices. Indeed, the use of questions is a favored Japanese tactic which they will use against you.

2. *Re-explain* your company's situation, needs, and preferences.

3. Use *other positive influence tactics*.

4. If still dissatisfied with the Japanese response, try *silence*. Let them think about your proposal and give them an opportunity to change their position. Be aware, however, that the Japanese are the world's experts at the use of silence and that your Japanese clients are likely to use it frequently.

5. If tactics 1 through 4 produce no concessions, change the subject or call a recess and put the *informal communication channel* to work. At this level, it would be appropriate, rather than going directly to more aggressive tactics, to try tactics 1 through 4 again. Continuing to ask questions and offer explanations may cause new information to surface that could not be broached at the negotiation table.

6. Only in special circumstances and with an awareness of the great risk involved should *aggressive tactics* be used with Japanese. They should be used only when the American company is clearly in the stronger position (e.g., monopoly power, larger size, the Japanese company has come courting), and they must be carried out only via the informal channel in the most indirect manner possible. Rather than an American saying, "If your company can't lower its price, then we'll go to another supplier," it would be better if he said, "Lower prices on the part of your company would go a long way toward our not having to consider other options available to us."

Even then, the use of aggressive persuasion tactics probably will damage *wa*, which in the long run may be to the American company's disadvantage. If power relations ever shift, the Japanese will be quick to exploit the change of events. If the American side exercises restraint and maintains the *wa*, then the Japanese, if and when power relations shift, will consider the American company's interests.

This latter point is difficult for most Americans to believe. "Why should they consider our interests?" We have, however, witnessed Japanese executives behave in this way several times. For example, some years ago, International Multi-Food Company (IMFC) sold franchise rights for the Mr

364

Donut chain to Duskin Ltd. in Japan. Initially, IMFC provided the know-how (operations and marketing) for a successful venture in Japan. Indeed, ten years later the franchise revenues from Duskin exceeded the total profits IMFC made from its US operations. When, IMFC executives met with Duskin to re-negotiate the franchise agreement, they anticipated changes in the agreement (reduced royalties, etc.) to reflect the change in power relations. Certainly, an American franchisee would have demanded such an adjustment. However, because IMFC initially had been careful to maintain *wa* with the Japanese clients, the president of Duskin simply offered to renew the agreement. Needless to say, the IMFC executives were pleasantly surprised.

7. If tactics 1 through 6 have not produced concessions by the Japanese, we suggest that they employ the *use of time*. This tactic requires the cooperation and understanding of the American home office.

    Given the Japanese time to consider new information and time to reach a consensus. They almost never make concessions immediately following persuasive appeals, because the entire group must consult and agree. This takes time. Unfortunately, American bargainers seem to find the use of the time tactic most difficult. "Letting things hang" goes against their nature, but it may be necessary, in the hope that the Japanese will run into their time limits before you run into yours. Consensus decision making and their long-term approach to business deals seem to enhance the effectiveness of tactical delays for Japanese bargaining with Americans.

8. The next persuasive tactic that can be used with Japanese clients is asking the *shokai-sha* to arbitrate differences by calling the Japanese clients and serving as a go-between. Though *shokai-sha* often successfully settles otherwise irreconcilable differences, serious consideration should be given to making concessions before calling in *shokai-sha*, because third-party arbitration ordinarily will work *only once*.

9. As a last resort, bring together top executives of the two companies to see if that will stimulate more cooperation using a *top-down approach*. Such a tactic is, however, fraught with danger, particularly if negative influence tactics have been used in the past. A refusal at this stage means the business is finished.

To conclude our discussion of persuasive tactics, we want to emphasize the importance of our recommendations. A mistake at this stage, even a minor one, can have serious consequences for Japanese/American cooperation. American managers will have to be doubly conscientious to avoid blunders here because the Japanese style of persuasion is so different and, apparently, cumbersome.

Remember that the Japanese are looking to establish a long-term business relationship of mutual benefit. Threats and the like do not fit into their understanding of how such a relationship should work. They are not in a hurry, because they are concerned about *wa* and cooperation in the long run. We recommend, moreover, that you adopt a Japanese approach to persuasion when bargaining with Japanese clients and business partners. Such an approach may take longer, but, in the end both companies will benefit by using it. Finally, smart American negotiators will anticipate the Japanese use of the nine persuasive tactics described in this section of the chapter.

Concessions and Agreement

The final stage of business negotiations involves concession making, building toward agreement. Negotiation requires compromise. Usually, both sides give up something to get even more.

However, the approaches used for compromise differ on the two sides of the Pacific. Americans and other Western business executives tend to take a *sequential* approach to solving complex problems. That is, "Let's discuss and settle quantity, then price, then delivery, then after-sale service," and so on. Alternatively, the Asian approach is more *holistic* — looking at all issues simultaneously and not agreeing on any single issue until the end. Americans often are very upset by such differences in style of concession making.

American managers report great difficulty in measuring progress. "After all, in America you're half done when half the issues are settled." In Japan, nothing seems to get settled. Then — surprise — the negotiation is done. Frequently, impatient Americans make unnecessary concessions right before agreements are announced by the Japanese.

These difficulties reflect more differences than just in decision-making styles (sequential versus holistic). The differences go deeper than that. In the American view, a business negotiation is a problem-solving activity, the solution being a deal that suits both parties. From the Japanese standpoint, a business negotiation is a time to develop a business relationship with the goal of long-term mutual benefit. For the Japanese the economic issues are the *context*, not the *content*, of the talks. Settling any one issue is not really so important. Such details will take care of themselves once a viable, harmonious business relationship is established. Once the relationship has been established, signaled by the first "agreement," then the other "details" are settled quickly.

American bargainers in Japan should expect this holistic approach and should be prepared to discuss all issues simultaneously and in what may appear to be a haphazard order. Progress in the talks should not be measured by how many issues have been settled. Rather, Americans must try to gauge the quality of the business relationship by watching for the following important signals of progress:

- higher-level Japanese executives being included in the discussions
- their questions beginning to focus on specific areas of the deal
- a softening of their attitudes and positions on some of the issues, such as, "Let us take some time to study this issue;"
- at the negotiation table increased talk among themselves in Japanese, which may often mean they're trying to decide something; and

- increased bargaining and use of the lower-level, informal channels of communication.

A crucial part of preparing for negotiations is *deciding upon and writing down* planned concession strategies. Americans need to follow such strategies with care, because "trading" concessions will not work with Japanese bargainers who will settle nothing until everything can be settled. After all issues and interests have been exposed and discussed fully, to help establish the relationship, make concessions on *minor issues first.*

Besides following a plan in making concessions, American negotiators in Japan should take care that concessions are made following recesses in the talks, not at the negotiation table the first time the topic is broached. It is better to reconsider each concession away from the social pressures of the formal negotiations. Again, this is a Japanese practice. Because of the nature of their consensus decision-making process, you will find that the Japanese frequently "have to check with the home office." This is a negotiation practice which Americans would do well to emulate, particularly in Japan. Having limited authority can be an important check on "run-away" concession making.

In conclusion, American managers will spend more time putting deals together with Japanese clients or partners than with other Americans. If the negotiation processes are handled adroitly, the US negotiators can look forward to long, mutually beneficial business relationships with Japanese partners.

CHAPTER 18

Negotiating with East Asians

ROSALIE TUNG

Introduction

There is a consensus of opinion among business leaders that the twenty-first century will be the "Century of the Pacific". Many believe that economic challenges and opportunities in the decades ahead will emanate from the countries in the Pacific Rim Basin, particularly those in East Asia, where phenomenal strides have been made in terms of economic and technological developments. For this reason, business ought to have a presence in East Asia.

The difference in cultural and value systems between North America and western Europe (referred to as the west, in short), on the one hand, and East Asia, on the other, is significant. Given such difference, western businesspeople could not approach business negotiations with East Asian partners with the same attitude and perspective they would assume for a domestic or western counterpart. East Asian businesspeople are generally more versed in western business practices because the former have been assiduous students of western industrial and management practices for several decades. Western businesspeople, on the other hand, have only recently discovered East Asia, and consequently have little knowledge about the East Asian way of doing business and their approach to business negotiations.

In this chapter, the focus is on China, Japan and Korea. An assumption is often made that the Chinese, Japanese and Koreans are similar. This is not true, however. During a visit to Seoul, a Korean professor of international business asked for my response to the following hypothetical situations: The cars driven by two Korean males approach each other at opposite ends of a narrow bridge. Only one vehicle can pass at a time. What would the two Koreans do? If the drivers were Japanese, what would they do? If the drivers were Chinese, what would they do?

My response was as follows: "The two Koreans would most probably step out of their cars and fight it out." "Correct", said my Korean colleague. "In the case of the two Japanese drivers, each person would most probably ask the other to go first", I continued. "Right you are again", nodded the Korean professor.

Rosalie Tung

I hesitated about the response to the possible reaction of the Chinese because China is a much larger country and there can be lots of regional differences. I told my Korean friend that I will venture an answer which is more characteristic of inhabitants in southern China. "Each driver will most probably pull out his newspaper and start reading". "Correct again", my Korean friend said.

Regardless of what the correct answers to the Korean professor's question were, this exercise highlights one important factor — despite certain similarities, differences do abound among the Koreans, Japanese and Chinese. Hence, it would be erroneous to assume that one can adopt a uniform approach to business transactions in these three countries.

This chapter will examine the dynamics, processes and outcomes of cross-cultural negotiations between westerners, on the one hand, and the Chinese, Japanese and Koreans, on the other. Specifically, it will focus on three areas: the issues under negotiation, the differences in decision-making and negotiating styles, and keys to success in negotiating with the Chinese, Japanese and Koreans.

Methodology

The findings here are based on a study of US–Japan, US–China and US–Korean cooperative ventures (Tung 1982, 1984, 1989, 1991). The ventures in these studies came from a diverse range of industries and services, including telecommunications, automotive parts and equipments, aerospace, computers and electronics, electrical parts and components, hotels, pharmaceutical, petrochemicals, cosmetics, and specialty materials.

Issues Under Negotiation

While the specific issues under negotiation varied from venture to venture, two common themes pervaded all the joint venture agreements included in these studies. They were: equity share and management control. Each issue is examined briefly below.

Equity share

Equity share is perhaps one of the most sensitive and contentious issues in negotiations with Japanese, Chinese and Korean partners. For purpose of consolidating their worldwide profit and loss statements, American firms generally insist on 51 per cent equity ownership. In Japan, while there is virtually no legal restriction on the percentage of foreign equity ownership, the issue of equity is still sensitive. According to several companies included in the US–Japan study, all kinds of problems developed if the American partner insisted on majority equity ownership. These problems somehow miraculously disappeared as soon as the American partner agreed to equal or minority partnership. In the case of China, with some exception, the 1979 China Joint Venture Law allows for a minimum of 25 per cent and maximum of 99 per cent foreign equity ownership. The Chinese partner, however, often desires majority or equal equity ownership for fear of exploitation by the foreign partner. The Korean partner also desires majority equity ownership. Jang (1988) ascribed this insistence on the part of the Koreans to a "deep-seated emotional response" resulting from a history of "repeated war and domination by neightboring powers. ... Therefore ... it is natural that [the Koreans] are sensitive and concerned about the degree of control which they can maintain".

Furthermore, in the case of China and Korea, since the local partner can play a very crucial role in building and maintaining relationships with the respective governmental ministries, suppliers, and customers, some American partners prefer to enter into a joint venture arrangement even when 100 per cent foreign equity ownership is permitted. In fact, virtually all the American firms engaged in the retail business do not believe that they can operate successfully in the Korean market without a local partner. However, even in these cases, the American partner will strive for majority equity ownership, where possible. Aside from the desire to consolidate their worldwide profit and loss statements, American firms seek at least 51 per cent equity ownership because they are afraid they will be relegated to the role of a passive partner if they do not have a majority position.

Management control

In general, management control is reflected in two areas: representation on the board and staffing of senior management positions. Representation on the board is usually commensurate with the percentage of equity ownership, although in ventures with a 51/49 split, there is almost always an equal number of directors from either side. Until recently, the chairman of a Chinese joint venture, regardless of equity split, has to be a Chinese. Most decisions in such joint venture operations are made through mutual discussions rather than through votes. This is why building and nurturing good relationships with the local partner is so important to the success of a venture. This point will be elaborated upon subsequently.

The more contentious issue in terms of management control is the staffing of senior management positions. In general, the American partner feels that it is imperative to use expatriates to staff certain key positions for two primary reasons. (Expatriates include nationals of the country who are US citizens and/or who have worked with the American company for some time prior to assignment to the foreign operation.) A first reason for insisting upon the use of expatriates is to protect one's technology. Where technology is being transferred from the American partner, the latter wants to maintain adequate control over its use. Many American companies feel that, despite change, there is inadequate protection of intellectual property rights in China and Korea. A second reason for insisting upon the use of expatriates is that in the case of Japan and Korea, the American partner fears that if the local partner exercises management control, the latter would seek to coordinate its joint venture activities, particularly in the areas of finance and personnel, with the rest of the local group. In terms of financing, this coordination could be in the form of intra-company loans and borrowing. In the area of personnel, the joint venture company can become a "dumping ground" for excess personnel from the local partner.

Besides nationalistic reasons, the Japanese, Chinese and Korean partners, in general, feel that they should exercise management control because they are more familiar with the unique aspects of managing and operating in the local environment.

Besides the issues of equity ownership and management control, in the case of China and Korea, there is usually an additional bone of contention between the American and East Asian partners, that of export requirement. In the case of China, because of the principle of foreign exchange equilibrium to prevent an unnecessary drain on China's balance-of-payment position, there is generally an insistence that a certain percentage of the products manufactured by the joint venture be exported. However, because many of the American companies may already have operations elsewhere in the region which manufacture similar types of products, or because of their concern about the inferior quality of Chinese manufactures, the American partner may desire that the products manufactured in the joint venture operation be sold exclusively in China. In the case of Korea, because of the export promotion policy espoused by the government which helped fuel economic growth in the country in the first three decades since the end of the Korean war, the issue of export requirement is still a very sensitive one. Despite the rising per capita income in the country, the Korean government still perceives the country to be a developed nation.

In 1991, a Korean tour company, Ajou Tours, wanted to mount an advertising campaign to market ocean cruises to Koreans. The Korean Ministry of Transportation sent a "warning letter" to the tour company that such trips "[encourage] lavish and extravagant consumption and [cause] a sense of incompatibility among classes". As a result, Ajou Tours had to revise their strategies. The cruises were oversubscribed in three days time.

Decision-making and Negotiating Styles

The difference in decision-making and negotiating styles and processes is examined under four major categories: first, the relative speed of decision making; second, personal considerations versus western logic; third, the role of the profit motive; and fourth, the role of the government.

Relative speed of decision making

Most westerners who have negotiated with the Japanese and Chinese will readily acknowledge that the experience is unique. Although the negotiations can generally be characterized as cordial, they can also tax one's patience. While conducting business in China and Japan, westerners have to abandon their usual time frame and allow matters to proceed at their own pace, which is character-istically unhurried. A number of factors have contributed to the general slowness in the progress of negotiations. First, human relations are fundamental to any kind of transaction, including business agreements, in Japan and China. These are usually developed over years of personal association. Second, in the case of Japan, approximately 90 per cent of decisions at the middle- and lower-management levels are made through consensus. In the case of China, there is a massive government bureaucracy and an inertia at each of the levels. Third, both the Japanese and Chinese have a longer-term orientation in planning; they look at what will happen ten or twenty years in the future. Hence delays of a few months, or sometimes even years, may appear inconsequential from their perspective. Fourth, since language barriers usually exist, interpreters are often used. This means that the negotiations may take twice as long with all the translations to and from a given language. In the case of Korea, since many Korean companies are still run by the owner/founder of the company or his family, decision making tends to be more centralized. As such, decisions can generally be made more quickly in the Korean context, as compared to Japanese and Chinese companies.

Despite the relative speed with which decisions can be made in Korea, it is important to note that, as in Japan and China, relationships are pivotal to all aspects of societal functioning. It takes time and patience to build and nurture these relationships.

Furthermore, in business negotiations, the Korean partner, like their Japanese and Chinese counterparts, may often use stalling as a negotiating ploy to arrive at a desired outcome. The use of this stalling technique may stem from the perception that Americans are generally more anxious to obtain closure within a relatively short period of time. By stalling, the Korean partner may hope to wear the American counterpart down and thus make more concessions.

The Korean partners explained that in negotiations delays may occur because Korean companies generally do not send their most senior people to the negotiating table. As such, the members of the Korean negotiating team often have to defer to members of senior management to make major decisions. This situation is similar to that in China. It is important to realize this aspect because convincing the members of the negotiation team does not mean that the decision makers will agree to certain proposals. This is where socialization with the decision makers over dinner and drinking bars in the evenings, and on the golf course at weekends could facilitate the process. This after-hours socializing can promote closer personal ties between prospective partners that are fundamental to business relations in East Asia.

Personal considerations vs. western logic

In comparing their experiences in Japan and China, many American executives included in these studies felt that their Korean counterparts were illogical, such

373

as being adamant over trivial matters while glossing over the major ones. The Koreans acknowledged that western logic or reasoning, by itself, may not be adequate to persuade a Korean into adopting a certain course of action. Personal considerations can be equally important, if not more so. The Koreans may often respond to *kilbun*. Jang (1988) explains *kilbun* as the "personal feeling, the attitude, the mood, the mental state ... which is an extremely important factor in ego fulfillment".

Compared to their Japanese and Chinese counterparts, the Koreans can often become quite emotional during the course of negotiations. According to several American executives, Koreans can become "abusive" during the course of negotiations and there can be "shouting matches, desk pounding, and chest beating". In a similar vein, as compared to their Japanese and Chinese counterparts, the Koreans are generally more direct in addressing issues which may be regarded as sensitive. A Korean executive recounted an incident of an American technician who was assigned as a trouble-shooter to their operations in the Far East. This American technician had to speak through an artificial voice box. He worked for three months in Japan but nobody there asked why he sounded different. In less than three days after his arrival in Seoul, he indicated that virtually every Korean he came into contact with had raised the question.

However, while Americans feel that their Japanese and Chinese counterparts are more logical, it is important to realize that linear logic alone cannot fully account for people's behavior and actions in East Asia. According to Hall and Hall (1987) there are two types of logic in Japan. One is linear logic, which is akin to Greek Aristotelian logic. The other is indirection. Indirection can be illustrated by the Japanese saying: "When the wind blows, it is good for the makers of wooden tubs". The logic runs something like this: When the wind blows, it kicks up dust which makes people sad and uncomfortable. To overcome their depression, they play a stringed instrument which is made of catgut. To make these stringed instruments, people kill cats. This results in a reduction in the population of cats, thus leading to a proliferation of mice. The mice gnaw at the wooden tubs in which grain is stored, thus resulting in an increased demand for wooden tubs. Hence, the saying "When the wind blows, it is good for the makers of wooden tubs". While the logic may seem convoluted and incomprehensible to westerners, it highlights two important points: First, the Japanese preoccupation with long-term implications of actions; and second, their ability to "perceive relationships between apparently unrelated systems", the wind blowing and the demand for wooden tubs. The use of spiral logic is fairly common in East Asia.

Significance of the profit motive

To many Japanese and Korean companies, profit may not be the most important objective nor motivator for entering into a particular project or venture. They may be more concerned with market share and growth. Given the Japanese and

Korean partner's concern with establishing market share and materializing growth, the venture may not be able to realize a quick return on its investment. In the case of China, until quite recently, the primary concern of state-owned enterprises was not profits nor profitability.

As far as the motivation of Korean workers is concerned, status and ego fulfillment may be a more significant motivator than money in spurring workers to heighten their performance. Consequently, status symbols such as titles, the use of a company car, the assignment of a personal chauffeur to the individual, the size of the office, and the use of a corporate charge card, can become powerful motivators to bring about desired objectives in the Korean context. Western investors have to take these factors into consideration in their investment decision.

Role of the government

While it is erroneous to characterize the relationship among government, business and labor in Japan as that of "Japan Inc.", the working relationship between government and business is more harmonious and much closer than that prevalent in North America. Professor Robert Ballon, a Belgian Jesuit priest who has lived in Japan for over 40 years and is a noted Japanologist, perhaps captured the essence of this relationship best. According to him: "Japanese social dynamics operate on the basis of interdependence. Whereas Western interaction tends to be $1 + 1 = 2$, in Japan the formula would be $1 \times 1 = 1$. Thus, in Japan the reality of government and business is not that of two entities to be somehow added up but rather the reality of one coin with two faces. In other words, two distinct but interdeppendentinstitutions, namely the government and business, form one reality: Japan. In Japan, the western notion of *laissez-faire* which supposes a gap between the public and private sectors, has never made sense. Although for Japan, the private is not the public, the dividing line between the two is not always clear" (Ballon 1987). In the case of China, government directives and approvals pervade virtually all aspects of societal and economic functionings. In Korea, government approvals are required on many aspects of the company's functioning. To compound the situation, in China and Korea, laws are often vague and hence subject to varied interpretations. This can be very frustrating and confusing from a western investor's perspective.

Keys to Success in Negotiating with East Asians

Based on these studies, six common denominators to success can be identified. These are: (i) complementarity of product/service provided by the foreign partner; (ii) patience; (iii) respect for cultural differences; (iv) need to build and nurture relationships; (v) long-term commitment to the market; and (vi) need to understand the system and work within it. Each factor is discussed below.

Complementarity of product/service

In China, Japan and Korea, a primary motive for the East Asian partner to enter into joint venture agreements with a foreign entity is to gain access to advanced foreign technology. Given the policy of industrial targeting in Japan and Korea and the role of central planning in China, foreign investments which can facilitate the development of targeted industries and sectors are favorably received. Consequently, if a foreign investor fails to sustain a technological lead, then the motive which brought the two partners together can dissipate, leading to the demise of the venture. Consider, for example, the case of the joint production program entered into between Boeing Aircraft and Civil Transport Development Corporation, a quasi Japanese government entity for the manufacture of Boeing 767s. Since the early 1980s, the Japanese government has designated aerospace as a targeted industry. This may stem, in part, from the US insistence that the Japanese should increase its defense budget. Since there is much complementarity between the production of civilian and military aircraft in terms of technological know-how and equipment, the production of commercial aircraft represents a viable route for recovering the costs of research and development on military defense. For this reason, the Japanese have decided to enter into commercial aircraft manufacturing. Hence, the Japanese eagerness to enter into a joint production relationship with Boeing Corporation on the manufacture of Boeing's 767s.

Consider, for example, the role of foreign banks in the Korean economy. After the Korean War, the country needed foreign capital to fund projects for industrial growth and development. In those days, foreign banks received preferential status treatement and were able to reap substantial profits. However, beginning in the 1990s, since domestic banks are now capable of financing many of the projects at home, the Korean banking authorities have enacted legislation to restrict the activities and operations of foreign banks in Korea. As a result, the growth in profits of foreign banks has fallen from a high of 30 per cent in 1987 to 3.8 per cent in 1989 (*Wall Street Journal*, September 4, 1990).

In the case of China, investment projects which do not fall within the purview of the current five-year plan or which do not meet certain stated government objectives, such as the generation of foreign exchange, have little chance of success.

Patience

As noted earlier, negotiations progress very slowly in both Japan and China. While the Koreans, as compared with their Japanese and Chinese counterparts, can generally arrive at decisions more quickly, an inordinate amount of patience is necessary to succeed in the Korean market for two primary reasons. One, the need to establish relationships with the appropriate authorities. Two, the Korean economy is still very much in a transitional phase. As such, proposed changes to restructure various sectors of the domestic market may take a long period of time to implement.

For these reasons, matters generally do not progress as rapidly as many westerners would like or expect. Foreign investors who fly to East Asia and expect to conclude an agreement within three or four weeks will be disappointed because things simply do not happen that way in that part of the world.

Respect for cultural differences

In her studies of US–Japan and US–China business negotiations, Tung (1982, 1984, 1989) found that knowledge of cultural differences is a necessary but insufficient condition for success. In other words, while "the ability to bridge cultural differences" was less important in explaining for the success of business negotiations, its absence was perceived as a major contributing factor to failure. All American partners involved in joint venture arrangements with the Koreans also drew the same conclusion with regard to Korea. The Korean partners went one step further by stating that knowledge of the Korean culture and language is imperative to success in Korea. Unfortunately, facility in exotic East Asian languages, and knowledge of cross-cultural differences, are not the forte of most North American business people.

Many Americans included in these studies considered Korea to be a very difficult country to live and work in, even more so than Japan and China. According to an American executive: "I would say this country rates number one (in terms of stress generation). I have talked to a fair number of people who have had experiences in other places, they would put Korea right at the top". This comment was echoed by several others, including some who have lived in the country for a long time and who are married to Korean nationals. Many Americans ascribed this difficulty to the different value system of Korean society and what westerners perceived as illogical ways of doing business, an issue discussed earlier in the chapter.

While it is impossible to enumerate all the cultural differences that can exist between westerners and East Asia in the context of this chapter, it may be useful to examine one area where the gap can be significant. This pertains to the attitude toward the sanctity of a written contract. The typical western view is that a contract defines the rights and responsibilities of the parties. There can be no deviations from the contract since it is considered as a legal document which binds both parties. The Japanese, Chinese and Koreans, on the other hand, believe that contracts are organic documents which can change as conditions evolve. Confucius' emphasis on governance by ethics over governance by law may account for the general aversion to law and litigation in East Asia and their penchant to view contracts as organic documents that can be varied (Tung, 1996).

This cultural gap is exacerbated by the fact that bribery, such as the giving of expensive gifts and the use of lavish entertainment, is common in Japan, China and Korea. Research has shown that there is a strong correlation between

Rosalie Tung

high-context culture and the use of questionable payments. Given the predominance of the world's people who belong to high-context cultures, there are only twelve "clean" countries — these are the United States, Canada, the Scandinavian and north European countries (Gladwyn and Walters, 1980).

Need to build and nurture relationships

There is a general saying in East Asia that "who you know is more important than what you know". This is referred to as *guanxi* in China, *kankei* in Japan, and *kwankye* in Korea. In China, Japan and Korea, building and maintaining relationships with the appropriate authorities and individuals are paramount to success (Yeung and Tung, in press). Most of these relationships are formed on the basis of one or a combination of the following three factors: (i) blood, i.e., members of one's immediate and extended families; (ii) school ties, i.e., attending the same grade school, high school, university, and/or organizational unit; and (iii) geography, i.e., members from the same clan or village to which one's ancestors belong. These relationships are reinforced through after-hours socializing. Such after-hours socializing is considered a "necessary carry-over" from the regular business hours from 9 to 5. In the case of China, this may be particularly important since the key decision makers are generally not present at the formal negotiation sessions. The after-hours socializing thus becomes an important forum for meeting and convincing these key decision makers about the merit of a given project. In general, it is difficult for westerners to break into the system, particularly when they are anxious to separate their professional from their personal lives. Another factor which can compound the difficulty of developing the necessary relations with the East Asian partner is the general practice among American firms to assign their expatriates on a short-term basis. The relatively short duration of these overseas assignments is not conducive to the development of such relations which are perceived to be crucial to success.

To maintain the right contacts with the appropriate authorities, it is imperative that western companies hire local nationals into senior executive positions who can manage these relationships. However, in both Japan and Korea, it is not easy to recruit competent local nationals with the proper connections to work for foreign companies. The reluctance of the graduates of elite Japanese universities to work for foreign firms has often been cited as a non-tariff barrier to trade. In the case of Korea, in the 1950s and 1960s, many Koreans preferred to work for foreign companies because of their higher wages. This situation began to change in the late 1970s when indigenous companies were able to match foreign companies in terms of salary. As in Japan, in Korea, there is a growing stigma associated with working for a foreign firm. Part of the reluctance stems from the college graduates' perception that foreign companies may not have a long-term commitment to remaining in Korea.

Japanese and Korean employees do differ in at least one important respect, however. In Japan, the loyalty is generally to the company, whereas in Korea, the loyalty is usually toward the person for whom one works. The employee is attracted to a particular boss because of special attributes possessed by the person, such as strong leadership skills, technical abilities, or intelligence. As such, if a foreign firm can manage to hire a Korean national who possesses one or more of such attributes, the recruitment of other competent Korean nationals should not be too problematic.

The social stigma associated with working for foreign companies, coupled with the vast differences between the English and Japanese and Korean languages, have led some foreign companies to recruit local nationals primarily on the basis of English language proficiency. However, a mere linguist may not be the best person for the position because he/she may not have the necessary connections to work within the local system.

In China, the graduates of elite Chinese universities are very eager to work for foreign firms. However, recruitment is regulated by governmental authorities. Foreign investors have complained that there is a tendency for the state employment agencies to transfer these employees into other wholly-owned Chinese enterprises once they have been trained in the joint venture operation.

Long-term commitment

As noted earlier, short-term profitability may not be the most important motive from the East Asian partner's standpoint. Market share and growth are often the primary objectives, in the case of Japan and Korea. In the case of China, given the relatively underdeveloped state of its economy at present, it may take years before foreign investors can hope to see a reasonable return on their investment.

In light of this difference, a foreign investor who seeks to enter into Japan, China or Korea for short-term gains may be disappointed. The East Asian partner expects the foreign investor to have a long-term commitment to remaining in the country. One Korean partner compared the joint venturing process to that of child-rearing: "It has to be long-term... It is like raising your children. You don't give up on raising children when they are only three or four years old. It is a continual process, and you must really look forward to the time when the children become successful, wholesome people. Companies are the same — there are going to be ups and downs. There are going to be difficult times, but this is all part of the learning process".

Need to understand the system and work within it

Besides significant cultural differences between the west and East Asia, the Japanese, Chinese and Korean markets are unique in their respective ways. In the case of Japan, its system of marketing and distribution is very different from that of the United States. There are almost as many wholesalers and retailers in Japan as there are in the United States, a country with twice the population of

Japan. There is a tendency to confuse modernization with westernization — an assumption is often made that since Japan is highly industrialized and modernized, it is also westernized. Hence what sells in the United States will also find a niche in the Japanese market. This is a flawed assumption, however. There are substantial differences between the lifestyles and buying behavior of American and Japanese consumers. Given the highly developed Japanese economy, unoriginal products do not sell well in the country. A foreign investor has to research the Japanese market thoroughly to determine whether there is a demand for its products and, if so, what types of modifications need to be made. For example, large refrigerators, which are the norm in North America, do not suit Japanese needs because of the smaller size of the houses and the shopping patterns of families. Since many of these practices are steeped in centuries of traditions, it may be difficult for foreign firms to change them. Rather, they should understand such differences and work within them.

In the case of Korea, the military still plays a very important role in the country. These relationships have to be understood and contended with.

In the case of China, the political system is so vastly different that it is often difficult for the foreign investor to understand who the key decision makers are. The party structure pervades all aspects of societal functioning. For example, Deng Xiaoping who is the most powerful man in China does not occupy the position of Chairman of the Party nor President or Premier of the land. There are many stories of how mayors from Chinese cities may be assigned the seat of honor while the party secretary, who is usually the more powerful person in China's socio-political structure, will be relegated to a position of lesser honor during their visit to an American City. In addition, China still is a centrally planned economy where national economic plans dictate what should be imported and exported, and in what quantities. Besides knowledge of China's national economic plans, in light of continued changes to the structure and management of foreign trade, investors should try to find out which agencies they should be dealing with. The investor should also be thoroughly familiar with the latest laws promulgated and changes implemented which affect the operations of joint ventures and other economic forms of arrangements. In addition, they should be knowledgeable about the problems and issues involved in conducting business with a planned market economy.

Conclusion and Discussion

In light of the increasing incidence of global economic cooperation among business entities from different nations, the need to identify strategies which can maximize the probability of positive outcomes in a negotiation situation is indeed great. Joint cooperative agreements between western firms, on the one hand, and entities from China, Japan and Korea, on the other, have mushroomed in the past decade and are expected to increase further in the years ahead. Such agreements are attractive to western companies for two reasons: first, the fast-growing East

Asian market, and second, the viability of the joint venture as an entry vehicle that leapfrogs market barriers and which gives the western partner more management control than licensing does.

The findings of the studies presented here suggest that mere possession of the right or technically advanced product and/or technology cannot always guarantee success in the international economic arena. Even in situations where technology alone may be the primary motivating force to draw the two partners to collaborate initially, the continuation of the venture still depends on the ability of the parties to work differences out when they arise and to coexist peacefully with each other. This chapter has highlighted the significant role that different value systems can play in affecting the partner's perception of what are important issues in a negotiation, how decisions are usually made, and how to proceed in the negotiation.

CHAPTER 19

Some General Guidelines for Negotiating International Business

JEAN-CLAUDE USUNIER AND PERVEZ GHAURI

This final chapter deals with a series of normative recommendations for negotiating international business successfully. It builds on the previous chapters in the book and provides the international business negotiator with some basic rules which have been organized in three distinct, but interrelated sets: (i) rules dealing with the preparation of the negotiation; (ii) a second set deals with how to manage the negotiation process itself, taking into account one's own and the other party's basic interests, time, people involved, communication processes etc. and (iii) the third part is dedicated to "negotiating beyond negotiation", that is, that part of the whole exercise which extends beyond what is generally considered as the "normal" task of the negotiators. The last part deals with the ethical aspects of IBNs.

Preparing for the Negotiation

General aspects

The first and foremost rule of international business negotiation is to be prepared, if need be, to renounce a negotiation. This may be necessary because the stakes are too low or when sending lower level, less expensive executives would not even match the expected benefits. Most international deals incur transaction costs which are disproportionate to the costs related to domestic deals: people in the domestic market usually share the same language and cultural background which acts as a common knowledge base. For instance, it is much easier within the native cultural setting to guess who will be a good payer, a reliable partner or a trustworthy supplier. Negotiation, as any strategic activity, lies even more in what one does *not* do than what one actually does.

Thus, it would be a mistake to go flitting about like a butterfly on the international market: always looking for new partners, new customers and new ventures, without following up. This results in a great deal of "one-off" business. Business people and companies perform poorly if they do not understand the golden rule of international business negotiations which is: have few partners and conduct few negotiations, but make the stakes meaningful.

Another set of guidelines is to consider that the negotiatior's tasks start largely before people sit around the table: be well prepared; define in advance your basic interests, objectives, bottom line and room for manoeuvre. Before participating in a negotiation, learn the basics about the behavioural norms of your partner's culture, especially concerning appointments, punctuality and planning.

Gathering factual information

Tung (1982) identified the preparation of the US team as a major factor for the success of their business negotiations with the Chinese. Key information must be collected prior to the negotiation and the lack of such information (or the fact that only part of the scope is covered by the information search) has often been noted as a reason for the failure of negotiation. The negotiators should thus create and demonstrate willingness to exchange information with each other.

Getting down to the facts implies searching for relevant data on the matter of the negotiation, both objective and more subjective; namely:

- operations-related information (costs, possible locations, inputs etc.)
- learning about the future partner: people- and networking-related information; team composition, who is who in the team (background, status etc.)
- expectations of the other party; their constraints (especially in terms of performance thresholds or mandate given by their superiors),
- the other party's decision-making process: general style of decision making (centralized, decentralized, committee, etc.); Who decides? How? Is decision strongly related to implementation? To what extent does it fit with our own decision-making style?
- environmental data: government; regulatory authority (including multinational ones, see EU commission's role in Chapter 14);
- competition-related data (especially in case of a sales negotiations but this may extend beyond; for instance to rival companies for a take-over, or different possible partners for a joint venture, or a licensing agreement): who are the possible competitors? What is their status in the process; (shortlist or final face-to-face negotiations)
- information about third parties: trade-unions, environmental groups, NGOs; all those who are generally not direct participants in the negotiation process as such but may influence the principals on either side, and/or participate in auxiliary negotiations or only in certain phases of the main negotiation.

The above-mentioned information will help us in defining the problem and basic facts about the process at hand. It is important to ascertain pieces of information, sorting them out and assessing which information needs to be sought, clarified; how additional data should be looked for, etc. It is a key requirement to have identified important information loopholes, that is, information which was not possible to obtain before arriving at the negotiation table and which needs to be gathered as soon as possible when starting the negotiation itself. It is important to comprehend the other side's needs and objectives which may change during the process.

Strategy formulation

An essential factor in the definition of a strategy is the concept of basic interests (Pruitt 1983). Basic interests are a limited set of core outcomes which are consciously expected by a party as a result of the negotiation process. This may concern a reservation price, a certain type of contractual arrangement, keeping a technology etc. The main characteristics of basic interests are that (i) they cover only a limited range of favourable outcomes: it is not "all the cake" which is desired but just a certain part of it which is significant to a party; (ii) they allow a clear definition of what is negotiable and what is not negotiable; (iii) clearly defined basic interests enable a party to signal firmness to the other party without offending them; and (iv) basic interests facilitate the scheduling of concessions and enable a party to avoid yielding too much.

A basic interests sheet is a one- or two-page memo discussed within the negotiation team and sent to the top executives who will be involved at the start and at the finish and who will often only actually come at the end of the process. Its preparation requires a quasi-pre-negotiation within one party's people, both between the negotiators and all people who will be affected by the consequences of the deal if it is agreed upon. There may be — and most often there are — organizational conflicts and divergence of interests within the company — and all the more so when it is a consortium of companies which deals with turnkey projects world-wide.

Copeland and Griggs give some rules for drafting a basic interests sheet: (i) "define what 'winning the negotiation' means to you"; and (ii) "be ambitious but set a realistic walk-away". What do we want: a fair price, a target profit, learning from the potential partner, getting access to resources, accessing a technology, or a combination of these achievements and which combination? Defining precisely what it means to a party to win or lose the negotiation is part of the "brainstorming" which is necessary for preparing the basic interests (Copeland and Griggs 1986, pp. 74–5).

While defining basic interests, it is also important to identify the common ground and, more precisely, the perceived common ground; take the true measure of the overlap between one's own basic interests and the other party's expected outcomes, as far as one can envisage them (Pruitt 1983). During the process and argumentation, parties should emphasize the common interest and not the conflicting objectives. One must give an impression that one is primarily looking for a solution that helps both parties to achieve their objectives.

The importance of walk-away possibilities is not readily apparent in the preparation phase. Future negotiators, on both sides, tend to over-emphasize a joint positive outcome, being inspired by a quite legitimate wishful thinking. In business, parties go to negotiation on a rather free basis: they often have alternative partners and/or alternative deals, ventures and projects. However, it may appear as the negotiation proceeds, that, despite favourable initial conditions, there is some deep mismatch between the parties. Thus, it is important to define what winning means to you as well as what *not winning* means to you. Being able to walk away without a deal is a scenario which has to be envisaged prior to the negotiation itself.

Once again: strategy is a lot about what one chooses not to do. Walk-away routes are an integral part of the strategy formulation. This may occur for many reasons, for instance: (i) a negotiation has started on definite premises which have changed in the meantime (take-over, price increase of key inputs or outputs); (ii) key people who were assets to the process have left; and (iii) little by little, the partners discover that they do not fit together (because of different corporate cultures for instance) and even though the deal itself would be profitable on paper, the relationship would not work and joint implementation would be difficult.

It is important also to elicit, prior to the face-to-face negotiation, the degree of toughness which a party will adopt towards the other. This issue has been widely discussed by Ghauri (1986). For example, a "tough" strategy is one in which a party starts with a high initial offer and avoids making concessions. A "soft" strategy is one in which the granting of concessions enhances trust and facilitates negotiations. In a "fair strategy", the negotiators appreciate that a certain settlement would be fair to both parties (50/50 split) and as soon as one of them suggests such a settlement the other party agrees, rather than holding out to obtain more concessions. In managing the process of yielding, on both sides, it is useful to have an understanding of the other's basic interests and strategic orientation. If one of the parties realises, once again before the face-to-face negotiation, that there is considerable overlap between its own and the other party's position, the negotiator should be ready to wait and not agree at once for a settlement.

Preparing for tactical moves

Some precautions will allow larger margins of manoeuvre for the tactical aspects of negotiation; for instance:

1. Controlling location: if a party negotiates on his own terrain (possibly by inviting the other party, bearing the full cost of accommodation locally, and treating the other party as honoured guests), it will have a competitive advantage over the foreign partner in terms of time control and agenda, and it will feel quite comfortable while negotiating face to face. Negotiate at home whenever you have the possibility.
2. It may be quite useful to simulate the margins of manoeuvre on both sides, the leeway of the negotiators on both sides, and investigate the other party's basic interests: how will they react to some of your proposals and, on the

other hand, how will you react to some of their proposals? Here, the history of the relationship between the two parties can play an important role. In the case where the parties have no previous relationship, expectations on each others behaviour can lead to competitive, co-operative or defensive behaviour.

3. Preparing a negotiation sketch allowing for both distributive/competitive and co-operative/integrative phases. Don't always use the same style. Allow people in your own negotiation team to play different roles (in a way which has been planned jointly beforehand) so that your team is never considered as being completely distributive or integrative. The nature of distributive vs. integrative phases may depend upon the type of issues discussed.

4. Be prepared for some rough style. This relates to the possibility that the other party might start with a quite "tough strategy", as defined above; in this case, one should be ready to signal firmness without directly applying a tough strategy (as a matter of straightforward retaliation) which may lead the negotiation process to an early deadlock. For instance, the Soviet style of business negotiations, still a part of the Russian style even after the Communist regime has fallen, has been described as fairly tough and unilateral. Negotiators tend to make extreme initial demands, to view concessions from the adversary as weakness, to be stingy with concessions, and to ignore deadlines (Cohen 1980). Graham *et al.* (1992) note the consensus of description of the Soviet negotiators as "competitive" and "uncompromising". They show in a laboratory experiment, that Russian negotiators tend to prefer a distributive strategy, and this with minimum regard to their partner's satisfaction, which tends to suggest that such competitive behaviour is considered locally as standard practice.

5. Plan to control your concessions. Concessions can be viewed and interpreted in rather opposite ways: either as a sign of openness, willingness to cooperate, or as a sign of weakness and readiness to yield considerably. For instance, coming back to the example of Russians, their ethical system widely differs from that of Americans according to Lefebvre (1992 p. 396): "Something that an American considers normative positive behaviour (for example, negotiating and reaching a compromise with an enemy, and even any deal with another individual), a Soviet man perceives as showing Philistine cowardice, weakness, as something unworthy (the word "deal" itself has a strong negative connotation in contemporary Russian)".

Managing the Negotiation Process

Good preparation for negotiation is both necessary and often disappointing: a lot of what has been prepared, thought out in advance, planned, will be lost in the process which will never take the expected form. Among the key issues in the management of the negotiation process, we distinguish between: (i) people; (ii) time; (iii) issues; (iv) communication; and (v) the expected outcomes.

Dealing with people

As emphasized in several chapters (4, 5, 7, 8, 17 and 18), it is crucial to take time for adequate preliminaries: getting to know the other party, not only as professionals but also as people, is most often crucial. More time is needed than in domestic business negotiations, since cultural as well as personal knowledge has to be acquired. Even though the non-task sounding-out part of the negotiation process may appear a waste of time to strongly economic-time-minded negotiators, it is seen by others as a prerequisite to good negotiation (see Chapter 4 and others).

In this process, it is important to "give face" to the people in front of you. As Copeland and Griggs (1986 p. 91) phrase it: "Almost every negotiation is a face-saving situation, and the successful international negotiator will avoid making people uncomfortable." In order to give face, avoid arrogance, be careful in the choice of words so as not to offend the other party; treat your adversaries with respect. This will help you generate trust. When people trust one another they communicate more openly and are more receptive to each other's arguments and point of view.

Respect towards the sensitivities of your partners is especially significant in two areas: (i) personal status; and (ii) national pride. Many societies, as diverse as the French, Japanese and Mexican, are strongly status-oriented. In Mexico, for instance, personal leverage — *palanca* — is important: influential Mexican negotiators tend to be well positioned in their society, expressively showing their status and stamina. Their personal status must be acknowledged in some way, even though they may seem arrogant to other people. On the other hand, Mexicans have an identity problem with their powerful neighbour, the United States, and there is high sensitivity "to their perceived dependent relationship with the United States and their long memory of patronizing and demeaning actions taken by the US as a government, by American companies and by Americans as individuals (Fisher 1980, p. 40). A US negotiation team will therefore need to take into account the national pride issue in their negotiations with Mexicans.

Monitoring time

As already mentioned — and illustrated — in Chapter 8: never tell the other side when you are leaving because this gives them control over your time. Allow yourself plenty of time, and even more. In particular, give yourself time to think: do not respond too quickly to new propositions; even small interruptions of negotiations may prove useful in order to think over confused issues or to define a common position within a negotiation team. It is important to show your dissatisfaction over session issues and discuss the reasons and possible solutions to that. The timing of verbal exchange is crucial in negotiations. Some Westerners find gaps or pauses in conversations to be disturbing, while people from other cultures prefer to leave a moment of silence between the statements.

Patience is an asset to negotiation and it is destroyed by time pressure. Do not give time-related information to the other party: your flight time, important deadlines within your company, etc. Your opposite numbers will use it to put your team under pressure, especially when you do not negotiate at home. When planning together, do not get fooled by the other party seemingly sharing your time pattern: try to set realistic dates and deadlines. Plan modestly and realistically: tight deadlines may result in enormous delays that ruin the credibility of the whole planning process.

Managing issues

Be flexible with the negotiation agenda if the other party does not stick to it. It may be somewhat frustrating to see that a negotiation agenda has been agreed upon and is eroded bit by bit. It may mean that the other party prefers a global to a step-by step negotiation, and that they do not see negotiation as a linear process in which issues are addressed one after the other and settled before proceeding to the next.

In face-to-face negotiation, the maintenance of flexibility of parties and issues is important, especially as concerns issues like terms of payment, credit facilities, delivery time, and of course, price. However, flexibility margins must always remain strictly monitored within the boundaries of basic interests. The process of give and take usually occurs after both sides have tested the commitment, and have sent and received signals to move on. For example, price can often be reduced if the party offers better terms of payment. It is also important to include in the margins of flexibility some elements which can be traded off but which cannot be evaluated in accounting terms, such as obtaining a reference project or market access where the potential is much larger than the present sale.

Key information should be kept under strict control: the release of strategic information in the negotiation must be monitored so that one party does not unnecessarily disclose data about costs, strategic plans, or a possible change in the company's corporate structure. Controlling key information and choosing the appropriate time to disclose it must be a constant concern of a good international negotiator: it is like playing cards, a hand is always kept out of sight of the other players until the appropriate time comes for playing a particular card. In the same manner, the timing of concessions is also crucial. A premature concession on price might lead to contrary results.

Managing the communication process

Face-to-face negotiation implies intensive communication flows the efficiency of which is often impaired by language and culture differences. Chapter 7 has reviewed the role of cross-cultural communication on business negotiations. The basic guideline for effective communication in international business is to be ready for different communication styles and be cautious in interpreting silence, emotionality, threats, and any kind of manipulative, instrumental communication. This general recommendation can be broken down into more detailed advice, which takes into account the kind of communication taking place (speaking, listening, using interpreters, speaking directly in the other party's language even if it is not your own native language etc.). They are listed below.

1. Start by assessing as accurately as possible the intercultural obstacles, such as language and problems of communication in general. Business people often underestimate or even completely overlook this point, since they often share a technical culture with their conversation partner. They are also deceived by an almost international atmosphere that can be quite misleading. Glen Fisher (1980 p. 8) emphasizes: "Obviously, the modern intensity of international interaction, especially in business and in technological, communication and educational fields, has produced something of an internationalized 'culture' which reduces the clash of cultural backgrounds and stereotyped images. Happily for us, this modus vivendi is largely based on Western practices and even on the English language, so many otherwise 'foreign' counterparts are accommodating to the American style of negotiation." Unfortunately, in the real world, the person who does not feel the need to adapt, especially as far as language is concerned, may be indulging in indolence. The result will be the mistaken impression that one's partner is just like oneself. That is to say that often similarities are illusions, especially when foreigners seemingly share the same "international culture". Those who adapt are aware of differences, whereas those who don't stay unaware.

2. Beware that what is explicitly said is not necessarily what is implicitly meant. Check, verify. Spend time on checking communication accuracy, especially when the stakes are high (orders, delivery dates, contractual involvement in general). Check the ambiguous messages directly, for example, by asking "Do we understand correctly that...". According to Foster (1995 p. 249), "The effective international negotiator knows how to probe, how to ask questions and how to listen."

3. Learning the non-verbal communication style of another culture may prove very difficult. Deep cultural learning in this area is very hard after childhood. As elaborated in Chapter nine, be careful and observant on non-verbal communication and read the real message between the lines. It is better to aim at a state of alertness so that one does not decode non-verbal messages erroneously, rather than try to gain full command of different types of non-verbal communication.

4. Interpreters are often used in the process of international business negotiations. In many cases, interpreters may serve a crucial purpose, that of transposers of meaning. They do not work "like a dictionary", translating literally. They may translate better from one language to another than in the reverse direction, and this will depend not only on which their native language is, but also on some personal leaning toward one party. It is also necessary to

make sure that they are truly loyal to the party which has hired them. It may be advisable to hire several interpreters when the business at stake justifies it. The role of interpreters may be crucial: verify that they really work for you, are on your side, inform you properly; interpreters sharing the same nationality as your adversaries may be tempted unconsciously to favour their countrymen.

5. It must be clearly appreciated that there is always a part of the language which cannot be translated. Culture-specific meaning is conveyed by language as it reflects the culture. Always keep in mind the Italian adage, cited above, *traduttore/traditore* (translator/traitor). The language and terminology used in the contract should be simple and clear.

6. Develop a "bomb squad" ability to defuse a conflict based on negative stereotypes. Subjective misunderstandings in intercultural communication often snowball and mix with purely interest-based (objective) conflicts, resulting in confrontations that may not be productive. There are sometimes necessary conflicts and even good ones, where confrontation should not be avoided. But in many other cases, cultural misunderstandings may have a purely negative influence on the dealings that follow, possibly even leading to the breaking-off of negotiations.

7. Keep in mind that all this depends on advance preparation, and unfortunately cannot be improvised. An effort to help the other intelligently and agreeably to understand one's own culture is a prerequisite, and it may often be "wine and dine" related. When formal business negotiations or even preliminary business talks start and one side lacks minimal knowledge of the partner's culture, the relations will often turn sour. It will soon be too late to approach basic issues affected by common understandings and cultural differences. Then the only way to negotiate is to discuss on the solid ground of "business is business". In this light, training in intercultural business seems more like a preliminary investment to improve the effectiveness of business deals than a way of resolving urgent problems. In medical terms, cultural understanding in business appears as the prevention rather than the cure.

Managing expected outcomes

What is a good outcome? A good agreement is one which leads to successful implementation. A good outcome is a deal which benefits both parties, and neither feels that it has a less advantageous contract. The main purpose of the contract is to avoid misunderstanding and trouble in the future and thus business negotiation is a process through which parties interact to reach an agreement which provides terms and conditions for the future behaviour of the parties involved. Both parties must in some way agree about what is a good joint outcome and on the significance of what is signed. As noted earlier, managing expected outcomes is a lot about managing concessions, preparing for the give-and-take part of the face-to-face negotiation, and being ready to face misunderstandings about the very meaning of trade-off and compromise (Box 19.1 below).

> **Box 19.1** Persian compromise
>
> In Persian, the word "compromise" does not have the English meaning of a midway solution which both sides can accept, but only the negative meaning of surrendering one's principles. Also, a "mediator is a meddler," someone who is barging in uninvited. In 1980, United Nations Secretary General Kurt Waldheim flew to Iran to deal with the hostage situation. National Iranian radio and television broadcast in Persian a comment he was said to have made upon his arrival in Tehran: "I have come as a mediator to work out a compromise." Less than an hour later, his car was being stoned by angry Iranians. (*Source:* Fisher and Ury (1983, p. 34).)

Clarity of Agreement

A number of authors on negotiations suggest that it is necessary to have a signed agreement before you leave (Copeland and Griggs 1986 p. 93). This is however debatable, because you may be at a risk of yielding too much or of signing an agreement which will afterwards be considered detrimental to one party. A simple memorandum of understanding which allows further refinement may be better when the parties have not reached full agreement within a negotiation round. The idea that "a deal closed is better than none" may be somewhat dangerous. To sign an ambiguous contract can lead to enormous problems in the implementation stage. It is thus wiser to spend one more session to discuss and clear the ambiguity than to sign the contract too early.

Negotiating beyond negotiation

This phrase captures a significant part of the paradox that negotiating business is clearly about deal-making and, at the same time, goes far beyond the simple drafting of final contract provisions. A relationship often develops through a series of successive negotiation rounds, with implementation phases in the meantime. Negotiation is often a continuous rather than discontinuous activity; although certain rituals such as the signature of a contract seem to place definite time boundaries, it is not so clear in the real world. In some cultures, the written agreement is very valuable and is followed literally, in others it has a symbolic value and is never referred to during the implementation. The negotiators should know about the importance of the written contract.

Formal versus informal agreements

In several chapters, the degree of formality of agreements has been mentioned as a key issue in international business negotiations. The presence of lawyers, especially early in the process, and a very punctilious attitude when drafting clauses may be interpreted by the other party as a sign of distrust. On the other hand, the role of lawyers in formalising the final agreement is standard in the world of international business. The advice would be, therefore, to exclude lawyers and accountants from the negotiation table in the early stages of the negotiation (and probably even in face-to-face negotiation; see Chapters 17 and 18); they may, however, be quite important doing a counselling job and working behind the scenes. They should show up only in the last phases of the negotiation process when the parties are finalizing the agreement. (See Chapters 11 and 14 written by lawyers. See also Chapter 5.)

Developing relationships and persuasion

The agreement should foster the development of the relationship and be flexible enough to deal with expected and unexpected changes. A major concern is to balance *relationship-* and *deal-orientation*: wait for the negotiation process to extend beyond the signature of the deal. The ultimate goal of negotiation is to establish a mutually trustworthy business relationship. This is particularly important in cases where you expect to have future business selling spare parts etc. Moreover, if you want this transaction to serve as a reference project, you should be sure about the other party's satisfaction or dissatisfaction with the deal. In many cultures, for example in China and the Middle East, parties do give great value to relationship/friendships and any previous positive relationship when looking for new business deals. It is evident that the better the relationship between the parties, the more they trust each other and prefer to do business with each other than with strangers. And the more the parties trust each other, the easier it is to persuade and be receptive to each other's messages and agreements. The persuasion is an essential part of communication exchanged in a negotiation process. But for persuasion to work properly, a previous relationship and a positive atmosphere (see Chapter nine) are very crucial. By persuasion we mean changing another person's opinions and perceptions through convincing him. It has to do with the presentation of facts and information in a way that makes it easier for the other party to be convinced. The contents and the formulation of a particular message and the communication as a whole is thus of the utmost importance. One important aspect here is to emphasize and let the other party see the advantages of the deal for him/her. The attractiveness of our arguments is, in other words, more important to the other party than to ourselves. While preparing communication and penetration, it is important to look at the issues at hand from the other party's point of view. The persuasion should be prepared in a rather successive or step-by-step approach: first getting their agreement on smaller, less crucial issues and saving the issues most crucial to the other party for later. When the party has agreed to one or more issues, it is more likely that they will accept the later issues more easily.

Managing conflicts as part of the whole process

Litigation does major damage to the relationship, which generally does not survive the legal process. Discussions, even tough ones, are always preferable to court settlements. Even very detailed contracts can never be fully perfect. Sometimes, the issue is simply that a clause has not been written precisely enough and the partners need to clarify it. In this very process, there is always an element of "re-negotiation", which may be resented by the party who fears losing as a result of the clarification of the clause. However, avoiding litigation, and even the threat of it, must be a major concern: since going to court means the dissolution of the relationship and quite often a "lose-lose" solution. A court settlement must be used only when the expected losses from litigation are substantially smaller than the solution without litigation (a rare case in practice).

Exercise of power

Negotiation process is typically a situation in which parties are mutually dependent. In other words, parties to a negotiation process need to find a solution which is acceptable to both of them. This interdependence relationship is quite complex, especially if one of the parties has more power than the other, due to their superior technology or access to a wide market or any other reason. Chapter nine discussed the power/dependence relationship in terms of perceptions of the other parties involved.

Ethical concerns in international business negotiations

"Mouth smiles, money smiles better" runs a Ghanean saying. Money is always at the very centre of business negotiations, as price is discussed as well as "side price". This is all the more important when the whole process takes place across borders, that is, with a much more limited control by national regulatory authorities than on the domestic scene. Most laws, including tax and anti-corruption regulations, do not apply beyond national borders. It is always tempting to win a deal by offering *baksheesh* rather than by fair competition. Moreover, significant price and performance advantages over competitors are sometimes not enough to win: some bribes or backhanders may be discreetly asked for by the buyers.

After reviewing the basic ethical standpoints for international business negotiations, we shall examine the main ethical issues confronted by the negotiators in the international arena. Finally, some recommendations for actions will try to propose a reasonable compromise between the moral/legal and the pragmatic/competitive perspectives.

Basic ethical standpoints: relativism versus universalism

With respect to ethical issues in international business negotiations, there are two extreme positions: relativism and universalism. Relativism is based on the view that rules are basically local and do not apply elsewhere; universalism, on the other hand, favours the view that most rules cross borders and apply everywhere because they are based on universal moral principles.

The first ethical position is that of cultural relativism: what is right or wrong, good or bad, depends on one's culture. This is based on the view that rules are applicable locally in the ingroup territory and thus "When in Rome, do as Romans do". There are some strong arguments in favour of relativism, such as in the case of Africa where corrupt money is largely, but not completely, redistributed in society. However, one cannot ignore the negative consequences of such widespread corrupt practices. Galtung (1994) and others show the heavy burden placed by corruption on economic development: for instance, the property of President Mobutu Sese Seko of Zaire is said to be equivalent to the whole of the foreign debt of the country.

A second position is therefore cultural universalism, which is based on the view that there are core ethical principles which are universally applicable, whenever and to whoever, regardless of territory and group membership. The US Foreign Corrupt Practices Act of 1977, revised in 1988, is an example of this type of universalist approach to ethics and rules. It applies extraterritorially, that is, American anti-bribery legislation applies to American companies whenever the illegal action take place outside US territory and with foreign companies and individuals. This legislation typifies the universalist orientation of US culture. However, Foster (1995, p. 212) outlines the limitations of such a view in the following terms:

"We need to recognize that this process of developing 'universal standards' of searching for and relying on objectifiable fact, is not universal, that it is, in part, a uniquely Western process and that many other cultures neither subscribe to this world view of ethics nor have histories and traditions supportive of it. In fact, it is precisely because of the profoundly opposite world view held by traditional Asian cultures in this regard that Americans find themselves in the mystifying position of having Chinese associates 'change' contract terms on them right after they've signed the deal."

In between lies a third possible view which is a pragmatic and respectful view of how ethical behaviour can be developed in a cross-cultural context. It implies the development of a specific set of ethical concerns and attitudes related to the situation, given the legality and the legitimacy of a definite action, both of which can differ in the home and the host country. Let us call it "moral pragmatism"; it is based on the Confucian view of *Shu*, emphasizing the importance of reciprocity in establishing human relationships and the cultivation of "like-heartedness" (cf Goldman 1994; see Box 5.1) and it is concerned with the welfare of the global collectivity, directing human relationships to the betterment of the common good. It is not a strictly pragmatic perspective which would involve a somewhat cynical analysis of the effectiveness of these practices in the winning of contracts. This approach avoids the risks of the simplistic attitudes whereby illegal payments are either roundly condemned or alternatively unequivocally accepted on the basis of merely being "realistic".

Bribery is considered by most business people as the key ethical issue in international business negotiations. According to Mayo *et al.* (1991), more than one third of a sample of US executives ranked bribery as the top ethical concern out of ten possible ethical problems that may arise in international marketing operations. However, there are other ethical concerns in international business negotiations; apart from buying the contract (through bribes), a party can:

- buy information in order to get strategic insight into the other party's basic interests, situation and organization.
- buy the influence of members of the adversary negotiation team or of their principals;
- use instrumental communication to mislead the other party and gain advantage in the process, for instance by disclosing erroneous information on costs, investments, dates, etc.;
- negotiate and sign clauses which, although legal in principle, will grossly disadvantage the other party in the future (is the ignorance of the other party a reason for exploiting them?);
- negotiate, knowing in advance that they will not respect their commitments toward their partners.

In the following sections, we explain why, in our opinion, a certain ethical concern arising from international business must be appreciated with universalism, cultural relativism or moral pragmatism.

Bribery in international business negotiations

Bribery is widespread and takes various forms.

- Small and large gifts: for instance, a multinational company offers a leading foreign politician a two-week stay in a nice resort; the whole affair, including receptions, restaurants and pretty hostesses for the evenings, quickly reaches a cost of $50,000.
- Percentages based on the contract value itself. Here the form of illegal payments result in much larger sums being paid because of the size of the contract such as the sale of a turnkey plant. Indeed, in the United States, in the public disclosure of the illegal payments involving American multinationals in the 1970s, sums of up to 70 million dollars were mentioned. The companies involved were, amongst others, Lockheed, United Brands, Gulf Oil. There were many other firms implicated, principally in the mining, aeronautic and engineering sectors.
- Tips: when civil servants are poorly paid, but hold authority and responsibility, it may be "implicitly understood" that in exchange for carrying out poorly rewarded public duties, such officials may supplement their income. Thus, obtaining information for the negotiation process or a tax form for a mandatory declaration may require some backhander, which can be assimilated to an implicit salary, in as much as the authorities are perfectly well aware of the existence of such practices. In China in 1993, more than

60,000 cases of civil servant corruption were unveiled, with more than a half million people being under investigation and more than 10,000 having already been tried by a court of law (Galtung, 1994).

Whether illegal payments are made and what sums are involved varies very widely from one country and one industry to another. Bribes will be much more substantial for example, in the construction industry or in Nigeria than in electronics or in Australia. Also the important caveat must be added that not everyone is corrupt. There is nothing worse than attempting to bribe someone who strongly disapproves of such immoral behaviour. This last point is clearly illustrated by Agpar (1977) who quotes the case of the Managing Director of a large American multinational who offered 500 Saudi Rials in cash to a Saudi police officer (about 140 dollars) to ensure that a decision on a fairly minor offence against labour law would be favourable. In a fury, the officer reported the attempted bribe to his superiors. After spending 20 days in prison, the businessman was sentenced to a fine of 25,000 Rials and was fortunate to escape a more serious penalty.

The direct method of passing cash from one hand to another is dangerous and ineffective; accordingly, more indirect methods exist instead.

- Slush funds are set up to effect small payments by cheque, nominally as payment for services rendered. In the 1980s, for instance, Braniff Airlines sold 3,500 plane tickets in South America for a total of 900,000 dollars without making any record of the transactions in their accounts. This money was used to set up a slush fund that in turn fed a secret bank account. This money was neither mentioned in the parent company accounts, nor in those of the subsidiary. This secret account was used to pay additional commissions to organisers and travel agents in clear breach of the Federal Aviation Act.

- Selected and local consultancy companies, to whom "phoney" consulting contracts are given, may be used in different ways. For example, an approach may be made to an advisor of the Transport Minister for country X who is well placed to influence the decision on an underground railway project in town Y. It will be suggested that he be made a part-time employee of the Luxembourg-based selected company. Without having to move an inch, he will receive a salary each month which, for reasons of discretion and convenience, will be paid into an account in Switzerland. When going skiing with his family, the advisor/consultant will take the money out of his bank account in Geneva, then discreetly spend it in an exclusive ski-resort. Money spent abroad is less compromising than money brought back home.

- Two other solutions are frequently employed: the over-invoicing of certain transactions, expenditure or receipts, and the recording of fictitious transactions. For example, the American Hospital Supply company was obliged to pay a 10 per cent commission to obtain the contract for the construction of a hospital in Saudi Arabia. AHS artificially inflated the price of the contract, then recorded a commission for consultancy fees, even though no service of this type had been rendered. This allowed the 10 per cent commission to become tax deductible expenditure, and made the payment apparently legitimate, whereas in fact it remained illegal (Daniels *et al.* 1982).

The process of illegal payments

When analysing the process of secret payments, one may focus either on the negotiators (briber/bribed), the way their relation is sealed, the authorities to whom they report, or even the messages and style of communication they use in this sensitive and precarious business. In business negotiations, one of the basic questions is: what is this remuneration supposed to be buying? How should the "service" be defined, its price determined or, in other words, what should be the level of the baksheesh?

Another aspect centres on the individual, either the donor or the recipient of the illegal payment. People are taking risks, even sometimes risking the death penalty. Donors, as individual negotiators, are poorly rewarded for these risks as they may be prosecuted and punished, whereas their organization may win a big contract. On the other side, the reward for the recipient of the payment depends on the ultimate allocation of the money. If it goes into his own pocket, the risk-taking can be viewed from the perspective of individual interest. If the money goes into a political party's funds, it is more difficult to assess the individual risks taken. In the latter case, personal risks are minimized by the power of political influence and the lack of strictly direct and personal benefit.

Givers and takers of bribes are not isolated individuals. They work in negotiating teams and report to higher authorities. Whenever they personally request the bribe, they have to share it with other people. In turnkey contracts, both the contractor and the owner are often complex organisations which assemble hundreds of representatives of various companies, ministries, utilities and agencies, all of whom are involved in the decision making. The methods of dividing up the illegal payment within the owner's group which acquires the project is a key issue in keeping it secret. A single individual rarely receives everything, for it would be difficult to avoid this fact becoming known and disclosed because of jealousy. Anyone who could potentially exert blackmail, such as a secretary who types a compromising letter or a minister who has to sign the letter, must therefore be "paid off".

The messages will never be straightforward. At first, meta-communication between the negotiator(s)/corruptor(s) and the negotiator(s)/corrupted will serve to establish the rules of the game, and ensure that the relationships are "fair" (if fairness can ever exist in such affairs). Potential recipients may discreetly signal their willingness to be bribed by casually mentioning, with a certain emphasis, their personal acquaintances and the influence they have over them, and the information they can obtain. This will be worded softly, without once raising the subject of money. It is even explicitly stated that there is no question of any money. As a result, the offer of becoming a bribed "business agent" is implicit.

Other potential recipients will complain about the poor salary earned as a customs officer; they will further hint at a missing document, and ultimately, mention their effectiveness at granting customs clearance to goods or obtaining any kind of compulsory administrative allowance. All this constitutes an implicit call for remuneration to the business negotiators who are seeking to obtain imported equipment for the factory whose construction they are negotiating. Negotiators on the buying side may state authoritatively that they are responsible civil servants, not motivated by money, and are seeking only to select the best supplier, adding that the choice is ultimately theirs. This may be a concealed reminder to the foreign contractor of an implicit property right over the signing of the deal.

Implicit economic explanations for illegal payments

"Economic" explanations for bribery are not excuses for unacceptable practices. However, there must be some strong economic and social reasons why bribing, although unlawful, remains in existence. Verna and Usunier (1994) have developed a framework for assessing the cultural relativity of ethical conceptions. They consider both the legal and regulatory point of view (*legality*) and the acceptability in terms of social practices (*legitimacy*). Legitimacy is the quality of what is just and equitable, conforming to established standards of usage and behaviour. It helps to settle disputes more by reference to personal evaluations of the requirements of natural justice than by reliance on the strict letter of the law. The notion of legitimacy is therefore much more indistinct because it is based on individual assessments. One might expect that where the citizens of a nation share a common system of values, they would also share at least the same general conception of natural law. Natural law, with its moral underpinning, is much more suffused with conceptions of legitimacy than positive law, which is founded on the formalism of law and its different sources. In this way, we can distinguish between four categories of activity:

- "normal activities" which are both legal and legitimate;
- "unofficial activities", at the margin of legality but often legitimate: underground economy and moonlighting in developed countries, parallel economy in developing countries;
- "criminal activities" which are those that are intentionally carried out in breach of the law, and are totally devoid of legitimacy;
- "legal violence" which designates those areas where an action is legal but not legitimate: forcing the population of a district to accept a hazardous factory, certain expropriations nominally in the public interest, the export of toxic waste to Third World countries, etc.

The arguments that will be considered further contend that: (i) illegal payments constitute an implicit agency contract (normal to unofficial activity); (ii) illegal payments are related to an implicit property right when the person(s) who has (have) the final say on a contract also feel entitled to exercise this right in return for money (a form of legal violence); (iii) illegal payments are an implicit salary, that is, they are fringe benefits for poorly paid civil servants and managers, particularly in developing countries where some officials may go months without receiving their salary (unofficial to criminal activity, depending on the degree). This last situation is tolerated as long as bribes do not exceed a "fair" level. If the employees are poorly paid, but hold authority and responsibility (e.g. a police officer, a customs officer or a tax inspector) it may be implicitly understood that in exchange for carrying out poorly rewarded public duties, such officials may supplement their income. Thus when passing through customs, obtaining a tax form (for a mandatory declaration) may require the greasing of someone's palm. That can be assimilated to an implicit salary, in as much as the authorities are perfectly well aware of the existence of such practices and consider this implicit salary as justified by the low level of the official salary.

The three implicit economic explanations for illegal payments that have just been described actually correspond to the three most common bribery scenarios in international business negotiations: (i) the agent who penetrates relational networks, supplies information and exerts influences; (ii) the "dictator" in its wider sense, namely someone very important, who sells his right to award deals; (iii) small-scale everyday corruption of poorly paid (if paid) public civil servants who supplement their income by exploiting their bureaucratic power. Far from being mutually exclusive, these forms of remuneration combine to reduce social rivalries in societies where most people, on their own level, sell their personal power of influence.

Buying influence

Negotiators are often led to buy "big influence", on the signature of large contracts, rather than "small influence" which is more important when implementing such contracts. It is not rare to see the ruler of a country (e.g., a president for life or a dictator) appear almost astonished when reproached in an interview for having accumulated huge sums of money as a result of illegal payments whilst in power. Some dictators have transferred the equivalent of a large part of their country's foreign debt to foreign bank accounts (e.g., Marcos or Mobutu). Almost unconsciously, these rulers are convinced that the state belongs to them personally and often also to their family. At the very least, they implicitly hold the opinion that power entitles them to use their influence for personal enrichment.

This situation can almost be compared to one of a property right. Demsetz (1967) suggests that property rights permit individuals to know *a priori* what they can reasonably expect in their dealings with the other members of the community. He claims that these expectations manifest themselves in the laws, customs and morals of a society. In the case of international bribery, the right, originally based on customary law, therefore unwritten and implicit, consists of deriving personal profit from a position of power over the signature of public deals. Property rights should be exclusive and transferable. An exclusive right occurs when one single individual receives all the profits, but also has to bear all the adverse consequences that may arise. These rights must be assignable and transferable since the individual must be able to proceed to effective arbitrage. He must be permanently in a position to exchange property rights on efficient markets on which these rights are quoted. Except for dictators who establish a quasi-ownership over their country, rights over the signature of deals are rarely exclusive. Moreover, in most cases, these rights are not transferable, or only in a very limited way, to an heir in dictatorship (e.g., the dictator Duvalier in Haiti was succeeded by his son Jean-Claude).

To maintain such "property rights" over the signature of deals, costs have to be accepted in two areas: (i) transaction costs: in other words, the costs that must be borne to ensure respect of one's rights by others (bodyguards, secret agents, repression of enemies, elimination of economic and political opponents, etc.); (ii) costs of information: to improve the efficiency of one's property rights, each agent must personally bear a certain amount of information costs. This may even extend to paying for a sophisticated information network (i.e., spies). As far as these last two characteristics occur in international bribery, these rights are only temporarily and partially exclusive. The property right over the signature of the deal can only really be considered as subjective and implicit.

This fact leads on to two real dangers incurred by business negotiators who are led to accept the practice of making illegal payments internationally:

- letting oneself be dragged along by the megalomaniac subjectivity of an authoritative ruler who, seeing the country as his personal property, sells the right to win business there. These rights are not transferable and no dictator rules for ever.
- Property rights over the signature of deals have never been legally recognised; most countries prohibit the use of any position of authority for personal enrichment. Even when it is clear that in reality the baksheesh is a widespread practice throughout a particular society, it must not be forgotten that it is forbidden by law and, accordingly, the most stringent precautions must be taken.

Ethical universalism is best in this area. The big loser from the system of baksheesh is the recipient country. In the end it is always the recipient country that pays for the received bribes, since they are inevitably included in the full contract price. This practice provokes numerous adverse consequences such as factories or equipment that are either idle or surplus to market needs, and the discouragement of the use of purely professional skills in recipient countries where skilled professionals see their expertise poorly rewarded. As a consequence, they will spend most of their time trying to attain those political positions where illegal payments enable significant personal enrichment. When bribery is a major background topic in the negotiation process and outcome, it significantly reduces the level of commitment of the negotiators to technical quality and to the respect of standards and dates. Bribes may ultimately be powerful motivators of under-performance: for example, a technical advisor, participating to the negotiating team of the buyer, is bribed by being made a fictitious employee of a fake consultancy company situated in Luxembourg. His objective interest is that his salary should be paid for as long as possible, therefore the contract should be negotiated slowly and the factory itself should be constructed over a long period of time. Such persons may be unconcerned with adhering to deadlines, because it would terminate their bribes.

Personal connections, networking, buying information

Often in international tenders, the organisational links within the "owner" consortium are poorly defined: a state-owned utility acquires a turnkey factory, under the supervision of different ministries and banks; various consultants also intervene. The areas of responsibility of each body are in fact vaguely defined. As influences can be so diverse and relational networks so complex, someone may offer a chance to escape the labyrinth, by identifying the relevant officials, assessing the extent of their influence, and may ultimately influence them. The tasks for the potential recipient of the baksheesh may therefore include the following: (i) supplying the briber with confidential information on the client organisation; (ii) supplying the briber with information on the competitors (warning: the recipient, or the one who is tantalised by the prospect of a baksheesh, may be a double agent!); (iii) manipulation: he/she can spread false information to the briber's benefit, so as to discredit a competitor. He may even seek to cloud the issue so that the imminent signature of the contract with a competing company can be avoided; (iv) implement baksheesh redistribution: by sharing out part of the illegal payment he/she can influence the necessary authorities or a certain decision.

The originators of the agency theory, Jensen and Meckling (1976), define the agency relationship as a contract in which one (or more) person(s) make(s) use of the services of another person to accomplish some task. This involves a delegation of decision-making from the principal to the agent. Agency costs arise in every situation where principal-agent cooperation is involved, even if the principal-agent relationship is not clearly defined. Originally, agency theory was applied to rather different relationships, mainly those between shareholders and the managerial teams which govern businesses they do not own. It rests on two behavioural hypotheses: (i) everyone acts so as to maximise his or her own utility function (in our case this can realistically be assumed to be true); (ii) everyone is capable of rationally calculating the impact of agency relationships on the future value of his personal wealth.

Although the recipient of the baksheesh will inevitably act fairly rationally by balancing high risk against high return, the donor (e.g. the executive of an engineering company) has to offset high risk against low return. He/she may simply be fulfilling his/her role in the company hierarchy (obeying his/her superiors), or acting out certain fears (precisely that failure to win the contract will result in him/her losing his/her job). These attitudes are not always based on purely rational criteria.

Agent–principal relationships can give rise to opportunistic behaviour. Each individual may seek to extract personal profit from any flaws in the contracts. These flaws will be very major in our case, since the "contracts of bribery" are never written down. It is not unheard of for baksheesh to be given to intermediaries without the contract being ultimately won. The risks thereby incurred when hiring an agent necessitate that one of the principal areas of expenditure in agency costs will relate to control of the agent. There must be some incentive for him to succeed and some measures of retaliation against him, should he fail to achieve his set objectives. Such retaliation has sometimes extended, in extreme cases, as far as hiring a paid assassin and making the agent aware of this. Conversely, a bonus on the signature of the deal may dissuade the agent from opportunism.

That also means that the commission must be paid at the last possible moment, once the signature of the deal is imminent and the selection of the final contracting party is effectively decided and cannot be changed. Games akin to hide-and-seek will often be played between the contractor and his agent in this final stage. As a result, it may be worth considering an extension of the agency relationship. Providing for the continuation of the relationship after the signature of the deal will ensure that the agent has an interest in carefully controlling his behaviour in the hope of future gains.

These issues of personal connections, networking, buying information and hiring agents and intermediaries for smoothing the negotiation process is an area where cultural relativism can be used to a large extent. However, moral pragmatism is better in any circumstance where things are intentionally hidden, suggesting that even local people are not certain about the legitimacy of what they do. Nepotism, for instance, which is considered evil in some places may be normal, and even necessary, in others, because of difference in the level of ingroup orientation (Triandis 1983, 1994). Any society combines, to various degrees, ingroup and outgroup orientation and organizes them around specific patterns. The ingroup bonds involve relationships of loyalty which can be based on kinship or patronage. The concrete virtue manifested in loyalty is maintaining allegiance, even in the face of conflicts with other members of the ingroup or when experiencing unfair treatment from the most powerful members.

Strong ingroup orientation increases loyalty as an insider but decreases at the same time, the feeling of obligation towards outsiders. Morality is space-related. It might, for instance, be considered as perfectly virtuous to lie to or steal from people to whom no loyalty is owed. The "mafia" is a good illustration of an ingroup-oriented society. Morality is based on a set of values favouring strict loyalty, treason being punished by the death sentence; the godfather who has ordered it goes to the burial ceremony because he still "loves" the betrayer. Ingroup versus outgroup orientations have a deep influence on the actual system of ethics and morality in a particular society. Impersonal rules applied by judges to people, regardless of their affiliation, is typical of low ingroup orientation. Outgroup orientation values universal rules, applied to everybody: human rights ethics are a typical feature of outgroup orientation. Objectivity and reciprocity are preferred above loyalty; or stated differently: loyalty is not to the group, not to people, but to the impersonal rules and values that govern the society as a whole, that is, largely "personalization" (people-orientation) versus "depersonalization" (rule-orientation). These differences have a major impact on international business negotiations and personal selling: how to make contacts? What information is required if we are to understand connections between people facing our negotiation team? How are decisions made in a particular negotiation group? Etc.

Gifts and bribes

Often in international business negotiations, the seller's team (in an export or a turnkey contract) or the party who has initiated the deal (the foreign partner in a joint venture) may find it useful and pleasant to offer gifts to their negotiation partners at the first meeting. It may make sense especially if they are hosted by their partners who spend time and effort accommodating them comfortably. Gifts are part of universal traditions of courtesy.

However, the border between gift and bribe is obviously not a very clear one; for instance: are twelve bottles of Champagne or a cask of Bordeaux wine — worth $250 — a gift or a bribe? Small gifts, say less than $50, are not considered as bribes in most contexts, but they can also be perceived as somewhat ridiculous presents, that is, offensive to receivers, their small size possibly suggesting a lack of true commitment towards and even disdain of, the receiver(s). Another area of difference is whether gifts are products or services. Gifts such as a sea cruise around the world or a paid ski holiday are generally more difficult to put into the "bribe" category. There is no direct money involved (it is paid for) or physical gift implied, although the receiver of this real bribe would have had to pay several thousand dollars for the trip.

To try and define a border between gift and bribe, it is necessary to list basic criteria for distinction:

1. *size*: obviously the larger the gift the more it tends to become a bribe; FCPA, for instance, allows gifts of small value as well as "lubrication payments";
2. *intent:* a gift is not meant to be made in exchange for a favour whereas a bribe compensates for illegal action; a gift takes place within a legal transaction whereas a bribe takes place within an illegal transaction (the favour traded is not for sale, neither legally nor morally); intentionality is a basic element of the bribing process, either on the donor's or the receiver's side;
3. who is the *recipient*? A bribe given to a head of state for a turnkey deal cannot be directly compared with that given to a custom officer for easing the custom process or obtaining a visa;

4. *nature* of the "object" being given (tangible versus intangible) — as noted above, intangible gifts, offering travel, favours to relatives or near acquaintances, etc. — are more difficult to consider as bribes, although they may be just as much so as tangibles;

5. *circumstances* in which the gift is given; if openly done, in official and public circumstances, it is less likely to be perceived as a bribe and more as a gift, than if the whole process is secret and hidden;

6. degree and nature of *reciprocity*: is there any reciprocation, that is, after receiving a gift a party reciprocates by giving a *fairly similar gift* later on to the initial giver? In the case of a bribe, there is no such reciprocation: money is given in exchange for various services such as key information, the awarding of contracts, etc., which are not of the same kind. Reciprocation for gifts very often takes places instantly by the practice of return gifts;

7. existence of a legal definition of *business gifts* (*cadeaux d'affaires*), that is the size and nature of gifts legally permitted to be given by companies to their customers, especially those who underwrite contracts;

8. *local customs:* in some countries, traditional gift economy is still very strong; for instance, in Japan gift rituals remain central in social life;

9. "*Poisonous gifts*" are a very special case. In order to be able to exert pressure on a person, the briber sends a gift to somebody who has not asked for bribes or gifts and feel embarrassed by the "gift". The receiver is surprised and cannot complain about having received it, because he/she would be under even more suspicion of having asked for it.

The border is obviously difficult to define: a universalist perspective must be avoided in judging such matters and moral pragmatism must be adopted instead. A maximum amount of legally-defined donation is probably the most operational solution, if it exists locally and if it is realistic enough to be respected.

Ethical aspects of disclosing information to the other party

There are various ways to reach outcomes in negotiation by manipulating the other party: (i) spreading intentionally false information (highly instrumental communication in the sense of Angelmar and Stern 1978), for instance, a seller's negotiation team that incidentally discloses alleged technical problems experienced by a well-placed competitor; (ii) hiding key information (e.g., a new technology is about to make totally obsolete the patent for which a licensing agreement is now being negotiated); (iii) falsifying information, that is, willingly alter figures, data, information in order to influence the other party's decision-making process; (iv) putting pressure on the other party by invoking false arguments ("our new Chief Executive Officer will be under pressure from the shareholders and will be obliged to refuse such deals: sign now or it will be too late!").

Taken at first glance, all these tactics seem to be unethical from a universalist point of view. However they are used in actual international business negotiations, at least on the fringe, because the true reality is never so clear-cut. When the (future) buyer states that one of your competitors is ready to offer the same performance for a price 10 per cent lower, it is quite difficult to check whether it is a pure lie, a simple bluff or a slightly transformed truth. As we have seen in Part II of this book, different cultures do not value to the same degree the very notions of honesty and sincerity, especially when it relates to information exchange. Americans value the exchange of representative information as a key to trust-building between the parties. Many other people do not and, for them, cheating a little bit — with words — is acceptable even between good business partners. That is why cultural relativism is necessary in this area.

An important aspect of information disclosure is who asks for it. There is an ethic of asking questions and giving answers in international business negotiations. Issues have to be addressed such as: (i) Is it fair to ask any question of the other party including questions which would involve the disclosure of proprietary information? (ii) Consequently, does it make sense to feel obliged to give answers to any question? The answer to both questions is obviously "No". However, one should be aware that there is always less ethical pressure on asking questions than on responding to them and people who value sincerity and talking can be unfairly exploited by partners who mostly ask questions. Cohen (1980 p. 103) phrases it in the following way:

> Some of us assume that the more intimidating or flawless we appear to others, the more they will tell us. Actually, the opposite is true. The more confused and defenseless you seem, the more readily they will help you with information and advice... With this approach you will find it easy to listen more than talk. You should prefer asking questions to giving answers. In fact, you ask questions even when you think you know the answers, because, by doing so, you test the credibility of the other side.

Commitment ethics

Commitment is a wide area of ethics of business negotiations, dealing not so much with the process itself but with what follows, that is, the real outcomes after the contract has been implemented. As explained in earlier chapters of this book, cultural relativism in this area is absolutely necessary. It is better to discuss as early as possible the common views about what commitment means in certain areas. A number of areas of commitment must be considered flexibly although firmly.

- Time commitments (deadlines, delay, delivery dates, common planning etc.); ethics in this field must be agreed upon more or less during the negotiation process and not be discovered too late; since attitudes toward time differ, delivery dates, construction time and the treatment of possible delays have to be considered with a view on how both parties can be *jointly* committed.

- Sticking to clauses: the renegotiation of clauses may seem normal to a party and an outright violation of one's signature to the other party.
- Escaping responsibilities by using the argument of exceptional circumstances, a change of government or something similar; not fulfilling obligations in terms of payments, penalty clauses, etc. Unless this is clearly forecasted in a *force majeure* clause or a hardship clause, this leads to an ethical issue.
- The ethics of words and deeds: "Do I say what I do and do I do what I say?", that is, the kind of link which is established by each party between its speech and promises and its real commitment towards the other party and the fulfilment of its obligations.

Moral pragmatism in this area is also necessary as a complement to cultural relativism: a party may exploit the other party by using the argument of its alleged "difference" in order to gain advantage after the contract has been signed. Although some flexibility with the letter of the contract is obviously needed (because there are always loopholes and minor inconsistencies even in the best drafted contracts), a party which does not stick to its obligations must in some way be forced to do so. A way to find adequate corrective measures is discreetly to take local advice about what happens locally when a company, an individual or a sponsor does not fulfil a certain part of its commitments: how is the issue raised and addressed, how is the conflict managed and what are the preferred ways to solution? Who are possible intermediaries for problem solving?

Some recommendations for action

1. Do not propose (as a negotiator on the seller's side) bribes: not only is this contrary to universal principles, but this actually has adverse consequences for the bribe-recipients' country, while also not being a normal way of winning business.
2. If asked for a bribe by the other party, you have to decide with your company whether this should be included in the (backstage) negotiation process or not; as an individual negotiator, always keep in mind that: (i) this is illegal; (ii) profits are for the bribing organization and not for the individual briber who takes considerable personal risks.
3. Remember that the ethical issue in international business negotiations is both organizational and personal (companies never go to jail whereas negotiators may be jailed).
4. Do not try to win over competitors by offering a larger bribe to a greedy buyer. This just feeds the "inflation" of bribes.
5. "Lubrication" payments can be acceptable provided that the gift does not unduly border on a bribe.
6. Do not confuse real ethical issues with a misled view of your partner's honesty, due principally to cultural and communication misunderstandings.

References

ABRAMS, S. T. *et al.* (1994) "Game theory" in Zartman, ed. *International Multilateral Negotiation* Jossey-Bass.

ACUFF, F. (1992) *How to Negotiate Anything Anywhere* Amacom, New York.

ADLER, N. J. (1980) "Cultural synergy: the management of cross-cultural organizations" in Burke W. W. and Goodstein L. D. (eds) *Trends and Issues in OD: Current theory and practice* pp.163–84 University Associates: San Diego, CA.

ADLER, N. J. (1986) *International Dimensions of Organizational Behavior* PWS-Kent: Boston.

ADLER, N. J., BRAHM, R. and GRAHAM, J. L. (1992) "Strategy implementation: A Comparison of Face-to-Face Negotiations in the People's Republic of China and the United States" *Strategic Management Journal* vol. 13, no. 6, pp. 449–66.

ADLER, N. J. and GRAHAM, J. L. (1989) "Cross-cultural comparison: The international comparison fallacy" *Journal of International Business Studies* vol. xx, no. 3, pp. 515–37.

ADLER, N. J., GRAHAM, J. L. and SCHWARZ-GEHRKE, T. (1987) "Business negotiations in Canada, Mexico and the United States" *Journal of Business Research* vol. 15, pp. 411–29.

AGPAR, M. (1977) "Succeeding in Saudi Arabia" *Harvard Business Review* January/February, App. 14–33.

AHMED, M. M. (1993) *International Marketing and Purchasing of Projects : Interactions and Paradoxes* The Swedish School of Economics and Business Administration, Helsinki.

ALLISON, G. T. (1971) *Essence of decision* Little, Brown and Co. Boston.

ALLIX-DESFAUTAUX, E. (1994) *Le processus des négociacions d'affaires internationales face aux comportements opportunistes des acteurs : une approche exploratoire par la théorie des coûts de transaction* no. 46, W. P. IAE de Caen.

ANGELMAR, R. and STERN, L. W (1978) "Development of a content analysis scheme for analysis of bargaining communication in marketing" *Journal of Marketing Research* vol. 15, February, pp. 93–102.

ANSLINGER, P. and COPELAND, T. (1996) "Growth Through Acquisitions: A Fresh Look" *Harvard Business Review*, 1/1996: 126–35.

ANSOFF, H. I. (1979) *Strategic Management* John Wiley & Sons, New York.

APASU, Y., ICHIKAWA, S. and GRAHAM, J. (1987) "Corporate Culture and Sales Force Management in Japan and America" *Journal of Personal Selling & Sales Management* vol. 7, no. 3, pp. 51–62.

ATTALI, J. (1982) *Histoires du Temps* Librairie Arthème Fayard, Paris.

AUDEBERT, P. (1995) *Profession Négociateur* Editions d'Organisation.

AXELROD, R. (1984) *The Evolution of Cooperation* Basic Books, New York.

AXELROD, R. (1992) *Donnant - Donnant, Théorie du comportement coopératif.* Jacob, Paris. Traduit de *The Evolution of Cooperation* (1984), Basic Books, New York.

BACHARACH, S. and LAWLER, E. (1980) *Power and politics in organisations* Jossey-Bass Publishers.

BALENBOIS, T. (1981) "Le marketing et l'exportation d'équipements lourds" *Direction et Gestion*, no. 6, pp. 54–62.

References

BALLON, R. J. (1987) "Japan: The government-business relationship" in Tung R. L. (ed.) *Strategic Management in the United States and Japan: A Comparative Analysis* Ballinger: 3–14 Cambridge, Ma.

BARTLETT, C. H. and GHOSHAL, S. (1989) *Managing Across Borders* Harvard Business School Press, Boston.

BARTLETT, S. (1989) "A vicious circle keeps Latin America in debt" *New York Times*, January 15: E5.

BARTOS, O. J. (1974) *Process and Outcome of negotiation* Columbia University Press.

BAZERMAN, M. and NEALE, M. (1992) *Negotiating rationally* The Free Press. New York.

BEAMISH, P. W. and INKPEN, A. C. (1995) "Keeping International Joint Ventures Stable and Profitable" *Long Range Planning* vol. 28, no. 3, pp. 26–36.

BEAUFORT, V. de (1994) *Acquérir une Enterprise en Europe* Editions Comptables Malesherbes, ANCE, Paris.

BEAUFORT, V. de (1995a) "L'acquisition d'une entreprise: Outil d'un développement a l'échelle européenne" *Cahiers Juridiques et Fiscaux de l'Exportation*, 3/95: 521–7.

BEAUFORT, V. de (1995b) *L'acquisition des sociétés en Suède* working paper, ESSEC.

BECKERS, L. (1989) "Post Acquisition, Post Merger, and Post Restructuring Consequences" RDAI, 4–5/1989 pp. 441–65.

BELIAEV, E., MULLEN, T. and PUNNET, J. P. (1985) "Understanding the Cultural Environment: U.S.–U.S.S.R. Trade Negotiations" *California Management Review*, vol. XXVII, no. 2, pp. 100–12.

BELK, R. W. and COON, G. S. (1993) "Gift Giving as Agapic Love: An Alternative to the Exchange Paradigm Based on Dating Experience" *Journal of Consumer Research* vol. 20, December, pp. 393–417.

BENNETT, D. C. and SHARPE, K. E. (1979) "Agenda-setting and bargaining power: The Mexican state versus transnational automobile corporations" *World Politics*, October: 57–89.

BENNETT, D. C. and SHARPE, K. E. (1985) *Transnational corporations versus the state* Princeton University Press, Princeton.

BERKO, R. M., WOLVIN, A. D. and CURTIS, R. (1980) *This Business of Communicating* Wm. C. Brown Company Publishers, Dubuque, Iowa.

BISTA, D. B. (1990) *Fatalism and Development* Orient Longman, Calcutta.

BJORKMAN, I. and KOCK, S. (1995) "Social Relationships and Business Networks: the Case of Western Companies in China" *International Business Review* vol. 4, no. 4, pp. 519–35.

BOND, M. H. (1987) "Chinese Values and the Search for Culture-Free Dimensions of Culture: The Chinese Culture Connection" *Journal of Cross-Cultural Psychology*.

BOOZ-ALLEN ACQUISITIONS SERVICES (1989) *Study on Obstacles to Takeovers Bids in the European Community*. Study for the DGXV.

BRADLEY, P. H. and BAIRD, J. E. jr (1980) *Communication for Business and the Professions* Wm. C. Brown Company Publishers, Dubuque, Iowa.

BRAKE, T., WALKER, D. and WALKER, T. (1995) *Doing Business Internationally ; The Guide to Cross-Cultural Success* Irwin, Burr Ridge, Illinois.

BROUTHERS, K. D., BROUTHERS, L. E. and WILKINSON, T. (1955) "Strategic Alliances: Choose Your Partners" in *Long Range Planning*, vol. 28, no. 3, pp. 18–25.

BUCKLEY, P. and GHAURI, P. (1994) *The Economics of Change in East and Central Europe: Its Impact on International Markets* Academic Press, London.

BURT, D. N. (1984) "The nuances of negotiating overseas" *Journal of Purchasing and Materials Management* (Winter), pp. 2–8.

BUSINESS INTERNATIONAL (1985a) "IBM in Mexico: The real changes that the PC will make" *Business Latin America*, August 21 pp. 265–7.

BUSINESS INTERNATIONAL (1985b) "IBM in Mexico: What the 'rejection' means for other firms" *Business Latin America*, February 6 pp. 41–3.

Business Week (1981) "No. 1's awesome strategy" June 8 p. 85.

Business Week (1983) "Why Apple wants a Mexican branch" June 13 p. 51.

Business Week (1984a) "Why an IBM PC plant is stalled at the border" August 6 p. 35.

Business Week (1984b) "Will Mexico make it?" October 1 pp. 74–88.

Business Week (1985) "A fire sale in personal computers" March 25 pp. 28–9.

CAMPBELL, N. C. G., GRAHAM, J. L., JOLIBERT, A. and MEISSNER, H. G. (1988) "Marketing negotiations in France, Germany, the United Kingdom and United States" *Journal of Marketing*, vol. 52, April, pp. 49–62.

CASSE, P. (1994) "Revisiting Communication: A 'New Way' to Manage It" *European Management Journal* vol. 12, no. 3 pp. 253–9.

CATEORA, P. R. (1993) *International Marketing* 8th edn, Richard D. Irwin, Homewood, IL.

CATHELINEAU, M. (1991) *Négocier gagnant* Interéditions.

CAVUSGIL, S. T. and GHAURI, P. N. (1990) *Doing Business in Developing Countries: Entry and Negotiation Strategies* Routledge, London.

CAVUSGIL, S. T., GHAURI, P. N. and AGGARWAL, M. (1992) *Doing Business in Emerging Markets* Addison & Wesley (forthcoming) London.

CHINESE CULTURE CONNECTION (1987) "Chinese values and the search for culture-free dimensions of culture", *Journal of Cross-Cultural Psychology* vol. 18, no. 2 (June), pp. 143–64.

CLARK, K. (1985) "Prospects for high-tech growth in Mexico fuel computer company objectives, boss says" *Mexico City News* September 26 pp. 23–4.

CLARK, T. (1990) "International Marketing and National Character: A Review and Proposal for an Integrative Theory" *Journal of Marketing*, vol. 54, no. 4, pp. 66–79.

CLINE, W. R. (1987) *Informatics and development: Trade and industrial policy in Argentina, Brazil, and Mexico* Economics International, Inc. Washington, D.C.

CNUCED (1978) "Monograph on the transfer of technology at Boccaro Plant, Geneva" *CNUCED/UNCTAD* TD/B/C 6/27.

COHEN, H. (1980) *You Can Negotiate Anything* Bantam, New York.

COLOMBO, M. and MARIOTTI, S. (1995) "Fusions et acquisitions transnationales: Avantages des entreprises européennes" in Noel *et al.* (eds) *Perspectives en Management stratégique* Economica, Paris.

CONOLLY, S. G. (1984) "Joint Ventures with Third World Multinationals: a New Form to Entry to International Markets" *Columbia Journal of World Business* vol. 19, no. 2 pp. 18–22.

CONTRACTOR, F. J. and LORANGE, P. (1988) *Cooperative Strategies in International Business; Joint Ventures and Technology Partnerships between Firms* Lexington Books, Lexington MA.

COOPERS and LYBRAND (1989) *Barriers to Takeovers in the European Community* Department of Trade and Industry, vol. 1–3, London.

COOPERS and LYBRAND (1995) *Joint-Ventures : étude internationale de l'experience des entreprises, et Guide pour une joint-venture réussie* 32 rue Guersant, 75017 Paris.

COPELAND, L. and GRIGGS, L. (1986) *Going International* Plume Books/New American Library; New York.

COPELAND, M. J. (1987) "International Training" in *Training and Development Handbook*, Craig, R. L. ed. McGraw-Hill Book Company, p. 1717–25, New York.

COPELAND, M. J. (1988) "Cross-Cultural Dynamics in the Workplace" presentation for Procter & Gamble Managers (December) Istanbul, Turkey.

COPELAND, M. J. (1983) "Managing in a Multicultural Workplace" presentation delivered for Procter & Gamble Managers (June) Hong Kong.

CORIAT, B. and WEINSTEIN, O. (1995) *Les nouvelles théories de l'entreprise* Librairie générale française, Références, Paris.

COVA, B. and HOLSTIUS, K. (1993) "How to Create Competitive Advantage in Project Business" *Journal of Marketing Management* March-April, 9.2, pp. 105–21.

References

COVA, B., MAZET, F. and SALLE, R. (1993) "Towards Flexible Anticipation: the Challenge of Project Marketing" in Baker M. J. (ed.) *Perspectives on Marketing Management*, vol. 3, John Wiley & Sons, pp. 375–400, Chichester.

COVA, B., MAZET, F. and SALLE, R. (1994) "From Competitive Tendering to Strategic Marketing: An Inductive Approach to Theory-Building" *Journal of Strategic Marketing*, vol. 2, pp. 1–19.

COVA, B., MAZET, F. and SALLE, R. (1995) "The Concept of Milieu: In Search of Network Boundaries" proceedings of the 11th IMP Conference, Sept. Manchester.

COVEY, S. and COVEY, R. (1989) *The 7 Habits of Highly Effective People* Simon & Schuster, New York.

CROSS, J. G. (1969) *The economics of bargaining* Basic Books.

CROZIER, M. and FRIEDBERG, E. (1977) *L'acteur et le système* Seuil, Paris.

DANIELS, J. D., OGRAM, E. W. and RADEBAUGH, L. H. (1982) *International Business: Environments and Operations* 3rd edn, Addison-Wesley, Reading, Ma.

DANIELS, J. D. and RADEBAUGH, L. H. (1995) *International Business: Environments and Operations* 7th edn, Addison, Reading, Mass.

DAVID, R. (1987) *Le Droit du commerce international, réflexions d'un comparatiste sur le droit international privé* Economica: Paris.

DE JONQUIERES, G. (1984) "IMB, E.C. settle competition case" *Europe* September/October pp. 18–19.

DE LA MADRID, H. M. (1984) "Mexico: The new challenges" *Foreign Affairs* Fall pp. 62–76.

DE LA TORRE, J. (1981) "Foreign investment and economic development: Conflict and negotiation" *Journal of International Business Studies* Fall pp. 9–32.

DE MENTE, B. (1987) *How to do Business with the Japanese* N.T.C. Publishing, Chicago, IL.

DEAL, T. and KENNEDY, A. A. (1982) *Corporate Culture* Addison-Wesley Publishing Company, Reading.

DEMSETZ, H. (1967) "Toward a theory of Property Rights" *American Economic Review* vol. 57, May, pp. 347–59.

DESHPANDE, R. and PARASURAMAN, A. (1986) "Linking Corporate Culture to Strategic Planning" *Business Horizons* vol. 29, no. 3, pp. 28–37.

DESHPANDE, R. and WEBSTER, F. jr (1989) "Organizational Culture and Marketing: Defining the Research Agenda" *Journal of Marketing* vol. 53, no. 1, pp. 3–15.

DEUTSCH, M. (1973) *The Resolution of Conflict* Yale University Press, New Haven.

DIETL, J. (1992) "Determinants of Private Business Activities in Poland" *Journal of Business Research* 24, pp. 27–35.

DOMANSKY, T. (1992) "Development of Small Private Companies and Their Marketing Activities" *Journal of Business Research* 24, pp. 57–65.

DOWNS, C. W., BERG, D. M. and LINKUGEL, W. A. (1977) *The Organizational Communicator* Harper & Row Publishers, New York.

DOWNS, L., DOWNS, B. and TACEY, W. S. (1980) *Business and Professional Speaking* 3rd edn, Wm. C. Brown Company Publishers, Dubuque, Iowa.

DOZ, Y. L. (1980) "Strategic management in multinational companies" *Sloan Management Review*, Winter, pp. 27–46.

DRUCKMAN, D. (1977) *Negotiations* Sage Publications.

DRUCKMAN, D., BENTON, A. A., ALI, F. and BAGUR, J. S. (1976) "Culture differences in bargaining behavior" *Journal of Conflict Resolution* vol. 20, pp. 413–49.

DUNNING, J. H. (1994) "The Prospects for Foreign Direct Investment in Central and Eastern Europe" in Buckley, P. and Ghauri, P. (eds), *The Economics of Change in East and Central Europe: Its Impact on International Business* Academic Press, pp. 373–88 London.

DUPONT, C. (1995) *La négociation: conduite, théorie, applications*, 4th edn, Dalloz, Paris.

DUPONT, C. (1996) "Negotiation as coalition-building" in *International Negotiation* vol. I, no. 1, pp. 47–64.

ECONOMIST (1985a) "Mexico woos foreign investors—And rejects them" February 9, pp. C61–2.

ECONOMIST (1985b) "What big teeth" May 4, p. 15.

EGELHOFF, W. G. (1984) "Patterns of control in US, UK and European MNCs" *Journal of International Business Studies*, Fall, pp. 73–83.

EISELE, J. (1995) *Erfolgsfaktoren des Joint Venture Management* Gabler, Wiesbaden.

EITEMAN, D. K. (1990) "American executives" perceptions of negotiating joint ventures with the People's Republic of China: Lessons learned" *Columbia Journal of World Business* (Winter), pp. 59–67.

ELGSTROM, O. (1990) "Norms, Culture, and Cognitive Patterns in Foreign-Aid Negotiations" *Negotiation Journal – On the Process of Dispute Settlement* vol. 6, no. 2, pp. 147–59.

EMERSON, R. M. (1962) "Power/dependence relationship" *American Sociological Review* vol. 27, February, pp. 31–40.

ENCARNATION, D. J. and WELLS, L. T. jr (1985) "Sovereignty en garde: Negotiating with foreign investors" *International Organization*, 39(1): 47–78.

EVANS, F. B. (1963) "Selling as a dyadic relationship: A new approach" *American Behavioral Scientist* vol. 6, May, pp. 76–9.

EZER, S. (1993) *International Exporting Agreements* Matthew Bender, New York.

FABRE, P. and MAROIS, B. (1992) *Comment Acquérir une entreprise en France ou à l'étranger* Dunod, Paris.

FAGRE, N. and WELLS, L. T. jr (1982) "Bargaining power of multinationals and host governments" *Journal of International Business Studies*, Fall, 9–23.

FAUQUET, P. (1995) "Le financement du dévelopement international des PME/PMI" *Cahiers Juridiques et Fiscaux de l'Exportation*, 3/95 pp. 529–36.

FAURE, G. O. (1991) "Négociation : de la théorie au réel" in *Encyclopedia Universalis*.

FAURE, G. O. and RUBIN, J. (eds) (1993) *Culture and Negotiation* Sage, Newbury Park.

FAYERWEATHER, J. and KAPOOR, A. (1976) *Strategy and Negotiation for the International Corporation* Ballinger Pub. Co. Cambridge, Mass.

FERRARO, G. P. (1990) *The Cultural Dimension of International Business* Prentice-Hall: Englewood Cliffs, NJ.

FISHER, G. (1980) *International Negotiation: A cross-cultural perspective* p. 50 Intercultural Press: Yarmouth, Maine.

FISHER, G. (1988) *Mindsets* Intercultural Press: Yarmouth, Maine.

FISHER, R., URY, W. and PATTON, B. (1991) *Getting to Yes. Negotiating Agreement Without Giving In* Penguin, New York.

FLETCHER, K. and WHEELER, C. (1989) "Market Intelligence for International Markets" *Marketing Intelligence and Planning*, 7, 5/6, pp. 30–4.

FOSTER, D. (1995) *Bargaining Across Borders. How to Negotiate Business Successfully Anywhere in the World* McGraw-Hill, New York.

FOSTER, G. M. (1965) "Peasant society and the image of limited good" *American Anthropologist* vol. 67, pp. 293–315.

FRANK, G. (1989) "OPA: Le facteur humain est decisif" *Revue Francaise de Gestion*, 9-10/1989: pp. 98–104.

FRAZIER, S. (1984a) "Mexico lures personal computer makers but IBM tries to change rules of the game" *Wall Street Journal*, August 21: 33.

FRAZIER, S. (1984b) "Mexico to decide soon on whether to allow computer venture 100% owned by IBM" *Wall Street Journal*, October 29: 37.

FRAZIER, S. (1985a) "Mexico gambles IBM will alter plans for factory" *Wall Street Journal*, January 21: 27.

FRAZIER, S. (1985b) "Plans to expand plant in Mexico revised by IBM" *Wall Street Journal*, March 11.

FRAZIER, G. and KALE, S. (1989) "Manufacturer-Distributor Relationships: A Sellers'

References

versus Buyers' Market Perspective" *International Marketing Review*, vol. 6, no. 6, pp. 7–26.

FUENTES, C. (1986) "To see ourselves as others see us" *Time Magazine* 16 June, p. 52.

FULBRIGHT, J. W. (1979) "We're Tongue Tied" *Newsweek* 30 June, p. 15.

GALTUNG, F. (1994) *Korruption* Lamuv Verlag, Göttingen.

GALTUNG, J. (1981) "Structure, culture and intellectual style: An essay comparing Saxonic, Teutonic, Gallic and Nipponic Approaches" *Social Science Information*, vol. 20, no. 6, pp. 817–56.

GARDNER, D. (1984) "IBM seeks concessions for Mexico plant" *Financial Times*, July 20: 4.

GARRETTE, B. and DUSSAUGE, P. (1995) *Les stratégies d'alliance* Ed. d'Organisation, Paris.

GHAURI, P. (1981) "The Development of a Model for Package Deal Negotiations" Uppsala Cif, Working Paper 1981/4.

GHAURI, P. (1982) "International Business Negotiations: a Turn-Key Project" Uppsala Cif, Working Paper, 1982/5.

GHAURI, P. N. (1983) *Negotiating International Package Deals* Almqvist & Wissell, Uppsala.

GHAURI, P. N. (1986) "Guidelines for international business negotiations" *International Marketing Review*, vol. 3, no. 6, Autumn, pp. 72–82.

GHAURI, P. N. (1994) "Negotiating projects with China (PRC)" 4th Seminar of the European Network on Project Marketing and Systems Selling, 21–3 April, Pisa.

GHAURI, P. N. (1995) "Marketing to Eastern Europe" in Baker, M. J. (ed.), *Marketing Theory and Practice* London Macmillan, pp. 379–89.

GHAURI, P. N. and HOLSTIUS, K. (1996) "The role of Matching in the Foreign Market Entry Process in the Baltic States" *European Journal of Marketing* vol. 30, no. 2, pp. 75–88.

GHAURI, P. N. and JOHANSON, J. (1979) "International Package Deal Negotiations: The role of the atmosphere" *Organisation, Marknad och Samhalle*, vol. 16, no. 5, pp. 335–64.

GLADWYN, T. and WALTER, I. (1980) *Multinationals under Fire* John Wiley, New York.

GLENN, E. (1981) *Man and Mankind: conflict and communication between cultures* Ablex: Horwood, N.J.

GODBOUT, J. T. and CAILLÉ, A. (1992) *L'esprit du don* La Découverte, Paris.

GOLDMAN, A. (1994) "The Centrality of 'Ningensei' to Japanese Negotiating and Interpersonal Relationships: Implications for U.S.–Japanese Communication" *International Journal of Intercultural Relations* vol. 18, no. 1, pp. 29–54.

GOODENOUGH, W. H. (1971) *Culture, language and society* Modular Publications, no. 7, Addison-Wesley, Reading, MA.

GRAHAM, J. L. (1981) "A hidden cause of America's trade deficit with Japan" *Columbia Journal of World Business* (Fall), pp. 5–15.

GRAHAM, J. L. (1983) "Brazilian, Japanese and American business negotiations" *Journal of International Business Studies*, Spring/Summer, pp. 47–61.

GRAHAM, J. L. (1985) "Cross-cultural marketing negotiations: A laboratory experiment" *Marketing Science* vol. 4, no. 2, pp. 130–46.

GRAHAM, J. L. (1993) "Business negotiations: Generalizations about Latin America and East Asia are dangerous" *UCINSIGHT* University of California Irvine GSM, Summer, pp. 6–23.

GRAHAM, J. L. and HERBERGER, R. A. jr (1983) "Negotiators abroad: Don't shoot from the hip" *Harvard Business Review* vol. 61, no. 4, pp. 160–8.

GRAHAM, J. L., IVENKO, L. I. and RAJAN, M. N. (1992) "An empirical comparison of Soviet and American business negotiations" *Journal of International Business Studies* vol. 23, no. 3, pp. 387–418.

GRAHAM, J., KIM, D., LIN, C. and ROBINSON, M. (1988) "Buyer-Seller Negotiations Around the Pacific Rim" *Journal of Consumer Research* vol. 15, no. 1, pp. 48–54.

GRAHAM, J. L. and LIN, C. Y. (1987) "A comparison of marketing negotiations in the Republic of China (Taiwan) and the United States" in *Advances in International Marketing* vol. 2, pp. 23–46, JAI Press, Greenwich, CT.

GRAHAM, J. L. and MEISSNER, H. G. (1986) "Content analysis of business negotiations in Five countries" Working Paper, University of Southern California.

GRAHAM, J. L., MINTU, A. T. and RODGERS, W. (1994) "Explorations of Negotiation Behaviors in Ten Foreign Cultures Using a Model Developed in The United States" *Management Science*, vol. 40, no. 1 (January), pp. 72–95.

GRAHAM, J. L. and SANO, Y. (1990) *Smart bargaining: Doing business with the Japanese* 2nd edn, Ballinger: Cambridge, MA.

GRAHAM, R. J. (1981) "The role of perception of time in consumer research" *Journal of Consumer Research* vol. 7, March, pp. 335–42.

GRAYSON, G. W. (1987) "Mexico: A love-hate relationship with North America" in Binnendijk, H. ed. *National negotiating styles* USGPO.

GRIECO, J. M. (1982) "Between dependency and autonomy: India's experience with the International computer industry" *International Organisation* 36(3): 609–32.

GROSSE, R. and ARAMBURU, D. (1989) "A bargaining view of government/MNE relations" International Business & Banking Institute Paper Series no. 89–1, University of Miami.

GROUPE, E. (ed.) (1996) *Négocier: Entreprise et négociations* Ellipses, Paris.

GULLIVER, P. H. (1979) *Disputes and negotiations* Academic Press, New York.

GUNTER, B. (1986) "Risk Management in Industrial Marketing-Project-Cooperations: some Comments on Joint Risk Handling" in Backhaus, K. and Wilson, D. T. (eds) *Industrial Marketing: a German-American Perspective* pp. 274–93, Springer Verlag, Berlin.

GUREVITCH, A. J. (1976) "Time as a problem of cultural history" in Gardner, L. *et al.* (eds) *Cultures and Time: At the crossroads of cultures* Unesco Press, Paris.

HADJIKHANI, A. and HAKANSSON, H. (1995) "Connected Effects Due to Political Actions Against a Business Firm – The Case of Bofors" Proceedings of the 11th IMP Conference, Manchester.

HÂKANSSON, H. (ed.) (1982) *Industrial Marketing and Purchasing: an Interaction Approach.* John Wiley, Chichester.

HALL, E. T. (1959) *The Silent Language* Doubleday: Garden-City, NY.

HALL, E. T. (1960) "The Silent Language in Overseas Business" *Harvard Business Review*, May-June, pp. 87–96.

HALL, E. T. (1976) *Beyond Culture* Anchor Press/Doubleday: Garden City, NY.

HALL, E. T. (1981) *Beyond Culture.* Doubleday, New York.

HALL, E. T. (1983) *The Dance of Life* Anchor Press/Doubleday: Garden City, NY.

HALL, E. T. and HALL, M. R. (1987) *Hidden Differences: Doing Business with the Japanese.* Garden City, Anchor Press, New York.

HALL, R. (1984) *The International Joint Venture* Praeger, New York.

HAMPDEN-TURNER, C. and TROMPENAARS, F. (1994) *The Seven Cultures of Capitalism* Piatkus.

HARNETT, D. L. and CUMMINGS, L. L. (1980) *Bargaining Behavior: an international study* Dame Publications: Houston, TX.

HARRIS, P. R. and MORAN, R. T. (1987) *Managing Cultural Differences* 2nd edn, Gulf Publishing Company: Houston, TX.

HARRISON, G. W. and SAFFER, B. H. (1980) "Negotiating at 30 Paces" *Management Review*, April, pp. 51–4.

HARRISON, R. (1978) "Questionnaire on the Cultures of Organizations" in Handy, C. (ed.) *The Gods of Management* pp. 83–8. Souvenir, London.

HARSANYI, J. C. and SELTEN, R. (1988) *A general theory of equilibrium selection* MIT Press.

HARVARD BUSINESS SCHOOL (1984) *Note on the personal computer industry*, January, 1983.

HASPESLAGH, P. and JEMISON, D. (1991) *Managing Acquisitions. Creating Value Through Corporate Renewal* The Free Press, New York.

HAWRYSH, B. M. and ZAICHKOWSKY, J. L. (1990) "Cultural approaches to negotiations: Understanding the Japanese" *International Marketing Review* vol. 7, no. 2, pp. 28–42.

References

HAY, M. and USUNIER, J. C. (1993) "Time and Strategic Action : A Cross-Cultural View" *Time and Society* vol. 2, no. 3, (September).

HAYASHI, S. (1988) *Culture and Management in Japan* University of Tokyo Press, Tokyo.

HENDON, D. W. and HENDON, R. A. (1990) *World-Class Negotiating; Deal making in the Global Market Place* John Wiley & Sons, New York.

HERTZFELD, J. M. (1991) "Joint Ventures: Saving the Soviets from Perestroika" *Harvard Business Review*, January-February, pp. 80–91.

HOCKER, J. L. and WILMOT, W. W. (1985) *Interpersonal Conflict* 2nd edn, Wm. C. Brown Publishers, Dubuque, IA.

HOFSTEDE, G. (1980) *Culture's Consequences: International differences in work-related values* Sage Publications: Beverly Hills, CA.

HOFSTEDE, G. (1983) "Dimensions of National Cultures in Fifty Countries and Three Regions" in Deregowski, J., Dziurawiec, S. and Annis, R. C. (eds) *Expectations in Cross-Cultural Psychology* Swets & Zeitlinger, pp. 335–55, Lisse, Netherlands.

HOFSTEDE, G. (1984) "Cultural Dimensions in Management and Planning" *Asia Pacific Journal of Management* vol. 2, no. 2, pp. 81–9.

HOFSTEDE, G. (1989) "Cultural Predictors of National Negotiation Styles" in Frances Mautner-Markhof" *Processes of International Negotiations* pp. 193–201, Westview Press, Boulder, Colorado.

HOFSTEDE, G. (1991) *Cultures and Organizations: Software of the Mind* McGraw-Hill: Maidenhead, Berkshire.

HOLDEN, N. (1995) "A Diachronic View of Russian Misconceptions of Marketing" *Proceedings of the Second Conference on the Cultural Dimension of International Marketing* May 27-31, pp. 30–52, Odense.

HOLT, J. B. (1978) "Decline of U.S. computer company bargaining power in Eastern Europe" *Columbia Journal of World Business*, Fall: pp. 95–112.

HOSKINS, S. (1996) "Current Concepts in Project Marketing" unpublished MBA dissertation, Henley Management College, UK.

HYDER, S. A. and GHAURI, P. N. (1993) "Joint Venture Relationship between Swedish Firms and Developing Countries", in Buckley, P. J. and Ghauri, P. N. (eds) *Internationalisation of the Firm: A Reader* pp. 322–36, Academic Press, London.

IBM CORPORATION (1983) IBM 1983 *annual report.*

IBM MEXICO (1984) Press release (final version) 8 October, Mexico City.

IKLE, F. (1964) *How Nations Negotiate* p. 53, Praeger, New York.

INFOTEXT (1985) *The personal computer industry in Mexico: The challenge of growth* Palo Alto, Calif.

INTERNATIONAL CHAMBER OF COMMERCE (1990) *Incoterms 1990* ICC Publishing, Paris.

INTERNATIONAL M&A LAW (1991) "Euromoney Books & The International Financial Law Review".

JACOBSEN, M. P. (1983) "Mexico"s computer decree: The problem of performance requirements and a U.S. response" *Law and Policy in International Business*, 14: pp. 1159–95.

JAIN, S. and TUCKER, L. R. (1994) "Market Opportunities in Eastern Europe: MNCs Response" in Buckley, P. and Ghauri, P. (eds) *The Economics of Change in East and Central Europe: Its Impact on International Business* pp. 389–461, Academic Press, London.

JANG, S. H. (1988) "Managing joint venture partnership in Korea" paper presented at the Korea–America Business Institute, Annual Seminar on Doing Business in Korea, May 3-4.

JANSSON, H. (1989) "Marketing to Projects in South-East Asia" in Cavusgil, (ed.) *Advances in International Marketing*, 3, pp. 259–276, JAI Press, Greenwich.

JEFFREY, B. (1984) "With a little help from some friends" *Datamation* February pp. 147–50.

JENSEN, M. C. and MECKLING, W. H. (1976) "Theory of the Firm: Managerial Behavior, Agency Costs and Ownership Structure" *Journal of Financial Economists* vol. 3, October, pp. 305–60.

JOHANSON, J. and MATTSON, L. G. (1993) "Internationalization in Industrial Systems. A Network Approach" in Buckley, P. J. and Ghauri, P. N. (eds) *Internationalisation of the Firm: A Reader* Academic Press, New York.

JOLIBERT, A. (1988) "Le Contexte culturel de la négociation commerciale" *Revue Francaise de Gestion* November–December, pp. 15–24.

JONSSON, C. (1991) "Cognitive theory" in Kremenyuk, V. (1991) *International negotiation* Jossey-Bass, San Francisco.

JOY, R. O. (1989) "Cultural and Procedural Differences That Influence Business Strategies and Operations in the People's Republic of China" *SAM Advanced Management Journal* (Summer) pp. 29–33.

JUNCO, A. (1985) "Computer-hungry Mexicans vs. power-hungry bureaucrats" *Wall Street Journal*, March 22: 25.

KALE, S. (1986) "Dealer Perceptions of Manufacturer Power and Influence Strategies in a Developing Country" *Journal of Marketing Research* vol. 23, No. 4, pp. 387–93.

KALE, S. (1995) "Grouping Euroconsumers: A Culture-Based Clustering Approach" *Journal of International Marketing* vol. 3, no. 3, pp. 37–50.

KALE, S. and BARNES, J. (1992) "Understanding the Domain of Cross-National Buyer-Seller Interactions" *Journal of International Business Studies* vol. 23, no. 1, pp. 101–32.

KAO, J. (1993) "The worldwide web of Chinese business" *Harvard Business Review* (March-April) pp. 24–96.

KAPOOR, A. (1970) *International Business Negotiations: a study in India.* New York University Press, New York.

KARRASS, C. A. (1970) *The Negotiating Game* Crowell: New York.

KARRASS, C. L. (1974) *Give and Take* (p. 191) Thomas Y. Crowell, New York.

KEEGAN, W. J. (1984) *Multinational Marketing Management* Prentice Hall: Englewood Cliffs, NJ.

KEIRSEY, D. and BATES, M. (1978) *Please Understand Me: Character and Temperament Types* Prometheus Nemesis, Del Mar.

KELLEY, H. H. (1966) "A classroom study of the dilemmas in interpersonal negotiations" in Archibald, K. (ed.) *Strategic Interaction and Conflict* Institute of International Studies, University of California, Berkeley, CA.

KERDELLANT, C. (1990) "Profits ici, Pertes au-delà" *L'Entreprise*, 63/December 1990: pp. 78–9.

KINDEL, S. and TEITEIMAN, R. (1988) "The best companies of the eighties" *Financial World*, 27 December, pp. 22–30.

KIRKBRIDE, P. S., TANG, S. F. Y. and WESTWOOD, R. I. (1991) "Chinese Conflict Preferences and Negotiating Behavior – Cultural and Psychological Influences" *Organization Studies*, vol. 12, no. 3, pp. 365–86.

KISSINGER, H. (1979) *White House years* Little, Brown, Boston.

KLUCKHOHN, F. R. and STRODTBECK, F. L. (1961) *Variations in Value Orientations* Row-Peterson: Evanston, IL.

KNITTEL, B. and STEFANINI, A. (1993) "Indian Joint Venture: Les Leçons de l'Expérience" *Annales des Mines – Gérer et Comprendre* March, pp. 17–23.

KOBRIN, S. J. (1987) "Testing the bargaining hypothesis in the manufacturing sector in developing countries" *International Organization*, 41: pp. 609–38.

KOGUT, B. (1988) "A Study of the Life Cycle of Joint Ventures" in Contractor, F. J. and Lorange, P. *Cooperative Strategies in International Business; Joint Ventures and Technology Partnerships between Firms* pp. 169–198, Lexington Books, Lexington, MA.

KRALJIC, A. P. (1990) "The Economic Gap Separating East and West" *Columbia Journal of World Business* Winter, pp. 14–19.

KREMENYUK, V. (ed.) (1991) *International Negotiation* Jossey-Bass Inc. Publishers. San Francisco.

References

KUHN, R. (1988) *Deal Maker* John Wiley, New York.

LANGENSCHEIDT (1989) *Compact Dictionary French-English/English-French* by Kenneth Urwin.

LAURENT, A. (1983) "The Cultural Diversity of Western Management Conceptions" *International Studies of Management and Organization* vol. 8, no. 1, pp. 75–96.

LAX, D. A. and SIBENIUS, J. K. (1986) *The Manager as Negotiator* The Free Press, New York.

LAYNARD, R. (1995) "Four Reasons for Gloom" in *The Economist* 21 January, p. 32.

LEBAS, M. and WEIGENSTEIN, J. (1986) "Management Control: The Role of Rules, Markets, and Culture" *Journal of Management Studies* vol. 23, no. 3, pp. 259–72.

LECRAW, D. J. (1984) "Bargaining power, ownership and profitability of transnational corporation in developing countries" *Journal of International Business Studies* Spring/Summer: pp. 27–43.

LEE, J. A. (1966) "Cultural analysis in overseas operations" *Harvard Business Review* March-April, pp. 106–11.

LEFEBVRE, VICTORIA D. (1983) "Ethical features of the normative hero in Soviet children's literature of the 1960s-70s" *Studies of Cognitive Sciences* vol. 20, School of Social Sciences: Irvine, CA.

LESIKAR, R. V. and PETTIT, J. D. (1989) *Business Communications: Theory and Application* 6th edn, Irwin, Homewood, IL.

LEWICKI, R. J., LITTERER, J. A., MINTON, J. W. and SAUNDERS, D. M. (1994) *Negotiation: Readings, Exercises and Cases* 2nd edn, Irwin, Burr Ridge, IL.

LINCOLN, Y. S. and GUBA, E. G. (1985) *Naturalistic inquiry* Sage: Beverly Hills, Calif.

LINDSEY, J. (1989) *Joint Ventures and Corporate Partnerships* Probus, Chicago.

LINTON, R. (1945) *The Cultural Background of Personality* D. Appleton-Century: New York.

LINTON, R. (1947) *The Cultural Background of Personality* Appleton-Century: New York.

LITTLER, D. and LEVERICK, F. (1995) "Joint Ventures for Product Development: Learning from Experience" *Long Range Planning* vol. 28, no. 3, pp. 58–67.

LUCE, R. D. and RAIFFA, H. (1957) *Games and decisions* Wiley.

LYLES, M. A. (1994) "The Impact of Organization Learning on Joint Venture Formations" *International Business Review* vol. 3, no. 4, pp. 459–67.

McCALL, J. B. and COUSINS, J. (1990) *Communication Problem Solving: The Language of Effective Management.* John Wiley, Chichester.

McCALL, J. B. and WARRINGTON, M. B. (1990) *Marketing By Agreement: A cross-cultural approach to business negotiations* 2nd edn, John Wiley: Chichester.

McCARTHY, W. (1991) "*The role of power and principle in 'getting to yes'*" in Brislin, J. W. and Rubin, J. Z. *Negotiation theory and practice* Harvard Law School.

McINTYRE, R. and KALE, S. (1988) "Buyer-Seller Productivity and Economic Development" *Journal of Macromarketing* vol. 8, no. 2, pp. 15–28.

McKENNA, R. (1995) "Real-Time Marketing" *Harvard Business Review* July-August, pp. 87–95.

MacMILLAN, I. C. (1978) *Strategy Formulation: Political Concepts* West Publishing, New York.

MAGENAU, J. M. and PRUITT, D. G. (1979) "The Social Psychology of Bargaining" in Stephenson, G. M. and Brotherton, C. J. (eds) *Industrial Relations: A Psychological Approach* John Wiley, Chichester.

MARBACH, W. D. *et al.* (1983) "The giant takes command" *Newsweek* July 11: pp. 38–40.

MARCH, R. M. (1982) "Business Negotiation as Cross-Cultural Communication: The Japanese Western Case" *Cross Currents* 9, 1 (Spring).

MARTINEZ, E. G. (1984) "Capital: IBM threatens Miguel de la Madrid's government" [translation] *Excelsior* September 27.

MASTENBROEK, W. (1989) *Negotiate* Basic Blackwell.

MATSUMOTO, M. (1988) *The unspoken way: Haragei – silence in Japanese business and society* Kodansha International, New York.

MATTHEWS, H. L., WILSON, D. T. and MONOKY, J. F. jr (1972) "Bargaining behavior in a Buyer-Seller Dyad" *Journal of Marketing Research* vol. 9, February, pp. 103–5.

MATTSSON, L. G. (1985) "An Application of Network Theory to Marketing: Defending and Changing Market Position" in Dholakia, N. and Arndt, J. (eds) *Changing the Course of Marketing: Alternative Paradigms for Widening Marketing Theory. Research in Marketing, Suppl.* 2, pp. 263–288, JAI Press, Greenwich.

MAYO, M. A., MARKS, L. J. and RYANS, J. K. jr (1991) "Perceptions of Ethical Problems in International Marketing" *International Marketing Review* vol. 8, no. 3, 61–75.

M'BITI, J. (1968) "African concept of time" *Africa Theological Journal*, 1, pp. 8–20.

MEISLIN, R. J. (1984) "I.B.M. deal on Mexico seen" *New York Times*, October p. 26: D1-D3.

MEISLIN, R. J. (1985a) "Mexico in reversal, to let I.B.M. build and own a computer plant" *New York Times*, July 24: A1.

MEISLIN, R. J. (1985b) "Mexico rejects I.B.M. control for new plant" *New York Times*, January 19: 1.

MEXICAN EMBASSY in the U.S.A. (MEU) (198) *$600 million export boost seen; IBM investment "vote of confidence"* Press release, February 4.

MICHAELS, J. S. (1984) "IBM mounts publicity drive in Brazil, hoping computer restrictions will end" *Wall Street Journal*, January 13: 27.

MILLER, D. L. (1986) "Mexico" in Rushing, F. W. and Brown, C. G. (eds) *National policies for developing high technology industries: International comparisons.* Westview Press, Boulder, Col.

MILLER, S. (1987) *Painted in Blood: Understanding Europeans* Atheneum, New York.

MINTZBERG, H. (1991) "Five Ps for Strategy" in Mintzberg, H. and Quinn, J. B. (eds) *The Strategy Process: Concepts, Contexts, Cases* 2nd edn Prentice Hall, Englewood Cliffs.

MNOOKIN, R., PEPPET, S. and TULUMELLO, D. (1995b) *Bargaining In the Shadow of the Law: The Lawyer As Negotiator* (forthcoming).

MNOOKIN, R. and ROSS, L. (1995a) "Introduction" in Arrow, K., Mnookin, R., Ross, L., Tversky, A. and Wilson, R. (eds) *Barriers to Conflict Resolution* Norton, New York.

MNOOKIN, R. and WILSON, R. (1989) "Rational Bargaining and Market Efficiency: Understanding *Pennzoil v. Texaco. Virginia Law Review* 75/1989: pp. 295–334.

MONTES, C. (1985) "Actions and reactions: Definitions around IBM's project" [translation]. *El Financiero*, July 30.

MORTENSON, E. A. (1992) "Business Opportunities in the Pacific Rim for Americans in Small Business: The Importance of Cultural Differences in Doing Business" in *1992 Conference on U.S. Competitiveness in the Global Marketplace* Braaten, D. O. and Anders, G. (eds) Thunderbird Publishing Group, Phoenix.

MUNA, F. A. (1980) *The Arab Executive* Macmillan, Basingstoke.

NADEL, J. (1987) *Cracking the Global Market* pp. 89–116, Amacom, New York.

NAKANE, C. (1970) *Japanese society* University of California Press, Berkeley, CA.

NANDA, A. and WILLIAMSON, P. J. (1995) "Use Joint Ventures to Ease the Pain of Restructuring" in *Harvard Business Review* vol. 73, no. 6, pp. 119–28.

NAOR, J. (1986) "Towards a Socialist Marketing Concept – The Case of Romania" *Journal of Marketing* vol. 50 (January), pp. 28–39.

NASH, J. F. (1950) *The bargaining problem* in *Econometrica* 18; pp. 155–62.

NEW YORK TIMES (City Edition) (1984a) "Mexico bar on I.B.M. seen" 28 November.

NEW YORK TIMES (1984b) "Mexico says I.B.M. plant is permissible" 28 November D8.

NEW YORK TIMES (1985) "The daunting power of I.B.M." 20 January E1.

NEWMAN, L. R. (1989) "Acquisition in Europe" in Bibler, R. (ed.) *The Arthur Young Management Guide to Mergers and Acquisitions* John Wiley & Sons, New York.

NOER, D. M. (1975) *Multination People Management* Bureau of National Affairs, Washington, DC.

OH, T. K. (1984) "Selling to the Japanese" *Nation's Business*, October, pp. 37–8.

OLLIVIER, A. and DE MARICOURT, R. (1990) *Pratique du marketing en Afrique* Edicef/Aupelf: Paris.

References

ORIEUX, J. (1970) *Talleyrand* Flammarion.

PEAR, R. (1990) "Jobless to Soar in East CIA Says" *New York Times* 17 May p. A6.

PEN, J. (1952) "A general theory of bargaining" in *American Economic Review* 42; pp. 24–42.

PEREZ, M. (1995) "Acquérir une entreprise: Obtenir, évaluer, auditer l'information financière" *Cahiers Juridiques et Fiscaux de l'Exportation*, 3/95: 547–57.

PERKINS, A. G. (1993) "Diversity" *Harvard Business Review* (September–October), p. 14.

PETERS, T. and WATERMAN, R. (1982) *In Search of Excellence* Harper & Row, New York.

PHILIPPS-MARTINSSON, J. (1981) *Swedes as Others See Them: Fact, Myth or Communication Complex* Affars Forlaget, Stockholm.

PLANTEY, A. (1994) *La négociation internationale. Principes et méthodes* (2nd edn) Editions du CNRS. Paris.

PONSSARD, J. P. (1977) *Logique de la négociation et théorie des jeux.* Les Editions d'Organisation.

PORTER, M. (1985) *Competitive Advantage; Creating and Sustaining Superior Performance* The Free Press, New York.

PORTER, M. (1990) *The Competitive Advantage of Nations* Macmillan, London.

POULAIN DE SAINT-PÈRE, A. (1995) "Acquérir une entreprise: Négocier et contracter" *Cahiers Juridiques et Fiscaux de l'Exportation*, 3/95: pp. 537–46.

PRAHALAD, C. K. and DOZ, Y. L. (1981) "An approach to strategic control in MNCs" *Sloan Management Review*, Summer: 5–13.

PRATT, J. W. and ZECKHAUSER (eds) (1985) *Principals and Agents: The Structure of Business* Harvard Business School Press, Boston.

PRUITT, D. G. (1981) *Bargaining Behavior* Academic Press, New York.

PRUITT, D. G. (1983) "Strategic choice in negotiation" *American Behavioral Scientist* vol. 27, no. 2, pp. 167–94.

PRUITT, D. G. and LEWIS, S. A. (1975) "Development of integrative solutions in bilateral negotiations" *Journal of Personality and Social Psychology* vol. 31, no. 4, pp. 621–33.

PRUITT, D. G. and RUBIN, J. Z. (1986) *Social Conflict: Escalation, Stalemate and Settlement* Random House, New York.

PYE, L. (1982) *Chinese Commercial Negotiating Style* Oelgeschlager, Gunn and Hain: Cambridge, MA.

PYE, L. (1986) "The China trade: making the deal" *Harvard Business Review*, vol. 46, no. 4 (July–August), pp. 74–84.

RADWAY, R. J. (1980) "Doing business in Mexico: A practical legal analysis" *International Lawyer*, 14(2): pp. 361–76.

RAIFFA, H. (1982) *The art and science of negotiation* The Belknap Press of Harvard University Press.

REED, S. F. (1989) *The Art of M&A. A Merger Acquisition Buyout Guide* Business One Irwin, Homewood, Ill.

REIX, R. (1995) *Systèmes d'information et management des organisations* Vuibert, Paris.

REYNOLDS, P. (1986) "Organizational Culture as Related to Industry, Position, and Performance: A Preliminary Report" *Journal of Management Studies* vol. 23, no. 3, pp. 333–45.

ROJOT, J. (1994) *La négociation* Vuibert, Paris.

ROOT, F. D. (1987) *Entry Strategies for International Markets* Lexington Books, Lexington.

ROSTAND, A. (1993) "Facteurs de réussite et causes d'échec" *Fusions & Acquisitions* December, pp. 55–9.

ROUT, L. (1982) "Mexico limits U.S. makers of computers" *Wall Street Journal*, 29 January p. 31.

ROWE, M. (1989) *Countertrade* Euromoney Books, London.

RUBIN, J. Z. and BROWN, B. R. (1975) *The Social Psychology of Bargaining and Negotiations* Academic Press: New York.

RUBIN, P. A. and CARTER, J. R. (1990) "Joint optimality in buyer-seller negotiations"

Journal of Purchasing and Materials Management (Spring) pp. 20–6.

RUBIN, J. Z. and FAURE, G. O. (1993) *Culture and negotiation* Sage.

SAHLIN-ANDERSSON, K. (1992) "The Social Construction of Projects: A Case Study of Organizing an Extraordinary Building Project – the Stockholm Globe Arena" *Scandinavian Housing and Planning Research* vol. 9, pp. 65–78.

SALACUSE, J. (1991) *Making Global Deals* Houghton Mifflin Company, Boston.

SALANCIK, G. R. and PFEFFER, J. (1977) "Who gets power and how they hold on to it: A strategic contingency model of power" *Organisational Dynamics*, vol. 5, pp. 3–21.

SALK, J. (1994) "Generic and Type-Specific Challenges in the Strategic Legitimation and Implementation of Mergers and Acquisitions" *International Business Review* vol. 3, no. 4, pp. 491–512.

SALLE, R. and SILVESTRE, H. (1992) *Vendre a l'industrie: approche stratégique de la relation business-to-business* Liaisons, Paris.

SANCHEZ, M. (1984) "Next month they will approve the IBM investment project" [translation] *El Universal*, October 26.

SANCHEZ, V. (1994) "Empathy and Assertiveness" Working Paper, Harvard Law School.

SANGER, D. E. (1985) "I.B.M. concessions to Mexico" *New York Times* 25 July.

SAPORITO, B. (1986) "IBM's No-hands assembly line" *Fortune*, 15 September pp. 105–7.

SATHE, V. (1984) "Implications of Corporate Culture: A Manager's Guide to Action" *Organizational Dynamics* vol. 12, no. 2, pp. 4–23.

SAUVANT, K. P. (1986) *Trade and foreign direct investment in data services* Westview Press, Boulder, Col.

SAVAGE, G. T., BLAIR, J. D. and SORENSON, P. L. (1989) "Consider both Relationships and Substance when Negotiating Strategically" *Academic of Management Executive*, 3/1, pp. 37–48.

SAWYER, J. and GUETZKOW, H. (1965) "Bargaining and negotiation in international relations" in Kelman, H. (ed.) *International Behavior* Holt, Rinehart and Winston: New York.

SCANZONI, J. (1979) "Social exchange and behavioral interdependence" in Burgess R. L. and Huston, T. L. (eds) *Social Exchange in Developing Relationships* Academic Press: New York.

SCHELLING, T. (1960) *The strategy of conflict* Harvard University Press.

SCHIFFMAN, J. R. (1984) "IBM mulls a computer making venture in South Korea, government sources say" *Wall Street Journal*, 26 June p. 38.

SCHMIDT, K. D. (1979) *Doing Business in Taiwan and Doing Business in Japan* Business Intelligence Program, SRI International, Menlo Park.

SCHRAMM, W. (1980) "How Communication Works" in *Messages: A Reader in Human Communication* Weinberg, S. B. (ed.) Random House, New York.

SCHUSTER, C. P. and COPELAND, M. J. (1996) *Global Business: Planning for Sales and Negotiations* Dryden Press, Fort Worth.

SCHUSTER, C. P. and KEITH, J. (1993) "Factors That Affect the Sales Force Choice Decision in International Market Entry Strategies" *Journal of Global Marketing* vol. 7, no. 2, pp. 29–47.

SCOTT, B. (1981) *The Skills of Negotiating* Gover, Brookfield.

SHAKUN, M. (1988) *Evolutionary systems design* Holden-Day, Oakland, California.

SHENKAR, O. and RONEN, S. (1987) "The Cultural Context of Negotiations – The Implications of Chinese Interpersonal Norms" *Journal of Applied Behavioral Science* vol. 23, no. 2, pp. 263–75.

SHETH, J. (1976) "Buyer-Seller Interaction: A Conceptual Framework" in Anderson, B. B. (ed.) *Advances in Consumer Research* pp. 382–6. Association for Consumer Research, Cincinnati.

SHETH, J. (1983) "Cross-Cultural Influences on the Buyer-Seller Interaction/Negotiation

References

Process" *Asia Pacific Journal of Management* vol. 1, no. 1, pp. 46–55.

SHOUBY, E. (1951) "The Influence of the Arabic Language on the Psychology of the Arabs" *Middle East Journal*, 5.

SIEBE, W. (1991) *Game theory* in Kremenyuk *International negotiation* Jossey-Bass.

SIMON, H. A. (1965) *Administrative Behavior*, (2nd edn) The Free Press, New York.

SIMURDA, S. (1988) "Finding an International Sales Manager" *Northeast International Business* vol. 1, no. 3, pp. 15–16.

SOROKIN, P. and MERTON, R. (1937) "Social Time: A Methodological and Functional Analysis" *American Journal of Sociology* vol. 42, pp. 615–29.

SPERBER, P. (1983) *Fail-safe Business Negotiations* Prentice Hall, N.J.

STOEVER, W. A. (1979) "Renegotiations: The cutting edge of relations between MNCs and LDCs" *Columbia Journal of World Business*, Spring: pp. 5–13.

STORY, D. (1982) "Trade politics in the Third World: A case study of the Mexican GATT decision" *International Organization*, 36(4): pp. 767–94.

STRAUSS, A. (1978) *Negotiations* Jossey-Bass Publishers, San Francisco.

SULLIVAN, J. J. and KAMEDA, N. (1982) "The Concept of Profit and Japanese-American Problems in Managerial Communications" *Journal of Business Communications*.

SZYBILLO, J., JACOB, G. J. and BERNING, C. K. (1976) "Time and consumer behavior: an interdisciplinary overview" *Journal of Consumer Research* vol. 2, pp. 320–39.

TACEY, W. S. (1980) *Business and Professional Speaking* (3rd edn) Wm. C. Brown Company Publishers, Dubuque, Iowa.

TANNEAU, C. (1993) "Une nouvelle génération de fusions-acquisitions: Les facteurs-clés de succès de l'integration" *Fusions & Acquisitions* December 1993: pp. 61–8.

THE ECONOMIST (1994) "Russia's Bankruptcy Bears" 19 March pp. 73–4.

THE WORLD FACTBOOK (1994) *Central Intelligence Agency (CIA)*, US Government, Washington DC.

THOMAS, K. (1977) "Conflict and management" in Dunnette M. (ed.) *Handbook of industrial and organizational psychology* Rand McNally, Chicago.

THORELLI, H. B. (1990) *Networks : Between Markets and Hierarchies* Academic Press, London.

TIANO, A. (1981) *Transfert de technologie industrielle* Editions Economica: Paris.

TIETZ, B. (1994) "The Opening up of Eastern Europe: The Implications for Western Business" in Buckley, P. and Ghauri, P. (eds) *The Economics of change in East and Central Europe: Its Impact on International Business* Academic Press, London.

TIME (1981) "Long Workdays" 12 January.

TOUZARD, H. (1977) *La médiation et la résolution des conflits* PUF.

TRAORÉ, SÉRIÉ R. (1986) "La promotion du Livre en Côte d'Ivoire" paper presented to the conference on Marketing and Development, Abidjan (Ivory Coast).

TROMPENAARS, F. (1993) *Riding the waves of culture* Nicholas Brealey: London.

TRIANDIS, H. (1982) "Review of Culture's Consequences: International Differences in Work-Related Values" *Human Organization* vol. 44, no. 1, pp. 86–90.

TRIANDIS, H. C. (1983) "Dimensions of cultural variation as parameters of organizational theories" *International Studies of Management and Organization* vol. XII, no. 4, pp. 139–69.

TRIANDIS, H. C. (1994) *Culture and Social Behavior* McGraw-Hill: New York.

TSE, D. K., FRANCIS, J. and WALLS, J. (1994) "Cultural Differences in Conducting Intra- and Inter-Cultural Negotiations: A Sino-Canadian perspective" *Journal of International Business Studies* vol. 25, no. 3, pp. 537–55.

TUCKER, M. (1982) Lecture presented to Procter & Gamble Managers, (October), Cincinnati, Ohio.

TUNG, R. L. (1982) "U.S.-China trade negotiations: Practices, procedures and outcomes" *Journal of International Business Studies*, Fall: pp. 25–37.

TUNG, R. L. (1984a) "How to negotiate with the Japanese" *California Management Review* vol. XXVI, no. 4 pp. 62–77.

TUNG, R. L. (1984b) *Business Negotiations with the Japanese* Lexington Books: Lexington, MA.

TUNG, R. L. (1989) "A longitudinal study of United States-China business negotiations" *China Economic Review* vol. 1, no. 1, 57–71.

TUNG, R. L. (1991) "Handshakes across the sea: Cross-cultural negotiating for business success" *Organizational Dynamics* vol. 19, no. 3: pp. 30–40.

TUNG, R. L. (1996) "Managing in Asia" in Joynt, P. D. and Warner, M. (eds) *Managing across Cultures: Issues and Perspectives* Routledge, London.

URBAN, S. (1992) "Strategies d'internationalisation" in *Encyclopédie du Management*, pp. 896–906, Vuibert, Paris.

URBAN, S. (1993) *Management international* Litec, Paris.

URBAN, S. and VENDEMINI, S. (1992) *European Strategic Alliances* B. Blackwell, Oxford.

U.S. DEPARTMENT OF COMMERCE (USDoC) (1981) *Computers and peripheral equipment-Mexico*, Washington, DC.

USUNIER, J-C. (1989) "Interculturel: La Parole et L'Action" *Harvard-L'Expansion*, no. 52, March, pp. 84–92.

USUNIER, J-C. (1991) "Business time perceptions and national cultures: A comparative survey" *Management International Review* vol. 31, no. 3, pp. 197–217.

USUNIER, J-C. (1992) *Commerce entre cultures: une approche culturelle du marketing international* P.U.F.: Paris.

USUNIER, J-C. (1996) *Marketing Across Cultures* (2nd edn) Prentice-Hall: Hemel Hempstead.

USUNIER, J-C. and VALETTE-FLORENCE, P. (1994) "Perceptual Time Patterns (Time Styles): A Psychometric Scale" *Time and Society* vol. 3, no. 2, May.

USUNIER, J-C. and VERNA, G. (1994) "Ethique des Affaires et Relativité Culturelle" *Revue Française de Gestion*, no. 99, June-July-August 1994, pp. 23–40.

VAN ZANDT, H. R. (1970) "How to negotiate with the Japanese" *Harvard Business Review*, November-December.

VÉRY, P. (1995) "Différences culturelles dans les acquisitions internationales" in Noël *et al.* (eds) *Perspectives en Management stratégique* Economica, Paris.

WALL STREET JOURNAL (1984) "Adolfo Hegewisch on foreign investment" 24 September: p. 24.

WALL STREET JOURNAL (1990) 4 September.

WALLACE, S. C. *et al.* (1988) *Profile of mini and micro computer systems market* June, Mexico City.

WALTON, R. E. and McKERSIE, R. B. (1965) *A Behavioral Theory of Labor Negotiations: An Analysis of a Social Interaction System* McGraw Hill, New York.

WALTON, R. E. and McKERSIE, R. B. (1992) "A retrospective on the behavioral Theory of Negotiation" *Journal of Organizational Behavior* vol. 13, no. 3, pp. 277–88.

WASNAK, L. (1986) "Knowing When To Bow" *Ohio Business* (March), p. 31–8.

WEISS, S. E. (1987) "Creating the GM-Toyota joint venture: A case in complex negotiation" *Columbia Journal of World Business* Summer: pp. 23–37.

WEISS, S. E. (1988) Beyond forests or trees in international business negotiations: An integrative framework with applications. Paper presented at annual conference of the Academy of Management, Anaheim, California.

WEISS, S. E. and STRIPP, W. G. (1985) "Negotiating with foreign businesspersons: An introduction with propositions on six cultures" GBA Working Paper Series nos 85–6, New York University.

WEISS, S. E. (1993) "Analysis of Complex Negotiations in International Business - The RBC Perspective" *Organization Science* vol. 4, no. 2, pp. 269–300.

WEISS, S. E. (1994) "Negotiating with Romans, no. 2" *Sloan Management Review* vol. 35, no. 3, pp. 85–9.

WEITZ, B. (1978) "Relationships Between Salesperson Performance and Understanding of Customer Decision Making" *Journal of Marketing Research* vol. 15, no. 4, pp. 501–16.

WEITZ, B. (1979) "A Critical review of personal selling research: the need for contingency approaches" in Albaum, G. and Churchill, G. A. jr (eds) *Critical Issues in Sales Management: State of the art and future needs* University of Oregon: Eugene.

WEITZ, B. (1981) "Effectiveness in Sales Interactions: A Contingency Framework" *Journal of Marketing* vol. 45, no. 1, pp. 85–103.

WEITZ, B., SUJAN, H. and SUJAN, M. (1986) "Knowledge, Motivation, and Adaptive Behavior: A Framework for Improving Selling Effectiveness" *Journal of Marketing*, vol. 50, no. 4, pp. 174–91.

WENBURG, J. and WILMOT, W. (1973) *The Personal Communication Process* John Wiley and Sons, New York.

WHITING, V. R. and SHANK, J. B. (1986) "Mexico's policy on the computer industry: The case of IBM" *Case Studies in Public Policy* Brown University.

WILKIE, W. L. (1986) *Consumer Behavior* John Wiley & Sons, New York.

WILLIAMSON, O. W. and WINTER, S. G. (1991) *The Nature of the Firm: Origins, Evolution and Development* Oxford University Press.

WILSON, I. (1980) "An American Success Story: Coca-Cola in Japan" in Winchester, M. B. (ed.) *The International Essays for Business Decision Makers* vol. 8, pp. 119–23. The Center for Business, Dallas.

YEUNG, I. Y. M. and TUNG, R. L. (in press). "*Guanxi* (connections) and business success in Confucian societies" *Organizational Dynamics*.

YIN, R. K. (1984) *Case study research: Design and methods* Applied social research methods series, Vol. 5, Sage, Beverly Hills.

YOSHINO, M. Y. and RANGAN, U. S. (1995) *Strategic Alliances, An Entrepreneurial Approach to Globalization* Harvard Business School Press, Boston.

YOUNG, S. and HOOD, N. (1977) "Multinationals and host governments: Lessons from the case of Chrysler-UK" *Columbia Journal of World Business*, 12(2): pp. 97–106.

ZAHRA, S. and ELHAGRASEY, G. (1994) "Strategic Management of International Joint Ventures" in *European Management Journal* vol. 12, no. 1, pp. 83–93.

ZARTMAN, I. W. (1977) *The negotiation process* Sage Pub. Co.

ZARTMAN, I. W. (1988) "Common elements in the analysis of the negotiation process" *Negotiation Journal* 4, no. 1, (January 1988).

ZARTMAN, I. W. (1994) *International multilateral negotiation* Jossey-Bass.

ZARTMAN, I. W. and BERMAN, M. (1982) *The practical negotiator* Yale University Press.

ZELDIN, T. (1977) *France 1848-1945* vol. 11, Oxford University Press: Oxford.

ZEUTHEN, F. (1930) *Problems of monopoly and economic warfare* Routledge and Kegan Paul, London.

Author Index

Subject Index

Subject Index

temperaments, 26–9, 32, 34
temporal behavior, 169–70
temporal clashes, 164–5
temporal orientations, 156, 160–2, 163
tender offers, 274, 279–83
Teutonic intellectual style, 111–12
theory (argumenting styles), 111–12
thinking (personality type), 26–9, 32, 34
thinking process (cultural difference), 87–8
third party, 5–6
    introducer (*shokai-sha*), 357, 365
    joint ventures, 238, 245–6, 247
    patents, 216, 218, 227
threat, 16
time, 12, 45, 64, 96, 365
    commitments, 406
    culture classification mode, 133–41
    frame (negotiation partners), 167–70
    monitoring, 388–9
    patience, 19–20, 376–7, 389
    relative speed of decision-making, 372–3
    role of, 153–72
tips (paid to civil servants), 396–7
tit for tat approach, 64
top-down approach, 365
top executives (non–task sounding), 356–7
tough strategies, 13, 54, 63, 107, 386, 387
trade secrets, 229
trademarks, 228, 244
trading-off (in agreements), 193–4, 391
Traditional cultures, 110, 139–40, 161–2
training of salespeople, 34
transaction costs, 383, 401
transactional analysis, 49
transformation, 55
transmission (in selling sequence), 35, 36
Treaty of Rome, 199
"Treuepflicht", 241
trust, 66, 99, 106–7, 114–15, 131, 141, 171, 393
truth, 122
turnkey projects, 56, 169, 253, 385, 396, 398, 402, 404

uncertainty avoidance, 22–3, 28–30, 103, 122, 123, 126
United Nations, 43, 47, 120, 195
universalism, 109
    ethics, 394–6, 401, 405–6
unlimited liability, 242
Uppsala model, 237
Uruguay Round, 50–1

value systems, 96, 120–2
    role (in East Asia), 369–81
values, 23, 41–4, 54–5, 64, 119, 251
    cultural differences, 84–7
venture culture, 109
verbal negotiation tactics, 78–81
virtue (argumenting styles), 111–12
voting rights clauses, 299

walk-away possibilities, 385–6
Warman, Plan, 310, 314, 316–17, 319, 321, 324–5
Warsaw stock exchange, 348
Waste Management, 264
weekly division system, 159
Weltanschauung, 155
Western economies, Eastern and (gaps), 338–9
westernization (of East Asia), 380
white knight defence (mergers and acquisitions), 277
win-lose negotiation, 3, 20, 104, 167, 175
win-win negotiation, 3, 4, 86, 174, 175
words (communication implications), 142, 146
written agreements, 114–18, 171–2, 392–4

Zeitanschauung, 155
Zen, 153, 163
zero-sum game, 52, 101, 103, 167